ESSAYS IN HONOR OF SUBAL KUMBHAKAR

ADVANCES IN ECONOMETRICS

Series editors: Thomas B. Fomby, R. Carter Hill, Ivan Jeliazkov, Juan Carlos Escanciano, Eric Hillebrand, Daniel L. Millimet, Rodney Strachan

Recent Volumes:

Volume 28	DSGE Models in Macroeconomics: Estimation, Evaluation and New Developments – Edited by Nathan Balke, Fabio Canova, Fabio Milani and Mark Wynne
Volume 29	Essays in Honor of Jerry Hausman – Edited by Badi H. Baltagi, Whitney Newey, Hal White and R. Carter Hill
Volume 30	30th Anniversary Edition – Edited by Dek Terrell and Daniel Millmet
Volume 31	Structural Econometric Models – Edited by Eugene Choo and Matthew Shum
Volume 32	VAR Models in Macroeconomics — New Developments and Applications: Essays in Honor of Christopher A. Sims – Edited by Thomas B. Fomby, Lutz Kilian and Anthony Murphy
Volume 33	Essays in Honor of Peter C. B. Phillips – Edited by Thomas B. Fomby, Yoosoon Chang and Joon Y. Park
Volume 34	Bayesian Model Comparison – Edited by Ivan Jeliazkov and Dale J. Poirier
Volume 35	Dynamic Factor Models – Edited by Eric Hillebrand and Siem Jan Koopman
Volume 36	Essays in Honor of Aman Ullah – Edited by Gloria Gonzalez-Rivera, R. Carter Hill and Tae-Hwy Lee
Volume 37	Spatial Econometrics – Edited by Badi H. Baltagi, James P. LeSage and R. Kelley Pace
Volume 38	Regression Discontinuity Designs: Theory and Applications – Edited by Matias D. Cattaneo and Juan Carlos Escanciano
Volume 39	The Econometrics of Complex Survey Data: Theory and Applications – Edited by Kim P. Huynh, David T. Jacho-Chávez and Guatam Tripathi
Volume 40A	Topics in Identification, Limited Dependent Variables, Partial Observability, Experimentation, and Flexible Modelling Part A – Edited by Ivan Jeliazkov and Justin L. Tobias
Volume 40B	Topics in Identification, Limited Dependent Variables, Partial Observability, Experimentation, and Flexible Modelling Part B – Edited by Ivan Jeliazkov and Justin L. Tobias
Volume 41	Essays in Honor of Cheng Hsiao – Edited by Tong Li, M. Hashem Pesaran and Dek Terrell
Volume 42	The Econometrics of Networks – Edited by Áureo de Paula, Elie Tamer and Marcel-Cristian Voia
Volume 43A	Essays in Honor of M. Hashem Pesaran – Edited by Alexander Chudik, Cheng Hsiao and Allan Timmermann
Volume 43B	Essays in Honor of M. Hashem Pesaran – Edited by Alexander Chudik, Cheng Hsiao and Allan Timmermann
Volume 44A	Essays in Honour of Fabio Canova – Edited by Juan J. Dolado, Luca Gambetti and Christian Matthes
Volume 44B	Essays in Honour of Fabio Canova – Edited by Juan J. Dolado, Luca Gambetti and Christian Matthes
Volume 45A	Essays in Honor of Joon Y. Park – Edited by Yoosoon Chang, Sokbae Lee and J. Isaac Miller
Volume 45B	Essays in Honor of Joon Y. Park – Edited by Yoosoon Chang, Sokbae Lee and J. Isaac Miller

ADVANCES IN ECONOMETRICS, VOLUME 46

ESSAYS IN HONOR OF SUBAL KUMBHAKAR

EDITED BY

CHRISTOPHER F. PARMETER
University of Miami, USA

MIKE G. TSIONAS
University of Lancaster, UK

and

HUNG-JEN WANG
National Taiwan University, Taiwan

emerald PUBLISHING

United Kingdom – North America – Japan
India – Malaysia – China

Emerald Publishing Limited
Emerald Publishing, Floor 5, Northspring, 21-23 Wellington Street, Leeds LS1 4DL.

First edition 2024

British Library Cataloguing in Publication Data
A catalogue record for this book is available from the British Library

ISBN: 978-1-83797-874-8 (Print)
ISBN: 978-1-83797-873-1 (Online)
ISBN: 978-1-83797-875-5 (Epub)

ISSN: 0731-9053 (Series)

Printed and bound by CPI Group (UK) Ltd, Croydon, CR0 4YY

This book is dedicated to the memory of Mike Tsionas who passed away shortly after the completion of this volume. He was an amazing colleague and brilliant thinker.

CONTENTS

LIST OF CONTRIBUTORS

Inmaculada Álvarez-Ayuso	Universidad Autónoma de Madrid, Spain
Christine Amsler	Michigan State University, USA
Badi H. Baltagi	Syracuse University, USA
Corey Fuller	Southwest Airlines, USA
Ziwen Gao	Academy of Mathematics and Systems Science, Chinese Academy of Sciences, China; University of Chinese Academy of Sciences, China
Bruce E. Hansen	University of Wisconsin, USA
Daniel J. Henderson	University of Alabama, USA
Robert James	University of Sydney, Australia
Kajal Lahiri	University at Albany, State University of New York, USA
Hung-pin Lai	National Chung Cheng University, Taiwan; Research Center of Humanities and Social Sciences, Academia Sinica, Taiwan
Steven F. Lehrer	Queen's University, Canada; NBER, USA
Qinling Lu	Risk Modeling & Analysis, KeyBank, USA
Emir Malikov	University of Nevada, Las Vegas, USA
Paul Noroski	University at Albany, State University of New York, USA
Luis Orea	University of Oviedo, Spain
Alecos Papadopoulos	Athens University of Economics and Business, Greece
Christopher F. Parmeter	University of Miami, USA
Artem Prokhorov	University of Sydney Business School, Australia; Center for Econometrics and Business Analytics, Russia
Jeffrey S. Racine	McMaster University, Canada; La Trobe University, Australia; American University, USA; Rimini Center for Economic Analysis, Italy

Peter Schmidt	Michigan State University, USA
Luis Servén	Centro de Estudios Monetarios y Financieros, Spain
Robin C. Sickles	Rice University, USA
Yiguo Sun	University of Guelph, Canada
Mike G. Tsionas	Lancaster University, UK
Hung-Jen Wang	National Taiwan University, Taiwan
Taining Wang	Capital University of Economics and Business, China
Zhichao Wang	University of Queensland, Australia
Tian Xie	Shanghai University of Finance and Economics, China
Feng Yao	West Virginia University, USA; Shenzhen University, China
Valentin Zelenyuk	University of Queensland, Australia
Jingfang Zhang	Alcorn State University, USA
Junsen Zhang	Zhejiang University, China
Xinyu Zhang	Academy of Mathematics and Systems Science, Chinese Academy of Sciences, China
Shunan Zhao	Oakland University, USA

CHAPTER 1

EDITORS' INTRODUCTION

Christopher F. Parmeter[a], Mike G. Tsionas[b] and Hung-Jen Wang[c]

[a]*University of Miami, Miami, FL, USA*
[b]*Lancaster University, UK*
[c]*National Taiwan University, Taiwan*

Deciding to put together this special issue in honor of Subal Kumbhakar was easy. Subal has been, and remains, a great colleague, mentor, friend, and coauthor to all of us. His influence on the applied productivity and efficiency profession is legion, as evidenced by the attendance of sessions where he is presenting (or most usually his coauthors are presenting, since despite all of Subal's many gifts, he still cannot be in two places at the same time). Subal's oeuvre continues to grow, his ability to move the applied econometric and productivity literature forward never stalling, and his charismatic smile always there to cheer up colleagues and friends on a gloomy day. It is our distinct honor to have put together this collection of research that honors Subal's many accomplishments and draws further attention to the various areas of scholarship that he has touched. We hope this volume will be useful for future researchers and serve as a beacon of respect and admiration for Subal.

The present volume is composed of 14 chapters, many of which are from Subal's peers and coauthors. The contributions cover a wide array of applied econometric domains, from model averaging to panel data methods, stochastic frontier analysis to productivity decompositions and ending on the two-tier frontier. The applied topics also cover a broad range: homelessness, underreporting of satisfaction, production, cryptocurrency and healthcare to name a few. This vast array of topics speaks to the impact that Subal continues to have. We thank all of the contributors for putting up with us as we went through the review process

Essays in Honor of Subal Kumbhakar
Advances in Econometrics, Volume 46, 1–12

Published under exclusive licence by Emerald Publishing Limited
ISSN: 0731-9053/doi:10.1108/S0731-905320240000046001

and asked for countless changes. But when the honoree has such high standards, we had quite a lot to live up to as editors. We would also like to thank those contributors who participated in a special session at the recent North American Productivity Workshop at the Miami Herbert Business School[1] in honor of Subal. Nearly half of the contributors to this volume were in attendance and it was moving to see Subal honored with such a large audience present.

We would also like to thank all of the external reviewers who took time away from their schedules to rigorously peer review all of the submissions to ensure the highest quality. Referees are routinely overlooked and underappreciated, but play a critical role in affecting the quality and clarity of submissions. To them, we offer our thanks and perhaps a beer or coffee at the next conference (on Subal of course). We would also like to thank the editorial team at *Advances in Econometrics* for entertaining our proposal and enthusiastically giving us the go-ahead with this project.

We have ordered the contributions in this volume by those who are closest to Subal, followed by those chapters that tie in closely to his various treks into productivity, ending on an area that has always interested Subal, the two-tier frontier. Here, our goal is to simply highlight the individual contributions, hoping to draw distinct interest in them but still leaving the desire for the reader to dig into the meat of each chapter on their own.

When we started putting together this special volume in honor of Subal, we reached out to his dissertation adviser, Dennis Aigner, who had moved from the University of Southern California (where Subal received his PhD) to the University of California at Irvine, to see if he could provide some remarks on Subal, the graduate student. We were delighted that he took us up on our offer and has provided some fantastic insight into the younger version of Subal that we all know now. We also found it fascinating that Subal and Dennis had not seen each other in over 35 years until this past June at the University of Southern California for the First USC PhD Alumni Conference (a photo of the two of them at the conference appears in Fig. 1.1). Fitting, in our opinion, that this volume is coming out after this event.

Baltagi's "Hausman's Specification Test for Panel Data: Practical Tips" discusses the case of interpreting the Hausman test when faced with a rejection of the null hypothesis. It is well known that Hausman's (1978) test is a general specification test and a rejection does not necessarily imply what is wrong, only that something is wrong. In the panel data case, this test is most commonly deployed to assess whether a fixed effects or a random effects framework is adequate for the data at hand. But when one rejects the null hypothesis of the random effects framework, what is the implication? Baltagi's work is a step in this direction, highlighting various deficiencies that might arise for which practitioners should be aware of.

An interesting point which Baltagi draws attention to is that if the random effects framework is rejected (thereby throwing support toward a fixed effects framework) one can test the restrictions that are inherent in the fixed effects framework. This can be done following Chamberlain (1982), for example, but as Baltagi rightly notes, it is rarely taken up in practice. A key takeaway from

Fig. 1.1. Subal and Dennis, Together Again.

Baltagi's contribution is that a rejection of the random effects estimator using the Hausman (1978) test does not automatically imply that the fixed effects estimator is correct. While this seems simple to write and state, it occurs so frequently in practice that it is useful to have these reminders.

Lahiri and Noroski's "Do Federal Disability Insurance Participants Exaggerate Their Health Problems? A Study Using Anchoring Vignettes" uses anchoring vignettes to examine whether or not applicants and recipients of federal disability insurance inflate their self-assessed health problems relative to others. This is a self-styled measurement error study, which has deep connections to the composite error structure of the stochastic frontier model, as recently described in Millimet and Parmeter (2022). Generally, survey data are used in place of revealed preference data, but concerns exist over respondents' ability to accurately convey the information being asked of them. This is especially important when designing policies where the survey answers are used to justify moving forward (or holding back) on a given agenda.

For Social Security Administration survey data, no consensus exists in the academic literature on the truthfulness of self-reports of disability. Anchoring vignettes, developed by King, Murray, Salomon, and Tandon (2004), provide a way of examining whether recipients of federal disability treat health-related survey questions any differently than non-recipients. Lahiri and Noroski use a parametric form of this approach to estimate a model of self-reported disability that is free of differential item functioning. A key finding is that reporting heterogeneity has the potential to affect the magnitude and significance of various components of self-reported disability.

Fuller and Sickles' "Homelessness on the West Coast and the Role of Health: Inefficiency and Productivity Loss in American Society" tackles a difficult empirical problem, homelessness. Homelessness is a stark example of the inefficient use of resources, which exemplifies nearly all of Subal's research. Homelessness is hard to address for many reasons, but one is the lack of data on the exact number of individuals who are homeless. Among the homeless, the prevalence of substance abuse and/or mental health disorders is significantly higher than those that live in a place fit for habitation. A lack of adequate habitation can negatively impact an individual's health, having the potential to create a negative feedback loop that can make exiting homelessness arduous. This suggests that a simple empirical model to unravel these effects is likely to be limited and a more formal approach is needed.

The model that Fuller and Sickles work with includes the potential consequences of poor health and healthcare access on homelessness within a two-period consumption framework developed originally by Glomm and John (2002). An individual's health is integrated directly into the model through an assumption that health directly impacts the skills a worker brings into the labor market. These skills in turn affect their earnings potential. The theoretical predictions of this model are then tested econometrically using an array of data from West Coast states.

As anyone who has met (or knows) Subal can attest, he has developed a lot of models. So many models in fact that it is difficult to know which model Subal might prefer. So what can be done when confronted with a multitude of models? Two competing approaches to adjudicate across models are model selection and model averaging. Since the seminal work of Hansen (2007), a large literature on model averaging has cropped up to combat the issues associated with model selection. They range from simple applications of regression models to more sophisticated frameworks in nonparametric settings (Henderson & Parmeter, 2016) and the full distribution theory (Liu, 2015).

In this volume, we are fortunate to have two contributions associated with model averaging. First, Hansen and Racine's "Bootstrap Model Averaging Unit Root Inference" provides a model averaging procedure to deal with model uncertainty when one is interested in testing for the presence of a unit root. These methods are preferable to inference based on model selection where a hard thresholding rule creates an inherently discontinuous choice of the selected model, and hence a discontinuous change in the test statistic. Beyond the construction of a model average test statistic, Hansen and Racine also deploy a model-free, automatic, time series bootstrap procedure which avoids issues with the selection of a model from which to bootstrap from. From the extensive Monte Carlo simulations provided, the proposed bootstrap model average approach emerges as the procedure of choice. We certainly believe that practitioners will find it a useful addition to their toolkit.

Our second model averaging piece is Gao, Lehrer, Xie, and Zhang's "Averaging Heterogeneous Autoregression Models with Heteroskedastic Errors: Theory and an Application to Cryptocurrency Volatility Forecasting." This chapter complements nicely with Hansen and Racine's, focusing on model averaging in a time series setting, but here with an eye on estimation rather than inference. They propose a heteroskedastic model averaging heterogeneous autoregressive (H-MAHAR) estimator to develop a forecasting strategy that can account for both model uncertainty and heteroskedasticity of unknown form. This estimator is studied theoretically and also applied to learn about realized volatility in the cryptocurrency arena.

Yao, Lu, Sun, and Zhang's "Efficient Estimation in Varying Coefficient Panel Data Model with Different Smoothing Variables and Fixed Effects" proposes a semiparametric smooth coefficient panel data model that allows for different smoothing variables across the various smooth coefficients. Smooth coefficient models are crafty modeling devices as, conditional on a given set of covariates, they can be interpreted as linear in parameter models (Hartarska, Parmeter, & Nadolnyak, 2011). Traditionally, varying coefficient models restrict the smooth coefficients to depend on the same smoothing variables, but in Yao et al.'s application, they have different variables which influence production and technical efficiency, making a model of this ilk necessary to modify. Naturally, the presence of fixed effects stemming from the panel data framework makes estimation more challenging than in a cross-sectional setup, but Yao et al. deploy a two-stage estimator, beginning first with a series based profile least squares estimator (Su & Ullah, 2006) and then use backfitting in a second stage to recover the smooth coefficients.

The approach of Yao et al. follows a recent set of work by Subal (Parmeter, Wang, & Kumbhakar, 2017; Zhou, Parmeter, & Kumbhakar, 2020) that seeks to allow determinants of inefficiency to enter into a panel data stochastic frontier model in a fully nonparametric setup. The difference however is the earlier papers that Subal coauthored always modeled the production technology in a parametric framework. Yao et al. further relax this assumption by allowing the production frontier to be semiparametric in nature, which has obvious appeal.

Next, a collection of the chapters focuses on some of Subal's recent contributions related to the difference between structural models of productivity (such as Gandhi, Navarro, & Rivers, 2020; Levinsohn & Petrin, 2003) and the stochastic frontier model (Aigner, Lovell, & Schmidt, 1977). This is highlighted by Tsionas and Kumbhakar (2023) and Subal's keynote address at the recent New York Camp Econometrics XVII in Bolton's Landing.[2] This line of research seeks to bridge the gap between these two styles of models (unobserved inefficiency vs unobserved productivity).

Tsionas' "The Role of Management in Efficient Production: Theoretical and Statistical Implications" attempts to understand how a simple model of production with managerial inefficiency can lead to statistical insights that link to the stochastic production frontier model. More specifically, Tsionas constructs a dynamic model of the firm under the assumption that managerial skill contributes to technical efficiency. There are several important implications from Tsionas' contribution. First, it turns out that it is not optimal for the firm to be fully efficient (in the information-processing sense) even if this possibility is an option. Second, his model shows that it is not optimal for the firm to be efficient even in the long-run. Beyond these theoretical insights, an econometric model of the inefficiency–management nexus is proposed that is nonparametric in nature and is applied to the well-known Bloom and Van Reenen (2007) dataset on managerial practice. A key finding is a nonlinear but positive relationship between estimated managerial compensation and effort. The relationship is concave, suggesting a turning point, where additional effort actually leads to reduced compensation, further evincing the lack of optimality of becoming fully efficient (at least by management standards).

Malikov, Zhao, and Zhang's "A System Approach to Structural Identification of Production Functions with Multi-Dimensional Productivity" extends Gandhi et al.'s (2020) proxy variable framework for structurally identifying production functions to a more general case when latent firm productivity is multi-dimensional, with both factor-neutral and (biased) factor-augmenting components. A novelty of their model is that it can be identified under weaker data requirements than are commonly required, eschewing reliance on cross-sectional variation in input prices, which are typically unavailable for a large swath of datasets. This identification comes at the expense of migrating from a fully nonparametric framework to a parametric framework. However, this setup also produces the identification of key model parameters that only depend on the cost-to-revenue ratio, which is typically observable in micro level.

A further benefit of Malikov et al.'s approach is that it is robust to the critique of Ackerberg, Caves, and Frazer (2015). Specifically, this critique draws into question the ability of a common class of structural "proxy" estimators to identify both the production function itself and a Hicksian productivity component, given the additive nature that arises in the construction of the model. The model proposed here does not fall under this critique since no endogenous variable input appears on the right-hand side of their final estimating equation, having been removed at an earlier stage. This new model, and subsequent estimation approach, are then demonstrated using both simulated data and an application to Chinese manufacturing firms. In their simulations, with a modestly large sample size, their methodology recovers the true parameters fairly well, however, those in the third stage are estimated the least precisely, which is to be expected.

Orea, Álvarez-Ayuso, and Servén's "The Structural and Productivity Effects of Infrastructure Provision in Developed and Developing Countries" provides evidence on the effects of infrastructure provision on aggregate productivity using industry-level data across a group of developed and developing countries. They do this by deploying a two-level decomposition of aggregate productivity.

First, the approach of Diewert (2015) is leveraged, (which breaks total factor productivity (TFP) into its constituent pieces) and then measures aggregate TFP improvements directly attributable to infrastructure provision (and other productivity drivers as well). That such a decomposition is feasible hinges on the two different channels through which infrastructure provision may promote aggregate productivity gains: a within effect and a reallocation effect.

Their decomposition has important implications for policy. A key finding from the empirical analysis is that public infrastructure capital improves within-firm productivity while also facilitating the efficient reallocation of inputs across both firms and industries. This suggests that the promotion of enhanced infrastructure investments should be a public policy priority in developing countries.

Our last set of chapters are perhaps the most apt to honor Subal, focusing on various aspects of the stochastic frontier model proposed by Aigner et al. (1977). It is this specific class of models that has served as the backbone of Subal's research agenda over the past four decades. Subal has made far too many contributions here to successfully highlight all of them, but each of the chapter in this area that appear here is predicated on insights that Subal has made. These chapters span the spectrum from predicting efficiency to new estimators and novel applications related to healthcare.

Amsler, James, Prokhorov, and Schmidt's "Improving Predictions of Technical Inefficiency" considers the classic Jondrow, Lovell, Materov, and Schmidt's (1982) estimator of technical efficiency and asks if this measure can be improved. In essence, Amsler et al. argue that what helps to improve the prediction of technical inefficiency is enlarging the conditioning set. This stems from the well-known decomposition of the variance of a random variable into distinct explained and unexplained components. In the most basic version of the prediction of inefficiency, only the residuals from maximum likelihood estimation enter the conditioning set. However, there typically arise many empirical settings where more information is available: a cost function with share equations (Schmidt & Lovell, 1979, 1980), panel data (Amsler, Prokhorov, & Schmidt, 2014), or endogeneity (Amsler, Prokhorov, & Schmidt, 2016), for example.

Here the authors go a step further and examine the impact that estimated objects entering the conditioning set have on the overall predictive power of the estimator. They suggest two alternative nonparametric estimators for this endeavor (the textbook local constant estimator and a local linear random forest). Their simulations reveal that, in the panel data setting, conditioning on all of the errors, not just the contemporaneous error, leads to reductions for the local linear random forest estimator.

That the local constant estimator does not result in improvements is due to the curse of dimensionality; as the number of time periods goes up, the size of the conditioning set increases and the finite sample bias dwarfs the reduction in variance, leading to increases in mean squared error.[3] A similar story emerges from their simulations incorporating cost shares. Conditioning on allocative inefficiency dramatically improves the estimation of technical inefficiency as the correlation between these two increases. Interestingly, reductions in mean square error are similar regardless of the number of inputs in the production function;

this suggests that even conditioning on a single allocative inefficiency term has the potential to substantially improve estimates of technical inefficiency scores.

Wang and Henderson's "A Semiparametric Constant Elasticity of Substitution Stochastic Frontier Model for Panel Data" begins with a classical constant elasticity of substitution (CES) production frontier, but proposes estimation of the model without resorting to log-linearization, which is known to induce substantial finite sample biases (Santos Silva & Tenreyro, 2006). They further enhance the model by allowing a set of covariates to impact efficiency levels and do so in a nonparametric fashion. Lastly, their model allows the technological shift parameter in the traditional CES model to depend on a set of covariates as well, and in a single index fashion. This model is then extended to the panel data setting to allow for unobserved firm level heterogeneity. They propose a two-step estimation procedure to estimate all the constituent components of the model. They provide theoretical results establishing identification as well as a set of high level assumptions that are conjectured to lead to the overall consistency of the estimator.

Beyond their theory, Wang and Henderson showcase their estimator using both simulations and an interesting empirical application. Their simulations reveal that their estimator can recover all of the primitives of the model with little concern over accuracy. The application focuses on the impact that trade has on cross-country productive efficiency levels. To facilitate comparisons, Wang and Henderson estimate four benchmark parametric stochastic frontier panel data models with different structures. The estimate of ρ, which measures elasticity of substitution, across the three different CES specifications, is statistically significant at the 1% level, casting some doubt on the Cobb–Douglas specification that is more common in applied frontier studies. Their proposed model reveals a significant nonlinear structure of the technology function, clearly deviating from the commonly assumed exponential functional form. As a result of this finding, the impact of the share of merchandising exports that a country has on technology deviates substantially from the proposed CES model compared to more rigid parametric frameworks. As Wang and Henderson note, for this finding the ability to model technology nonparametrically is vital to avoid misleading inferences on the effect of environment variables stemming from model misspecification.

Wang and Zelenyuk's "Random Versus Explained Inefficiency in Stochastic Frontier Analysis: The Case of Queensland Hospitals" is a *ne plus ultra* application of stochastic frontier methods. They apply several of the most well-known models to learn about hospital efficiency in Queensland, Australia. This analysis is then sistered with an array of model selection devices to help understand some of the interesting divergences that arise between models. Specifically, using a classic cross-sectional stochastic frontier model, Queensland hospitals are found to be nearly fully efficient, yet, accounting for a range of determinants (such as if it is a teaching hospital, located in a rural area, the occupancy rate and the number of beds), these high efficiency levels fade away.

To facilitate further confidence in their model selection findings, Wang and Zelenyuk use a novel approach: designing a recovery test based on their preferred model findings. The idea is to take the parameter estimates from a previously estimated model, use the actual data, and take random draws from the error terms to create new outputs. These new outputs can then be analyzed in a variety of ways. Wang and Zelenyuk's discussion on efficiency levels highlights the differences in what impacts hospital level efficiency based on specific model specifications. Their preferred specification, the Kumbhakar, Ghosh, and McGuckin (1991) model, presents several interesting patterns of technical inefficiency: "teaching hospitals" tend to have higher technical efficiency estimates than "non-teaching hospitals" while hospitals in remote areas are more likely to have higher estimates of technical inefficiency. These results are not just cursory either. A broad view of the preferred estimates suggests that in order for small, non-teaching, or remote hospitals in Queensland to improve their performance, they should be encouraged to increase their occupancy and turnover rates, while maintaining length of stay.

Lai's "Indirect Inference of Stochastic Frontier Models" is a fascinating approach to the estimation of the stochastic frontier model. It is well known that one of the appealing features of the Aigner et al.'s (1977) setup is that with the assumption of noise being normally distributed and inefficiency being Half Normally distributed, their convolution produces a random variable that possesses a skew normal distribution. But beyond the simplicity afforded by these assumptions, there is always the constant wonder if the distributional assumptions on either the noise or inefficiency are correct. With more flexible distributional assumptions come more complicated (even intractable) likelihood functions. There already exist several approaches in this scenario, from maximum simulated likelihood estimation (Greene, 1990) to the fast Fourier transform (Tsionas, 2012). Lai's framework, following from the inference approach of Chen and Wang (2012), uses a series of moment conditions that stem from the characteristic function of the composite error term, which is easy to construct if noise and inefficiency are assumed independent.

Since the characteristic function of a density is unique, this provides a continuum of moment conditions that can be used to recover the unknown parameters from each of the two distributions. Further, Lai shows that all that is needed is residuals estimated via ordinary least squares (OLS). The procedure essentially entails generating simulated datasets for a range of parameter values from the assumed distributions for noise and inefficiency and selecting the parameter values which are closest (in weighted quadratic norm) to the OLS estimates. The challenge here is that one has to engage in simulation to produce these datasets, but all that is needed to estimate the model is the repeated use of OLS.

Our final contribution offers a unique extension to a model that Subal worked on in the late aughts that served as the basis for Parmeter's dissertation, the two-tier stochastic frontier model (Polachek & Yoon, 1987, 1996). This model was initially proposed to capture information deficiencies in models of labor market search for both workers and firms. This led to shortfalls for each side from the optimal level (workers being paid more than the minimum they would work for and firms paying less than the maximum they would pay). An issue with these models is that there was a subtle flavor of bargaining (see Kumbhakar & Parmeter, 2009, 2010), but this was never fully expounded upon in a structural manner. Papadopoulos' "The Nash Bargaining Two-tier Stochastic Frontier Model" is an excellent step in formalizing the usefulness of the two-tier stochastic frontier model in situations where bargaining arises. Rather than treat these two one-sided forces as distinct entities, this model shows how they are connected and arise from a game-theoretic perspective.

Papadopoulos' empirical model brings together elements from axiomatic and strategic bargaining theory and combines static and dynamic aspects of bargaining. A further strength of his model is that he keeps relative bargaining power distinct from private information. This allows econometric identification of both sides of the market and provides an avenue for estimation. This model is tested using separate matched employer–employee datasets from Ghana and Zambia. A useful empirical feature of the model proposed by Papadopoulos is that both intra-error dependence and endogeneity of covariates can be handled, opening up a potentially larger array of applications.

Our brief review here cannot adequately do justice to each of the chapters that appear in this volume. We encourage readers to sit down and properly digest the research here, hopefully with a view toward the remarkable contributions that Subal has made (and will inevitably continue making). All of us have been profoundly inspired by Subal and hope that we have sufficiently portrayed his depth of skill and unique econometric vision in this collection of chapters. Though it is just three simple words, "thank you Subal," we hope that it sums up our appreciation for our mentor, friend, colleague, and coauthor. Enjoy!

NOTES

1. Event: North American Productivity Workshop (NAPW 2023) (iseapa.org).
2. See here https://surface.syr.edu/cpr_campecon/17/.
3. The local linear random forest estimator exploits a random forest model's ability to fit high dimensional non-linear signals to generate adaptive weights for use in a standard local linear regression, thus allaying concerns over dimensionality.

REFERENCES

Ackerberg, D. A., Caves, K., & Frazer, G. (2015). Identification properties of recent production function estimators. *Econometrica*, *83*(6), 2411–2451.

Aigner, D. J., Lovell, C. A. K., & Schmidt, P. (1977). Formulation and estimation of stochastic frontier production functions. *Journal of Econometrics*, *6*(1), 21–37.

Amsler, C., Prokhorov, A., & Schmidt, P. (2014). Using copulas to model time dependence in stochastic frontier models. *Econometric Reviews*, *33*(5–6), 497–522.

Amsler, C., Prokhorov, A., & Schmidt, P. (2016). Endogeneity in stochastic frontier models. *Journal of Econometrics*, *190*, 280–288.

Bloom, N., & Van Reenen, J. (2007). Measuring and explaining management practices across firms and countries. *The Quarterly Journal of Economics*, *122*(4), 1351–1408.

Chamberlain, G. (1982). Multivariate regression models for panel data. *Journal of Econometrics*, *18*(1), 5–46.

Chen, Y.-T., & Wang, H.-J. (2012). Centered-residuals-based moment tests for stochastic frontier models. *Econometric Reviews*, *31*, 625–653.

Diewert, W. E. (2015). Decompositions of productivity growth into sectoral effects. *Journal of Productivity Analysis*, *43*(3), 367–387.

Gandhi, A., Navarro, S., & Rivers, D. A. (2020). On the identification of gross output production functions. *Journal of Political Economy*, *128*(8), 2973–3016.

Glomm, G., & John, A. (2002). Homelessness and labor markets. *Regional Science and Urban Economics*, *32*(5), 591–606.
Greene, W. H. (1990). A gamma-distributed stochastic frontier model. *Journal of Econometrics*, *46*(1–2), 141–164.
Hansen, B. E. (2007). Least squares model averaging. *Econometrica*, *75*(4), 1175–1189.
Hartarska, V., Parmeter, C. F., & Nadolnyak, D. (2011). Economies of scope of lending and mobilizing deposits in microfinance institutions: A semiparametric analysis. *American Journal of Agricultural Economics*, *93*(2), 389–398.
Hausman, J. A. (1978). Specification tests in econometrics. *Econometrica*, *46*(6), 1251–1271.
Henderson, D. J., & Parmeter, C. F. (2016). Model averaging over nonparametric estimators. In R. C. Hill, G. Gonzalez-Rivera, & T.-H. Lee (Eds.), *Advances in econometrics* (Vol. 36, pp. 539–560). Bingley: Emerald.
Jondrow, J., Lovell, C. A. K., Materov, I. S., & Schmidt, P. (1982). On the estimation of technical efficiency in the stochastic frontier production function model. *Journal of Econometrics*, *19*(2–3), 233–238.
King, G., Murray, C. J. L., Salomon, J. A., & Tandon, A. (2004). Enhancing the validity and cross-cultural comparability of measurement in survey research. *American Political Science Review*, *98*, 191–207.
Kumbhakar, S. C., Ghosh, S., & McGuckin, J. T. (1991). A generalized production frontier approach for estimating determinants of inefficiency in US diary farms. *Journal of Business & Economic Statistics*, *9*(1), 279–286.
Kumbhakar, S. C., & Parmeter, C. F. (2009). The effects of match uncertainty and bargaining on labor market outcomes: Evidence from firm and worker specific estimates. *Journal of Productivity Analysis*, *31*(1), 1–14.
Kumbhakar, S. C., & Parmeter, C. F. (2010). Estimation of hedonic price functions with incomplete information. *Empirical Economics*, *39*(1), 1–25.
Levinsohn, J., & Petrin, A. (2003). Estimating production functions using inputs to control for unobservables. *The Review of Economic Studies*, *70*(2), 317–341.
Liu, C.-A. (2015). Distribution theory of the least squares averaging estimator. *Journal of Econometrics*, *186*(1), 142–159.
Millimet, D. L., & Parmeter, C. F. (2022). Accounting for skewed or one-sided measurement error in the dependent variable. *Political Analysis*, *30*(1), 66–88.
Parmeter, C. F., Wang, H.-J., & Kumbhakar, S. C. (2017). Nonparametric estimation of the determinants of inefficiency. *Journal of Productivity Analysis*, *47*, 205–221.
Polachek, S. W., & Yoon, B. J. (1987). A two-tiered earnings frontier estimation of employer and employee information in the labor market. *The Review of Economics and Statistics*, *69*(2), 296–302.
Polachek, S. W., & Yoon, B. J. (1996). Panel estimates of a two-tiered earnings frontier. *Journal of Applied Econometrics*, *11*(2), 169–178.
Santos Silva, J. M. C., & Tenreyro, S. (2006). The log of gravity. *Review of Economics and Statistics*, *88*, 641–658.
Schmidt, P., & Lovell, C. A. K. (1979). Estimating technical and allocative inefficiency relative to stochastic production and cost frontiers. *Journal of Econometrics*, *9*(3), 343–366.
Schmidt, P., & Lovell, C. A. K. (1980). Estimating stochastic production and cost frontiers when technical and allocative inefficiency are correlated. *Journal of Econometrics*, *13*(1), 83–100.
Su, L. and Ullah, A. (2006). Profile likelihood estimation of partially linear panel data models with fixed effects. *Economics Letters*, *92*, 75–81.
Tsionas, E. G. (2012). Maximum likelihood estimation of stochastic frontier models by the Fourier transform. *Journal of Econometrics*, *170*(2), 234–248.
Tsionas, M. G., & Kumbhakar, S. C. (2023). Proxy variable estimation of productivity and efficiency. *Southern Economic Journal*, *89*(3), 885–923.
Zhou, J., Parmeter, C. F., & Kumbhakar, S. C. (2020). Nonparametric estimation of the determinants of inefficiency in the presence of firm heterogeneity. *European Journal of Operational Research*, *286*, 1141–1152.

LETTER FROM DENNIS J. AIGNER

In 1968, I published an article in the *AER* on the theme of the "industry production function." Its primary contribution was to estimate the production function as an envelope of cross-sectional observations on output, labor, and capital rather than the usual "average" that derives from a regression approach. The method used was quadratic programming. This subsequently became known as the production "frontier," with broad applicability to the estimation of technical and economic (allocative) efficiency. And the estimation approach was ultimately shown to be equivalent to a maximum likelihood method applied to a stochastic production function with a one-sided distribution of residuals.

As a graduate student at USC, where I was serving as Department Chair, Subal became interested in this topic. Subsequently, he developed four separate papers that expanded on the efficacy of the stochastic frontier approach for estimating technical and allocative efficiency and its applications. These formed his doctoral dissertation and all were subsequently published in prestigious journals.

Since then, via professorships at UT Austin and SUNY Binghamton, Subal has distinguished himself as the preeminent scholar in his field. His publication record is voluminous, with papers appearing in some of the very best journals devoted to theoretical and applied econometrics, statistics, and productivity analysis. His methodological contributions include dynamic stochastic frontier models and panel stochastic frontier models. With various co-authors, he has tackled a variety of applications of the stochastic frontier model to industries as wide-ranging as the US railroads and airlines; the US, Spanish and Indian banks; Norwegian fisheries and electricity distribution; and Swedish, Finnish, and Norwegian agriculture, to name a few.

Subal continues to be extremely productive in his published research, conference and seminar presentations, professional involvement, and mentoring of international doctoral students. I am grateful for whatever part I may have played in launching his illustrious career but in the final analysis it was his brilliance and drive that explains it all.

Dennis J. Aigner
Professor Emeritus of Economics and Management
University of California, Irvine,
USA

CHAPTER 2

HAUSMAN'S SPECIFICATION TEST FOR PANEL DATA: PRACTICAL TIPS

Badi H. Baltagi

Department of Economics and Center for Policy Research, Syracuse University, USA

ABSTRACT

This chapter revisits the Hausman (1978) test for panel data. It emphasizes that it is a general specification test and that rejection of the null signals misspecification and is not an endorsement of the fixed effects estimator as is done in practice. Non-rejection of the null provides support for the random effects estimator which is efficient under the null. The chapter offers practical tips on what to do in case the null is rejected including checking for endogeneity of the regressors, misspecified dynamics, and applying a nonparametric Hausman test, see Amini, Delgado, Henderson, and Parmeter (2012, chapter 16). Alternatively, for the fixed effects die hard, the chapter suggests testing the fixed effects restrictions before adopting this estimator. The chapter also recommends a pretest estimator that is based on an additional Hausman test based on the difference between the Hausman and Taylor estimator and the fixed effects estimator.

Keywords: Panel data; fixed and random effects; Hausman test; Mundlak regression; Hausman and Taylor estimator; misspecification

JEL classification: C33

Essays in Honor of Subal Kumbhakar
Advances in Econometrics, Volume 46, 13–24

Published under exclusive licence by Emerald Publishing Limited
ISSN: 0731-9053/doi:10.1108/S0731-905320240000046002

1. INTRODUCTION[1]

Hausman's (1978) specification test has been so influential in econometrics and generated a lot of research in economics. Google scholar has more than 25,000 citations as of December 2023. In his seminal paper, Hausman (1978) used endogeneity, measurement error, and panel data as three major applications for his test.

Much has been written on the Hausman test, see early papers like Holly (1982) for a discussion of what null hypothesis is actually being tested using the Hausman test, and 34 years later, the special issue in honor of Hausman in the *Advances of Econometrics* edited by Baltagi, Hill, Newey, and White (2012) and the papers published there. In fact, chapter 1 of that volume by Zapata and Caminita (2012) examines the diffusion of Hausman's econometric ideas using citation counts, citing authors, and source journals of his most referenced citers. They find that his seminal paper (Hausman, 1978) has been cited in over 300 journals and by more than 1,000 authors of various nationalities and languages.

An extensive survey of the Hausman test literature, especially for panel data, is given in chapter 16 of that volume by Amini et al. (2012). This chapter also focuses on the use of the Hausman test in panel data adding some warnings and critiques on how it has been used and giving practical tips for empirical researchers on what to do in case the test rejects the null.

We start by siding with Davidson and MacKinnon (1993) who emphasize that the Hausman test is useful when it does not reject the null, in which case the efficient estimator under the null is supported by the data. If we reject the null, we are detecting misspecification and neither estimator used in the Hausman test is supported by the data. In essence, we do not know what the true model is under the alternative, or equivalently, what is causing the misspecification when the null is not satisfied.

Consider the panel data regression with

$$y_{it} = \alpha + X'_{it}\beta + u_{it} \quad i = 1,\ldots,N; \quad t = 1,\ldots,T \tag{1}$$

where i denotes households, individuals, firms, or countries, while t denotes time. α is a scalar, β is $K \times 1$ and X_{it} is the itth observation on K explanatory variables. Most panel data applications utilize a one-way error component model for the disturbances, with

$$u_{it} = \mu_i + \nu_{it} \tag{2}$$

where μ_i denotes the *unobservable* individual specific effect and v_{it} denotes the remainder disturbance which is independent and identically distributed $\text{IID}(0, \sigma_\nu^2)$. We start by emphasizing that Hausman's (1978) test is a specification test and not a test to choose between fixed and random effects as most panel data applications have used it for. Remember that the null being tested by Hausman is H_0; $E(u_{it} \mid X_{it}) = 0$. This seems like a well-known point, but the practice continues in choosing fixed effects when the Hausman test rejects the null, see, for example, Glick and Rose (2002) for an application to a gravity model examining whether common currency enhances trade.[2] Also, choosing random effects when the Hausman test does not reject the null hypothesis, see, for example, Owusu-Gyapong (1986) for an application to strike activity in 60 Canadian manufacturing industries for the period 1967–1979, to mention only two examples. Although the latter choice is supported by the Hausman test, the former is not necessarily supported by the Hausman test results, as will be clear below.

Under H_0, the random effects estimator, yields a GLS estimator $\hat{\beta}_{GLS}$ which is efficient, see Baltagi (2021, chapter 2) for details. This assumes that μ_i is independent and identically distributed IID $\left(0,\sigma_\mu^2\right)$ and independent of the X_{it} and the v_{it}. However, if $E(u_{it} \mid X_{it}) \neq 0$, $\hat{\beta}_{GLS}$ is inconsistent for β. The null could be violated when the individual effects (the μ_i) are correlated with the X_{it}. For example, in an earnings equation, the μ_i may denote unobservable ability of the individual and this may be correlated with the schooling variable included on the right-hand side of this equation. In this case, the fixed effects estimator or the within estimator $\tilde{\beta}_{Within}$ wipes out these μ_i whether correlated with X_{it} or not, and render the within estimator consistent for β whether H_0 is true or not, see Baltagi (2021, chapter 2) for details. These estimators can be obtained using Stata with the *xtreg* command using the options *re* for random effects and *fe* for fixed effects.[3] The within transformation is denoted by $\tilde{X}_{it,k} = (X_{it,k} - \bar{X}_{i.,k})$ where $\bar{X}_{i.,k} = \sum_{t=1}^{T} X_{it,k} / T$ is the time average for the kth regressor, $k = 1,2,\ldots,K$. The Hausman test statistic is based upon the contrast $\hat{q}_1 = \hat{\beta}_{GLS} - \tilde{\beta}_{Within}$. Under H_0, $\text{plim}\,\hat{q}_1 = 0$, and $\text{cov}(\hat{q}_1, \hat{\beta}_{GLS}) = 0$. The test statistic is given by

$$m_1 = \hat{q}_1'[\text{var}(\hat{q}_1)]^{-1}\hat{q}_1 \tag{3}$$

with

$$\text{var}(\hat{q}_1) = \text{var}(\tilde{\beta}_{Within}) - \text{var}\ (\hat{\beta}_{GLS}). \tag{4}$$

Under H_0, m_1 is asymptotically distributed as χ_K^2 where K denotes the dimension of slope vector β. This test statistic can be obtained using the *hausman* command in Stata after saving the fixed effects and random effects estimates. If the null is not rejected, the Hausman test for panel data supports the random effects efficient estimator, see the Grunfeld (1958) investment application illustrated in Baltagi (2021, pp. 94–96) where the random effects estimator is not rejected by the null. However, if the null is rejected, one does not know the true model under the alternative, that is, what is causing the misspecification. It could be due to the correlation between μ_i and X_{it}, but it could also be due to omitted variables, dynamics, nonlinearities or endogeneity, to mention a few of the causes of misspecification. Hence, under misspecification, the fixed effects estimator is not necessarily consistent. Yet, despite preaching this point in my book on panel data and lectures around the world, one still finds many papers arguing that the fixed effects estimator is supported by the rejection of the Hausman test.

Let us look at specific empirical applications. Cornwell and Trumbull (1994) estimated an economic model of crime using panel data on 90 counties in North Carolina over the period 1981–1987. They rejected the null using the Hausman test based on fixed effects versus random effects and their preferred estimator was the fixed effects estimator. However, when they instrumented for police which is suspected of being endogenous with crime, their fixed effects 2sls estimator yielded insignificant estimates. Baltagi (2006a) applied the Hausman test for fixed effects 2sls versus random effects 2sls to this crime data using the same instruments used by Cornwell and Trumbull (1994) and the null was not rejected. This yielded results that were significant for the efficient random effects 2sls supporting the Cornwell and Trumbull model for crime. This empirical application illustrates that rejecting the usual Hausman test ignoring the endogeneity of police and crime does not necessarily support the fixed effects estimator. Accounting for endogeneity of police, renders fixed effects inconsistent. In this case, instrumenting for police and applying the proper Hausman test, see Baltagi (2004), based on fixed effects 2sls versus random effects 2sls does not reject the null finding significant results for the efficient random effects 2sls estimator for the crime model. This is implemented using Stata commands in Baltagi (2021, pp. 161–166).

Amini et al. (2012) reconsider the static version of the gasoline demand study by Baltagi and Griffin (1983) and show that the random effects estimator which was rejected by the Hausman test could be due to the restrictive parametric specification of the gasoline demand. They show that once neglected nonlinearities are allowed in the model, a nonparametric Hausman test fails to reject the random effects model as the appropriate specification. In fact, they go on to add that while Baltagi and Griffin (1983) opted for dynamic misspecification, Amini et al. (2012) opted for a nonparametric specification. They conclude that: "In either case, when model misspecification is of concern, the outcome of the Hausman test may be misleading." Amini et al. (2012) emphasize the dependence of the Hausman test on the correct parametric specification of the regression function and argue persuasively that one should apply the nonparametric Hausman test developed by Henderson, Carroll, and Li (2008) which does not depend on a priori (correct) parametric specification of the model. Because the nonparametric estimator does not require a priori specification of the conditional mean, the nonparametric Hausman test is robust to model misspecification.

Keane and Runkle (1992) estimate a simple version of the rational expectations life-cycle consumption model using the Panel Study on Income Dynamics (PSID). Due to the dynamics, the within estimator is inconsistent and the standard Hausman test based on the difference between the standard within and GLS estimators is inappropriate. Keane and Runkle show that if one uses the inconsistent within estimates for inference one would get misleading evidence against the life-cycle model. However, based on the Keane and Runkle-2sls estimates which is not rejected by the data, the authors cannot reject the simple life-cycle model.

Hausman (1978) suggested an alternative way of obtaining his contrast test as an artificial OLS regression that yields the Hausman test as a standard F test for the omission of the fixed effects regressors when they are included as additional regressors in the random effects regression. This artificial regression can be used to obtain a Hausman test that is robust to heteroskedasticity and serial correlation, see Baltagi (2021, p. 92). Note that Stata has an *xtoverid* command that computes the Hausman test after running the random effects using the *xtreg* command. However, the robust version produced by this command does not yield the same results as the robust artificial regression described above. Arellano (1993) also provided an alternative variable addition test which results in a Hausman test which is robust to autocorrelation and heteroskedasticity of arbitrary form. However, this version of the robust Hausman test is not commonly used in empirical applications, albeit because the Hausman artificial regression is simpler to apply and robustify, see Baltagi (2021, chapter 4) for several demonstrations of the robust Hausman test using many empirical examples. See also Baltagi and Liu (2007) who give alternative artificial regressions that generate the Hausman test allowing for endogeneity of the regressors. These artificial regressions can be easily robustified to yield robust Hausman tests to autocorrelation and heteroskedasticity of arbitrary form.

Hausman and Taylor (1981) showed that H_0 can be tested using any of the following three paired differences: $\hat{q}_1 = \hat{\beta}_{GLS} - \tilde{\beta}_{Within}$; $\hat{q}_2 = \hat{\beta}_{GLS} - \hat{\beta}_{Between}$; or $\hat{q}_3 = \tilde{\beta}_{Within} - \hat{\beta}_{Between}$. $\hat{\beta}_{Between}$ is the between regression based on averaging the panel regression over time. The corresponding test statistics can be computed as $m_i = \hat{q}_i' V_i^{-1} \hat{q}_i$, where $V_i = \text{var}(\hat{q}_i)$. Under H_0, these Hausman tests are asymptotically distributed as χ^2_K for $i = 1,2,3$. Hausman and Taylor (1981) showed that these tests are numerically exactly identical. One has to be careful in applying these tests in practice. For example, m_3 is based on two estimators, none of which is efficient under the null. This is in fact the test suggested by Mundlak (1978) and in this case, $V_3 = \text{var}(\hat{q}_3) = \text{var}(\tilde{\beta}_{Within}) + \text{var}(\hat{\beta}_{Between})$ and not the difference in variances which is what Stata will report if the *hausman* command is wrongly applied after storing the within and between estimators. Also, m_2 is based on two estimators, none of which is consistent under the alternative, but the test is valid because one is efficient and the other is consistent under the null, and the variance of the difference is the difference in variances under the null, so computing m_2 in Stata yields the right test statistic when the *hausman* command is applied to the between and random effects estimators. Note though, that the Stata output will claim that the between estimator is consistent under the alternative, which is not true. But, this consistency under the alternative is not needed. Remember, the test statistic has the proper distribution only under the null.

2. WHEN DO I SETTLE ON THE FIXED EFFECTS ESTIMATOR IF THE HAUSMAN TEST REJECTS THE NULL?

Section 1 emphasized that rejection of the null means that there is misspecification and one ought to consider it seriously in the analysis. We showed examples where it could have been due to endogeneity, or misspecified dynamics, or due to the restrictive parametric functional form. In these cases, correcting for endogeneity or dynamics or using a nonparametric specification could be the alternative way to proceed rather than reporting the fixed effects estimator as many empirical panel data applications do.

In this section, we argue that if one is intent on reporting the fixed effects estimator as the preferred estimator, why not test the fixed effects restrictions? In fact,

Chamberlain (1982) allowed the unobserved individual effects μ_i to be correlated with X_{it} as follows:

$$\mu_i = X'_{i1}\lambda_1 + .. + X'_{iT}\lambda_T + \varepsilon_i \tag{5}$$

where each λ_t is of dimension $K \times 1$ for $t = 1,2,\ldots,T$. Let $y'_i = (y_{i1},\ldots,y_{iT})$ and $X'_i = (X'_{i1},\ldots,X'_{iT})$ and denote the "reduced form" regression of y'_i on X'_i by

$$y'_i = X'_i\pi + \eta_i \tag{6}$$

The restrictions between the reduced form and structural parameters are given by

$$\pi = (I_T \otimes \beta) + \lambda\iota'_T \tag{7}$$

with $\lambda' = (\lambda'_1,\ldots,\lambda'_T)$. Chamberlain (1982) suggested that estimation and testing be carried out using the minimum chi-square method where the minimand is a χ^2 goodness of fit statistic for the restrictions on the reduced form, see Baltagi (2021, chapter 4). Angrist and Newey (1991) showed that this minimand can be obtained as the sum of T terms. Each term of this sum is simply the degrees of freedom times the R^2 from a regression of the within residuals for a particular period on all leads and lags of the independent variables. Angrist and Newey (1991) illustrate this test using two examples finding the fixed effects restrictions are not rejected for a union-wage empirical application using the National Longitudinal Survey of Youth (NLSY). However, they find that the fixed effects assumption may be inappropriate for a conventional human capital earnings function using the NLSY. Unfortunately, this careful testing of the fixed effects restrictions is not common in practice for those that adopt the fixed effects estimator.

Baltagi, Bresson, and Pirotte (2009) argue that one should run the Chamberlain (1982) test or its simpler Angrist and Newey (1991) alternative to check that the restrictions imposed by a fixed effects model are valid. Their Monte Carlo results show that these tests yield the same decision and are in conflict at most 2.2% of the time. One caveat, is that like the Sargan over-identification test for dynamic panels, the minimum chi-square test tends to understate the true variance of the test statistic as T gets large. This is because as T gets large, the number of testable restrictions increase and the variance of the test statistic is understated. They suggest careful examination of which regressors may or may not be correlated with the individual effects. In this case, one should be willing to entertain a more restricted model where only a subset of the regressors are correlated with the individual effects as proposed by Hausman and Taylor (1981), see Baltagi (2021, chapter 7). This would impose less restrictions than the general Chamberlain model and is also testable with a Hausman test. This will be taken up in the next section.

3. THE MUNDLAK (1978) AND THE HAUSMAN AND TAYLOR (1981) ESTIMATORS

Mundlak (1978) considered the one-way error component regression model given in equations (1) and (2), but he specified a simpler reduced form than that given by Chamberlain (1982) in equation (5). More specifically, Mundlak assumed that the individual effects are a linear function of the averages of *all* the explanatory variables across time:

$$\mu_i = \bar{X}_{i.}'\pi + \varepsilon_i \tag{8}$$

where $\varepsilon_i \sim \text{IIN}(0, \sigma_\varepsilon^2)$ and $\bar{X}_{i.}'$ is $1 \times K$ vector of observations on the explanatory variables averaged over time. Clearly, μ_i is uncorrelated with the explanatory variables if and only if $\pi = 0$. Mundlak (1978) showed that random effects ignore the extra regressors $\bar{X}_{i.}'$, and if $\pi \neq 0$, omission bias renders the random effects estimator biased and inconsistent. In this case, the regression in (1) has to be augmented with the extra regressors $\bar{X}_{i.}'$ and performing OLS or GLS on the resulting augmented regression yields the *fixed effects* (within) estimator for β and the estimator for π yields the contrast $\hat{q}_3 = \tilde{\beta}_{Within} - \hat{\beta}_{Between}$. Hence, a test for $H_0; \pi = 0$ yields another natural derivation for the Hausman test from an artificial regression which adds $\bar{X}$ to equation (1). This is remarkable, since this is published in the same journal *Econometrica* as Hausman's (1978) paper and in the same year. Note that Mundlak applied GLS to this augmented regression since the ε_i replaces the μ_i as the random individual effect. However, Baltagi (2006b) showed that OLS and GLS are equivalent for this augmented regression and researchers use OLS rather than GLS for applying the Mundlak specification in practice.

Mundlak (1978) assumes that *all* the explanatory variables are related to the individual effects. The random effects model on the other hand assumes *no* correlation between the explanatory variables and the individual effects. The random effects model generates the GLS estimator, whereas Mundlak's formulation produces the within estimator. Instead of this "*all* or *nothing*" correlation among the X and the μ_i, Hausman and Taylor (1981) consider a model where some of the explanatory variables are related to the μ_i. In particular, they consider the following model:

$$y_{it} = X_{it}'\beta + Z_i'\gamma + \mu_i + \nu_{it} \tag{9}$$

where the Z_i are cross-sectional *time-invariant* variables. Hausman and Taylor (1981) split X and Z into two sets of variables: $X = [X_u; X_c]$ and $Z = [Z_u; Z_c]$ where X_u is $n \times k_1, X_c$ is $n \times k_2, Z_u$ is $n \times g_1, Z_c$ is $n \times g_2$ and $n = NT$. X_u and Z_u are assumed exogenous in that they are not correlated with μ_i, and ν_{it} while X_c and Z_c are endogenous because they are correlated with the μ_i, but not the ν_{it}. The within transformation would sweep the μ_i and remove the bias, but in the process it would also remove the Z_i and hence the within estimator will not give an estimate of γ. To get around that, Hausman and Taylor suggest an instrumental variable GLS estimator which uses as instruments $[\tilde{X}, \bar{X}_u, Z_u]$. Note that X_u is used twice, once in within form as $\tilde{X}_u$ and another time in averaged form $\bar{X}_u$. This is an advantage of panel data not needing external instruments because of the within and between variation over time of the exogenous X_u. The order condition for identification requires that k_1 the number of variables in X_u must be at least as large as g_2 the number of variables in Z_c. If $k_1 < g_2$, then the equation is under-identified. In this case, the Hausman and Taylor estimator of β is $\tilde{\beta}_{Within}$

and one cannot estimate γ. If $k_1 > g_2$, then the equation is over-identified and the Hausman and Taylor estimator of β is more efficient than the within estimator, and yields an estimator of γ, which was wiped out by the within transformation.

A test for over-identification is obtained by computing the Hausman test based on the contrast between the fixed effects estimator and the Hausman and Taylor estimator. The resulting statistic is distributed as $\chi^2_{k_1-g_2}$ under the null. If the null is not rejected, the Hausman and Taylor estimator is more efficient than the within estimator and the choice of the uncorrelated regressors is not rejected by the data. If the null is rejected, then the Hausman and Taylor estimator is not consistent and the choice of the uncorrelated regressors is not supported by the data.

See extensions of the Hausman and Taylor estimator by Amemiya and MaCurdy (1986) and Breusch, Mizon, and Schmidt (1989). The *xthtaylor* command in Stata computes the standard Hausman and Taylor estimator. If one adds the option *amacurdy* one gets the Amemiya and MaCurdy (1986) estimator. Stata does not compute the Breusch et al. (1989) estimator. If one applies the Hausman test in Stata after storing the fixed effects and Hausman and Taylor estimators, the reported degrees of freedom of the resulting test statistic are incorrect and they should be the degree of over-identification, so the *p*-values reported by Stata are incorrect. One can force the degrees of freedom of the resulting test statistic to be the degree of over-identification by adding the option *df*$(k_1 - g_2)$ in the *hausman* command where you enter the $(k_1 - g_2)$ degrees of freedom by hand. Alternatively, you could issue the *xtoverid* command which yields the proper degrees of freedom after performing the *xthtaylor* command. One could also do the same for the Hausman test after performing the Amemiya and MaCurdy (1986) estimator.

There are several examples of the Hausman and Taylor estimator and its extensions in empirical economics. The first being Cornwell and Rupert (1988) who applied the Hausman & Taylor (1981) as well as the Amemiya and MaCurdy (1986) and the Breusch et al. (1989) methods to a returns to schooling example using the PSID. This empirical example is used to illustrate the *xthtaylor* command in Stata. Baltagi and Khanti-Akom (1990) replicate this study. This application shows that the Hausman test based on the difference between random and fixed effects rejects the null and hence the random effects estimator is not consistent. However, selecting regressors that are uncorrelated with the individual effects yield a Hausman and Taylor estimator that passes Hausman test based on the contrast of these estimates with the fixed effects estimates. This means that the choice of uncorrelated regressors is supported by the data and the Hausman and Taylor estimator is more efficient than the within estimator. Another advantage is that estimates of time-invariant variables like race, gender, and education which are wiped out by the fixed effects estimator are now available using the Hausman and Taylor estimator. This is important, because this gives estimates of the gender wage gap, and allows one to check whether there is race or gender discrimination, and also provides estimates of the returns to schooling, see the implementation of this empirical example in Baltagi (2021, pp. 173–177).

Other applications of the Hausman–Taylor estimator include Contoyannis and Rice (2001) who study the impact of health on wages using the British Household Panel Survey. Egger and Pfaffermayr (2004) who study of the effects of distance as a common determinant of exports and foreign direct investment in a three-factor new trade theory model. Serlenga and Shin (2007) who study the effect of common language on trade using a gravity equation of bilateral trade flows among European countries over the period 1960–2001.

Baltagi, Bresson, and Pirotte (2003) suggest that one should consider the Hausman and Taylor (1981) estimator if one restricts the model misspecification to the correlation between the regressors and the individual effects. This can be done using a *pretest* estimator that reverts to the random effects estimator if the standard Hausman test based on the fixed effects versus the random effects estimators is not rejected. It reverts to the Hausman and Taylor estimator if the choice of strictly exogenous regressors is not rejected by a second Hausman test based on the difference between the fixed effects and Hausman and Taylor estimators. Otherwise, this pretest estimator reverts to the fixed effects estimator which is consistent in this setting since the only misspecification considered is that of correlation between the regressors and individual effects, not endogeneity of another kind or misspecified dynamics or nonlinearities, etc. Monte Carlo experiments showed that this pretest estimator performs well in root mean squared error performance and is always second best to the efficient estimator whether it is fixed effects, random effects, or Hausman and Taylor. See also the extension of this pretest estimator to allow for spatial correlation in the remainder error by Baltagi, Egger, and Kesina (2012). Having recommended the pretest estimator, there is a literature against pretesting including Guggenberger (2010) who argues that if one uses a Hausman test, inference in the second stage will be misleading. Guggenberger (2010) recommends refraining from this pretesting in favor of inference based on the fixed effects estimator. This presumes that the fixed effects estimator is the correct estimator to use no matter what type of misspecification is implied by the rejection of the Hausman test.

An extension of the Hausman and Taylor estimator to allow for serial correlation of the AR(1) type in the remainder disturbances is given by Baltagi and Liu (2012). See also Baltagi, Egger, and Kesina (2016) for an application of the spatial Hausman and Taylor model to firm-level productivity spillovers in China's chemical industry. For an extension of the Hausman and Taylor (1981) estimator using panel data methods that are robust to influential observations, see Baltagi and Bresson (2012). Applying this to the Cornwell and Rupert (1988) earnings equation, Baltagi and Bresson (2012) find that the returns to education estimate seem to be robust to influential observations, while the magnitude and significance of the female coefficient is sensitive to influential observations.

4. CONCLUSION

This chapter warns researchers using the Hausman (1978) test for panel data not to automatically choose the fixed effects estimator when the null is rejected. This estimator is valid when the misspecification is due to the correlation of the individual effects and the regressors. But the null of the Hausman test could be rejected due to other types of misspecification including endogeneity say of police and crime, dynamic misspecification in gasoline demand, or choosing the wrong parametric functional for the estimated equation, to mention a few examples. Section 1 provides alternative solutions to apply in case the null is rejected including correcting for endogeneity using instrumental variables, or adding dynamics to the model which render fixed effects biased especially for short T, or using a Hausman nonparametric test which does not depend on a priori (correct) parametric specification of the model. Section 2 is for the die hard that prefer fixed effects over checking for alternative forms of misspecification. We recommended testing the fixed effects restrictions as suggested by Chamberlain (1982) and Angrist and Newey (1991). Alternatively, Section 3 argues that rather than choosing between fixed effects which assumes that *all* the regressors are correlated with the individual effects and random effects which assumes *none* of the regressors is correlated with the individual effects, one can compute a Hausman and Taylor (1981) estimator that assumes only a subset of the regressors are correlated with the individual effects and this is testable with another Hausman test. We cited empirical examples and left the econometric theory details supporting these results for textbooks like Baltagi (2021) and Hsiao (2003).

Alternatively, Hsiao and Sun (2000, chapter 9) argue that fixed versus random effects specification is better treated as an issue of model selection rather than hypothesis testing. They suggest a recursive predictive density ratio as well as the Akaike and Schwartz information criteria for model selection. Monte Carlo results indicate that all three criteria perform well in finite samples. However, the Schwartz criterion was found to be more reliable of the three.

NOTES

1. This chapter is written in honor of Subal Kumbhakar for his many contributions to econometrics especially in productivity and panel data. On a personal note, I met Subal in Texas when he was at UT-Austin and I was at Texas A&M. We met regularly at Texas Camp econometrics and when we moved to New York, we continued to meet at NY Camp econometrics. We also spent a lot of time together as co-editors of *Empirical Economics* especially at the editorial meetings in Vienna.
2. The Stata commands along with the data set implementing the Hausman test for the gravity equation are given on Rose's website: http://faculty.haas.berkeley.edu/arose.
3. Several examples of the Hausman test are given in Baltagi (2021, chapter 4) using Stata as well as EViews. These include Grunfeld's (1958) investment application, Baltagi and Griffin's (1983) gasoline demand equation, Munnell's (1990) public capital productivity puzzle, to mention a few.

REFERENCES

Amemiya, T., & MaCurdy, T. E. (1986). Instrumental-variable estimation of an error components model. *Econometrica*, *54*, 869–881.

Amini, S., Delgado, M. S., Henderson, D. J., & Parmeter, C. F. (2012). Fixed vs random: The Hausman test four decades later. In B. H. Baltagi, R. Carter Hill, W. K. Newey, & H. L. White (Eds.), *Essays in honor of Jerry Hausman* (Advances in Econometrics, Vol. 29, pp. 479–513). Bingley: Emerald Group Publishing Limited.

Angrist, J. D., & Newey, W. K. (1991). Over-identification tests in earnings functions with fixed effects. *Journal of Business and Economic Statistics*, *9*, 317–323.

Arellano, M. (1993). On the testing of correlated effects with panel data. *Journal of Econometrics*, *59*, 87–97.

Baltagi, B. H. (2004). A Hausman test based on the difference between fixed effects two-stage least squares and error components two-stage least squares, problem 04.1.1. *Econometric Theory, 20*, 223–224.

Baltagi, B. H. (2006a). Estimating an economic model of crime using panel data from North Carolina. *Journal of Applied Econometrics, 21*, 543–547.

Baltagi, B.H. (2006b). An alternative derivation of Mundlak's fixed effects results using system estimation. *Econometric Theory, 22*, 1191–1194.

Baltagi, B. H. (2021). *Econometric analysis of panel data* (6th ed.). Cham: Springer.

Baltagi, B.H. & Bresson, G. (2012). A Robust Hausman–Taylor Estimator. In B. H. Baltagi, R. Carter Hill, W. K. Newey & H. L. White (Eds.), *Essays in honor of Jerry Hausman (Advances in Econometrics, Vol. 29, pp. 175–214)*. Leeds: Emerald Group Publishing Limited.

Baltagi, B. H., Bresson, G., & Pirotte, A. (2003). Fixed effects, random effects or Hausman–Taylor? A pretest estimator. *Economics Letters, 79*, 361–369.

Baltagi, B. H., Bresson, G., & Pirotte, A. (2009). Testing the fixed effects restrictions? A Monte Carlo study of Chamberlain's minimum chi-squared test. *Statistics and Probability Letters, 79*, 1358–1362.

Baltagi, B. H., Egger, P., & Kesina, M. (2012). Small sample properties and pretest estimation of a spatial Hausman–Taylor model. *Advances in Econometrics, 29*, 219–241.

Baltagi, B.H., Egger, P., & Kesina, M. (2016). Firm-level productivity spillovers in China's chemical industry: A spatial Hausman–Taylor approach. *Journal of Applied Econometrics, 31*, 214–248.

Baltagi, B. H., & Griffin, J. M. (1983). Gasoline demand in the OECD: An application of pooling and testing procedures. *European Economic Review, 22*, 117–137.

Baltagi, B. H., Hill, R. C., Newey, W., & White, H. (Eds.). (2012). *Essays in honor of Jerry Hausman* (Advances in Econometrics, Vol. 29). Bingley: Emerald Group Publishing Limited.

Baltagi, B. H., & Khanti-Akom, S. (1990). On efficient estimation with panel data: An empirical comparison of instrumental variables estimators. *Journal of Applied Econometrics, 5*, 401–406.

Baltagi, B. H., & Liu, L. (2007). Alternative ways of obtaining Hausman's test using artificial regressions. *Statistics and Probability Letters, 77*, 1413–1417.

Baltagi, B. H., & Liu, L. (2012). The Hausman–Taylor panel data model with serial correlation. *Statistics and Probability Letters, 82*, 1401–1406.

Breusch, T. S., Mizon, G. E., & Schmidt, P. (1989). Efficient estimation using panel data. *Econometrica, 57*, 695–700.

Chamberlain, G. (1982). Multivariate regression models for panel data. *Journal of Econometrics, 18*, 5–46.

Contoyannis, P., & Rice, N. (2001). The impact of health on wages: Evidence from the British Household Panel Survey. *Empirical Economics, 26*, 599–622.

Cornwell, C., & Rupert, P. (1988). Efficient estimation with panel data: An empirical comparison of instrumental variables estimators. *Journal of Applied Econometrics, 3*, 149–155.

Cornwell, C., & Trumbull, W. N. (1994). Estimating the economic model of crime with panel data. *Review of Economics and Statistics, 76*, 360–366.

Davidson, R., & MacKinnon, J. G. (1993). *Estimation and inference in econometrics*. New York, NY: Oxford University Press.

Egger, P., & Pfaffermayr, M. (2004). Distance, trade and FDI: A Hausman–Taylor SUR approach. *Journal of Applied Econometrics, 19*, 227–246.

Glick, R., & Rose, A. K. (2002). Does a currency union affect trade? The time series evidence. *European Economic Review, 46*, 1125–1151.

Grunfeld, Y. (1958). *The determinants of corporate investment*. Unpublished Ph.D., University of Chicago, Chicago.

Guggenberger, P. (2010). The impact of a Hausman pretest on the size of a hypothesis test: The panel data case. *Journal of Econometrics, 156*, 337–343.

Hausman, J. A. (1978). Specification tests in econometrics. *Econometrica, 46*, 1251–1271.

Hausman, J. A., & Taylor, W. E. (1981). Panel data and unobservable individual effects. *Econometrica, 49*, 1377–1398.

Henderson, D. J., Carroll, R. J., & Li, Q. (2008). Nonparametric estimation and testing of fixed effects panel data models. *Journal of Econometrics, 144*, 257–275.

Holly, A. (1982). A remark on Hausman's specification test. *Econometrica, 50*, 749–759.

Hsiao, C. (2003). *Analysis of panel data*. Cambridge: Cambridge University Press.

Hsiao, C., & Sun, B. (2000). To pool or not to pool panel data. In J. Krishnakumar & E. Ronchetti (Eds.), *Panel data econometrics: Future directions* (pp. 181–198). Amsterdam: North-Holland.

Keane, M. P., & Runkle, D. E. (1992). On the estimation of panel-data models with serial correlation when instruments are not strictly exogenous. *Journal of Business and Economic Statistics*, *10*, 1–9.

Mundlak, Y. (1978). On the pooling of time series and cross-section data. *Econometrica*, *46*, 69–85.

Munnell, A. (1990). How does public infrastructure affect regional economic performance? *New England Economic Review* (September), 3–22.

Owusu-Gyapong, A. (1986). Alternative estimating techniques for panel data on strike activity. *Review of Economics and Statistics*, *68*, 526–531.

Serlenga, L., & Shin, Y. (2007). Gravity models of intra-EU trade: Application of the CCEP-HT estimation in heterogeneous panels with unobserved common time-specific factors. *Journal of Applied Econometrics*, *22*, 361–381.

Zapata, H. O., & Caminita, C. M. (2012). The diffusion of Hausman's econometric ideas. In B. H. Baltagi, R. Carter Hill, W. K. Newey, & H. L. White (Eds.), *Essays in honor of Jerry Hausman* (Advances in Econometrics, Vol. 29, pp. 1–29). Bingley: Emerald Group Publishing Limited.

CHAPTER 3

DO FEDERAL DISABILITY INSURANCE PARTICIPANTS EXAGGERATE THEIR HEALTH PROBLEMS? A STUDY USING ANCHORING VIGNETTES

Kajal Lahiri and Paul Noroski*

Department of Economics, University at Albany: SUNY, Albany NY, USA

ABSTRACT

The authors examine whether or not applicants and recipients of federal disability insurance (DI) inflate their self-assessed health (SAH) problems relative to others. To do this, the authors employ a technique which uses anchoring vignettes. This approach allows them to examine how various cohorts of the population interpret survey questions associated with subjective self-assessments of health. The results of the analysis suggest that DI participants do *inflate the severity of a given health problem, but by a small but significant degree. This tendency to exaggerate the severity of disability problems is much more apparent among those with more education (especially those with a college degree). In contrast, racial minorities tend to underestimate severity ratings for a given disability vignette when compared to their white peers.*

*Paul Noroski, PhD (University at Albany: SUNY) passed away before he could see his publication. At the time of writing this chapter, he was a Lecturer of Economics and Statistics at the University of Pittsburgh.

Essays in Honor of Subal Kumbhakar
Advances in Econometrics, Volume 46, 25–44

ISSN: 0731-9053/doi:10.1108/S0731-905320240000046003

Keywords: Disability insurance; self-assessed health; anchoring vignettes; CHOPIT model; differential item functioning; Health and Retirement Study

JEL classifications: C25; C83; I12; I19

1. INTRODUCTION

While measures of SAH have been lauded for their simplicity and predictive power, they also carry with them several drawbacks.[1] Aside from being prone to random measurement errors, it is not always clear what the self-assessment data measures. Another issue with self-assessment questions on surveys is the difficulty associated with interpersonal comparison of responses. Lack of interpersonal comparability is generally referred to as differential item functioning (or DIF). This phenomenon has been observed and analyzed in various fields, including political science, educational testing, economics, and health. In statistical models of ordered choice (e.g., ordered probit and ordered logit), DIF can be modeled as threshold variation across respondents, see Greene and Hensher (2010). That is, the boundary cut-points between categories can be assumed to vary from one person to the next according to the characteristics of the respondents. However, to identify and estimate threshold heterogeneity without making restrictive assumptions, additional information from the respondent is required. In an influential paper from *Political Science*, King, Murray, Salomon, and Tandon (2004) have suggested techniques using anchoring vignettes for this purpose. A vignette is a short, fictional scenario related to the concept (e.g., health) being measured. Because of their objectivity and impersonal framing of the questions, the vignettes are assumed to be understood in the same way across the population, implying that differences in the ratings of a vignette from person to person are a result of DIF that can be used to adjust the estimation of the main response variable.

Self-reports of health in socio-economic surveys have been routinely used to help estimate models of retirement and disability behavior. Organizations such as the Social Security Administration (SSA) and Health and Human Services are interested study involving the efficacy of their screening process, many of which use self-reported survey data. The SSA's procedure for awarding benefits has been studied directly by Lahiri, Vaughan, and Wixon (1995), Hu, Lahiri, Vaughan, and Wixon (1997), and Benítez-Silva, Buchinsky, and Rust (2005) to name a few. As a result of these and other efforts to model disability, the reliability of self-reported health data has been closely scrutinized. In the context of disability behavior, self-reported health by disability recipients and perspective applicants may understandably suffer from justification bias.[2]

Various efforts to examine the truthfulness of self-reports of disability have been undertaken, but no consensus has been reached. Dwyer, Hu, Vaughan, and Wixon (2003) use SSA earnings data to find that only 55.6% of applicants are correctly classified based upon simple self-assessments. Bound and Burkhauser (1999) suggest that applicants and recipients of DI might have obvious incentives to exaggerate the extent of their work limitations (a form of rationalization bias). Kreider (1999) constructs two measures of the probability of reporting a work limiting disability; one that controls for over-reporting by non-workers and one that does not. He reports that self-reported disability status tends to be over-reported by non-working women, high school dropouts, non-whites, and blue-collar workers. Kerkhofs and Lindeboom (1995) find that among Dutch respondents receiving disability allowances reporting errors are large and systematic.

However, other studies argue that self-reports of disability are likely unbiased, especially in non-governmental surveys where the respondents are sufficiently convinced that their responses will be anonymous and disconnected from granting agencies. For example, Benítez-Silva, Buchinsky, Man Chan, Cheidvasser, and Rust (2004) match self-reported disability from the Health and Retirement Study (HRS) to the SSA's actual award decision to formally test a "rational unbiased reporting" hypothesis which they cannot reject. They find that a large fraction of the population reports truthfully, and that self-reported disability is underestimated as often as it is inflated.

Aside from these concerns, reasons for these disagreements may stem from the nature of the self-reported data itself. SAH data have certain drawbacks due to its subjective nature. Crossley and Kennedy (2002) provide evidence that reliability of self-reported health is associated with income, age, and occupation. Baker, Stabile, and Deri (2004) argue that there is a high degree of error associated with self-assessments of health when compared to matched medical records. Kreider and Pepper (2008) compare subjective self-assessments of work limitation with objective measures of functional limitation. They find that the two indicators "appear to measure markedly different aspects of health status." Sandner and Jungmann (2016) found that the concordance between maternal ratings and children's true health decreases with mother's morbidity and other risk burdens.

Anchoring vignettes have been used to enhance the comparability of self-reported survey responses across various populations. Techniques developed by King et al. (2004) that use information from anchoring vignettes provide a way of examining whether recipients of federal disability treat health-related survey questions any differently than non-recipients. Heiland and Yin (2015), using data from the HRS, find that health professionals (excluding nurses) and disability recipients "tend to classify identical work limitations as more severe" when comparing against other respondents to the survey. They surmise that, having first-hand experience with health and work limitations, recipients of DI "may be more empathetic" than other respondents. But the inclusion of health professionals in the disability group makes the justification bias argument in the self-reports tenuous.

In this chapter, we estimate a model of self-reported disability status which allows the cut-points between response categories (none, mild, moderate, etc.) to vary across individuals. We implement the parametric approach of King et al. (2004) to estimate a model of self-reported disability that is free of DIF including justification bias. Respondents' vignette ratings allow us to estimate the cut-points in each category of individuals to depend on their personal characteristics. This approach simultaneously accomplishes two things. First, it tells us whether being a disability recipient or applicant affects the response scales in reporting their disability levels. Second, it uses this information to estimate the so-called compound hierarchical ordered probit (CHOPIT) model of self-reported disability that produces estimates that are purged of this reporting bias.

The chapter proceeds as follows: In Section 2, we introduce the data including nine disability vignettes used. Section 3 introduces the CHOPIT model that delivers the ordered probit estimates that are robust to DIF. Section 4 reports and interprets our estimates. Finally, conclusions are summarized in Section 5.

2. DATA

The HRS is sponsored by the National Institute on Aging (grant number NIA U01AG009740) and is conducted by the University of Michigan, see HRS (2006). The HRS Disability and Vignette Study (DVS; Health and Retirement Study, 2007) collected information on self-reported disability levels and corresponding vignettes. The self-assessed disability question asked by the DVS is: *Do you have any impairment or health problem that limits the kind or amount of work you can do?* Each respondent answers categorically on the five-point ordered Likert scale: none, mild, moderate, severe, or extreme. After providing this self-assessment, the respondent rates the severity of disability for nine vignettes that exhibit varying degrees of work-limiting disability problems.[3] The complete list of the HRS disability vignettes is as follows:

Disability Vignettes

V1: *Kevin/Lisa suffers from back pain that causes stiffness in his back especially at work but is relieved with low doses of medication. He does not have any pains other than this generalized discomfort.*

V2: *Alice/Charles has almost constant pain in her back and this sometimes prevents her from doing her work.*

V3: *Lisa/Kevin has pain in her back and legs, and the pain is present almost all the time. It gets worse while she is working. Although medication helps, she feels uncomfortable when moving around, holding, and lifting things at work.*

V4: *Anthony/Tamara generally enjoys his work. He gets depressed every three weeks for a day or two and loses interest in what he usually enjoys but is able to carry on with his day-to-day activities on the job.*

V5: *Tom/Sue feels worried all the time. He gets depressed once a week at work for a couple of days in a row, thinking about what could go wrong and that his boss will disapprove of his condition. But he is able to come out of this mood if he concentrates on something else.*

V6: *Tamara/Anthony has mood swings on the job. When she gets depressed, everything she does at work is an effort for her and she no longer enjoys her usual activities at work. These mood swings are not predictable and occur two or three times during a month.*

V7: *Eve/Rob has had heart problems in the past and she has been told to watch her cholesterol level. Sometimes if she feels stressed at work she feels pain in her chest and occasionally in her arms.*

V8: *Mark/Anna has been diagnosed with high blood pressure. His blood pressure goes up quickly if he feels under stress. Mark does not exercise much and is overweight.*

V9: *Anna/Mark has undergone triple bypass heart surgery. She is a heavy smoker and still experiences severe chest pain sometimes.*

Upon reading each vignette, the respondent is asked: "How much is [name] limited in the kind or amount of work he/she could do?" The respondent then marks one of same five categories: none, mild, moderate, severe, or extreme. Note that, compared with the self-assessment, the vignettes questions are not asked in a personal frame of reference to avoid self-justification.

The remaining data used in this chapter were obtained by matching the DVS data with the core of the Health and Retirement Study (2006; see Table 3.1 for variable definitions). These data include information on whether the respondent is an applicant or recipient for supplemental security income (SSI)/DI, gender, chronic health conditions, information on activities of daily living's (ADL), maximum educational attainment, household income, and other demographic controls. After merging the vignette data with the core, the resulting data set contains $N = 4{,}639$ records. Sample averages for the key variables are given for the full sample and for the subsample of disability recipients/applicants separately in Table 3.2.

The HRS identifies if a respondent is either a recipient or applicant of federal DI in the form of DI or SSI. We combine both recipients and applicants for either program into one group of disability behavior. Due to continuing disability reviews, where recipients are often checked for the continuation of the disabling

Table 3.1. Variable Definitions.

RECIP	1 if the respondent is a recipient of (or applicant for) SSI or DI
AGE	Age of respondent in years as of fall 2007
MALE	1 if respondent is male, 0 otherwise
log(INCOME)	log of household income (real US. dollars)
EDU1	1 if highest academic qualification is a high school diploma, 0 otherwise
EDU2	1 if highest academic qualification is some college, 0 otherwise
EDU3	1 if respondent graduated college and possibly attended graduate school, 0 otherwise
MALE	1 if respondent is male, 0 otherwise
RACEBLACK	1 if respondent's race is black, 0 otherwise
RACEOTHER	1 if respondent's race is neither black nor white, 0 otherwise
SINGLE	1 if respondent has never married, 0 otherwise
WID	1 if respondent is widowed, 0 otherwise
DIV\SEP	1 if respondent is divorced or separated, 0 otherwise
HOSP	1 if respondent stayed overnight in hospital in previous two years, 0 otherwise
NUMDOCVIS	Number of doctor's visits the respondent had in the previous two years
HBP	1 if respondent presently has high blood pressure or hypertension, 0 otherwise
DBT	1 if respondent ever had diabetes or high blood sugar, 0 otherwise
CANCER	1 if respondent ever had cancer or a malignant tumor (excluding skin cancer), 0 otherwise
LUNG	1 if respondent has ever had a chronic lung disease (excluding asthma), 0 otherwise
HEART	1 if respondent has ever had a heart attack, angina, or other heart problems, 0 otherwise
STROKE	1 if respondent has ever had a stroke, 0 otherwise
PSY	1 if respondent has ever had emotional, nervous, or psychiatric problems, 0 otherwise
ARTH	1 if respondent is troubled with arthritis, 0 otherwise
SIT	1 if respondent has difficulty sitting for two hours, 0 otherwise
CHAIR	1 if respondent has difficulty getting up from chair, 0 otherwise
STAIRS	1 if respondent has difficulty climbing one flight of stairs, 0 otherwise
DRESS	1 if respondent has difficulty getting dressed, 0 otherwise
WALK	1 if respondent has difficulty walking across room, 0 otherwise
EAT	1 if respondent has difficulty eating (e.g., cutting food), 0 otherwise
BED	1 if respondent has difficulty getting out of bed, 0 otherwise

Table 3.2. Variable Means for Full Sample and Subsample of Disability Recipients.

Variable	Disabled Only ($N = 250$)	Full Sample ($N = 4,639$)
SSI/SSDI Status		
RECIP	1.00	0.054
Demographic/socioeconomic		
Age	61.8	64.2
Male	0.392	0.396
Household income	$35,940	$79,666
Highest Edu: high school	0.296	0.345
Highest Edu: some college	0.264	0.237
Highest Edu: college plus	0.096	0.252
Race: Black	0.248	0.114
Race: Other	0.076	0.053
Medical activity		
Hospital overnight (prev two years)	0.456	0.227
Num doctor visits (prev two years)	17.32	8.962
Chronic health problems		
High blood pressure	0.676	0.514
Diabetes	0.320	0.169
Cancer	0.136	0.128
Chronic lung disease	0.236	0.081
Heart condition	0.400	0.207
Stroke	0.156	0.056
Psychological problems	0.424	0.149
Arthritis	0.776	0.537
ADL		
Trouble sitting for two hours	0.500	0.165
Trouble getting up from chair	0.672	0.357
Trouble climbing one flight of stairs	0.400	0.123
Trouble getting dressed	0.220	0.063
Trouble walking around room	0.184	0.040
Trouble eating	0.072	0.015
Trouble getting out of bed	0.176	0.037

conditions, successful applicants of the DI and SSI programs may have similar incentives to exaggerate their health conditions like the applicants, see Hemmeter and Stegman (2013) for an analysis of continuing disability reviews. Thus, we define a binary indicator RECIP which equals 1 if the respondent is a recipient/applicant of SSI, DI, or both (and equals 0 otherwise). Of the 4,639 sample members in the DVS data set, 250 (or about 5.4%) fall into the category RECIP.[4]

The chronic health conditions are binary variables corresponding to whether or not the sample member has ever had diabetes, a heart condition, a lung condition, an emotional or psychological condition, a stroke, cancer, arthritis, or high blood pressure. Table 3.2 reveals that the subsample of disabled individuals' reports having a higher proportion of these problems than the non-disabled for all eight conditions. The same is true with respect to the ADL controls, the number of doctors' visits, and the binary indicator of overnight hospital stay.

Race is captured with the binary indicators RACEBLACK, RACEOTHER, and WHITE. It's worth mentioning that although respondents who identify themselves as being black make up about 11% of the data set, they make up nearly 25% of the recipient group. Marital status dummies include DIVSEP (divorced/separated), WIDOW (widowed), SINGLE, and MARRIED.

Maximum educational attainment is divided into the four groups NOQUAL, EDU1, EDU2, and EDU3, corresponding to individuals without high school diploma, a high school diploma but no further schooling, some college courses but no college degree, and a college degree or more. An interesting point here is that in the full sample, over 25% of respondents graduated from college, but in the subsample of disability recipients this number drops to 9.6%.

The income variable is the sum total of all household income over the previous calendar year and is measured in real US dollars. Table 3.2 reveals that the sample as a whole has an average household income of \$79,666, which is over twice the average household income of the disabled subsample (\$35,940). To allow for concavity in the relationship between health and income, the natural log of income is used in all regressions.

Table 3.3 shows preliminary evidence of reporting heterogeneity by the sample as a whole (in the first column) and by disability group subsamples (no disability and disabled in the second and third columns). The table reveals how the different groups rate themselves on average, as well as how they rate the problems associated with the vignettes. Note that the ratings of disability severity are scaled from 1 to 5 as none, mild, moderate, severe, or extreme.

As expected, disability recipients report higher average disability problems than non-recipients (3.47 and 1.87 respectively). However, the ratings of the vignettes reveal an interesting pattern. In particular, the members of the disability recipient group report higher severity levels than the non-recipients for seven of the nine vignettes. In other words, the survey respondents who are involved with the SSI/DI programs overestimate the degree of work-limiting problems associated with the vignettes *relative* to the non-recipients. However, unlike in many vignette studies that use multi-country data like SHARE, we do not find huge differences in reporting

Table 3.3. Average Vignette Ratings by Group (SSI/SSDI Recipients and Applicants pooled).

	Full Sample ($N = 4{,}639$)	Not Disabled ($N = 4{,}389$)	SSI/SSDI ($N = 250$)
Self-assessed work-limiting problems	1.958	1.872	3.470
Vignettes: Back problems			
V1	2.459	2.447	2.654
V2	3.685	3.678	3.805
V3	3.629	3.624	3.707
Vignettes: Depression			
V4	2.345	2.334	2.526
V5	2.955	2.957	2.923
V6	3.009	3.009	3.020
Vignettes: Other			
V7 (high cholesterol)	3.177	3.176	3.191
V8 (high blood pressure)	3.202	3.197	3.294
V8 (bypass surgery)	3.858	3.865	3.744

scales of DIF in respondents' assessments. Thus, controlling for DIF is expected to have limited effect on the CHOPIT estimates. It is important to remember that this table provides only a simple comparison without any control for health conditions, demographic and socioeconomic information. The analysis below aims to explore this phenomenon in greater detail.

3. THE MODEL

The overriding objective in this chapter is to examine whether federal disability recipients and non-recipients use different scales when providing categorical self-assessments of their health and disability status. Also, if they do use different scales, we want to explore the consequences of ignoring reporting heterogeneity in a baseline ordered probit model of self-reported disability status.

Both of these goals can be accomplished simultaneously by implementing the parametric approach of King et al. (2004) using a hierarchical ordered probit model. To implement the model, two key assumptions must be made. The first is *vignette equivalence* (VE), which is the assumption that the level of the variable represented by a particular vignette is perceived by all respondents in the same way and on the same scale (apart from random measurement error). The second is *response consistency* (RC), which is the assumption that everyone uses the response categories for a particular survey question in the same way when providing a self-assessment as they do when assessing each of the hypothetical vignette characters. Note that whereas VE is an assumption across respondents, RC is an assumption within each respondent across the vignettes.

King et al. (2004) propose two models (one parametric and one non-parametric) that use the information from anchoring vignettes to identify and estimate DIF in the context of ordered choice models. In this framework, the self-assessments become interpersonally comparable once variation in individual thresholds are controlled for and estimated. Their parametric model, and variants thereof (see e.g., Peracchi & Rossetti 2009) have since been used to control for reporting differences in various applications at relatively low administration costs (Greene, Harris, Knott, & Rice, 2021; King & Wand 2007). Peracchi and Rossetti (2009), and more recently Greene et al. (2021), have suggested two alternative large sample tests for the validity of VE and RC.

King et al. (2004) control for DIF in a model of self-reported political efficacy and show how their method corrects bias resulting from incomparability between Mexican and Chinese response scales. Bonsang and van Soest (2012a, 2012b) use European vignette data to compare self-rated satisfaction levels in the domains of income, jobs, social contracts, and daily activities across 11 countries. After controlling for reporting heterogeneity, they find substantive scaling differences between the countries. Kapteyn, Smith, and van Soest (2007) use internet survey data from the USA and the Netherlands to find that a large part of observed differences in self-reported work disability is due to the difference in response scales between the two countries. Kapteyn et al. (2007) find that, although the raw data implies Americans are significantly less satisfied with their income, after correcting for response scale heterogeneity this difference disappears.

Other applications of vignettes have been conducted in the context of socioeconomic health inequalities. For example, Etilé and Milcent (2006) find substantial evidence of income related reporting heterogeneity with respect to SAH data in France. They suggest collapsing the self-reports of health to two categories ("poor" and "other") to minimize the effects of reporting bias. More recently, Schneider et al. (2012) find socioeconomic and gender related reporting bias with German data.

Using data from the Survey of Health, Ageing, and Retirement in Europe (SHARE), Bago d'Uva, Van Doorslaer, Lindeboom, and O'Donnell (2008) find that higher-educated older Europeans are more likely to rate a given health state negatively and that correcting for these differences generally increases health inequalities. Peracchi and Rossetti (2009) also analyzed the European SHARE data and discovered both gender and regional variation in reported health. However, their analysis revealed that these variations were substantially reduced after controlling for differences in response scales via anchoring vignette analysis. Vonková and Hullegie (2010) and van Kapteyn et al. (2007) argue that techniques which use anchoring vignettes are useful in bringing subjective ratings and their objective counterparts closer together.

Effects of threshold heterogeneity on modeling health disparities have also been examined using data from Asia. For example, Bago d'Uva et al. (2008) find that correcting for threshold heterogeneity tends to reduce estimated disparities in health by education in India and Indonesia and tends to increase these disparities by income in Indonesia, India, and China. Salomon et al (2004) use vignette data from China, Myanmar, Sri Lanka, Pakistan, Turkey, and the UAE to conclude that expectations for mobility decline with age.

In this chapter, the dependent variable is the self-assessed level of work-limiting disability reported in five-category ordered Likert scale. A rich set of regressors are then chosen to maximize the explanatory power of the disability model.[5] Denoting the actual level of unobserved disability for respondent i as y_i^*, we assume that the respondent perceives this level with random standard normal error ε_i, conditional on a set of covariates $\mathbf{x}_i$:

$$y_i^* = \beta_0 + \boldsymbol{\beta}'\mathbf{x}_i + \varepsilon_i, \quad \varepsilon_i \sim N[0,1] \tag{1}$$

Following the notations from Greene and Hensher (2010), the heterogeneity and ordering of the thresholds are specified as:

$$\begin{aligned} &\mu_{i,0} = -\infty, \quad \mu_{i,J} = +\infty \\ &\mu_{i,1} = \lambda_1 + \boldsymbol{\gamma}_1'\mathbf{z}_i \\ &\mu_{i,j} = \mu_{i,j-1} + \exp\left(\lambda_j + \boldsymbol{\gamma}_j'\mathbf{z}_i\right), \quad j = 2,\ldots,J-1 \end{aligned} \tag{2}$$

The self-assessed response is recorded on a J point scale, $j = 1, 2, \ldots, J$. In the absence of more specific information, the set of covariates $\mathbf{z}_i$ is generally assumed to be the same as $\mathbf{x}_i$. The measurement equation is a discrete mapping:

$$y_i = j \quad \text{if} \quad \mu_{i,j-1} < y_i^* \le \mu_{i,j}, \quad j = 1,\ldots,J \tag{3}$$

The assumptions on $\mu_{i,0,\ldots,\mu i,J}$ and variance of σ are standard in the heteroskedastic ordered probit model. Greene and Hensher (2010) have shown that the above model can be rewritten in the following form, incorporating individual heterogeneity in the thresholds by using a set of k exogenous factors $\mathbf{z}_i$ which can be same as $\mathbf{x}_i$:

$$\begin{aligned} y_i^* &= \beta_0 + \boldsymbol{\beta}'\mathbf{x}_i - (\lambda_0 + \boldsymbol{\gamma}_0'\mathbf{z}_i) + \varepsilon_i \\ \tau_{i,-1} &= -\infty, \tau_{i,0} = 0, \tau_{i,J} = +\infty \\ \tau_{i,j} &= \tau_{i,j-1} + \exp(\lambda_j + \boldsymbol{\gamma}_j'\mathbf{z}_i), \quad j = 1,\ldots,J-1 \\ y_i &= j \quad \text{if} \quad \tau_{i,j-1} < y_i^* \leq \tau_{i,j}, \quad j = 1,\ldots,J \end{aligned} \tag{4}$$

The log likelihood function of the self-assessment model can be written as:

$$\log L_A = \sum_{i=1}^{N} \log \sum_{j=0}^{J} B_{i,j} \begin{bmatrix} \Phi(\tau_{i,j} - (\beta_0 + \boldsymbol{\beta}'\mathbf{x}_i - \lambda_0 - \boldsymbol{\gamma}_0'\mathbf{z}_i)) - \\ \Phi(\tau_{i,j-1} - (\beta_0 + \boldsymbol{\beta}'\mathbf{x}_t - \lambda_0 - \boldsymbol{\gamma}_0'\mathbf{z}_i)) \end{bmatrix} \tag{5}$$

where $B_{i,j}$ equals 1 if $y_i = j$, and 0 otherwise.

The model containing the vignettes is as follows: Let the actual level for the hypothetical individual described in the vignette m be θ_m, $m = 1, \ldots, M$. The assumption VE means $\theta_m = \theta$ for all m. The latent regression using all the vignettes is:

$$w_{m,q}^* = \theta_m + \sigma e_{mq} \quad \text{where} \quad e_{mq} \sim N[0, 1] \tag{6}$$

The vignettes are assumed to have the same set of responses as the self-assessment model. The responses to the vignette questions are specified as follows:

$$\begin{aligned} w_{m,q}^* &= \theta_m - (\lambda_0 + \boldsymbol{\gamma}_0'\mathbf{z}_m) + \sigma e_{mq} \\ \tau_{-1,q} &= -\infty, \quad \tau_{0,q} = 0, \quad \tau_{J,q} = +\infty \\ \tau_{j,q} &= \tau_{j-1,q} + \exp(\lambda_j + \boldsymbol{\gamma}_j'\mathbf{z}_q), \quad j = 1,\ldots,J-1 \\ w_{m,q} &= j \quad \text{if} \quad \tau_{j-1,q} < w_{m,q}^* \leq \tau_{j,q}, \quad j = 1,\ldots,J \end{aligned} \tag{7}$$

The thresholds are constrained to match those for the self-assessment equation. The anchoring aspect of the vignettes is obtained by the constraint that the same (λ_j, γ_j) appears in the vignettes and the self-assessment models. The log likelihood for the vignettes part of the model is:

$$\log L_V = \sum_{q=1}^{Q} \sum_{m=1}^{M} \log \sum_{j=0}^{J} B_{q,j,m} \begin{bmatrix} \Phi\left\{\frac{1}{\sigma}\left[\tau_{j,q} - (\theta_m - (\lambda_0 - \boldsymbol{\gamma}_0'\mathbf{z}_q))\right]\right\} - \\ \Phi\left\{\frac{1}{\sigma}\left[\tau_{j-1,q} - (\theta_m - (\lambda_0 - \boldsymbol{\gamma}_0'\mathbf{z}_q))\right]\right\} \end{bmatrix} \tag{8}$$

with parameters $(\theta_1,\ldots,\theta_M, \sigma)$. We can now put together the likelihood functions of the self-assessment equation and that of the vignettes in order to exploit the anchoring vignettes restrictions in terms of the cross-equation restrictions for the parameter vector $(\lambda_j, \gamma_j, j = 0, 1, \ldots, J-1)$.

$$\log L = \sum_{i=1}^{N} \log \sum_{j=0}^{J} B_{i,j} \left[\begin{array}{l} \Phi\left(\tau_{i,j} - (\beta_0 - \lambda_0) - \left(\boldsymbol{\beta}'^{\mathbf{x}_t} - \gamma_0'^{\mathbf{z}_i}\right)\right) - \\ \Phi\left(\tau_{i,j-1} - (\beta_0 - \lambda_0) - \left(\boldsymbol{\beta}'\mathbf{x}_t - \gamma_0'\mathbf{z}_i\right)\right) \end{array} \right]$$

$$+ \sum_{q=1}^{Q} \sum_{m=1}^{M} \log \sum_{j=0}^{J} B_{q,j,m} \left[\begin{array}{l} \Phi\left\{\frac{1}{\sigma}\left[\tau_{j,q} - (\theta_m - \lambda_0) - \gamma_0'\mathbf{z}_q\right]\right\} - \\ \Phi\left\{\frac{1}{\sigma}\left[\tau_{j-1,q} - (\theta_m - \lambda_0) - \gamma_0'\mathbf{z}_q\right]\right\} \end{array} \right] \tag{9}$$

In this model, γ_0 and $\boldsymbol{\beta}$ are identifiable and estimable. However, as long as β_0 is non-zero, λ_0 is not identifiable, see Greene and Hensher (2010). In our estimation, we set $\beta_0 = 0$, and instead estimated the intercepts for the threshold equations.

We estimate the above model with maximum likelihood methods in R using the *anchors* package (Wand, King, & Lao, 2016). Finally, a traditional ordered probit (which uses no information from the vignettes) is run as a baseline model for comparison. The coefficients between the ordered probit and CHOPIT models are directly comparable since the two models are scaled in the same way.

4. ESTIMATION RESULTS

To reiterate, we study the reporting behavior of federal disability recipients, we estimate a model of self-reported disability with categorical cut-points that vary with respondent characteristics. Identification is achieved through the use of anchoring vignettes. Among the covariates that determine the cut-point estimates is an indicator of whether or not the respondent is a recipient or applicant of SSI or DI. The estimates of the model are presented in Tables 3.4 and 3.5, with graphs of the cut-point distributions in Figs. 3.1 and 3.2.[6]

4.1. The Effects of DIF Correction

The columns of estimates given in Table 3.4 correspond to a traditional ordered probit (where thresholds between categories are assumed to be identical for all respondents) and a CHOPIT (where thresholds may vary with a respondent's characteristics). The estimates of the parameters in the CHOPIT specification may be viewed as being adjusted for DIF or "DIF-free" estimates in the sense that reporting heterogeneity has been controlled for, making the self-reports of disability comparable across individuals.

Since the dependent variable is self-reported disability, a positive sign on the coefficient of a covariate in Table 3.4 corresponds to a positive association with

Table 3.4. Coefficient Estimates for Ordered Probit and HOPIT Models of Self-reported Disability.[a]

Variable	Ordered Probit		CHOPIT	
	Coefficient	*S.E.*	*Coefficient*	*S.E.*
Fed DI				
RECIP	0.790	0.077***	0.738	0.079***
Socioeconomic status				
Log(INCOME)	−0.099	0.021***	−0.111	0.022***
EDU1	−0.008	0.051	−0.131	0.053**
EDU2	0.009	0.056	−0.062	0.058
EDU3	−0.125	0.059**	−0.242	0.061***
Demographic				
MALE	0.263	0.038***	0.194	0.039***
AGE	0.013	0.002***	0.013	0.002***
RACEBLACK	−0.019	0.056	−0.031	0.059
RACEOTHER	0.061	0.081	0.040	0.085
SINGLE	0.003	0.116	0.009	0.122
WIDOW	0.047	0.057	−0.027	0.060
DIVSEP	−0.082	0.062	−0.030	0.065
Health controls				
HBP	0.101	0.037***	0.062	0.039
DBT	0.133	0.046***	0.144	0.048***
CANCER	0.075	0.051	0.122	0.053**
LUNG	0.410	0.060***	0.410	0.063***
HEART	0.182	0.044***	0.233	0.046***
STROKE	0.125	0.072*	0.197	0.075***
PSYCHE	0.276	0.049***	0.257	0.051***
ARTHRITIS	0.342	0.038***	0.292	0.040***
SIT	0.272	0.049***	0.232	0.052***
CHAIR	0.372	0.041***	0.333	0.043***
STAIRS	0.568	0.057***	0.638	0.059***
DRESS	0.296	0.075***	0.259	0.078***
WALK	0.298	0.094***	0.232	0.097**
EAT	0.196	0.139	0.163	0.144
BED	0.026	0.094	−0.056	0.097
HOSP	0.264	0.042***	0.268	0.044***
DOCVIS	0.004	0.001***	0.004	0.001***

[a] In both models, the dependent variable is the ordered categorical self-reported work-limiting disability level of the HRS respondent. A traditional ordered probit is used as the baseline to compare with the DIF-corrected CHOPIT estimates. CHOPIT refers to the CHOPIT (i.e., the parametric method used in King et al., 2004).

* indicates significance at the 10% level, ** at the 5% level, and *** at the 1% level.

disability. Notice that most of the coefficients have the expected signs in both models. In particular, chronic health problems, difficulty with ADL's, and being a recipient of SSI/DI have a positive association with self-reported disability, while the opposite is true for household income and maximum educational status. With respect to the demographic variables, the two versions of the model agree that being a male is positively and significantly associated with disability level, as is respondent age.

Table 3.5. Threshold Model Coefficients for Self-reported Disability.

Variable	Threshold Coefficients							
	Cut 1		*Cut 2*		*Cut 3*		*Cut 4*	
	COEF	*S.E.*	*COEF*	*S.E.*	*COEF*	*S.E.*	*COEF*	*S.E.*
RECIP	**−0.082**	**0.042**	0.043	0.046	0.007	0.032	0.026	0.035
Log(INCOME)	−0.014	0.010	0.001	0.012	0.010	0.008	**0.020**	**0.010**
EDU1	**−0.175**	**0.024**	**0.071**	**0.029**	**0.051**	**0.020**	**0.086**	**0.024**
EDU2	**−0.112**	**0.026**	0.057	0.031	0.006	0.022	**0.104**	**0.026**
EDU3	**−0.217**	**0.027**	**0.211**	**0.032**	0.044	0.023	**0.118**	**0.027**
MALE	**−0.060**	**0.018**	−0.023	0.021	−0.022	0.015	0.020	0.017
AGE	**0.003**	**0.001**	**−0.009**	**0.001**	0.001	0.001	**0.003**	**0.001**
RACEBLACK	**0.096**	**0.026**	**−0.170**	**0.032**	**−0.168**	**0.023**	**−0.125**	**0.025**
RACEOTHER	**0.071**	**0.036**	**−0.202**	**0.046**	**−0.069**	**0.032**	**−0.087**	**0.035**
SINGLE	**0.103**	**0.051**	**−0.242**	**0.069**	−0.003	0.045	0.018	0.049
WIDOW	−0.017	0.028	0.000	0.033	0.003	0.023	0.018	0.027
DIVSEP	**0.100**	**0.028**	**−0.118**	**0.034**	−0.010	0.024	0.020	0.028
HBP	**−0.063**	**0.017**	**0.051**	**0.020**	0.012	0.014	0.030	0.017
DBT	−0.007	0.022	0.010	0.026	0.027	0.018	0.022	0.021
CANCER	**0.077**	**0.024**	−0.054	0.029	−0.024	0.020	0.042	0.023
LUNG	−0.047	0.031	0.024	0.035	**0.065**	**0.024**	0.018	0.029
HEART	**−0.053**	**0.022**	0.002	0.025	0.000	0.017	−0.021	0.021
STROKE	0.049	0.036	0.029	0.041	−0.004	0.029	0.053	0.034
PSYCHE	−0.033	0.024	0.028	0.027	−0.021	0.019	0.026	0.023
ARTHRITIS	**−0.089**	**0.018**	**0.089**	**0.021**	**0.043**	**0.015**	0.015	0.017
SIT	−0.028	0.025	−0.039	0.029	0.003	0.020	**0.084**	**0.023**
CHAIR	**−0.062**	**0.021**	**0.061**	**0.023**	−0.010	0.017	−0.035	0.019
STAIRS	**0.093**	**0.029**	−0.052	0.033	0.019	0.023	−0.016	0.027
DRESS	−0.035	0.040	−0.002	0.045	0.012	0.030	−0.020	0.035
WALK	**−0.194**	**0.054**	**0.138**	**0.057**	**0.072**	**0.037**	−0.086	0.044
EAT	−0.011	0.077	0.091	0.081	−0.101	0.058	−0.120	0.065
BED	−0.087	0.052	0.031	0.055	0.022	0.038	−0.067	0.044
HOSP	0.010	0.021	0.014	0.023	**−0.045**	**0.017**	−0.003	0.019
DOCVIS	0.000	0.001	0.000	0.001	−0.001	0.000	−0.001	0.001
CONSTANT	0.406	0.275	0.217	0.148	**−0.275**	**0.107**	**−0.483**	**0.125**

Note: Bold type indicates significance at the 5% level.

Comparing the columns of Table 3.4, we see that the DIF correction does not lead to any changes in the signs of coefficient estimates (except in a few cases where the coefficient estimates are insignificant). However, the magnitudes change in several cases. The most notable example occurs with the variable EDU1, which is significant only under the CHOPIT specification, implying that the negative association between disability levels and having a high school diploma is masked when reporting heterogeneity is not controlled for. In general, the coefficients on log of household income and the education indicators increase in magnitude under the CHOPIT specification; notably, the coefficient for having a college

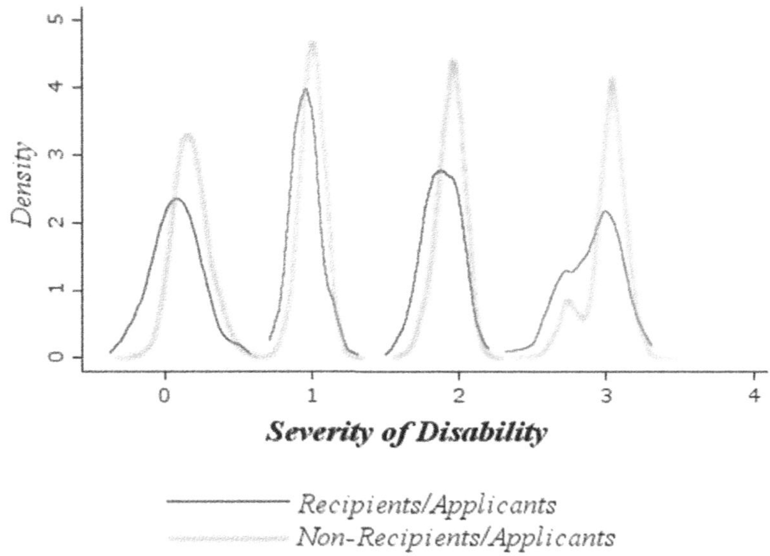

Fig. 3.1. Comparison of Disability Ratings for DI/SSI Recipients and Non-recipients.

degree nearly doubles. In contrast, DIF correction *decreases* the magnitude of the coefficient estimates for RECIP and MALE, indicating that models which fail to control for reporting differences may overestimate the effect of gender and receipt status on self-reported health.

4.2. Threshold Analysis

The differences in the columns of Table 3.4 can be explained (at least in part) by the threshold equation coefficient estimates in Table 3.5. Since the categories in the dependent variable represent severity levels of work-limiting problems (with higher values associated with greater disability), the signs of the estimates in Table 3.5 have the following interpretation: A positive coefficient on a covariate for the first cut-point equation (corresponding to the difference between *no problem* and *mild problem*) indicates that this covariate pushes the threshold to the right, which in turn translates to a less severe rating of a given disability problem. Because of the exponential specification of the threshold equations, the interpretation of cut-points 2–4 is somewhat different.

The covariate RECIP from the threshold model is of particular interest. Recall that this is a binary variable that equals 1 if the respondent is a recipient/applicant of SSI or DI, and 0 otherwise. The main observation in Table 3.5 is that the coefficient on RECIP is negative and significant at the 5% level for the first threshold (between categories *no problem* and *mild problem*). This substantiates the preliminary evidence from Table 3.3 which showed a tendency of disability recipients to over-report a given disability on average. This covariate, however, does not

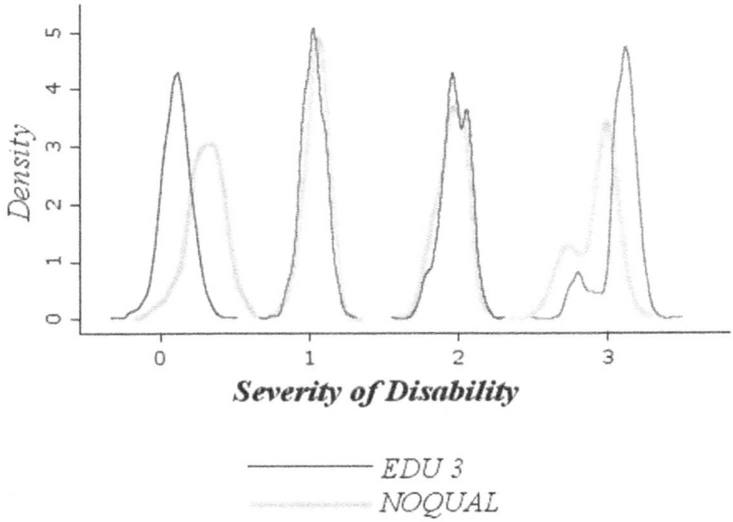

Fig. 3.2. Comparison of Disability Ratings for College Grads and High School Non-Grads.

appear to have any significant effects on any of the other thresholds. Kapteyn et al. (2007) argue that in the simple binary sense of disability (i.e., disabled vs not disabled), there surely is not much difference between being severely disabled and being extremely disabled. However, the difference between having no disability and having a mild disability could be consequential. By this reasoning, recipients and applicants of federal disability *do* appear to over-report a given disability problem in the region where it counts most, but only by a small amount.

To get a clearer picture of the CHOPIT estimation results, Fig. 3.1 overlays the distributions of the threshold estimates for the two groups: RECIP = 1 and RECIP = 0. The significance in the threshold coefficient estimates (mentioned above) substantiate the difference between the two distributions in Fig. 3.1. For each threshold, the CHOPIT gives very similar distribution estimates for both groups. Overall, the thresholds of the disabled are positioned only slightly to the left of those for the non-disabled, indicating perhaps a small tendency of the disabled to over-report. However, the small (and mostly insignificant) coefficients on RECIP in Table 3.5 suggest that the variable is relatively unimportant in explaining reporting differences.

Other variables that have significant effects on reporting behavior in this model include education, gender, age, and race. For parsimony, we concentrate on the first cut-point equation estimates in Table 3.5. The education variables (EDU1–EDU3) have significantly negative (and relatively large) coefficients on the first threshold, implying that the educated are more likely to rate a given disability scenario as being at least a mild problem as opposed to being no problem at all. Having a college degree (EDU3) has a particularly large effect on this first threshold, a result that is reinforced by the corresponding threshold distributions plotted in Fig. 3.2. This finding that higher education is associated with lower disability thresholds is in agreement with the analysis of Kapteyn et al. (2007) who arrive at this conclusion in their comparison of the USA and Dutch self-reported disability.

Being a male also has a negative effect on the first threshold, but to a lesser degree than we see with education. In contrast, being a racial minority has an estimated positive effect on the first cut-point. That is, respondents who identify their race as non-white are more likely to rate a given disability problem as being "no problem" as opposed to being a "mild problem." This result may seem to contradict the results in Table 3.2 where we found that relatively more blacks (25%) are on the disability rolls compared to blacks in the general population (11%). Lahiri, Song, and Wixon (2008) have shown that this is explained by their vulnerable economic circumstances and relative bad health. Income appears to have little effect on reporting behavior in this sample.

Testing the validity of the VE and RC assumptions are important for the credibility of the DIF-adjusted estimates. Both Peracchi and Rossetti (2013) and Greene et al. (2021) found evidence against these critical assumptions in their CHOPIT models for pain using European SHARE data. Peracchi and Rossetti (2013) suggested a χ^2 test for the overidentifying restrictions in a minimum distance estimation implied by the VE and RC assumptions. The χ^2 statistic is simply the sample size times the minimum distance criterion evaluated at the optimal parameter value. Greene et al. (2021) suggested an alternative χ^2 score test but needs alternative normalizations to ensure full identification under the alternative. The code is conveniently available as a GAUSS program in http://github.com/aptech/chopitlib. Given number of explanatory variables (6), number of vignettes (3) and number of ordered response categories (4), the number of overidentifying restrictions is around 30 in their models given alternative scaling and normalizations.

The dimensions of our disability CHOPIT model is considerably larger with 9 vignettes, 29 explanatory variables, and 5 response categories giving over 1,033 overidentifying restrictions. This is because the 10 reduced form regressions (9 vignettes and 1 SAH response) with 29 covariates in each yields 1,200 reduced form estimates. The imposition of VE and RC implies that there are 167 free parameters that can be recovered from the minimum distance estimation. This gives 1,033 overidentifying restrictions, given the usual required location and scale normalizations. In our empirical case, the χ^2 values were calculated as 559.45 and 600.35 for the Peracchi–Rossetti and Green et al. χ^2 test statistics respectively for testing VE and RC jointly. But, with this high degrees of freedom over 1,000, the validity of the VE and RC assumptions in our empirical context is accepted easily at any reasonable levels of significance. Our conclusion remained unchanged even when we dropped vignettes V5 and V9 for which the disability recipients underestimated the extent of disability compared with the non-disabled and used only the remaining seven vignettes in estimating the CHOPIT model and testing the validity of VE and RC jointly. As both Peracchi and Rossetti (2013) and Greene et al. (2021) have the found, in empirical applications, the assumption of VE tend to be more restrictive than RC because the former involves interpersonal comparisons often across different cultures. Our positive result can be explained in view of our well specified response and vignettes equations using 29 widely used variables defined over a sample of only one country.

5. CONCLUSIONS

This chapter examines differences in the reporting behavior of US self-assessed disability status between respondents who have applied for and recipients of US. disability programs and those who are not involved with the programs. Adjustments using anchoring vignettes are applied to a standard self-reported disability model to examine and control for the effects of reporting heterogeneity using the HRS's Disability Vignette Survey. Included in the analysis is an indicator of whether a respondent is a recipient (or an applicant) of federal DI programs as a shifter of threshold variation.

The main results presented in this research suggest that applicants and recipients of federal disability tend to slightly over-report the severity of a given work-limiting condition, especially in the milder regions of disability continuum. Based on their vignette ratings alone, recipients of federal disability give higher severity ratings to 7 of 9 disability vignette scenarios when compared to other respondents. A parametric model of disability reveals that this tendency of DI/SSI recipients to over-report the level of their problems persists even after controlling for socio-economic status, chronic health conditions, and difficulties associated with ADL. Respondents receiving or applying for DI have an increased probability of rating a given condition as being mildly disabling as opposed to being not at all disabling. However, it should be noted that this tendency to exaggerate the severity of disability problems is much more apparent among those with more education (and especially among those with a college degree). The more educated workers are possibly better positioned to represent their disabilities to the social security adjudicators, often using disability lawyers. In contrast, and most remarkably, the analysis suggests that racial minorities tend to underestimate severity ratings for a given disability vignette when compared to their white peers. This evidence seems to contradict popular myth that the minorities game the system because relatively more minorities apply and receive disability benefits.

In addition to measuring the effects of personal characteristics on threshold variation, the model allows us to estimate the way in which reporting differences affect estimates in a general model of self-reported disability. In this regard, it is found that having a high school diploma has a positive association with health (i.e., a negative association with disability) that goes unnoticed under traditional specifications which do not control for threshold variation. In general, the simpler models of self-reported disability (i.e., those with constant thresholds) tend to underestimate the contributions of income and education but overestimate the contributions of respondent gender and federal disability recipient status.

The analysis of this chapter reveals that reporting heterogeneity has the potential to affect the magnitude and significance of various components of self-reported disability. Future models of self-reported disability should consider controlling for reporting bias before making any conclusions.

NOTES

1. See Lahiri and Pulungan (2007) for an early summary of the use of SAH in health economics, and Lahiri and Pulungan (2021) for a recent application. Sen (2002) has argued that public health decisions should be responsive to patients' own understanding of their health, and not merely only on alternative external views.

2. When systematic underestimation or overestimation in a response variable is suspected like the number of infections and deaths during the COVID-19 pandemic, Millimet and Parmeter (2022a) have worked a novel extension of the Susceptible-Infected-Recovered (SIR) epidemiological model with one-sided measurement errors that resemble that of the classic stochastic frontier analysis (SFA), see also Millimet and Parmeter (2022b). Kumbhakar and Lovell (2000) includes a classic introduction to the SFA literature.

3. The vignette information was not asked in any other HRS survey wave.

4. Preliminary analysis keeping these two groups separate produced very similar results. Since the percentages of disabled are quite small, combining recipients and applicants of federal aid results in a more respectable total count.

5. In this regard, we largely follow the specification of Benítez-Silva (2004), which was based on HRS, to facilitate comparison with that work.

6. Of the 5,678 HRS sample members that were initially selected to participate in the vignette study, we noticed that the 1,039 who opted not to return the survey had somewhat different socioeconomic characteristics than the 4,639 who did return them. To buffer the effects of selection bias, we ran all regressions with an inverse Mills ratio term included among the covariates. These regressions indicated that the effects of the selection bias were negligible. As a result, the estimates presented in this chapter are those obtained without the inverse Mills ratio term.

ACKNOWLEDGMENTS

This research was supported by the National Institute on Minority Health and Health Disparities, National Institutes of Health (grant number 1 P20 MD003373). The content is solely the responsibility of the authors and does not represent the official views of the National Institute on Minority Health and Health Disparities or the National Institutes of Health.

REFERENCES

Bago d'Uva, T., Van Doorslaer, E., Lindeboom, M., & O'Donnell, O. (2008). Does reporting heterogeneity bias the measurement of health disparities? *Health Economics*, *17*, 351–375.

Baker, M., Stabile, M., & Deri, C. (2004). What do self-reported, objective measures of health measure? *The Journal of Human Resources*, *39*(4), 1067–1093.

Benítez-Silva, H., Buchinsky, M., Man Chan, H., Cheidvasser, S., & Rust, J. (2004). How large is the bias in self-reported disability? *Journal of Applied Econometrics*, *19*(6), 649–670.

Benítez-Silva, H., Buchinsky, M., & Rust, J. (2005). *How large are the classification errors in the social security disability award process?*. NBER Working Paper 10219.

Bonsang, E. & Van Soest, A. (2012a). Satisfaction with job and income among older individuals across European countries, *Social Indicators Research*, *105*, 227–254.

Bonsang, E. & Van Soest, A. (2012b). Satisfaction with social contacts of older Europeans, *Social indicators research*, *105*, 273–292.

Bound, J., & Burkhauser, R. (1999). Economic analysis of transfer programs targeted on people with disabilities. In O. Ashenfelter & D. Card (Eds.), *Handbook of labor economics* (Vol. 3C, pp. 3417–3528). Amsterdam: Elsevier Science.

Crossley, T. F., & Kennedy, S. (2002). The reliability of self-assessed health status. *Journal of Health Economics*, *21*(4), 643–658.

Dwyer, D., Hu, J., Vaughan, D. R., & Wixon, B. (2003). Counting the disabled: Using survey self-reports to estimate medical eligibility for social security's disability programs. *Journal of Economics and Social Measurement*, *20*(2002/2003), 109–142.

Etilé, F. & Milcent, C. (2006). Income-related reporting heterogeneity in self-assessed health: evidence from France. *Health Economics, 15*(9), 965–81.

Greene, W. H., Harris, M. N., Knott, R. J., & Rice, N. (2021). Specification and testing of hierarchical ordered response models with anchoring vignettes. *Journal of the Royal Statistical Society, Series A*, *184*, 31–64.

Greene, W., & Hensher, D. A. (2010). *Modeling ordered choices: A primer*. Cambridge: Cambridge University Press.

Health and Retirement Study. (2006). *Core data 2006 (Final V1.0) public use data set*. Produced and distributed by the University of Michigan with funding from the National Institute on Aging (grant number NIA U01AG009740). Ann Arbor, MI (2007).

Health and Retirement Study. (2007). *Disability Vignette Survey (DVS) (Final V1.0) public use data set*. Produced and distributed by the University of Michigan with funding from the National Institute on Aging (grant number NIA U01AG009740). Ann Arbor, MI (2007).

Heiland, F., & Yin, N. (2015). Anchoring vignettes in the Health and Retirement Study: How do medical professionals and disability recipients characterize the severity of work limitation? *PLoS One*, *12*(5), e0126218.

Hemmeter, J. & Stegman, M. (2013). Subsequent Program Participation of Former Social Security Disability Insurance Beneficiaries and Supplemental Security Income Recipients Whose Eligibility Ceased Because of Medical Improvement. *Social Security Bulletin 73*(2), 1–38.

Hu, J., Lahiri, K., Vaughan, D. R., & Wixon, B. (1997). A structural model of social security's disability determination process. *The Review of Economics and Statistics*, *83*(2), 348–361.

Kapteyn, A., Smith, J. P., & van Soest, A. (2007). Vignettes and self-reported work disability in the US and the Netherlands. *American Economic Review*, *97*(1), 461–473.

Kerkhofs, M., & Lindeboom, M. (1995). Subjective health measures and state dependent reporting errors. *Health Economics*, *4*(3), 221–235.

King, G., Murray, C. J. L., Salomon, J. A., & Tandon, A. (2004). Enhancing the validity and cross-cultural comparability of measurement in survey research. *American Political Science Review*, *98*(1), 191–207.

King, G. & Wand, J. (2007). Comparing Incomparable Survey Responses: New Tools for Anchoring Vignettes." *Political Analysis*, *15*, 46–66.

Kreider, B. (1999). Latent work disability and reporting bias. *Journal of Human Resources*, *34*(4), 734–769.

Kreider, B., & Pepper, J. (2008). Inferring disability status from corrupt data. *Journal of Applied Econometrics*, *23*(3), 329–349.

Kumbhakar, S., & Lovell, K. (2000). *Stochastic frontier analysis*. Cambridge: Cambridge University Press (Paperback version, 2003).

Lahiri, K., & Pulungan, Z. (2007). Income related health disparity and its determinants in New York State: Racial/ethnic and geographical comparisons. In B. Wallace (Ed.), *Toward equity in health: A new global approach to inequities in health* (pp. 97–127). New York, NY: Springer.

Lahiri, K., & Pulungan, Z. (2021). Racial/ethnic health disparity in the U.S.: A decomposition analysis. *Econometrics*, *9*, 22. https://doi.org/10.3390/econometrics9020022

Lahiri, K., Vaughan, D. R., & Wixon, B. (1995). Modeling SSA's sequential disability determination process using matched SIPP data. *Social Security Bulletin*, *58*(4), 3–42.

Lahiri, K., Song, J., & Wixon, B. (2008). A model of social security disability insurance using matched SIPP/administrative data. *Journal of Econometrics*, *145*, 4–20.

Millimet, D. L., & Parmeter, C. F. (2022a). COVID-19 severity: A new approach to quantify global cases and deaths. *Journal of the Royal Statistical Society Series A: Statistics in Society*, *185*(3), 1178–1215.

Millimet, D. L., & Parmeter, C. F. (2022b). Accounting for skewed or one-sided measurement error in the dependent variable. *Political Analysis*, *30*(1), 66–88.

Perrachi, F. & Rossetti, C. (2009). Gender and regional differences in self-rated health in Europe. CEIS Working Paper No.142. Available at: http://dx.doi.org/10.2139/ssrn.1434488.

Peracchi. F. & Rossetti, C. (2013). The heterogeneous thresholds ordered response model: identification and inference. *Journal of the Royal Statistical Society. Series A (Statistics in Society)*, *176*(3), 703–722.

Sandner, M., & Jungmann, T. (2016). How much can we trust maternal ratings of early child development in disadvantaged samples? *Economics Letters*, *141*(April), 73–76.

Salomon, J. A., Tandon, A., Murray, C. J. (2004). Comparability of self rated health: cross sectional multi-country survey using anchoring vignettes. *BMJ (Clinical research ed.)*, *328* (7434), 258.

Schneider, U., Pfarr, C., Schneider, B. S., & Ulrich, V. (2012). I Feel Good! Gender Differences and Reporting Heterogeneity in Self-Assessed Health. *European Journal of Health Economics*, *13*(3), 251–65.

Voňková, H., & Hullegie, P. (2011). Is the anchoring vignette method sensitive to the domain and choice of the vignette? *Journal of the Royal Statistical Society. Series A (Statistics in Society)*, *174*(3), 597–620.

Sen, A. (2002). Health: Perception versus observation. *British Medical Journal*, *324*, 860–861.

Wand, J., King, G., & Lao, O. (2016). Anchors: Software for anchoring vignette data. *Journal of Statistical Software*, *42*(3), 1–25.

CHAPTER 4

HOMELESSNESS ON THE WEST COAST AND THE ROLE OF HEALTH: INEFFICIENCY AND PRODUCTIVITY LOSS IN AMERICAN SOCIETY

Corey Fuller[a] and Robin C. Sickles[b]

[a]*Southwest Airlines, Dallas, TX, USA*
[b]*Department of Economics, Rice University, Houston, TX, USA*

ABSTRACT

Homelessness has many causes and also is stigmatized in the United States, leading to much misunderstanding of its causes and what policy solutions may ameliorate the problem. The problem is of course getting worse and impacting many communities far removed from the West Coast cities the authors examine in this study. This analysis examines the socioeconomic variables influencing homelessness on the West Coast in recent years. The authors utilize a panel fixed effects model that explicitly includes measures of healthcare access and availability to account for the additional health risks faced by individuals who lack shelter. The authors estimate a spatial error model (SEM) in order to better understand the impacts that systemic shocks, such as the COVID-19 pandemic, have on a variety of factors that directly influence productivity and other measures of welfare such as income inequality, housing supply, healthcare investment, and homelessness.

Essays in Honor of Subal Kumbhakar
Advances in Econometrics, Volume 46, 45–80

Published under exclusive licence by Emerald Publishing Limited
ISSN: 0731-9053/doi:10.1108/S0731-905320240000046004

Keywords: Homelessness; health; inequality; spatial spillovers; panel data; COVID-19

JEL classifications: C21; C23; C42; C81; I1; I32; I38

1. INTRODUCTION

1.1. Inefficiency and Productivity Losses from Homelessness and Subal Kumbhakar's Scholarly Legacy

Subal Kumbhakar and the second author of this contribution in honor of Subal have had a working relationship for almost 40 years. As a junior colleague, Subal's brilliance, dedication to the field of productivity and efficiency, his singular drive, and remarkable work ethic have propelled him to hard-to-fathom ranks in the pantheon of iconic contributors to the field of productivity and efficiency analysis. He is no longer a junior colleague but of course has become a most revered and respected senior colleague.

Throughout his career, Subal has had to deal with an economics profession that has a substantial bias against the notion that markets are not efficient, which of course is the hallmark of our most iconic construct: inefficient and measurable production levels. Subal of course has focused on the contributions of his (and Sickles) PhD advisor, the regression-based Aigner–Lovell–Schmidt (ALS) stochastic frontier model (SFA). Others have focused on the linear programming-based characterization of production and measurement of frontier and non-frontier production activities data envelopment analysis (DEA). In both cases, the orthodox neoclassical perspective to this vast literature has been at best indifferent and at worst unscientifically prejudiced against such inefficiency constructs. Glimmers of hope that the glacial tempo of academic acceptance of new ideas our field has been promoting for half a century do exist. One such example is the recent Special Symposium in the *International Productivity Monitor (IPM)*, originated in large part by academic leaders in the field of productivity at the time from Harvard (the late Dale Jorgenson), University of Manchester (Bart van Ark), and the University of Ottawa (Andrew Sharpe) (Sharpe, Sichel, & van Ark, 2022).

The recent IPM symposium notwithstanding, acceptance by the orthodox economics community is rather rare and in cases in which efficiency is acknowledged, structural approaches completely ignoring the methods we have developed are the mainstay of accepted research in main-line economics journals.

We can think of no better example of a failure of economic modeling and economic science to come to terms with its fundamental shortsightedness on the issue of the long-term existence of inefficiency and its accurate measurement than how it has ignored the massive inefficiencies inherent in inequality, discrimination, and the institutions that perpetuate their long-run existence. We also can think of no better example of the massive costs of the results of inequality and discrimination in our country than the existence of our growing homeless population.

Our contribution to this volume is meant to point researchers in the direction of better understanding and measuring the true costs of homelessness, its many dimensions, and its persistence over time and over generations. Such a massive problem, with its economic, health, and social justice dimensions needs to be better understood and modeled as what it truly is, a failure of our economy to provide for the basic welfare of its population, to acknowledge a self-evident truth that unalienable rights are denied to those whose basic housing needs are not being met. Homelessness is at its core an inefficient use of our country's resources, which has been the focus of the entirety of Subal Kumbhakar's career contributions in the field of productivity and efficiency analysis.

1.2. Homelessness and Its Correlates in America[1]

The COVID-19 pandemic notwithstanding, the United States until early 2020 was under the longest economic expansion in its history. Unemployment had been at its lowest in 50 years and stock market indices like the Dow Jones Industrial Average hit record highs. And yet, at the same time, it is estimated that more than 550,000 people across the country experienced homelessness on any given night, either in a shelter or in a place unfit for habitation.

The 2019 Annual Homeless Assessment Report, submitted to Congress by the Department of Housing and Urban Development (HUD), noted that homelessness in America declined 12% from 2007 to 2019. However, homelessness increased in 2017 for the first time since 2010, and has continued to go up since then. Though homelessness decreased in 37 states over the last decade or so, this decline was offset by the rapid growth of homeless populations along the West Coast. Cities such as Los Angeles, Seattle, and San Francisco continue to struggle to combat the increasing visibility of the problem, despite increases in government spending and additional taxes proposed to address the crisis. Given the success of many of the country's macroeconomic indicators pre-COVID-19, this upward trend was alarming and seemingly counterintuitive.

Rising homelessness on the West Coast is most severe in California, which saw a 16% increase in its homeless population from 2018 to 2019 (Henry, Wiatt, Mahathey, Ouelette, & Sitler, 2020). California and Oregon had the highest and second highest rates of unsheltered homelessness in the country, respectively. In fact, more than 70% of California's observed homeless population in 2019 was unsheltered, and 1 in 2 unsheltered homeless Americans lived in California.

Various issues, including income inequality and housing shortages, have been proposed as contributing factors to rising levels of homelessness on the West Coast. However, the sheer complexity of the issue makes any attempt to identify one particular "cause" misguided. Many studies examine the link between income and homelessness, but economist Brendan O'Flaherty (2004) noted that the interaction of personal *and* structural challenges matters most in influencing homelessness risk. Unlike income, the relationship between health and homelessness has not been as extensively studied in the economics literature. However, the prevalence of health issues (such as substance abuse or mental health disorders) is significantly higher among the homeless than among the general population. Just as a health shock can negatively impact future earnings potential or increase the proportion of income spent on healthcare, a lack of shelter can negatively impact one's health. This has the potential to create a negative feedback loop that, when compounded with a debilitating addiction or mental illness, makes exiting homelessness even more arduous.

Health, or by extension access to healthcare resources, is one of the many issues that could affect homelessness risk, and the purpose of this analysis is to test its importance relative to other factors. The maps in Fig. 4.1 (all color figures, including Fig. 4.1, can be found at http://rsickles.rice.edu/) help visualize the potential relationship between homelessness and health. On the left, percentage changes in homeless populations from 2015 to 2019 are colored in terms of severity. This map is divided into districts called continuums of care (CoCs), which manage homeless services in a region and are discussed in more detail in Section 4. The picture on the right uses geolocations of Health Professional Shortage Areas, designated as such by the United States Health Resources and Services Administration (HRSA), to create a heat map of healthcare insufficiencies. A cursory comparison of these images suggests that a potential connection may exist between homelessness and healthcare access, which this analysis attempts to examine in greater detail through the use of spatial econometric techniques.

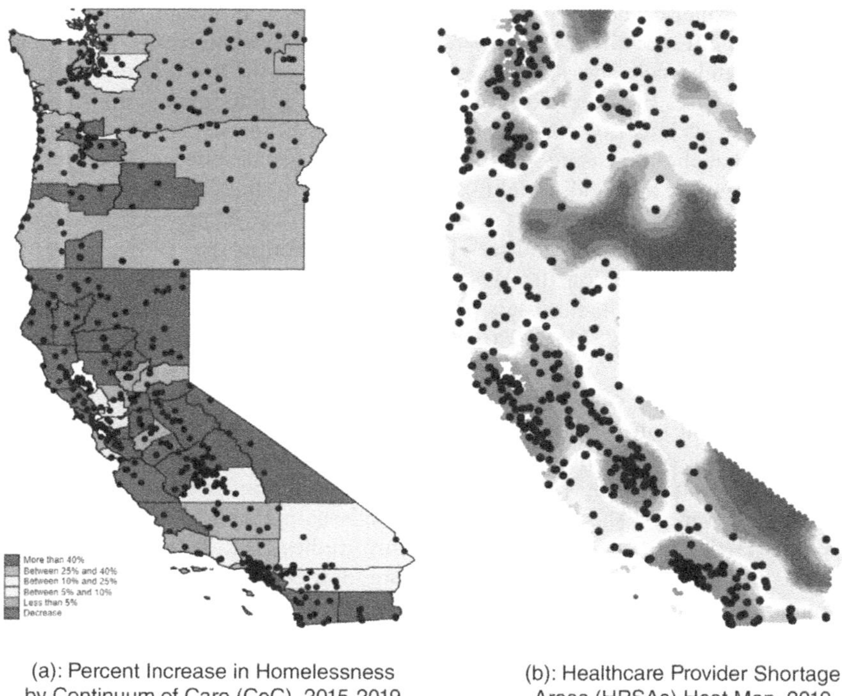

(a): Percent Increase in Homelessness by Continuum of Care (CoC), 2015-2019

(b): Healthcare Provider Shortage Areas (HPSAs) Heat Map, 2019

Fig. 4.1. Maps of Homelessness Changes and Healthcare Shortages. (a) Percent increase in homelessness by CoC, 2015–2019. (b) Healthcare provider shortage areas Heat Map, 2019.

This chapter is outlined as follows. Section 2 of our chapter discusses the relevant economics literature on homelessness. Section 3 details the theoretical framework and approach that will be used to interpret the results from our analysis. Following this, Section 4 is a detailed discussion of our data sources, which is succeeded by an introduction of the econometric models being used in Section 5. This chapter ends with a discussion of results in Section 6, followed by a brief conclusion in Section 7.

2. PREVIOUS STUDIES OF HOMELESSNESS

In this section, we provide an overview of the economics literature on homelessness in America. Both structural and personal factors contribute to homelessness, and we detail studies that view the problem both at the individual and aggregate level, comparing differences in their results. Specifically, we discuss studies that focus on the problem of homelessness through the lenses of income and health. We continue with a short discussion of the relationship between health and future outcomes and then move to studies that have examined homelessness from a spatial perspective.

2.1. Homelessness in America

"Homeless" is an umbrella term that describes the poorest and most marginalized individuals in our society. Over time, the composition and structure of the homeless population has changed, as events like the Great Depression, the de-institutionalization movement in the 1970s, the HIV/AIDS crisis in the 1980s, and the recent opioid epidemic have affected broad swaths of individuals (Evans, Phillips, & Ruffini, 2019). Though the makeup of homeless populations has changed, modern homelessness in America is generally defined by the growing presence and visibility of street populations in urban areas (O'Flaherty, 1996).

Two major roadblocks have hampered past economic research on homelessness: unreliable (or non-existent) data and difficulty defining what homelessness actually means. However, as data collection and availability have improved – a major advancement has been the Annual Homelessness Assessment Report to Congress, which HUD has produced since 2007 – and homeless populations in metropolitan areas have grown in visibility, research on homelessness in America has proliferated. Potential factors contributing to homelessness that have been studied can be grouped into two broad categories: those relating to income and those relating to health.

2.2. Income and Homelessness

The "bread and butter" of literature on homelessness analyzes the problem through an income lens. When viewed purely as an economic decision, homelessness occurs when an individual exits the housing market. Various papers have been written to frame this housing choice decision. O'Flaherty (1993) models the household consumption problem, arguing that individuals spend income on both housing and a non-housing numeraire good in order to maximize their utility, subject to a budget constraint. In this setup, an individual "chooses" to enter into homelessness when their utility from homelessness (spending nothing on housing) is greater than the utility received from spending a sizeable portion of their income on the lowest-quality housing available. O'Flaherty (1996) subsequently applies this framework to study homeless populations in three American cities – New York City, Newark, and Chicago. Comparing changes in homelessness with changes in the slope of the income distribution, O'Flaherty concludes that growing income inequality can explain much of the rise in homelessness in these cities. According to his analysis, growing income inequality increases demand, and subsequently rental costs, of housing for the poor, causing homelessness to rise farther into the income distribution. Quigley and Raphael (2001) test the predictions of O'Flaherty's (1993) housing market model, using the rent-to-income ratio and vacancy rates as measures of inequality and the tightness of the housing market. They find that both have large, significant effects on the presence of homelessness in North America, and argue that modest adjustments to ease rent burdens would be effective in reducing the incidence of homelessness.

Several other studies have examined community economic characteristics and their impact on aggregate homelessness levels. Honig and Filer (1993) use data from the first point-in-time homeless count conducted by HUD in 1984. They regress a variety of economic indicators to test their relationship with the associated homeless counts, finding that the rent level at the tenth percentile of the cost distribution has the most significant impact on homelessness. However, the presence of rent-control laws and the poverty rate did not have statistically significant effects on homelessness levels in their results. This is similar to the findings of Hanratty (2017), who uses HUD data from 2007 to 2014 in a community fixed effects model. Investigating median rent, poverty rate, and rental rate, she concludes that only median rent has a noteworthy impact on homelessness. In other studies of housing affordability, the Zillow Rent Index (ZRI), produced by the real estate website of the same name, has been used as a proxy for living costs. Combining these data with recent HUD counts, Glynn and Fox (2019) observe that homelessness in Los Angeles, Seattle, New York, and Washington DC is severely impacted by changes in ZRI, much more so than in other American cities. In Glynn, Byrne, and Culhane (2018), the expected homeless rate increases sharply once rent payments reach a third of total income. Unlike the aforementioned studies, which assume a linear relationship between community measures of affordability and homelessness, Glynn et al. (2018) identify an inflection point whereupon larger changes in homelessness occur. Other works have also linked stricter zoning laws (Raphael, 2010) and higher eviction rates (Collinson & Reed, 2018) with homelessness.

Microeconomic analyses of homelessness tend to find that individual characteristics hold more weight in impacting homelessness than do broad economic measures like median rent. For example, several papers by Early (1999, 2005) have studied homelessness using individual-level observations. Early (1999) modifies O'Flaherty's (1996) housing market model, using maximum likelihood estimation to determine the conditional probability of homelessness. This study finds that the marginal propensity to consume housing is reduced by being male, suffering from depression, and being older. Looking specifically at street homelessness, Early (2005) uses data from the 1996 National Survey of Homeless Assistance Providers and Clients and finds housing market factors and income are not statistically significant. Instead, drug or alcohol abuse, age of the head of the household, and lack of children significantly impacted the chance of experiencing homelessness outside of the traditional shelter system.

It is important to note the theoretical reasoning for why aggregate and individual level studies can reach seemingly contradictory conclusions. As witnessed above, studies using aggregate counts of homelessness tend to find that housing affordability is a key driver; on the other hand, studies using data on individuals tend to find that personal characteristics are much more important in determining housing status. O'Flaherty (2004) notes that homelessness occurs due to the combination of structural and personal challenges working in tandem. As such, regressions examining only individual characteristics or aggregate measures of housing affordability are misspecified. This is because aggregate level studies lack a sufficient level of variation in personal characteristics, and the opposite is true for studies at the individual level. Thus, O'Flaherty (2004) argues that the interaction between personal and market factors should be explicitly modeled in order to get a clear picture of the homelessness issue.

A more limited, dated literature exists that focuses solely on West Coast cities and states. Quigley, Raphael, and Smolensky (2002) obtain results that are similar to other aggregate level studies. Analyzing homelessness in California specifically, they find that median rent and rent-to-income levels are significant determinants of homelessness. In terms of the current West Coast crisis, various contributing factors have been hypothesized. These include high construction costs, resident animosity toward the construction of shelters or affordable housing ("not in my backyard" or NIMBY-ism), and restrictive zoning laws, to name a few (Ohanian, 2019). Regulatory stringency in California (Quigley & Raphael, 2005) has been shown to be correlated with decreased construction and higher housing prices. Proposition 13, which passed in 1978 and capped property tax growth rates in California, has also been shown to have inflated housing prices in coastal cities and disincentivized selling in the state (Imrohoroglu, Matoba, & Tuzel, 2018; Wasi & White, 2005). Yu (2018) finds strong correlations between median home value, housing supply growth, and homelessness, which he uses to explain California's recent homeless surge relative to the rest of the country. However, Evans et al. (2019) find that changes in rent levels in Los Angeles hold little influence in determining changes in the homeless count. Given that Los Angeles has the largest homeless population on the West Coast, this result suggests that individual factors may be compounding issues of housing affordability. A discussion of one of these factors, health, is pursued next.

2.3. Health and Homelessness

Rather than viewing homelessness as a consequence of rising inequality, stagnant wages, tight housing markets, or other income-related variables, some have analyzed homelessness from a personal health perspective. Untreated mental illness, substance abuse disorders, and HIV/AIDS prevalence are all much higher among the homeless than they are among the general population (Evans et al., 2019). These subpopulations suffer disproportionately from health problems (Baumohl, 1996) that make escaping homelessness even more arduous without some sort of specialized intervention.

One of the first studies to directly test O'Flaherty's assertion – that homelessness is a result of structural barriers and personal challenges working together – examines the impacts of exogenous health shocks on homelessness. Curtis, Corman, Noonan, and Reichman (2012) use survey data from the Fragile Families and Child Wellbeing study to investigate the impact that the birth of a child with a severe illness or health condition has on increasing the risk of homelessness. To do this, Curtis et al. examine economically disadvantaged families who experience a negative health shock, tracking housing status over time. Using a variety of probit models, they find robust results indicating that the risk of homelessness increases after having a child with a severe health issue. Controlling for housing market factors, they also find that the effect of this shock is exacerbated in markets with higher rents, as measured by HUD's Fair Market Rents index. The inability to recover from a negative shock to personal income or health, then, can be made worse depending upon the strictness of the housing market in which an individual finds oneself.

Links between healthcare access and homelessness are well-documented, in economics and public health literature alike. Early (2004), using data from the Survey of Income and Program Participation, models the probability of homelessness, conditional on receiving a voucher or other form of housing subsidy. He concludes that, all else equal, households in states with higher per capita spending on community healthcare were less likely to experience homelessness. Schanzer, Domingues, Shrout, and Caton (2006) documented the health status of persons in the New York City shelter system, both upon entry and eighteen months later. They note that a majority of individuals in their study made use of emergency health services in the year before becoming homeless, and they found those who remained homeless at the conclusion of the study had worse health outcomes than those who were able to find housing, although this difference was not statistically significant. Homeless persons, particularly outside the shelter system, are more likely to make use of costly emergency medical services. In a study of 10,000 homeless persons in Los Angeles, Flaming, Matsunaga, and Burns (2009) find healthcare to be the largest public cost associated with the homeless population. For single men in ages 46–65, with no recent employment and a history of mental illness or substance abuse, monthly public costs totaled more than $4,500 per person. More than half of these costs were for healthcare services, a majority of which resulted from hospitalizations. As homeless populations continue to grow, so do sheltering and healthcare costs for individuals who cannot afford to pay for these services themselves.

Given the large social and healthcare costs, various attempts have been made by economists to connect growing homeless populations with health challenges like mental illness and drug addiction. For example, the widespread closure of state and county mental institutions in the 1960s and 1970s was theorized as an explanation for the rise in urban homelessness visibility in the 1980s. O'Flaherty (1996) finds little correlation between the two events, arguing that growth in homeless populations was too far removed in time from the de-institutionalization movement for facility closures to be at fault. Similarly, Quigley et al. (2002) find no statistically significant evidence for de-institutionalization augmenting homeless counts in California. More recently, the opioid epidemic is speculated to be a contributing factor to homelessness via increasing mortality risks for street populations (Marzilli, 2017). Although there is anecdotal evidence to suggest opioid addiction has played a role in expanding rural homelessness in places like rural Northern California (Del Real, 2018), we are unaware of any study that formally tests the relationship between homelessness and the current opioid crisis. Clearly, health factors compound the challenges faced by homeless populations. With that being said, there is little economic evidence to suggest that homelessness is entirely a result of personal health struggles, addictions, or mental health issues.

The notion of a "health–poverty trap" is traditionally applied in development economics to discuss macroeconomic stagnation in poorer countries (Sala-i-Martin, 2005). However, this same idea of a negative feedback loop can be applied in the context of homelessness in wealthy nations. Just as a lack of investment in one's physical and mental health today can increase the future risk of homelessness, homeless people suffer from increased morbidity rates and healthcare accessibility challenges. The relationship between health and homelessness is a two-way street, and this endogeneity can skew econometric estimates of the relationship that do not address it. Dai and Zhou (2019) use a structural equations framework to address this mutual causality problem, analyzing the health of the homeless population in Wales. Taking this interaction into account, they conclude that the feedback loop between homelessness and health problems is stronger than what previous studies suggest. Meyer et al. (2021) utilized linked survey and administrative data sources, many of them underused, to look closer into the transitory and permanent components of factors that lead to homelessness – low material well-being, access to transfers and coverage via the social safety net, as well as the exclusion of such individuals and families from official statistics. They found that health factors, such as physical and cognitive limitations, are more prevalent among the homeless, relative to the housed population and relative to those with similar economic means. However, they also found that Supplemental Nutrition Assistance Program (SNAP) and Medicaid reached at least 88% of the sheltered and 78% of the unsheltered receiving at least one benefit.

The negative feedback loop between homelessness and health is likely further compounded by the impacts of climate change, though we are unaware of any study that formally examines the relationship between temperature and the health of homeless individuals. Unsheltered populations are directly exposed to adverse weather events and air pollution, and warming global temperatures have helped to increase the severity and frequency of natural disasters such as floods, forest fires, and extreme heat. For example, drought conditions helped to turn the 2018 Camp Fire into one of the deadliest wildfires in California's history, which, in addition to destroying thousands of homes, left unsheltered individuals across

Northern California exposed to wildfire smoke and dangerous air (Hidalgo, 2020). A majority of California's homeless population is unsheltered, and despite much of the West Coast having a moderate climate, it is theorized that warming global temperatures will leave these individuals at a greater risk of worse health outcomes. California already contains five of the ten most ozone-polluted metropolitan areas in the country (Shonkoff, Morello-Frosch, Pastor, & Sadd, 2011), and major heat waves leave homeless individuals in urban areas, which trap warmth due to the "heat island effect," at greater risk of morbidities such as dehydration and heat stroke (Ramin & Svoboda, 2009). Though warming temperatures may help mitigate mortality from cold exposure during winter months, this is unlikely to outweigh the negative impacts of climate change on the health and safety of unsheltered homeless populations. The inherent randomness of natural disasters would make quantifying a statistical relationship with health outcomes difficult, but nonetheless, extreme heat and air pollution pose significant health risks to these vulnerable populations.

2.3.1. Health Production and Future Outcomes

Future outcomes have been shown to be highly correlated to investments made in personal health. Among others, Sickles and Taubman (1986, 1997) and Sickles and Yazbeck (1998) incorporate health investment into the standard economic utility framework, arguing that individuals maximize their utility with respect to consumption, leisure, and health. The maximal utility is, in turn, subject to a budget constraint as well as a health production function. Given the higher prevalence of substance abuse and mental health problems in homeless populations, it is reasonable to question whether a standard utility maximization framework would hold among vulnerable persons who may lack the agency to make health-conscious decisions. However, Becker and Murphy's (1988) seminal paper on rational addiction modeling finds that, even in the presence of addictive behavior, individuals maximize lifetime utility instead of discounting future utility more heavily, as previously theorized. Other research supports the notion that homeless individuals are acting as rational economic agents. A study by Flato and Johannessen (2010) of 10 chronically homeless individuals in Oslo, Norway, all suffering from drug addiction or alcoholism, theorizes that these individuals participate in a "harvesting economy" as a means of managing their daily lives that differs from modern society's traditional economic framework and that maintains alternative incentives. In this "harvesting economy," consumption is more immediate out of necessity, while saving and property accumulation are disincentivized because they increase the risk of becoming a victim of theft or impairing one's mobility. Similarly, Quigley and Raphael (2001) conclude that their statistical findings "support models of homelessness that emphasize rational choice among the extremely poor."

Conceptually, the concept of a health production function has been used to quantify individual investments in health and their impact on an individual's health "stock" over time. The idea of a health stock was first theorized in the literature by Grossman (1972), who argued that individual health level is analogous to capital stock, in that investments or disinvestments can be made in one's health, with corresponding effects on future outcomes. In the economic literature on retirement, personal health is a crucial determinant in the decision to stop working. Sickles and Taubman (1986) define health stock in this context as a function of age, healthcare spending, and personal and job characteristics. Their limited dependent variable model links health status to the decision to retire or not; a similar framework could be applied to the "decision" to enter into homelessness.

2.4. Spatial Analyses of Homelessness

Fewer works use spatial methods and techniques to analyze the issue of homelessness in America. Spatial econometric methods are used to identify dependencies resulting from geographic connections and also within networks of economic agents. From a health economics perspective, spatial analysis can be used to examine variations in healthcare access, outcomes, and spillover effects. Failure to account for the spatial structure of data can ultimately lead to biased conclusions (Baltagi, Moscone, & Santos, 2018). Given the interactions between homelessness, geography, and healthcare access, detailed spatial modeling would give a much clearer picture of homelessness in America. However, potential issues related to unknown migration patterns of homeless individuals could challenge the robustness of these results.[2] Climate change may also play an increasingly relevant role in the migration patterns of homeless individuals over time, if more moderate temperatures and environments are increasingly sought out.

Mast (2014) uses a Theil index to identify spatial mismatching of resources for homeless individuals. Comparing accessible shelter beds with homeless counts in individual CoCs, Mast finds that large misallocations of shelter beds relative to the concentrations of homeless individuals exist across the country. Abraham, Goetzmann, and Wachter (1994) used *K*-means clustering to compare housing price fluctuations across the United States. Their research notes that West Coast housing markets in California and Washington had similar returns on price from 1977 to 1992. Similarly, Glynn et al. (2018) use a Dirichlet process mixture model to test for peer groups of CoCs in need of similar policy solutions. Their clustering techniques group together many urban CoCs on the West Coast (including Seattle, San Francisco, and Los Angeles), although it should be mentioned that spatial interactions are not evaluated in their model. These analyses suggest that similar challenges are putting poor individuals at increased risk for homelessness all along the Pacific Coast. Making use of spatial econometric techniques could more clearly specify these dependencies.

3. ECONOMIC THEORY

Economic models tend to view homelessness as a utility-maximizing housing choice for poor individuals, who prefer homelessness to spending a large proportion of their income on the cheapest available housing. O'Flaherty's (1993) model is built on this assumption. Its main finding is that an increase in homelessness occurs as income inequality worsens, due to the demand for lower-quality housing increasing with supply failing to increase at the same time. This occurs through the following mechanism: as income inequality worsens, the middle class shrinks, reducing demand for medium quality housing. Over time, this causes the supply of medium quality housing to shrink. However, O'Flaherty's model assumes that all housing deteriorates over time, so this smaller supply of mid-tier housing eventually becomes a smaller supply of low-quality housing. Consequently, the demand for low-quality housing has increased as a result of growing inequality, but the supply of low-quality housing has shrunk, and this mismatch causes homelessness to rise.

Although O'Flaherty's model makes an interesting prediction, for this analysis we will need a more flexible model that can include the potential consequences of poor health and healthcare access on homelessness. In order to do this, we examine a two-period consumption model developed by Glomm and John (2002) and test its conclusions in the econometric analysis section. Health is integrated into this framework by assuming that health directly impacts the skills that a worker can offer in the labor market, in turn affecting earnings potential. Thus, Glomm and John view housing not only as a consumption good but also as an investment good in the context of personal health.

To set up this model, we consider a population of size n. Each individual lives for two periods, which we label "today" and "tomorrow." As in any standard consumption model, all individuals look to maximize their lifetime utility, which is the sum of their utility in both periods, discounting the future period to the present.

Define the utility of individual i in period t to be $U_{it}(H,X) = \ln(X_t(H_t + \hat{h}))$, where H is housing consumption, and X is a numeraire non-housing good which encompasses all other spending. The constant $\hat{h}$ is positive, and is included in order to ensure that the utility function is still well-defined in the event that an individual is homeless ($H = 0$) in a given time period. Given the linkage between homelessness and poverty, we focus mainly on the housing choices of the "marginally homeless" consumer. Thus, housing consumed by individual i in period t takes on one of two values: 0 or h, where 0 represents homelessness and h represents the minimum quality of housing available on the market. Unlike O'Flaherty (1993), who views housing quality as a continuum with homelessness as the lower bound, in this model homelessness is viewed as a separate state of nature from the minimum housing quality available on the market. Given the presence of building codes which effectively set minimum housing quality standards, this discontinuity assumption makes sense. In this model, consumption in each period is limited by the budget constraint:

$$\begin{aligned} x_1 + h_1 + s &= w_1 \\ x_2 + h_2 &= g_2 w_2 + s \end{aligned} \tag{1}$$

In (1), s represents today's savings, and g_2 represents the effective units of labor that an individual possesses in period 2. If an individual is housed today

($h_1 = h$), then $g_2 = 1$. Otherwise, $g_2 = \theta$, where θ is a fraction between 0 and 1. The parameter θ represents the negative health consequences of homelessness, with a smaller value implying that homelessness is more detrimental to future earnings potential. Wage earned per effective unit of labor in period i is denoted by w_i, so $g_i w_i$ represents earned income in period i. We assume $g_1 = 1$ for all individuals.

Given that individuals have two housing choices in each period (homeless or housed), there are four potential outcomes in this model. We define $U_{ab}(s)$ to be individual utility as a function of savings, where $a, b \in \{0,1\}$, a denotes housing choice in period 1, and b denotes the housing choice in period 2. A subscript of 0 indicates homelessness, and 1 indicates being housed. Thus, individual utility can be represented as follows:

$$U_{ab}(s) = \ln(w_1 - h_1 - s) + \ln(y_1) + \beta \ln(g_2 w_2 - h_2 + s) + \beta \ln(y_2) \tag{2}$$

In this setup, $y_i = h_i + \hat{h}$. For our four cases, we have:

Homeless today and tomorrow

$$U_{00}(s) = \ln(w_1 - s) + \beta \ln(\theta w_2 + s) + (1 + \beta)\ln(\hat{h})$$

Homeless today and housed tomorrow

$$U_{01}(s) = \ln(w_1 - s) + \ln(\hat{h}) + \beta \ln(\theta w_2 - h + s) + \beta \ln(h + \hat{h})$$

Housed today and homeless tomorrow

$$U_{10}(s) = \ln(w_1 - h - s) + \ln(h + \hat{h}) + \beta \ln(w_2 + s) + \beta \ln(\hat{h})$$

Housed today and tomorrow

$$U_{11}(s) = \ln(w_1 - h - s) + \beta \ln(w_2 - h + s) + (1 + \beta)\ln(h + \hat{h}).$$

Maximizing consumer utility over both periods, we can determine the optimal savings rate in terms of x_1 and x_2, where $x_1 = w_1 - h_1$ and $x_2 = g_2 w_2 - h_2$. Taking the derivative of (2) with respect to s:

$$\frac{\delta}{\delta s} U_{ab}(s) = -\frac{1}{x_1 - s} + \frac{\beta}{x_2 + s} = 0$$

$$\frac{\beta}{x_2 + s} = \frac{1}{x_1 - s}$$

$$s = \frac{\beta x_1 - x_2}{1 + \beta}$$

Depending upon how heavily the future is discounted, consumers will choose to save when $\beta x_1 > x_2$, and borrow when the opposite is true. Using this result, we can write the indirect utility function, which we derive as follows:

$$U_{ab} = \ln\left(x_1 - \frac{\beta x_1 - x_2}{1+\beta}\right) + \ln(y_1) + \beta \ln\left(x_2 + \frac{\beta x_1 - x_2}{1+\beta}\right) + \beta \ln(y_2)$$

$$U_{ab} = \ln\left(\frac{x_1 + x_2}{1+\beta}\right) + \ln(y_1) + \beta \ln\left(\frac{\beta x_1 + \beta x_2}{1+\beta}\right) + \beta \ln(y_2) \tag{3}$$

$$U_{ab} = (1+\beta)\ln(x_1 + x_2) + \ln(y_1) + \beta \ln(y_2) + \beta \ln(\beta) - (1+\beta)\ln(1+\beta)$$

$$U_{ab} = (1+\beta)\ln(x_1 + x_2) + \ln(y_1) + \beta \ln(y_2)$$

In (3), our simplified indirect utility function, we omit the constant terms at the end. In order to determine a consumer's optimal housing pattern over the two time periods, we compare the utilities in each case. Since there are four potential housing patterns (housed both periods, homeless both periods, housed only in the first, and housed only in the second), we make six pairwise comparisons between the utilities in each scenario. These are graphed in Fig. 4.2, with the shaded region indicating the set of exogenous wage rates (w_1, w_2) wherein one housing choice is strictly preferred over the other. For illustrative purposes only, we have assumed the following parameter values in creating the following figures: $\beta = 1$; $\theta = 0.75$, $h = 3$, and $\hat{h} = 1$. Note also that these plots are meant purely as a visual exercise, and the graphed values do not correspond to a specific dollar value.

Looking at these plots, we see that, when incomes are low enough, individuals strictly prefer homelessness in both periods, and when incomes are high, individuals strictly prefer being sheltered in both periods. For individuals with intermediate wage levels we see that, when incomes are low enough, individuals may only be able to afford housing in one period although they prefer to be housed today and homeless tomorrow rather than be homeless today and housed tomorrow. As seen in Fig. 4.2, the area where $U_{10} > U_{01}$ is the entire graph.

Due to the added health challenges that homelessness presents, it is never optimal for an individual to be homeless in the first period and housed in the second period. Although this is shown graphically, it can also be seen mathematically, as the parameter θ reduces earnings in period 2 if an individual is homeless today. However, if they are housed today and homeless tomorrow, their wage tomorrow is not adversely affected by having been homeless. Thus, depending on today's earnings and tomorrow's earnings, only three of the four potential housing choices are willingly chosen by consumers. Fig. 4.3 combines the results of the pairwise comparisons into one chart. The labels represent the utility function with the highest value for that region of exogenous wage rates in the graph.

The line separating the U_{00} and U_{10} regions in Fig. 4.3 represents the set of exogenous wage rates (w_1, w_2) such that individuals are indifferent between being homeless in both periods and homeless only in the second period. The equation of the line where $U_{00} = U_{10}$ is:

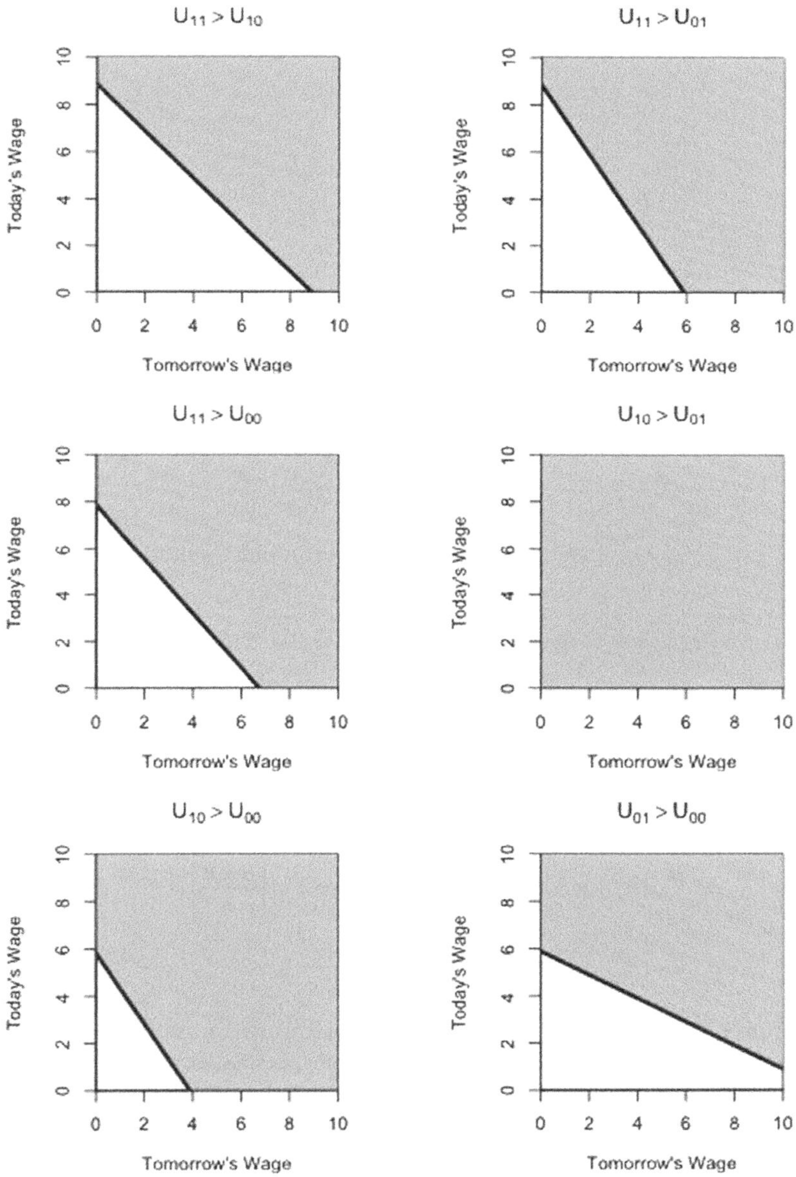

Fig. 4.2. Pairwise Housing Choice Utility Comparison.

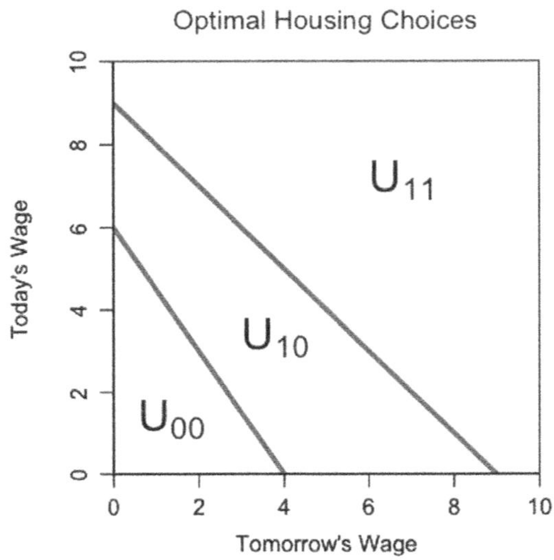

Fig. 4.3. Income and Preferred Housing Choices.

$$
\begin{aligned}
(1+\beta)\ln(w_1+w_2-h)+\ln(h+\hat{h})+\beta\ln(\hat{h}) &= (1+\beta)[\ln(w_1+\theta w_2)+\ln(\hat{h})] \\
\ln\left(\frac{h+\hat{h}}{\hat{h}}\right) &= (1+\beta)\ln\left(\frac{w_1+\theta w_2}{w_1+w_2-h}\right) \\
\left(\frac{h+\hat{h}}{\hat{h}}\right)^{1/(1+\beta)} &= \left(\frac{w_1+\theta w_2}{w_1+w_2-h}\right) \\
\phi(w_1+w_2-h) = w_1+\theta w_2,\ \text{where } \phi &= \left(\frac{h+\hat{h}}{\hat{h}}\right)^{1/(1+\beta)} \\
w_1 &= \frac{(\theta-\phi)w_2+\phi h}{\phi-1}
\end{aligned}
\tag{4}
$$

From (4), we see that θ affects the slope of this curve. As the health consequences of homelessness become more severe, θ gets smaller and the slope steepens. As these consequences become worse, more individuals will prefer to be housed today rather than be homeless in both periods, expanding the U_{10} area and shrinking the U_{00} one.

This model does have some limitations, as it is an oversimplification of real life and the plethora of factors that lead to housing insecurity. This result is derived under the assumption that all individuals have knowledge today of what their earnings will be both now and in the future, and that they make their housing choices based on this information. As a result, it does not account for the possibility of random, personal shocks that may drastically lower future income or force someone into homelessness. Just because more individuals would strictly prefer being housed in the first period on account of the health and economic consequences of homelessness being more severe, that does not necessarily mean that all of those individuals would be able to avoid homelessness on their own.

Additionally, the above model has been evaluated under the assumption that all individuals are able to save and borrow freely. This assumption may not be entirely realistic for poorer individuals, who may lack access to credit if lending institutions see them as too risky. In a more restricted context, where individuals cannot borrow freely, the picture becomes more complicated, as seen in Fig. 4.4.

In the setting where borrowing is restricted, certain groups that would have been able to avoid homelessness are suddenly no longer able to do so, and the possibility of a "homelessness trap" emerges. For certain individuals who would've chosen to be housed in both periods, being unable to borrow to pay for housing forces them into homelessness in period 1. However, being homeless today lowers their income in period 2 due to the negative health consequences of homelessness. As a result, they experience homelessness in period 2 as well. This result – that homelessness can "trap" certain individuals, in the absence of direct intervention – seems like a realistic possibility given the growing unsheltered and chronically homeless populations on the West Coast. If we were to extend this setup to be a multi-period model, we could see how this trap would force more and more individuals into housing insecurity. Additionally, in the event that the health consequences for homelessness are more severe (either due to a shortage of readily available healthcare resources or, say, a lack of shelter beds which increases the proportion of the homeless population that is unsheltered), it is expected that this phenomenon would impact more at-risk individuals, and homeless populations would grow over time.

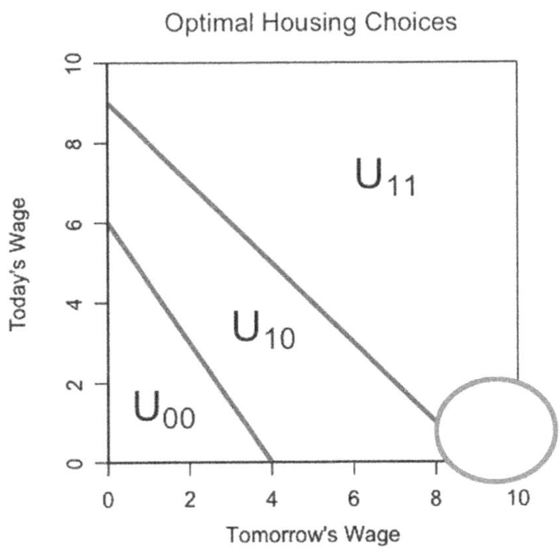

Fig. 4.4. Homelessness as a "Trap" When Borrowing Is Restricted.

4. DATA SOURCES

4.1. Homelessness Data

Before beginning the econometric analysis, it is important to clarify what is exactly meant by the word "homelessness" in the context in which the term is defined. Homeless individuals fall into two groups according to the Department of HUD's definition: sheltered and unsheltered. These definitions are what will be used in the context of this analysis.

Sheltered: An individual or family living in a supervised, publicly, or privately operated shelter designated to provide temporary living arrangement (including congregate shelters, transitional housing, and hotels and motels paid for by charitable organizations or by federal, state, or local government programs for low-income individuals).

Unsheltered: An individual or family with a primary nighttime residence that is a public or private place not designed for or ordinarily used as a regular sleeping accommodation for human beings, including a car, park, abandoned building, bus or train station, airport, or camping ground.

Total homelessness then is simply the sum of all sheltered and unsheltered homeless individuals. Note that the above definitions are fairly strict sets of criteria. Other government organizations have more expansive definitions that, in turn, produce larger homelessness estimates. For example, the United States Department of Education counts children who are "doubling up," or living with another family in a single-family housing unit, as homeless, whereas HUD does not. Similarly, HUD's definition does not include individuals residing in jails, hospitals, or foster care.

Homeless counts used in this analysis are from HUD's Annual Point-In-Time Counts for 2010–2019. These homeless counts are conducted during the last two weeks of January each year and are reported by individual CoCs. CoCs are local homeless service management organizations that have trained volunteers who count homeless individuals in their district. These CoCs tend to vary in size; for rural, less populous regions, one CoC may cover several counties. However, for more populated, urban areas, a CoC may only manage homeless services for one county.

The federal government does not have one standardized training or methodology that all CoCs must follow when conducting their annual counts. As a result, counts of unsheltered individuals are often done by simple observation, where volunteers count the number of individuals they see that appear to be homeless. Thus, it is almost certain that these reported numbers are an undercount of the true unsheltered population, given the sheer difficulty of completing a full count. Tables 4.1(a)–(c) provide summary statistics regarding homeless counts within each of the CoC in four states: California, Hawaii, Oregon, and Washington. We have also included maps of homelessness across CoCs for 2019. See the Appendix[3] for a labeled map and complete list of CoCs included in this analysis.

4.2. Healthcare Data

To measure the availability of healthcare resources, we use data on primary care physicians per 1,000 people from the United States HRSA's Area Health

Table 4.1(a). Summary Statistics for Total Homelessness Counts by Year.

Year	*N*	Mean	Std. Dev.	Min	Max
2010	52	3,301	5,569	146	38,717
2011	52	3,242	5,628	170	39,414
2012	52	3,120	5,203	217	35,926
2013	52	3,009	5,604	180	39,461
2014	52	2,913	5,403	195	38,089
2015	55	2,836	6,108	53	44,359
2016	55	2,911	6,440	115	46,874
2017	55	3,210	7,871	121	57,794
2018	55	3,151	7,226	125	52,765
2019	55	3,548	8,042	192	58,936

Table 4.1(b). Summary Statistics for Unsheltered Homelessness Counts by Year.

Year	*N*	Mean	Std. Dev.	Min	Max
2010	52	1,799	3,170	83	21,722
2011	52	1,773	3,068	37	20,827
2012	52	1,751	3,028	37	20,500
2013	52	1,693	3,530	49	24,969
2014	52	1,664	3,510	49	24,977
2015	55	1,674	4,189	45	31,025
2016	55	1,803	4,684	60	34,701
2017	55	2,036	5,776	56	42,828
2018	55	2,047	5,328	56	39,396
2019	55	2,396	5,989	150	44,214

Table 4.1(c). Summary Statistics for the Unsheltered Proportion of the Homeless Population by Year.

Year	*N*	Mean	Std. Dev.	Min	Max
2010	52	0.5416	0.1931	0.05491	0.9368
2011	52	0.5278	0.1960	0.09724	0.9025
2012	52	0.5281	0.2063	0.09614	0.9119
2013	52	0.5170	0.2052	0.05825	0.9003
2014	52	0.5301	0.1985	0.1302	0.8969
2015	55	0.5744	0.1614	0.1277	0.9143
2016	55	0.5922	0.1591	0.1753	0.9084
2017	55	0.5975	0.1691	0.1266	0.9587
2018	55	0.6241	0.1565	0.2490	0.9936
2019	55	0.6551	0.1429	0.2406	0.9363

Resource File, which is reported for the years 2010–2017. Additionally, to measure investment in healthcare resources we utilize HRSA grant funding data, which is given to counties annually and reported for 2010–2019. These data have then been converted to 2010 dollars. We have made use of both of these measures, one as a measure of stock and another as a measure of investment flows, to mirror Grossman's (1972) consideration of health as a capital good with a stock that can be augmented over time.

4.3. Income and Demographic Data

Economic variables in our analyses include income inequality, median rent, and available housing units per capita. Income inequality is measured using the United States Census Bureau's Gini index calculations from the American Community Survey (ACS) for 2010–2017. Data on housing units per 100 persons are also from the ACS, and median rent data are from HUD.

Other demographic variables used in this analysis are measures of age, ethnicity, and health risk. Proportions of the population that are black, male, and 65+ come from the Census Bureau, and the uninsured rate comes from the Census Bureau's Small Area Health Insurance Estimates. Lastly, data on opioid prescriptions per 100 persons for the years 2010–2017 come from the Center for Disease Control. This is included in this analysis to address the potential impact of the recent opioid epidemic that has affected broad swaths of the country over the last decade. Summary statistics for the explanatory variables are in Table 4.2.

4.4. Reconciling Homeless Counts with Other Data

Before beginning the econometric analysis, modifications to the data needed to be made. Since homeless counts are reported at the CoC level, but data for the various independent variables in this analysis are all reported at the county level, it was necessary to aggregate the county-level data and put it into terms of each CoC. For certain variables, such as population or grant funding, the value at the CoC level is simply the sum of the values for each county making up that CoC. However, for other variables, such as the Gini index and median rent, this same summation approach does not make sense. For those variables, the values at the CoC level are population-weighted sums of the values for each county making up each CoC. Los Angeles County is the only county in the previously mentioned four states that has more than one CoC inside of it. As a result, homeless counts for those CoCs (Los Angeles County CoC, Glendale CoC, Long Beach CoC, and Pasadena CoC) were combined into one so that this analysis could be conducted.

Table 4.2. Summary Statistics for Explanatory Variables.

Variable	*N*	Mean	Std. Dev.	Min	Max
Population	550	931,574	1,459,056	33,255	10,253,716
Physicians	440	0.79154	0.263393	0.20525	1.592228
Grant funding	550	27.2719	29.59313	0	165.932
Gini	440	0.45234	0.023630	0.38393	0.5263
Median rent	550	1,026.80	396.236	554.105	2,704
Housing units	495	40.6650	7.396118	31.2107	76.51329
Opioid	440	73.9209	31.24375	20.7	176.4
% Uninsured	440	0.11308	0.048289	0.03055	0.228903
% Black	495	0.03731	0.032381	0.00419	0.153332
% Male	495	0.49896	0.007676	0.48431	0.521164
% 65+	495	0.14745	0.033769	0.08947	0.269735

It should be clear that a study such as ours that is based on aggregate community data cannot address the plethora of issues relating to causes and consequences of homelessness such as substance abuse and food insecurity, to name but a very few, that vary on an individual-specific basis. Our measure of health is meant to address in part the extent of substance abuse but again, at the individual level, these proxies are incomplete. For a more extensive discussion of these issues at the individual level see, among others, Herault and Ribar (2017), McVicar, Moschion, and van Ours (2015, 2018), and Sickles and Taubman (2019).

5. ECONOMETRIC MODEL AND EMPIRICAL FINDINGS

The theoretical model discussed in Section 3 predicts that, in regions where healthcare access is worse, more people would enter into homelessness over time due to the heightened negative consequences of being homeless, which leads to a decline in future earnings potential. In order to analyze the relationship between homelessness and measures of healthcare access, income, and demographic traits described in the previous section, we first examine variations on a general least squares model where the dependent variable (our measure of homelessness) changes. The second part of the analysis extends this model to include a spatial component, accounting for potential dependencies between nearby CoCs and how that may impact homelessness levels across the West Coast.

For our model, we have drawn from the work of Hanratty (2017), who analyzes a panel dataset of homeless counts across the United States for 2007–2014 and estimates a least squares regression model with CoC fixed effects in her regression of homelessness counts on an array of socioeconomic variables. However, we have modified this approach to include interactions terms, motivated by findings in O'Flaherty (2004). O'Flaherty notes that since homelessness is a result of both personal and structural factors working against individuals, the interactions between these variables must be modeled and a failure to do so would seriously misspecify the econometric model. Additionally, given the ability of health and homelessness status to impact each other, reverse causality was a concern when setting up our econometric model. However, we believe that we have addressed any potential issues by proxying health with variables which measure access to healthcare resources, as well as by lagging specific demographic and health variables such as the uninsured rate, which we discuss in more detail below.

5.1. Fixed Effects Analysis

The general fixed effects model that we estimate is[4]:

$$HL_{it} = \alpha_i + \beta_1 Grnt_{it} + \beta_2 Gini_{i,t-2} + \beta_3 MR_{it} + \beta_4 H_{i,t-2} + \beta_5 D_{i,t-1} + \beta_6 X_{it} + \mu_{it} \quad (5)$$

Here, the dependent variable HL_{it} will take on three separate values: the number of homeless individuals per 1,000 in a CoC in a given year, the number of unsheltered homeless individuals per 1,000 in a CoC in a given year, and the proportion of the homeless population that is unsheltered in a CoC in a given year. α_i is a CoC-fixed effect term, encompassing characteristics specific to each CoC that may impact homelessness. $Grnt_{it}$ is HRSA grant funding per person (in 2010 dollars), $Gini_{i,t-2}$ is the Census Bureau's Gini index calculation, and MR_{it} is HUD's median rent value for a two-bedroom housing unit. $H_{i,t-2}$ is a matrix of health and healthcare variables, and includes physicians per 1,000 people, the percentage of uninsured individuals, and opioid prescriptions per 100 people. $D_{i,t-1}$ is a matrix of demographic variables, including the number of housing units per 100 people, as well as the proportions of the population in a CoC that are black, male, and older than 65. X_{it} contains a set of interaction terms.

In our analysis, we have also included lags of some of the variables to account for the time that it may take for specific factors to potentially influence homelessness levels in an area. We chose a 2 year lag for the uninsured rate, the Gini index, the opioid prescribing rate, and the number of primary care physicians per 1,000 people. Additionally, demographic characteristics in the matrix $D_{i,t-1}$ have all been lagged by one year.

5.2. Spatial Analysis

The second component of this analysis is an extension of the previous model to examine spatial dependencies that exist between adjacent CoCs.[5] We examine both a spatial autoregressive (SAR) model and a SEM and compare the two for goodness-of-fit. The SAR is (6), and the SEM is (7):

$$HL_{it} = \alpha_i + \beta_1 Grnt_{it} + \beta_2 Gini_{i,t-2} + \beta_3 MR_{it} + \beta_4 H_{i,t-2} + \beta_5 D_{i,t-1} + \beta_6 X_{it} + \rho \sum_{j=1}^{n} w_{ij} HL_{it} + \mu_{it} \tag{6}$$

$$HL_{it} = \alpha_i + \beta_1 Grnt_{it} + \beta_2 Gini_{i,t-2} + \beta_3 MR_{it} + \beta_4 H_{i,t-2} + \beta_5 D_{i,t-1} + \beta_6 X_{it*} + \mu_{it}$$
$$\text{where } \mu_{it} = \lambda_m \sum_{j=1}^{n} w_{ij} \mu_{jt} + \pi_{it} \tag{7}$$

The spatial component of the SAR model measures how homelessness in a CoC is influenced by homelessness in nearby CoCs. The spatial component is represented as a statistical noise term in the SEM specification. We estimate two different versions based on two different weighting matrices. The first uses a k-nearest-neighbors approach ($k = 5$). The second uses the inverse distance-squared approach and both are row standardized.

The spatial panels are based on data for the years 2015–2019.[6] Three CoCs in California (Lake County CoC, Tehama County CoC, and the Alpine/Inyo/Mono Counties CoC) are missing homeless count data for certain years. As a result, these three CoCs have been excluded from this spatial modeling. Fig. 4.5 is a map of all West Coast CoCs and their geometric centroids, which were used to create the spatial weights matrices.[7] The CoCs excluded from this spatial analysis are highlighted in orange.

6. RESULTS

6.1. Fixed Effects

Table 4.3 provides estimates from several different specifications of fixed effects regressions. In the cases where the dependent variable is the number of homeless or unsheltered homeless per 1,000 people, the estimates are based on two time periods, 2012–2019 and 2015–2019. We have included only those results from 2012 to 2019 for specifications using the unsheltered share of the homeless population as the dependent variable as the restricted regression from limited period 2015–2019 did not have enough within variation for estimates to be informative.[8]

Given that the rise in homelessness on the West Coast is a relatively recent phenomenon, we first focus on the results for more recent time period (2015–2019). Looking at these results in Table 4.3 for regressions 2 and 4, we see several clear relationships that emerge. There is a positive, statistically significant relationship between the Gini index and homelessness, both in the overall and unsheltered cases. This mirrors the conclusions of the O'Flaherty (1993) housing supply model discussed earlier. We also see a positive, significant relationship between homelessness and the percentage of the population that is male. In the unsheltered case, a positive relationship exists for the size of the senior population. Further, we see that interactions the Gini index has with housing availability and physicians per capita are both negative and significant.

Table 4.3. Model 1 Regression Results.

	Total HL		Unsheltered HL		% Un HL
	2012–2019 (1)	2015–2019 (2)	2012–2019 (3)	2015–2019 (4)	2012–2019 (5)
Grant money	−0.0365*** (0.0097)	−0.0017 (0.0125)	−0.0366*** (0.0088)	−0.0169 (0.0123)	−0.0005 (0.0008)
Physicians	−42.971** (17.1421)	71.11522*** (27.0371)	−38.319** (15.5125)	60.2527** (26.5971)	−2.6312* (1.3892)
Gini	−105.3924 (72.148)	364.7684*** (91.9001)	−72.913 (65.2891)	304.1258*** (90.4042)	−7.1332 (5.847)
Median Rent	−0.0061* (0.0036)	−0.0018 (0.0042)	−0.0064* (0.0033)	−0.0003 (0.0041)	−0.0007** (0.0003)
Housing	0.1431 (0.6221)	2.1445*** (0.7637)	0.3950 (0.5629)	1.785** (0.7513)	−0.0099 (0.0504)
Opioid	−0.0379*** (0.0103)	−0.014 (0.0133)	−0.0383*** (0.0093)	−0.0117 (0.0131)	−0.0017** (0.0008)
% Uninsured	−15.9533*** (5.7101)	0.6669 (6.7329)	−19.2044*** (5.1672)	−1.6417 (6.6233)	−1.6922*** (0.4628)
% Black	−257.5593* (141.294)	134.804 (252.6515)	−242.0142* (127.8616)	97.0286 (248.539)	−37.2957*** (11.4507)
% Male	186.3306** (79.33126)	263.382** (107.2984)	246.6127*** (71.7895)	238.9577** (105.5519)	20.6656*** (6.4292)
% 65+	10.6966 (13.5361)	38.6951 (24.5957)	15.0631 (12.2493)	41.8520* (24.1954)	2.4545** (1.097)

(Continued)

Table 4.3. *(Continued)*

	Total HL		Unsheltered HL		% Un HL
	2012–2019 (1)	2015–2019 (2)	2012–2019 (3)	2015–2019 (4)	2012–2019 (5)
(Physicians × uninsured)	23.1264***	3.2391	28.4172***	6.2031	2.7496***
	(7.8377)	(9.0850)	(7.0926)	(8.9372)	(0.6352)
(Physicians × Black)	−91.6825	13.9879	−90.4101	−4.3080	−10.7184*
	(77.3036)	(101.5564)	(69.9546)	(99.9034)	(6.2648)
(Median rent × Black)	0.0071	0.0030	0.0100	0.0016	0.0014
	(0.0142)	(0.0169)	(0.0129)	(0.0167)	(0.0012)
(Housing × median rent)	0.0001	−0.00001	0.0001	−0.00004	0.00002*
	(0.0001)	(0.0001)	(0.0001)	(0.0001)	(0.00001)
(Housing × Gini)	0.1207	−4.8557***	−0.2615	−4.0520**	0.0789
	(1.3990)	(1.731)	(1.2660)	(1.702)	(0.1134)
(Gini × Black)	367.3555	−617.1436	421.6887	−462.527	92.7323***
	(365.2022)	(511.2364)	(330.4834)	(502.915)	(29.5967)
(Physicians × Gini)	101.9004***	−155.5766**	90.2777***	−128.9356**	6.5975**
	(37.9605)	(61.6045)	(34.3517)	(60.6018)	(3.0764)
(Physicians × median rent)	−0.0007	0.0012	−0.0001	0.0014	−0.0001
	(51.5789)	(0.0021)	(0.0016)	(0.0021)	(0.0001)
N	431	275	431	275	431
R-2 – within	0.1252	0.2597	0.1668	0.254	0.2835
R-2 – between	0.0494	0.0488	0.071	0.0585	0.089
R-2 – overall	0.0443	0.0481	0.057	0.056	0.0566
F-Statistic	17.99	16.29	16.65	11.91	16.24
Prob > *F*	0.0000	0.0000	0.0000	0.0000	0.0000

* denotes 10% significance, ** denotes 5% significance, and *** denotes 1% significance.

There also appears to be a positive and statistically significant association between housing units per capita and homelessness. Though it seems counter-intuitive to suggest that homelessness is worse in CoCs with more housing units per capita, it is possible that this additional housing that is being built is more expensive, raising property values and subsequently crowding out lower-quality housing.

From a health perspective, we see that grant funding per person is negatively related to homelessness in regressions 1–4, although that relationship is only significant for the 2012–2019 panels. Additionally, the number of primary care physicians per 1,000 people is statistically significant in every regression. However, the sign of the relationship changes depending upon the time frame we are examining. The relationship between the two variables is negative over the longer time frame (regressions 1 and 3), but then becomes positive when our panel length is constrained to the shorter 2015–2019 period (regressions 2 and 4). Looking at regression 5, we see a negative, statistically significant relationship between the unsheltered proportion of homeless individuals and the number of primary care physicians per capita.

Due to the presence of interaction terms that complicate the interpretation of individual variable effects, we compute marginal effects at the mean of all other

Table 4.4. Marginal Effects at Means of Other Variables.

	Total HL		Unsheltered HL		% Un HL
	2012–2019 (1)	2015–2019 (2)	2012–2019 (3)	2015–2019 (4)	2012–2019 (5)
Grant money	−0.0365***	−0.0017	−0.0366***	−0.0169	−0.0005
	(0.0097)	(0.0125)	(0.0088)	(0.0123)	(0.0008)
Physicians	1.522	2.3754	2.3019	3.4518	0.1811*
	(2.4699)	(3.1528)	(2.235)	(3.1014)	(0.2002)
Gini	−5.5683	20.5191	4.3349	19.531	4.8023***
	(13.3239)	(18.3433)	(12.0573)	(18.0447)	(1.078)
Median rent	−0.0006	−0.0011	−0.0006	−0.0009	−0.00002
	(0.0008)	(0.0009)	(0.0007)	(0.0009)	(0.00006)
Housing	0.3481*	−0.0809	0.4165**	−0.1134	0.0438***
	(0.1917)	(0.2601)	(0.1734)	(0.2558)	(0.0155)
Opioid	−0.0379***	−0.014	−0.0383***	−0.0117	−0.0017**
	(0.0103)	(0.0133)	(0.0093)	(0.0131)	(0.0008)
% Uninsured	2.4428	3.2604	3.4004	3.3251	0.495*
	(3.2479)	(3.4430)	(2.9391)	(3.3869)	(0.2632)
% Black	−156.6981***	−132.0816	−112.5236**	−115.5901	−2.3527
	(60.0975)	(83.7874)	(54.3842)	(82.4236)	(4.8704)
% Male	186.3307**	263.382**	246.6127***	238.9577**	20.6656***
	(79.33126)	(107.2984)	(71.7895)	(105.5519)	(6.4292)
% 65+	10.6966	38.6951	15.0631	41.8520*	2.4545**
	(13.5361)	(24.5957)	(12.2493)	(24.1954)	(1.097)
N	431	275	431	275	431

* denotes 10% significance, ** denotes 5% significance, and *** denotes 1% significance.

covariates. These results are in Table 4.4, and can be interpreted as the impact on the dependent variable (homeless per 1,000, unsheltered homeless per 1,000, or percentage of homeless unsheltered) that a change in that independent variable has, holding all others at their mean values. Looking at these results, we see that the marginal effect of the number of physicians per 1,000 people is positive in all cases, but only has a statistically significant effect on the unsheltered proportion of homeless persons. Additionally, the marginal effect of grant funding per person is negative and significant in regressions 1 and 3. Every additional 100 dollars of grant funding per person lowers the number of sheltered (unsheltered) homeless persons per 1,000 by 3.65 (3.66). The marginal effect of the proportion of the population that is male is significant and positive in all cases, and the marginal effect of the senior population is positive in all cases as well. For example, in regression 1, increasing the proportion of the population that is male by 1% would increase the number of homeless individuals by 1.86 per 1,000. Although we observe that income inequality and the uninsured rate have positive impacts in regressions 1–4 as well, those marginal effects are not statistically significant. We see a positive, statistically significant relationship between housing units per capita and homelessness in regressions 1, 3, and 5, potentially due to the crowding out of lower-quality housing discussed earlier.

Looking at the marginal effects in regression 5, we see statistically significant marginal effects for physicians per capita, income inequality, and the uninsured rate, among others. Having one more primary care physician per 1,000 increases the unsheltered proportion of the homeless population by 18%, while an increase in the Gini index by one basis point would increase the unsheltered proportion by 4.8%. Additionally, a 1% increase in the uninsured rate would raise the unsheltered proportion by 0.5%.

Although some noteworthy conclusions can be drawn, this model has produced some mixed results. It is unexpected that a positive relationship between physicians per capita and homelessness would exist. However, this could be due to constraints of the model setup. Physicians per capita is being used to proxy the stock of healthcare resources, but the presence of more physicians does not necessarily imply that those physicians are easily accessible, and also does not speak to issues in regard to quality of care. Additionally, we implicitly assume that those individuals who are already at risk of homelessness would actively seek out care. We also do not find a positive link between opioid prescriptions and homelessness in any version of this model.

Similarly, the variables included in this model represent some, but not all, of the many variables that impact homelessness. To double-check this model setup, we have run the Hausman–Wu test for fixed and random effects. The results of those tests are listed in Table 4.5. We include these Durbin–Hausman–Wu results as they are the usual specification error criteria used in applied econometrics. That said, Guggenberger (2010) has shown that any inference done after model selection via the Hausman test is corrupted with pretest bias. In order to address this issue we would need to have taken a random sample from the data we have used in order to avoid such a pretest bias in our results. Data limitations and problems with conceptualizing how one would randomly sample from a spatially correlated SAR or SEM model utilized in our simulations is beyond the scope of this contribution. Only in regression 4, where unsheltered homeless per 1,000 is our dependent variable and the panel is restricted to 2015–2019, do we fail to reject the null hypothesis that a random effects model is preferred. However, given the low power of the test and our desire to account for specific characteristics that could impact homelessness and are unique to each CoC, we take the fixed effects approach as our default panel estimator.

Table 4.5. Hausman Test for Fixed Versus Random Effects.

	Total HL		Unsheltered HL		% Un HL
	2012–2019 (1)	2015–2019 (2)	2012–2019 (3)	2015–2019 (4)	2012–2019 (5)
p-Value	0.0038*	0.0428*	0.0016*	0.1817	0.001*

A significant *p*-value indicates a rejection of the null hypothesis (that the random effects setup is preferred).

6.2. Spatial Analysis

Both the SAR model and SEM produced similar results. In the SAR model, we see that the spatial component, ρ, is negative and statistically significant when we use total homelessness and unsheltered homelessness per 1,000 as the dependent variable. The negative coefficient suggests that levels of homelessness in contiguous communities are not similar. With that being said, we prefer the fit of the regressions run using the SEM, due to the lower Akeike information criterion (AIC) and Bayesian information criterion (BIC) values produced. We discuss those results in this section, but a table of results for the SAR model also has been included in the Appendix.

Table 4.6 details our results from the SEM. A total of 6 regressions have been run, where each dependent variable (total homeless per 1,000, unsheltered homeless per 1,000, and the unsheltered proportion) has been evaluated using the two

Table 4.6. SEM Results.

	Total HL		Unsheltered HL		% Un HL	
	K-N-N (1)	Inv-D2 (2)	K-N-N (3)	Inv-D2 (4)	K-N-N (5)	Inv-D2 (6)
Grant money	0.0038	−0.0021	−0.0130	−0.0162	−0.0017*	−0.0017*
	(0.0104)	(0.0112)	(0.0101)	(0.0109)	(0.0009)	(0.0009)
Physicians	42.9863*	45.0910*	24.1235	29.9581	2.5390	2.1426
	(25.4984)	(26.1530)	(25.0713)	(25.2841)	(2.2548)	(2.2171)
Gini	2.9022***	3.0359***	2.4346***	2.6764***	0.1836**	0.1763**
	(0.9649)	(0.9606)	(0.9447)	(0.9338)	(0.0841)	(0.0837)
Median rent	−0.0049	−0.0042	−0.0050	−0.0036	−0.0002	−0.0003
	(0.0037)	(0.0039)	(0.0037)	(0.0038)	(0.0003)	(0.0003)
Housing	1.8887**	1.9596**	1.8652**	1.9537**	0.1218*	0.1224*
	(0.8152)	(0.8252)	(0.7948)	(0.8023)	(0.0724)	(0.0721)
Opioid	−0.0274**	−0.0196	−0.0202*	−0.0120	0.0002	0.0001
	(0.0120)	(0.0123)	(0.0117)	(0.0118)	(0.0011)	(0.0011)
% Uninsured	−1.4228	−1.5145	−3.3242	−3.6805	−0.4743	−0.4268
	(5.6281)	(5.5672)	(5.4799)	(5.3769)	(0.5052)	(0.4991)
% Black	−6.0470	55.4913	−55.3973	22.3812	−22.8291	−25.7077
	(216.9466)	(223.5114)	(213.1579)	(218.0473)	(19.4570)	(19.5761)
% Male	395.4110***	324.7136***	379.6812***	308.5832***	5.6424	7.5210
	(95.5972)	(92.9970)	(93.2316)	(90.6650)	(8.2394)	(8.1312)
% 65+	10.6804	19.4355	20.4974	30.9293	2.8601	3.0549
	(22.5369)	(22.4811)	(21.9381)	(21.6580)	(2.0668)	(2.0281)
(Physicians ×	6.3643	6.6869	9.0373	10.0897	0.9325	0.9352
uninsured)	(7.7096)	(7.6759)	(7.5024)	(7.4279)	(0.6818)	(0.6764)
(Physicians ×	−3.3030	−18.6921	−15.2417	−42.4297	−2.7662	−1.6330
Black)	(90.9654)	(91.1332)	(88.9497)	(89.0464)	(7.7592)	(7.7859)
(Median rent	0.0004	0.0019	0.0008	0.0016	0.0007	0.0008
× Black)	(0.0139)	(0.0137)	(0.0135)	(0.0133)	(0.0012)	(0.0012)
(Housing ×	0.0001	0.0001	0.0002	0.0001	0.0000	0.0000
median rent)	(0.0001)	(0.0001)	(0.0001)	(0.0001)	(0.0000)	(0.0000)
(Housing ×	−0.0424**	−0.0438**	−0.0419**	−0.0443**	−0.0031*	−0.0031*
Gini)	(0.0187)	(0.0188)	(0.0182)	(0.0182)	(0.0016)	(0.0016)
(Gini × Black)	−3.8314	−4.6856	−2.2879	−3.1466	0.4252	0.4717
	(4.2996)	(4.5096)	(4.1979)	(4.3985)	(0.3926)	(0.3953)

(Continued)

Table 4.6. (*Continued*)

	Total HL		Unsheltered HL		% Un HL	
	K-N-N (1)	Inv-D2 (2)	K-N-N (3)	Inv-D2 (4)	K-N-N (5)	Inv-D2 (6)
(Physicians × Gini)	−0.8271 (0.5700)	−0.8873 (0.5808)	−0.3680 (0.5605)	−0.5121 (0.5610)	−0.0358 (0.0501)	−0.0277 (0.0492)
(Physicians × median rent)	−0.0011 (0.0019)	−0.0011 (0.0020)	−0.0019 (0.0019)	−0.0015 (0.0019)	−0.0002 (0.0002)	−0.0002 (0.0002)
Spatial lambda (λ)	−0.3690*** (0.1287)	−0.2460** (0.1135)	−0.3855*** (0.1284)	−0.2881** (0.1175)	0.0630 (0.1129)	−0.0586 (0.1134)
Variance E^2	0.4434*** (0.0392)	0.4517*** (0.0399)	0.4218*** (0.0373)	0.4277*** (0.0379)	0.0034*** (0.0003)	0.0034*** (0.0003)
N	260	260	260	260	260	260
R-2	0.0929	0.0808	0.0779	0.0692	0.0028	0.0042
AIC	568.717	572.2884	556.0895	559.2324	−701.0057	−700.9672
BIC	636.3699	639.9414	623.7424	626.8853	−633.3548	−633.3143
LL	−265.3585	−267.1442	−259.0447	−260.6162	369.5039	369.4836

different weighting matrices (*k*-nearest neighbors and inverse distance-squared).[9] Compared with results from the standard fixed effects models in Section 6.1, we see the fits improve when evaluating both total homelessness and unsheltered homelessness. However, the fits for the unsheltered share model appear to be very poor, with R^2 values less than 0.01, so for this reason we focus our discussion on regressions 1–4 in Table 4.6. Our results indicate similar outcomes to those from the original fixed effects specifications. They can be interpreted in a similar way, as the spatial component is within the error term so it has no bearing on the coefficients of the explanatory variables. There are positive, significant relationships among the Gini index, housing units, and the proportion of the population that is male, with both total and unsheltered homelessness in all four regression outputs. We also once again see a positive relationship coefficient on physicians per capita, although this is only significant in impacting total homelessness.

From a spatial perspective, we find that the spatial autocorrelation coefficient, λ, is negative and significant in all four cases. This negative spatial dependence implies that the error terms of nearby CoCs tend to be dissimilar to one another, suggesting that shocks to variables outside of our model, or outside of the level of homelessness itself, tend to affect homelessness levels in nearby regions in different ways. Further examination of this conclusion is presented below by examining the spatial effects of unforeseen shocks to SEM error.

6.2.1. Analysis of SEM Propagation Due to an Unforeseen Shock such as COVID-19 Contagion

The outbreak of coronavirus across the globe is an example of an unforeseen and exogenous factor that can impact homelessness. We use this interpretation to study how such a shock can have spatial effects throughout communities impacted by homelessness. To do this, we test a multiple standard deviation change in the error component for each CoC, and see how that shock would affect homelessness across regions. The approach we take is similar to that taken in Le Gallo,

Baumont, Dall'erba, and Ertur (2005), using the intuition for the SEM formulated by Glass, Kenjegalieva, and Sickles (2012).

Recall the equation for the SEM from Section 6.2:

$$HL_{it} = \alpha_i + \beta_1 Grnt_{it} + \beta_2 Gini_{i,t-2} + \beta_3 MR_{it} + \beta_4 H_{i,t-2} + \beta_5 D_{i,t-1} + \beta_6 X_{it*} + \mu_{it}$$

where

$$\mu_{it} = \rho_m \sum_{j=1}^{n} w_{ij} \mu_{jt} + \pi_{it}.$$

We focus on spatial impacts for 2019, the most recent year in our study, by allowing for various shocks π_{it} equal to two and five standard deviations in the error terms listed in the SEM output in Table 4.6. The error term for each CoC takes on the value of $\pi_{it} + 2\sigma$ or $\pi_{it} + 5\sigma$. The error term draws are from a normal distribution with zero mean and variance specified by the size of each scenario's shock that are used to determine the new value of the dependent variable within every geographic unit. We develop a $(n \times n)$ matrix Y^*, where each column j of Y^* represents the new values of the dependent variable in every CoC resulting from the shock occurring in the jth CoC.

The impacts of a shock on each CoC can be evaluated by constructing the matrix $D = (Y^* - Y)$ and a matrix V, which allow us to evaluate the spatial shocks in percentage terms specified below:

$$Y^* = \alpha + \beta X + (I - \lambda W)^{-1} \text{diag}(b\sigma)$$

$$D = Y^* - Y = (I - \lambda W)^{-1} \text{diag}(b\sigma)$$

$$[V]_{ij} = \frac{[D]_{ij}}{[Y]_{ij}}.$$

The diagonal elements of V represent the direct impact of a shock, occurring in a CoC, on the CoC itself while each column of V gives the impact of a shock in a CoC on all other CoC's and each row of V provides a similar measure of how each CoC is impacted by shocks in every other CoC.

Given the poor fit of the SEM where the dependent variable is the share of homeless that are unsheltered, we only consider the versions of this model where the dependent variable is the number of homeless or unsheltered homeless per 1,000. These are from regressions 1–4 in Table 4.6. Since shocks of two different sizes are being considered, this generates eight different V matrices. Results across these models are fairly similar. For the sake of brevity, we focus our discussion on shocks calculated for cases wherein the spatial weights matrix was created using the inverse distance-squared method. Other results are available on request.

Table 4.7 lists the diagonal elements of four different V matrices. These numbers represent the direct effect that a shock happening in a CoC has on that CoC itself. So, for example, a 2 standard deviation shock on CA-501 (San Francisco County CoC) is predicted to raise the number of homeless persons per 1,000 there by 14.9%.

Table 4.7. Direct Effects of a Shock in Each CoC.

	Total HL (%)		Unsheltered HL (%)	
	Shock = 2σ	Shock = 5σ	Shock = 2σ	Shock = 5σ
CA-500	27.2	68.0	32.5	81.2
CA-501	14.9	37.4	22.7	56.6
CA-502	28.3	70.8	35.2	88.0
CA-503	37.6	94.0	52.3	130.7
CA-504	23.0	57.4	33.8	84.5
CA-505	68.7	171.8	94.9	237.2
CA-506	25.3	63.2	33.3	83.3
CA-507	34.5	86.2	49.1	122.8
CA-508	17.1	42.8	21.3	53.2
CA-509	15.3	38.2	21.7	54.4
CA-510	39.3	98.4	67.8	169.6
CA-511	39.6	99.1	65.3	163.2
CA-512	69.5	173.8	113.9	284.8
CA-513	80.6	201.5	108.0	270.0
CA-514	63.3	158.3	74.8	187.0
CA-515	65.2	163.1	120.2	300.6
CA-516	31.3	78.2	51.0	127.4
CA-517	59.0	147.4	123.3	308.2
CA-518	52.1	130.1	62.8	156.9
CA-519	24.2	60.6	35.7	89.3
CA-520	62.9	157.2	129.5	323.6
CA-521	46.0	114.9	73.9	184.8
CA-522	10.7	26.8	12.7	31.7
CA-523	45.6	113.9	56.8	142.0
CA-524	33.0	82.4	44.7	111.8
CA-525	42.5	106.4	53.1	132.7
CA-526	24.9	62.3	29.8	74.6
CA-600	23.7	59.2	30.9	77.2
CA-601	56.0	140.0	98.9	247.2
CA-602	63.9	159.7	108.1	270.4
CA-603	34.1	85.3	52.9	132.3
CA-604	93.8	234.4	151.4	378.5
CA-608	119.9	299.7	162.0	404.9
CA-609	115.2	287.9	153.2	383.0
CA-611	69.5	173.7	89.9	224.8
CA-613	18.3	45.7	20.6	51.5
CA-614	25.6	63.9	31.6	78.9
HI-500	17.3	43.2	27.8	69.5
HI-501	31.6	79.1	58.0	145.0
OR-500	23.6	59.0	30.5	76.2
OR-501	28.6	71.6	55.7	139.3
OR-502	41.9	104.7	79.8	199.5
OR-503	37.1	92.7	51.9	129.8
OR-505	29.4	73.5	40.5	101.1
OR-506	156.0	389.9	347.0	867.6
OR-507	121.8	304.4	250.9	627.3
WA-500	27.5	68.8	58.0	144.9
WA-501	63.9	159.8	149.2	373.1
WA-502	53.0	132.6	214.7	536.7
WA-503	81.2	202.9	187.3	468.2
WA-504	100.8	251.9	184.1	460.3
WA-508	71.0	177.5	137.7	344.2

Fig. 4.9 maps the direct effects on total homelessness per 1,000 in the event of either a two standard deviation or 5 standard deviation shock (the first two columns in Table 4.7). As expected, the direct impacts are larger in the event of a more drastic shock. Additionally, suburban and rural areas of Washington and California appear to be hit particularly hard by a shock affecting every CoC. However, it is important to note that these maps do not consider any spatial dependencies between CoCs. Given the presence of significant spatial autocorrelation found in the SEM, it is important that this be considered. One way to investigate these interactions or spillover effects is to examine how a shock hitting one CoC would diffuse through the rest of the map.

As the coronavirus pandemic continues, different parts of the United States have emerged as "hotspots": New York, Michigan, and Louisiana, among others. In light of the fallout from this outbreak, both from an economic and a public health perspective, it is reasonable to guess that a wide-scale outbreak in a city or county could facilitate a short-term rise in homelessness in that area. Given that the columns of the matrix V contain information regarding how a shock in one CoC would affect all others, these data can be mapped to examine how a shock, such as the birth of a COVID-19 hotspot, might dissipate across the West Coast.

In Fig. 4.10, we have mapped the effects of specific shocks to four CoCs: CA-600 (Los Angeles County), CA-501 (San Francisco County), OR-501 (Portland/Multnomah County), and WA-500 (Seattle/King County). Given that these effects were determined using the inverse distance-squared spatial weights matrix, there were no measurable impacts to either CoC in Hawaii, so the state is excluded from the following mappings.

Looking at these results, the negative spatial relationships predicted by the SEM are clearly visible. In all four cases, a shock to that CoC leads to an increase in homelessness in the CoC itself, and a decrease in homelessness in the surrounding CoCs. This result is seemingly counterintuitive, as it seems reasonable to suspect that a shock such as this would have positive spillover effects. However, an alternative explanation could be the following. In the context of the COVID-19 pandemic, the emergence of a hotspot in a city, and the resulting economic and health challenges that it brings, could serve as a signal to nearby regions of the potential struggles that they may face should they also suffer a shock. In a time of crisis, outreach to those in need in nearby CoCs could potentially increase as surrounding regions take mitigating steps, companies make donations, and governments take preventative action to contain the spread. As a result, it is possible that homelessness could decline in the short term as outreach and aid to the vulnerable increase. With that being said, evidence is mixed on the efficacy of increased funding and outreach on homelessness levels, and success is influenced by the nature of any specific intervention. When examining the impact of federal funding, Lucas (2017) finds a positive relationship with sheltered homelessness levels and a negative one with unsheltered homelessness levels, but only the former relationship is statistically significant. In practice, more targeted outreach programs and aid have been used to positive effect. For example, the city of Houston has significantly reduced its chronically homeless population over the last decade by adopting a "housing first" approach that identifies vulnerable individuals to place directly into rapid rehousing, pairing shelter with a case manager to help give access to employment programs or substance abuse treatment services, if needed (Kimmelman, 2022). Of the individuals placed into rapid rehousing, which covers rent for a year, the success rate for remaining housed after that year is almost 75%.

7. CONCLUSIONS

The results of this analysis demonstrate the complexity of homelessness and the difficulty of understanding its underlying causes. We did not find one single "determinant" to account for the sudden growth of homeless populations on the West Coast. However, this was to be expected, given the sheer number of factors that can influence an individual's housing status. Even though many individuals may be living in poverty, suffering from health conditions, or struggling to make ends meet, those circumstances alone do not cause homelessness on their own. However, they increase a person's risk of experiencing housing insecurity. When this insecurity is amplified in a more unforgiving economic environment, it is only natural that smaller shocks would push more and more people into homelessness.

We have examined the impacts of a variety of socioeconomic variables on homelessness on the West Coast using two versions of a fixed effects framework – one simple, and one testing for spatial dependencies. Though results were mixed, we did find positive links between income inequality, housing units per capita, and homelessness. In particular, a statistically significant relationship exists between growing income inequality and the proportion of the homeless population that is unsheltered. However, unlike Hanratty (2017), our results did not indicate that the median rent level played a significant role in affecting homelessness levels. From a health perspective, investment via grant funding was found to have a positive effect on mitigating homelessness, but the relationship between homelessness and physicians per capita was unclear. Additionally, there was no positive relationship found between opioid prescriptions and homelessness. Negative and significant spatial dependencies were found, suggesting that homelessness levels in nearby CoCs are more dissimilar from one another and that homeless populations may tend to cluster in certain regions or areas.

Due to the SEM's ability to incorporate shocks occurring outside of our model framework, and in light of the recent coronavirus pandemic, we also tested how the overall effect of a shock would permeate through all CoCs across the West Coast. Results suggest that homelessness does not have a positive spillover effect. Simulated shocks in major cities predict a decrease in homelessness in nearby geographic areas, suggesting that a shock in one area could signal nearby areas to expand outreach and take preventative action in the face of a crisis.

This framework is not without limitations. For example, the variables used to measure healthcare investment and stock are constrained in their ability to say anything about quality and accessibility of care for poor individuals. We also are implicitly assuming that all individuals would make use of healthcare resources if they had them available. In terms of data quality, the homeless counts produced by HUD are almost certainly an undercount of the true size of the unsheltered population. Additionally, these counts do not include individuals who are "doubling up," or living with relatives or friends in overcrowded housing. Extensions of this model, perhaps that include more complicated spatial frameworks, that include variables like shelter beds or average temperature, or that make use of individual-level data, could paint a clearer picture of the homelessness problem.

Clearly, the struggles that local governments on the West Coast have faced highlight how much more difficult it is to reduce homelessness than it is to increase it. From an individual perspective, it is easy to see how, in the absence of external intervention, it is possible to become trapped by homelessness, as predicted in Glomm and John (2002). The transition to homelessness entails a loss of possessions, social capital, and sense of belonging (Baumohl 1996). Additionally, the homeless face added health complications, employment discrimination, and housing market challenges as they look to re-enter the traditional economy (O'Flaherty, 1993). When compounded with a health issue, breaking the cycle of homelessness could become almost impossible without some sort of intervention.

Freeman and Hall (1986), in a study of homeless individuals in New York City, found that a majority were chronically without shelter, and predicted that, without major changes to the housing market or economic position of the poor, homelessness would be a permanent fixture of American cities. More than 30 years later, despite the recent success of the American economy, the issue of homelessness (particularly on the West Coast) is timelier than ever. Now, in light of the coronavirus epidemic, intervention is crucial in order to protect those who lack shelter, as they and the working poor are most at risk. The homeless already receive a majority of their medical care via emergency hospitalizations (Flaming et al., 2009), and this cost burden on hospitals is likely to worsen as coronavirus spreads and the capacity of the healthcare system is tested. However, it is clear, both from this analysis as well as from the permanence of homelessness in America, that no simple solutions to this problem exist.

NOTES

1. Our chapter is based in part on Fuller (2020).
2. That said, Meyer Wyse, Grunwaldt, Medalia, and Wu (2021) have corroborated the relatively low rates of migration out of states in which they became homeless, with their estimates indicating, for example, that about 9% of sheltered homeless adults moved in the past year to a new state (2011–2018).
3. Due to space constraints in this volume, the Appendix can be found at http://rsickles.rice.edu/.
4. Our modeling framework can be more closely tied to the SFA literature generally and Subal Kumbhakar's contributions in particular by specifying (5) with a one-sided error, to pick up the possibility of undercounts, much like the models introduced by Millimet and Parmeter (2022a, 2022b). In their context, it was COVID-19 deaths and infections that are undercounted. In our chapter, the natural implication is that the number of homeless is surely an undercount. Such a model that formalizes the undercount into the econometric specification as well as possible skewed versions of it (see also Almanidis & Sickles, 2012; Almanidis et al., 2014; Sickles & Zelenyuk, 2019) is a natural link between the statistical literature on undercounts and the production econometric literature on SFA modeling and

this link is just beginning to get traction in the econometrics literature. Subal Kumbhakar's influence on this emergent use of SFA methods in addressing undercounts is not only felt by way of his theoretical contributions but also by way of one of his most well-known and published mentees, co-editor Christopher Parmeter.

5. Appendices 1 and 2 provide additional details on the West Coast CoC used in our analyses. These appendices also can be found at http://rsickles.rice.edu/.

6. In order to use the "xsmle" command in Stata to run these spatial models, the panel of data must be strongly balanced.

7. Due to space constraints in the volume Figs. 4.5–4.10 can be found at http://rsickles.rice.edu/.

8. All of these models have been estimated using Stata's "xtreg" command for panel data.

9. Appendix 3 provides detailed results for the SAR model estimates.

ACKNOWLEDGMENTS

The authors would like to thank the editors and a referee for comments that substantially improved the chapter.

REFERENCES

Abraham, J. M., Goetzmann, W. N., & Wachter, S. M. (1994). Homogeneous groupings of metropolitan housing markets. *Journal of Housing Economics*, *3*(3), 186–206.

Almanidis, P., Qian, J., & Sickles, R. C. (2014). Stochastic frontier models with bounded inefficiency. In R. C. Sickles & W. C. Horrace (Eds.), *Festschrift in honor of Peter Schmidt: Econometric methods and applications* (pp. 47–82). New York, NY: Springer.

Almanidis, P., & Sickles, R. C. (2012). The skewness problem in stochastic frontier models: Fact or fiction? In I. Van Keilegom & P. W. Wilson (Eds.), *Exploring research frontiers in contemporary statistics and econometrics: A Festschrift in honor of Leopold Simar* (pp. 201–227). New York, NY: Springer.

Baltagi, B. H., Moscone, F., & Santos, R. (2018). Spatial health econometrics. In B. H. Baltagi & F. Moscone (Eds.),*Health Econometrics* (pp. 305–326). Bingley: Emerald Publishing Limited.

Baumohl, J. (1996). *Homelessness in America*. Phoenix, AZ: Oryx Press.

Becker, G. S., & Murphy, K. M. (1988). A theory of rational addiction. *Journal of Political Economy*, *96*(4), 675–700.

Collinson, R., & Reed, D. (2018). *The effects of evictions on low-income households*. Working Paper, New York University Wagner School of Public Service, New York, NY. Retrieved from https://www.law.nyu.edu/sites/default/files/upload_documents/evictions_collinson_reed.pdf

Curtis, M. A., Corman, H., Noonan, K., & Reichman, N. (2012). *Life shocks and homelessness*. NBER Working Paper 16826, National Bureau of Economic Research, Cambridge, MA.

Dai, L., & Zhou, P. (2019). *The health issues of the homeless and the homeless issues of the ill-health*. Cardiff Economics Working Paper E2019/12, Cardiff Business School, Economics Section, Cardiff, UK.

Del Real, J. A. (2018, May 8). Needle by needle, a heroin crisis grips California's rural north. *New York Times*. https://www.nytimes.com/2018/05/08/us/california-heroin-opioid.html

Early, D. (1999). A microeconomic analysis of homelessness: An empirical investigation using choice-based sampling. *Journal of Housing Economics*, *8*(4), 312–327.

Early, D. (2004). The determinants of homelessness and the targeting of housing assistance. *Journal of Urban Economics*, *55*, 195–214.

Early, D. (2005). An empirical analysis of the determinants of street homelessness. *Journal of Housing Economics*, *14*, 27–47.

Evans, W. N., Philips, D. C., & Ruffini, K. J. (2019). *Reducing and preventing homelessness: a review of the evidence and charting a research agenda*. NBER Working Paper 26232, National Bureau of Economic Research, Cambridge, MA.

Flaming, D., Matsunaga, M., & Burns, P. (2009, November 1). *Where we sleep: Costs when homeless and housed in Los Angeles*. Economic Roundtable, Los Angeles Homeless Services Authority. Retrieved from https://economicrt.org/publication/where-we-sleep/

Flato, M., & Johannessen, K. (2010). Economic strategies among long-term homeless people: The concept of harvesting economy. *European Journal of Homelessness*, *4*, 89–109.

Freeman, R. B., & Hall, B. (1986). *Permanent homelessness in America?* NBER Working Paper 2013, National Bureau of Economic Research, Cambridge, MA.

Fuller, C. (2020). *Homelessness on the West Coast: What role does health play?*. Unpublished Honors Thesis, Rice University, TX, USA.

Glass, A. J., Kenjagalieva, K., & Sickles, R. (2012). *The economic case for the spatial error model with an application to state vehicle usage in the U.S.* Working Paper. Retrieved from http://www.ruf.rice.edu/~rsickles/paper/the%20economic%20case%20for%20the%20spatial%20error%20model.pdf

Glomm, G., & John, A. (2002). Homelessness and labor markets. *Regional Science and Urban Economics*, *32*, 591–606.

Glynn, C., Byrne, T., & Culhane, D. P. (2018). *Inflection points in community-level homeless rates*. Working Paper. Retrieved from https://wp-tid.zillowstatic.com/3/Homelessness_InflectionPoints-27eb88.pdf

Glynn, C., & Fox, E. B. (2019). Dynamics of homelessness in urban America. *Annals of Applied Statistics*, *13*(1), 573–605.

Grossman, M. (1972). On the concept of health capital and the demand for health. *The Journal of Political Economy*, *80*(2), 223–255.

Guggenberger, P. (2010). The impact of a Hausman pretest on the asymptotic size of a hypothesis test. *Econometric Theory*, *26*(2), 369–382.

Hanratty, M. (2017). Do local economic conditions affect homelessness? Impact of area housing market factors, unemployment, and poverty on community homeless rates. *Housing Policy Debate*, *27*(4), 640–655.

Henry, M., Wiatt, R., Mahathey, A. Ouelette, J., & Sitler, A. (2020, January). *The 2019 annual homeless assessment report (AHAR) to Congress, Part 1: Point-in-time estimates of homelessness*. U.S. Department of Housing and Urban Development. Retrieved from https://files.hudexchange.info/resources/documents/2019-AHAR-Part-1.pdf

Herault, N., & Ribar, D. C. (2017). Food insecurity and homelessness in the Journeys Home survey. *Journal of Housing Economics*, *37*, 52–66.

Hidalgo, S. (2020, November 13). The health of the homeless: A climate change problem. *The Climate Change Review*. Retrieved from https://www.theclimatechangereview.com/post/the-health-of-the-homeless-a-climate-change-problem

Honig, M., & Filer, R. K. (1993). Causes of intercity variation in homelessness. *American Economic Review*, *83*(1), 248–255.

Imrohoroglu, A., Matoba, K., & Tuzel, S. (2018). Proposition 13: an equilibrium analysis. *American Economic Journal*, *10*(2), 24–51.

Kimmelman, M. (2022, June 24). How Houston moved 25,000 people from the streets into homes of their own. *New York Times*. Retrieved from https://www.nytimes.com/2022/06/14/headway/houston-homeless-people.html

Le Gallo, J., Baumont, C., Dall'erba, S., & Ertur, C. (2005). On the property of diffusion in the spatial error model. *Applied Economics Letters*, *12*, 533–536.

Lucas, D. S. (2017). The impact of federal homelessness funding on homelessness. *Southern Economic Journal*, *84*(2), 548–576.

Marzilli, A. (2017). *Homeless and housing services providers confront opioid overdose*. United States Substance Abuse and Mental Health Services Administration. Retrieved from https://www.samhsa.gov/homelessness-programs-resources/hpr-resources/homeless-housing-services-providers-confront-opioid

Mast, B. D. (2014). Measuring spatial mismatch between homelessness and homeless resources with a Theil index and statistical inference. *Cityscape*, *16*(1), 339–350.

McVicar, D., Moschion, J., & van Ours, J. (2015). From substance use to homelessness or vice versa? *Social Science and Medicine*, *136–137*, 89–98.

McVicar, D., Moschoin, J., & van Ours, J. (2018). Early illicit drug use and the age of onset of homelessness. *Journal of Royal Statistical Society: Series A (Statistics in Society)*, *182*(1), 345–372.

Meyer, B. D., Wyse, A., Grunwaldt, A., Medalia, C., & Wu, D. (2021, June 23). Learning about homelessness using linked survey and administrative data. *Economic Finding*, Becker Friedman Institute for Economics, University of Chicago. Retrieved from https://bfi.uchicago.edu/insight/finding/learning-about-homelessness-using-linked-survey-and-administrative-data/

Millimet, D. L., & Parmeter, C. F. (2022a). Accounting for skewed or one-sided measurement error in the dependent variable. *Political Analysis*, *30*(1), 66–88.

Millimet, D. L., & Parmeter, C. F. (2022b). COVID-19 severity: A new approach to quantifying global cases and deaths. *Journal of the Royal Statistical Society: Series A Statistics in Society*, *185*(3), 1178–1215.

O'Flaherty, B. (1993). An economic theory of housing and homelessness. *Journal of Housing Economics*, *4*(1), 13–49.

O'Flaherty, B. (1996). *Making room: The economics of homelessness*. Cambridge, MA: Harvard University Press.

O'Flaherty, B. (2004). Wrong person and wrong place: For homelessness, the conjunction is what matters. *Journal of Housing Economics*, *13*(1), 1–15.

Ohanian, L. (2019, June 18). *The economics of why homelessness worsens as governments spend even more on the problem*. Hoover Institution. Retrieved from https://www.hoover.org/research/economics-why-homelessness-worsens-governments-spend-even-more-problem

Quigley, J., & Raphael, S. (2001). The economics of homelessness: The evidence from North America. *European Journal of Housing Policy*, *1*(3), 323–336.

Quigley, J., & Raphael, S. (2005). Regulation and the high cost of housing in California. *American Economic Review*, *95*(2), 323–328.

Quigley, J., Raphael, S., & Smolensky, E. (2002). *Homeless in America, homeless in California*. Working Paper #W99-001, Berkeley Program on Housing and Urban Policy, Berkeley, CA.

Ramin, B., & Svoboda, T. (2009). Health of the homeless and climate change. *Journal of Urban Health*, *86*(4), 654–664.

Raphael, S. (2010). Housing market regulation and homelessness. In I. Gould Ellen & B. O'Flaherty (Eds.), *How to house the homeless* (pp. 110–140). New York, NY: Russell Sage Foundation.

Sala-i-Martin, X. (2005). On the health-poverty trap. In G. López-Casasnovas, B. Rivera, & L. Currais (Eds.), *Health and economic growth: Findings and policy implications* (pp. 95–97). Cambridge, MA: The MIT Press.

Schanzer, B., Dominguez, B., Shrout, P. E., & Caton, C. L. M. (2007). Homelessness, health status, and health care use. *American Journal of Public Health*, *97*, 464–469.

Sharpe, A., Sichel, D., & van Ark, B. (2022). Symposium on productivity and well-being – Part II. *International Productivity Monitor*, no. 43.

Sickles, R. C., & Taubman, P. (1986). An analysis of the health and retirement status of the elderly. *Econometrica*, *54*(6), 1339–1356.

Sickles, R. C., & Taubman, P. (1997). Mortality and morbidity among adults and the elderly. In M. R. Rosenzweig & O. Stark (Eds.), *Handbook of population and family economics* (pp. 559–643). Amsterdam: North-Holland.

Sickles, R. C., & Yazbeck, A. S. (1998). On the dynamics of demand for leisure and production of health: Evidence from the retirement history survey. *Journal of Business and Economic Statistics*, *16*, 187–197.

Sickles, R. C., & Zelenyuk, V. (2019). *Measurement of productivity and efficiency*. New York, NY: Cambridge University Press.

Shonkoff, S. B., Morello-Frosch, R., Pastor, M., & Sadd, J. (2011). The climate gap: environmental health and equity implications of climate change and mitigation policies in California – A review of the literature. *Climatic Change*, *109*(1), 485–503.

Wasi, N., & White, M. J. (2005). *Property tax limitations and mobility: the lock-in effect of California's Proposition 13*. NBER Working Paper 11108, National Bureau of Economic Research, Cambridge, MA.

Yu, W. (2018). *Homelessness in the U.S., California, and Los Angeles*. The UCLA Anderson Forecast for the Nation and California, University of California at Los Angeles. Retrieved from https://www.anderson.ucla.edu/documents/areas/ctr/forecast/reports/uclaforecast_June2018_Yu.pdf

CHAPTER 5

BOOTSTRAP MODEL AVERAGING UNIT ROOT INFERENCE

Bruce E. Hansen[a] and Jeffrey S. Racine[b,c,d,e]

[a]*Department of Economics, University of Wisconsin, USA*
[b]*Department of Economics and Graduate Program in Statistics, McMaster University, Canada*
[c]*Department of Economics and Finance, La Trobe University, Australia*
[d]*Info-Metrics Institute, American University, USA*
[e]*Rimini Center for Economic Analysis, Italy*

ABSTRACT

Classical unit root tests are known to suffer from potentially crippling size distortions, and a range of procedures have been proposed to attenuate this problem, including the use of bootstrap procedures. It is also known that the estimating equation's functional form can affect the outcome of the test, and various model selection procedures have been proposed to overcome this limitation. In this chapter, the authors adopt a model averaging procedure to deal with model uncertainty at the testing stage. In addition, the authors leverage an automatic model-free dependent bootstrap procedure where the null is imposed by simple differencing (the block length is automatically determined using recent developments for bootstrapping dependent processes). Monte Carlo simulations indicate that this approach exhibits the lowest size distortions among its peers in settings that confound existing approaches, while it has superior power relative to those peers whose size distortions do not preclude their general use. The proposed approach is fully automatic, and there are no nuisance parameters that have to be set by the user, which ought to appeal to practitioners.

Essays in Honor of Subal Kumbhakar
Advances in Econometrics, Volume 46, 81–98

Published under exclusive licence by Emerald Publishing Limited
ISSN: 0731-9053/doi:10.1108/S0731-905320240000046005

Keywords: Inference; lag uncertainty; model selection; power; size distortion; time series

JEL classifications: C12; C32

1. INTRODUCTION

Unit root tests, developed initially for univariate time series data, have widespread potential application beyond this setting including but not limited to panel data settings by way of illustration (Kumbhakar, 1990). Though unit root tests were developed over four decades ago, problems with the various approaches that have been proposed persist and, perhaps surprisingly, there remains room for improvement. When testing for a unit root, the null is that the series contains a unit root, with rejection of the null in one direction indicating that a series is stationary, and rejection in the other direction indicating explosiveness. If these tests exhibit large upwards size distortions, practitioners may wrongly conclude that a time series is stationary (or explosive) when in fact it is not, which can render subsequent inference invalid. Size distortions surface surprisingly often in this setting since practitioners must select from among a range of candidate estimating equations when testing for the presence of a unit root, and estimating equation mis-specification leads to bias in estimated parameters. To deal with the size distortions arising from mis-specification, bootstrap procedures have been proposed (Palm, Smeekes, & Urbain, 2008; Park, 2003). However, for many of these tests, size distortions and sub-optimal power concerns persist in part because they rely on a model specification which must be selected by the practitioner from amount a set of mis-specified candidate models. In order to attenuate the size distortions arising from the choice of a mis-specified estimating equation, the use of model selection criteria such as the Bayes Information Criterion (BIC) (Schwarz, 1978) has been advocated (Ng & Perron, 2001). Ng and Perron (2001) assert that the BIC selects overly parsimonious models and propose a Modified Information Criteria (MIC). For Ng and Perron's (2001) approach, size distortions are attenuated as the dimension of the selected model increases, however, this is not without cost as power falls as the dimension increases. Furthermore, the maximum lag that must be set by the practitioner affects the outcome of the test and ad hoc rules are frequently adopted for its selection (Schwert, 1989).

Model selection methods, however, are limited by the fact that they are *hard thresholding* rules, and are hence inherently discontinuous functions of the data. Small changes in a time series can induce a discontinuous change in the selected model, and hence a discontinuous change in the test statistic. Such hard threshold rules inflate sampling variance and distort finite sample sampling distributions.

As an alternative to model selection, we exploit recent developments in (frequentist) model averaging (Hansen's, 2007, Mallows Model Averaging, MMA; Hansen, 2014; Hansen & Racine's, 2012, Jackknife Model Averaging, JMA), as it is known that model averaging can overcome limitations associated with the use of model selection methods. In the present context, we propose a unit root statistic that is a weighted average of unit root statistics taken from a set of candidate estimating equations that are the same as those used for the Ng and Perron (2001) or Dickey and Fuller (1979) approaches. We also adopt an automatic, model-free, time series bootstrap procedure for constructing the null distribution of the proposed statistic, from which nonparametric critical values or nonparametric *P*-values can be obtained. Most existing bootstrap unit root procedures are model-based, and one problem with model-based resampling is that the data generating process (DGP) is unknown and must be identified from the series at hand. In order to ensure that the bootstrap samples have the same structure as the series at hand, this identification must be correct. Swensen (2003) considers model-based and model-free bootstrap approaches and demonstrates that a difference-based model-free approach (along the lines of that proposed herein) delivers a bootstrap distribution that approaches the true asymptotic distribution under the null of a unit root (see also Palm et al., 2008, Section 2.4).

We will see that when model averaging is combined with a model-free, automatic, time series bootstrap procedure (Politis & Romano 1994; Politis & White 2004; Patton, Politis & White 2009), we can obtain a fully automatic data-driven procedure that has superior size *and* power relative to those peers whose size distortions do not preclude their general use, while the sensitivity to the dimension of the model (i.e., the maximum lag that must be set by the practitioner) is attenuated by averaging over a set of candidate estimating equations in a particular manner. Furthermore, unlike its peers, the procedure is very robust to the number of and maximum dimension of the candidate estimating equations over which the averaging is performed (size and power are largely unaffected whether you use augmented Dickey–Fuller, ADF, models with, e.g., one through two, four, eight, sixteen, or twenty four differenced lags of the time series). To the best of our knowledge, ours is the first to consider model averaging procedures in the unit root setting.

We compare the proposed bootstrap model average approach with the classic Dickey and Fuller (1979) method, Phillips and Perron (1988) procedure, and with Ng and Perron (2001) procedure (using the detrending approach of Perron & Qu, 2007) which is a state-of-the-art procedure that appears to be the go-to method for most practitioners. The proposed bootstrap model average approach emerges as the procedure of choice based upon a fairly extensive Monte Carlo comparison with the existing go-to and classical approaches. Ng and Perron's (2001) procedure is based on the same estimating equations as Dickey and Fuller (1979), but they first detrend the series (this reduces size distortions when there is a large negative moving average root in the differenced series) and then use a novel lag selection procedure that chooses a larger lag length than traditional lag selection procedures. The Dickey and Fuller (1979) and Ng and Perron (2001) tests use a parametric autoregression to approximate the ARMA structure of the errors in the test regression, while Phillips and Perron's (1988) procedure instead corrects for any serial correlation and heteroskedasticity in the errors of the estimating equation by directly modifying the test statistic. We direct the reader to the original references for further details.

It has been established that the classical approach (Dickey & Fuller, 1979) which uses tabulated critical values sometimes suffers from crippling size distortions. MacKinnon's (1996) improved tabulated critical values do not attenuate such size distortions, unfortunately. Schwert (1989) conducted extensive Monte Carlo simulations and demonstrated how there can exist considerable bias present in a mis-specified estimating equation for unit root testing in the presence of a moving average error process (i.e., in the presence of a large negative moving average root). In such cases, the critical values depend on the unknown parameters hence tabulated Dickey–Fuller critical values should be avoided, and appropriate bootstrap procedures may be necessary for sound inference in this setting. DeJong, Nankervis, Savin, and Whiteman (1992), again via extensive simulations, demonstrate that the ADF tests have low power in the presence of a large autoregressive (AR) root. One important practical aspect for ADF unit root tests is the specification of the lag length. If it is too small, then the remaining serial correlation in the errors will bias the test. If it is too large, then the power of the test will suffer. Hansen (1995) demonstrates how large power gains can be achieved by including correlated stationary covariates in the estimating equation (this could be incorporated in our proposed bootstrap model average approach). Ng and Perron (2001) point out that a high order augmented autoregression is often necessary for unit root tests to have good size, but that information criteria such as the BIC tend to select a truncation lag that is small, and propose a MIC along with generalized least squares (GLS), detrended data and demonstrate how this improves size but can lead to a loss in power. Perron and Qu (2007) propose an improved method for detrending for the Ng and Perron (2001) approach. We direct the interested reader to Choi (2015) who presents a state-of-the art treatment of unit root inference.

This chapter explores the use of frequentist model averaging for the purpose of inference. This is a relatively unexplored and technically difficult topic. For existing theory, see Hjort and Claeskens (2003) for a local mis-specification approach, and Liu (2015), Zhang and Liu (2019), and Zhang, Zou, Liang, and Carroll (2020) for an approach based on the convergence of random weights.

We would be remiss if we did not point out the strong connections between the modern stochastic frontier/productivity literature (as exemplified by Kumbhakar, 1990) and the model averaging literature; see by way of illustration Sickles (2005), Huang and Lai (2012), Parmeter, Wan, and Zhang (2019), and Isaksson, Shang, and Sickles (2021), to name but a few.

The rest of this chapter proceeds as follows. Section 2 presents some background on unit root inference and presents theoretical underpinnings and the distribution of the weighted average ADF statistic with fixed weights. Section 3 outlines the proposed approach. Section 4 presents results from a Monte Carlo simulation that compares the proposed approach with the classic Dickey and Fuller (1979) procedure, that of Ng and Perron (2001), and a bootstrap BIC model selection procedure. An R Core Team (2018) package exists that implements the proposed method (Racine, 2018).

2. TESTING FOR A UNIT ROOT

Consider a time series y_t which satisfies an AR equation

$$y_t = \rho y_{t-1} + u_t \tag{1}$$

for $t = 1,\ldots,T$, where u_t is a stationary $I(0)$ process. The latter includes i.i.d. processes, white noise, and mean-reverting stationary processes. When $\rho = 1$ then y_t is $I(1)$ and we say that y_t has a unit root in its AR representation. On the other hand when $|\rho| < 1$ then y_t is $I(0)$, is stationary, and does not have a unit root. When $\rho > 1$ then y_t is explosive. Testing $H_0 : \rho = 1$ versus either $H_1 : \rho \neq 1$ or $H_1 : \rho < 1$ are important practical issues in applied time series modeling.

The most common method for testing the unit root hypothesis is to use the ADF statistic, which is based on the least-squares estimation of an AR model for y_t. The test can be described as follows. For some lag order k, estimate by least squares the kth order autoregression

$$\Delta y_t = \hat{\gamma}(k) y_{t-1} + \sum_{j=1}^{k-1} \hat{a}_j(k) \Delta y_{t-j} + \hat{\beta}(k) + \hat{\epsilon}_t(k)$$

Form a t-statistic for the null that $\gamma = 0$, that is,

$$ADF(k) = \frac{\hat{\gamma}(k)}{s(\hat{\gamma}(k))}$$

where $s(\hat{\gamma}(k))$ is a standard error for $\hat{\gamma}(k)$. The test rejects in favor of a stationary alternative for large negative values of $ADF(k)$ and in favor of non-stationary explosive alternatives for positive (or small negative) values. For stationary trend alternatives a linear time trend is also included in the regression.

The conventional asymptotic distribution theory approximates the null distribution of $ADF(k)$ by either assuming that k is the true AR order (so that the estimated model is correctly specified) or by assuming that $k \to \infty$ as $T \to \infty$ so that the model is approximately correct. We take a different approach and derive the asymptotic distribution without either of these assumptions.

We use the following regularity condition on the fundamental errors u_t defined in (1).

Assumption 2.1. For some $p > r > 2$, u_t is a strictly stationary, zero mean, strong mixing process of size $-pr/(p-r)$, $E|u_i|^p < \infty$, and $\omega^2 > 0$ where

$$\omega^2 = \sum_{j=-\infty}^{\infty} E\left(u_t u_{t-j}\right).$$

Assumption 2.1 is a mild set of standard mixing conditions which allow for broad $I(0)$ processes, and encompasses standard AR and ARMA processes. The assumption that the long-run variance ω^2 is positive excludes over-differenced processes.

Our representation of the asymptotic distribution of the ADF statistic will be written in terms of the approximating models. For each k define the approximate model

$$u_t = \sum_{j=1}^{k-1} a_j(k) u_{t-j} + \epsilon_t(k)$$

by projection. That is, the coefficients $a_j(k)$ are defined so that $E\left(u_{t-j}\epsilon_t(k)\right) = 0$ for $j = 1,\ldots,k-1$. This defines the AR(k) approximate model and error. Given the error $\epsilon_t(k)$, we can define its variance, autocovariance, and long-run variance

$$\sigma^2(k) = E\left(\epsilon_t(k)^2\right) \tag{2}$$

$$\lambda(k) = \sum_{j=1}^{\infty} E\left(\epsilon_t(k)\epsilon_{t-j}(k)\right) \tag{3}$$

$$\nu^2(k) = \sigma^2(k) + 2\lambda(k). \tag{4}$$

The parameter $\sigma^2(k)$ is the variance of $\epsilon_t(k)$, $\lambda(k)$ is the sum of its autocovariances, and $\nu^2(k)$ is its long-run variance. Under mis-specification, the error $\epsilon_t(k)$ has serial correlation so that $\lambda(k) \neq 0$ and $\sigma^2(k) \neq \nu^2(k)$. Under correct specification, the error is white noise so $\lambda(k) = 0$ and $\sigma^2(k) = \nu^2(k)$. Thus, for small k we expect $\lambda(k) \neq 0$ and $\sigma^2(k) \neq \nu^2(k)$, but for large k we expect $\lambda(k) \simeq 0$ and $\sigma^2(k) \simeq \nu^2(k)$, though there is no reason to expect equality for any finite k.

Theorem 2.1. Under Assumption 2.1 and $H_0 : \rho = 1$, jointly over $k = 1,\ldots,K$, as $T \to \infty$

$$ADF(k) \xrightarrow{d} \frac{\nu(k)}{\sigma(k)} \frac{\int_0^1 W^* dW}{\left(\int_0^1 W^{*2}\right)^{1/2}} + \frac{\lambda(k)}{\omega\sigma(k)\left(\int_0^1 W^{*2}\right)^{1/2}} \tag{5}$$

where $W(r)$ is a standard Brownian motion, and $W^*(r) = W(r) - \int_0^1 W(r)dr$ (or a detrended Brownian motion if a time trend is included).

Theorem 2.1 shows that the ADF t-statistics converge jointly to mis-specified versions of the classic Dickey–Fuller t-distribution. The distortions are due to mis-specified serial correlation. When the autoregression is correctly specified so that the error is white noise, then $\lambda(k) = 0$ in which case the distribution in (5) simplifies to the classical $\int_0^1 W^* dW / \left(\int_0^1 W^{*2}\right)^{1/2}$ found by Dickey and Fuller (1979).

Theorem 2.1 also shows that the sequence of t-statistics (for different AR orders) converge jointly, and are all functions of the same Brownian motion process W®.

The asymptotic distribution in Theorem 2.1 is generally unknown as it depends on the unknown parameters $\sigma(k)$ and $\lambda(k)$. However, the distribution can be approximated by bootstrap methods since these parameters can be consistently estimated.

By picking a suitably large AR order k the distributional distortions can be minimized. Larger values of k, however, reduce the power of unit root tests in finite samples. Thus, it has been viewed as desirable to use an AR order k which is large enough to minimize the size distortions but not so large as to reduce the power of the test. This requires a data-dependent rule $\hat{k}$ for selection of k. One popular method is BIC selection. However, Ng and Perron (2001) argued that this produces a $\hat{k}$ which is too small to alleviate the size distortion, and proposed instead a MIC designed for the unit root testing problem.

A data-dependent selection rule $\hat{k}$ leads to a data-dependent ADF test $ADF(\hat{k})$. The appropriate null distribution for $ADF(\hat{k})$ is unclear, however, as the use of a selected lag length invalidates the conventional limit theory unless used with an ad hoc assumption that $\hat{k}$ diverges with T. Bootstrap critical values could be used instead though no formal justification has been provided in the previous literature.

Instead of selection rules, we propose an averaging statistic. For $k = 1, \ldots, K$ let $w(k)$ be a set of non-negative weights which sum to one, and set $w = (w(1), \ldots, w(K))$. Then an averaging ADF statistic is

$$ADF(w) = \sum_{k=1}^{K} w(k) ADF(k).$$

The asymptotic distribution of the averaging ADF statistic can be deduced directly from Theorem 2.1.

Theorem 2.2. As $T \to \infty$

$$ADF(w) \xrightarrow{d} \left(\sum_{k=1}^{K} w(k) \frac{\nu(k)}{\sigma(k)} \right) \frac{\int_0^1 W^* dW}{\left(\int_0^1 W^{*2} \right)^{1/2}} + \left(\sum_{k=1}^{K} w(k) \frac{\lambda(k)}{\omega\sigma(k)} \right) \frac{1}{\left(\int_0^1 W^{*2} \right)^{1/2}}.$$

Theorem 2.2 provides the asymptotic distribution of the averaging ADF statistic for fixed weights. Like the distribution in Theorem 2.1, it is a distorted version of the classic Dickey–Fuller t-distribution.

While the distribution in Theorem 2.2 is generally unknown, and dependent on the unknown serial correlation properties of the series Δy_t, it can be approximated by standard bootstrap methods since the serial correlation properties can be consistently estimated.

Proof of Theorem 2.1. For simplicity, we omit the deterministic components from the exposition. By the Herrndorf (1984) functional central limit theorem

$$\frac{1}{\sqrt{T}} \sum_{t=1}^{[Tr]} u_t \Rightarrow \omega W(r)$$

$$\frac{1}{\sqrt{T}} \sum_{t=1}^{[Tr]} \epsilon_t(k) \Rightarrow \nu(k) W(r)$$

where $W(r)$ is standard Brownian motion. This convergence holds jointly over both equations and over k since the $\epsilon_t(k)$ are linear transformations of the errors u_t. Applying Theorem 4.1 of Hansen (1992)

$$\frac{1}{T}\sum_{t=1}^{T} y_{t-1}\epsilon_t(k) \xrightarrow{d} \omega\nu(k)\int_0^1 W dW + \lambda(k)$$

jointly over k.

Let $\hat{a}(k) = (\hat{a}_1(k), \ldots, \hat{a}_{k-1}(k))'$ and $a(k) = (a_1(k), \ldots, a_{k-1}(k))'$. Define $x_t(k) = (y_{t-1}, \ldots, y_{t-k+1})'$, $Q(k) = E(x_t(k)x_t(k)')$ and

$$\Omega(k) = \sum_{j=-\infty}^{\infty} E(x_t(k)\epsilon_t(k)x_{t-j}(k)'\epsilon_{t-j}(k))$$

By standard manipulations for the asymptotic theory of integrated processes

$$\begin{pmatrix} T\hat{\gamma}(k) \\ \sqrt{T}(\hat{a}(k) - a(k)) \end{pmatrix} \xrightarrow{d} \begin{pmatrix} \omega^2 \int_0^1 W^2 & 0 \\ 0 & Q(k) \end{pmatrix}^{-1} \begin{pmatrix} \omega\nu(k)\int_0^1 W dW + \lambda(k) \\ \xi(k) \end{pmatrix}$$

where $\xi(k) \sim N(0, \Omega(k))$. This convergence is joint across k.

Furthermore, the standard errors satisfy

$$T\left(s(\hat{\gamma}(k))\right)^2 \xrightarrow{d} \left(\omega^2 \int_0^1 W^2\right)^{-1} \sigma^2(k).$$

Together, we find

$$ADF(k) \xrightarrow{d} \frac{\omega\nu(k)\int_0^1 W dW + \lambda(k)}{\left(\omega^2 \int_0^1 W^2\right)^{1/2} \sigma(k)} = \frac{\nu(k)}{\sigma(k)} \frac{\int_0^1 W dW}{\left(\int_0^1 W^2\right)^{1/2}} + \frac{\lambda(k)}{\omega\sigma(k)\left(\int_0^1 W^2\right)^{1/2}}$$

as claimed.

3. A MODEL AVERAGING BOOTSTRAP PROCEDURE

3.1. Model Average Estimators

The goal in model averaging is to reduce estimation variance while controlling mis-specification bias. The Mallows (1973) criterion for the model average estimator (Hansen, 2007) is

$$C_n(w) = w'\hat{E}'\hat{E}w + 2\sigma^2\mathcal{K}'w$$

where $\hat{E}$ is the $T \times M$ matrix with columns containing the residual vector from the mth candidate estimating equation, $\mathcal{K}$ the $M \times 1$ vector of the number of parameters in each model, and σ^2 the variance from the largest dimensional model.[1] This criterion is used to select the weight vector $\hat{w}$, that is,

$$\hat{w} = \arg\min_{w} C_n(w)$$

Because $\arg\min_w C_n(w)$ has no closed-form solution, the weight vector is found numerically. The solution involves constrained minimization subject to non-negativity and summation constraints, which constitutes a classic quadratic programming problem. This criterion involves nothing more than computing the residuals for each candidate estimating equation, obtaining the rank of each candidate estimating equation, and solving a simple quadratic program. The MMA $C_n(w)$ criterion provides an estimate of the average squared error from the model average fit, and has been shown to be asymptotically optimal in the sense of achieving the lowest possible squared error in a class of model average estimators. See Hansen (2007) for further details in the cross-section case, and Zhang, Wan, and Zou (2013) for the time series case. See also Hansen (2014) who explores the use of the Mallows criterion in a time series autoregression setting and notes that averaging estimators have reduced risk relative to unconstrained estimation when the covariates are grouped in sets of four or larger so that a Stein shrinkage effect holds, and suggests that averaging estimators be restricted to models in which the regressors have been grouped in this manner. See also the related work of Hansen (2010) who uses a Mallows criterion for combining forecasts local to a unit root. In our procedure we use Schwert's (1989) rule for determining the dimension of the largest ADF model that is averaged over (i.e., the integer part of $12\times(T/100)^{1/4}$ obtained using the R function ceiling()), and group candidate models per Hansen (2014).

Hansen and Racine (2012) propose an alternative JMA criterion for the model average estimator given by

$$CV_n(w) = \frac{1}{n}(y - \tilde{X}w)'(y - \tilde{X}w),$$

where $\tilde{X}$ is the $T \times M$ matrix with columns containing the jackknife estimator from the mth candidate estimating equation formed by deleting the t observation when constructing the tth prediction. Like its Mallows counterpart, this involves solving a quadratic program where we minimize $(y-\tilde{X}w)'(y-\tilde{X}w) = y'y + w'\tilde{X}'\tilde{X}w - 2y'\tilde{X}w$ and the first term is ignorable. The simulations presented in Hansen and Racine (2012) and the theory of Zhang and Liu (2019) suggest that in the presence of homoskedastic errors, JMA and MMA are nearly equivalent, but when the errors are heteroskedastic, JMA has significantly lower MSE.

To obtain a model average test statistic, we take the *ADF*(k) statistic from each of the K candidate estimating equations and average them using the weight vector $\hat{w}$, and call this averaged statistic $ADF(w) = \sum_{k=1}^{K} \hat{w}(k) ADF(k)$. In order to obtain the null distribution of this statistic, we use a time series bootstrap with automatic choice of the expected block length.

3.2. A Unit Root Model Average Bootstrap Procedure

We consider a first-difference-based bootstrap procedure for obtaining the sampling distribution of $ADF(w)$ under the null of a unit root along the lines of Swensen (2003), who proves the consistency of the standard (non-averaged) test without deterministic components based on the stationary bootstrap (deterministic components can be added in the same manner as in Psaradakis, 2001; see Palm et al., 2008, p. 382). The bootstrap procedure is as follows:

(1) Take the first difference of the series at hand $\epsilon_t = \Delta y_t, t = 1,\ldots,T$ (ε_t could be, e.g., an ARMA process).
(2) Apply a time series bootstrap with automated block length choice to ε_t, $t = 1,\ldots,T$ (l is the expected block length obtained for the geometric bootstrap; see Patton, Politis, & White, 2009; Politis & White, 2004; Politis & Romano, 1994).
(3) Take the cumulative sum of this bootstrap residual ϵ_t^*, $t = 1,\ldots,T$ initializing the sum to the first realization of the series, which will generate a bootstrap series containing a unit root, that is, $y_t^* = y_1 + \sum_{i=2}^{t} \epsilon_i^* = y_{t-1}^* + \epsilon_t^*$.
(4) Next, take the bootstrap $ADF(k)^*$ statistics from each of the K candidate estimating equations and average them using the weight vector for the original series $\hat{w}$, which delivers a bootstrap model average statistic $ADF(w)^*$ generated under the null.
(5) Repeat this process B times to obtain the B bootstrap statistics $ADF(w)_{1,K}^*,\ldots,ADF(w)_{B,K}^*$.
(6) For the one-sided stationary alternative $H_1 : \rho < 1$ compute the α empirical quantile q_α from the bootstrap statistics. Reject $H_0 : \rho = 1$ in favor of $H_1 : \rho < 1$ if $ADF(w) < q_\alpha$.
(7) For the two-sided alternative $H_1 : \rho \neq 1$ compute the $\alpha/2$ and $1-\alpha/2$ empirical quantiles $q_{\alpha/2}$ and $q_{1-\alpha/2}$ from the bootstrap statistics. Reject $H_0 : \rho = 1$ in favor of $H_1 : \rho \neq 1$ if $ADF(w) < q_{\alpha/2}$ or $ADF(w) > q_{1-\alpha/2}$.

4. MONTE CARLO SIMULATION FOR BOOTSTRAP UNIT ROOT TEST

In order to assess the finite-sample performance of the proposed approach relative to its peers, we conduct a series of Monte Carlo simulation experiments. In particular, we construct power curves for a handful of procedures based upon three DGPs, one a simple AR(1), one an ARMA(1,1), and one an ARMA(1,2). The ARMA(1,1) DGP was used in simulations appearing in Palm et al. (2008) ($y_t = \rho y_{t-1} + \epsilon_t - 0.8\epsilon_{t-1}$) and is known to confound existing tests. It is noteworthy that Phillips and Perron (1988, p. 344) point out a limitation of their approach writing that their tests "have significant size distortions and are too liberal to be useful for $\theta = -0.5, -0.8$" (here $\theta = -0.8$ is the

MA coefficient in the ARMA(1,1) model). For the ARMA(1,2) DGP, we use $y_t = \rho y_{t-1} + \epsilon_t + 0.3\epsilon_{t-1} - 0.2\epsilon_{t-1}$, while for the AR(1) DGP, we use $y_t = \rho y_{t-1} + \epsilon_t$.

We conduct $B = 399$ bootstrap replications and $M = 2{,}500$ Monte Carlo replications for sample sizes $T = (50, 100, 200, 400)$. We then conduct the two-sided bootstrap test described above using the MMA and JMA weighting scheme and report the empirical rejection frequency of it and the one-sided tests of Ng and Perron (2001), Phillips and Perron (1988), and Dickey and Fuller (1979), where each test is conducted using a 5% nominal level. When $\rho = 1$ we can assess each test's empirical size. We examine power against stationary alternatives $\rho < 1$, and we consider $\rho \in [0.75, 1]$ using a grid of 15 equally spaced values for ρ when constructing each power curve.

It might seem odd that we compare our proposed two-sided tests with existing one-sided tests. We select our two-sided test as we believe it is important to be agnostic about the alternative. We use existing one-sided tests as these are the common implementation. If we replace the latter tests by two-sided versions this substantially decreases their power, so this is a fair comparison regarding power.

The legends in the figures follow use the following abbreviations: MMA (proposed bootstrap model average ADF test with Hansen's 2007 weight selection); JMA (proposed test with Hansen & Racine's, 2012 weight selection); N-P (Ng & Perron's, 2001 with MIC model selection using Perron & Qu's, 2007 detrending based on asymptotic critical values); P-P (Phillips & Perron, 1988) based on asymptotic critical values); and ADF (Dickey & Fuller, 1979, with BIC model selection based on MacKinnon's, 1996 asymptotic critical values). The N-P and ADF tests are from the R package CADFtest (Lupi, 2009) while the P-P test is from the R package tseries Trapletti & Hornik, 2018). The proposed test is from the R package hr (Racine, 2018).

Among all tests considered, the preferred test would have a power curve that would exhibit correct size (i.e., when $\rho = 1$ would have an empirical rejection frequency that is approximately 5% or otherwise exhibit the lowest size distortions), and otherwise would have uniformly higher power than its peers (i.e., when $\rho < 1$ its power curve would lie above those of its peers). Any test procedure exhibiting large upwards size distortions in standard settings in good conscience cannot be recommended to practitioners since it could lead to the rejection of the null at levels far in excess of the nominal level of the test when the null is in fact correct. Results for each DGP and a brief discussion follow.

4.1. AR(1) DGP

Fig. 5.1 presents power curves generated under the AR(1) DGP. For the proposed test, we present results using both the MMA or JMA weight selection schemes outlined in Section 3 based upon the bootstrap procedure outlined in Section 3. For the remaining tests, we use asymptotic critical values as outlined above.

Fig. 5.1 reveals that this is a textbook case where all tests are approximately correctly sized, though it is evident that the proposed approach dominates in terms of power. As expected, for a given value of ρ (< 1), power increases as the sample size increases for all tests. For the proposed test, Hansen's (2007)

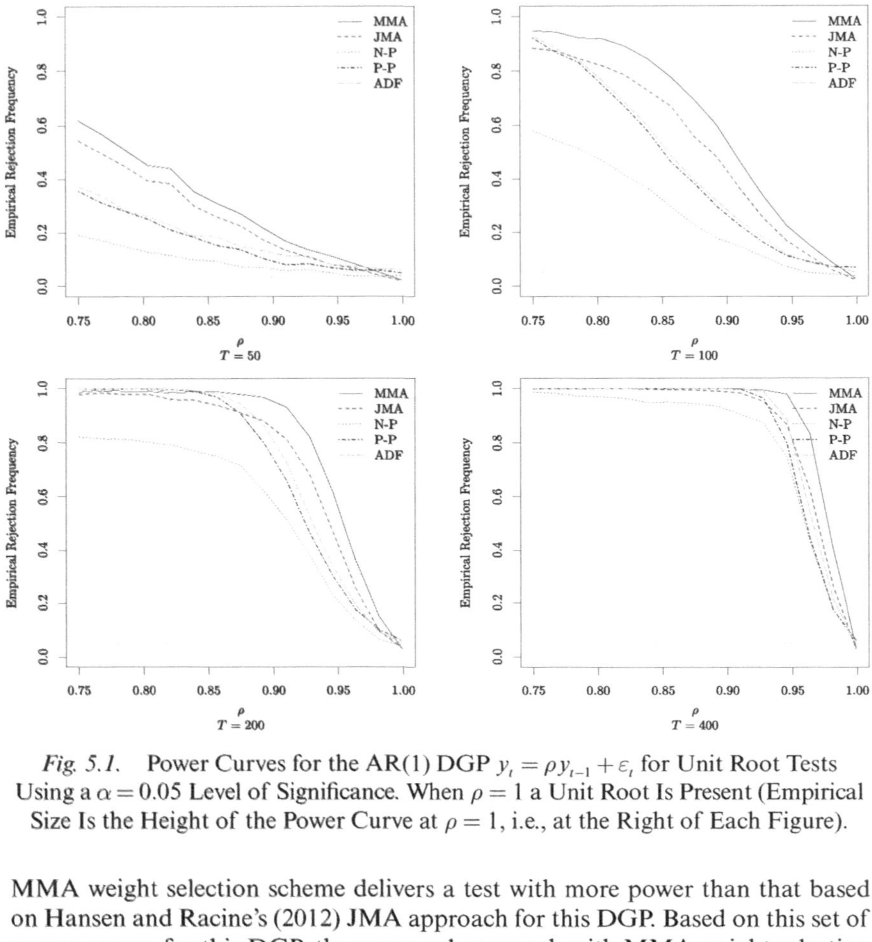

Fig. 5.1. Power Curves for the AR(1) DGP $y_t = \rho y_{t-1} + \varepsilon_t$ for Unit Root Tests Using a $\alpha = 0.05$ Level of Significance. When $\rho = 1$ a Unit Root Is Present (Empirical Size Is the Height of the Power Curve at $\rho = 1$, i.e., at the Right of Each Figure).

MMA weight selection scheme delivers a test with more power than that based on Hansen and Racine's (2012) JMA approach for this DGP. Based on this set of power curves, for this DGP, the proposed approach with MMA weight selection dominates its peers.

Next, we address the question of the fact that there are two comparisons being made, one between model selection and model averaging, and one between asymptotic and bootstrap inference. To assess these interplay of these issues, we report both the asymptotic and bootstrapped versions of the N-P approach in Fig. 5.2. We report this simply because the reader might reasonably wonder whether the power gains associated with the proposed procedure arise from the use of the bootstrap procedure rather than from the use of model averaging.

By way of illustration, compare the performance of the asymptotic and bootstrapped MIC model selected using Ng and Perron's (2001) test (N-P and N-P*, respectively) with the bootstrapped model averaged ADF test (MMA or JMA) in Fig. 5.2. A comparison of the asymptotic and bootstrapped versions of Ng and Perron's (2001) MIC model selected test reveals no consequential power gains

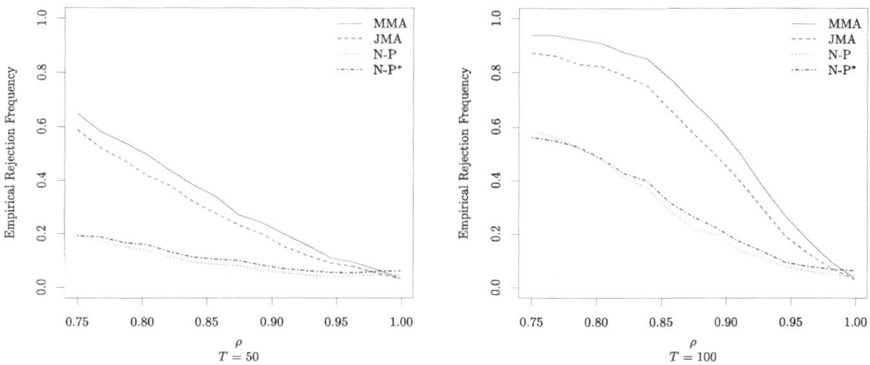

Fig. 5.2. Power Curves for the AR(1) DGP $y_t = \rho y_{t-1} + \varepsilon_t$ for Unit Root Tests Using a $\alpha = 0.05$ Level of Significance. When $\rho = 1$ a Unit Root Is Present (Empirical Size Is the Height of the Power Curve at $\rho = 1$, i.e., at the Right of Each Figure). The Power Curve N-P Is Based on Asymptotic Critical Values, While N-P* Is Based on Bootstrapped Critical Values.

associated with bootstrapping the process using the identical bootstrap procedure that underpins the proposed approach (we present results for $T = 50$ and $T = 100$ only as results do not differ qualitatively for $T = 200$ and $T = 400$). We can therefore safely conclude that any power gains associated with the proposed approach arise from the use of model averaging versus model selection and cannot be attributed to the use of a bootstrap procedure.

4.2. ARMA(1,1) DGP

Fig. 5.3 presents power curves generated under the ARMA(1,1) DGP containing a coefficient of −0.8 on the lagged MA component that is known to confound existing tests.

It is evident from Fig. 5.3 that the Phillips and Perron (1988) and Dickey and Fuller (1979) approaches completely fail for this DGP as was pointed out by Phillips and Perron (1988) and Palm et al. (2008). In particular, for this DGP, the Phillips and Perron (1988) test has empirical size equal to 1.00 for any T when $\alpha = 0.05$ thereby rejecting 100% of the time when in fact the null is true, while the Dickey and Fuller (1979) approach displays similarly crippling upward size distortions that very slowly approach nominal size as T increases but otherwise remain unacceptably high.

In light of the extreme size distortions that surface for this (and similar) DGPs when using the Phillips and Perron (1988) and Dickey and Fuller (1979) tests, it is difficult to recommend either test to practitioners, therefore the choice of tests therefore comes down to either Ng and Perron's (2001) procedure or the proposed bootstrap model averaging approach.

For this DGP, the proposed approach is slightly over-sized for $T \leq 100$ (for the MMA weighting scheme the empirical rejection frequencies are approximately

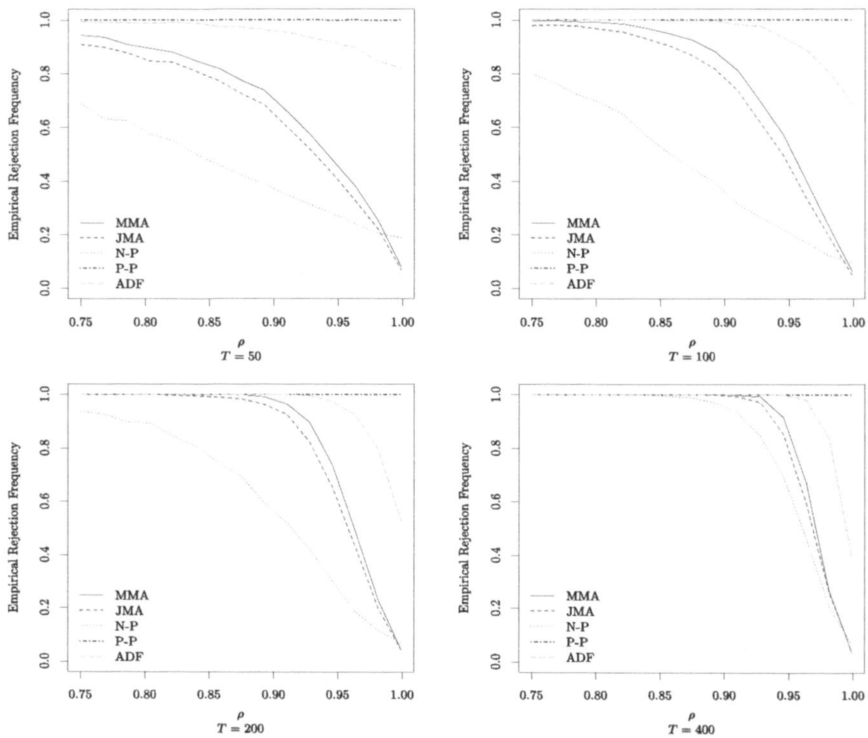

Fig. 5.3. Power Curves for the ARMA(1,1) DGP $y_t = \rho y_{t-1} + \varepsilon_t - 0.8\varepsilon_{t-1}$ for Unit Root Tests Using a $\alpha = 0.05$ Level of Significance. When $\rho = 1$ a Unit Root Is Present (Empirical Size Is the Height of the Power Curve at $\rho = 1$, i.e., at the Right of Each Figure).

8% for $T = 50$ and 6% for $T = 100$, respectively; for the JMA weighting scheme the empirical rejection frequencies are approximately 7% for $T = 50$ and 5% for $T = 100$, respectively) while Ng and Perron's (2001) approach exhibits substantially larger size distortions for samples of size $T \leq 100$ (approximately 18% and 10% for $T = 50$ and $T = 100$, respectively), while both tests are approximately correctly sized for $T \geq 200$. In addition, the proposed approach has substantially higher power than Ng and Perron's (2001) approach for this DGP, size distortions notwithstanding, regardless of whether the MMA or JMA weighting schemes are adopted. For this DGP, the proposed approach is first among its peers when judged by its power curve.

4.3. ARMA(1,2) DGP

Fig. 5.4 presents power curves generated under the ARMA(1,2) DGP. Given that neither the Phillips and Perron (1988) nor Dickey and Fuller (1979) tests

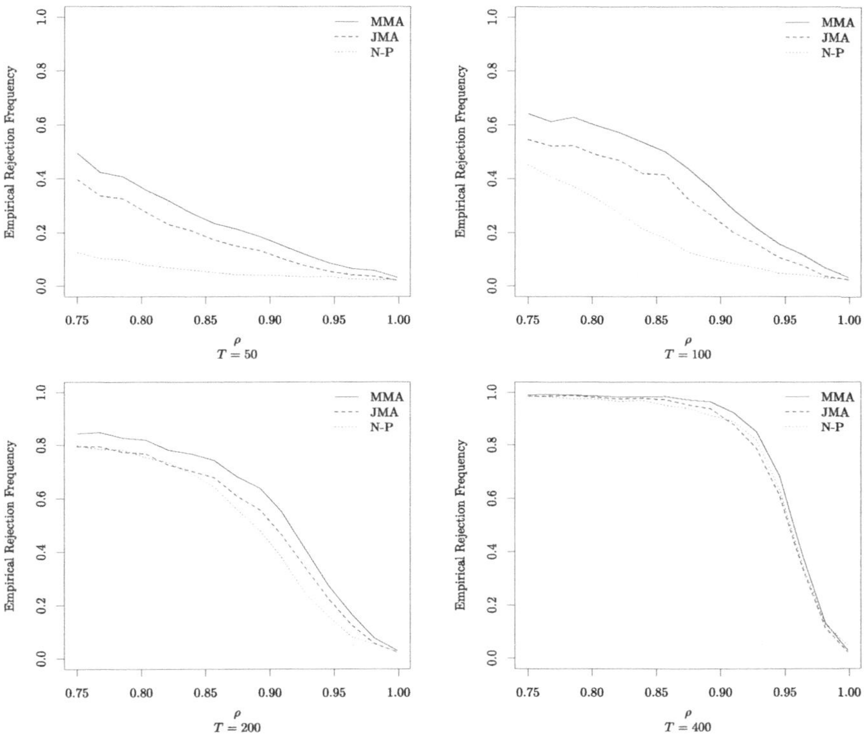

Fig. 5.4. Power Curves for the DGP $y_t = \rho y_{t-1} + \varepsilon_t + 0.3\varepsilon_{t-1} - 0.2\varepsilon_{t-2}$ for Unit Root Tests Using a $\alpha = 0.05$ Level of Significance. When $\rho = 1$ a Unit Root Is Present (Empirical Size Is the Height of the Power Curve at $\rho = 1$, i.e., at the Right of Each Figure).

can be recommended to practitioners given their failure for the ARMA(1,1) DGP above and for a range of similar DGPs, we drop them in the power analysis that follows.

Fig. 5.4 reveals that, for this DGP, all three procedures are approximately correctly sized for all T while the proposed approach that employs the MMA weight scheme dominates in terms of power.

4.4. Discussion

On the basis of our simulation results, we feel confident recommending the proposed procedure for testing for the presence of a unit root (extensive simulations that examine the effect of the largest dimension model that is averaged over, the distribution of the weight vector and so forth are available upon request). Our approach attenuates the large size distortions that can arise when using the classical approach (Dickey & Fuller, 1979) that relies on tabulated critical values, distortions that can also arise when using in Ng and Perron's (2001) approach. Furthermore, the proposed approach exhibits higher power, does not require specification of the model from which the bootstrap resamples are drawn, and uses and an automatic block length selection procedure for the dependent bootstrap method. Though the MMA procedure has higher power than the JMA procedure for the DGPs considered above, extensive simulations not reported here indicate that the JMA procedure exhibits lower size distortions, when present, than the MMA approach, particularly when a trend is included in the model. A conservative approach would therefore be to use the JMA weight selection scheme for this reason, which we recommend in practice. This JMA-based procedure ought to appeal to practitioners as there are no unknown parameters that must be specified by the user, an R implementation exists, and the procedure is not computationally demanding.

5. CONCLUSION

We propose a bootstrap model averaging procedure capable of attenuating large upward size distortions that can arise when testing for the presence of a unit root while possessing power that dominates its peers. We adopt a model-free bootstrap procedure where the null is imposed by simple differencing, exploit recent developments in automatic block length selection for the geometric bootstrap procedure invoked, and adopt a novel model averaging procedure to address model uncertainty. Theoretical support is provided, and a set of simulation exercises underscore its advantages relative to its peers. An R Core Team (2018) package exists that implements the proposed method (Racine, 2018). Since there are no nuisance parameters to be set by the user, and in light of its performance in a range of simulated scenarios, we are optimistic that the proposed approach will appeal to practitioners.

NOTE

1. Note that the residual vectors will be of different lengths when the model incorporates lags, so some care must be exercised when populating $\hat{E}$, that is, the first $k - 1$ elements from the residual vector for the estimating equation models not containing lags must be discarded.

ACKNOWLEDGMENTS

Racine would like to gratefully acknowledge support from the Natural Sciences and Engineering Research Council of Canada (NSERC: www.nserc.ca), the Social Sciences and Humanities Research Council of Canada (SSHRC: www.sshrc.ca), and the Shared Hierarchical Academic Research Computing Network (SHARCNET: www.sharcnet.ca). Hansen thanks the National Science Foundation and the Phipps Chair for research support. We would like to thank but not implicate James MacKinnon, Rob Hyndman, and In Choi for their insight and encouragement.

REFERENCES

Choi, I. (2015). *Almost all about unit roots: Foundations, developments, and applications*. Cambridge: Cambridge University Press.

DeJong, D. N., Nankervis, J. C., Savin, N., & Whiteman, C. H. (1992). The power problems of unit root test in time series with autoregressive errors. *Journal of Econometrics*, *53*(1), 323–343.

Dickey, D. A., & Fuller, W. A. (1979). Distribution of the estimators for autoregressive time series with a unit root. *Journal of the American Statistical Association*, *74*(366), 427–431.

Hansen, B. E. (1992). Convergence to stochastic integrals for dependent heterogeneous processes. *Econometric Theory*, 8, 489–500.

Hansen, B. E. (1995). Rethinking the univariate approach to unit root testing: Using covariates to increase power. *Econometric Theory*, *11*(5), 1148–1171.

Hansen, B. E. (2007). Least squares model averaging. *Econometrica*, *75*, 1175–1189.

Hansen, B. E. (2010). Averaging estimators for autoregressions with a near unit root. *Journal of Econometrics*, *158*(1), 142–155.

Hansen, B. E. (2014). Model averaging, asymptotic risk, and regressor groups. *Quantitative Economics*, *5*(3), 495–530.

Hansen, B. E., & Racine, J. S. (2012). Jackknife model averaging. *Journal of Econometrics*, *167*(1), 38–46.

Herrndorf, N. (1984). A functional central limit theorem for weakly dependent sequences of random variables. *The Annals of Probability*, *12*, 141–153.

Hjort, N. L., & Claeskens, G. (2003). Frequentist model averaging estimators. *Journal of the American Statistical Association*, *98*(464), 900–916.

Huang, C. J., & Lai, H.-p. (2012). Estimation of stochastic frontier models based on multimodel inference. *Journal of Productivity Analysis*, *38*, 273–284.

Isaksson, A., Shang, C., & Sickles, R. C. (2021). Nonstructural analysis of productivity growth for the industrialized countries: A jackknife model averaging approach. *Econometric Reviews*, *40*(4), 321–358.

Kumbhakar, S. C. (1990). Production frontiers, panel data, and time-varying technical inefficiency. *Journal of Econometrics*, *46*(1), 201–211.

Liu, C.-A. (2015). Distribution theory of the least squares averaging estimator. *Journal of Econometrics*, *186*(1), 142–150.

Lupi, C. (2009). Unit root cadf testing with R. *Journal of Statistical Software*, *32*(2), 20.

MacKinnon, J. (1996). Numerical distribution functions for unit root and cointegration tests. *Journal of Applied Econometrics*, *11*, 601–618.

Mallows, C. L. (1973). Some comments on c_p. *Technometrics*, *15*, 661–675.

Ng, S., & Perron, P. (2001). Lag length selection and the construction of unit root tests with good size and power. *Econometrica*, *69*(6), 1519–1554.

Palm, F. C., Smeekes, S., & Urbain, J.-P. (2008). Bootstrap unit-root tests: Comparison and extensions. *Journal of Time Series Analysis*, *29*(2), 371–401.

Park, J. Y. (2003). Bootstrap unit root tests. *Econometrica*, *71*(6), 1845–1895.

Parmeter, C. F., Wan, A. T. K., & Zhang, X. (2019). Model averaging estimators for the stochastic frontier model. *Journal of Productivity Analysis*, *51*, 91–103.

Patton, A., Politis, D. N. & White, H. (2009). Correction to "Automatic block-length selection for the dependent bootstrap" by D. Politis and H. White. *Econometric Reviews*, *28*(4), 372–375.

Perron, P., & Qu, Z. (2007). A simple modification to improve the finite sample properties of Ng and Perron's unit root tests. *Economics Letters*, *94*(1), 12–19.

Phillips, P. C. B., & Perron, P. (1988). Testing for a unit root in time series regression. *Biometrika*, *75*(2), 335–346.

Politis, D. N., & Romano, J. P. (1994). Limit theorems for weakly dependent Hilbert space valued random variables with applications to the stationary bootstrap. *Statistica Sinica*, *4*, 461–476.

Politis, D. N., & White, H. (2004). Automatic block-length selection for the dependent bootstrap. *Econometric Reviews*, *23*, 53–70.

Psaradakis, Z. (2001). Bootstrap tests for an autoregressive unit root in the presence of weakly dependent errors. *Journal of Time Series Analysis*, *22*(5), 577–594.

R Core Team. (2018). *R: A language and environment for statistical computing*. Vienna: R Foundation for Statistical Computing. Retrieved from https://www.R-project.org/

Racine, J. S. (2018). hr: Bootstrap model average unit root test. R package version 1.0-2. Retrieved from https://github.com/JeffreyRacine/R-Package-hr

Schwarz, G. (1978). Estimating the dimension of a model. *The Annals of Statistics*, *6*, 461–464.

Schwert, G. W. (1989). Tests for unit roots: A Monte Carlo investigation. *Journal of Business & Economic Statistics*, *7*(2), 147–159.

Sickles, R. C. (2005). Panel estimators and the identification of firm-specific efficiency levels in parametric, semiparametric and nonparametric settings. *Journal of Econometrics*, *126*(2), 305–334 (Current developments in productivity and efficiency measurement).

Swensen, A. R. (2003). Bootstrapping unit root tests for integrated processes. *Journal of Time Series Analysis*, *24*(1), 99–126.

Trapletti, A., & Hornik, K. (2018). *tseries: Time series analysis and computational finance. R package version 0.10-43*. Retrieved from https://CRAN.R-project.org/package=tseries

Zhang, X., & Liu, C.-A. (2019). Inference after model averaging in linear regression models. *Econometric Theory*, *35*(4), 816–841.

Zhang, X., Wan, A. T. K., & Zou, G. (2013). Model averaging by jackknife criterion on models with dependent data. *Journal of Econometrics*, *174*(2), 82–94.

Zhang, X., Zou, G., Liang, H., & Carroll, R. J. (2020). Parsimonious model averaging with a diverging number of parameters. *Journal of the American Statistical Association*, *115*(530), 972–984.

CHAPTER 6

AVERAGING HETEROGENEOUS AUTOREGRESSION MODELS WITH HETEROSKEDASTIC ERRORS: THEORY AND AN APPLICATION TO CRYPTOCURRENCY VOLATILITY FORECASTING

Ziwen Gao[a,b], Steven F. Lehrer[c,d], Tian Xie[e] and Xinyu Zhang[a]

[a]*Academy of Mathematics and Systems Science, Chinese Academy of Sciences, China*
[b]*University of Chinese Academy of Sciences, China*
[c]*Queen's University, Canada*
[d]*NBER, USA*
[e]*College of Business, Shanghai University of Finance and Economics, China*

ABSTRACT

Motivated by empirical features that characterize cryptocurrency volatility data, the authors develop a forecasting strategy that can account for both model uncertainty and heteroskedasticity of unknown form. The theoretical investigation establishes the asymptotic optimality of the proposed heteroskedastic model averaging heterogeneous autoregressive (H-MAHAR) estimator under mild conditions. The authors additionally examine the convergence rate of the estimated weights of the proposed H-MAHAR estimator. This analysis sheds new light on the asymptotic properties of the least squares model averaging estimator under alternative complicated data generating

Essays in Honor of Subal Kumbhakar
Advances in Econometrics, Volume 46, 99–131

Published under exclusive licence by Emerald Publishing Limited
ISSN: 0731-9053/doi:10.1108/S0731-905320240000046006

processes (DGPs). To examine the performance of the H-MAHAR estimator, the authors conduct an out-of-sample forecasting application involving 22 different cryptocurrency assets. The results emphasize the importance of accounting for both model uncertainty and heteroskedasticity in practice.

Keywords: Model uncertainty; model averaging; asymptotic optimality; heterogeneous autoregression; cryptocurrency; volatility forecasting

JEL classifications: C31; C32; G12; G17

1. INTRODUCTION

As a newer asset class, cryptocurrencies are widely considered to be volatile, with the potential for significant upward and downward movements over short time periods. While other investment classes also experience upward and downward swings, their movements have historically been less dramatic than cryptocurrencies. While cryptocurrency assets remain a small part of the overall financial system, their market capitalization grew 3.5 times in 2021 to a value of $3.0trn. Not only are the regulators in the financial industry requiring that time-varying volatility is included in their risk mark management models, but it is also crucial for risk management or hedging to be able to accurately forecast the volatility of cryptocurrency.[1]

While a voluminous literature has developed and assessed many empirical strategies to forecast volatility for financial assets, their applicability to cryptocurrencies can face additional challenges. These challenges arise from two well-documented empirical features that are present in cryptocurrency data. First, investors face significant uncertainty concerning which factors influence cryptocurrency movements, and their relative importance may vary sharply even across short periods of time. This implies that there is likely model specification uncertainty. Second, heteroskedasticity is prominent in the underlying data, in part resulting from rapid changes in sentiment and other explanatory variables in the aggregate economy. Heteroskedasticity is known to both bring challenges to financial forecasting as well as being quite prominent in most financial data since the economic climate can change rapidly.

In this chapter, we propose and develop an empirical strategy to forecast cryptocurrency volatility that accounts for both heteroskedasticity and model uncertainty. Model uncertainty is necessary to handle situations when the specification of a model does not apply across all observations. It is plausible that both the set of and how individual explanatory variables affect cryptocurrency asset prices differ across meme-based crypto assets from crypto asset leaders such as Bitcoin and Ethereum. The idea that different inputs affect outcomes is not unique to our setting, and for example, Wang and Kumbhakar (2009) show the importance of allowing for heterogeneous relationships and find that seven different subgroups of banks each have different inputs included in their cost functions.

Motivated by this potential specification uncertainty, we propose a model averaging heterogeneous autoregressive (HAR) realized volatility model that is robust to heteroskedasticity of unknown form. Model averaging allows the researcher to estimate multiple specifications and takes a weighted average thereby providing an alternative to using a model selection method, for which Kumbhakar, Heshmati, and Hjalmarsson (1999) provide mixed evidence in their application of productivity growth. Our proposed estimator (henceforth H-MAHAR) also can solve specification issues related to the lag index of the HAR model of Corsi (2009).

Thus, we contribute to the literature examining both the properties and performance of model averaging estimators. On the former, we establish the asymptotic optimality of the proposed estimator and theoretically examine the convergence rate to optimal weights under mild conditions. Specifically, we innovate upon the techniques used in Liao, Zong, Zhang, and Zou (2019) to demonstrate that even in settings characterized by a restricted autoregressive and heteroskedastic DGP, a least squares model averaging estimator can be asymptotically optimal. A special case of H-MAHAR is the estimator proposed by Lehrer, Xie, and Zhang (2021) that only considers homoskedastic error terms. Our approach can be applied to more general settings and sheds new light on proving the asymptotic optimality of a least squares model averaging estimator under complicated DGPs.

Second, we examine the performance of our proposed H-MAHAR estimator using an out-of-sample forecasting application where we independently explore 22 different cryptocurrency assets. These results emphasize the importance of accounting for model uncertainty in practice. In addition, we find that while there are small benefits for accounting for the presence of heteroskedasticity when forecasting over a very short time horizon, the H-MAHAR estimator has dominating performance when forecasting over either a one week, or one month, ahead horizon relative to model averaging strategies that do not consider heteroskedasticity. In other words, assuming that the variance of the error term is constant over time is more likely to under- or over-estimate volatility, since these assets can experience their prices rapidly grow or decline in their prices within periods that are as short as one week.

The remainder of the chapter is set up as follows. In the next section, we provide a more detailed overview of existing strategies that could be used to forecast the volatility of cryptocurrency assets. In Section 3, we propose the H-MAHAR estimator and present several theoretical results including asymptotic optimality. Our theoretical examination is inspired by Zhang, Wan, and Zou (2013) and presents several innovations to the techniques introduced in Liao et al. (2019) to shed new light on the asymptotic properties of the least squares model averaging estimator. Formal proofs of the theoretical results are contained in the Appendix. Section 4 introduces the data and simulation exercise to examine the finite sample performance of the H-MAHAR estimator. Section 5 introduces our empirical application. We contrast the H-MAHAR estimator to common alternatives to forecast the realized volatility for 22 different cryptocurrency assets. The results from this out-of-sample forecasting application provide strong evidence of the benefits of both accounting for model uncertainty and heteroskedasticity when forecasting longer horizons. Our conclusions are presented in Section 6.

2. A REVIEW OF REFERENCE MODELS TO FORECAST VOLATILITY

Volatility is the most important variable in the pricing of derivative securities. Given the interest in having accurate volatility forecasts, a burgeoning literature has developed estimators that often include lagged values of the dependent variable to forecast financial market volatility. The inclusion of lagged dependent variables is motivated by the well established property that volatility possesses a slow decaying autocorrelation function, usually termed long memory.[2] In this section, we provide a brief review of forecasting strategies that have been developed based on the HAR model of Corsi (2009), where we focus on estimator that incorporates both model uncertainty and heteroskedasticity in this framework.

The HAR model of Corsi (2009) has gained substantial popularity to forecast financial assets in part since it is easy to implement. This estimator can also approximate the long memory and multiscaling properties of realized volatility.[3] Following Andersen and Bollerslev (1998), the M-sample daily realized variance (RV) at day t can be calculated by summing the corresponding M equally spaced intra-daily squared returns $r_{t,j}$. Here, the subscript t indexes the day, and j indicates the time interval within day t,

$$\mathrm{RV}_t \equiv \sum_{j=1}^{M} r_{t,j}^2, \quad \text{for } t = 1,2,\ldots,T,\ j = 1,2,\ldots,M, \tag{1}$$

where $r_{t,j} = p_{t,j} - p_{t,j-1}$ with $p_{t,j}$ being the log-price at time (t, j).

To model realized volatility, the HAR model in Corsi (2009) postulates that the h-step-ahead daily RV_{t+h} can be modeled by

$$\mathrm{RV}_{t+h} = \beta_0 + \beta_d \mathrm{RV}_t^{(1)} + \beta_w \mathrm{RV}_t^{(5)} + \beta_m \mathrm{RV}_t^{(22)} + \varsigma_{t+h}, \tag{2}$$

where the explanatory variables can take the general form of $\mathrm{RV}_t^{(l)}$. It is defined by

$$\mathrm{RV}_t^{(l)} \equiv l^{-1} \sum_{s=1}^{l} \mathrm{RV}_{t-s}$$

as the l period averages of daily RV, the βs are the coefficients, and $\{\varsigma_t\}_t$ is the error term. Each $\mathrm{RV}_t^{(l)}$ can be regarded as a volatility cascade, generated by the actions of distinct types of market participants trading at daily, weekly or monthly frequencies (Müller et al., 1993). Generally, the lag structure in the HAR model is fixed at some lag index vector $\boldsymbol{l} = [1,5,22]$.

Prior research has found that most significant jumps in financial asset prices are readily associated with specific macroeconomic news announcements. Thus,

Andersen, Bollerslev, and Diebold (2007) extend the standard HAR model and add the daily jump component J_t to Equation (2) to explicitly capture the impacts of jumps, or discontinuities. The extended model is denoted as the HAR-J model,

$$\mathrm{RV}_{t+h} = \beta_0 + \beta_d \mathrm{RV}_t^{(1)} + \beta_w \mathrm{RV}_t^{(5)} + \beta_m \mathrm{RV}_t^{(22)} + \beta^j J_t + \varsigma_{t+h},$$

where the empirical measurement of the squared jumps is $J_t = \max(\mathrm{RV}_t - \mathrm{BPV}_t, 0)$, and the realized bipower variation (BPV) is defined as $\mathrm{BPV}_t \equiv (2/\pi)^{-1} \sum_{j=2}^{M} |r_{t,j-1}||r_{t,j}|$.

Future volatility may not be influenced in an identical manner to the volatility of past negative returns than to the volatility of positive returns. To allow for heterogeneous impacts of past volatility, Patton and Sheppard (2015) develop a series of realized semivariance HAR (HAR-RS) models that can capture the information from signed high-frequency variation. The first one, HAR-RS-I model, completely decomposes the $\mathrm{RV}_t^{(1)}$ in Equation (2) into two asymmetric semivariances, RS_t^+ and RS_t^-,

$$\mathrm{RV}_{t+h} = \beta_0 + \beta_d^+ \mathrm{RS}_t^+ + \beta_d^- \mathrm{RS}_t^- + \beta_w \mathrm{RV}_t^{(5)} + \beta_m \mathrm{RV}_t^{(22)} + \varsigma_{t+h},$$

where $\mathrm{RS}_t^- = \sum_{j=1}^{M} r_{t,j}^2 \cdot \mathbb{I}(r_{t,j} < 0)$ and $\mathrm{RS}_t^+ = \sum_{j=1}^{M} r_{t,j}^2 \cdot \mathbb{I}(r_{t,j} > 0)$.

The second model developed by the authors includes not only the effects of sign-variations but also the term $\mathrm{RV}_t^{(1)} \cdot \mathbb{I}(r_t < 0)$, which can be interpreted as the leverage effect. This model, denoted as HAR-RS-II, can be expressed as follows:

$$\mathrm{RV}_{t+h} = \beta_0 + \beta_1 \mathrm{RV}_t^{(1)} \cdot \mathbb{I}(r_t < 0) + \beta_d^+ \mathrm{RS}_t^+ + \beta_d^- \mathrm{RS}_t^- + \beta_w \mathrm{RV}_t^{(5)} + \beta_m \mathrm{RV}_t^{(22)} + \varsigma_{t+h}. \quad (3)$$

The third and fourth models developed in Patton and Sheppard (2015), denoted as HAR-SJ-I (Equation (4)) and HAR-SJ-II (Equation (5)), respectively examine the role that decomposing RVs into signed jump variations and BPV can play in forecasting volatility:

$$\mathrm{RV}_{t+h} = \beta_0 + \beta_d^j \mathrm{SJ}_t + \beta_d^{bpv} \mathrm{BPV}_t + \beta_w \mathrm{RV}_t^{(5)} + \beta_m \mathrm{RV}_t^{(22)} + \varsigma_{t+h}, \quad (4)$$

$$\mathrm{RV}_{t+h} = \beta_0 + \beta_d^{j-} \mathrm{SJ}_t^- + \beta_d^{j+} \mathrm{SJ}_t^+ + \beta_d^{bpv} \mathrm{BPV}_t + \beta_w \mathrm{RV}_t^{(5)} + \beta_m \mathrm{RV}_t^{(22)} + \varsigma_{t+h}, \quad (5)$$

where $\mathrm{SJ}_t = \mathrm{RS}_t^+ - \mathrm{RS}_t^-$, $\mathrm{SJ}_t^+ = \mathrm{SJ}_t \cdot \mathbb{I}(\mathrm{SJ}_t > 0)$, and $\mathrm{SJ}_t^- = \mathrm{SJ}_t \cdot \mathbb{I}(\mathrm{SJ}_t < 0)$. The HAR-SJ-II model further extends the HAR-SJ-I model by distinguishing the effect of a positive jump variation from that of a negative jump variation.

Theorems in Barndorff-Nielsen and Shephard (2002) point out that asymptotically RV contains some degrees of estimation error, characterized by

$$\mathrm{RV}_t = \mathrm{IV}_t + \eta_t, \quad \eta_t \sim \mathrm{MN}(0, 2\Delta \mathrm{IQ}_t).$$

IV_t stands for the true latent integrated volatility, η_t is the measurement error from proxying IV with RV, and MN stands for the mixture normal distribution. The variance of MN is $2\Delta IQ_t$, in which the term $IQ_t = \int_{t-1}^{t} \sigma_s^4 ds$ denotes the integrated quarticity (IQ) and σ_s represents the instantaneous volatility in a stochastic differential equation for the price process of the asset. In practice, IQ_t can be approximated by the realized quarticity (RQ):

$$RQ_t = \frac{M}{3}\sum_{j=1}^{M} r_{t,j}^4.$$

The RQ term plays a crucial rule in the HARQ-type models. Bollerslev, Patton, and Quaedvlieg (2016) show that the HARQ model fully adjusted to measurement errors of RV can be characterized by

$$RV_{t+h} = \beta_0 + \left(\beta_d + \beta_{dQ}\sqrt{RQ_t^{(1)}}\right)RV_t^{(1)} + \left(\beta_w + \beta_{wQ}\sqrt{RQ_t^{(7)}}\right)RV_t^{(7)}$$
$$+ \left(\beta_m + \beta_{mQ}\sqrt{RQ_t^{(30)}}\right)RV_t^{(30)} + \varsigma_{t+h},$$

where the RQ_t approximates the IQ, $RQ_t = 3^{-1}M\sum_{i=1}^{M} r_{t,i}^4$, and $RQ_t^{(l)} \equiv l^{-1}\sum_{s=1}^{l} RQ_{t-s}$. In practice, RV_{t+h} is unobservable at time t. However, the expression for RV_{t+h} includes a set of interaction terms that adjust each coefficient in proportion to the magnitude of the measurement error in the corresponding explanatory variable.

Recently, Lehrer, Xie, and Zhang (2021) propose a model averaging estimator under the HAR framework that assumes the error in the estimating equation is homoskedastic. The authors additionally contrast the performance of this estimator to various HAR-type models with and without a social media sentiment predictor constructed from Twitter messages in VIX forecasting applications. In the next section, we propose a new estimator that relaxes the assumption of homoskedasticity to allow for asymmetric returns among other features that are common in most financial asset data including those of cryptocurrencies.

3. ASYMPTOTIC OPTIMALITY OF THE H-MAHAR ESTIMATOR

In this section, we propose a new model averaging estimator under the HAR framework that is heteroskedasticity robust. We denote the new method as H-MAHAR and theoretically derive its asymptotic properties. The H-MAHAR estimator relaxes the assumption of a homoskedastic error term that underlies the model averaging coefficient (MAC) method developed in Qiu, Wang, Xie, and Zhang (2021). A special case of the MAC estimator is the extension of the prediction model averaging (PMA) approach of Xie (2015) to the dynamic HAR framework in order to combat the model specification uncertainty is considered in Lehrer, Xie, and Zhang (2021).

We consider the following DGP:

$$y_t = \sum_{l=1}^{\infty} a_l y_{t-l} + \varsigma_t \equiv \mu_t + \varsigma_t, \quad t = \ldots, -1, 0, 1, \ldots, \tag{6}$$

where $\mu_t = \mathbb{E}(y_t \mid y_{t-1}, y_{t-2}, \ldots)$ is the conditional mean, $\sum_{l=1}^{\infty} |a_l| < \infty$, $1 - \sum_{l=1}^{\infty} a_l v^l$ is bounded away from zero for $|v| \leq 1$, and ς_t follows an independent process with mean 0 and variance $\sigma_t^2 < \infty$. The above DGP in Equation (6) is very common in time series analysis and allows y_t to depend on an infinite lag, following Zhang et al. (2013) and Liao et al. (2019). However, it does not consider nonlinear time series. Equation (6) follows a stationary AR(∞) process if we limit $\sigma_t^2 \equiv \sigma^2$. Following Ing and Wei (2003), y_t has a one-sided infinite moving-average representation:

$$y_t = \sum_{l=0}^{\infty} b_l \varsigma_{t-l},$$

where b_l's are absolutely summable with $b_0 = 1$, and the polynomial $(1 - \sum_{l=1}^{\infty} a_l v^l)^{-1} = \sum_{l=0}^{\infty} b_l v^l$ is bounded away from zero for $|v| \leq 1$.

The analyst or researcher is interested in calculating a forecast of y and has access to data with T observations. We assume that there is a regressor matrix that contains potentially predetermined explanatory variables, and there are M_T potential candidate models that could approximate the DGP in Equation (6). Let d be the maximal lag order in all candidate models and observations of y_t be available for $t = -d+1, \ldots, T$, so that $\mathbf{y} = [y_1, \ldots, y_T]^\top$ is the vector of observations of the dependent variable in every candidate model. The regressor matrix $\mathbf{X}_m$ of the mth candidate model is formed by combining columns in $\mathbf{X} = [\mathbf{1}, \overline{\mathbf{y}}^{(1)}, \ldots, \overline{\mathbf{y}}^{(d)}, \mathbf{F}]$, where $\overline{\mathbf{y}}^{(l)} = [\mathrm{RV}_1^{(l)}, \ldots, \mathrm{RV}_T^{(l)}]^\top$ and $\mathbf{F} = [\mathbf{f}_1, \ldots, \mathbf{f}_T]^\top$ is a $T \times q$ matrix containing exogenous explanatory regressors. Suppose there is a candidate model such that the regressor matrix is $\mathbf{X}$, and $\mathbf{X}$ has the full column rank. When T increases, we allow d to increase but assume that q is fixed. The mth candidate model can be written as

$$\mathbf{y} = \mathbf{X}_m \boldsymbol{\beta}_m^o + \varsigma_m,$$

where $\boldsymbol{\beta}_m^o$ and ς_m are the parameter and error term of the mth candidate model, respectively. The least squares estimate of $\boldsymbol{\beta}_m^o$ is $\widehat{\boldsymbol{\beta}}_m = (\mathbf{X}_m^\top \mathbf{X}_m)^{-1} \mathbf{X}_m^\top \mathbf{y}$. Thus, $\widehat{\boldsymbol{\mu}}_m = \mathbf{X}_m \widehat{\boldsymbol{\beta}}_m = \mathbf{P}_m \mathbf{y}$ is defined as the vector of the estimated conditional means from model m, where $\mathbf{P}_m = \mathbf{X}_m (\mathbf{X}_m^\top \mathbf{X}_m)^{-1} \mathbf{X}_m^\top$ is the projection matrix by model m. The model averaging estimator $\widehat{\boldsymbol{\mu}}(\mathbf{w})$ of the conditional mean $\boldsymbol{\mu} = [\mu_1, \ldots, \mu_T]^\top$ is defined as

$$\widehat{\boldsymbol{\mu}}(\mathbf{w}) \equiv \sum_{m=1}^{M_T} w_m \widehat{\boldsymbol{\mu}}_m,$$

where $\mathbf{w} = [w_1, \ldots, w_{M_T}]^\top$ is a weight vector in the unit simplex in $\mathbb{R}^{M_T}$:

$$\mathcal{H} \equiv \left\{ \mathbf{w} \in [0,1]^{M_T} : \sum_{m=1}^{M_T} w_m = 1 \right\}.$$

Let $\boldsymbol{\Omega} \equiv \text{diag}\{\sigma_1^2,\ldots,\sigma_T^2\}$, and we adopt the method proposed by Zhao, Zhang, and Gao (2016) to estimate $\boldsymbol{\Omega}$ by

$$\widehat{\boldsymbol{\Omega}}(\mathbf{w}) = \text{diag}\{\widehat{\varsigma}_1^2(\mathbf{w}),\ldots,\widehat{\varsigma}_T^2(\mathbf{w})\},$$

where $\widehat{\varsigma}(\mathbf{w}) \equiv [\widehat{\varsigma}_1(\mathbf{w}),\ldots,\widehat{\varsigma}_T(\mathbf{w})]^\top = \mathbf{y} - \widehat{\boldsymbol{\mu}}(\mathbf{w})$.

The performance of model averaging forecast crucially depends on the criterion used to estimate the weight vector $\mathbf{w}$. The H-MAHAR criterion aims to balance the fit and the complexity of a model:

$$\text{H-MAHAR}(\mathbf{w}) = \| \mathbf{A}(\mathbf{w})\mathbf{y} \|^2 + 2\text{tr}\{\mathbf{P}(\mathbf{w})\widehat{\boldsymbol{\Omega}}(\mathbf{w})\}, \tag{7}$$

where $\mathbf{P}(\mathbf{w}) = \sum_{m=1}^{M_T} w_m \mathbf{P}_m$, $\mathbf{A}(\mathbf{w}) = \mathbf{I}_T - \mathbf{P}(\mathbf{w})$, and $\mathbf{I}_T$ is a $T \times T$ identity matrix. The empirical weight vector $\widehat{\mathbf{w}}$ is obtained from the H-MAHAR criterion

$$\widehat{\mathbf{w}} = \text{argmin}_{\mathbf{w}\in\mathcal{H}} \text{H-MAHAR}(\mathbf{w}).$$

Note that the MAHAR method of Lehrer, Xie, and Zhang (2021) is a special case of the proposed H-MAHAR. If the error term is assumed to be homoskedastic, the H-MAHAR criterion in Equation (7) is identical to the PMA criterion in Xie (2015) under the HAR framework as in Lehrer, Xie, and Zhang (2021).

Each candidate model that we consider with our H-MAHAR estimator is a linear model. This may appear dissatisfying and recent developments of model averaging methods now consider the possibility of semiparametric candidate models (see e.g., Li, Li, Racine, & Zhang, 2018; Zhang & Wang, 2019; Zhu, Wan, Zhang, & Zou, 2019) as well as nonparametric candidate models (Racine, Li, Yu, & Zheng, 2022). Those extensions to the candidate model set each involves an assumption that the error is homoskedastic. We believe that the extension of our H-MAHAR estimator to accommodate either semiparametric or nonparametric candidate models is a promising direction for future research.

3.1. Asymptotic Optimality of H-MAHAR

To demonstrate the asymptotic optimality of the H-MAHAR estimator, we consider the following squared error loss:

$$L_T(\mathbf{w}) = \| \widehat{\boldsymbol{\mu}}(\mathbf{w}) - \boldsymbol{\mu} \|^2 .$$

Let $R_T(\mathbf{w}) = \| \mathbf{A}(\mathbf{w})\boldsymbol{\mu} \|^2 + \text{tr}\{\mathbf{P}(\mathbf{w})\mathbf{P}(\mathbf{w})\boldsymbol{\Omega}\}$ and $\xi_T = \inf_{\mathbf{w}\in\mathcal{H}} R_T(\mathbf{w})$. We will establish optimality under a handful of mild technical assumptions. All limiting processes discussed in the chapter assume the limit as $T \to \infty$.

Let $\mathbf{Q}_m \equiv \text{diag}\{h_{11}^{(m)},\ldots,h_{TT}^{(m)}\}$ and $\mathbf{Q}(\mathbf{w}) = \sum_{m=1}^{M_T} w_m \mathbf{Q}_m$, where $h_{tt}^{(m)}$ is the tth diagonal element of $\mathbf{P}_m$. We define $\bar{h} = \max_{1\le m\le M_T} \max_{1\le t\le T} h_{tt}^{(m)}$, $\bar{k} = \max_{1\le m\le M_T} k_m$, and $k_m = \text{rank}(\mathbf{X}_m)$. Let $\mathbf{y}^{(-i)} = [y_{1-i},\ldots,y_{T-i}]^\top$, $\mathbf{y}_L = [\mathbf{y}^{(-1)},\ldots,\mathbf{y}^{(-d)}]$, and $\mathbf{M}_0 = \mathbf{I}_T - \mathbf{y}_L(\mathbf{y}_L^\top\mathbf{y}_L)^{-1}\mathbf{y}_L^\top$.

Assumption 1. $\bar{h} = o_p(1)$ and $h_{tt}^{(m)} \leq c_0 k_m T^{-1}$ for $t = 1,\ldots,T$ and $m = 1,\ldots,M_T$, where c_0 is a constant.

Assumption 2. There exist two positive constants c_1 and c_2, such that

$$0 < c_1 \leq \zeta_{\min}\{T^{-1}(\mathbf{y}_L^\top \mathbf{y}_L)\} \leq \zeta_{\max}\{T^{-1}(\mathbf{y}_L^\top \mathbf{y}_L)\} \leq c_2 < \infty$$

in probability, where $\zeta_{\min}(\cdot)$ / $\zeta_{\max}(\cdot)$ denote the minimum/maximum singular value.

Assumption 3. $\zeta_{\max}(T^{-1}\mathbf{F}^\top \mathbf{F}) = O_p(1)$ and $\zeta_{\max}\left\{(T^{-1}\mathbf{F}^\top \mathbf{M}_0 \mathbf{F})^{-1}\right\} = O_p(1)$

Assumption 4. $\bar{k}^4 \xi_T^{-1} = o_p(1)$ and $\bar{k}^4 \boldsymbol{\mu}^\top \mathbf{P} \boldsymbol{\mu} \xi_T^{-2} = o_p(1)$, where $\mathbf{P} = \mathbf{X}(\mathbf{X}^\top \mathbf{X})^{-1}\mathbf{X}^\top$

Assumption 1 is commonly used in the literature. The first part of Assumption 1 is the same as Condition (A.9) of Hansen and Racine (2012). The second part of Assumption 1 prohibits highly unbalanced designs and is equivalent to requiring the ratio of the maximum to the average diagonal element of $\mathbf{P}_m$ to be bounded above by some $c_0 < \infty$ for all m, and this assumption is widely used, for example, Li (1987) and Andrews (1991).

Assumption 2 implies that $T^{-1}\mathbf{y}_L^\top \mathbf{y}_L$ is an invertible matrix, and $T\zeta_{\max}\{(\mathbf{y}_L^\top \mathbf{y}_L)^{-1}\} = O_p(1)$ can be obtained. Note that assumption $T\zeta_{\max}\{(\mathbf{y}_L^\top \mathbf{y}_L)^{-1}\} = O_p(1)$ is identical to Condition (C.2) of Liao et al. (2019) and Liao et al. (2019) who each argue is a reasonable assumption.

Assumption 3 is the same as Condition (C.2) of Zhang et al. (2013), and Zhang et al. (2013) have given a reasonable argument. The first part of Assumption 3 is very mild, which can be derived from Condition (C1) of Fang and Liu (2020), and similar assumptions can also be found in Shao (1993), Zou and Zhang (2009), among others. The second part of Assumption 3 holds when $T^{-1}\mathbf{F}^\top \mathbf{M}_0 \mathbf{F}$ converges to a positive definite matrix in probability.

Assumption 4 places restrictions on the orders of $\bar{k}$ and ξ_T. The first part of Assumption 4 requires ξ_T to diverge at a faster speed than $\bar{k}^4$, and the second part of Assumption 4 is similar to Equation (25) of Zhang et al. (2013).

Theorem 1. If Assumptions 1-4 hold, then

$$\frac{L_T(\widehat{\mathbf{w}})}{\inf_{\mathbf{w}\in\mathcal{H}} L_T(\mathbf{w})} \to_p 1. \tag{8}$$

The proof of Theorem 1 is provided in the Appendix. This theorem states that our proposed estimator of the model averaging is asymptotically optimal, in the sense of achieving the lowest possible mean squared error.

We next establish the consistency of the weight-based H-MAHAR estimator. Let the optimal weight $\mathbf{w}^* = \operatorname{argmin}_{\mathbf{w}\in\mathcal{H}} L_T(\mathbf{w})$, $\tilde{\xi}_T = \inf_{\mathbf{w}\in\mathcal{H}} L_T(\mathbf{w})$ and $\boldsymbol{\Lambda} = [\widehat{\boldsymbol{\mu}}_1,\ldots,\widehat{\boldsymbol{\mu}}_{M_T}]$. We assume that $\mathbf{w}^*$ is an interior point of $\mathcal{H}$. We need to introduce the following assumptions to derive the asymptotic theory.

Assumption 5. There exist two positive constants κ_1 and κ_2, such that

$$0 < \kappa_1 < \zeta_{\min}(\boldsymbol{\Lambda}^\top \Lambda / T) \leq \zeta_{\max}(\boldsymbol{\Lambda}^\top \Lambda / T) < \kappa_2 < \infty$$

in probability tending to 1.

Assumption 6. $\tilde{\xi}_T^{-1} T^{-2\delta} M_T \bar{k}^4 = o_p(1)$, where δ is a positive constant.

Assumption 5 requires that the eigenvalues of $\Lambda^\top \boldsymbol{\Lambda} / T$ be bounded in probability and excludes the case of a degenerate eigenvalue. This assumption is commonly used in the literature, for example, Shao (1997), Liao et al. (2019), among others.

Assumption 6 constrains the divergence velocity of M_T and $\bar{k}$, which requires that $M_T \bar{k}^4$ does not increase faster than $\tilde{\xi}_T T^{2\delta}$. Similar assumptions can be found in Liao et al. (2019), Feng, Liu, Yao, and Zhao (2022), among others.

Theorem 2. If Assumptions 1–3 and 5–6 hold, then there exists a local minimizer $\widehat{\mathbf{w}}$ of H-MAHAR such that

$$\| \widehat{\mathbf{w}} - \mathbf{w}^* \| = O_p(\tilde{\xi}_T^{1/2} T^{-1/2+\delta}), \tag{9}$$

where the definition of δ is given in Assumption 6.

The proof of Theorem 2 is provided in the Appendix. Theorem 2 provides the rate at which the H-MAHAR based weight converges to the optimal weight $\mathbf{w}^*$. If $\tilde{\xi}_T$ does not diverge to infinity, the rate of $\widehat{\mathbf{w}}$ converging to $\mathbf{w}^*$ is at least $O_p(T^{-1/2+\delta})$. If $\tilde{\xi}_T$ diverges to infinity, the rate of $\widehat{\mathbf{w}}$ converging to $\mathbf{w}^*$ will increase as the rate of $\tilde{\xi}_T$ diverges to infinity slows down.

4. DATA AND SIMULATION EXERCISE

To examine the performance of the H-MAHAR estimator as well as explore how it compares to alternative approaches used in financial econometrics, we use the following data in both our simulation exercise and empirical application. We collected the 5-minute closing price for 22 cryptocurrencies as measured by the USD (**/USD) from the Bitfinex exchange for the period August 27, 2019 to August 31, 2021. We selected this 5-minute closing price as the benchmark following evidence in Liu, Patton, and Sheppard (2015) that alternative measures do not significantly outperform 5-minute RV. The Bitfinex exchange was founded in 2012 and is an online platform that acts as an intermediary between buyers and sellers of numerous cryptocurrencies.[4] We generated measures of daily RV of each of these cryptocurrencies using the intraday prices. In total, we have a balanced panel consisting of 736 daily RV observations for each cryptocurrency.

The descriptive statistics for daily RV are reported in Table 6.1. To conserve space, we present the statistics of six representative cryptocurrencies (i.e., BTC/USD, EOS/USD, ETC/USD, ETH/USD, LTC/USD, and XRP/USD). These reflect the six individual cryptocurrencies with the highest trading volume on the Bitfinex exchange during this period, conditional on having been launched prior to our sample period. As shown clearly, all the cryptocurrencies in our sample period exhibit positive skewness, as well as excess kurtosis. The Jarque–Bera statistics and the ADF test further demonstrate that the distributions of these series are asymmetric and leptokurtic, rejecting both the normality and unit-root property.

Table 6.1. Descriptive Statistics for RVs of Six Representative Cryptocurrencies.

Statistic	BTC/USD	EOS/USD	ETC/USD	ETH/USD	LTC/USD	XRP/USD
Mean	20.8816	45.8263	59.9163	30.6213	42.4205	55.2119
Median	9.2405	17.9710	25.1937	14.4313	21.2266	15.7851
Maximum	988.7351	2,606.1455	2,827.8540	1,237.7685	1,677.4124	1,868.3587
Minimum	0.5056	0.1206	1.4302	1.4555	1.8030	1.0701
Std. Dev.	52.5629	123.9428	147.6550	74.5580	93.2699	135.6291
Skewness	11.8498	13.8661	11.5333	11.4523	11.8070	7.2698
Kurtosis	187.7325	262.3409	189.5615	168.9939	182.3381	76.2189
Jarque–Bera	0.0010	0.0010	0.0010	0.0010	0.0010	0.0010
ADF test	0.0010	0.0010	0.0010	0.0010	0.0010	0.0010

Notes: The table reports mean, median, maximum, minimum, standard deviation, skewness, and kurtosis for the daily RV on Bitcoin/USD (BTC/USD), EOS/USD, EthereumClassic/USD (ETC/USD), Ethereum (ETH/USD), Litecoin/USD (LTC/USD), and Ripple/USD (XRP/USD). Data are daily for the period August 27, 2019 to August 31, 2021 from Bifinex. The last two rows report the Jarque–Bera test and the augmented Dickey–Fuller test. We set the lower bound of the p-values of the two tests at 0.001. Values less than 0.001 are truncated at 0.001.

4.1. Simulation Exercise

To evaluate the performance of the H-MAHAR approach relative to other competitors, we use a block-bootstrap type DGP for our simulation. We used BTC/USD as an example to generate the bootstrap data. Our procedure involves several steps. First, split the data into many clusters in sequence with equal cluster size $N = 25$ and omit the remainder sample at the end to serve as the test sample.[5] We then randomly pick the clusters to form a T data sample for the exercise. We consider $T = 50, 100, 200, 400, 800$, and 1,600.

We use $T - 1$ observations as training data to make the one-step-ahead forecast. We consider the following estimation strategies: (i) HAR_{full}; (ii) HAR; (iii) SAIC; (iv) SBIC; (v) MAHAR; and (vi) H-MAHAR. Here the HAR_{full} model stands for a HAR model utilizing all the 30 lagged components and the HAR model represents the conventional HAR model proposed by Corsi (2009) with daily, weekly, and monthly components. The SAIC and SBIC are the forecast combination methods proposed by Buckland, Burnham, and Augustin (1997) that utilize the following smoothed AIC and smoothed BIC weights:

$$\hat{w}_j^{xIC} = \exp(-xIC_m/2) \Big/ \sum_{m=1}^{M} \exp(-xIC_m/2),$$

where xIC_m stands for the AIC or BIC score by the candidate model m. In Lehrer, Xie, and Zhang (2021), the authors compare MAHAR to other strategies and find that their performance is dominated by MAHAR according to mean squared forecast error (MSFE). Thus, to conserve space we consider fewer strategies as our focus is not solely on model uncertainty, but also accounting for heteroskedasticity.

We use the model screening method of Yuan and Yang (2005) to construct the candidate model set. Yuan and Yang (2005) proposed an adaptive regression by

Table 6.2. Relative Forecasting Performance to HAR_{full}.

T	HAR	HAR_{full}	SAIC	SBIC	MAHAR	H-MAHAR
50	1.0000	35.6408	1.0319	1.0053	0.9701	0.7866
100	1.0000	8.6446	0.9859	0.9479	0.8775	0.7117
200	1.0000	1.5040	0.9558	0.9661	0.7643	0.7141
400	1.0000	1.3099	0.9703	0.9451	0.8880	0.6840
800	1.0000	1.3122	0.9532	0.9472	0.9579	0.6596
1,600	1.0000	1.2835	0.9472	0.9566	0.9794	0.6902

mixing with model screening. We denote the associated model screening method as ARMS. The ARMS method explores the full model set and ranks all models from the best to the worst according to the Akaike information criterion. Then, the top M' models are selected. In this chapter, we set $M' = 10$ in all the exercises.[6]

We calculate the averaged MSFE for all estimation strategies under all values of T across $B = 10{,}000$ repetitions. For comparison, we standardize all MSFEs by the MSFE of HAR. Results are reported in Table 6.2 and since the results are normalized relative to the MSFE of HAR that column has values of 1. We note that HAR_{full} has the worst performance in all cases. It is particularly inaccurate when the sample size is small, since the HAR_{full} method is over-parameterized. Our H-MAHAR has better performance than HAR in all cases. Relative to HAR, the MAHAR estimator acknowledges model uncertainty and deals with this challenge using least squares model averaging techniques. However, MAHAR does not consider the influence of heteroskedasticity, which explains why the performance of this estimator is worse relative to H-MAHAR. The H-MAHAR approach has the best performance in all cases, as it utilizes the information on heteroskedasticity and circumvents the model uncertainty issue by averaging across various candidate models.

5. EMPIRICAL APPLICATION

Our empirical exercise examines the relative prediction efficiency of different HAR estimators by conducting an h-step-ahead rolling window exercise of forecasting the volatility of 22 cryptocurrencies. We consider different forecasting horizons with each of the following estimators in the exercise[7]:

(i) HAR_{full}: the HAR model with all 30 lagged components;
(ii) HAR: the conventional HAR method of Corsi (2009);
(iii) HAR-J: the HAR model with jump component of Andersen et al. (2007);
(iv) HAR-RS-I: the first HAR-type method proposed in Patton and Sheppard (2015);
(v) HAR-RS-II: the second HAR-type method proposed in Patton and Sheppard (2015);
(vi) HAR-SJ-I: the third HAR-type method proposed in Patton and Sheppard (2015);

(vii) HAR-SJ-II: the fourth HAR-type method proposed in Patton and Sheppard (2015);
(viii) HARQ: the HAR method with RQ component of Bollerslev et al. (2016);
(ix) MAHAR: the model averaging HAR method proposed in Lehrer, Xie, and Zhang (2021);
(x) H-MAHAR: the heteroskedasticity-robust MAHAR method proposed in Section 3.

We use a rolling window forecasting approach to forecast RV_{t+h} for $h = 1, 7, 30$ with window length $L = 300$.[8] We compute the MSFE as the evaluation criterion.

We first demonstrate the relative performance of all the forecasting strategies using BTC/USD, ETH/USD, and LTC/USD. These cryptocurrencies are widely popular among investors and roughly account for 60% of the overall crypto market capitalization according to *coinmarketcap.com*. Table 6.3 presents results from this application where we report the MSFE of each strategy relative to the MSFE of HAR_{full}. Forecasting strategies are listed in the first row and rows 2–4 correspond to results under $h = 1, 7$, and 30, respectively. We note that the HAR_{full} and HARQ methods do not perform well due to the over-parameterization problem. Moreover, the more complicated HAR-type models (including HAR-J, HAR-RS-I, HAR-RS-II, HAR-SJ-I, HAR-SJ-II, and HARQ) do not always outperform the basic HAR model in forecasting the crypto RVs. The model averaging estimators always yield superior forecasting accuracy. Among all forecasting strategies, the H-MAHAR has dominating performance, as it acknowledges both model specification uncertainty and heteroskedasticity.

To further examine whether the advantage of accounting for model uncertainty is statistically important, we conduct the modified Giacomini–White (GW) test (Giacomini & White, 2006).[9] Results from these tests are presented in Tables 6.4–6.6 where each table corresponds to a specific cryptocurrency.

Table 6.3. Relative MSFE of All Forecasting Strategies on BTC/USD, ETH/USD, and LTC/USD.

h	HAR_{full}	HAR	HAR-J	HAR-RS-I	HAR-RS-II	HAR-SJ-I	HAR-SJ-II	HARQ	MAHAR	H-MAHAR
Panel A: BTC/USD										
1	1.0000	0.7449	0.7764	0.7914	0.8522	0.8134	0.8445	6.7112	0.6729	0.6662
7	1.0000	0.8934	0.9835	0.9323	0.9790	0.9605	0.9683	5.6491	0.8071	0.7964
30	1.0000	0.8704	0.9902	0.8957	0.9454	0.9234	0.9339	5.9791	0.7824	0.7754
Panel B: ETH/USD										
1	1.0000	0.5610	0.5824	0.6031	0.5775	0.6085	0.5950	5.1487	0.5085	0.5179
7	1.0000	0.7819	0.8248	0.8427	0.8232	0.8650	0.8304	8.6041	0.7159	0.7070
30	1.0000	0.8893	0.9308	0.9552	0.9318	0.9814	0.9393	2.5731	0.8271	0.8232
Panel C: LTC/USD										
1	1.0000	0.6870	0.7308	0.6820	0.6999	0.6963	0.7165	1.9276	0.5907	0.5901
7	1.0000	0.7954	0.9581	0.8919	0.8956	0.9306	0.9954	2.1106	0.6960	0.6947
30	1.0000	0.9261	1.1375	1.0288	1.0636	1.0789	1.2423	2.3986	0.8228	0.8205

Table 6.4. GW Test Results of All Forecasting Strategies on BTC/USD.

Method	HAR_{full}	HAR	HAR-J	HAR-RS-I	HAR-RS-II	HAR-SJ-I	HAR-SJ-II	HARQ	MAHAR
Panel A: h = 1									
HAR_{full}	–	–	–	–	–	–	–	–	–
HAR	0.0000	–	–	–	–	–	–	–	–
HAR-J	0.0040	0.0000	–	–	–	–	–	–	–
HAR-RS-I	0.0003	0.0944	0.0570	–	–	–	–	–	–
HAR-RS-II	0.0023	0.0500	0.4391	0.1734	–	–	–	–	–
HAR-SJ-I	0.0006	0.0506	0.1142	0.2336	0.3823	–	–	–	–
HAR-SJ-II	0.0014	0.0549	0.2604	0.2588	0.7127	0.3695	–	–	–
HARQ	0.4521	0.1135	0.1829	0.1414	0.1583	0.1409	0.1384	–	–
MAHAR	0.0000	0.0000	0.0000	0.0000	0.0000	0.0000	0.0000	0.0333	–
H-MAHAR	0.0000	0.0000	0.0000	0.0000	0.0000	0.0000	0.0000	0.0361	0.0288
Panel B: h = 7									
HAR_{full}	–	–	–	–	–	–	–	–	–
HAR	0.0506	–	–	–	–	–	–	–	–
HAR-J	0.7781	0.0013	–	–	–	–	–	–	–
HAR-RS-I	0.1726	0.2171	0.0722	–	–	–	–	–	–
HAR-RS-II	0.3185	0.0982	0.1296	0.3082	–	–	–	–	–
HAR-SJ-I	0.2414	0.0909	0.1091	0.2258	0.6170	–	–	–	–
HAR-SJ-II	0.2229	0.1562	0.1182	0.5063	0.5557	0.4426	–	–	–
HARQ	0.0929	0.0416	0.0707	0.0495	0.0534	0.0478	0.0458	–	–
MAHAR	0.0000	0.0000	0.0000	0.0000	0.0000	0.0000	0.0000	0.0137	–
H-MAHAR	0.0000	0.0000	0.0000	0.0000	0.0000	0.0000	0.0000	0.0155	0.2547
Panel C: h = 30									
HAR_{full}	–	–	–	–	–	–	–	–	–
HAR	0.0467	–	–	–	–	–	–	–	–
HAR-J	0.7553	0.0083	–	–	–	–	–	–	–
HAR-RS-I	0.1251	0.4294	0.0283	–	–	–	–	–	–
HAR-RS-II	0.1804	0.2787	0.0376	0.2594	–	–	–	–	–
HAR-SJ-I	0.1708	0.2474	0.0408	0.1710	0.8020	–	–	–	–
HAR-SJ-II	0.1814	0.2315	0.0721	0.2121	0.9857	0.6604	–	–	–
HARQ	0.1060	0.0711	0.1091	0.0782	0.0808	0.0779	0.0768	–	–
MAHAR	0.0002	0.0001	0.0005	0.0019	0.0031	0.0013	0.0010	0.0357	–
H-MAHAR	0.0003	0.0001	0.0006	0.0025	0.0040	0.0019	0.0014	0.0380	0.0477

Table 6.5. GW Test Results of All Methods on ETH/USD.

Method	HAR_{full}	HAR	HAR-J	HAR-RS-I	HAR-RS-II	HAR-SJ-I	HAR-SJ-II	HARQ	MAHAR
Panel A: h = 1									
HAR_{full}	–	–	–	–	–	–	–	–	–
HAR	0.0001	–	–	–	–	–	–	–	–
HAR-J	0.0004	0.0319	–	–	–	–	–	–	–
HAR-RS-I	0.0009	0.0010	0.1883	–	–	–	–	–	–
HAR-RS-II	0.0004	0.0434	0.8214	0.4144	–	–	–	–	–
HAR-SJ-I	0.0012	0.0004	0.0795	0.0020	0.2308	–	–	–	–
HAR-SJ-II	0.0003	0.0076	0.7391	0.0513	0.9804	0.0096	–	–	–
HARQ	0.4991	0.2484	0.2707	0.2773	0.2773	0.2820	0.2703	–	–
MAHAR	0.0000	0.0000	0.0000	0.0000	0.0000	0.0000	0.0000	0.1755	–
H-MAHAR	0.0000	0.0000	0.0000	0.0000	0.0000	0.0000	0.0000	0.1821	0.0165
Panel B: h = 7									
HAR_{full}	–	–	–	–	–	–	–	–	–
HAR	0.0140	–	–	–	–	–	–	–	–
HAR-J	0.0537	0.0386	–	–	–	–	–	–	–
HAR-RS-I	0.0883	0.0054	0.1721	–	–	–	–	–	–
HAR-RS-II	0.0479	0.1049	0.3961	0.0105	–	–	–	–	–
HAR-SJ-I	0.1174	0.0033	0.0744	0.0211	0.0085	–	–	–	–
HAR-SJ-II	0.0475	0.0557	0.6652	0.0198	0.6928	0.0064	–	–	–
HARQ	0.2098	0.1263	0.1410	0.1449	0.1381	0.1471	0.1361	–	–
MAHAR	0.0001	0.0000	0.0000	0.0000	0.0000	0.0000	0.0000	0.0845	–
H-MAHAR	0.0001	0.0000	0.0000	0.0000	0.0000	0.0000	0.0000	0.0905	0.3507
Panel C: h = 30									
HAR_{full}	–	–	–	–	–	–	–	–	–
HAR	0.0986	–	–	–	–	–	–	–	–
HAR-J	0.2219	0.0695	–	–	–	–	–	–	–
HAR-RS-I	0.3466	0.0183	0.0283	–	–	–	–	–	–
HAR-RS-II	0.2223	0.0435	0.7494	0.0241	–	–	–	–	–
HAR-SJ-I	0.4197	0.0152	0.0192	0.0318	0.0209	–	–	–	–
HAR-SJ-II	0.2040	0.0270	0.8690	0.0900	0.9532	0.0386	–	–	–
HARQ	0.1844	0.1667	0.1759	0.1814	0.1763	0.1833	0.1741	–	–
MAHAR	0.0027	0.0000	0.0001	0.0001	0.0000	0.0001	0.0000	0.1366	–
H-MAHAR	0.0073	0.0000	0.0000	0.0001	0.0000	0.0001	0.0000	0.1429	0.4820

Table 6.6. GW Test Results of All Methods on LTC/USD.

Method	HAR_{full}	HAR	HAR-J	HAR-RS-I	HAR-RS-II	HAR-SJ-I	HAR-SJ-II	HARQ	MAHAR
Panel A: h = 1									
HAR_{full}	–	–	–	–	–	–	–	–	–
HAR	0.0000	–	–	–	–	–	–	–	–
HAR-J	0.0008	0.0005	–	–	–	–	–	–	–
HAR-RS-I	0.0000	0.6315	0.0044	–	–	–	–	–	–
HAR-RS-II	0.0001	0.1188	0.0616	0.0019	–	–	–	–	–
HAR-SJ-I	0.0000	0.2666	0.0051	0.0744	0.1377	–	–	–	–
HAR-SJ-II	0.0010	0.0046	0.8802	0.0001	0.0142	0.0001	–	–	–
HARQ	0.5997	0.0713	0.2574	0.1203	0.1682	0.1316	0.2804	–	–
MAHAR	0.0000	0.0000	0.0000	0.0000	0.0000	0.0000	0.0000	0.0011	–
H-MAHAR	0.0000	0.0000	0.0000	0.0000	0.0000	0.0000	0.0000	0.0016	0.0046
Panel B: h = 7									
HAR_{full}	–	–	–	–	–	–	–	–	–
HAR	0.0179	–	–	–	–	–	–	–	–
HAR-J	0.7926	0.0036	–	–	–	–	–	–	–
HAR-RS-I	0.2283	0.2545	0.0007	–	–	–	–	–	–
HAR-RS-II	0.3553	0.1333	0.0144	0.0261	–	–	–	–	–
HAR-SJ-I	0.3167	0.1454	0.0010	0.0739	0.8641	–	–	–	–
HAR-SJ-II	0.9257	0.0164	0.6423	0.0007	0.0030	0.0012	–	–	–
HARQ	0.1879	0.0411	0.1546	0.0843	0.1024	0.0902	0.1824	–	–
MAHAR	0.0000	0.0000	0.0000	0.0000	0.0000	0.0000	0.0000	0.0041	–
H-MAHAR	0.0000	0.0000	0.0000	0.0000	0.0000	0.0000	0.0000	0.0045	0.8412
Panel C: h = 30									
HAR_{full}	–	–	–	–	–	–	–	–	–
HAR	0.1037	–	–	–	–	–	–	–	–
HAR-J	0.5852	0.0566	–	–	–	–	–	–	–
HAR-RS-I	0.6945	0.4440	0.0001	–	–	–	–	–	–
HAR-RS-II	0.9834	0.2681	0.0583	0.0142	–	–	–	–	–
HAR-SJ-I	0.8481	0.3177	0.0000	0.0470	0.2570	–	–	–	–
HAR-SJ-II	0.4927	0.1173	0.3883	0.0126	0.0193	0.0249	–	–	–
HARQ	0.0919	0.0575	0.1700	0.1062	0.1432	0.1138	0.2513	–	–
MAHAR	0.0001	0.0000	0.0004	0.0041	0.0041	0.0032	0.0049	0.0145	–
H-MAHAR	0.0001	0.0000	0.0006	0.0053	0.0050	0.0042	0.0055	0.0155	0.5333

The results in each table confirm that the improvement from the H-MAHAR model is statistically significant at 5% for most of the cases. The only exception is when $h = 7$, results between MAHAR and H-MAHAR are statistically indistinguishable. The above findings illustrate the importance of considering heteroskedasticity while controlling for model uncertainty when forecasting Bitcoin's RV.

As a robustness check, we compare the H-MAHAR method with the following homoskedastic and heteroskedastic model averaging estimators using the BTC/USD data as an example: (i) SAIC; (ii) SBIC; (iii) the jackknife model averaging (JMA) of Hansen and Racine (2012); and (iv) the HRCp approach of Liu and Okui (2013). Relative MSFE results are presented in Table 6.7. Forecast horizons are listed in the first column. We keep the results of HAR_{full} in the second column as the benchmark and H-MAHAR in the last column for comparisons within and across columns and tables. Columns 3–6 represent the relative MSFEs of SAIC, SBIC, JMA, and HRCp, respectively.

All the averaging estimators deliver relative MSFEs that are smaller than 1, which implies their superior out-of-sample performance relative to the benchmark HAR_{full}. SAIC and SBIC perform relatively worse compared to the other averaging estimators. This is due to the fact that the estimations of SAIC and SBIC weights rely on the homoskedastic assumption of the error terms. On the other hand, the heteroskedasticity-robust JMA and HRCp outperform H-MAHAR when the forecast horizon is short. Whether there are further gains from extending the H-MAHAR estimator to the JMA and HRCp frameworks presents a direction for future research. At present, H-MAHAR can handle heteroskedasticity within the Zhao et al. (2016) framework.

We additionally compare the out-of-sample performance of all forecasting strategies utilizing each of the 22 cryptocurrency RVs. We average the relative MSFEs across all cryptos and report the results in Panel A of Table 6.8. The results exhibit a very similar pattern as those in Table 6.3. Our H-MAHAR demonstrates the best performance among all forecasting strategies considered for all forecasting horizons examined.

To further investigate the results among different cryptocurrencies, we calculate the winning rate of each forecasting strategy under each forecasting horizon. For each case, only one method is defined as the winner if it yields the smallest MSFE among rival forecasting strategies. The winning rate is calculated as the frequency of one specific method being the winner among all 22 cryptos for each case. Results are presented in Panel B of Table 6.8. As we can see, only the model averaging forecasting strategies have a nonzero winning rate. When $h = 1$, we note that MAHAR wins 40.91% of the time. That being said, the H-MAHAR forecasting strategy has the dominating winning rate for the rest of the cases.

Table 6.7. Relative MSFE of Averaging Forecasting Strategies on BTC/USD.

h	HAR_{full}	SAIC	SBIC	JMA	HRCp	H-MAHAR
1	1.0000	0.7073	0.7020	0.6641	0.6379	0.6662
7	1.0000	0.7806	0.7812	0.7642	0.7572	0.7964
30	1.0000	0.8271	0.8349	0.8067	0.8163	0.7754

Table 6.8. Forecasting Performance of the Methods Among 22 Crypto RVs.

h	HAR_{full}	HAR	HAR-J	HAR-RS-I	HAR-RS-II	HAR-SJ-I	HAR-SJ-II	HARQ	MAHAR	H-MAHAR
Panel A: Averaged Relative MSFE										
1	1.0000	0.5616	0.6180	0.8063	1.1409	0.8072	0.9029	1.4534	0.4970	0.4830
7	1.0000	0.6106	0.7149	0.7203	0.7153	0.7208	0.7646	7.8009	0.5443	0.5289
30	1.0000	0.8729	0.9991	0.9311	0.9810	0.9382	0.9814	6.1553	0.7525	0.7396
Panel B: Winning Rate										
1	0.0000	0.0000	0.0000	0.0000	0.0000	0.0000	0.0000	0.0000	0.4091	0.5909
7	0.0000	0.0000	0.0000	0.0000	0.0000	0.0000	0.0000	0.0000	0.0909	0.9091
30	0.0000	0.0000	0.0000	0.0000	0.0000	0.0000	0.0000	0.0000	0.1364	0.8636

The importance of model uncertainty may not be a large surprise since investors face uncertainty about the factors driving cryptocurrency movements and their relative importance. Investors have imperfect knowledge and to date, a unifying underlying theory that guides the modeling of cryptocurrencies has not been developed. An alternative explanation for the importance of model uncertainty arises from the heterogeneous market hypothesis that suggests market participants interpret the same information in different ways according to their trading preferences and opportunities. This heterogeneity creates additive volatility with various different trading activities duration such as short-, medium-, and long-term investments. Our empirical analysis cannot separate if it is due to different investors or different information sets, and note the decentralized and volatile nature of the cryptocurrency provides an additional rationale for why both of these explanations for model uncertainty are likely to present for forecasters in this asset market.

6. CONCLUSION

Motivated by empirical features that characterize cryptocurrency volatility data, we develop a forecasting strategy that can account for both model uncertainty and heteroskedasticity of unknown form. We argue that this strategy may have significant value to practitioners since heteroskedasticity is known to bring challenges to financial forecasting and the heterogeneous market hypothesis would suggest that there is significant model uncertainty. After all, this hypothesis suggests that financial market volatility arises since market participants interpret the same information in different ways according to their trading preferences and opportunities. Our theoretical investigation establishes the asymptotic optimality and examines the convergence rate of the weight of the proposed H-MAHAR estimator under mild conditions. Our theoretical investigation additionally offers a means to shed new light on the asymptotic properties of the least squares model averaging estimator under alternative complicated DGPs.

To investigate whether these proposed gains occur with financial data, we conduct an out-of-sample forecasting application where we independently explore 22 different cryptocurrency assets. These results emphasize the importance of accounting for model uncertainty in practice. In addition, we find that while there are small benefits for accounting for the presence of heteroskedasticity when forecasting over a very short time horizon, the H-MAHAR estimator has dominating performance when forecasting over either a one week or one month, ahead horizon relative to model averaging strategies that do not consider heteroskedasticity. Strategies that neglect the increased swings in cryptocurrency prices over these time periods are more likely to under- or over-estimate volatility. Taken together, we believe the proposed strategy has potential benefits for empirical practice and the theoretical contributions may be useful to researchers who wish to further explore the least squares model averaging estimator in alternative settings.

There are numerous directions for future research including extending the H-MAHAR strategy to consider semiparametric and nonparametric candidate models. Further, the theory underlying the H-MAHAR estimator applies only to stationary time series. Extensions of econometric methods that consider model uncertainty with nonstationary time series data remain few. Recently, Sun, Hong, Lee, Wang, and Zhang (2021) propose a time-varying model averaging estimator, but their candidate models are not allowed to include lagged dependent variables among the set of explanatory variables. While our H-MAHAR estimator does not share this limitation, we believe that developing a time-varying model averaging estimator that can both account for heteroskedasticity in a nonstationary time series setting and include lagged dependent variables among its regressors presents another promising direction for future work.

A final direction of interest for future research is to extend earlier work on stochastic frontier models where concerns related to both heteroskedasticity and specification model uncertainty have been noted. For example, prior research examining stochastic frontier models have pointed to the importance of model uncertainty by considering either the properties of competing estimators (Sickles, 2005) or discussing the consequences to statistical inference if researchers select a preferred model among competing alternatives (see e.g., Huang & Lai, 2012). To the best of our knowledge only two studies have considered model averaging with stochastic frontier models. Isaksson, Shang, and Sickles (2021) illustrate how to apply existing model averaging estimators to a set of competing stochastic frontier estimators, whereas Parmeter, Wan, and Zhang (2019) propose two new distinct model averaging estimators for this empirical setting and study their finite sample performance. While the two new estimators proposed respond to issues stemming from model specification uncertainty as well as the proper distributional specification of the error components of a stochastic frontier model, the authors assumed homoskedasticity. Thus, based on our empirical findings and the prominence of heteroskedasticity in empirical data, we suggest that future research may wish to consider the development of new model averaging strategies that can account for both model uncertainty and heteroskedasticity with the stochastic frontier model.

NOTES

1. At the time of writing this chapter, the cryptocurrency industry remains unregulated. However, firms within the broader financial industry that invest in cryptocurrency assets as a component of a broader portfolio are subject to such regulation.
2. This phenomenon has also been uncovered by Dacorogna, Müller, Nagler, Olsen, and Pictet (1993), Andersen, Bollerslev, Diebold, and Labys (2001) for the foreign exchange market and Andersen, Bollerslev, Diebold, and Ebens (2001) for stock market returns.
3. Fernandes, Medeiros, and Scharth (2014) perform a thorough statistical examination of the time series properties of the VIX index and propose using the HAR-type models for modeling and forecasting purposes. See Vortelinos (2017) for further discussion.
4. As noted above, we have data on 22 cryptocurrencies that include ATOM/USD, BTC/USD, DASH/USD, EOS/USD, ETC/USD, ETH/USD, FUN/USD, GTO/USD, IOTA/USD, LTC/USD, NULS/USD, ONT/USD, PAX/USD, PERL/USD, THETA/USD, TRX/USD, TUSD/USD, USDC/USD, VET/USD, XRP/USD, ZEC/USD, and ZIL/USD.
5. Our main results are robust to alternative values of $N = 15, 20,$ and 30.
6. As a robustness exercise, we also considered the heteroskedasticity-robust model screening (HRMS) method of Xie (2017). The results are qualitatively unchanged and available from the authors upon request.
7. We do not consider machine learning algorithms in this exercise to forecast volatility. Lehrer, Xie, and Yi (2021) present evidence when forecasting Bitcoin volatility machine learning algorithms can provide gains in forecast accuracy relative to variants of the HAR model that do not allow for model averaging, since the algorithms can account for nonlinearities.
8. In this way, it allows us to produce multi-step ahead forecasts without imposing additional assumptions about future realizations of the explanatory variables.
9. The modified GW test is implemented to test the null hypothesis that one model performs equally well as another model in terms of a certain loss function.

ACKNOWLEDGMENTS

We are very grateful to the editors and the referees for their insightful comments that greatly improved our chapter. Lehrer wishes to thank SSHRC for research support. Xie's research is supported by the Natural Science Foundation of China (No. 72173075), the Shanghai Research Center for Data Science and Decision Technology, and the Fundamental Research Funds for the Central Universities. Zhang gratefully acknowledges research support from the National Natural Science Foundation of China (71925007, 72091212, and 12288201) and the CAS Project for Young Scientists in Basic Research (YSBR-008).

REFERENCES

Andersen, T., Bollerslev, T., Diebold, F., & Ebens, H. (2001). The distribution of realized stock return volatility. *Journal of Financial Economics*, *61*(1), 43–76.

Andersen, T. G., & Bollerslev, T. (1998). Answering the skeptics: Yes, standard volatility models do provide accurate forecasts. *International Economic Review*, *39*(4), 885–905.

Andersen, T. G., Bollerslev, T., & Diebold, F. X. (2007). Roughing it up: Including jump components in the measurement, modeling, and forecasting of return volatility. *The Review of Economics and Statistics*, *89*(4), 701–720.

Andersen, T. G., Bollerslev, T., Diebold, F. X., & Labys, P. (2001). The distribution of realized exchange rate volatility. *Journal of the American Statistical Association*, *96*(453), 42–55.

Andrews, D. (1991). Asymptotic optimality of generalized C_L, cross-validation, and generalized cross-validation in regression with heteroskedastic errors. *Journal of Econometrics*, *47*(2), 359–377.

Barndorff-Nielsen, O. E., & Shephard, N. (2002). Econometric analysis of realized volatility and its use in estimating stochastic volatility models. *Journal of the Royal Statistical Society: Series B (Statistical Methodology)*, *64*(2), 253–280.

Bollerslev, T., Patton, A. J., & Quaedvlieg, R. (2016). Exploiting the errors: A simple approach for improved volatility forecasting. *Journal of Econometrics*, *192*(1), 1–18.

Buckland, S. T., Burnham, K. P., & Augustin, N. H. (1997). Model selection: An integral part of inference. *Biometrics*, *53*(2), 603–618.

Chen, J., Li, D., Linton, O., & Lu, Z. (2018). Semiparametric ultra-high dimensional model averaging of nonlinear dynamic time series. *Journal of the American Statistical Association*, *113*(522), 919–932.

Corsi, F. (2009). A simple approximate long-memory model of realized volatility. *Journal of Financial Econometrics*, *7*(2), 174–196.

Dacorogna, M. M., Müller, U. A., Nagler, R. J., Olsen, R. B. & Pictet, O. V. (1993). A geographical model for the daily and weekly seasonal volatility in the foreign exchange market. *Journal of International Money and Finance*, *12*(4), 413–438.

Fan, J., & Peng, H. (2004). Nonconcave penalized likelihood with a diverging number of parameters. *The Annals of Statistics*, *32*(3), 928–961.

Fang, F., & Liu, M. (2020). Limit of the optimal weight in least squares model averaging with non-nested models. *Economics Letters*, *196*, 109586.

Feng, Y., Liu, Q., Yao, Q., & G. Zhao (2022). Model averaging for nonlinear regression models. *Journal of Business & Economic Statistics*, *40*(2), 785–798.

Fernandes, M., Medeiros, M. C., & Scharth, M. (2014). Modeling and predicting the CBOE market volatility index. *Journal of Banking & Finance*, *40*, 1–10.

Gao, Y., Zhang, X., Wang, S., Chong, T. T.-L., & Zou, G. (2019). Frequentist model averaging for threshold models. *Annals of the Institute of Statistical Mathematics*, *71*(2), 275–306.

Giacomini, R., & White, H. (2006). Tests of conditional predictive ability. *Econometrica*, *74*(6), 1545–1578.

Hansen, B. E., & Racine, J. S. (2012). Jackknife model averaging. *Journal of Econometrics*, *167*(1), 38–46.

Huang, C. J., & Lai, H.-p. (2012). Estimation of stochastic frontier models based on multimodel inference. *Journal of Productivity Analysis*, *38*(2), 273–284.

Ing, C.-K., & Wei, C.-Z. (2003). On same-realization prediction in an infinite-order autoregressive process. *Journal of Multivariate Analysis*, *85*(1), 130–155.

Isaksson, A., Shang, C., & Sickles, R. C. (2021). Nonstructural analysis of productivity growth for the industrialized countries: A jackknife model averaging approach. *Econometric Reviews*, *40*(4), 321–358.

Kumbhakar, S. C., Heshmati, A., & Hjalmarsson, L. (1999). Parametric approaches to productivity measurement: A comparison among alternative models. *The Scandinavian Journal of Economics*, *101*(3), 405–424.

Lehrer, S., Xie, T., & Zhang, X. (2021). Social media sentiment, model uncertainty, and volatility forecasting. *Economic Modelling*, *102*, 105556.

Lehrer, S. F., Xie, T., & Yi, G. (2021). Do the hype of the benefits from using new data science tools extend to forecasting extremely volatile assets?. In S. Consoli, D. R. Recupero & M. Saisana (Eds.), *Data science for economics and finance* (pp. 287–330). Cham: Springer.

Li, C., Li, Q., Racine, J. S., & Zhang, D. (2018). Optimal model averaging of varying coefficient models. *Statistica Sinica*, *28*(4), 2795–2809.

Li, K.-C. (1987). Asymptotic optimality for C_p, C_L, cross-validation and generalized cross-validation: Discrete index set. *The Annals of Statistics*, *15*(3), 958–975.

Liao, J., Zong, X., Zhang, X., & Zou, G. (2019). Model averaging based on leave-subject-out cross-validation for vector autoregressions. *Journal of Econometrics*, *209*(1), 35–60.

Liu, L. Y., Patton, A. J., & Sheppard, K. (2015). Does anything beat 5-minute RV? A comparison of realized measures across multiple asset classes. *Journal of Econometrics*, *187*(1), 293–311.

Liu, Q., & Okui, R. (2013). Heteroscedasticity-robust C_p model averaging. *The Econometrics Journal*, *16*(3), 463–472.

Müller, U. A., Dacorogna, M. M., Davé, R. D., Pictet, O. V., Olsen, R. B., & Ward, J. R. (1993). *Fractals and intrinsic time: A challenge to econometricians* (Unpublished manuscript, p. 130). Zürich: Olsen & Associates.

Parmeter, C. F., Wan, A. T. K., & Zhang, X. (2019). Model averaging estimators for the stochastic frontier model. *Journal of Productivity Analysis*, *51*(2), 91–103.

Patton, A. J., & Sheppard, K. (2015). Good volatility, bad volatility: Signed jumps and the persistence of volatility. *The Review of Economics and Statistics*, *97*(3), 683–697.

Qiu, Y., Wang, Z., Xie, T., & Zhang, X. (2021). Forecasting Bitcoin realized volatility by exploiting measurement error under model uncertainty. *Journal of Empirical Finance*, *62*, 179–201.

Racine, J. S., Li, Q., Yu, D., & Zheng, L. (2022). Optimal model averaging of mixed-data Kernel-weighted spline regressions. *Journal of Business & Economic Statistics*, *41*(4), 1251–1261.

Shao, J. (1993). Linear model selection by cross-validation. *Journal of the American statistical Association*, *88*(422), 486–494.

Shao, J. (1997). An asymptotic theory for linear model selection. *Statistica Sinica*, *7*(2), 221–242.

Sickles, R. C. (2005). Panel estimators and the identification of firm-specific efficiency levels in parametric, semiparametric and nonparametric settings. *Journal of Econometrics*, *126*(2), 305–334.

Sun, Y., Hong, Y., Lee, T.-H., Wang, S., & Zhang, X. (2021). Time-varying model averaging. *Journal of Econometrics*, *222*(2), 974–992.

Vortelinos, D. I. (2017). Forecasting realized volatility: HAR against principal components combining, neural networks and GARCH. *Research in International Business and Finance*, *39*(Part B), 824–839.

Wang, D., & Kumbhakar, S. C. (2009). Strategic groups and heterogeneous technologies: An application to the US banking industry. *Macroeconomics and Finance in Emerging Market Economies*, *2*(1), 31–57.

Wei, C. (1987). Adaptive prediction by least squares predictors in stochastic regression models with applications to time series. *The Annals of Statistics*, *15*(4), 1667–1682.

Xie, T. (2015). Prediction model averaging estimator. *Economics Letters*, *131*, 5–8.

Xie, T. (2017). Heteroscedasticity-robust model screening: A useful toolkit for model averaging in big data analytics. *Economics Letters*, *151*, 119–121.

Yuan, Z., & Yang, Y. (2005). Combining linear regression models: When and how?. *Journal of the American Statistical Association*, *100*(472), 1202–1214.

Zhang, X., Wan, A. T., & Zou, G. (2013). Model averaging by jackknife criterion in models with dependent data. *Journal of Econometrics*, *174*(2), 82–94.

Zhang, X., & Wang, W. (2019). Optimal model averaging estimation for partially linear models. *Statistica Sinica*, *29*(2), 693–718.

Zhao, S., Zhang, X., & Gao, Y. (2016). Model averaging with averaging covariance matrix. *Economics Letters*, *145*, 214–217.

Zhu, R., Wan, A. T., Zhang, X., & Zou, G. (2019). A Mallows-type model averaging estimator for the varying-coefficient partially linear model. *Journal of the American Statistical Association*, *114*(526), 882–892.

Zou, H., & Zhang, H. H. (2009). On the adaptive elastic-net with a diverging number of parameters. *Annals of Statistics*, *37*(4), 1733–1751.

APPENDIX

A.1. PROOF OF THEOREM 1

Let $\boldsymbol{\varsigma} = [\varsigma_1, \ldots, \varsigma_T]^{\mathrm{T}}$. It is seen that

$$\begin{aligned}\text{H-MAHAR}(\mathbf{w}) - L_T(\mathbf{w}) &= \| \widehat{\boldsymbol{\mu}}(\mathbf{w}) - \mathbf{y} \|^2 + 2\mathrm{tr}\{\mathbf{P}(\mathbf{w})\widehat{\boldsymbol{\Omega}}(\mathbf{w})\} - \| \widehat{\boldsymbol{\mu}}(\mathbf{w}) - \boldsymbol{\mu} \|^2 \\ &= \| \boldsymbol{\varsigma} \|^2 + 2\boldsymbol{\varsigma}^{\top}\boldsymbol{\mu} - 2\boldsymbol{\varsigma}^{\top}\mathbf{P}(\mathbf{w})\boldsymbol{\mu} \\ &\quad + 2\mathrm{tr}\{\mathbf{P}(\mathbf{w})\widehat{\boldsymbol{\Omega}}(\mathbf{w})\} - 2\boldsymbol{\varsigma}^{\top}\mathbf{P}(\mathbf{w})\boldsymbol{\varsigma},\end{aligned}$$

where the terms $\| \boldsymbol{\varsigma} \|^2$ and $\boldsymbol{\varsigma}^{\mathrm{T}}\boldsymbol{\mu}$ are unrelated to $\mathbf{w}$, and

$$\begin{aligned}R_T(\mathbf{w}) - L_T(\mathbf{w}) &= \| \mathbf{A}(\mathbf{w})\boldsymbol{\mu} \|^2 + \mathrm{tr}\left\{\mathbf{P}^2(\mathbf{w})\boldsymbol{\Omega}\right\} - \| \widehat{\boldsymbol{\mu}}(\mathbf{w}) - \boldsymbol{\mu} \|^2 \\ &= 2\boldsymbol{\varsigma}^{\top}\mathbf{P}(\mathbf{w})\mathbf{A}(\mathbf{w})\boldsymbol{\mu} + \mathrm{tr}\{\mathbf{P}^2(\mathbf{w})\boldsymbol{\Omega}\} - \boldsymbol{\varsigma}^{\top}\mathbf{P}^2(\mathbf{w})\boldsymbol{\varsigma}.\end{aligned}$$

Then, we have

$$\begin{aligned}&\sup_{\mathbf{w}\in\mathcal{H}} | \mathrm{tr}\{\mathbf{P}(\mathbf{w})\widehat{\boldsymbol{\Omega}}(\mathbf{w})\} | / R_T(\mathbf{w}) \\ &= \sup_{\mathbf{w}\in\mathcal{H}} | \{\mathbf{y} - \mathbf{P}(\mathbf{w})\mathbf{y}\}^{\top}\mathbf{Q}(\mathbf{w})\{\mathbf{y} - \mathbf{P}(\mathbf{w})\mathbf{y}\} | / R_T(\mathbf{w}) \\ &= \sup_{\mathbf{w}\in\mathcal{H}} | \{\boldsymbol{\mu} + \boldsymbol{\varsigma} - \mathbf{P}(\mathbf{w})\mathbf{y}\}^{\top}\mathbf{Q}(\mathbf{w})\{\boldsymbol{\mu} + \boldsymbol{\varsigma} - \mathbf{P}(\mathbf{w})\mathbf{y}\} | / R_T(\mathbf{w}) \\ &\le \sup_{\mathbf{w}\in\mathcal{H}} | \boldsymbol{\varsigma}^{\top}\mathbf{Q}(\mathbf{w})\boldsymbol{\varsigma} | / R_T(\mathbf{w}) + 2\sup_{\mathbf{w}\in\mathcal{H}} | \boldsymbol{\varsigma}^{\top}\mathbf{Q}(\mathbf{w})\{\mathbf{P}(\mathbf{w})\mathbf{y} - \boldsymbol{\mu}\} | / R_T(\mathbf{w}) \\ &\quad + \sup_{\mathbf{w}\in\mathcal{H}} | \{\mathbf{P}(\mathbf{w})\mathbf{y} - \boldsymbol{\mu}\}^{\top}\mathbf{Q}(\mathbf{w})\{\mathbf{P}(\mathbf{w})\mathbf{y} - \boldsymbol{\mu}\} | / R_T(\mathbf{w}).\end{aligned}$$

Hence, from Gao, Zhang, Wang, Chong, and Zou (2019), to prove Theorem 1, it is sufficient to verify that

$$\sup_{\mathbf{w}\in\mathcal{H}} | \boldsymbol{\varsigma}\mathbf{P}^{\top}(\mathbf{w})\boldsymbol{\varsigma} | / R_T(\mathbf{w}) = o_p(1), \tag{A.1}$$

$$\sup_{\mathbf{w}\in\mathcal{H}} | \boldsymbol{\varsigma}^{\top}\mathbf{P}(\mathbf{w})\boldsymbol{\mu} | / R_T(\mathbf{w}) = o_p(1), \tag{A.2}$$

$$\sup_{\mathbf{w}\in\mathcal{H}} | \mathrm{tr}\{\mathbf{P}^2(\mathbf{w})\boldsymbol{\Omega}\} | / R_T(\mathbf{w}) = o_p(1), \tag{A.3}$$

$$\sup_{\mathbf{w}\in\mathcal{H}} | \boldsymbol{\varsigma}^{\top}\mathbf{P}^2(\mathbf{w})\boldsymbol{\varsigma} | / R_T(\mathbf{w}) = o_p(1), \tag{A.4}$$

$$\sup_{\mathbf{w}\in\mathcal{H}} | \boldsymbol{\varsigma}^{\top}\mathbf{P}(\mathbf{w})\mathbf{A}(\mathbf{w})\boldsymbol{\mu} | / R_T(\mathbf{w}) = o_p(1), \tag{A.5}$$

$$\sup_{\mathbf{w}\in\mathcal{H}} | \boldsymbol{\varsigma}^{\top}\mathbf{Q}(\mathbf{w})\boldsymbol{\varsigma}\} | / R_T(\mathbf{w}) = o_p(1), \tag{A.6}$$

$$\sup_{\mathbf{w}\in\mathcal{H}} |\boldsymbol{\varsigma}^{\top}\mathbf{Q}(\mathbf{w})\{\mathbf{P}(\mathbf{w})\mathbf{y}-\boldsymbol{\mu}\}| / R_T(\mathbf{w}) = o_p(1), \tag{A.7}$$

$$\sup_{\mathbf{w}\in\mathcal{H}} |\{\mathbf{P}(\mathbf{w})\mathbf{y}-\boldsymbol{\mu}\}^{\top}\mathbf{Q}(\mathbf{w})\{\mathbf{P}(\mathbf{w})\mathbf{y}-\boldsymbol{\mu}\}| / R_T(\mathbf{w}) = o_p(1). \tag{A.8}$$

Proof of (A.1): To verify (A.1), we first show that $\mathbb{E}|y_{t-v}|^{q_0} \leq C$ for some $q_0 \geq 2$. According to $y_t = \sum_{l=0}^{\infty} b_l \varsigma_{t-l}$, note that $\sum_{l=0}^{\infty} |b_l| < \infty$, we have, uniformly in t and v with $1 \leq t \leq T$ and $1 \leq v \leq d$,

$$\mathbb{E}|y_{t-v}|^{q_0} = \mathbb{E}\left|\sum_{l=0}^{\infty} b_l \varsigma_{t-v-l}\right|^{q_0} \leq K\left(\sum_{l=0}^{\infty} b_l^2\right)^{q_0/2} \leq C, \tag{A.9}$$

where K and C are positive constants, and the first inequality is yielded from Lemma 2 of Wei (1987).

Then, let $\mathbf{U} = [\mathbf{1}, \mathbf{y}_L, \mathbf{F}]$, and we show that $\boldsymbol{\varsigma}^{\top}\mathbf{U}\mathbf{U}\boldsymbol{\varsigma}^{\top} = O_p(Td)$. Defining f_{ti} as the (ti)th element of $\mathbf{F}$ and $\bar{k} = d+1+q$, for some $q_0 \geq 2$, we have

$$\begin{aligned}
&\mathbb{E}\left(\left\|\mathbf{U}^{\top}\boldsymbol{\varsigma}\right\|^{q_0}\right)\\
&= \mathbb{E}\left|\sum_{v=1}^{d}\left(\sum_{t=1}^{T} y_{t-v}\varsigma_t\right)^2 + \left(\sum_{t=1}^{T}\varsigma_t\right)^2 + \sum_{i=1}^{q}\left(\sum_{t=1}^{T} f_{ti}\varsigma_t\right)^2\right|^{q_0/2}\\
&\leq (3\bar{k})^{q_0/2-1}\sum_{v=1}^{d}\mathbb{E}\left|\sum_{t=1}^{T} y_{t-v}\varsigma_t\right|^{q_0} + (3\bar{k})^{q_0/2-1}\mathbb{E}\left|\sum_{t=1}^{T}\varsigma_t\right|^{q_0} + (3\bar{k})^{q_0/2-1}\sum_{i=1}^{q}\mathbb{E}\left|\sum_{t=1}^{T} f_{ti}\varsigma_t\right|^{q_0} \qquad \text{(A.10)}\\
&\leq (3\bar{k})^{q_0/2-1} K\left(\sum_{v=1}^{d}\mathbb{E}\left|\sum_{t=1}^{T} y_{t-v}^2\right|^{q_0/2} + |T|^{q_0/2} + \sum_{i=1}^{q}\mathbb{E}\left|\sum_{t=1}^{T} f_{ti}^2\right|^{q_0/2}\right)\\
&\leq (3\bar{k}T)^{q_0/2-1} K\left(\sum_{v=1}^{d}\sum_{t=1}^{T}\mathbb{E}|y_{t-v}|^{q_0} + T + \sum_{i=1}^{q}\sum_{t=1}^{T}\mathbb{E}|f_{ti}|^{q_0}\right),
\end{aligned}$$

where the first and third inequalities are obtained by the convexity of $x^{q_0/2}$ for $x > 0$, and the second inequality is obtained by Lemma 2 of Wei (1987). Combining (A.9) and the fact that both q and f_{ti} are finite, we have

$$\mathbb{E}(\boldsymbol{\varsigma}^{\top}\mathbf{U}\mathbf{U}^{\top}\boldsymbol{\varsigma}) = O_p(Td). \tag{A.11}$$

So, by Markov's inequality, $\boldsymbol{\varsigma}^{\top}\mathbf{U}\mathbf{U}^{\top}\boldsymbol{\varsigma} = O_p(Td)$.

Finally, we show that $\zeta_{\max}\{(\mathbf{X}^{\top}\mathbf{X})^{-1}\} = O_p(T^{-1}d^2)$. According to Assumption 3, the proof of (A.63) of Zhang et al. (2013), and $T\zeta_{\max}\{(\mathbf{y}_L{}^{\top}\mathbf{y}_L)^{-1}\} = O_p(1)$ derived from Assumption 2, we have

$$\zeta_{\max}\{(\mathbf{U}^{\top}\mathbf{U})^{-1}\} = O_p(T^{-1}). \tag{A.12}$$

Let

$$\mathbf{B}^* = \begin{pmatrix} 1 & 1 & 1 & 1 & \cdots & 1 \\ 0 & 1 & 1/2 & 1/3 & \cdots & 1/d \\ 0 & 0 & 1/2 & 1/3 & \cdots & 1/d \\ 0 & 0 & 0 & 1/3 & \cdots & 1/d \\ \vdots & \vdots & \vdots & \vdots & \ddots & \vdots \\ 0 & 0 & 0 & 0 & \cdots & 1/d \end{pmatrix} \quad \text{and} \quad \mathbf{B} = \begin{pmatrix} \mathbf{B}^* & 0 \\ 0 & \mathbf{I}_q \end{pmatrix},$$

then $\mathbf{X} = \mathbf{U}\mathbf{B}$. It is easy to see that

$$\zeta_{\max}(\mathbf{B}\mathbf{B}^\top) = O_p(d). \tag{A.13}$$

From (A.12) and (A.13), we have

$$\begin{aligned} &\zeta_{\max}\{(\mathbf{X}^\top\mathbf{X})^{-1}\} \\ &= \zeta_{\max}\{(\mathbf{B}^\top\mathbf{U}^\top\mathbf{U}\mathbf{B})^{-1}\} \\ &= \zeta_{\max}\{\mathbf{B}^{-1}(\mathbf{U}^\top\mathbf{U})^{-1}\mathbf{B}^{\top-1}\} \\ &\le \zeta_{\max}(\mathbf{B}^{-1})\zeta_{\max}\{(\mathbf{U}^\top\mathbf{U})^{-1}\}\zeta_{\max}(\mathbf{B}^{\top-1}) \\ &= O_p(T^{-1}d^2). \end{aligned} \tag{A.14}$$

Combining (A.11), (A.13), and (A.14), we have

$$\begin{aligned} &\sup_{\mathbf{w}\in\mathcal{H}} \frac{|\varsigma^\top \mathbf{P}(\mathbf{w})\varsigma|}{R_T(\mathbf{w})} \\ &\le \xi_T^{-1} |\varsigma^\top \mathbf{P}\varsigma| \\ &= \xi_T^{-1}\varsigma^\top \mathbf{X}(\mathbf{X}^\top\mathbf{X})^{-1}\mathbf{X}^\mathrm{T}\varsigma \\ &\le \zeta_{\max}\{(\mathbf{X}^\top\mathbf{X})^{-1}\}\xi_T^{-1}\varsigma^\top\mathbf{X}\mathbf{X}^\top\varsigma \\ &= \zeta_{\max}\{(\mathbf{X}^\top\mathbf{X})^{-1}\}\xi_T^{-1}\varsigma\mathbf{U}\mathbf{B}\mathbf{B}^\top\mathbf{U}\varsigma \\ &\le \zeta_{\max}\{(\mathbf{X}^\top\mathbf{X})^{-1}\}\zeta_{\max}(\mathbf{B}\mathbf{B}^\top)\xi_T^{-1}\varsigma^\top\mathbf{U}\mathbf{U}^\top\varsigma \\ &= O_p(\xi_T^{-1}d^4) \\ &= o_p(1), \end{aligned} \tag{A.15}$$

where the last step is from Assumption 4.

Proof of (A.2): To verify (A.2), we first show

$$|\varsigma^\top \mathbf{P}(\mathbf{w})\boldsymbol{\mu}| = |\varsigma^\top \mathbf{P}(\mathbf{w})\mathbf{P}\boldsymbol{\mu}| \le \{\varsigma^\top \mathbf{P}(\mathbf{w})\varsigma\boldsymbol{\mu}\mathbf{P}\boldsymbol{\mu}\}^{1/2} \le (\varsigma^\top \mathbf{P}\varsigma\boldsymbol{\mu}^\top\mathbf{P}\boldsymbol{\mu})^{1/2}. \tag{A.16}$$

Moreover, according to (A.15), we have

$$d^{-4}\varsigma^\top\mathbf{P}\varsigma = O_p(1). \tag{A.17}$$

Then,

$$\begin{aligned}\sup_{\mathbf{w}\in\mathcal{H}}\frac{|\varsigma^{\top}\mathbf{P}(\mathbf{w})\boldsymbol{\mu}|}{R_T(\mathbf{w})} &\leq \xi_T^{-1}(\varsigma^{\top}\mathbf{P}\varsigma\boldsymbol{\mu}^{\top}\mathbf{P}\boldsymbol{\mu})^{1/2} \\ &= (d^{-4}\varsigma^{\top}\mathbf{P}\varsigma d^{4}\boldsymbol{\mu}^{\top}\mathbf{P}\boldsymbol{\mu}\xi_T^{-2})^{1/2} \\ &= o_p(1),\end{aligned} \tag{A.18}$$

where the last step is from (A.17) and Assumption 4.

Proof of (A.3):

$$\begin{aligned}\sup_{\mathbf{w}\in\mathcal{H}}\frac{|\operatorname{tr}\{\mathbf{P}^2(\mathbf{w})\boldsymbol{\Omega}\}|}{R_T(\mathbf{w})} &\leq \xi_T^{-1}\max_{1\leq t\leq T}\sigma_t^2\sup_{\mathbf{w}\in\mathcal{H}}|\operatorname{tr}\{\mathbf{P}^2(\mathbf{w})\}| \\ &\leq \xi_T^{-1}\max_{1\leq t\leq T}\sigma_t^2\sup_{\mathbf{w}\in\mathcal{H}}|\operatorname{tr}\{\mathbf{P}(\mathbf{w})\}| \\ &\leq \xi_T^{-1}\bar{k}\max_{1\leq t\leq T}\sigma_t^2 \\ &= o_p(1),\end{aligned}$$

where the last step is from Assumption 4.

Proof of (A.4):

$$\begin{aligned}\sup_{\mathbf{w}\in\mathcal{H}}\frac{|\varsigma^{\top}\mathbf{P}^2(\mathbf{w})\varsigma|}{R_T(\mathbf{w})} &\leq \xi_T^{-1}\sup_{\mathbf{w}\in\mathcal{H}}|\varsigma^{\top}\mathbf{P}(\mathbf{w})\varsigma| \\ &= o_p(1),\end{aligned}$$

where the last step is from (A.1).

Proof of (A.5): Since

$$|\varsigma^{\top}\mathbf{P}(\mathbf{w})\mathbf{A}(\mathbf{w})\boldsymbol{\mu}| = |\varsigma^{\top}\mathbf{P}(\mathbf{w})\boldsymbol{\mu} - \varsigma^{\top}\mathbf{P}(\mathbf{w})\mathbf{P}(\mathbf{w})\boldsymbol{\mu}|, \tag{A.19}$$

and we already proved (A.2), to prove (A.5), we only need to verify

$$\sup_{\mathbf{w}\in\mathcal{H}}\frac{|\varsigma^{\top}\mathbf{P}(\mathbf{w})\mathbf{P}(\mathbf{w})\boldsymbol{\mu}|}{R_T(\mathbf{w})} = o_p(1).$$

It is seen that

$$|\varsigma^{\top}\mathbf{P}(\mathbf{w})\mathbf{P}(\mathbf{w})\boldsymbol{\mu}| = |\varsigma^{\top}\mathbf{P}(\mathbf{w})\mathbf{P}(\mathbf{w})\mathbf{P}\boldsymbol{\mu}| \leq \{\varsigma^{\top}\mathbf{P}(\mathbf{w})\varsigma\boldsymbol{\mu}^{\top}\mathbf{P}\boldsymbol{\mu}\}^{1/2} \leq (\varsigma^{\top}\mathbf{P}\varsigma\boldsymbol{\mu}^{\top}\mathbf{P}\boldsymbol{\mu})^{1/2} \tag{A.20}$$

Following the proof of (A.2) and (A.20), we obtain (A.5).

Proof of (A.6):

$$
\begin{aligned}
\sup_{\mathbf{w}\in\mathcal{H}} \frac{|\varsigma^{\top}\mathbf{Q}(\mathbf{w})\varsigma|}{R_T(\mathbf{w})} &\leq \xi_T^{-1} \sup_{\mathbf{w}\in\mathcal{H}} |\varsigma^{\top}\mathbf{Q}(\mathbf{w})\varsigma| \\
&= \xi_T^{-1} \sup_{\mathbf{w}\in\mathcal{H}} \left| \sum_{m=1}^{M_T} w_m \left(\sum_{t=1}^{T} h_{tt}^{(m)} \varsigma_t^2 \right) \right| \\
&\leq \xi_T^{-1} \bar{h} \, \| \varsigma \|^2 \\
&= O_p(\xi_T^{-1} \bar{k}) \\
&= o_p(1),
\end{aligned}
$$

where the fourth step is from $\| \varsigma \|^2 = O_p(T)$ and Assumption 1, and the last step is from Assumption 4.

Proof of (A.7):

$$
\begin{aligned}
&\sup_{\mathbf{w}\in\mathcal{H}} \frac{|\varsigma^{\top}\mathbf{Q}(\mathbf{w})\{\mathbf{P}(\mathbf{w})\mathbf{y}-\boldsymbol{\mu}\}|}{R_T(\mathbf{w})} \\
&\leq \sup_{\mathbf{w}\in\mathcal{H}} \frac{\left\|\mathbf{Q}^{1/2}(\mathbf{w})\varsigma\right\| \cdot \left\|\mathbf{Q}^{1/2}(\mathbf{w})\{\mathbf{P}(\mathbf{w})\mathbf{y}-\boldsymbol{\mu}\}\right\|}{R_T(\mathbf{w})} \\
&\leq \sup_{\mathbf{w}\in\mathcal{H}} \left\{ \frac{\left\|\mathbf{Q}^{1/2}(\mathbf{w})\varsigma\right\|^2}{R_T(\mathbf{w})} \right\}^{1/2} \sup_{\mathbf{w}\in\mathcal{H}} \left\{ \frac{\left\|\mathbf{Q}^{1/2}(\mathbf{w})\{\mathbf{P}(\mathbf{w})\mathbf{y}-\boldsymbol{\mu}\}\right\|^2}{R_T(\mathbf{w})} \right\}^{1/2} \\
&\leq \sup_{\mathbf{w}\in\mathcal{H}} \left\{ \frac{\left\|\mathbf{Q}^{1/2}(\mathbf{w})\varsigma\right\|^2}{R_T(\mathbf{w})} \right\}^{1/2} \sup_{\mathbf{w}\in\mathcal{H}} \left\{ \frac{\bar{h} L_T(\mathbf{w})}{R_T(\mathbf{w})} \right\}^{1/2} \\
&= o_p(1) \cdot \bar{h}^{1/2} \\
&= o_p(1),
\end{aligned}
$$

where the fourth step is from (A.3)–(A.6).

Proof of (A.8): It is seen that

$$
\begin{aligned}
&\sup_{\mathbf{w}\in\mathcal{H}} |\{\mathbf{P}(\mathbf{w})\mathbf{y}-\boldsymbol{\mu}\}^{\top}\mathbf{Q}(\mathbf{w})\{\mathbf{P}(\mathbf{w})\mathbf{y}-\boldsymbol{\mu}\}| / R_T(\mathbf{w}) \\
&\leq \bar{h} \sup_{\mathbf{w}\in\mathcal{H}} \frac{L_T(\mathbf{w})}{R_T(\mathbf{w})} \\
&= o_p(1),
\end{aligned}
$$

where the last step is from (A.3)–(A.5) and Assumption 1. We have established (A.1)–(A.8) which are sufficient for Equation (8).

A.2. PROOF OF THEOREM 2

Let $\varepsilon_T = \tilde{\xi}_T^{1/2} T^{-1/2+\delta}$. To verify Equation (9) of Theorem 2, following Fan and Peng (2004) and Chen, Li, Linton, and Lu (2018), it suffices to show that, there is a constant C such that, for the $M_T \times 1$ vector $\tilde{\mathbf{v}} = [v_1, \ldots, v_{M_T}]^\top$,

$$\lim_{T\to\infty} \Pr\left(\inf_{\|\tilde{\mathbf{v}}\|=C, (\mathbf{w}^* + \varepsilon_T \tilde{\mathbf{v}}) \in \mathcal{H}} \text{H-MAHAR}(\mathbf{w}^* + \varepsilon_T \tilde{\mathbf{v}}) > \text{H-MAHAR}(\mathbf{w}^*) \right) = 1, \quad \text{(A.21)}$$

which means that there exists a minimum $\widehat{\mathbf{w}}$ in the set $\{\mathbf{w}^* + \varepsilon_T \tilde{\mathbf{v}} : \| \tilde{\mathbf{v}} \| = C, (\mathbf{w}^* + \varepsilon_T \tilde{\mathbf{v}}) \in \mathcal{H}\}$ such that $\| \widehat{\mathbf{w}} - \mathbf{w}^* \| = O_p(\varepsilon_T)$.

It is seen that

$$\begin{aligned}
&\text{H-MAHAR}(\mathbf{w}^* + \varepsilon_T \tilde{\mathbf{v}}) - \text{H-MAHAR}(\mathbf{w}^*) \\
&= \| \mathbf{y} - \widehat{\boldsymbol{\mu}}(\mathbf{w}^* + \varepsilon_T \tilde{\mathbf{v}}) \|^2 - \| \mathbf{y} - \widehat{\boldsymbol{\mu}}(\mathbf{w}^*) \|^2 \\
&\quad + 2\text{tr}\{\mathbf{P}(\mathbf{w}^* + \varepsilon_T \tilde{\mathbf{v}}) \widehat{\boldsymbol{\Omega}}(\mathbf{w}^* + \varepsilon_T \tilde{\mathbf{v}})\} - 2\text{tr}\{\mathbf{P}(\mathbf{w}^*) \widehat{\boldsymbol{\Omega}}(\mathbf{w}^*)\} \\
&= \| \widehat{\boldsymbol{\mu}}(\varepsilon_T \tilde{\mathbf{v}}) \|^2 - 2\{\mathbf{y} - \widehat{\boldsymbol{\mu}}(\mathbf{w}^*)\}^\top \widehat{\boldsymbol{\mu}}(\varepsilon_T \tilde{\mathbf{v}}) \\
&\quad + 2\text{tr}\{\mathbf{P}(\mathbf{w}^*) \widehat{\boldsymbol{\Omega}}(\varepsilon_T \tilde{\mathbf{v}})\} + 2\text{tr}\{\mathbf{P}(\varepsilon_T \tilde{\mathbf{v}}) \widehat{\boldsymbol{\Omega}}(\mathbf{w}^*)\} + 2\text{tr}\{\mathbf{P}(\varepsilon_T \tilde{\mathbf{v}}) \widehat{\boldsymbol{\Omega}}(\varepsilon_T \tilde{\mathbf{v}})\} \\
&= \| \widehat{\boldsymbol{\mu}}(\varepsilon_T \tilde{\mathbf{v}}) \|^2 - 2\{\boldsymbol{\mu} - \widehat{\boldsymbol{\mu}}(\mathbf{w}^*)\}^\top \widehat{\boldsymbol{\mu}}(\varepsilon_T \tilde{\mathbf{v}}) - 2\boldsymbol{\varsigma}^\top \widehat{\boldsymbol{\mu}}(\varepsilon_T \tilde{\mathbf{v}}) \\
&\quad + 2\text{tr}\{\mathbf{P}(\varepsilon_T \tilde{\mathbf{v}}) \widehat{\boldsymbol{\Omega}}(\varepsilon_T \tilde{\mathbf{v}})\} + 2\text{tr}\{\mathbf{P}(\mathbf{w}^*) \widehat{\boldsymbol{\Omega}}(\varepsilon_T \tilde{\mathbf{v}})\} + 2\text{tr}\{\mathbf{P}(\varepsilon_T \tilde{\mathbf{v}}) \widehat{\boldsymbol{\Omega}}(\mathbf{w}^*)\} \\
&\equiv \Delta_1 - \Delta_2 - \Delta_3 + \Delta_4 + \Delta_5 + \Delta_6.
\end{aligned} \quad \text{(A.22)}$$

For Δ_1, we have

$$\begin{aligned}
\Delta_1 &= \| \widehat{\boldsymbol{\mu}}(\varepsilon_T \tilde{\mathbf{v}}) \|^2 \\
&= \left\| \sum_{m=1}^{M_T} \varepsilon_T v_m \widehat{\boldsymbol{\mu}}_m \right\|^2 \\
&= \varepsilon_T^2 \| \boldsymbol{\Lambda} \tilde{\mathbf{v}} \|^2 \\
&\geq \varepsilon_T^2 T \zeta_{\min}(\boldsymbol{\Lambda}^\top \boldsymbol{\Lambda} / T) \| \tilde{\mathbf{v}} \|^2 \\
&> \varepsilon_T^2 T \kappa_1 \| \tilde{\mathbf{v}} \|^2 > 0,
\end{aligned} \quad \text{(A.23)}$$

where the fifth step is from Assumption 5.

For Δ_2, we have

$$\begin{aligned}
|\Delta_2 / 2| &= \left| \{\boldsymbol{\mu} - \widehat{\boldsymbol{\mu}}(\mathbf{w}^*)\}^\top \widehat{\boldsymbol{\mu}}(\varepsilon_T \tilde{\mathbf{v}}) \right| \\
&= \varepsilon_T \left| \{\boldsymbol{\mu} - \widehat{\boldsymbol{\mu}}(\mathbf{w}^*)\}^\top \left(\sum_{m=1}^{M_T} v_m \widehat{\boldsymbol{\mu}}_m \right) \right| \\
&= \varepsilon_T \left| \{\boldsymbol{\mu} - \widehat{\boldsymbol{\mu}}(\mathbf{w}^*)\}^\top \boldsymbol{\Lambda} \tilde{\mathbf{v}} \right| \\
&\leq \varepsilon_T \| \boldsymbol{\mu} - \widehat{\boldsymbol{\mu}}(\mathbf{w}^*) \| \cdot \| \boldsymbol{\Lambda} \tilde{\mathbf{v}} \| \\
&< \varepsilon_T L_T^{1/2}(\mathbf{w}^*) T^{1/2} \kappa_2 \| \tilde{\mathbf{v}} \| \\
&= O_p(\varepsilon_T \tilde{\xi}_T^{1/2} T^{1/2}) \| \tilde{\mathbf{v}} \|,
\end{aligned} \quad \text{(A.24)}$$

where the fifth step is from Assumption 5. It is clear to see that $|\Delta_2|$ is dominated by Δ_1 asymptotically.

Next, we consider Δ_3. Making use of (A.9), we have $\|\mathbf{y}\|^2 = O_p(T)$. Further,

$$
\begin{aligned}
|\Delta_3/2| &= \varsigma^\top \widehat{\boldsymbol{\mu}}(\varepsilon_T \tilde{\mathbf{v}}) \\
&= \varepsilon_T \left| \varsigma^\top \sum_{m=1}^{M_T} v_m \widehat{\boldsymbol{\mu}}_m \right| \\
&= \varepsilon_T \left| \varsigma^\top \boldsymbol{\Lambda} \tilde{\mathbf{v}} \right| \\
&\le \varepsilon_T \, \| \boldsymbol{\Lambda}^\top \varsigma \| \cdot \| \tilde{\mathbf{v}} \| \\
&= \varepsilon_T \left(\sum_{m=1}^{M_T} \varsigma^\top \widehat{\boldsymbol{\mu}}_m \widehat{\boldsymbol{\mu}}_m^\top \varsigma \right)^{1/2} \| \tilde{\mathbf{v}} \| \\
&= \varepsilon_T \left(\sum_{m=1}^{M_T} \| \mathbf{y}^\top \mathbf{P}_m \varsigma \|^2 \right)^{1/2} \| \tilde{\mathbf{v}} \| \\
&\le \varepsilon_T \left(\sum_{m=1}^{M_T} \| \mathbf{P}_m \varsigma \|^2 \| \mathbf{y} \|^2 \right)^{1/2} \| \tilde{\mathbf{v}} \| \\
&\le \varepsilon_T \left(M_T \| \mathbf{P} \varsigma \|^2 \| \mathbf{y} \|^2 \right)^{1/2} \| \tilde{\mathbf{v}} \| \\
&= O_p(\varepsilon_T M_T^{1/2} \bar{k}^2 T^{1/2}) \| \tilde{\mathbf{v}} \|,
\end{aligned} \tag{A.25}
$$

where the last step is from (A.15). From Assumption 6, we see that $|\Delta_3|$ is dominated by Δ_1 asymptotically.

For Δ_4, we have

$$
\begin{aligned}
|\Delta_4/2| &= \left| \mathrm{tr}\{\mathbf{P}(\varepsilon_T \tilde{\mathbf{v}}) \widehat{\boldsymbol{\Omega}}(\varepsilon_T \tilde{\mathbf{v}})\} \right| \\
&= \left| \{\mathbf{y} - \mathbf{P}(\varepsilon_T \tilde{\mathbf{v}})\mathbf{y}\}^\top \mathbf{Q}(\varepsilon_T \tilde{\mathbf{v}}) \{\mathbf{y} - \mathbf{P}(\varepsilon_T \tilde{\mathbf{v}})\mathbf{y}\} \right| \\
&\le | \varsigma^\top \mathbf{Q}(\varepsilon_T \tilde{\mathbf{v}}) \varsigma | + 2 | \varsigma^\top \mathbf{Q}(\varepsilon_T \tilde{\mathbf{v}}) \{\boldsymbol{\mu} - \mathbf{P}(\varepsilon_T \tilde{\mathbf{v}})\mathbf{y}\} | \\
&\quad + \left| \{\boldsymbol{\mu} - \mathbf{P}(\varepsilon_T \tilde{\mathbf{v}})\mathbf{y}\}^\top \mathbf{Q}(\varepsilon_T \tilde{\mathbf{v}}) \{\boldsymbol{\mu} - \mathbf{P}(\varepsilon_T \tilde{\mathbf{v}})\mathbf{y}\} \right| \\
&\equiv \Delta_4^1 + \Delta_4^2 + \Delta_4^3.
\end{aligned} \tag{A.26}
$$

As for Δ_4^1, we have

$$
\begin{aligned}
|\Delta_4^1| &= | \varsigma^\top \mathbf{Q}(\varepsilon_T \tilde{\mathbf{v}}) \varsigma | \\
&= \varepsilon_T \left| \varsigma^\top \sum_{m=1}^{M_T} v_m \mathbf{Q}_m \varsigma \right| \\
&= \varepsilon_T \left| \sum_{m=1}^{M_T} v_m \left(\sum_{t=1}^{T} h_{tt}^{(m)} \varsigma_t^2 \right) \right| \\
&\le \varepsilon_T \| \tilde{\mathbf{v}} \| \left\{ \sum_{m=1}^{M_T} \left(\sum_{t=1}^{T} h_{tt}^{(m)} \varsigma_t^2 \right)^2 \right\}^{1/2} \\
&\le \varepsilon_T \| \tilde{\mathbf{v}} \| \left(M_T \bar{h}^2 \| \varsigma \|^4 \right)^{1/2} \\
&= O_p(\varepsilon_T M_T^{1/2} \bar{k}) \| \tilde{\mathbf{v}} \|,
\end{aligned} \tag{A.27}
$$

where the last step is from $\| \varsigma \|^2 = O_p(T)$ and Assumption 1. As for Δ_4^2, making use of (A.9), we have $\| \boldsymbol{\mu} \|^2 \le \| \mathbf{y} \|^2 + \| \varsigma \|^2 = O_p(T)$. Further,

$$\begin{aligned}
|\Delta_4^2/2| &= |\varsigma^\top \mathbf{Q}(\varepsilon_T \tilde{\mathbf{v}})\{\boldsymbol{\mu} - \mathbf{P}(\varepsilon_T \tilde{\mathbf{v}})\mathbf{y}\}| \\
&= \varepsilon_T |\varsigma^\top \mathbf{Q}(\tilde{\mathbf{v}})\{\boldsymbol{\mu} - \mathbf{P}(\varepsilon_T \tilde{\mathbf{v}})\mathbf{y}\}| \\
&\le \varepsilon_T \| \mathbf{Q}(\tilde{\mathbf{v}})\varsigma \| \cdot \| \boldsymbol{\mu} - \mathbf{P}(\varepsilon_T \tilde{\mathbf{v}})\mathbf{y} \| \\
&= \varepsilon_T \left\{ \sum_{t=1}^{T} \varsigma_t^2 \left(\sum_{m=1}^{M_T} v_m h_{tt}^{(m)} \right)^2 \right\}^{1/2} \cdot \| \varepsilon_T \boldsymbol{\Lambda} \tilde{\mathbf{v}} - \boldsymbol{\mu} \| \\
&\le \varepsilon_T \left\{ \max_{1 \le t \le T} \left(\sum_{m=1}^{M_T} v_m h_{tt}^{(m)} \right)^2 \| \varsigma \|^2 \right\}^{1/2} \\
&\quad \times \left(\varepsilon_T^2 \| \boldsymbol{\Lambda} \tilde{\mathbf{v}} \|^2 + \| \boldsymbol{\mu} \|^2 + 2 \| \varepsilon_T \boldsymbol{\Lambda} \tilde{\mathbf{v}} \| \| \boldsymbol{\mu} \| \right)^{1/2} \\
&\le \varepsilon_T \left[\max_{1 \le t \le T} \| \tilde{\mathbf{v}} \|^2 \left\{ \sum_{m=1}^{M_T} (h_{tt}^{(m)})^2 \right\} \| \varsigma \|^2 \right]^{1/2} \\
&\quad \times \left(\varepsilon_T^2 T \kappa_2 \| \tilde{\mathbf{v}} \|^2 + \| \boldsymbol{\mu} \|^2 + 2 \| \varepsilon_T \boldsymbol{\Lambda} \tilde{\mathbf{v}} \| \| \boldsymbol{\mu} \| \right)^{1/2} \\
&\le \varepsilon_T \left(\| \tilde{\mathbf{v}} \|^2 M_T \bar{h}^2 \| \varsigma \|^2 \right)^{1/2} \\
&\quad \times \left(\varepsilon_T^2 T \kappa_2 \| \tilde{\mathbf{v}} \|^2 + \| \boldsymbol{\mu} \|^2 + 2 \| \varepsilon_T \boldsymbol{\Lambda} \tilde{\mathbf{v}} \| \| \boldsymbol{\mu} \| \right)^{1/2} \\
&= O_p(\varepsilon_T M_T^{1/2} \bar{k} T^{-1/2}) \| \tilde{\mathbf{v}} \| \cdot O_p(\varepsilon_T T^{1/2} \| \tilde{\mathbf{v}} \| + T^{1/2} + \varepsilon_T^{1/2} T^{1/2} \| \tilde{\mathbf{v}} \|^{1/2}) \\
&= O_p(\varepsilon_T M_T^{1/2} \bar{k}) \| \tilde{\mathbf{v}} \|,
\end{aligned} \tag{A.28}$$

where the sixth step is from Assumption 5, and the eighth step is from $\| \varsigma \|^2 = O_p(T)$ and Assumption 1. According to (A.28), we obtain $\| \boldsymbol{\mu} - \mathbf{P}(\varepsilon_T \tilde{\mathbf{v}})\mathbf{y} \|^2 = O_p(T)$. As for Δ_4^3, we have

$$\begin{aligned}
|\Delta_4^3| &= \left| \{\boldsymbol{\mu} - \mathbf{P}(\varepsilon_T \tilde{\mathbf{v}})\mathbf{y}\}^\top \mathbf{Q}(\varepsilon_T \tilde{\mathbf{v}}) \{\boldsymbol{\mu} - \mathbf{P}(\varepsilon_T \tilde{\mathbf{v}})\mathbf{y}\} \right| \\
&\le \varepsilon_T \| \mathbf{Q}(\tilde{\mathbf{v}}) \{\boldsymbol{\mu} - \mathbf{P}(\varepsilon_T \tilde{\mathbf{v}})\mathbf{y}\} \| \cdot \| \boldsymbol{\mu} - \mathbf{P}(\varepsilon_T \tilde{\mathbf{v}})\mathbf{y} \| \\
&\le \varepsilon_T \left\{ \max_{1 \le t \le T} \left(\sum_{m=1}^{M_T} v_m h_{tt}^{(m)} \right)^2 \| \boldsymbol{\mu} - \mathbf{P}(\varepsilon_T \tilde{\mathbf{v}})\mathbf{y} \|^2 \right\}^{1/2} \\
&\quad \times \| \boldsymbol{\mu} - \mathbf{P}(\varepsilon_T \tilde{\mathbf{v}})\mathbf{y} \| \\
&\le \varepsilon_T \left(\| \tilde{\mathbf{v}} \|^2 M_T \bar{h}^2 \| \boldsymbol{\mu} - \mathbf{P}(\varepsilon_T \tilde{\mathbf{v}})\mathbf{y} \|^2 \right)^{1/2} \| \boldsymbol{\mu} - \mathbf{P}(\varepsilon_T \tilde{\mathbf{v}})\mathbf{y} \| \\
&= O_p(\varepsilon_T M_T^{1/2} \bar{k}) \| \tilde{\mathbf{v}} \|,
\end{aligned} \tag{A.29}$$

where the third step is similar to the fifth step of (A.28), the fourth step is similar to the seventh step of (A.28), and the last step is from $\| \boldsymbol{\mu} - \mathbf{P}(\varepsilon_T \tilde{\mathbf{v}})\mathbf{y} \|^2 = O_p(T)$ and Assumption 1. Combining (A.26)–(A.29) and Assumption 6, we obtain $|\Delta_4| = O_p(\varepsilon_T M_T^{1/2} \bar{k}) \| \tilde{\mathbf{v}} \|$, which is dominated by Δ_1 asymptotically.

For Δ_5, we have

$$\begin{aligned}
|\Delta_5/2| &= |\operatorname{tr}\{\mathbf{P}(\mathbf{w}^*)\widehat{\boldsymbol{\Omega}}(\varepsilon_T\tilde{\mathbf{v}})\}| \\
&= \left|\{\mathbf{y}-\mathbf{P}(\varepsilon_T\tilde{\mathbf{v}})\mathbf{y}\}^\top \mathbf{Q}(\mathbf{w}^*)\{\mathbf{y}-\mathbf{P}(\varepsilon_T\tilde{\mathbf{v}})\mathbf{y}\}\right| \\
&\le |\boldsymbol{\varsigma}^\top \mathbf{Q}(\mathbf{w}^*)\boldsymbol{\varsigma}| + 2|\boldsymbol{\varsigma}^\top \mathbf{Q}(\mathbf{w}^*)\{\boldsymbol{\mu}-\mathbf{P}(\varepsilon_T\tilde{\mathbf{v}})\mathbf{y}\}| \\
&\quad + \left|\{\boldsymbol{\mu}-\mathbf{P}(\varepsilon_T\tilde{\mathbf{v}})\mathbf{y}\}^\top \mathbf{Q}(\mathbf{w}^*)\{\boldsymbol{\mu}-\mathbf{P}(\varepsilon_T\tilde{\mathbf{v}})\mathbf{y}\}\right| \\
&\equiv \Delta_5^1 + \Delta_5^2 + \Delta_5^3.
\end{aligned} \tag{A.30}$$

As for Δ_5^1, let $\mathbf{w}^* = [w_1^*, \ldots, w_{M_T}^*]^\top$, we have

$$\begin{aligned}
|\Delta_5^1| &= |\boldsymbol{\varsigma}^\top \mathbf{Q}(\mathbf{w}^*)\boldsymbol{\varsigma}| \\
&= \left|\boldsymbol{\varsigma}^\top \sum_{m=1}^{M_T} w_m^* \mathbf{Q}_m \boldsymbol{\varsigma}\right| \\
&= \left|\sum_{m=1}^{M_T} w_m^* \left(\sum_{t=1}^{T} h_{tt}^{(m)} \varsigma_t^2\right)\right| \\
&\le \max_{1\le m\le M_T} \sum_{t=1}^{T} h_{tt}^{(m)} \varsigma_t^2 \\
&\le \bar{h}\,\|\boldsymbol{\varsigma}\|^2 \\
&= O_p(\bar{k}),
\end{aligned} \tag{A.31}$$

where the last step is from $\|\boldsymbol{\varsigma}\|^2 = O_p(T)$ and Assumption 1. As for Δ_5^2, we have

$$\begin{aligned}
|\Delta_5^2/2| &= |\boldsymbol{\varsigma}^\top \mathbf{Q}(\mathbf{w}^*)\{\boldsymbol{\mu}-\mathbf{P}(\varepsilon_T\tilde{\mathbf{v}})\mathbf{y}\}| \\
&\le \|\mathbf{Q}^{1/2}(\mathbf{w}^*)\boldsymbol{\varsigma}\|\cdot\|\mathbf{Q}^{1/2}(\mathbf{w}^*)\{\boldsymbol{\mu}-\mathbf{P}(\varepsilon_T\tilde{\mathbf{v}})\mathbf{y}\}\| \\
&\le \|\mathbf{Q}^{1/2}(\mathbf{w}^*)\boldsymbol{\varsigma}\|\,\zeta_{\max}{}^{1/2}\{\mathbf{Q}(\mathbf{w}^*)\}\,\|\boldsymbol{\mu}-\mathbf{P}(\varepsilon_T\tilde{\mathbf{v}})\mathbf{y}\| \\
&= \|\mathbf{Q}^{1/2}(\mathbf{w}^*)\boldsymbol{\varsigma}\| \left(\max_{1\le t\le T} \sum_{m=1}^{M_T} w_m^* h_{tt}^{(m)}\right)^{1/2} \|\boldsymbol{\mu}-\mathbf{P}(\varepsilon_T\tilde{\mathbf{v}})\mathbf{y}\| \\
&\le \|\mathbf{Q}^{1/2}(\mathbf{w}^*)\boldsymbol{\varsigma}\|\,\bar{h}^{1/2}\,\|\boldsymbol{\mu}-\mathbf{P}(\varepsilon_T\tilde{\mathbf{v}})\mathbf{y}\| \\
&= O_p(\bar{k}),
\end{aligned} \tag{A.32}$$

where the last step is from $\|\boldsymbol{\mu}-\mathbf{P}(\varepsilon_T\tilde{\mathbf{v}})\mathbf{y}\|^2 = O_p(T)$, (A.31), and Assumption 1. As for Δ_5^3, we have

$$\begin{aligned}
|\Delta_5^3| &= \left|\{\boldsymbol{\mu}-\mathbf{P}(\varepsilon_T\tilde{\mathbf{v}})\mathbf{y}\}^\top \mathbf{Q}(\mathbf{w}^*)\{\boldsymbol{\mu}-\mathbf{P}(\varepsilon_T\tilde{\mathbf{v}})\mathbf{y}\}\right| \\
&\le \zeta_{\max}\{\mathbf{Q}(\mathbf{w}^*)\}\,\|\boldsymbol{\mu}-\mathbf{P}(\varepsilon_T\tilde{\mathbf{v}})\mathbf{y}\|^2 \\
&\le \bar{h}\,\|\boldsymbol{\mu}-\mathbf{P}(\varepsilon_T\tilde{\mathbf{v}})\mathbf{y}\|^2 \\
&= O_p(\bar{k}),
\end{aligned} \tag{A.33}$$

where the third step is similar to the fifth step of (A.32), and the last step is from $\| \boldsymbol{\mu} - \mathbf{P}(\varepsilon_T \tilde{\mathbf{v}})\mathbf{y} \|^2 = O_p(T)$ and Assumption 1. Combining (A.30)–(A.33) and Assumption 6, we obtain $|\Delta_5| = O_p(\bar{k})$, which is dominated by Δ_1 asymptotically.

For Δ_6, we have

$$\begin{aligned}
|\Delta_6/2| &= |\operatorname{tr}\{\mathbf{P}(\varepsilon_T \tilde{\mathbf{v}})\widehat{\boldsymbol{\Omega}}(\mathbf{w}^*)\}| \\
&= \left|\{\mathbf{y} - \mathbf{P}(\mathbf{w}^*)\mathbf{y}\}^\top \mathbf{Q}(\varepsilon_T \tilde{\mathbf{v}})\{\mathbf{y} - \mathbf{P}(\mathbf{w}^*)\mathbf{y}\}\right| \\
&\le |\boldsymbol{\varsigma}^\top \mathbf{Q}(\varepsilon_T \tilde{\mathbf{v}})\boldsymbol{\varsigma}| + 2|\boldsymbol{\varsigma}^\top \mathbf{Q}(\varepsilon_T \tilde{\mathbf{v}})\{\boldsymbol{\mu} - \mathbf{P}(\mathbf{w}^*)\mathbf{y}\}| \\
&\quad + \left|\{\boldsymbol{\mu} - \mathbf{P}(\mathbf{w}^*)\mathbf{y}\}^\top \mathbf{Q}(\varepsilon_T \tilde{\mathbf{v}})\{\boldsymbol{\mu} - \mathbf{P}(\mathbf{w}^*)\mathbf{y}\}\right| \\
&\equiv \Delta_6^1 + \Delta_6^2 + \Delta_6^3,
\end{aligned} \tag{A.34}$$

where $\Delta_6^1 = \Delta_4^1 = O_p(\varepsilon_T M_T^{1/2}\bar{k}) \| \tilde{\mathbf{v}} \|$. As for Δ_6^2, we have

$$\begin{aligned}
|\Delta_6^2/2| &= |\boldsymbol{\varsigma}^\top \mathbf{Q}(\varepsilon_T \tilde{\mathbf{v}})\{\boldsymbol{\mu} - \mathbf{P}(\mathbf{w}^*)\mathbf{y}\}| \\
&= \varepsilon_T |\boldsymbol{\varsigma}^\top \mathbf{Q}(\tilde{\mathbf{v}})\{\boldsymbol{\mu} - \mathbf{P}(\mathbf{w}^*)\mathbf{y}\}| \\
&\le \varepsilon_T \| \mathbf{Q}(\tilde{\mathbf{v}})\boldsymbol{\varsigma} \| \cdot \| \boldsymbol{\mu} - \mathbf{P}(\mathbf{w}^*)\mathbf{y} \| \\
&= \varepsilon_T \left\{ \sum_{t=1}^{T} \varsigma_t^2 \left(\sum_{m=1}^{M_T} v_m h_{tt}^{(m)} \right)^2 \right\}^{1/2} \cdot \| \boldsymbol{\Lambda}\mathbf{w}^* - \boldsymbol{\mu} \| \\
&\le \varepsilon_T \left\{ \max_{1\le t\le T} \left(\sum_{m=1}^{M_T} v_m h_{tt}^{(m)} \right)^2 \| \boldsymbol{\varsigma} \|^2 \right\}^{1/2} \\
&\quad \times \left(\| \boldsymbol{\Lambda}\mathbf{w}^* \|^2 + \| \boldsymbol{\mu} \|^2 + 2 \| \boldsymbol{\Lambda}\mathbf{w}^* \| \| \boldsymbol{\mu} \| \right)^{1/2} \\
&\le \varepsilon_T \left[\max_{1\le t\le T} \| \tilde{\mathbf{v}} \|^2 \left\{ \sum_{m=1}^{M_T} (h_{tt}^{(m)})^2 \right\} \| \boldsymbol{\varsigma} \|^2 \right]^{1/2} \\
&\quad \times \left(T\kappa_2 \| \mathbf{w}^* \|^2 + \| \boldsymbol{\mu} \|^2 + 2 \| \boldsymbol{\Lambda}\mathbf{w}^* \| \| \boldsymbol{\mu} \| \right)^{1/2} \\
&\le \varepsilon_T \left(\| \tilde{\mathbf{v}} \|^2 M_T \bar{h}^2 \| \boldsymbol{\varsigma} \|^2 \right)^{1/2} \\
&\quad \times \left(T\kappa_2 \| \mathbf{w}^* \|^2 + \| \boldsymbol{\mu} \|^2 + 2 \| \boldsymbol{\Lambda}\mathbf{w}^* \| \| \boldsymbol{\mu} \| \right)^{1/2} \\
&= O_p(\varepsilon_T M_T^{1/2} \bar{k} T^{-1/2}) \| \tilde{\mathbf{v}} \| \cdot O_p(T^{1/2} \| \mathbf{w}^* \| + T^{1/2} + T^{1/2} \| \mathbf{w}^* \|^{1/2}) \\
&= O_p(\varepsilon_T M_T^{1/2} \bar{k}) \| \tilde{\mathbf{v}} \|,
\end{aligned} \tag{A.35}$$

where the sixth step is from Assumption 5, and the eighth step is from $\| \boldsymbol{\varsigma} \|^2 = O_p(T)$ and Assumption 1. According to (A.35), we obtain $\| \boldsymbol{\mu} - \mathbf{P}(\mathbf{w}^*)\mathbf{y} \|^2 = O_p(T)$. As for Δ_6^3, we have

$$
\begin{aligned}
|\Delta_6^3| &= \left|\{\boldsymbol{\mu} - \mathbf{P}(\mathbf{w}^*)\mathbf{y}\}^\top \mathbf{Q}(\varepsilon_T \tilde{\mathbf{v}})\{\boldsymbol{\mu} - \mathbf{P}(\mathbf{w}^*)\mathbf{y}\}\right| \\
&\le \zeta_{\max}\{\mathbf{Q}(\varepsilon_T \tilde{\mathbf{v}})\} \| \boldsymbol{\mu} - \mathbf{P}(\mathbf{w}^*)\mathbf{y} \|^2 \\
&\le \varepsilon_T \left\{ \max_{1\le t\le T} \left(\sum\nolimits_{m=1}^{M_T} v_m h_{tt}^{(m)} \right)^2 \right\}^{1/2} \| \boldsymbol{\mu} - \mathbf{P}(\mathbf{w}^*)\mathbf{y} \|^2 \\
&\le \varepsilon_T \left\{ \max_{1\le t\le T} \| \tilde{\mathbf{v}} \|^2 \sum\nolimits_{m=1}^{M_T} \left(h_{tt}^{(m)} \right)^2 \right\}^{1/2} \| \boldsymbol{\mu} - \mathbf{P}(\mathbf{w}^*)\mathbf{y} \|^2 \\
&\le \varepsilon_T \| \tilde{\mathbf{v}} \| M_T^{1/2} \bar{h} \| \boldsymbol{\mu} - \mathbf{P}(\mathbf{w}^*)\mathbf{y} \|^2 \\
&= O_p(\varepsilon_T M_T^{1/2} \bar{k}) \| \tilde{\mathbf{v}} \|,
\end{aligned} \tag{A.36}
$$

where the last step is from $\| \boldsymbol{\mu} - \mathbf{P}(\mathbf{w}^*)\mathbf{y} \|^2 = O_p(T)$ and Assumption 1. Combining (A.34)–(A.36) and Assumption 6, we obtain $|\Delta_6| = O_p(\varepsilon_T M_T^{1/2} \bar{k}) \| \tilde{\mathbf{v}} \|$, which is dominated by Δ_1 asymptotically.

Combining (A.22)–(A.36), these imply that (A.21) is true, and thus we complete the proof of Equation (9) of Theorem 2.

CHAPTER 7

EFFICIENT ESTIMATION IN VARYING COEFFICIENT PANEL DATA MODEL WITH DIFFERENT SMOOTHING VARIABLES AND FIXED EFFECTS

Feng Yao[a,b], Qinling Lu[c], Yiguo Sun[d], Junsen Zhang[e]

[a]*Department of Economics, West Virginia University, USA*
[b]*China Center for Special Economic Zone Research, Shenzhen University, P.R. China*
[c]*Risk Modeling & Analysis, KeyBank, USA*
[d]*Department of Economics and Finance, University of Guelph, Canada*
[e]*School of Economics, Zhejiang University, P.R. China*

ABSTRACT

The authors propose to estimate a varying coefficient panel data model with different smoothing variables and fixed effects using a two-step approach. The pilot step estimates the varying coefficients by a series method. We then use the pilot estimates to perform a one-step backfitting through local linear kernel smoothing, which is shown to be oracle efficient in the sense of being asymptotically equivalent to the estimate knowing the other components of the varying coefficients. In both steps, the authors remove the fixed effects through properly constructed weights. The authors obtain the asymptotic properties of both the pilot and efficient estimators. The Monte Carlo simulations show that the proposed estimator performs well. The authors illustrate their applicability by estimating a varying coefficient production frontier using a panel data, without assuming distributions of the efficiency and error terms.

Essays in Honor of Subal Kumbhakar
Advances in Econometrics, Volume 46, 133–184

Published under exclusive licence by Emerald Publishing Limited
ISSN: 0731-9053/doi:10.1108/S0731-905320240000046007

Keywords: Varying coefficient model; panel; fixed effect; production frontier; efficiency; kernel-based backfitting

JEL classifications: C14; C23

1. INTRODUCTION

The availability of panel data allows researchers to track individual information over time, and conduct estimation and inference on models with more complexity than those in purely time-series or cross-section data (see Arellano, 2003; Baltagi, 2013; Hsiao, 2014 for an excellent review of parametric panel data analysis). As parametric panel data models may be misspecified, their analysis may give misleading inferences. To address this issue, nonparametric and semiparametric methods have been introduced in the panel data analysis, and recent studies include those on random effects (Henderson & Ullah, 2005; Li & Stengos, 1996; Lin & Carroll, 2006; Martins-Filho & Yao, 2009; Ruckstuhl, Welsh, & Carroll, 2000; Ullah & Roy, 1998; Wang, 2003), and fixed effects (Henderson, Carroll, & Li, 2008; Su & Ullah, 2006). Since the estimation of random effect models is appropriate only when the individual effects are not correlated with regressors, we focus on the fixed effect models.

A purely nonparametric multivariate regression cannot be estimated with reasonable accuracy due to the so-called "curse of dimensionality." A useful structural regression, the varying coefficient model, including the purely nonparametric, additive and partially linear regression models as special cases, allows the regression coefficients to depend on smoothing variables. It inherits the simplicity and easy interpretation of traditional linear models, yet is intrinsically nonparametric. Sun, Carroll, and Li (2009) propose an interesting estimator for the varying coefficient panel data model, removing the fixed effect with kernel-based weights. Rodriguez-Poo and Soberon (2014, 2015) propose different backfitting estimators for the varying coefficients in a panel, using a within and difference transformation, respectively (see Rodriguez-Poo & Soberon, 2017 for a survey on recent developments in semiparametric panel data models).

The traditional varying coefficient model restricts the coefficient function of each regressor to depend on the same smoothing variables. An important extension is to allow the coefficient functions to depend on different smoothing variables, so the partial impact of the regressors is allowed to be driven by different variables. For example, in our application in a production frontier estimation, the determinants of conditional mean of inefficiency term can be very different from the variables entering the frontier. With a varying coefficient frontier, we can rewrite the frontier model as a regression, in which the varying coefficients with different smoothing variables arise naturally. In terms of modeling for real dataset, this is more flexible than the traditional varying coefficient model (Park, Simar, & Zelenyuk, 2015, section 3). The estimation of these two models is totally different. A pointwise kernel-weighted local polynomial fit gives a direct estimation of the coefficient functions in the traditional case, but for the case of different smoothing variables, the procedure gives multivariate functions of all smoothing variables, not capturing the structure of different smoothing variables in different coefficient functions. In a regression model without fixed effects, two approaches have been proposed to estimate the coefficient functions with different smoothing variables. First approach applies marginal integration technique of Linton and Nielsen (1995) to recover each individual coefficient function, including Yang, Park, Xue, and Hardle (2006), Zhang and Li (2007), Feng, Huang, and Zhang (2012), and Xue and Yang (2006). The other approach is based on the smooth backfitting introduced by Mammen, Linton, and Nielsen (1999), including Lee, Mammen, and Park (2012a,[1] 2012b) and Roca-Pardinas and Sperlich (2010). To our knowledge, we are not aware of any estimation of the varying coefficient model with different smoothing variables using panel data with fixed effects.

Without the panel data and the fixed effects, the model that we consider in equation (1) below is the same as model (I) of Yang et al. (2006). Different from Sun et al. (2009), we allow for different smoothing variables Z_{jit} for different coefficient $\beta_j(\cdot)$, thus the marginal impact of X_{jit} can be driven by different variables, where $j = 1,\cdots,d, i = 1,\cdots,n$, and $t = 1,\cdots,T$. One strategy would be performing a backfitting or a smooth backfitting, extending the method in Henderson et al. (2008) to the varying coefficient setup, though its asymptotic property can be difficult to study. As mentioned before, direct estimation of $\beta_j(\cdot)$ following Sun et al. (2009) is not proper, as the procedure delivers multivariate functions of the whole smoothing vector Z_{it}, losing the structure of different smoothing variables. Another strategy will be performing a multivariate smoothing first on all $\beta_j(\cdot)$'s, then utilize the marginal integration idea as in Linton and Nielsen (1995) and Yang et al. (2006) to obtain estimates for each $\beta_j(\cdot)$. We do not pursue this idea here, as the marginal integration estimator may not maintain the oracle property and the associated multivariate smoothing can be very demanding when dimension d is large.

We propose a two-step estimator for the varying coefficients. In the first step, we model the fixed effect as in Su and Ullah (2006) and Sun et al. (2009), but construct a pilot estimator by approximating the varying coefficients with a series-based estimator. The pilot step consistently estimates the varying coefficients and it is computationally straightforward to implement, especially with different smoothing variables. Inspired by Linton (1997), in the second step we use the pilot estimates to perform a one-step kernel-based backfitting. We obtain the asymptotic distributions of the proposed estimators, and show that the second-step estimator has the oracle property, in the sense that each varying coefficient can be estimated with the same asymptotic accuracy as if all the other varying coefficients in the regression model were known.

The rest of the chapter gives the model and estimators in Section 2, asymptotic properties in Section 3, a Monte Carlo simulation in Section 4, an application in production frontier in Section 5, and a conclusion in Section 6.

2. ESTIMATION OF THE VARYING COEFFICIENT PANEL DATA MODEL WITH FIXED EFFECT AND DIFFERENT SMOOTHING VARIABLES

Let's consider the following varying coefficient panel data model with unknown fixed effects and different smoothing variables:

$$Y_{it} = \alpha_i + X_{1it}'\beta_1(Z_{1it}) + \cdots + X_{dit}'\beta_d(Z_{dit}) + \epsilon_{it}, i = 1,\cdots,n, t = 1,\cdots,T. \tag{1}$$

Here, for $j=1,\cdots,d$, $X_{jit}\in\Re^{r_j}$, and $Z_{jit}\in\Re$. We allow Z_{jit} in $\beta_j(\cdot)$ to change with j; thus, the smoothing variable is different. We denote the lth element in X_{jit} by $X_{jit,l}$. Correspondingly, $\beta_j(Z_{jit})=(\beta_{j1}(Z_{jit}),\cdots,\beta_{jr_j}(Z_{jit}))'$, where $\beta_{jl}(\cdot):\Re\rightarrow\Re$. We denote $r=\sum_{j=1}^{d}r_j$. We assume $E(\epsilon_{it}\mid X_{it},Z_{it},\alpha_i)=0$, and allow α_i to be arbitrarily correlated with X_{it} and Z_{it} for all $t=1,\cdots,T$. So α_i is the fixed effect in (1). In practice, we envision that the dimension of X_{jit} can be large, and that of Z_{jit} should be relatively small so that the curse-of-dimensionality issue will not be of severe concern. Here, we simply consider Z_{jit} to be univariate. We allow different subgroups of X to interact with smooth functions of each component of Z. By grouping our vectors of smooth coefficients that depend on the same smoothing variable, our X_{jit} are allowed to overlap. If we group the model with respect to each disjoint element of the vector X, the smooth coefficients are additive functions of Z.[2]

We note that if there exists nontrivial linear dependence among the variables $X_{jit,l}$ with corresponding functions of Z_{jit} as coefficients, functions $\beta_{jl}(\cdot)$ are unidentifiable. To be specific, if $\sum_{j=1}^{d}\sum_{l=1}^{r_j}X_{jit,l}\xi_{jl}(Z_{jit})=0\ a.s.$ for some nonzero measurable functions $\xi_{jl}(\cdot)$, then the regression function, excluding the fixed effect, equals $\sum_{j=1}^{d}\sum_{l=1}^{r_j}X_{jit,l}\{\beta_{jl}(Z_{jit})+\xi_{jl}(Z_{jit})\}$ as well. Hence, for identification, we follow Yang et al. (2006) to assume that $\sum_{j=1}^{d}\sum_{l=1}^{r_j}X_{jit,l}\xi_{jl}(Z_{jit})=0\ a.s.$ $\Rightarrow\xi_{jl}(z_j)\equiv 0$, $j=1,\cdots,d$, $l=1,\cdots,r_j$. The condition may be considered as an analog to the linear independence between covariates in linear models. Investigating the existence and uniqueness of the solutions to the additive model estimating equations and the convergence of the backfitting algorithm, Hastie and Tibishirani (1990, chapter 5) refer to the term *concurvity* in additive models as an analog of collinearity in linear models. Because our varying coefficient estimators below are defined through estimating equations, this condition is used to avoid the "concurvity" in the varying coefficient model. It is closely related to the invertibility of matrices in our first step estimator in equation (2) and the second step estimator in equation (3).

In estimating additive models, Horowitz and Mammen (2004) pioneered a two-step estimation procedure. They perform a series estimation of the nonparametric additive components, followed by a kernel-based backfitting step, and the resulted estimators are oracle efficient and free of the curse of dimensionality. This two-step estimation reduces the computation burden due to its simplicity, and exhibits attractive asymptotic properties. This idea appears also in Wang and Yang (2007) in additive autoregression model, and in several papers that deals with endogeneity using a control function approach (Delgado, Ozabaci, Sun, & Kumbhakar, 2020; Ozabaci, Henderson, & Su, 2014).

Inspired by this idea, we propose a two-step estimation. The first step is a series-based pilot estimation for each $\beta_j(\cdot)$. Let $\{\phi_l(\cdot),\ l=1,2,\cdots\}$ be a sequence of basis functions (B-spline series) and L_n be some integer such that $L_n\rightarrow\infty$ as $n\rightarrow\infty$. With $\Phi_{Ln}(v)=[\phi_1(v),\cdots,\phi_{L_n}(v)]'$, we approximate $\beta_{jl}(z_j)$ with $\Phi_{Ln}(z_j)'\lambda_{jl}$, where λ_{jl}

is an $L_n \times 1$ vector for each $l = 1,\cdots,r_j$ and $j = 1,\cdots,d$. Then for $\lambda_j = (\lambda_{j1}',\cdots,\lambda_{jr_j}')'$, an $(L_n * r_j)\times 1$ vector, we approximate $X_{jit}'\beta_j(Z_{jit})$ with $[X_{jit} \otimes \Phi_{L_n}(Z_{jit})]'\lambda_j \equiv \chi_{jit}'\lambda_j$, where χ_{jit} is also an $(L_n * r_j)\times 1$ vector. Thus,

$$Y_{it} \approx \alpha_i + \sum_{j=1}^{d} \chi_{jit}'\lambda_j + \epsilon_{it} = \alpha_i + \chi_{it}'\lambda + \epsilon_{it},$$

where $\chi_{it} = [\chi_{1it}',\cdots,\chi_{dit}']'$, $\lambda = [\lambda_1',\cdots,\lambda_d']'$, each an $(L_n * r)\times 1$ vector.

Following Sun et al. (2009), we impose the assumption that $\sum_{i=1}^{n}\alpha_i = 0$ for the fixed effects, which implies that $\alpha_1 = -\sum_{i=2}^{n}\alpha_i$. We let $\alpha_0 = (-\sum_{i=2}^{n}\alpha_i,\alpha_2,\cdots,\alpha_n)'$, $\alpha_{-1} = (\alpha_2,\cdots,\alpha_n)'$, then for I_n an $n \times n$ identity matrix, e_T a $T\times 1$ column of ones, and $D_M = [-e_{n-1}, I_{n-1}]'\otimes e_T$, we express the assumption on the fixed effects through $D_M\alpha_{-1} = \alpha_0 \otimes e_T$. For notation purpose, we let $Y_i = (Y_{i1},\cdots,Y_{iT})'$, $Y = (Y_1',\cdots,Y_n')'$, $X_{it} = (X_{1it}',\cdots,X_{dit}')'$, $Z_{it} = (Z_{1it},\cdots,Z_{dit})'$, $\epsilon = (\epsilon_1',\cdots,\epsilon_n')'$, $\epsilon_i = (\epsilon_{i1},\cdots,\epsilon_{iT})'$, and $\chi = \{\{\chi'_{it}\}_{t=1}^{T}\}_{i=1}^{n}$.[3] We estimate

$$(\hat{\alpha}_{-1},\hat{\lambda}) = \text{argmin}_{\alpha_{-1},\lambda}[Y - D_M\alpha_{-1} - \chi\lambda]'[Y - D_M\alpha_{-1} - \chi\lambda].$$

It is easy to see that for $M_D = I_{nT} - D_M(D_M'D_M)^{-1}D_M'$, $\hat{\lambda} = (\chi'M_D\chi)^{-1}\chi'M_DY$. We like to comment that the first step is very easy to carry through in computations. Thus, we estimate $\beta_{jl}(z_j)$ and $\beta_j(z_j)$ with

$$\hat{\beta}_{jl}(z_j) = \Phi_{L_n}(z_j)'\hat{\lambda}_{jl},\ \hat{\beta}_j(z_j) = [I_{r_j} \otimes \Phi_{L_n}(z_j)]'\hat{\lambda}_j. \tag{2}$$

Second, we propose a one-step backfitting estimator inspired by Linton (1997), based on the pilot estimates defined in equation (2). We utilize h as the bandwidth in the backfitting step. Let's define $(X'\hat{\beta})_{(-j)} = \{\{X_{(-j)it}'\hat{\beta}_{(-j)}(Z_{(-j)it})\}_{t=1}^{T}\}_{i=1}^{n}$, where

$$X'_{(-j)it}\hat{\beta}_{(-j)}(Z_{(-j)it}) = \sum_{q=1,q\neq j}^{d} X'_{qit}\hat{\beta}_q(Z_{qit}) = \sum_{q=1,q\neq j}^{d}\sum_{l=1}^{r_q} X_{qit,l}\hat{\beta}_{ql}(Z_{qit}).$$

We approximate $\beta_{jl}(Z_{jit}) \approx \beta_{jl}(z_{j0}) + (Z_{jit} - z_{j0})\beta_{jl}^{(1)}(z_{j0})$ for $(i,\ t)$ such that $|Z_{jit} - z_{j0}| = o(1)$. We define $b_{jl}(z_{j0}) = (\beta_{jl}(z_{j0}),\beta_{jl}^{(1)}(z_{j0}))'$ to be a 2×1 vector, $b_j(z_{j0}) = (b_{j1}(z_{j0}),\cdots,b_{jr_j}(z_{j0}))'$ a $r_j \times 2$ matrix, and $R_{jit} = (1,(Z_{jit} - z_{j0}))'$. Then with $X_{(-j)it}'\beta_{(-j)}(Z_{(-j)it})$ defined similarly with a true $\beta_{ql}(\cdot)$,

$$\begin{aligned} Y_{it} - X'_{(-j)it}\beta_{(-j)}(Z_{(-j)it}) &= \alpha_i + X'_{jit}\beta_j(Z_{jit}) + \epsilon_{it} \\ &= \alpha_i + X'_{jit}b_j(z_{j0})R_{jit} + \sum_{l=1}^{r_j} X_{jit,l}\tfrac{1}{2}\beta_{jl}^{(2)}(z_{j0}^{*})(Z_{jit} - z_{j0})^2 + \epsilon_{it} \\ &= \alpha_i + (R'_{jit} \otimes X'_{jit})\text{vec}(b_j(z_{j0})) \\ &\quad + \sum_{l=1}^{r_j} X_{jit,l}\frac{1}{2}\beta_{jl}^{(2)}(z_{j0}^{*})(Z_{jit} - z_{j0})^2 + \epsilon_{it}. \end{aligned}$$

Here, we perform the second-order Taylor expansion and z^*_{j0} is a point between Z_{jit} and z_{j0}. Below, we use local linear estimation, approximating $X_{jit}'\beta_j(Z_{jit})$ with $(R_{jit}'\otimes X_{jit}')\text{vec}(b_j(z_{j0}))$. The bias arising from ignoring the term $\sum_{l=1}^{r_j} X_{jit,l}\frac{1}{2}\beta_{jl}^{(2)}(z^*_{j0})(Z_{jit}-z_{j0})^2$ is controlled asymptotically through the kernel weight (see Theorem 2(i)(2) for details). Here $\text{vec}(b_j(z_{j0}))$ denotes a vector created by stacking columns of $b_j(z_{j0})$ on tops of one another. Note that the first r_j elements in $\text{vec}(b_j(z_{j0}))$ is $\beta_j(z_{j0})$. Let $R_{ji}(z_{j0})=[(R_{ji1}'\otimes X_{ji1}')',\cdots,(R_{jiT}'\otimes X_{jiT}')']'$ be a $T\times(2r_j)$ matrix, $R_j(z_{j0})=[R_{j1}(z_{j0})',\cdots,R_{jn}(z_{j0})']'$ be an $nT\times(2r_j)$ matrix. We define

$$\begin{aligned}M_h(z_{j0}) &= I_{nT}-D_M(D_M'W_h(z_{j0})D_M)^{-1}D_M'W_h(z_{j0}), S_h(z_{j0})\\ &= M_h(z_{j0})'W_h(z_{j0})M_h(z_{j0}),\end{aligned}$$

where $W_h(z_{j0})=\text{diag}\{\{K(\frac{Z_{jit}-z_{j0}}{h})\}_{t=1}^T\}_{i=1}^n$ is an $nT\times nT$ matrix, where $K(\cdot)$ is a univariate kernel function. We define the backfitting estimator as

$$\begin{aligned}(\text{vec}(\breve{b}_j(z_{j0})),\breve{\alpha}_{-1}(z_{j0})) = \underset{\text{vec}(b_j(z_{j0})),\alpha_{-1}}{\text{argmin}}\ & [Y-(X'\hat{\beta})_{(-j)}\\ & -R_j(z_{j0})\text{vec}(b_j(z_{j0}))-D_M\alpha_{-1}]'W_h(z_{j0})\\ & \times[Y-(X'\hat{\beta})_{(-j)}-R_j(z_{j0})\text{vec}(b_j(z_{j0}))-D_M\alpha_{-1}].\end{aligned}$$

We obtain

$$\breve{\alpha}_{-1}(z_{j0})=[D'_MW_h(z_{j0})D_M]^{-1}D'_MW_h(z_{j0})[Y-(X'\hat{\beta})_{(-j)}-R_j(z_{j0})\text{vec}(b_j(z_{j0}))],$$

$$\text{vec}(\breve{b}_j(z_{j0}))=[R'_j(z_{j0})S_h(z_{j0})R_j(z_{j0})]^{-1}R'_j(z_{j0})S_h(z_{j0})[Y-(X'\hat{\beta})_{(-j)}].$$

Specifically, for $e_{l,2r_j}$ a $2r_j\times 1$ vector of zeros, except that the *lth* position is one,

$$\breve{\beta}_{jl}(z_{j0})=e'_{l,2r_j}[R'_j(z_{j0})S_h(z_{j0})R_j(z_{j0})]^{-1}R'_j(z_{j0})S_h(z_{j0})[Y-(X'\hat{\beta})_{(-j)}]. \quad (3)$$

Indeed, we can follow Baltagi and Li (2002) to perform a first difference and remove the fixed effects (alternatively, we can also deduct each equation at time t from that for time 1, or deduct each equation from the cross-time average of the system). However, for each i, the right-hand side of equation (1) after differencing will contain linear combination of $X_{jit}'\beta_j(Z_{jit})$ for different time t. Specifically, if X_{jit} contains a time-invariant term in $X_{jit,1}$, then a first difference of $X_{jit,1}\beta_{j1}(Z_{jit})\equiv X_{ji,1}\beta_{j1}(Z_{jit})$ gives $X_{ji,1}(\beta_{j1}(Z_{jit})-\beta_{j1}(Z_{jit-1}))$, which is an additive function with the same function form for the two functions, evaluated at different observation points. If one uses kernel-based estimation, it usually requires a bivariate smoothing and some backfitting algorithms to recover the unknown function, which can be cumbersome. Moreover, if $\beta_{j1}(Z_{jit})$ contains an additive constant term, $\beta_{j1}(Z_{jit}) = c + \beta_{j10}(Z_{jit})$, where c is a constant, then the first differencing will wipe out the additive constant c. As a consequence, one cannot consistently estimate $\beta_{j1}(\cdot)$ in general without additional steps. Our transformation removes the fixed effects with properly constructed weights. This transformation will not wipe out the additive constant c in $\beta_{j1}(\cdot) = c + \beta_{j10}(Z_{jit})$. Therefore, we can consistently estimate $c + \beta_{j10}(\cdot)$ as well as other components of $\beta(\cdot)$ when at most one of the variables X is time invariant.

We comment that we remove the fixed effects in both steps, with properly constructed weights (M_D and $M_h(z_{j0})$ are such that $M_D D_M \alpha_{-1} = 0$ and $M_h(z_{j0}) D_M \alpha_{-1} = 0$). In our first step, there is no need to impose the restriction that $\sum_{i=1}^{n} \alpha_i = 0$, since $\chi_{jit} = [X_{jit} \otimes \Phi_{Ln}(Z_{jit})]$ are not time invariant. However, in the case that X_{jit} contains a constant, we need to impose the restriction to make the second step feasible since we perform a local linear expansion of the varying coefficient (see p. 169 of Lin, Li, & Sun, 2014 for a similar comment). Thus, we impose the restriction in both steps and we comment later that imposing this restriction changes the asymptotic result of $\hat{\beta}_{jl}(\cdot)$ and the resulted first step requires a less stringent assumption for identification.

We have considered the framework that both X and Z are exogenous. In the case that X contain endogenous regressors, we can follow Cai, Das, Xiong, and Wu (2006) and Cai and Xiong (2012) to extend our model and construct multiple-step estimates to handle the endogeneity. In the case of endogenous Z, we can possibly follow Centorrino and Racine (2017) to construct a consistent estimator.[4] We leave these topics for future research.

3. ASYMPTOTIC PROPERTIES

We characterize the asymptotic properties of our proposed estimators under the following assumptions, and we relegate all the proof to the Appendix. Below we denote a generic constant by C, the magnitude of which is inconsequential for the asymptotic analysis, and can vary from one place to another. Let's denote a generic function $\xi(\cdot) \in \mathcal{C}^{(j)}$ if $\xi(w): \Re^d \to \Re$ and all of its partial derivatives of order $\leq j$ are continuous and uniformly bounded on $\Re^d$. We define

$$K_{jit} \equiv K\left(\frac{Z_{jit} - z_{j0}}{h}\right),\ K_{ji.} \equiv \sum_{t=1}^{T} K_{jit}, \text{ and } \tilde{R}_{jit}{}' = \left(1, \frac{Z_{jit} - z_{j_0}}{h}\right).$$

The function $q(\cdot): \Re \to \Re$ satisfies Hölder condition with exponent $r \in [0,1]$ if there exists C_q such that $|q(v) - q(v')| \leq C_q |v - v'|^r$ for all v, v' on the support of $q(\cdot)$. $q(\cdot)$ is said to be ξ-smooth for $\xi = r + m$ if $q(\cdot)$ is m-times continuously differentiable on its support and $\frac{d^m q(\cdot)}{dv^m}$ satisfies Hölder condition with exponent r. For a vector x, $\|x\|$ is the Euclidean norm. For a matrix A, $\|A\| = [\mathrm{tr}(AA')]^{\frac{1}{2}}$ is the Frobenius norm, and $\|A\|_{sp} = \sqrt{\lambda_{max}(A'A)}$ is the spectral norm. Clearly, $\|a\| = \|a\|_{sp}$ for a being a vector. For a real symmetric matrix A, we denote A's smallest eigenvalue by $\lambda_{min}(A)$ and largest eigenvalue by $\lambda_{max}(A)$.

Assumptions

A1. For $i = 1,\cdots,n$ and $t = 1,\cdots,T$, $\{X_{1it},\cdots,X_{dit},Z_{1it},\cdots,Z_{dit},\epsilon_{it}\}$ are IID across *i*. n is sufficiently large and T is fixed.

A2. $E(X^2_{jit,l}X^2_{j'i\tau,l'}) < C$ for $j \neq j'$, $l \in \{1,\cdots,r_j\}$, $l' \in \{1,\cdots,r_{j'}\}$, for all *t* and τ.

A3. (1) ϵ_{it} is IID with $E(\epsilon_{it}) = 0$, $V(\epsilon_{it}) = \sigma^2_\epsilon$, $E|\epsilon_{it}|^{2+\delta} < C$ for some $\delta > 0$, and ϵ_{it} is independent of X_{it} and Z_{it}.

(2) Either $\sum_{i=1}^{n}\alpha_i = 0$, or α_i is IID with a zero mean and a finite variance.

A4. The $L_n * r$ variables in χ are linearly independent, where each variable is an $nT \times 1$ vector.

B1. (1) The functions $\{\beta_{jl}(z_j), j = 1,\cdots,d, l = 1,\cdots,r_j\}$ and $\{\phi_j(v) : j = 1,2,\cdots\}$ belong to the class of $\xi -$ smooth functions with $\xi \geq 2$.

(2) For any $j = 1,\cdots,d$, $l = 1,\cdots,r_j$, there exists λ_{jl}, an $L_n \times 1$ constant vector such that $\max_{1\le j\le d,\ 1\le l\le r_j}\max_{z_j\in G_j}|\beta_{jl}(z_j) - \Phi_{L_n}(z_j)'\lambda_{jl}| = O(L_n^{-\xi})$ for $\xi > 2$ and for any L_n, where G_j, the support of Z_{jit}, is a compact subset of $\Re$

(3) The set of basis functions $\{\phi_j(v) : j = 1,2,\cdots\}$ satisfies $\sup_{j>=1}|\phi_j(\cdot)| < C$.

B2. For every *n*, there exists $\underline{c}$ and $\overline{c}$ such that $0 < \underline{c} \leq \lambda_{min}(\Sigma_{\Phi\Phi}) \leq \lambda_{max}(\Sigma_{\Phi\Phi}) \leq \overline{c} < \infty$,

$$\Sigma_{\Phi\Phi} = \sum_{t=1}^{T} E\left[(\chi_{jit} - \frac{1}{T}\sum_{t=1}^{T}\chi_{jit})(\chi_{jit} - \frac{1}{T}\sum_{t=1}^{T}\chi_{jit})'\right]_{j,l=1}^{d} + \frac{1}{T}E\left[(\sum_{t=1}^{T}\chi_{jit})(\sum_{t=1}^{T}\chi_{jit})\right]_{j,l=1}^{d}$$

where $i \neq m$, $[\cdot]^d_{j,l=1}$ refers to a $rL_n \times rL_n$ matrix, whose (*j, l*) block matrix of dimension $L_n \times L_n$ is given in the $[\cdot]$. Note that $\Sigma_{\Phi\Phi}$ still depends on *n* and we suppress the dependence on *n* to simplify notation.

C1. (1) The marginal density of Z_{jit} at $Z_{jit} = z_{j0}$ is $f_{z_{jt}}(z_{j0})$ and $f_{z_{jt}}(\cdot) \in C^{(2)}$, and $\inf_{z_{j0}\in G_j} f_{z_{jt}}(z_{j0}) > 0$.

(2) The conditional density of Z_{jit} at $Z_{jit} = z_{j0}$ given X_{jit} is $f_{z_{jt}|x_{jt}}(z_{j0})$ and $f_{z_{jt}|x_{jt}}(\cdot) < C$ in the domain of Z_{jit} for all *j, t*.

(3) $\Sigma_{j0}(z_{j0}) = \lim_{n\to\infty}\Sigma_{j0n}(z_{j0})$, where $\Sigma_{j0n}(z_{j0}) = \frac{1}{h}\sum_{t=1}^{T}E\left[K_{jit}(1 - \frac{K_{jit}}{K_{ji.}})(\tilde{R}_{jit}\tilde{R}_{jit}{}' \otimes X_{jit}X_{jit}{}')\right]$ is a nonsingular matrix, and $\lambda_{min}(\Sigma_{j0}(z_{j0})) > C > 0$.

(4) For all $j \neq q$ and all *t*, the conditional density of (Z_{jit}, Z_{qit}) at $(Z_{jit}, Z_{qit}) = (z_{j0}, z_{q0})$ given (X_{jit}, X_{qit}) is $f_{z_{jt},z_{qt}|x_{jt},x_{qt}}(z_{j0}, z_{q0})$, $f_{z_{jt},z_{qt}|x_{jt},x_{qt}}(\cdot,\cdot) \in C^{(2)}$ in (Z_{jit}, Z_{qit}) only. Define the joint density of (X_{jit}, X_{qit}) at $(X_{jit}, X_{qit}) = (x_{j0}, x_{q0})$ as $f_{x_{jt},x_{qt}}(x_{j0}, x_{q0})$. Define the joint density of (Z_{jit}, Z_{qit}) at $(Z_{jit}, Z_{qit}) = (z_{j0}, z_{q0})$ as $f_{z_{jt},z_{qt}}(z_{j0}, z_{q0})$, we assume $f_{z_{jt},z_{qt}|x_{jt},x_{qt}}(\cdot,\cdot) < Cf_{z_{jt},z_{qt}}(\cdot,\cdot) < C$ in the domain of Z_{jit} and Z_{qit}.

(5) The conditional density of $(Z_{jit}, Z_{ji\tau})$ at $(Z_{jit}, Z_{ji\tau}) = (z_{j0}, z_{j1})$ conditioning on $(X_{it}, X_{i\tau})$ is $f_{z_{jt}, z_{j\tau}|x_{it}, x_{i\tau}}(z_{j0}, z_{j1})$. For all $j \neq q$ and $t \neq \tau$, the conditional density of $(Z_{jit}, Z_{ji\tau}, Z_{qi\tau})$ at $(Z_{jit}, Z_{ji\tau}, Z_{qi\tau}) = (z_{j0}, z_{j0'}, z_{q0'})$ given $(X_{jit}, X_{qi\tau})$ is $f_{z_{jt}, z_{j\tau}, z_{q\tau}|x_{jt}, x_{q\tau}}(z_{j0}, z_{j0'}, z_{q0'})$, $f_{z_{jt}, z_{j\tau}, z_{q\tau}|x_{jt}, x_{q\tau}}(\cdot,\cdot,\cdot) \in \mathcal{C}^{(2)}$ in $(Z_{jit}, Z_{ji\tau}, Z_{qi\tau})$ only. Define the joint density of $(Z_{jit}, Z_{ji\tau}, Z_{qi\tau})$ at $(Z_{jit}, Z_{ji\tau}, Z_{qi\tau}) = (z_{j0}, z_{j0'}, z_{q0'})$ as $f_{z_{jt}, z_{j\tau}, z_{q\tau}}(z_{j0}, z_{j0'}, z_{q0'})$, we assume $f_{z_{jt}, z_{j\tau}, z_{q\tau}|x_{jt}, x_{q\tau}}(\cdot,\cdot,\cdot) < Cf_{z_{jt}, z_{j\tau}, z_{q\tau}}(\cdot,\cdot,\cdot) < C$ in the domain of $(Z_{jit}, Z_{ji\tau}, Z_{qi\tau})$.

C2. The kernel function $K(\phi): \Re \to \Re$ is a symmetric function such that (1) $| K(\phi)\phi^j | \leq C$ for all $\phi \in \Re$ and $j = 0,1,2,3$. (2) $\int |\phi^j K(\phi)| \, d\phi \leq C$ for $j = 0,1,2,3$. (3) $\int K(\phi) d\phi = 1$, $\int \phi K(\phi) d\phi = 0$, $\int \phi^2 K(\phi) d\phi = \mu_{k,2} < \infty$. (4) $K(\phi)$ is continuously differentiable on $\Re$ with $| \phi^j \frac{d}{d\phi} K(\phi) | \leq C$ for all $\phi \in \Re$, and $j = 0,1,2,3$. (5) $\forall\, j,\, i,\, K_{ji.} = \sum_{t=1}^{T} K_{jit} > C > 0$.

C3. (1) Let $v_{ll',jt}(Z_{jit}) = E(X_{jit,l} X_{jit,l'} \mid Z_{jit}) \in \mathcal{C}^{(2)}$ for all t, j, and $l, l' = 1, \cdots, r_j$.

(2) $E | X_{jit,l} X_{jit,l'} |^s | Z_{jit}) < C$ almost surely for some $s > 2$, for all t and $l, l' \in \{1, \cdots,, r_j\}$.

C4. (1) $nh^3 \to \infty$, $h \to 0$, and $nh^5 \to C > 0$ as $n \to \infty$. (2) $L_n \to \infty$, $L_n h^2 < C$, $L_n (\frac{\log(n)}{n})^{\frac{1}{2}} \to 0$. (3) $\sqrt{nh} L_n^{-\xi} = o(1)$.

(4) $n^{-1} \mathcal{S}_{0L_n}^{2+\frac{4}{\delta}} \to 0$, where $\max_{1 \leq j \leq d} \sup_{z_j \in G_j} \| \Phi_{L_n}(z_j) \| \leq \mathcal{S}_{0L_n}$.

C5. $\{X_{jit,1}, \cdots, X_{jit,r_j}, X_{jit,1} Z_{jit}, \cdots, X_{jit,r_j} Z_{jit}\}$ are linearly independent for $j = 1, \cdots, d$.

We organize the assumptions to identify those needed for each estimation step. Specifically, Assumption *A* is used to regulate the raw data. Assumptions *A* and *B* are used to support the limit results of the first-step series estimator. In *A1*, we consider the panel data with a sufficiently large n and fixed T, so that appropriate handling of the fixed effects is important due to the incidental parameter problem. *A2* bounds the moment of X's, *A3*(1) requires that ϵ_{it} is IID random error, and *A3*(2) assumes either $\sum_{i=1}^{n} \alpha_i = 0$, or α_i is IID with zero mean and finite variance. It allows us to show that the fixed effects can be properly removed. *A4* allows us to calculate the first-step estimates. *B1* and *B2* give conditions to approximate, estimate $\beta_{jl}(\cdot)$ and obtain the uniform convergence rate for the first-step series estimates $\hat{\beta}(\cdot)$.

Assumption *C*, together with Assumptions *A* and *B*, allows us to study the asymptotic behavior of the second-step estimator. In *C1*(1) and (2), we require smoothness and boundedness on the marginal and conditional densities of Z_j conditioning on X. We also require a sufficient condition on the conditional density to be bounded, or bounded by a multiple of the marginal density in *C1*(4) and (5). They allow us to apply uniform convergence argument as in Lemma 1 in Martins-Filho, Yao, and Torero (2018). *C1*(3) is an asymptotic condition for identification for the backfitting estimator, compared to the asymptotic identification condition for the series estimator in *B2*. *C2* gives conditions on kernel functions to be used in the backfitting step, which are frequently used in kernel-based estimation, see Martins-Filho et al. (2018). Specifically, a Gaussian kernel can be used. *C3* requires smoothness on the conditional moments of X_j given Z_j, and boundedness on several conditional moments. Because the second-step kernel estimation is based on the first-step series estimates, *C4* gives the proper order for the bandwidth h and the number of basis functions that are required for the asymptotic analysis. Taylor expansions can be performed with the smoothness condition on $\beta_{jl}(\cdot)$ in *B1*. *A3*(1) gives the higher order moment condition for applying the central limit theorem. *C5* allow us to calculate the second-step $\beta(\cdot)$ estimates.

We argue that for at most one $l=\{1,2,\cdots,r_j\}$ and given j, $X_{jit,l}=1$ (time invariant) is allowed. If $X_{jit,l}=1$, then our first-step estimator for $\beta(\cdot)$ is estimable if $M_D\Phi_{Ln}(\mathbf{Z}_j)\neq \mathbf{0}_{nT\times 1}$ for $\Phi_{Ln}(\mathbf{Z}_j)=\{\{\Phi_{Ln}'(Z_{jit})\}_{t=1}^{T}\}_{i=1}^{n}$. Our second-step estimator for $\beta_{jl}(\cdot)$ is estimable if $S_h(z_{j0})(e_n\otimes e_T)\neq 0_{nT\times 1}$. Both conditions can be shown to be valid using our arguments in the proof of Theorem 1(i)(1) and Theorem 2(i)(1).

We consider the total number of time period T to be fixed in Assumption *A1*, but leave the distribution of variables $\{X_{jit}, Z_{jit}\}$ fairly unrestricted across the time period. Assumptions *C3, A2, A3*, and *B1* rule out the case of X_{jit}, or $\beta_{jl}(Z_{jit})$ being $I(1)$; other than these moment restrictions, we do not impose $I(0)$ structure on them across time.

We first characterize our first step pilot estimators.

Theorem 1. Under Assumptions A and B, we have (i) $\|\hat{\lambda}-\lambda\|=O_p(\sqrt{\frac{L_n}{n}}+L_n^{-\xi})$.

(ii) $\sup_{z_j\in G_j}\|\hat{\beta}_j(z_j)-\beta_j(z_j)\|=O_p(S_{0L_n}(\sqrt{\frac{L_n}{n}}+L_n^{-\xi}))$, for $j=1,\cdots,d$.

We can see that the uniform convergence rate obtained for $\hat{\beta}(\cdot)$ does not depend on d. It indicates that the first-step series estimation conveniently utilizes the additive structure in (1), alleviating the curse of dimensionality.

Next, we consider the infeasible estimator $\tilde{\beta}_{jl}(z_{j0})$, assuming the knowledge of true values of $(X'\beta)_{-j}$. Using the notation before, we define

$$\tilde{\beta}_{jl}(z_{j0})=e_{l,2r_j}'[R_j'(z_{j0})S_h(z_{j0})R_j(z_{j0})]^{-1}R_j'(z_{j0})S_h(z_{j0})[Y-(X'\beta)_{(-j)}]. \quad (4)$$

In Theorem 2 below, we first establish the asymptotic distribution of $\tilde{\beta}_j(z_{j0})=(\tilde{\beta}_{j1}(z_{j0}),\cdots,\tilde{\beta}_{jr_j}(z_{j0}))'$, then we show that the difference between the infeasible $\tilde{\beta}_j(z_{j0})$ and the feasible $\beta_j(z_{j0})$ is negligible; thus, $\beta_j(z_{j0})$ inherits the asymptotic characterization of $\tilde{\beta}_j(z_{j0})$ and is oracle.

Theorem 2. (i) Under Assumptions *A1, A3, C1*(1)–(3), *C2, C3, C4*(1), and *C5*, and with z_{j0} an interior point, we have $\sqrt{nh}[\tilde{\beta}_j(z_{j0})-\beta_j(z_{j0})-(B_{n0}(z_{j0})+o_p(h^2))]\xrightarrow{d}$

$N(0, e_{\cdot,2r_j}{}'\Sigma_{j0}^{-1}(z_{j0})\Omega_j(z_{j0})\Sigma_{j0}^{-1}(z_{j0})e_{\cdot,2r_j})$, where $e_{\cdot,2r_j} = [e_{1,2r_j}, \cdots, e_{r_j,2r_j}]$, $\Sigma_{j0}(z_{j0})$ is defined in Assumption *C1*(3), $B_{n0}(z_{j0}) = h^2 e_{\cdot,2r_j}{}'\Sigma_{j0}(z_{j0})^{-1}\frac{1}{h}\sum_{t=1}^{T} E \left[K_{jit}(1 - \frac{K_{jit}}{K_{ji\cdot}})(\tilde{R}_{jit} \otimes X_{jit})X_{jit}{}'\frac{1}{2}(\frac{Z_{jit} - z_{j0}}{h})^2 \beta_j^{(2)}(Z_{jit}) \right]$, and $\Omega_j(z_{j0}) = \lim_{n\to\infty} \Omega_{jn}(z_{j0})$ with $\Omega_{jn}(z_{j0}) = \frac{1}{h}\sum_{t=1}^{T} E \left[K_{jit}^2(1 - \frac{K_{jit}}{K_{ji\cdot}})^2(\tilde{R}_{jit} \otimes X_{jit})(\tilde{R}_{jit} \otimes X_{jit})' \right] \sigma_\epsilon^2$.

(ii) Under Assumptions *A*, *B* and *C*, we have $\| \sqrt{nh}(\beta_j(z_{j0}) - \tilde{\beta}_j(z_{j0})) \| = o_p(1)$.

We note that the sandwich format appears in the asymptotic variance, which will remain even with conditional homoskedasticity of ϵ. This is due to the special kernel weight used to construct the estimator.

4. MONTE CARLO SIMULATION

4.1. Finite Sample Performance of the Estimators

In this subsection, we present a Monte Carlo simulation to examine the finite sample performance of the proposed estimators. We design the simulation with two goals. First, we investigate the performance of both the series-based estimator and the kernel-based backfitting estimator with different sample sizes, across different coefficient functions. This will illustrate the consistency of the estimators. Second, we compare the relative performance of both estimators, illustrating the oracle efficiency of the kernel-based backfitting estimator. We consider the following data-generating process (DGP):

$$\text{DGP}: Y_{it} = \alpha_i + \sum_{j=1}^{d} X_{jit}\beta_j(Z_{jit}) + \epsilon_{it} \quad i = 1, \ldots, n, \quad t = 1, \ldots, T,$$

where $X_{jit} = 0.5X_{jit-1} + \xi_{it}$, and ξ_{it} is IID and drawn from a standard normal distribution *N*(0, 1) for each *j, i, t*. The smoothing variable $Z_{jit} = w_{it} + w_{it-1}$ and w_{it} is IID from a uniform distribution $\text{Unif}(0, 0.5)$ for each *j, i, t*. Here, we have followed Sun et al. (2009) to introduce time dependence in X_{jit} and Z_{jit}. In this simulation, we let $d = 6$ and specify the varying coefficient functions nonlinearly as $\beta_1(z_{1it}) = (2z_{1it})^3$, $\beta_2(z_{2it}) = 1 + e^{2z_{2it}-1}$, $\beta_3(z_{3it}) = 0.5e^{-2z_{3it}}$, $\beta_4(z_{4it}) = ln(5z_{4it})$, $\beta_5(z_{5it}) = 1 + z_{5it} + z_{5it}^2$, and $\beta_6(z_{6it}) = \sin(\pi z_{6it})$. We let the fixed effect be $\alpha_i = \frac{1}{T}\sum_{t=1}^{T} Z_{2it} - 0.5$, which has a zero mean and is correlated with Z_{2it}. The random error term ϵ_{it} is IID *N*(0, 1), independent of X_{jit} and Z_{jit}, which is consistent with the assumption $E(\epsilon_{it} \mid X_{it}, Z_{it}, \alpha_i) = 0$. ω_{jit}, ξ_{jit} and ϵ_{it} are independent of each other.

The proposed estimation requires selections of smoothing parameters in both steps, which are the number of knots in the first step and bandwidths in the second step. In the first step, we use the cubic B-splines which is based on the De Boor's algorithm. The number of total knots L_n in series estimation requires that for fixed *T*, as $n \to \infty$, $L_n \to \infty$ and $L_n(\frac{\log(n)}{n})^{\frac{1}{2}} \to 0$ (Li & Racine, 2007). Following

Wang and Yang (2007), we choose the number of evenly spaced interior knots as $N = \min([c(n*T)^{2/5}\log(n*T)],[((n*T)/2-1)d^{-1}])$, where the bracket represents taking the integer part of the number; $c = 0.5$ is a tuning constant. To ensure that the base functions of the cubic B-splines near the boundary are lined in the unit interval, three knots are added at both ends of the knots interval, which leads to the total number of knots $L_n = N + 6$. In the second-step of the local linear regression, given *C4*(1) and (2), the rate-optimal bandwidths for regression can be used. Though other data-driven methods to choose bandwidths can be used, we employ the rule-of-thumb bandwidths for computational simplicity. Define bandwidth $h = (h_1, \ldots, h_d)'$ and $h_j = c_j S_{z,j}(n*T)^{-1/(4+p_j)}$, where c_j is a constant set to be 2,[5] and $S_{z,j}$ represents sample standard deviation of $z_{j,it}$ for each j; $p_j = 1$ for all j in this case. We use the Gaussian kernel, let $T = 3$, $n = \{100, 200, 400\}$, and repeat each experiment 500 times.

The main criterion for evaluation is the average mean squared error (AMSE) across 500 repetitions. The evaluation is performed at 100 fixed grid points which are evenly spaced on (0, 1), the support of Z_{jit} for both steps.[6] We also report the average bias (ABIAS) and the average standard deviation (ASTD). Specifically,

$$AMSE[\hat{\beta}_j] = \frac{1}{100}\sum_{k=1}^{100}[\hat{\beta}_j(grid_k) - \beta_j(grid_k)]^2$$

$$AMSE[\breve{\beta}_j] = \frac{1}{100}\sum_{k=1}^{100}[\breve{\beta}_j(grid_k) - \beta_j(grid_k)]^2,$$

where $j = 1, \cdots, d$; $grid_k$ represents the 100 grid points; $\hat{\beta}_j(grid_k)$ and $\breve{\beta}_j(grid_k)$ are the first-step and the second-step estimators; $\beta_j(grid_k)$ is the true coefficient function at the 100 fixed grid points. ABIAS and ASTD are defined similarly.

Table 7.1 summarizes the performance of the two estimators across different sample size for each coefficient function. As shown in the first panel of Table 7.1, AMSE decreases when n increases for both the first-step and second-step estimators. The performance of the proposed estimators improves with large sample sizes, robust across different specifications of coefficient functions. It confirms the consistency for both estimators. Relative to the series-based first-step estimator, the kernel-based backfitting second-step estimator exhibits smaller AMSE across all experiment designs, which is consistent with our expectation that the second-step estimator is oracle efficient. We notice that the gain in terms of reduction in AMSE is substantial, especially for β_2, β_3 and β_5.

The ABIAS and ASTD are reported in the second and third panels in Table 7.1, respectively. The pattern of the change in ASTD for each coefficient function at different sample size roughly matches that observed in the AMSE. However, the ABIAS reported is slightly different. Though the ABIAS generally decreases in magnitude with a large sample size for both estimators, the first-step estimator has a relatively smaller ABIAS than the second-step estimator. We know that the two estimators are distinct in nature. The first step is series based, computationally convenient to approximate the coefficients with different smoothing variables, while the second step is kernel based, which makes a fair comparison across them to be challenging. Based on the proposed selection of smoothing

Table 7.1. The AMSE, ABIAS, and ASTD of the Two-step Estimator with $T = 3$.

			AMSE			
	$\hat{\beta}_1$	$\hat{\beta}_2$	$\hat{\beta}_3$	$\hat{\beta}_4$	$\hat{\beta}_5$	$\hat{\beta}_6$
$n = 100$	0.5185	0.8070	0.5087	0.5506	0.4212	0.4998
$n = 200$	0.1105	0.1478	0.1268	0.1157	0.2110	0.1973
$n = 400$	0.0690	0.0625	0.0625	0.0607	0.0664	0.0668
	$\check{\beta}_1$	$\check{\beta}_2$	$\check{\beta}_3$	$\check{\beta}_4$	$\check{\beta}_5$	$\check{\beta}_6$
$n = 100$	0.1510	0.0596	0.0546	0.1769	0.1108	0.1436
$n = 200$	0.0568	0.0232	0.0276	0.0314	0.0212	0.0251
$n = 400$	0.0355	0.0147	0.0123	0.0191	0.0125	0.0179
			ABIAS			
	$\hat{\beta}_1$	$\hat{\beta}_2$	$\hat{\beta}_3$	$\hat{\beta}_4$	$\hat{\beta}_5$	$\hat{\beta}_6$
$n = 100$	−0.0001	0.0133	−0.0125	−0.0040	0.0019	0.0066
$n = 200$	0.0001	−0.0074	0.0038	−0.0007	0.0007	−0.0037
$n = 400$	0.0000	0.0019	0.0022	0.0003	0.0046	−0.0026
	$\check{\beta}_1$	$\check{\beta}_2$	$\check{\beta}_3$	$\check{\beta}_4$	$\check{\beta}_5$	$\check{\beta}_6$
$n = 100$	0.0730	0.0225	−0.0065	−0.0534	0.0043	−0.0255
$n = 200$	0.0740	0.0106	0.0031	−0.0381	0.0052	−0.0311
$n = 400$	0.0840	0.0170	0.0062	−0.0307	0.0099	−0.0302
			ASTD			
	$\hat{\beta}_1$	$\hat{\beta}_2$	$\hat{\beta}_3$	$\hat{\beta}_4$	$\hat{\beta}_5$	$\hat{\beta}_6$
$n = 100$	0.4990	0.5322	0.4955	0.4943	0.4762	0.4954
$n = 200$	0.3022	0.3247	0.3140	0.3074	0.3321	0.3343
$n = 400$	0.2230	0.2199	0.2192	0.2187	0.2219	0.2202
	$\check{\beta}_1$	$\check{\beta}_2$	$\check{\beta}_3$	$\check{\beta}_4$	$\check{\beta}_5$	$\check{\beta}_6$
$n = 100$	0.2724	0.1624	0.1660	0.2083	0.1715	0.1836
$n = 200$	0.2008	0.1150	0.1132	0.1413	0.1092	0.1196
$n = 400$	0.1509	0.0909	0.0866	0.1135	0.0867	0.0970

parameters (knots and bandwidth), we only attempt to give some indication for their finite sample performance. We conclude that the gain observed in the AMSE in the second step estimator is mainly driven by its sharp decrease in the ASTD.

4.2. A Test for the Significance of the Coefficient Function

Practitioners frequently are interested in testing the function forms, or more specifically, testing the significance of the coefficient functions. We follow Sun et al. (2009) and Lin et al. (2014) to develop a significance test here for $H_0 : \beta_{jl}(\cdot) = 0$ for a given (j, l). As discussed in the introduction for our equation (1), when we group the model with respect to each disjoint element of the vector X, the smooth coefficients are additive function of Z. Thus, the DGP considered in Section 4.1 is a restrictive version, in the sense that X_{jit} does not have interaction with coefficient that varies with $Z_{j'it}$ for $j \neq j'$. Our test can be used to check the validity of this restriction, among other uses.

Because $W_{it} \equiv Y_{it} - X'_{(-j)it}\beta_{(-j)}(Z_{(-j)it}) - \sum_{l'=1,l'\neq l}^{r_j} X_{jit,l'}\beta_{jl'}(Z_{jit}) = \alpha_i + X_{jit,l}\beta_{jl}(Z_{jit}) + \epsilon_{it}$, we construct $\hat{W}_{it} = Y_{it} - X'_{(-j)it}\hat{\beta}_{(-j)}(Z_{(-j)it}) - \sum_{l'=1,l'\neq l}^{r_j} X_{jit,l'}\hat{\beta}_{jl'}(Z_{jit})$ by replacing the unknowns with our first-step estimates under the hypothesis H_0. To save on the notation and computing time, we propose the local constant estimator[7] for $\beta_{jl}(\cdot)$ as $\hat{\beta}_{jl}(z_{j0}) = (X_{jl}'S_h(z_{j0})X_{jl})^{-1}X_{jl}'S_h(z_{j0})\hat{W}$, where $\hat{W} = (\hat{W}_1', \cdots, \hat{W}_n')'$, $\hat{W}_i = (\widehat{W_{i1}}, \cdots, \hat{W}_{iT})'$, $X_{jl} = (X_{j1,l}', \cdots, X_{jn,l}')'$, and $X_{ji,l} = (X_{ji1,l}, \cdots, X_{jiT,l})'$. To test H_0, we construct the test statistic as

$$\int [\hat{\beta}_{jl}(z_j)]^2 dz_j.$$

Following Li, Huang, Li, and Fu (2002), we remove the random denominator of $\tilde{\beta}_{jl}(z_j)$ to construct

$$\begin{aligned} T_n &= \int \hat{\beta}_{jl}(z_j)'(X_{jl}'S_h(z_{j0})X_{jl})'(X_{jl}'S_h(z_{j0})X_{jl})\hat{\beta}_{jl}(z_j)dz_j \\ &= \hat{W}\int S_h(z_{j0})X_{jl}X_{jl}'S_h(z_{j0})dz_j\hat{W}. \end{aligned}$$

Note that $S_h(z_j) = M_h(z_j)'W_h(z_j)M_h(z_j)$, $M_h(z_j) = I_{nT} - D_M(D_M'W_h(z_j)D_M)^{-1}D_M'W_h(z_j)$ and $D_M = [-e_{n-1}, T_{n-1}]' \otimes e_T$. To overcome the complexity caused by the random denominator in $M_h(z_j)$, we replace it with $M_{D_0} = I_{nT} - \frac{1}{T}I_n \otimes (e_T e_T')$, so that the fixed effects will be removed as $M_{D_0}\alpha = 0$ where $\alpha = (\alpha_1, \cdots, \alpha_n)'$. We also remove the $i \neq j$ terms in T_n (since T_n contains two summations $\sum_{i=1}^{n}\sum_{j=1}^{n}$), so our test statistic is given by

$$\tilde{T}_n = \sum_{i=1}^{n}\sum_{\substack{m=1 \\ m\neq i}}^{n} \hat{W}_i'Q_T \int K_h(Z_{ji} - z_j)X_{ji,l}'X_{jm,l}K_h(Z_{jm} - z_j)dz_j Q_T \hat{W}_m,$$

where $Q_T = I_T - \frac{1}{T}e_T e_T'$, and $K_h(Z_{ji} - z_j) = \mathrm{diag}\{K(\frac{Z_{jit} - z_j}{h})\}_{t=1}^{T}$.

Next, consider a typical element in $\frac{1}{h}\int K_h(Z_{ji} - z_j)X_{ji,l}'X_{jm,l}K_h(Z_{jm} - z_j)dz_j$ as $\bar{K}(Z_{jit}, Z_{jms}) = \int K(\frac{1}{h}(Z_{jit} - Z_{jms}) + \omega)K(\omega)d\omega$. Without changing the nature of assigning local weight, we replace $\bar{K}(Z_{jit}, Z_{jms})$ with $K(\frac{1}{h}(Z_{jit} - Z_{jms}))$. It is also a weighting function such that only those Z_{jit} and Z_{jms} close to each other make a nonnegligible contribution to the test statistic. So the test statistic is

$$\hat{T}_n = \frac{1}{n^2 h}\sum_{i=1}^{n}\sum_{\substack{m=1 \\ i\neq m}}^{n} \hat{W}_i'Q_T A_{i,m} Q_T \hat{W}_m,$$

where $A_{i,m} = \{\{K(\frac{Z_{jit} - Z_{jms}}{h})X_{jit,l}X_{jms,l}\}_{t=1}^{T}\}_{s=1}^{T}$, a $T \times T$ matrix. Compared with equation (17) in Sun et al. (2009) and (3.4) in Lin et al. (2014), we conjecture that the test consistency statement similar to Theorem 3 in Sun et al. (2009) continues to hold.

To better approximate the finite sample null distribution of the $\hat{T}_n$ test, we propose a wild bootstrap procedure as below.

1. Because $\beta_{jl}(\cdot)=0$ for a given (j, l) under H_0, we simply let $\hat{u}_{it}=\hat{W}_{it}$ as the residuals.
2. Obtain the two-point wild bootstrap error by setting $u^*_{it}=a\hat{u}_{it}$ with probability r, and $u^*_{it}=b\hat{u}_{it}$ with probability $1-r$, where $a=\frac{1-\sqrt{5}}{2}$, $b=\frac{1+\sqrt{5}}{2}$, and $r=\frac{1+\sqrt{5}}{2\sqrt{5}}$. We obtain the bootstrap sample[8] as $\hat{W}^*_{it}=u^*_{it}$.
3. Compute $\hat{T}^*_n=\frac{1}{n^2h}\sum_{i=1}^{n}\sum_{\substack{m=1\\ i\neq m}}^{n}(\hat{W}^*_i)'Q_T A_{i,m} Q_T \hat{W}^*_m$, where $\hat{W}^*_i=(\hat{W}^*_{i1},\cdots,\hat{W}^*_{iT})'$.
4. We repeat steps 1-3 for B times. Use the empirical distribution of the B bootstrap statistics to obtain upper percentile values, which approximate the upper percentile values of the test statistic $\hat{T}_n$ under H_0.

Note that $Q_T\hat{W}^*_m=\{\hat{W}^*_{mt}-\frac{1}{T}\sum_{s=1}^{T}\hat{W}^*_{ms}\}_{t=1}^{T}$ performs the within transformation on $\hat{W}^*_m$. We conjecture that similar statements in Theorem 3.3 in Lin et al. (2014) continue to hold, and our test statistic can have reasonable size and power, which we illustrate in the simulation.

To illustrate the performance, we consider a simple DGP as

$$Y_{it}=\alpha_i+X_{1it}\cdot[\beta_{11}(Z_{1it})+\beta_{12}(Z_{2it})]+X_{2it}\cdot\beta_2(Z_{2it})+\epsilon_{it} \quad \text{for } i=1,\ldots,n,\ t=1,\ldots,T,$$

where $\beta_{11}(z)=1+z+z^2$, $\beta_{12}(z)=ln(5z)$, $\beta_2(z)=1+\exp(2z-1)$, $Z_{jit}=\omega_{jit}+\omega_{jit-1}$, ω_{jit} is IID uniformly distributed in $[0,1/2]$, $X_{jit}=0.5X_{jit-1}+\xi_{jit}$, ξ_{jit} is IID $N(0, 1)$ for $j = 1, 2$. In addition, $\alpha_i=\bar{Z}_{2i.}-0.5$ for $i=1,\cdots,n$, where $\bar{Z}_{2i.}=(1/T)\sum_{t=1}^{T}Z_{2it}$ and α_i and Z_{2it} are correlated. Moreover, ϵ_{it} is IID $N(0, 1)$, and ω_{jit}, ξ_{jit}, and ϵ_{it} are independent of each other.

We choose $n = 50, 100$, and $T = 3$, repeat the experiment 1,000 times and consider the bootstrap repetitions B to be 400. We construct the first step estimates as in Section 4.1 and select the bandwidth h for $\hat{T}_n$ as in Sun et al. (2009). Specifically, $h=C_h(nT)^{-2/7}\hat{\sigma}_{z_2}$, where $\hat{\sigma}_{z_2}$ is the sample standard deviation of Z_{2it} and $C_h=0.8,1$, and 1.2 to probe the sensitivity of the test performance on the magnitude of the bandwidth. Note that $(nT)^{-2/7}$ term in h is recommended in Sun et al. (2009), and we conjecture that this rate will be able to justify the asymptotic properties of our test. We report the percentage rejection rate in Table 7.2 to test the null $H_0:\beta_{12}(z_2)=0$ at the significance level $\alpha=10\%$, 5%, and 1%. With $T=3$ and $n = 50$ and 100, we have an effective sample size of 150 and 300, a small but moderate sample size. Although the bandwidth chosen may not be optimal, results in Table 7.2 indicate that the proposed test statistic is not very sensitive to the choice of h when C_h changes. We are glad to see that power of the test

Table 7.2. Percentage Rejection Ratio.

				$\beta_{12}(z_2)=0$ (size)					
	$C_h=0.8$			$C_h=1$			$C_h=1.2$		
	10%	5%	1%	10%	5%	1%	10%	5%	1%
$n=50$	0.048	0.012	0.003	0.036	0.013	0.002	0.038	0.014	0.001
$n=100$	0.057	0.020	0.001	0.041	0.020	0	0.053	0.017	0.002
				$\beta_{12}(z_2)=\ln(5z_2)$ (power)					
	$C_h=0.8$			$C_h=1$			$C_h=1.2$		
	10%	5%	1%	10%	5%	1%	10%	5%	1%
$n=50$	0.498	0.338	0.110	0.536	0.355	0.137	0.529	0.362	0.149
$n=100$	0.893	0.789	0.511	0.921	0.839	0.585	0.944	0.873	0.637

statistic improves quickly with a larger sample size. There is a bit of distortion of size being smaller than the targeted significance level, but the size does seem to improve with the sample size. We conjecture that a careful choice of the bandwidth might help to correct for it in a large sample setup.

5. SEMIPARAMETRIC ESTIMATION OF PRODUCTION FRONTIER AND INEFFICIENCY

Since the seminar work of Aigner, Lovell, and Schmidt (1977) and Meeusen and van den Broeck (1977), the stochastic frontier model becomes a popular tool to investigate the presence and magnitude of firm inefficiency. The distribution of the inefficiency can depend on a set of environment variables, that is, firm characteristics type determinants. A common approach is to model some of the parameters of the inefficiency distribution as function of firm characteristics and estimate them via maximum likelihood estimation (MLE, Caudill, Ford, & Gropper, 1995; Kumbhakar, Ghosh, & Mcguckin, 1991). Though attractive for the ease of incorporating determinants, it assumes an explicit and parametric distribution of inefficiency. Furthermore, the determinant of inefficiency is generally specified in a parametric fashion to facilitate MLE. Alvarez, Amsler, Orea, and Schmidt (2006) eliminate the need for distribution assumption and estimation can be performed via nonlinear least squares (see Wang & Schmidt, 2002), however, they need to specify a scaling function.

Utilizing the determinants of inefficiency which are separable from traditional inputs in production, our estimator proposed above estimates the stochastic frontier model without imposing either the distributional assumption, or the requirement of the scaling property. Recent work in Zhou, Parmeter, and Kumbhakar (2020) extends Parmeter, Wang, and Kumbhakar (2017) to allow for fixed effects following the profile lease squares approach as in Su and Ullah (2006). We allow for the presence of fixed effects in the frontier in a similar fashion, making it possible to separate the heterogeneous effect from the firm-specific inefficiency level. Different from them, we further relax the parametric frontier assumption, modeling it flexibly as a varying coefficient semiparametric frontier. Below, we estimate the production efficiency of US coal-fired power plants under the Acid Rain Program (ARP), which is a market-based environmental program.

We consider the following stochastic frontier model with fixed effects:

$$Y_{it} = \alpha_i + X_{it}'\beta(Z_{it}) + v_{it} - u_{it} = \alpha_i + \sum_{j=1}^{d} X_{jit}\beta_j(Z_{jit}) + v_{it} - u_{it} \quad \text{for } i = 1,2,\ldots,n, \quad t = 1,2,\ldots,T, \tag{5}$$

where α_i is the unobserved firm-specific fixed effects; $X_{it} = (X_{1it}, X_{2it}, \ldots, X_{dit})'$ is of dimension *d*, representing the traditional inputs, such as labor, capital, and fuel consumption in a power plant; $Z_{it}=[Z_{1it}, Z_{2it}, \ldots, Z_{dit}]T$ represents the variables with dimension *d* that can potentially impact the marginal output of traditional inputs, such as the number of generators in a power plant and the average age of the generators, where some Z_{jit} can overlap; $\beta(Z_{it}) = (\beta_1(Z_{1it}), \cdots, \beta_d(Z_{dit}))'$ collects the marginal outputs corresponding to the inputs; v_{it} refers to the random error, which is assumed to be IID with zero mean and finite variance $\sigma_v^2 > 0$; $u_{it} > 0$ represents the technical inefficiency which leads to the shortfall of actual production from the frontier, and its distribution depends generally on the determinants W_{it}.

To estimate equation (5), we assume that $E(u_{it} \mid \alpha_i, X_{it}, Z_{it}, W_{it}) = g(W_{it})$, where W_{it} are a $q \times 1$ vector of determinants of the inefficiency in the production process, such as the operation and maintenance cost for exhaust pollution control in a power plant. Clearly, we maintain that W_{it} can be separated from the traditional inputs X_{it} and variables Z_{it} that change the marginal outputs. Meanwhile, we also assume that $E(v_{it} \mid \alpha_i, X_{it}, Z_{it}, W_{it}) = 0$. Since $E((v_{it} - u_{it}) \mid \alpha_i, X_{it}, Z_{it}, W_{it}) \neq 0$, equation (5) is not a proper regression model. However, we can write

$$Y_{it} = \alpha_i + X_{it}^T\beta(Z_{it}) - g(W_{it}) + \epsilon_{it} \tag{6}$$

where the composite error $\epsilon_{it} = v_{it} - (u_{it} - g(W_{it}))$ satisfies $E(\epsilon_{it} \mid \alpha_i, X_{it}, Z_{it}, W_{it}) = 0$. Equation (6) is a varying coefficient panel data model with fixed effects and different smoothing variables as in equation (1). We can apply the proposed procedure to estimate both the coefficient function $\beta(\cdot)$ and the conditional mean of the technical inefficiency $g(\cdot)$.

We examine the production efficiency of 36 US coal-burning power plants that are covered under the ARP over the period of 2001–2005.[9] We follow the literature of power plant analysis and choose one output (net electricity generation) and three inputs – labor, physical capital, and coal consumption (Färe, Grosskopf, Noh, & Weber, 2005; Färe, Grosskopf, & Pasurka, 2007, 2014; Hampf, 2014; Kleit & Terrell, 2001; Knittel, 2002). The choice of determinant of inefficiency W_{it} is due to the following consideration. Coal was the primary energy source for electricity generation before 2015[10] and the combustion of coal generates harmful sulfur dioxide (SO_2), which is the culprit to blame for the formation of acid rain and particulate matter pollution. To curb the emission of sulfur dioxide from the power station, the Environmental Protection Agency (EPA) introduced the market-based ARP in 1995.[11] Since the EPA only requires a total reduction in SO_2 emission, the power plants can choose the most cost-effective method to control pollution. They have the option to reduce emissions by switching to low-sulfur coal, installing scrubber (flue-gas desulfurization, FGD, units),[12] and purchasing emission permits from other regulated units (Hancevic, 2016). Because properly designed environmental policy encourages innovation and improves the production process, the market-based environmental program enables electricity generating units to offset compliance costs and improve their efficiency (Porter & van der Linde, 1995). The impact of the ARP on the production efficiency of power plants can be potentially evaluated through the conditional mean of technical inefficiency $g(W_{it})$ in equation (5). We should keep the dimension of W_{it} low for a feasible nonparametric estimation. Here, we use the operation and maintenance costs of FGD technology as the determinant of inefficiency W_{it}, the impact of which on $g(\cdot)$ can be far from a linear one.

Besides inefficiency, other factors can indirectly change the output level, such as firm characteristics. Ignoring environment variables in the productivity analysis may lead to unreliable inference due to possible model misspecification. Firm characteristics are a typical example of environment variables, since they differ from traditional inputs and change the output level through the marginal product of inputs. Here, we choose the average age of generators (Age_{it}) and the total number of generators (Number_{it}) in each power plant as the environment variables. The functional forms of the varying coefficients are unknown, and we can estimate them without imposing functional form assumptions. The varying coefficient functions $\beta_L(\cdot)$ (labor), $\beta_K(\cdot)$ (capital), and $\beta_F(\cdot)$ (fuel) can depend on the same or different environment variables. In the panel data model of Heshmati, Kumbhakar, and Sun (2014), the age of the generators is positively related to the return on capital. Therefore, we allow $\beta_K(\text{Age}_{it})$ to vary with Age_{it}. The number of generators gives information on the size of power plants and also indicates the capital utilization. Thus, we consider $\beta_L(\text{Number}_{it})$ and $\beta_F(\text{Number}_{it})$ to vary with Number_{it}. Thus, we obtain

$$\begin{aligned} \ln Y_{it} &= \alpha_i + \ln L_{it} \cdot \beta_L(\text{Number}_{it}) + \ln K_{it} \cdot \beta_K(\text{Age}_{it}) \\ &\quad + \ln F_{it} \cdot \beta_F(\text{Number}_{it}) - g(\text{W}_{it}) + \epsilon_{it} \end{aligned} \tag{7}$$

Our equation (7) can be rewritten as

$$\begin{aligned} \ln Y_{it} &= \alpha_i + [\ln L_{it}, \ln F_{it}][\beta_L(\text{Number}_{it}), \beta_F(\text{Number}_{it})]' \\ &\quad + \ln K_{it} \cdot \beta_K(\text{Age}_{it}) - g(\text{W}_{it}) + \epsilon_{it} \\ &= \alpha_i + X_{1it}' \beta_1(\text{Number}_{it}) + X_{2it} \beta_K(\text{Age}_{it}) + X_{3it}(-g(\text{W}_{it})) + \epsilon_{it}, \end{aligned}$$

where $X_{1it} = [\ln \text{L}_{it}, \ln \text{F}_{it}]'$, $\beta_1(\text{Number}_{it}) = [\beta_{11}(\text{Number}_{it}), \beta_{12}(\text{Number}_{it})]' = [\beta_L(\text{Number}_{it}), \beta_F(\text{Number}_{it})]'$, $X_{2it} = \ln \text{K}_{it}$, and $X_{3it} = 1$.

For comparison purposes, we introduce a parametric model in equation (8) by assuming each coefficient function is a linear function of the environment variable. The coefficient functions are $\beta_L(\text{Number}_{it}) = c_1 + a_1$

$*\text{Number}_{it}$, $\beta_K(\text{Age}_{it}) = c_2 + a_2 * \text{Age}_{it}$, $\beta_F(\text{Number}_{it}) = c_3 + a_3 * \text{Number}_{it}$, and $-g(\text{W}_{it}) = c_4 + a_4 * \text{W}_{it}$.

$$\begin{aligned}\ln \text{Y}_{it} = \alpha_i + c_1 \ln \text{L}_{it} + c_2 \ln \text{K}_{it} + c_3 \ln \text{F}_{it} + c_4 + a_1 \text{Number}_{it} \ln \text{L}_{it} \\ + a_2 \text{Age}_{it} \ln \text{K}_{it} + a_3 \text{Number}_{it} \ln \text{F}_{it} + a_4 \text{W}_{it} + \epsilon_{it}.\end{aligned} \tag{8}$$

To give a better understanding of the overall performance of power plants, we also calculate the technical efficiency score (TE) in equation (9) (Li & Phillips, 2017)). TE is always between 0 and 1, with 0 being least efficient and 1 being fully efficient, where

$$\text{TE}_{it} = exp(-g(W_{it})) \tag{9}$$

Instead of using $E(u_{it})$, we have followed Jondrow, Lovell, Materov, and Schmidt (1982) to evaluate the performance of each individual unit. Here, we propose to use $E(u_{it} \mid W_{it})$, which is estimated by $\hat{g}(W_{it})$, and define $exp(-g(W_{it}))$ as the technical efficiency because it conveniently takes values between (0, 1).[13]

We obtain data from the Energy Information Administration (EIA), the Federal Energy Regulatory Commission (FERC), and the EPA. Since data are reported at different levels (boiler level, generator level, and plant level) from the above sources, it is aggregated to plant level for consistency. The output Y_{it} is measured as the annual net generation of electricity (MWh) in each power plant, and it is obtained from EIA form 767. The annual heat content (MMBtu) of coal (measurement of fuel F_{it}) and the total operation and maintenance costs on sulfur removal units FGD (determinant of inefficiency W_{it}) are also collected from EIA form 767. The generating capacity (MW) is introduced as a measurement of capital K_{it} (Hampf & Rødseth, 2015). We aggregate the generator-level data in EIA form 860 to plant level for all the generators that use coal as the primary energy source. EIA form 860 also offers data on the environment variables, which are the average age of generators Age_{it} and the total number of generators Number_{it}. The average number of employees in each plant is used as the measurement of labor L_{it}, and it is obtained from FERC Form 1. At last, we use the EPA Air Markets Program Data to ensure all the power plants in the observation are covered under the ARP. Summary statistics are reported in Table 7.3. The total number of power plants n is 35, and the number of years considered is $T = 5$.

In the empirical application, we need to choose the number of knots and bandwidths. For the first-step estimation, we adopt the formula in the simulation to choose the number of the knots, N, but we have to reduce it to $N - 9$ to avoid matrix singularity issue. For the second-step estimation, we follow the simulation section to utilize the rule-of-thumb bandwidths, with a constant of $cj = 3$ for all j to produce moderate variability in all coefficients estimates. Estimation results are reported in Table 7.4, which include the 25th, 50th, and 75th percentiles and mean of the coefficient estimates. The parametric estimates in Table 7.5 are mostly insignificant. We further plot the coefficient functions $\beta_L(\text{Number}_{it})$, $\beta_K(\text{Age}_{it})$, and $\beta_F(\text{Number}_{it})$ against the smoothing variables in Fig. 7.1 for illustration. The confidence interval for each coefficient estimate is constructed using the wild bootstrap technique; therefore, the 95% confidence interval is not necessarily

Table 7.3. Summary Statistics.

Variable	Def.	Mean	Std. Dev.	Min	Max
$\ln Y_{it}$	Log of net electricity generation (MWh)	15.40	0.81	13.34	16.93
$\ln L_{it}$	Log of average number of employees	4.83	0.76	2.40	6.33
$\ln K_{it}$	Log of nameplate capacity (MW)	6.70	0.80	4.75	8.11
$\ln F_{it}$	Log of heat content of coal (MMBtu)	12.58	0.63	11.00	13.85
Age_{it}	Average age of generators	31	10	12	53
Number_{it}	Total number of generators	2.7	1.4	1	7
W_{it}	O&M costs on FGD units (million dollars)	6.61	11.88	0	106.31
Number of observations	180 ($n = 36$, $T = 5$)				

Table 7.4. Estimation of the Semiparametric Model with Varying Coefficient.

	Q(25%)	Median	Q(75%)	Mean
$\hat{\beta}_L(\text{Number}_{it})$	0.1432	0.2600	0.2600	0.2190
	(0.1281)	(0.5306)	(0.5306)	(0.4170)
$\hat{\beta}_K(\text{Age}_{it})$	0.0424	0.0811	0.0937*	0.0608
	(0.0559)	(0.0510)	(0.0488)	(0.0672)
$\hat{\beta}_F(\text{Number}_{it})$	1.1070***	1.1070***	1.1291***	1.1116***
	(0.1989)	(0.1989)	(0.0600)	(0.1777)
$-\hat{g}(W_{it})$	−0.2835*	-0.2469	-0.2297	-0.2667
	(0.1697)	(0.1594)	(0.1574)	(0.1971)

***,**,* represent the significant level at the 1%, 5%, and 10%, respectively.

Table 7.5. Estimation of the Parametric Model with Linear Coefficient Functions.

	Estimates
$\ln L$	−0.0638
	(10.2051)
$\text{Number}_{it} \ln L_{it}$	0.0145
	(3.0452)
$\ln K_{it}$	−0.3386
	(55.3382)
$\text{Age}_{it} \ln K_{it}$	0.0024
	(0.1155)
$\ln F_{it}$	0.2996
	(10.4417)
$\text{Number}_{it} \ln F_{it}$	−0.0008
	(1.3117)
W_{it}	0.0004
	(0.1581)

***,**,* represent the significant level at the 1%, 5%, and 10%, respectively.

symmetric around the estimates. We also include the plot of the estimated parametric coefficient function in the upper two panels in Fig. 7.1. The plots of parametric estimates for $\beta_F(\text{Number}_{it})$ and $-g(W_{it})$ are not included in the bottom two panels, because the parametric estimates are much smaller than the lower bound of the confidence interval. In the lower right panel, we plot the inefficiency coefficient function $-g(W_{it})$ against W_{it}, which ranges from 0 to 20 million dollars, and it includes around 97% of the observations. Except for $\beta_L(\cdot)$, the parametric estimates generally fall out of the confidence intervals of the semiparametric alternatives, which indicates potential misspecification in the linear coefficient functions.

Our specification has used W as the variable that only impacts $g(\cdot)$, but not the frontier estimates. To further explore the possible dependence of the frontier estimates on W, we consider significance tests for $\beta_{L2}(W)$, $\beta_{K2}(W)$, and $\beta_{F2}(W)$, in equations (10) (11), and (12) below. Following Section 4.2, we specify the null hypothesis as $H_0 : \beta_{L2}(\cdot) = 0$; $H_0 : \beta_{K2}(\cdot) = 0$; and $H_0 : \beta_{F2}(\cdot) = 0$, separately. We adopt the bandwidth of W_{it} from Section 4.2 as $h_W = C_h(nT)^{-2/7}\hat{\sigma}_W$ with $C_h = 1$. In each hypothesis test, we repeat the wild bootstrap procedure B 400 times to obtain the empirical distribution of the bootstrap test statistics $\hat{T}_n^*$. We calculate the test statistics $\hat{T}_n$, compare with the empirical distribution of the bootstrap test statistics, and obtain the empirical p-values for the above mentioned null hypothesis as 0.408, 0.428, and 0.433, respectively. The large p-values all indicate that we cannot reject the null, partially supporting our specification that W does not enter the frontier.

$$\begin{aligned} \ln Y_{it} = \alpha_i + \ln L_{it}[\beta_{L1}(\text{Number}_{it}) + \beta_{L2}(W_{it})] + \ln K_{it}\beta_K(\text{Age}_{it}) \\ + \ln F_{it}\beta_F(\text{Number}_{it}) - g(W_{it}) + \epsilon_{it}, \end{aligned} \tag{10}$$

$$\begin{aligned} \ln Y_{it} = \alpha_i + \ln L_{it}\beta_L(\text{Number}_{it}) + \ln K_{it}[\beta_{K1}(\text{Age}_{it}) + \beta_{K2}(W_{it})] \\ + \ln F_{it}\beta_F(\text{Number}_{it}) - g(W_{it}) + \epsilon_{it}, \end{aligned} \tag{11}$$

$$\begin{aligned} \ln Y_{it} = \alpha_i + \ln L_{it}\beta_L(\text{Number}_{it}) + \ln K_{it}\cdot\beta_K(\text{Age}_{it}) \\ + \ln F_{it}[\beta_{F1}(\text{Number}_{it}) + \beta_{F2}(W_{it})] - g(\text{W}_{it}) + \epsilon_{it}, \end{aligned} \tag{12}$$

In Table 7.4, the estimated average conditional mean of inefficiency $-\breve{g}(W_{it})$ is –0.2667, which indicates that net electricity generation is reduced by 23.4% ($(1-e^{-0.2667})\times 100\%$) on average. It reduces net electricity generation by 1,141,645 MWh, considering the average electricity generation (4,876,801 MWh). In Fig. 7.2, we plot the technical efficiency against the determinant of inefficiency W_{it} and it reveals a nonlinear relationship between the technical efficiency and the costs of sulfur removal equipment. The efficiency score ranges from 0.65 to 0.9. When the costs W_{it} is below 20 (million dollars), the technical efficiency decreases with increasing FGD costs. The efficiency has an upward trend when the cost of FGD units is between 20 and 55 (million dollars). When the cost of FGD is beyond 80 (million dollars), the efficiency stays around 0.775.

The marginal product of labor is insignificant across all the percentiles in Table 7.4. In Fig. 7.1, we observe that the confidence bounds of $\beta_L(\text{Number}_{it})$ include zero

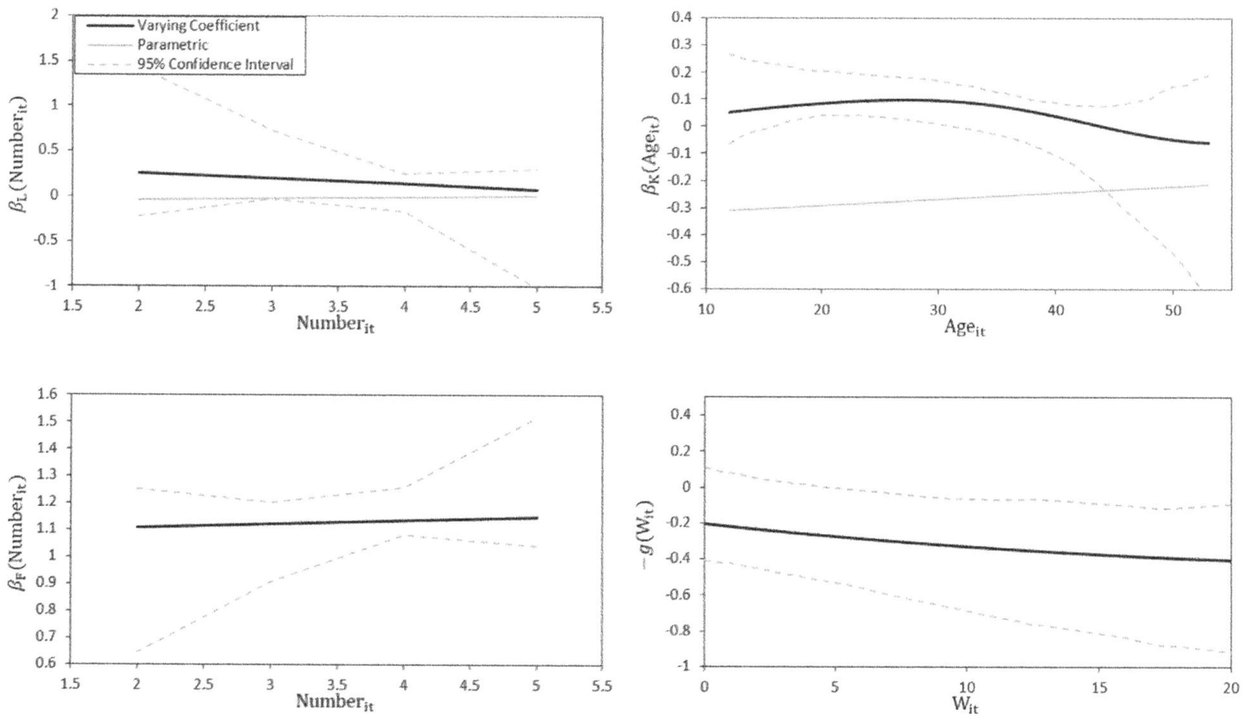

Fig. 7.1. Plots of Estimated $\beta_L(\text{Number}_{it})$, $\beta_K(\text{Age}_{it})$, $\beta_F(\text{Number}_{it})$, and $-g(W_{it})$ Against Environment Variables.

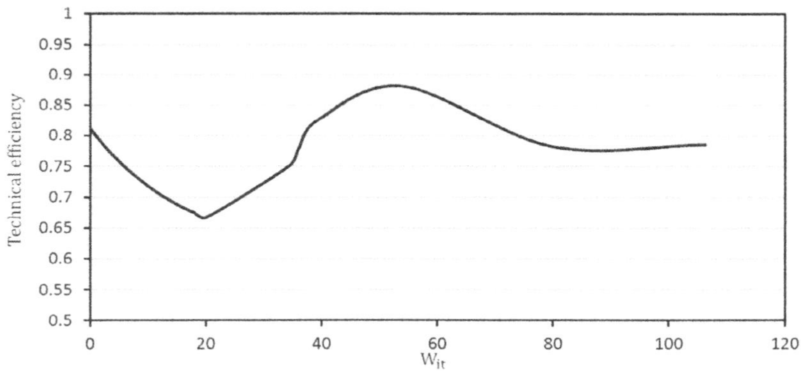

Fig. 7.2. Plot of Technical Efficiency Score TE_{it} Against W_{it}.

across all the Number_{it}. In other words, we do not find a significant change in the marginal return of labor with respect to the average number of generators in a power plant. The plot of $\beta_K(\text{Age}_{it})$ in Fig. 7.1 has an inverse U shape. The age of generators has a positive impact on the marginal product of capital when generators are new. However, when the operation reaches 30 years, the performance deterioration decreases marginal return on capital. In the early year of operation (25–30 years), regular maintenance of the power plants keeps the performance at the optimal level. However, when the equipment is 30 years or older, the substantial repair is required to keep the machine running at an efficient level (Campbell (2013)). The marginal return on fuel $\beta_F(\text{Number}_{it})$ is significant in Table 7.4 and we observe that the plot of coefficient function of fuel is relatively flat in Fig. 7.1. It indicates that the number of generators in a power plant has a negligible impact on the utilization of coal.

To give an overall assessment of the power plants' technical efficiency levels, we plot in Fig. 7.3, the kernel density of the technical efficiency scores. The parametric specification in equation (7) fails to yield significant estimate, making it hard to assess the efficiency level. Relying on our semiparametric model and estimated technical efficiency, we observe that its density hovers relatively tightly around 0.78, with a mean of 0.767, and a standard deviation of 0.041. The efficiency scores range from 0.667 to 0.881. Very few power plants achieve efficiency level above 0.84, indicating that there is still room for improvement in the industry.

6. CONCLUSION

We propose to estimate a varying coefficient panel data model with fixed effects that allows different smoothing variables with a two-step approach. We are able to remove the fixed effects in both steps through properly constructed weights. The first step is series based, which conveniently captures the varying coefficients with different smoothing variables. Using the first-step estimates, we construct a kernel-based backfitting estimator, which is shown to be oracle efficient and facilitates the inference. We obtain their asymptotic properties and through a

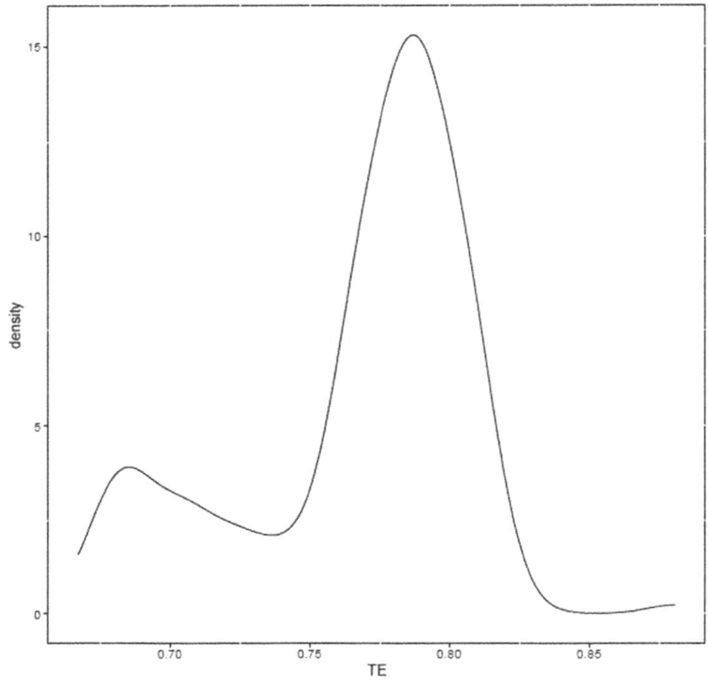

Fig. 7.3. Kernel Density of Technical Efficiency Score.

Monte Carlo study, we illustrate their encouraging finite sample performance. We demonstrate their empirical applicability by examining the efficiency of 36 US coal-burning power plants that are covered under the ARP from 2001 to 2005. We employ a stochastic varying coefficient frontier with fixed effects, and model the conditional mean of the inefficiency term nonparametrically. We conclude that there is still room for the US coal-burning power plants to improve their efficiency level.

REFERENCES

Aigner, D., Lovell, C. A. K., & Schmidt, P. (1977). Formulation and estimation of stochastic frontiers production function models. *Journal of Econometrics*, *6*, 21–37.

Alvarez, A., Amsler, C., Orea, L., & Schmidt, P. (2006). Interpreting and testing the scaling property in models where inefficiency depends on firm characteristics. *Journal of Productivity Analysis*, *25*, 201–212.

Arellano, M. (2003). *Panel data econometrics*. Oxford: Oxford University Press.

Baltagi, B. H. (2013). *Econometric analysis of panel data* (2nd ed.). New York, NY: Wiley.

Baltagi, B. H., & Li, D. (2002). Series estimation of partially linear panel data models with fixed effects. *Annals of Economics and Finance*, *3*, 103–116.

Cai, Z., Das, M., Xiong, H., & Wu, X. (2006). Functional coefficient instrumental variables models. *Journal of Econometrics*, *133*, 207–241.

Cai, Z., & Xiong, H. (2012). Partially varying coefficient instrumental variables models. *Statistica Neerlandica*, *66*, 85–110.
Campbell, R. J. (2013). *Increasing the efficiency of existing coal-fired power plants*. Retrieved from www.crs.gov
Caudill, S. B., Ford, J. M., & Gropper, D. M. (1995). Frontier estimation and firm-specific inefficiency measure in the presence of heteroskedasticity. *Journal of Business & Economic Statistics*, *13*(1), 105–111.
Centorrino, S., & Racine, J. (2017). Semiparametric varying coefficient models with endogenous covariates. *Annals of Economics and Finance*, *128*, 261–295.
Chan, H. R., Chupp, B. A., Cropper, M. L., & Muller, N. Z. (2018). The impact of trading on the costs and benefits of the Acid Rain Program. *Journal of Environmental Economics and Management*, *88*, 180–209.
Chen, X., & Pouzo, D. (2015). Sieve Wald and QLR Inferences on Semi/Nonparametric Conditional Moment Models. *Econometrica*, *83*(3), 1013–1079.
Delgado, M. S., Ozabaci, D., Sun, Y., & Kumbhakar, S. C. (2020). Smooth coefficient models with endogenous environmental variables. *Econometric Reviews*, *39*, 158–180.
Färe, R., Grosskopf, S., Noh, D.-W., & Weber, W. (2005). Characteristics of a polluting technology: Theory and practice. *Journal of Econometrics*, *126*(2), 469–492.
Färe, R., Grosskopf, S., & Pasurka, C. A. (2007). Pollution abatement activities and traditional productivity. *Ecological Economics*, *62*(3–4), 673–682.
Färe, R., Grosskopf, S., & Pasurka, C. A. (2014). Potential gains from trading bad outputs: The case of U.S. electric power plants. *Resource and Energy Economics*, *36*(1), 99–112.
Feng, J., Huang, Z., & Zhang, R. (2012). Estimation on varying-coefficient partially linear model with different smoothing variables. *Communications in Statistics – Theory and Methods*, *41*, 516–529.
Hampf, B. (2014). Separating environmental efficiency into production and abatement efficiency: A nonparametric model with application to US power plants. *Journal of Productivity Analysis*, *41*(3), 457–473.
Hampf, B., & Rødseth, K. L. (2015). Carbon dioxide emission standards for U.S. power plants: An efficiency analysis perspective. *Energy Economics*, *50*, 140–153.
Hancevic, P. I. (2016). Environmental regulation and productivity: The case of electricity generation under the CAAA-1990. *Energy Economics*, *60*, 131–143.
Hastie, T. J., & Tibishirani, R. J. (1990). *Generalized additive models*. London: Chapman and Hall.
Henderson, D. J., Carroll, R. J., & Li, Q. (2008). Nonparametric estimation and testing of fixed effects panel data model. *Journal of Econometrics*, *144*, 257–275.
Henderson, D. J., & Ullah, A. (2005). A nonparametric random effects estimator. *Economics Letters*, *88*, 403–407.
Heshmati, A., Kumbhakar, S. C., & Sun, K. (2014). Estimation of productivity in Korean electric power plants: A semiparametric smooth coefficient model. *Energy Economics*, *45*, 491–500.
Horn, R. A., & Johnson, C. R. (2013). *Matrix analysis* (2nd ed.). New York, NY: Cambridge University Press.
Horowitz, J. L., & Mammen, E. (2004). Nonparametric estimation of an additive model with a link function. *Annals of Statistics*, *32*(6), 2412–2443.
Hsiao, C. (2014). *Analysis of panel data* (Econometric Society Monographs, 3rd ed.). New York, NY: Cambridge University Press.
Jondrow, J., Lovell, C. A. K., Materov, I. S., & Schmidt, P. (1982). On the estimation of technical inefficiency in the stochastic frontier production function model. *Journal of Econometrics*, *19*, 233–238.
Kleit, A. N., & Terrell, D. (2001). Measuring potential efficiency gains from deregulation of electricity generation: A Bayesian approach. *Review of Economics and Statistics*, *83*(3), 523–530.
Knittel, C. R. (2002). Alternative regulatory methods and firm efficiency: Stochastic frontier evidence from the U.S. electricity industry. *Review of Economics and Statistics*, *84*(3), 530–540.
Kumbhakar, S. C., Ghosh, S., & Mcguckin, J. T. (1991). A Generalized production frontier approach for estimating determinants of inefficiency in U.S. dairy farms. *Journal of Business {&} Economic Statistics*, *9*(3), 279–286.
Lee, Y. K., Mammen, E., Park, B. U. (2012a). Flexible generalized varying coefficient regression models. *Annals of Statistics*, *40*, 1906–1933.
Lee, Y. K., Mammen, E., & Park, B. U. (2012b). Projection-type estimation for varying coefficient regression models. *Bernoulli*, *18*, 177–205.

Li, F., & Phillips, M. A. (2017). The influence of the regulatory environment on Chinese urban water utilities. *Water Resources Management*, *31*(1), 205–218.

Li, Q., Huang, C. J., Li, D., & Fu, T. (2002). Semiparametric smooth coefficient models. *Journal of Business & Economic Statistics*, *20*(3), 412–422.

Li, Q., & Racine, J. (2007). *Nonparametric econometrics: Theory and practice*. Princeton, NJ: Princeton University Press.

Li, Q., & Stengos, T. (1996). On the root-n-consistent semiparametric estimation of partially linear models. *Journal of Econometrics*, *71*, 389–397.

Lin, X., & Carroll, R. J. (2006). Semiparametric estimation in general repeated measures problems. *Journal of the Royal Statistical Society (Series B)*, *68*(1), 68–88.

Lin, Z., Li, Q., & Sun, Y. (2014). A consistent nonparametric test of parametric regression functional form in fixed effects panel data models. *Journal of Econometrics*, *178*(PART 1), 167–179.

Linton, O. B. (1997). Efficient estimation of additive nonparametric regression models. *Biometrika*, *84*, 469–473.

Linton, O. B., & Nielsen, J. P. (1995). A kernel method of estimating structured nonparametric regression based on marginal integration. *Biometrika*, *82*, 93–100.

Mammen, E., Linton, O. B., & Nielsen, J. P. (1999). The existence and asymptotic properties of a backfitting projection algorithm under weak conditions. *Annals of Statistics*, *27*, 1443–1490.

Martins-Filho, C., & Yao, F. (2009). Nonparametric regression estimation with general parametric error covariance. *Journal of Multivariate Analysis*, *100*, 309–333.

Martins-Filho, C., Yao, F., & Torero, M. (2018). Nonparametric estimation of conditional value-at-risk and expected shortfall based on extreme value theory. *Econometric Theory*, *34*(1), 23–67.

Meeusen, W., & van den Broeck, J. (1977). Efficiency estimation from Cobb–Douglas production functions with composed error. *International Economic Review*, *18*, 435–444.

Newey, W. K., Powell, J. L., & Vella, F. (1999). Nonparametric estimation of triangular simultaneous equations models. *Econometrica*, *67*, 565–603.

Ozabaci, D., Henderson, D. J., & Su, L. (2014). Additive nonparametric regression in the presence of endogenous regressors. *Journal of Business and Economic Statistics*, *32*(4), 555–575.

Park, B. U., Simar, L., & Zelenyuk, V. (2015). Categorical data in local maximum likelihood: Theory and applications to productivity analysis. *Journal of Productivity Analysis*, *43*, 199–214.

Parmeter, C. F., Wang, H. J., & Kumbhakar, S. C. (2017). Nonparametric estimation of the determinants of inefficiency. *Journal of Productivity Analysis*, *47*(3), 205–221.

Porter, M. E., & van der Linde, C. (1995). Toward a new conception of the environment–competitiveness relationship. *Journal of Economic Perspectives*, *9*(4), 97–118.

Roca-Pardinas, J., & Sperlich, S. (2010). Feasible estimation in generalized structured models. *Statistics and Computing*, *20*, 367–379.

Rodriguez-Poo, J. M., & Soberon, A. (2014). Direct semi-parametric estimation of fixed effects panel data varying coefficient models. *The Econometrics Journal*, *17*, 107–138.

Rodriguez-Poo, J. M., & Soberon, A. (2015). Nonparametric estimation of fixed effects panel data varying coefficient models. *Journal of Multivariate Analysis*, *133*, 95–122.

Rodriguez-Poo, J. M., & Soberon, A. (2017). Nonparametric and semiparametric panel data models: Recent developments. *Journal of Economic Surveys*, *31*, 923–960.

Ruckstuhl, A. F., Welsh, A. H., & Carroll, R. J. (2000). Nonparametric function estimation of the relationship between two repeatedly measured variables. *Statistica Sinica*, *10*, 51–71.

Seber, G. A. (2008). *A matrix handbook for statisticians*. Hoboken, NJ: John Wiley & Sons.

Su, L., & Ullah, A. (2006). Profile likelihood estimation of partially linear panel data models with fixed effects. *Economics Letters*, *92*, 75–81.

Sun, Y., Carroll, R. J., & Li, D. (2009). Semiparametric estimation of fixed effects panel data varying coefficient models. *Advances in Econometrics*, *25*, 101–130.

Ullah, A., & Roy, N. (1998). Nonparametric and semiparametric econometrics of panel data. In A. Ullah & D. E. Giles (Eds.), *Handbook of applied economic statistics* (pp. 579–604). New York, NY: Marcel Dekker.

Wang, H.-J., & Schmidt, P. (2002). One-step and two-step estimation of the effects of exogenous variables on technical efficiency levels. *Journal of Productivity Analysis*, *18*, 129–144.

Wang, L., & Yang, L. (2007). Spline-backfitted kernel smoothing of nonlinear additive autoregression model. *Annals of Statistics*, *35*, 2474–2503.
Wang, N. (2003). Marginal nonparametric kernel regression accounting for within-subject correlation. *Biometrika*, *90*(1), 43–52.
Xue, L., & Yang, L. (2006). Estimation of semiparametric additive coefficient model. *Journal of Statistical Planning and Inference*, *136*, 2506–2534.
Yang, L., Park, B. U., Xue, L., & Hardle, W. (2006). Estimation and testing for varying coefficients in additive models with marginal integration. *Journal of the American Statistical Association*, *101*, 1212–1227.
Zhang, R., & Li, G. (2007). Averaged estimation of functional-coefficient regression models with different smoothing variables. *Statistics & Probability Letters*, *77*, 455–461.
Zhou, J., Parmeter, C. F., & Kumbhakar, S. (2020). Nonparametric estimation of the determinants of inefficiency in the presence of firm heterogeneity. *European Journal of Operational Research*, *286*, 1142–1152.

NOTES

1. They consider a very flexible varying coefficient model in which the linear variables X and smoothing variables Z do not have to be disjoint.
2. We are grateful to an anonymous referee for this clarifying interpretation.
3. For a generic variable ξ, $\{\{\xi_{it}\}_{t=1}^{T}\}_{i=1}^{n} = (\xi_1{}', \cdots, \xi_n{}')'$, and $\xi_i = (\xi_{i1}{}', \cdots, \xi_{iT}{}')'$.
4. We are grateful to an anonymous referee for bringing these to our attention. Centorrino and Racine (2017) apply the sieve minimum distance estimator as in Chen and Pouzo (2015). Our method can be easily adapted to the endogeneity case if we apply the nonparametric control function approach (Newey, Powell, & Vella, 1999) with some modification for our future research, as the control function approach simply adds a nonparametric additive term of residuals from an IV regression of endogenous Z on its instruments.
5. With the Gaussian kernel used, we choose $c_j = 2$ in the simulation to avoid singularity of $R_j{}'(z_{j0})S_h(z_{j0})R_j(z_{j0})$ in equation (3) at different evaluation points across different sample sizes considered.
6. We avoid the upper and lower 5% of the support of Z_{jit} so that the boundary bias impact is not severe.
7. See also $\hat{\theta}_{FE}(z)$ on page 111 of Sun et al. (2009) and $\hat{\theta}(x)$ in (2.12) in Lin et al. (2014).
8. This is for the special case under which ϵ_{it} is IID in both i and t. Otherwise, if one assumes IID across index i, we will generate a vector of u_i^* (each element in the vector being $T \times 1$) from a vector of $\hat{u}_i$ (each element in the vector being $T \times 1$), to ensure independence across index i without affecting any possible correlation in index t.
9. The coal-burning power plant is defined as the plant in which at least one boiler consumes coal as the primary fuel (Chan, Chupp, Cropper, & Muller, 2018). Fuels, other than coal, are mainly used to heat the boiler instead of generating steam for electricity generation in a coal-burning power plant.
10. According to the US EIA, natural gas became the largest source (38%) for US electricity generation in 2021. Coal is the second largest energy source for electricity generation (22%).
11. The ARP was introduced by the EPA in 1995 as the first national cap-and-trade program, which is designed to reduce the overall level of air pollution, such as sulfur dioxide (SO_2) and nitrogen oxide (NO_x). As a market-based pollution control approach, the ARP allows power plants to purchase and sell emission permits based on their needs and costs.
12. Scrubber is also called FGD, which is a technology used to remove end-of-pipe SO_2 emission.
13. Alternatively, technical efficiency can be defined to be $E[\exp(U_{it}) \mid W_{it}]$, in which case our equation (9) is only a lower bound by Jensen's inequality.

APPENDIX

Lemma 1. Recall that $K_{jit} \equiv K(\frac{Z_{jit}-z_{j0}}{h})$, $K_{ji.} \equiv \sum_{t=1}^{T} K_{jit}$. Under Assumptions *A1*, *C1*(1), *C2*(2), and *C4*(1), we have $\sup_{z_{j0}\in G_j}[\sum_{i=1}^{n} K_{ji.}^{-1}]^{-1} = O_p(n^{-1}h)$.

Proof. For the convex function $\varphi(x)=\frac{1}{x}$ with $x>0$, by Jensen's inequality, we have

$$\varphi(\frac{1}{n}\sum_{i=1}^{n} x_i) \le \frac{1}{n}\sum_{i=1}^{n}\varphi(x_i).$$

Then $[\frac{1}{n}\sum_{i=1}^{n} K_{ji.}^{-1}]^{-1} \le \frac{1}{n}\sum_{i=1}^{n} K_{ji.}$.

So we have $\sup_{z_{j0}\in G_j}[\sum_{i=1}^{n} K_{ji.}^{-1}]^{-1} \le \frac{1}{n}\sup_{z_{j0}\in G_j}\frac{1}{n}\sum_{i=1}^{n} K_{ji.}$

$\le \frac{1}{n}\sup_{z_{j0}\in G_j}\frac{1}{n}\sum_{i=1}^{n} EK_{ji.} + \frac{1}{n}\sup_{z_{j0}\in G_j}|\frac{1}{n}\sum_{i=1}^{n}(K_{ji.}-EK_{ji.})|$ By Lemma 1 in Martins-Filho et al. (2018), $\sup_{z_{j0}\in G_j}|\frac{1}{nh}\sum_{i=1}^{n}(K_{ji.}-EK_{ji.})| \le \sum_{t=1}^{T}\sup_{z_{j0}\in G_j}|\frac{1}{nh}\sum_{i=1}^{n} K_{jit} - \frac{1}{nh}\sum_{i=1}^{n} EK_{jit}| = O_p((\frac{\log(n)}{nh})^{\frac{1}{2}})$. With *A1*, $\frac{1}{nh}\sum_{i=1}^{n} EK_{ji.} = \frac{1}{h}E\sum_{t=1}^{T} K_{jit} = \sum_{t=1}^{T}\int K(\psi) f_{z_{jt}}(z_{j0}+h\psi)d\psi = \sum_{t=1}^{T} f_{z_{jt}}(z_{j0}) + O(h^2)$, which is uniformly bounded under Assumption *C1*(1). So we have the claim that $\sup_{z_{j0}\in G_j}[\sum_{i=1}^{n} K_{ji.}^{-1}]^{-1} = O_p(n^{-1}h(\frac{\log(n)}{nh})^{\frac{1}{2}}) + O_p(n^{-1}h) = O_p(n^{-1}h)$.

Proof of. Theorem 1.

(i) Since $\chi\lambda = \{\{\chi_{it}'\lambda\}_{t=1}^{T}\}_{i=1}^{n} = \{\{\sum_{j=1}^{d} X_{jit}'(I_{r_j}\otimes\Phi_{L_n}(Z_{jit}))'\lambda_j)\}_{t=1}^{T}\}_{i=1}^{n}$, we define $X'\beta = \{\{\sum_{j=1}^{d} X_{jit}'\beta_j(Z_{jit})\}_{t=1}^{T}\}_{i=1}^{n}$, $Y = D_0\alpha + X'\beta + \epsilon$, with $D_0\alpha = (I_n\otimes e_T)\begin{bmatrix}\alpha_1\\ \vdots\\ \alpha_n\end{bmatrix}$, we have

$$\begin{aligned}
\hat{\lambda}-\lambda &= (\chi' M_D\chi)^{-1}\chi' M_D(Y-\chi\lambda)\\
&= (\frac{1}{n}\chi' M_D\chi)^{-1}\frac{1}{n}\chi' M_D(D_0\alpha + X'\beta - \chi\lambda + \epsilon)\\
&= \Sigma_{\Phi\Phi}^{-1}\frac{1}{n}\chi' M_D(D_0\alpha + X'\beta - \chi\lambda + \epsilon) + [\Sigma_{n,\Phi\Phi}^{-1} - \Sigma_{\Phi\Phi}^{-1}]\frac{1}{n}\chi' M_D\\
&\quad (D_0\alpha + X'\beta - \chi\lambda + \epsilon),
\end{aligned}$$

where $\Sigma_{n,\Phi\Phi} = \frac{1}{n}\chi' M_D \chi$. We show below that

(1) $\| \Sigma_{n,\Phi\Phi}^{-1} - \Sigma_{\Phi\Phi}^{-1} \|_{sp} = O_p(\frac{L_n}{\sqrt{n}})$.

(2) $\| \frac{1}{n}\chi' M_D \epsilon \|^2 = O_p(\frac{L_n}{n})$.

(3) $\| \frac{1}{n}\chi' M_D (X'\beta - \chi\lambda) \|_{sp}^2 = O_p(L_n^{-2\xi})$.

(4) $\| \frac{1}{n}\chi' M_D D_0 \alpha \| = O_p(n^{-\frac{1}{2}})$.

With Assumption *B2*, because $\|\cdot\|_{sp} \le \|\cdot\|$ and $\| \Sigma_{\Phi\Phi}^{-1} \|_{sp} < C$ as shown in (1) below:

$$
\begin{aligned}
&\| \hat{\lambda} - \lambda \| = \| \hat{\lambda} - \lambda \|_{sp} \\
\le\ & \| \Sigma_{\Phi\Phi}^{-1} \|_{sp} \left[\| \frac{1}{n}\chi' M_D D_0 \alpha \|_{sp} + \| \frac{1}{n}\chi' M_D (X'\beta - \chi\lambda) \|_{sp} + \| \frac{1}{n}\chi' M_D \epsilon \|_{sp} \right] \\
& + \| \Sigma_{n,\Phi\Phi}^{-1} - \Sigma_{\Phi\Phi}^{-1} \|_{sp} \left[\| \frac{1}{n}\chi' M_D D_0 \alpha \|_{sp} + \| \frac{1}{n}\chi' M_D (X'\beta - \chi\lambda) \|_{sp} + \| \frac{1}{n}\chi' M_D \epsilon \|_{sp} \right]
\end{aligned}
$$

we obtain the claimed result in (i) from (1)–(4) above.

(1) With $D_M = [-e_{n-1}, I_{n-1}]' \otimes e_T$, we obtain

$D_M{}' D_M = T(I_{n-1} + e_{n-1} e_{n-1}{}'), (D_M{}' D_M)^{-1} = \frac{1}{T}(I_{n-1} - \frac{1}{n} e_{n-1} e_{n-1}{}')$ and

$$
\begin{aligned}
D_M (D_{M'} D_M)^{-1} D_{M'} &= [(-e_{n-1}, I_{n-1})' \otimes e_T] \frac{1}{T}(I_{n-1} - \frac{1}{n} e_{n-1} e_{n-1'})[(-e_{n-1}, I_{n-1}) \otimes e_{T'}] \\
&= \frac{1}{T} Q_n \otimes (e_T e_{T'}),
\end{aligned}
$$

where Q_n is an $n \times n$ matrix, with its ith diagonal element being $Q_{ni,i} = 1 - \frac{1}{n}$ and its (*i*, *j*)-th element being $Q_{ni,j} = -\frac{1}{n}$ for $i \neq j$. So with $M_D = I_{nT} - D_M (D_{M'} D_M)^{-1} D_M' = I_{nT} - \frac{1}{T} Q_n \otimes (e_T e_T')$, we have

$$
\Sigma_{n,\Phi\Phi} = \frac{1}{n}\chi' M_D \chi = \frac{1}{n}\chi'\chi - \frac{1}{nT}\chi'[Q_n \otimes (e_T e_T')]\chi
$$

$$
\begin{aligned}
\frac{1}{n}\chi'\chi &= \frac{1}{n}\sum_{i=1}^{n}\sum_{t=1}^{T}\chi_{it}\chi_{it}' = \frac{1}{n}\sum_{i=1}^{n}\sum_{t=1}^{T}[[\chi_{jit}\chi_{lit}]_{j=1}^{d}]_{l=1}^{d} = \frac{1}{n}\sum_{i=1}^{n}\sum_{t=1}^{T}[[(X_{jit} \otimes \Phi_{L_n}(Z_{jit})) \\
&\quad (X_{lit}' \otimes \Phi_{L_n}'(Z_{lit}))]_{j=1}^{d}]_{l=1}^{d}.
\end{aligned}
$$

So $E\frac{1}{n}\chi'\chi = E\sum_{t=1}^{T}[[(X_{jit} \otimes \Phi_{L_n}(Z_{jit}))(X_{lit}' \otimes \Phi_{L_n}'(Z_{lit}))]_{j=1}^{d}]_{l=1}^{d}$. With $\chi_i = \{\chi_{it}'\}_{t=1}^{T}$,

$$\frac{1}{nT}\chi'[Q_n \otimes (e_T e_T')]\chi = \frac{1}{nT}[\chi_1', \cdots, \chi_n'][Q_n \otimes (e_T e_T')]\begin{bmatrix}\chi_1 \\ \vdots \\ \chi_n\end{bmatrix} = \frac{1}{nT}\sum_{i=1}^{n}\sum_{j=1}^{n} Q_{ni,j}\chi_i' e_T e_T' \chi_j$$

$$= \frac{1}{nT}\sum_{i=1}^{n}\sum_{j=1}^{n} Q_{ni,j}[[(\sum_{t=1}^{T} X_{lit} \otimes \Phi_{L_n}(Z_{lit}))(\sum_{t=1}^{T} X'_{mjt} \otimes \Phi_{L_n}(Z_{mjt})')]_{l=1}^{d}]_{m=1}^{d}$$

$$= \frac{1}{nT}\sum_{i=1}^{n} Q_{ni,i}[[(\sum_{t=1}^{T} X_{lit} \otimes \Phi_{L_n}(Z_{lit}))(\sum_{t=1}^{T} X'_{mit} \otimes \Phi_{L_n}(Z_{mit})')]_{l=1}^{d}]_{m=1}^{d}$$

$$+ \frac{1}{nT}\sum_{i=1}^{n}\sum_{\substack{j=1 \\ i\neq j}}^{n} Q_{ni,j}[[(\sum_{t=1}^{T} X_{lit} \otimes \Phi_{L_n}(Z_{lit}))(\sum_{t=1}^{T} X'_{mjt} \otimes \Phi_{L_n}(Z_{mjt})')]_{l=1}^{d}]_{m=1}^{d}$$

$$= I_{1n} + I_{2n}.$$

$$EI_{1n} = (1-\frac{1}{n})\frac{1}{T}E[[(\sum_{t=1}^{T} X_{lit} \otimes \Phi_{L_n}(Z_{lit}))(\sum_{t=1}^{T} X'_{mit} \otimes \Phi_{L_n}(Z_{mit})')]_{l=1}^{d}]_{m=1}^{d}$$

$$= \frac{1}{T}E[[(\sum_{t=1}^{T} X_{lit} \otimes \Phi_{L_n}(Z_{lit}))(\sum_{t=1}^{T} X'_{mit} \otimes \Phi_{L_n}(Z_{mit})')]_{l=1}^{d}]_{m=1}^{d} + O(\frac{L_n}{n}), \text{ since}$$

$$\| E[[(\sum_{t=1}^{T} X_{lit} \otimes \Phi_{L_n}(Z_{lit}))(\sum_{t=1}^{T} X'_{mit} \otimes \Phi_{L_n}(Z_{mit})')]_{l=1}^{d}]_{m=1}^{d} \|^2$$

$$= \sum_{l=1}^{d}\sum_{q=1}^{r_l}\sum_{p=1}^{L_n}\sum_{m=1}^{d}\sum_{q'=1}^{r_m}\sum_{p'=1}^{L_n} E[(\sum_{t=1}^{T} X_{lit,q}\phi_p(Z_{lit}))(\sum_{t=1}^{T} X_{mit,q'}\phi_{p'}(Z_{mit}))]^2$$

$$\leq C\sum_{t=1}^{T}\sum_{\tau=1}^{T}\sum_{l=1}^{d}\sum_{q=1}^{r_l}\sum_{p=1}^{L_n}\sum_{m=1}^{d}\sum_{q'=1}^{r_m}\sum_{p'=1}^{L_n} [EX_{lit,q}\phi_p(Z_{lit})X_{mit,q'}\phi_{p'}(Z_{mit})]^2$$

$= O(L_n^2)$ by $c-r$ inequality, assumption $A2$ and $B1(3)$.

$$EI_{2n} = -\frac{n(n-1)}{n^2}\frac{1}{T}E[[(\sum_{t=1}^{T} X_{lit} \otimes \Phi_{L_n}(Z_{lit}))(\sum_{t=1}^{T} X'_{mjt} \otimes \Phi_{L_n}(Z_{mjt})')]_{l=1}^{d}]_{m=1}^{d}$$

$$= -\frac{1}{T}E[[(\sum_{t=1}^{T} X_{lit} \otimes \Phi_{L_n}(Z_{lit}))(\sum_{t=1}^{T} X'_{mjt} \otimes \Phi_{L_n}(Z_{mjt})')]_{l=1}^{d}]_{m=1}^{d} + O\left(\frac{L_n}{n}\right), \text{ since}$$

$$\| E[[(\sum_{t=1}^{T} X_{lit} \otimes \Phi_{L_n}(Z_{lit}))(\sum_{t=1}^{T} X'_{mjt} \otimes \Phi_{L_n}(Z_{mjt})')]_{l=1}^{d}]_{m=1}^{d} \|^2 = O(L_n^2)$$

for similar reasons.

So we obtain $E\Sigma_{n,\Phi\Phi} = \Sigma_{\Phi\Phi} + O\left(\frac{L_n}{n}\right)$, since $\| E\Sigma_{n,\Phi\Phi} - \Sigma_{\Phi\Phi} \|^2 = O\left(\frac{L_n^2}{n^2}\right)$.

We show that $\| \Sigma_{n,\Phi\Phi} - E\Sigma_{n,\Phi\Phi} \|^2 = O_p\left(\frac{L_n^2}{n}\right)$. To this end, we show that $E\| \Sigma_{n,\Phi\Phi} - E\Sigma_{n,\Phi\Phi} \|^2 = O\left(\frac{L_n^2}{n}\right)$. Recall that for a symmetric matrix $A_{n\times n}$ with *(i, j)-th* element being A_{ij}, $\| A \|^2 = \sum_{i=1}^{n}\sum_{j=1}^{n} A_{ij}^2$. Then

$$
\begin{aligned}
E\|\Sigma_{n,\Phi\Phi}-E\Sigma_{n,\Phi\Phi}\|^2 &= E\|\frac{1}{n}\chi'\chi-\frac{1}{nT}\chi'Q_n\otimes e_Te_T'\chi-E\frac{1}{n}\chi'\chi+ \\
&\quad E\frac{1}{nT}\chi'Q_n\otimes e_Te_T'\chi\|^2 \\
&= E\sum_{j=1}^{d}\sum_{q=1}^{r_j}\sum_{p=1}^{L_n}\sum_{l=1}^{d}\sum_{q'=1}^{r_l}\sum_{p'=1}^{L_n}[\frac{1}{n}\sum_{i=1}^{n}\sum_{t=1}^{T}X_{jit,q}\phi_p(Z_{jit})X_{lit,q'}\phi_{p'}(Z_{lit})- \\
&\quad E\frac{1}{n}\sum_{i=1}^{n}\sum_{t=1}^{T}X_{jit,q}\phi_p(Z_{jit})X_{lit,q'}\phi_{p'}(Z_{lit}) \\
&\quad -\frac{1}{nT}\sum_{i=1}^{n}\sum_{m=1}^{n}Q_{ni,m}\sum_{t=1}^{T}X_{jit,q}\phi_p(Z_{jit})\sum_{t=1}^{T}X_{lmt,q'}\phi_{p'}(Z_{lmt}) \\
&\quad +E\frac{1}{nT}\sum_{i=1}^{n}\sum_{m=1}^{n}Q_{ni,m}\sum_{t=1}^{T}X_{jit,q}\phi_p(Z_{jit})\sum_{t=1}^{T}X_{lmt,q'}\phi_{p'}(Z_{lmt})]^2 \\
&\le C\sum_{j=1}^{d}\sum_{q=1}^{r_j}\sum_{p=1}^{L_n}\sum_{l=1}^{d}\sum_{q'=1}^{r_l}\sum_{p'=1}^{L_n}\{\frac{1}{n}V(\sum_{t=1}^{T}X_{jit,q}\phi_p(Z_{jit})X_{lit,q'}\phi_{p'}(Z_{lit})) \\
&\quad +\frac{1}{n^2T^2}V(\sum_{i=1}^{n}\sum_{m=1}^{n}Q_{ni,m}\sum_{t=1}^{T}X_{jit,q}\phi_p(Z_{jit})\sum_{t=1}^{T}X_{lmt,q'}\phi_{p'}(Z_{lmt}))\} \\
&= I_3+I_4.
\end{aligned}
$$

The last inequality is obtained by applying $c-r$ inequality and using *A1*. Since T is fixed, we apply $c-r$ inequality again with Assumption *B1*(3):

$$
I_3 \le C\frac{1}{n}\sum_{t=1}^{T}\sum_{j=1}^{d}\sum_{q=1}^{r_j}\sum_{p=1}^{L_n}\sum_{l=1}^{d}\sum_{q'=1}^{r_l}\sum_{p'=1}^{L_n}E(X_{jit,q}^2\phi_p^2(Z_{jit})X_{lit,q'}^2\phi_{p'}^2(Z_{lit}))
$$

$\le \quad \frac{C}{n}\sum_{t=1}^{T}\sum_{j=1}^{d}\sum_{q=1}^{r_j}\sum_{p=1}^{L_n}\sum_{l=1}^{d}\sum_{q'=1}^{r_l}\sum_{p'=1}^{L_n}EX_{jit,q}^2X_{lit,q'}^2=O(\frac{L_n^2}{n}),$ Where we apply *A2* in the last equality

For $i=m$, $Q_{ni,i}=1-\frac{1}{n}$. With $|\phi_p(Z_{jit})|<C$ in *B1*(3), and T finite,

$$
\begin{aligned}
I_4 &= C\sum_{j=1}^{d}\sum_{q=1}^{r_j}\sum_{p=1}^{L_n}\sum_{l=1}^{d}\sum_{q'=1}^{r_l}\sum_{p'=1}^{L_n}\frac{1}{n^2T^2}V(\sum_{i=1}^{n}(1-\frac{1}{n})(\sum_{t=1}^{T}X_{jit,q}\phi_p(Z_{jit}))(\sum_{t=1}^{T}X_{lit,q'}\phi_{p'}(Z_{lit}))) \\
&\le C\sum_{j=1}^{d}\sum_{q=1}^{r_j}\sum_{p=1}^{L_n}\sum_{l=1}^{d}\sum_{q'=1}^{r_l}\sum_{p'=1}^{L_n}\frac{n}{n^2T^2}(1-\frac{1}{n})^2E[(\sum_{t=1}^{T}X_{jit,q}\phi_p(Z_{jit}))(\sum_{t=1}^{T}X_{lit,q'}\phi_{p'}(Z_{lit}))]^2 \\
&\le \frac{C}{nT^2}\sum_{t=1}^{T}\sum_{\tau=1}^{T}\sum_{j=1}^{d}\sum_{q=1}^{r_j}\sum_{p=1}^{L_n}\sum_{l=1}^{d}\sum_{q'=1}^{r_l}\sum_{p'=1}^{L_n}EX_{jit,q}^2X_{li\tau,q'}^2=O\left(\frac{L_n^2}{n}\right).
\end{aligned}
$$

For $i\neq m$, $Q_{ni,m}=-\frac{1}{n}$.

$$I_4 = C\sum_{j=1}^{d}\sum_{q=1}^{r_j}\sum_{p=1}^{L_n}\sum_{l=1}^{d}\sum_{q'=1}^{r_l}\sum_{p'=1}^{L_n}\frac{1}{n^4T^2}V(\sum_{i=1}^{n}\sum_{t=1}^{T}X_{jit,q}\phi_p(Z_{jit})$$
$$\sum_{m=1}^{n}\sum_{\tau=1}^{T}X_{lm\tau,q'}\phi_{p'}(Z_{lm\tau}))$$
$$= C\sum_{j=1}^{d}\sum_{q=1}^{r_j}\sum_{p=1}^{L_n}\sum_{l=1}^{d}\sum_{q'=1}^{r_l}\sum_{p'=1}^{L_n}\frac{1}{n^4T^2}[\sum_{i=1}^{n}\sum_{m=1}^{n}V(\sum_{t=1}^{T}X_{jit,q}\phi_p$$
$$(Z_{jit})\sum_{\tau=1}^{T}X_{lm\tau,q'}\phi_{p'}(Z_{lm\tau}))]$$
$$+C\sum_{i=1}^{n}\sum_{m=1}^{n}\sum_{i'=1}^{n}\sum_{m'=1}^{n}cov(\sum_{t=1}^{T}X_{jit,q}\phi_p(Z_{jit})\sum_{\tau=1}^{T}X_{lm\tau,q'}\phi_{p'}(Z_{lm\tau}),$$
$$\sum_{t=1}^{T}X_{ji't,q}\phi_p(Z_{ji't})\sum_{\tau=1}^{T}X_{lm'\tau,q'}\phi_{p'}(Z_{lm'\tau}))]$$
$$= I_{41} + I_{42}.$$

$$I_{41} \leq \begin{array}{l} C\sum_{j=1}^{d}\sum_{q=1}^{r_j}\sum_{p=1}^{L_n}\sum_{l=1}^{d}\sum_{q'=1}^{r_l}\sum_{p'=1}^{L_n}\frac{1}{n^4T^2}\sum_{i=1}^{n}\sum_{m=1}^{n}E(\sum_{t=1}^{T}X_{jit,q}\phi_p(Z_{jit}) \\ \sum_{\tau=1}^{T}X_{lm\tau,q'}\phi_{p'}(Z_{lm\tau}))^2 = O(\frac{L_n^2}{n^2}) = o(\frac{L_n^2}{n}), \end{array}$$

with T fixed and *B1*(3) and *A2*. $I_{42} = 0$ when both indexes (i, m) are different from (i', m'). Consider one of the indices in (i, m) and (i', m') to be equal, that is, $i = m'$, since $cov(X,Y) \leq [V(X)V(Y)]^{\frac{1}{2}}$,

$$I_{42} = C\sum_{j=1}^{d}\sum_{q=1}^{r_j}\sum_{p=1}^{L_n}\sum_{l=1}^{d}\sum_{q'=1}^{r_l}\sum_{p'=1}^{L_n}\frac{1}{n^4T^2}\sum_{i=1}^{n}\sum_{m=1}^{n}\sum_{i'=1}^{n}$$
$$cov\left(\sum_{t=1}^{T}X_{jit,q}\phi_p(Z_{jit})\sum_{\tau=1}^{T}X_{lm\tau,q'}\phi_{p'}(Z_{lm\tau})\right),$$
$$\sum_{t=1}^{T}X_{ji't,q}\phi_p(Z_{ji't})\sum_{\tau=1}^{T}X_{li\tau,q'}\phi_{p'}(Z_{li\tau}))$$

$$I_{42} \leq \frac{C}{n^4T^2}\sum_{j=1}^{d}\sum_{q=1}^{r_j}\sum_{p=1}^{L_n}\sum_{l=1}^{d}\sum_{q'=1}^{r_l}\sum_{p'=1}^{L_n}\sum_{i=1}^{n}\sum_{m=1}^{n}\sum_{i'=1}^{n}[V(\sum_{t=1}^{T}X_{jit,q}\phi_p(Z_{jit})\sum_{\tau=1}^{T}X_{lm\tau,q'}\phi_{p'}(Z_{lm\tau}))$$
$$\times V(\sum_{t=1}^{T}X_{ji't,q}\phi_p(Z_{ji't})\sum_{\tau=1}^{T}X_{li\tau,q'}\phi_{p'}(Z_{li\tau}))]^{\frac{1}{2}}$$
$$= O\left(\frac{L_n^2}{n}\right) \text{ for similar reasons.}$$

With similar arguments we show that the other terms in $I_{42} = O\left(\frac{L_n^2}{n}\right)$. So $T_{42} = O\left(\frac{L_n^2}{n}\right)$ and $I_4 = O\left(\frac{L_n^2}{n}\right)$. Combining I_3 and I_4, we obtain that $E\|\Sigma_{n,\Phi\Phi} - E\Sigma_{n,\Phi\Phi}\|^2 = O\left(\frac{L_n^2}{n}\right)$. Given that $\|E\Sigma_{n,\Phi\Phi} - \Sigma_{\Phi\Phi}\|^2 = O\left(\frac{L_n^2}{n^2}\right)$, we obtain $E\|\Sigma_{n,\Phi\Phi} - \Sigma_{\Phi\Phi}\|^2 = O\left(\frac{L_n^2}{n}\right)$. Thus, $\|\Sigma_{n,\Phi\Phi} - \Sigma_{\Phi\Phi}\| = O_p\left(\frac{L_n}{\sqrt{n}}\right)$.

Note that $\|\cdot\|_{sp} \leq \|\cdot\|$ and we obtain that $\|\Sigma_{n,\Phi\Phi} - \Sigma_{\Phi\Phi}\|_{sp} = O_p\left(\frac{L_n}{\sqrt{n}}\right)$ from above. By the sub-multiplicative property of the spectral norm, $\|\Sigma_{n,\Phi\Phi}^{-1} - \Sigma_{\Phi\Phi}^{-1}\|_{sp} = \|\Sigma_{n,\Phi\Phi}^{-1}(\Sigma_{\Phi\Phi} - \Sigma_{n,\Phi\Phi})\Sigma_{\Phi\Phi}^{-1}\|_{sp} \leq \|\Sigma_{n,\Phi\Phi}^{-1}\|_{sp}\|\Sigma_{\Phi\Phi} - \Sigma_{n,\Phi\Phi}\|_{sp}\|\Sigma_{\Phi\Phi}^{-1}\|_{sp}$. Note that for any symmetric invertible matrix A, $\|A^{-1}\|_{sp} = [\lambda_{max}((A^{-1})'A^{-1})]^{\frac{1}{2}} = [\lambda_{max}((A'A)^{-1})]^{\frac{1}{2}} = [(\lambda_{min}(A'A))^{-1}]^{\frac{1}{2}} = (\lambda_{min}(A'A))^{-\frac{1}{2}}$. Because $\Sigma_{\Phi\Phi}$ is symmetric and invertible by *B2*, we have $\|\Sigma_{\Phi\Phi}^{-1}\|_{sp} = [\lambda_{min}(\Sigma_{\Phi\Phi}'\Sigma_{\Phi\Phi})]^{-\frac{1}{2}} = [\lambda_{min}(\Sigma_{\Phi\Phi}^2)]^{-\frac{1}{2}} = [\lambda_{min}(\Sigma_{\Phi\Phi})]^{-1} \leq \frac{1}{\underline{c}}$ By *B2*. $\|\Sigma_{n,\Phi\Phi}^{-1}\|_{sp} = [\lambda_{min}(\Sigma_{n,\Phi\Phi})]^{-1} - [\lambda_{min}(\Sigma_{\Phi\Phi})]^{-1} + [\lambda_{min}(\Sigma_{\Phi\Phi})]^{-1}$, and $[\lambda_{min}(\Sigma_{n\Phi\Phi})]^{-1} - [\lambda_{min}(\Sigma_{\Phi\Phi})]^{-1} = \frac{\lambda_{min}(\Sigma_{\Phi\Phi}) - \lambda_{min}(\Sigma_{n,\Phi\Phi})}{\lambda_{min}(\Sigma_{n,\Phi\Phi})\lambda_{min}(\Sigma_{\Phi\Phi})}$.

By Weyl's Theorem (page 117 of Seber, 2008)), $\lambda_{min}(B) \leq \lambda_{min}(A+B) - \lambda_{min}(A) \leq \lambda_{max}(B)$. So $\lambda_{min}(\Sigma_{\Phi\Phi} - \Sigma_{n,\Phi\Phi}) \leq \lambda_{min}(\Sigma_{\Phi\Phi}) - \lambda_{min}(\Sigma_{n,\Phi\Phi}) \leq \lambda_{max}(\Sigma_{\Phi\Phi} - \Sigma_{n,\Phi\Phi})$. Then by Theorem 5.6.9 in Horn and Johnson (2013), $|\lambda_{min}(\Sigma_{\Phi\Phi} - \Sigma_{n,\Phi\Phi})| \leq \|\Sigma_{\Phi\Phi} - \Sigma_{n,\Phi\Phi}\|_{sp}$, and $|\lambda_{max}(\Sigma_{\Phi\Phi} - \Sigma_{n,\Phi\Phi})| \leq \|\Sigma_{\Phi\Phi} - \Sigma_{n,\Phi\Phi}\|_{sp}$, so we obtain $\lambda_{min}(\Sigma_{\Phi\Phi}) - \lambda_{min}(\Sigma_{n,\Phi\Phi}) = o_p(1)$. Furthermore, $\lambda_{min}(\Sigma_{n,\Phi\Phi}) = \lambda_{min}(\Sigma_{\Phi\Phi}) + \lambda_{min}(\Sigma_{n,\Phi\Phi}) - \lambda_{min}(\Sigma_{\Phi\Phi}) = \lambda_{min}(\Sigma_{\Phi\Phi}) + o_p(1)$, so $[\lambda_{min}(\Sigma_{n,\Phi\Phi})]^{-1} - [\lambda_{min}(\Sigma_{\Phi\Phi})]^{-1} = o_p(1)$ and $\|\Sigma_{\Phi\Phi}^{-1}\|_{sp} = [\lambda_{min}(\Sigma_{\Phi\Phi})]^{-1} + o_p(1)$. So in all, $|\Sigma_{n,\Phi\Phi}^{-1} - \Sigma_{\Phi\Phi}^{-1}\|_{sp} \leq \frac{1}{\underline{c}}([\lambda_{min}(\Sigma_{\Phi\Phi})]^{-1} + o_p(1))\, O_p\left(\frac{L_n}{\sqrt{n}}\right) = O_p\left(\frac{L_n}{\sqrt{n}}\right)$.

(2) By Assumption *A3*(1) and the fact that MD is idempotent,

$$E\left\|\frac{1}{n}\chi' M_D\epsilon\right\|^2 = \frac{1}{n^2}Etr(\chi' M_D\epsilon\epsilon' M_D\chi) = \frac{\sigma_\epsilon^2}{n^2}Etr(\chi' M_D\chi) =$$

$$\frac{\sigma_\epsilon^2}{n^2}Etr\left[\chi'\chi - \frac{1}{T}\chi' Q_n \otimes e_T e_{T'}\chi\right] = \frac{\sigma_\epsilon^2}{n^2}\left[n\sum_{j=1}^{d}\sum_{q=1}^{r_j}\sum_{p=1}^{L_n}E\sum_{t=1}^{T}X_{jit,q}^2\phi_p^2\right.$$

$$(Z_{jit}) - n\left(1-\frac{1}{n}\right)T\sum_{j=1}^{d}\sum_{q=1}^{r_j}\sum_{p=1}^{L_n}E\left(\sum_{t=1}^{T}X_{jit,q}\phi_p(Z_{jit})\right)\left(\sum_{t=1}^{T}X_{jit,q}\phi_p(Z_{jit})\right)$$

$$\left.+n\frac{n(n-1)}{n^2}\frac{1}{T}\sum_{j=1}^{d}\sum_{q=1}^{r_j}\sum_{p=1}^{L_n}E\left(\sum_{t=1}^{T}X_{jit,q}\phi_p(Z_{jit})\right)\left(\sum_{t=1}^{T}X_{jmt,q}\phi_p(Z_{jmt})\right)\right] = O\left(\frac{L_n}{n}\right).$$

So by Markov's inequality, we obtain $\| \frac{1}{n}\chi' M_D \epsilon \|^2 = O_p\left(\frac{L_n}{n}\right)$.

(3) Note that for a matrix A, $\lambda_i(A)$ the *i-th* largest eigenvalue, x be an eigenvector, then $Ax = \lambda_i(A)x$, and $x'Ax = \lambda_i(A)\| x \|^2 \leq \lambda_{max}(A)\| x \|^2$. From Exercises on page 342 of Horn and Johnson (2013), when A is a vector, $\| A \|^2 = \| A \|_{sp}^2 = \lambda_{max}(AA') = max_{\|x\|=1} x'AA'x$, and it is also the Euclidean norm. Then

$$\begin{aligned}
\| \frac{1}{n}\chi' M_D(X'\beta - \chi\lambda) \|_{sp}^2 &= \| \frac{1}{n}\chi' M_D(X'\beta - \chi\lambda) \|^2 \\
&= \frac{1}{n^2}(X'\beta - \chi\lambda)' M_D \chi\chi' M_D (X'\beta - \chi\lambda) \text{ and we denote W=X}'\beta\text{-}\chi\lambda \\
&= \frac{\| W \|^2}{n^2} \frac{W'}{\| W \|} M_D \chi\chi' M_D \frac{W}{\| W \|} \leq \frac{\| W \|^2}{n^2} \lambda_{max}(M_D \chi\chi' M_D) \| \frac{W}{\| W \|} \|^2 \\
&= \frac{\| W \|^2}{n^2} \lambda_{max}(M_D \chi\chi' M_D) \\
&= \frac{\| W \|^2}{n} \lambda_{max}\left(\frac{1}{n}\chi' M_D \chi\right) = \frac{\| W \|^2}{n} \lambda_{max}(\Sigma_{n,\Phi\Phi}) \\
&= \frac{\| W \|^2}{n} (\lambda_{max}(\Sigma_{\Phi\Phi}) + O_p\left(\frac{L_n}{\sqrt{n}}\right),
\end{aligned}$$

where we obtain the last equality with the following arguments.

By *B2*, $\lambda_{max}(\Sigma_{\Phi\Phi}) \leq \bar{c} < \infty$.

$\lambda_{max}(\Sigma_{\Phi\Phi}) - \lambda_{max}(\Sigma_{n,\Phi\Phi}) = \lambda_{max}(\Sigma_{n,\Phi\Phi} + \Sigma_{\Phi\Phi} - \Sigma_{n,\Phi\Phi}) - \lambda_{max}(\Sigma_{n,\Phi\Phi})$. By Weyl's Theorem again, $\lambda_{min}(\Sigma_{\Phi\Phi} - \Sigma_{n,\Phi\Phi}) \leq \lambda_{max}(\Sigma_{\Phi\Phi}) - \lambda_{max}(\Sigma_{n,\Phi\Phi}) \leq \lambda_{max}(\Sigma_{\Phi\Phi} - \Sigma_{n,\Phi\Phi})$, and $|\lambda_{min}(\Sigma_{\Phi\Phi} - \Sigma_{n,\Phi\Phi})| \leq \| \Sigma_{\Phi\Phi} - \Sigma_{n,\Phi\Phi} \| = O_p\left(\frac{L_n}{\sqrt{n}}\right)$, $|\lambda_{max}(\Sigma_{\Phi\Phi} - \Sigma_{n,\Phi\Phi})| \leq \| \Sigma_{\Phi\Phi} - \Sigma_{n,\Phi\Phi} \| = O_p\left(\frac{L_n}{\sqrt{n}}\right)$.

Furthermore,

$\| W \|^2 = \| \{\{\sum_{j=1}^{d}\sum_{q=1}^{r_j} X_{jit,q}(\beta_{j,q}(Z_{jit}) - \Phi_{L_n}(Z_{jit})'\lambda_{jq})\}_{i=1}^{n}\}_{t=1}^{T} \|^2$ by *B1*(1) $\leq O(L_n^{-2\xi})$

$\sum_{i=1}^{n}\sum_{t=1}^{T} | \sum_{j=1}^{d}\sum_{q=1}^{r_j} X_{jit,q} |^2 = O_p(nL_n^{-2\xi})$ where the last equality follows from A2

So we obtain $\| \frac{1}{n}\chi' M_D(X'\beta - \chi\lambda) \|_{sp}^2 = O_p(L_n^{-2\xi})((\lambda_{max}(\Sigma_{\Phi\Phi}) + O_p(\frac{L_n}{\sqrt{n}})))$

$= O_p(L_n^{-2\xi})$.

(4) With simple algebra, we obtain $M_D D_0 \alpha = M_D(e_n \otimes e_T)\bar{\alpha} + M_D D_M (\alpha_{-1} - \bar{\alpha} e_{n-1}) = M_D(e_n \otimes e_T)\bar{\alpha}$, where $\bar{\alpha} = \frac{1}{n}\sum_{i=1}^{n}\alpha_i$. Note that if $\sum_{i=1}^{n}\alpha_i = 0$, then $\| \frac{1}{n}\chi' M_D D_0 \alpha \| = 0$. If $\sum_{i=1}^{n}\alpha_i \neq 0$, and *A3*(2) is valid, then

$$\frac{1}{n}\chi' M_D D_0 \alpha = \bar{\alpha}\frac{1}{n}\chi' M_D(e_n \otimes e_T) = O_p(n^{-1/2})\frac{1}{n}\chi' M_D(e_n \otimes e_T).$$

$$\begin{aligned}
\| \frac{1}{n}\chi' M_D(e_n \otimes e_T) \|_{sp}^2 =& \| \frac{1}{n}\chi' M_D(e_n \otimes e_T) \|^2 = \frac{1}{n^2}(e_n \otimes e_T)' M_D \chi\chi' M_D (e_n \otimes e_T) \\
=& \frac{nT}{n^2}\left(\frac{e_n \otimes e_T}{\| e_n \otimes e_T \|}\right)' M_D \chi\chi' M_D \left(\frac{e_n \otimes e_T}{\| e_n \otimes e_T \|}\right)' \\
\le& \frac{T}{n}\lambda_{max}(D_D \chi\chi' M_D) \| \frac{e_n \otimes e_T}{\| e_n \otimes e_T \|} \|^2 = T\lambda_{max}\left(\frac{1}{n}\chi' M_D \chi\right) \\
=& T\lambda_{max}(\Sigma_{n,\Phi\Phi}) = T\lambda_{max}(\Sigma_{\Phi\Phi}) + o_p(1),
\end{aligned}$$

where the last equality is from (3) above. So $\| \frac{1}{n}\chi' M_D D_0 \alpha \| = O_p(n^{-1/2})$.

(ii) It is sufficient to show that $\sup_{z_j \in G_j} | \hat{\beta}_{jl}(z_j) - \beta_{jl}(z_j) | = O_p(\mathcal{S}_{0L_n}(\sqrt{\frac{L_n}{n}} + L_n^{-\xi}))$, for $l = 1, \cdots, r_j$. Since $\hat{\beta}_{jl}(z_j) - \beta_{jl}(z_j) = \Phi_{L_n}(z_j)'(\hat{\lambda}_{jl} - \lambda_{jl}) + \Phi_{L_n}(z_j)'\lambda_{jl} - \beta_{jl}(z_j)$,

and $\sup_{z_j \in G_j} | \Phi_{L_n}(z_j)'\lambda_{jl} - \beta_{jl}(z_j) | = O(L_n^{-\xi})$ by *B1*(1), we use the result in (i) to have

$$\begin{aligned}
\sup_{z_j \in G_j} | \Phi_{L_n}(z_j)'(\hat{\lambda}_{jl} - \lambda_{jl}) | \le& \sup_{z_j \in G_j} \| \Phi_{L_n}(z_j) \| \| \hat{\lambda}_{jl} - \lambda_{jl} \| \\
=& \sup_{z_j \in G_j} \| \Phi_{L_n}(z_j) \| O_p\left(\sqrt{\frac{L_n}{n}} + L_n^{-\xi}\right) \\
=& O_p\left(\mathcal{S}_{0L_n}\left(\sqrt{\frac{L_n}{n}} + L_n^{-\xi}\right)\right),
\end{aligned}$$

where the last equality follows from Assumption *B1*(3). The claim in (ii) follows.

Proof of Theorem 2.

(i) We first investigate the properties of the infeasible estimator defined in (4). By Taylor expansion on $\beta_{jl}(\cdot)$ allowed in Assumption *B1*, with $Z_{jit}^* = \lambda z_{j0} + (1-\lambda)Z_{jit}$ for $\lambda \in (0.1)$, we obtain

$$\begin{aligned}
X_{jit}'\beta_j(Z_{jit}) =& \sum_{l=1}^{r_j} X_{jit,l}\beta_{jl}(Z_{jit}) \\
=& \sum_{l=1}^{r_j}[X_{jit,l}\beta_{jl}(z_{j0}) + X_{jit,l}(Z_{jit} - z_{j0})\beta_{jl}^{(1)}(z_{j0}) \\
&+ X_{jit,l}\frac{1}{2}(Z_{jit} - z_{j0})^2\beta_{jl}^{(2)}(Z_{jit}^*)].
\end{aligned}$$

Let $H=\text{diag}\{I_{r_j}, hI_{r_j}\}$ be a $2r_j \times 2r_j$ diagonal matrix. Then with $\beta_j^{(1)}(z_{j0}) = \left[\frac{d\beta_{j1}(z_{j0})}{dz_{j0}}, \cdots, \frac{d\beta_{jr_j}(z_{j0})}{dz_{j0}}\right]'$, and $\tilde{R}_{jit}{}' = \left[1, \frac{Z_{jit}-z_{j0}}{h}\right]$,

$$
\begin{aligned}
(X'\beta)_j &= \{\{X_{jit}{}'\beta_j(Z_{jit})\}_{t=1}^T\}_{i=1}^n \\
&= \{\{R_{jit}{}' \otimes X_{jit}{}'\}_{t=1}^T\}_{i=1}^n H^{-1} H \begin{bmatrix} \beta_j(z_{j0}) \\ \beta_j^{(1)}(z_{j0}) \end{bmatrix} \\
&+ \{\{\sum_{l=1}^{r_j} X_{jit,l} \frac{1}{2}(Z_{jit}-z_{j0})^2 \beta_{jl}^{(2)}(Z_{jit}^*)\}_{t=1}^T\}_{i=1}^n, \\
&= \{\{\tilde{R}_{jit}{}' \otimes X_{jit}{}'\}_{t=1}^T\}_{i=1}^n \begin{bmatrix} \beta_j(z_{j0}) \\ h\beta_j^{(1)}(z_{j0}) \end{bmatrix} + \pi_j = \tilde{R}_j(z_{j0}) \begin{bmatrix} \beta_j(z_{j0}) \\ h\beta_j^{(1)}(z_{j0}) \end{bmatrix} + \pi_j,
\end{aligned}
$$

where $\tilde{R}_j(Z_{j0}) = [\tilde{R}_{j1}(z_{j0})', \cdots, \tilde{R}_{jn}(z_{j0})']'$, and $\tilde{R}_{ji}(z_{j0}) = [(\tilde{R}_{ji1}{}' \otimes X_{ji1}{}')', \cdots, (\tilde{R}_{jiT}{}' \otimes X_{jiT}{}')']'$. $Y = D_0\alpha + (X'\beta)_{(-j)} + (X'\beta)_j + \epsilon = D_0\alpha + (X'\beta)_{(-j)}$

$+\tilde{R}_j(z_{j0}) \begin{bmatrix} \beta_j(z_{j0}) \\ h\beta_j^{(1)}(z_{j0}) \end{bmatrix} + \pi_j + \epsilon$. Thus, with $e_{\cdot,2r_j} = [e_{1,2r_j}, \cdots, e_{r_j,2r_j}]$,

$$
\begin{aligned}
\tilde{\beta}_j(z_{j0}) &= e'_{\cdot,2r_j}[\tilde{R}_j(z_{j0})'S_h(z_{j0})\tilde{R}_j(z_{j0})]^{-1}\tilde{R}_j(z_{j0})'S_h(z_{j0}) \\
&\quad (Y-(X'\beta)_{(-j)}) \text{ and} \\
\tilde{\beta}_j(z_{j0}) - \beta_j(z_{j0}) &= e'_{\cdot,2r_j}[\tilde{R}_j(z_{j0})'S_h(z_{j0})\tilde{R}_j(z_{j0})]^{-1}\tilde{R}_j(z_{j0})'S_h(z_{j0}) \\
&\quad (D_0\alpha + \pi_j + \epsilon) \\
&= e'_{\cdot,2r_j}[S_n(z_{j0})]^{-1}\tilde{R}_j(z_{j0})'S_h(z_{j0})(D_0\alpha + \pi_j + \epsilon).
\end{aligned}
$$

We show the following results:

(1) $\frac{1}{nh}S_n(z_{j0}) = \Sigma_{j0n}(z_{j0}) + o_p(1)$;

(2) $e'_{\cdot,2r_j}\Sigma_{j0}(z_{j0})^{-1}\frac{1}{nh}\tilde{R}_j(z_{j0})'S_h(z_{j0})\pi_j = B_{n0}(z_{j0}) + o_p(h^2)$

$= h^2 e'_{\cdot,2r_j}\Sigma_{j0}(z_{j0})^{-1}\frac{1}{h}\sum_{t=1}^T EK_{jit}(1-\frac{K_{jit}}{K_{ji\cdot}})(\tilde{R}_{jit} \otimes X_{jit})$

$X'_{jit}\frac{1}{2}(\frac{Z_{jit}-z_{j0}}{h})^2\beta_j^{(2)}(Z_{jit}) + o_p(h^2)$,

where $\beta_j^{(2)}(Z_{jit}) = (\beta_{j1}^{(2)}(Z_{jit})), \cdots, \beta_{jr_j}^{(2)}(Z_{jit}))'$;

(3) $\frac{1}{nh}\tilde{R}_j(z_{j0})'S_h(z_{j0})D_0\alpha = O_p(n^{-\frac{1}{2}})$;

(4) $\sqrt{nh}\frac{1}{nh}\tilde{R}_j(z_{j0})'S_h(z_{j0})\epsilon \xrightarrow{d} N(0,\Omega_j(z_{j0}))$, where $\Omega_j(z_{j0}) = \lim_{n\to\infty}\Omega_{jn}(z_{j0})$ and

$$\Omega_{jn}(z_{j0}) = \frac{1}{h}\sum_{t=1}^{T} EK_{jit}^2(1-\frac{K_{jit}}{K_{ji\cdot}})^2(\tilde{R}_{jit}\otimes X_{jit})(\tilde{R}_{jit}\otimes X_{jit})'\sigma_\epsilon^2.$$

Given (1) and Assumption *C1* (3), we have $\tilde{\beta}_j(z_{j0}) - \beta_j(z_{j0}) = e'_{\cdot,2r_j}\Sigma_{j0}^{-1}(z_{j0})$ $\frac{1}{nh}\tilde{R}_j(z_{j0})'S_h(z_{j0})(D_0\alpha + \pi_j + \epsilon)(1+o_p(1))$; thus, the claimed result in (i) follows from (2)–(4). So we show (1)–(4) below.

$$\begin{aligned} S_n(z_{j0}) &= \tilde{R}_j(z_{j0})'S_h(z_{j0})\tilde{R}_j(z_{j0}) \\ &= \tilde{R}_j(z_{j0})'[I_{nT} - D_M(D_M{}'W_h(z_{j0})D_M)^{-1}D_M'W_h(z_{j0})]'W_h(z_{j0}) \\ &\quad\times [I_{nT} - D_M(D_M{}'W_h(z_{j0})D_M)^{-1}D_M'W_h(z_{j0})]\tilde{R}_j(z_{j0}) \qquad (1)\\ &= \tilde{R}_j(z_{j0})'W_h(z_{j0})\tilde{R}_j(z_{j0}) - \tilde{R}_j(z_{j0})'W_h(z_{j0}) \\ &\quad D_M(D_M'W_h(z_{j0})D_M)^{-1}D_M'W_h(z_{j0})\tilde{R}_j(z_{j0}). \end{aligned}$$

With some algebra, we obtain that $D_M(D_M{}'W_h(z_{j0})D_M)^{-1}D_M = Q\otimes(e_Te_T{}')$, where Q is $n \times n$ symmetric matrix with its (i,i)th element being $q_{ii} = K_{ji.}^{-1} - K_{ji.}^{-2}/\left(\sum_{i=1}^{n}K_{ji.}^{-1}\right)$, and (i,l)th element $q_{il} = -K_{ji.}^{-1}K_{jl.}^{-1}/\left(\sum_{i=1}^{n}K_{ji.}^{-1}\right)$ for $i \neq l$.

Then

$$\begin{aligned} S_n(z_{j0}) &= \sum_{i=1}^{n}\tilde{R}'_{ji}(z_{j0})\text{diag}\{K_{jit}\}_{t=1}^{T}\tilde{R}_{ji}(z_{j0}) - \sum_{i=1}^{n}\sum_{l=1,l\neq i}^{n}q_{il}\tilde{R}_{ji}{}'(z_{j0}) \\ &\quad \text{diag}\{K_{jit}\}_{t=1}^{T}e_Te_T{}'\text{diag}\{K_{jlt}\}_{t=1}^{T}\tilde{R}_{jl}(z_{j0}) \\ &= \sum_{i=1}^{n}\tilde{R}'_{ji}(z_{j0})\text{diag}\{K_{jit}\}_{t=1}^{T}\tilde{R}_{ji}(z_{j0}) \\ &\quad -\sum_{i=1}^{n}q_{ii}\sum_{t=1}^{T}\sum_{\tau=1}^{T}K_{jit}K_{ji\tau}(\tilde{R}_{jit}\tilde{R}'_{ji\tau}\otimes X_{jit}X'_{ji\tau}) \\ &\quad -\sum_{i=1}^{n}\sum_{l=1,l\neq i}^{n}q_{il}\sum_{t=1}^{T}\sum_{\tau=1}^{T}K_{jit}K_{jl\tau}(\tilde{R}_{jit}\tilde{R}'_{jl\tau}\otimes X_{jit}X'_{jl\tau}) \\ &= S_{n1} - S_{n2} - S_{n3}. \end{aligned}$$

$$\frac{1}{nh}S_{n1}=\frac{1}{nh}\sum_{i=1}^{n}\sum_{t=1}^{T}K_{jit}(\tilde{R}_{jit}\tilde{R}_{jit}')\otimes(X_{jit}X_{jit}')=\frac{1}{nh}\sum_{i=1}^{n}\sum_{t=1}^{T}K_{jit}$$
$$\begin{bmatrix} 1 & \frac{Z_{jit}-z_{j0}}{h} \\ \frac{Z_{jit}-z_{j0}}{h} & (\frac{Z_{jit}-z_{j0}}{h})^2 \end{bmatrix}\otimes(X_{jit}X_{jit}')$$

Let $\frac{1}{nh}S_{n1,mll'}=\frac{1}{nh}\sum_{i=1}^{n}\sum_{t=1}^{T}K_{jit}\left(\frac{Z_{jit}-z_{j0}}{h}\right)^m X_{jit,l}X_{jit,l'}$, for $m=0,1,2,$ and $l,l'\in\{1,\cdots,r_j\}$. By Assumptions *A1*, *C1*(1), (2), *C2*(1)–(4), *C3*(1), (2), and *C4*(1), we can apply Lemma 1 in Martins-Filho et al. (2018) to obtain that $\sup_{z_{j0}\in G_j}|\frac{1}{nh}S_{n1,mll'}-E\frac{1}{nh}S_{n1,mll'}|=O_p\left(\left(\frac{\text{Log}(n)}{nh}\right)^{\frac{1}{2}}\right)$. $E\frac{1}{nh}S_{n1,mll'}=\sum_{t=1}^{T}\int K(\psi)\psi^m v_{ll',jt}$ $(z_{j0}+h\psi)f_{z_{jt}}(z_{j0}+h\psi)d\psi$, by *C1*(1), *C2*, and *C3* (1). So $E\frac{1}{nh}S_{n1,0ll'}=$ $\sum_{t=1}^{T}v_{ll',jt}(z_{j0})f_{z_{jt}}(z_{j0})+O(h^2)$, $E\frac{1}{nh}S_{n1,1ll'}=O(h)$, and $E\frac{1}{nh}S_{n1,2ll'}=\sum_{t=1}^{T}v_{ll',jt}(z_{j0})f_{z_{jt}}$ $(z_{j0})\mu_{k,2}+o(1)$. So we obtain that $\frac{1}{nh}S_{n1}=\frac{1}{h}\sum_{t=1}^{T}EK_{jit}(\tilde{R}_{jit}\tilde{R}_{jit}'\otimes X_{jit}X_{jit}')+o_p(1)$.

$$\frac{1}{nh}S_{n2}=\frac{1}{nh}\sum_{i=1}^{n}[\frac{1}{K_{ji.}}-\frac{K_{ji.}^{-2}}{\sum_{i=1}^{n}K_{ji.}^{-1}}]\sum_{t=1}^{T}\sum_{\tau=1}^{T}K_{jit}K_{ji\tau}(\tilde{R}_{jit}\tilde{R}_{ji\tau}'\otimes X_{jit}X_{ji\tau}')$$
$$=\frac{1}{nh}[S_{n21}-S_{n22}].$$

With Lemma 1, we obtain that $\frac{1}{\sum_{i=1}^{n}K_{ji.}^{-1}}=O_p(n^{-1}h)$ uniformly in $z_{j0}\in G_j$.

Together with the assumption that $K_{ji.}>C>0$, we have

$$\begin{aligned}\frac{1}{nh}S_{n22}\leq\ & O_p(n^{-1}h)\frac{1}{nh}\sum_{i=1}^{n}|\sum_{t=1}^{T}\sum_{\tau=1}^{T}\frac{K_{jit}}{K_{ji.}}\frac{K_{ji\tau}}{K_{ji.}}(\tilde{R}_{jit}\tilde{R}'_{ji\tau}{}'\otimes X_{jit}X'_{ji\tau})| \\ \leq\ & O_p(n^{-1}h)\frac{1}{nh}\sum_{i=1}^{n}\sum_{t=1}^{T}\sum_{\tau=1}^{T}|K_{jit}K_{ji\tau}(\tilde{R}_{jit}\tilde{R}'_{ji\tau}\otimes X_{jit}X'_{ji\tau})|.\end{aligned}$$

With assumption *C2*(1) that $|K(\phi)\phi^j|\leq C$ for $j=0,1,2,3$ and *C3*, $E|X_{jit,l}X_{ji\tau,l'}|\leq[E|X_{jit,l}|^2\,E|X_{ji\tau,l'}|^2]^{\frac{1}{2}}<C$, we obtain that $\frac{1}{nh}S_{n22}=$ $O_p(n^{-1}h)O_p(h^{-1})=O_p(n^{-1})$.

Consider S_{n21} for $t \neq \tau$. By assumption *C2*(5), we denote a typical element in S_{n21} by $S_{n21,mll'}$. Then

$$\frac{1}{nh} S_{n21,mll'} = \frac{1}{nh} \sum_{i=1}^{n} \sum_{\substack{t=1 \\ t \neq \tau}}^{T} \sum_{\tau=1}^{T} \frac{K_{jit} K_{ji\tau}}{K_{ji.}} \left(\frac{Z_{jit} - z_{j0}}{h}\right)^m X_{jit,l} X_{ji\tau,l'}$$
$$\leq C \frac{1}{nh} \sum_{i=1}^{n} \sum_{\substack{t=1 \\ t \neq \tau}}^{T} \sum_{\tau=1}^{T} \left| K_{jit} K_{ji\tau} \left(\frac{Z_{jit} - z_{j0}}{h}\right)^m X_{jit,l} X_{ji\tau,l'} \right|$$
$$= C \frac{1}{nh} S_{n21,b}.$$

Since $t \neq \tau$, with Assumptions *A1, C1*(1), (2), *A2*(1)–(4), and *C3*(2), we apply Lemma 1 in Martins-Filho et al. (2018) to obtain $\sup_{z_{j0} \in G_j} \left| \frac{1}{nh^2} S_{n21,b} - E \frac{1}{nh^2} S_{n21,b} \right| = O_p\left(\left(\frac{\text{Log}(n)}{nh^2}\right)^{\frac{1}{2}}\right)$. Furthermore, it is easy to show that $E \frac{1}{nh^2} S_{n21,b} = O(1)$. Thus, we conclude that $\frac{1}{nh} S_{n21,b} = O_p(h)$ uniformly over $z_{j0} \in G_j$, and thus $\frac{1}{nh} S_{n21} = O_p(h)$ element wise uniformly over $z_{j0} \in G_j$. For $t = \tau$, $\frac{1}{nh} S_{n21} = \frac{1}{nh} \sum_{i=1}^{n} \sum_{t=1}^{T} \frac{K_{jit}^2}{K_{ji.}} (\tilde{R}_{jit} \tilde{R}_{jit}' \otimes X_{jit} X_{jit}')$. Let $\lambda_{jit}(z_{j0}) = \frac{K_{jit}(z_{j0})}{K_{ji.}}$, where we make clear the dependence on z_{j0}, and we note that $|\lambda_{jit}(z_{j0})| \leq C$. With Assumptions *C2*(1)–(4) and triangle inequality, we can show that for $m = 0, 1, 2$, $\left| \lambda_{jit}(z_{j0}) K_{jit}(z_{j0}) \left(\frac{z_{jit} - z_{j0}}{h}\right)^m - \lambda_{jit}(z_{j0}') K_{jit}(z_{j0}') \left(\frac{z_{jit} - z_{j0}'}{h}\right)^m \right| \leq C \frac{1}{h} |z_{j0} - z_{j0}'|$. Again denote a typical element in S_{n21} as $S_{n21,mll'}$, and $\frac{1}{nh} S_{n21,mll'} = \frac{1}{nh} \sum_{i=1}^{n} \sum_{t=1}^{T} \frac{K_{jit}^2}{K_{ji.}} \left(\frac{Z_{jit} - z_{j0}}{h}\right)^m X_{jit,l} X_{jit,l'}$. We similarly obtain that $\sup_{z_{j0} \in G_j} \left| \frac{1}{nh} S_{n21,mll'} - E \frac{1}{nh} S_{n21,mll'} \right| = O_p\left(\left(\frac{\text{Log}(n)}{nh}\right)^{\frac{1}{2}}\right)$. So we have $\frac{1}{nh} S_{n21,mll'} = E \frac{1}{nh} S_{n21,mll'} + o_p(1)$. Thus, we conclude that $\frac{1}{nh} S_{n21} = \frac{1}{h} \sum_{t=1}^{T} E \frac{K_{jit}^2}{K_{ji.}} \tilde{R}_{jit} \tilde{R}'_{jit} \otimes X_{jit} X_{jit'} + o_p(1)$.

Given the result of S_{n22}, we have $\frac{1}{nh} S_{n2} = \frac{1}{h} \sum_{t=1}^{T} E \frac{K_{jit}^2}{K_{ji.}} \tilde{R}_{jit} \tilde{R}_{jit}' \otimes X_{jit} X_{jit'} + o_p(1)$.

$$\frac{1}{nh}S_{n3} = -\frac{1}{\sum_{i=1}^{n} K_{ji.}^{-1}} \frac{1}{nh}\sum_{i=1}^{n}\sum_{l=1,l\neq i}^{n}\sum_{t=1}^{T}\sum_{\tau=1}^{T}\frac{K_{jit}}{K_{ji.}}\frac{K_{jl\tau}}{K_{jl.}}(\tilde{R}_{jit}\tilde{R}'_{jl\tau}\otimes X_{jit}X'_{jl\tau})$$

$$= O_p(n^{-1}h)\frac{1}{nh}\sum_{i=1}^{n}\sum_{l=1,l\neq i}^{n}\sum_{t=1}^{T}\sum_{\tau=1}^{T}\frac{K_{jit}}{K_{ji.}}\frac{K_{jl\tau}}{K_{jl.}}(\tilde{R}_{jit}\tilde{R}'_{jl\tau}\otimes X_{jit}X'_{jl\tau})$$

$$= O_p(n^{-1}h)S_{n31}, \text{ by Lemma 1.}$$

Denote a typical element in S_{n31} by $S_{n31,mm'qq'} = \frac{1}{nh}\sum_{i=1}^{n}\sum_{l=1,l\neq i}^{n}\sum_{t=1}^{T}\sum_{\substack{\tau=1\\ t\neq\tau}}^{T}\frac{K_{jit}}{K_{ji.}}\frac{K_{jl\tau}}{K_{jl.}}(\frac{Z_{jit}-z_{j0}}{h})^{m}(\frac{Z_{jl\tau}-z_{j0}}{h})^{m'}X_{jit,q}X_{jl\tau,q'}$, for $m,m'=0,1$. For $t\neq\tau$, we follow the arguments in S_{n21} to obtain $\frac{1}{nh}\sum_{i=1}^{n}\sum_{t=1}^{T}\frac{K_{jit}}{K_{ji.}}(\frac{Z_{jit}-z_{j0}}{h})^{m}X_{jit,q} = O_p(1)$ uniformly over $z_{j0}\in G_j$. $S_{n31,mm'qq'} = nh\frac{1}{nh}\sum_{i=1}^{n}\sum_{t=1}^{T}\frac{K_{jit}}{K_{ji.}}(\frac{Z_{jit}-z_{j0}}{h})^{m}X_{jit,q}\frac{1}{nh}\sum_{l=1,l\neq i}^{n}\sum_{\tau=1}^{T}\frac{K_{jl\tau}}{K_{jl.}}(\frac{Z_{jl\tau}-z_{j0}}{h})^{m'}X_{jl\tau,q'} = O_p(nh)$. So we conclude that $\frac{1}{nh}S_{n3} = O_p(n^{-1}h)$ $O_p(nh) = O_p(h^2)$. For $t=\tau$, by Cauchy Schwatz inequality,

$$S_{n31,mm'qq'} = nh\sum_{t=1}^{T}\frac{1}{nh}\sum_{i=1}^{n}\sum_{l=1,l\neq i}^{n}\frac{K_{jit}}{K_{ji.}}(\frac{Z_{jit}-z_{j0}}{h})^{m}X_{jit,q}$$

$$\frac{1}{nh}\sum_{l=1,l\neq i}^{n}\frac{K_{jlt}}{K_{jl.}}(\frac{Z_{jlt}-z_{j0}}{h})^{m'}X_{jlt,q'}$$

$$\leq nh[\sum_{t=1}^{T}(\frac{1}{nh}\sum_{i=1}^{n}\sum_{l=1,l\neq i}^{n}\frac{K_{jit}}{K_{ji.}}(\frac{Z_{jit}-z_{j0}}{h})^{m}X_{jit,q})^{2}]^{\frac{1}{2}}$$

$$[\sum_{t=1}^{T}(\frac{1}{nh}\sum_{l=1,l\neq i}^{n}\frac{K_{jlt}}{K_{jl.}}(\frac{Z_{jlt}-z_{j0}}{h})^{m'}X_{jlt,q'})^{2}]^{\frac{1}{2}}$$

$$= O_p(nh),$$

since $\sup_{z_{j0}\in G_j}|\frac{1}{nh}\sum_{i=1}^{n}\sum_{l=1,l\neq i}^{n}\frac{K_{jit}}{K_{ji.}}(\frac{Z_{jit}-z_{j0}}{h})^{m}X_{jit,q}| = O_p(1)$, so we obtain $\frac{1}{nh}S_{n3} = O_p(n^{-1}h)O_p(nh) = O_p(h^2)$ as well.

In all, we obtain $\frac{1}{nh}S_n(z_{j0}) = \frac{1}{nh}[S_{n1}-S_{n2}-S_{n3}] = \frac{1}{h}\sum_{t=1}^{T}EK_{jit}(1-\frac{K_{jit}}{K_{ji.}})$ $(\tilde{R}_{jit}\tilde{R}_{jit}'\otimes X_{jit}X_{jit}') + o_p(1) = \Sigma_{j0n}(z_{j0}) + o_p(1)$. Relative to Sun et al. (2009), we obtain the uniform bound in probability and allow kernel functions to have a noncompact support in Lemma 1.

$$(2)\frac{1}{nh}\tilde{R}_j(z_{j0})'S_h(z_{j0})\pi_j = \frac{1}{nh}\tilde{R}_j(z_{j0})'W_h(z_{j0})\pi_j - \frac{1}{nh}\tilde{R}_j(z_{j0})'W_h(z_{j0})D_M(D_M{}'W_h(z_{j0})D_M)^{-1} D_M{}'W_h(z_{j0})\pi_j = B_{1n} - B_{2n}.$$

With the additional Assumption of *B1*, we follow (1) to obtain that

$$B_{1n} = \frac{1}{nh}\sum_{i=1}^{n}\sum_{t=1}^{T}(\tilde{R}_{jit}\otimes X_{jit})K_{jit}X'_{jit}\frac{1}{2}(Z_{jit}-z_{j0})^2\beta_j^{(2)}(Z^*_{jit})$$
$$= h^2\frac{1}{h}\sum_{t=1}^{T}EK_{jit}(\tilde{R}_{jit}\otimes X_{jit})X'_{jit}\frac{1}{2}(\frac{Z_{jit}-z_{j0}}{h})^2\beta_j^{(2)}(Z^*_{jit})+o_p(h^2).$$

$$B_{2n} = \frac{1}{nh}\tilde{R}_j(z_{j0})W_h(z_{j0})Q\otimes e_T e_T{}'W_h(z_{j0})\pi_j$$
$$= \frac{1}{nh}\sum_{i=1}^{n}[K_{ji.}^{-1} - \frac{K_{ji.}^{-2}}{\sum_{i=1}^{n}K_{ji.}^{-1}}]\sum_{t=1}^{T}\sum_{\tau=1}^{T}K_{jit}K_{ji\tau}(\tilde{R}_{jit}\otimes X_{jit})X'_{ji\tau} \frac{1}{2}(Z_{ji\tau}-z_{j0})^2\beta_j^{(2)}(Z^*_{ji\tau})$$
$$+\frac{1}{nh}\sum_{i=1}^{n}\sum_{l=1,l\neq i}^{n}[-\frac{K_{ji.}^{-1}K_{jl.}^{-1}}{\sum_{i=1}^{n}K_{ji.}^{-1}}]\sum_{t=1}^{T}\sum_{\tau=1}^{T}K_{jit}K_{jl\tau}(\tilde{R}_{jit}\otimes X_{jit})X'_{jl\tau} \frac{1}{2}(Z_{jl\tau}-z_{j0})^2\beta_j^{(2)}(Z^*_{jl\tau})$$
$$= (B_{2n1}-B_{2n2})+B_{2n3}.$$

$$\frac{1}{h^2}B_{2n1} = \frac{1}{nh}\sum_{i=1}^{n}K_{ji.}^{-1}\sum_{t=1}^{T}\sum_{\tau=1}^{T}K_{jit}K_{ji\tau}(\tilde{R}_{jit}\otimes X_{jit})X_{ji\tau}{}'\frac{1}{2}(\frac{Z_{ji\tau}-z_{j0}}{h})^2\beta_j^{(2)}(Z^*_{ji\tau})$$
$$= \begin{cases} O_p(h) \text{ for } t\neq\tau. \\ \frac{1}{h}\sum_{t=1}^{T}E\frac{K_{jit}^2}{K_{ji.}}(\tilde{R}_{jit}\otimes X_{jit})X_{jit}{}'\frac{1}{2}(\frac{Z_{jit}-z_{j0}}{h})^2\beta_j^{(2)}(Z^*_{jit})+o_p(1) \text{ for } t=\tau. \end{cases}$$

By Lemma 1, $B_{2n2} = O_p(n^{-1}h)\frac{1}{nh}\sum_{i=1}^{n}\sum_{t=1}^{T}\sum_{\tau=1}^{T}\frac{K_{jit}K_{ji\tau}}{K_{ji.}^2}(\tilde{R}_{jit}\otimes X_{jit})X_{ji\tau}{}'\frac{1}{2}(Z_{ji\tau}-z_{j0})^2$ $\beta_j^{(2)}(Z^*_{ji\tau}) = O_p(n^{-1}h^3)$, since $B_{2n2,mll'} = \frac{1}{nh}\sum_{i=1}^{n}\sum_{t=1}^{T}\sum_{\tau=1}^{T}\frac{K_{jit}K_{ji\tau}}{K_{ji.}^2}(\frac{Z_{jit}-z_{j0}}{h})^m$

$X_{jit,l} X_{ji\tau,l'} \frac{1}{2}(Z_{ji\tau} - z_{j0})^2 \beta_{jl'}^{(2)}(Z_{ji\tau}^*) = O_p(h^3)$ for $t \neq \tau$ and $B_{2n2,mll'} = O_p(h^2)$ for $t = \tau$.

$$B_{2n3} = O_p(n^{-1}h) \frac{1}{nh} \sum_{i=1}^{n} \sum_{l=1,l\neq i}^{n} \sum_{t=1}^{T} \sum_{\tau=1}^{T} \frac{K_{jit} K_{jl\tau}}{K_{ji.} K_{jl.}} (\tilde{R}_{jit} \otimes X_{jit}) X_{jl\tau}' \frac{1}{2}(Z_{jl\tau} - z_{j0})^2 \beta_j^{(2)}(Z_{jl\tau}^*)$$
$$= O_p(n^{-1}h) O_p(nh^2) = O_p(h^3),$$

since for $B_{2n3,mqq'} = \frac{1}{nh} \sum_{i=1}^{n} \sum_{l=1,l\neq i}^{n} \sum_{t=1}^{T} \sum_{\tau=1}^{T} \frac{K_{jit} K_{jl\tau}}{K_{ji.} K_{jl.}} (\frac{Z_{jit} - z_{j0}}{h})^m X_{jit,q} X_{jl\tau,q'}$ $\frac{1}{2}(Z_{jl\tau} - z_{j0})^2 \beta_{jq'}^{(2)}(Z_{jl\tau}^*)$, we can show that for $t \neq \tau$, $E \frac{1}{h^3} | B_{2n3,mqq'} | = O(n)$, and for $t = \tau$, $E \frac{1}{h^2} | B_{2n3,mqq'} | = O(n)$.

So combining the terms above, we obtain that $\frac{1}{nh} \tilde{R}_j(z_{j0})' S_h(z_{j0}) \pi_j = B_{1n} - B_{2n}$ $= h^2 \frac{1}{h} \sum_{t=1}^{T} E K_{jit} (1 - \frac{K_{jit}}{K_{ji.}})(\tilde{R}_{jit} \otimes X_{jit}) X_{jit}' \frac{1}{2} (\frac{Z_{jit} - z_{j0}}{h})^2 \beta_j^{(2)}(Z_{jit}^*) + o_p(h^2)$. We apply the Hölder condition to get the claimed result.

(3) Let's define $A_{-1} = \begin{bmatrix} \alpha_2 - \bar{\alpha} \\ \vdots \\ \alpha_n - \bar{\alpha} \end{bmatrix}$, then $D_M A_{-1} = \begin{bmatrix} -\sum_{i=2}^{n} \alpha_i + (n-1)\bar{\alpha} \\ \alpha_2 - \bar{\alpha} \\ \vdots \\ \alpha_n - \bar{\alpha} \end{bmatrix} \otimes e_T$, where $\bar{\alpha} = \frac{1}{n} \sum_{i=1}^{n} \alpha_i$. Then $D_0 \alpha = (e_n \otimes e_T)\bar{\alpha} + D_M A_{-1}$. So $M_h(z_{j0}) D_0 \alpha = \bar{\alpha} M_h(z_{j0}) e_n \otimes e_T$.

Then

$$\begin{aligned} \frac{1}{nh} \tilde{R}_j(z_{j0})' S_h(z_{j0}) D_0 \alpha &= \frac{1}{nh} \tilde{R}_j(z_{j0})' M_h(z_{j0}) W_h(z_{j0}) M_h(z_{j0}) D_0 \alpha \\ &= \bar{\alpha} \frac{1}{nh} \tilde{R}_j(z_{j0})' W_h(z_{j0}) M_h(z_{j0})(e_n \otimes e_T) \\ &= \bar{\alpha}[\frac{1}{nh} \tilde{R}_j(z_{j0})' W_h(z_{j0})(e_n \otimes e_T) - \frac{1}{nh} \tilde{R}_j(z_{j0})' W_h(z_{j0}) Q \\ &\quad \otimes (e_T e_T') W_h(z_{j0})(e_n \otimes e_T)] \\ &= \bar{\alpha}[D_{1n} - D_{2n}]. \end{aligned}$$

By *A3*(2), $\bar{\alpha} = O_p(n^{-\frac{1}{2}})$. $D_{1n} = \frac{1}{nh} \sum_{i=1}^{n} \sum_{t=1}^{T} K_{jit} \tilde{R}_{jit} \otimes X_{jit}$.

$$D_{2n} = \frac{1}{nh}\sum_{i=1}^{n}[K_{ji.}^{-1} - \frac{K_{ji.}^{-2}}{\sum_{i=1}^{n} K_{ji.}^{-1}}]\sum_{t=1}^{T}\sum_{\tau=1}^{T} K_{jit}K_{ji\tau}\tilde{R}_{jit}\otimes X_{jit}$$
$$-\frac{1}{nh}\sum_{i=1}^{n}\sum_{l=1,l\neq i}^{n}[\frac{K_{ji.}^{-1}K_{jl.}^{-1}}{\sum_{i=1}^{n} K_{ji.}^{-1}}]\sum_{t=1}^{T}\sum_{\tau=1}^{T} K_{jit}K_{jl\tau}\tilde{R}_{jit}\otimes X_{jit}.$$

We follow previous arguments to have $D_{1n} = O_p(1), D_{2n} = O_p(1)$ as well. So $\frac{1}{nh}\tilde{R}_j(z_{j0})'S_h(z_{j0})D_0\alpha = O_p(n^{-\frac{1}{2}})$.

(4) Now Consider

$$\frac{1}{nh}\tilde{R}_j(z_{j0})'S_h(z_{j0})\epsilon = \frac{1}{nh}\tilde{R}_j(z_{j0})'W_h(z_{j0})\epsilon - \frac{1}{nh}\tilde{R}_j(z_{j0})'W_h(z_{j0})$$
$$D_M(D_M'W_h(z_{j0})D_M)^{-1}D_M'W_h(z_{j0})\epsilon$$
$$= \frac{1}{nh}\sum_{i=1}^{n}\sum_{t=1}^{T}(\tilde{R}_{jit}\otimes X_{jit})K_{jit}\epsilon_{it} - \frac{1}{nh}\sum_{i=1}^{n}[K_{ji.}^{-1}$$
$$-\frac{K_{ji.}^{-2}}{\sum_{i=1}^{n} K_{ji.}^{-1}}]\sum_{t=1}^{T}\sum_{\tau=1}^{T}(\tilde{R}_{jit}\otimes X_{jit})K_{jit}K_{ji\tau}\epsilon_{i\tau}$$
$$-\frac{1}{nh}\sum_{i=1}^{n}\sum_{l=1,l\neq i}^{n}[-\frac{K_{ji.}^{-1}K_{jl.}^{-1}}{\sum_{i=1}^{n} K_{ji.}^{-1}}]\sum_{t=1}^{T}\sum_{\tau=1}^{T}(\tilde{R}_{jit}\otimes X_{jit})K_{jit}K_{jl\tau}\epsilon_{l\tau}$$
$$= C_{1n} - C_{2n} - C_{3n}.$$

$$C_{2n} = \frac{1}{nh}\sum_{i=1}^{n}\sum_{t=1}^{T}\sum_{\tau=1}^{T}\frac{K_{jit}K_{ji\tau}}{K_{ji.}}(\tilde{R}_{jit}\otimes X_{jit})\epsilon_{i\tau} + O_p(n^{-\frac{3}{2}}h^{\frac{1}{2}})$$
$$= \frac{1}{nh}\sum_{i=1}^{n}\sum_{t=1}^{T}\sum_{\substack{\tau=1\\ t\neq\tau}}^{T}\frac{K_{jit}K_{ji\tau}}{K_{ji.}}(\tilde{R}_{jit}\otimes X_{jit})\epsilon_{i\tau}$$
$$+\frac{1}{nh}\sum_{i=1}^{n}\sum_{t=1}^{T}\frac{K_{jit}^2}{K_{ji.}}(\tilde{R}_{jit}\otimes X_{jit})\epsilon_{it} + +O_p(n^{-\frac{3}{2}}h^{\frac{1}{2}})$$
$$= C_{2n1} + C_{2n2} + O_p(n^{-\frac{3}{2}}h^{\frac{1}{2}}).$$

We obtain the above result as

$$\frac{1}{nh}\sum_{i=1}^{n}[\frac{K_{ji.}^{-2}}{\sum_{i=1}^{n} K_{ji.}^{-1}}]\sum_{t=1}^{T}\sum_{\tau=1}^{T}(\tilde{R}_{jit}\otimes X_{jit})K_{jit}K_{ji\tau}\epsilon_{i\tau} = O_p(n^{-1}h)$$
$$\sum_{t=1}^{T}\sum_{\tau=1}^{T}\frac{1}{nh}\sum_{i=1}^{n}\frac{K_{jit}K_{ji\tau}}{K_{ji.}^2}(\tilde{R}_{jit}\otimes X_{jit})\epsilon_{i\tau} = O_p(n^{-\frac{3}{2}}h^{\frac{1}{2}}).$$

Define $C_{2n3,ml} = \frac{1}{nh}\sum_{i=1}^{n}\frac{K_{jit}K_{ji\tau}}{K_{ji.}^2}\left(\frac{Z_{jit}-z_{j0}}{h}\right)^m X_{jit,l}\epsilon_{i\tau} = O_p(n^{-\frac{1}{2}}h^{-\frac{1}{2}})$. By $A3(1)$, $E(C_{2n3,ml}) = 0$, and $V(C_{2n3,ml}) = \frac{1}{nh^2}E\frac{K_{jit}^2K_{ji\tau}^2}{K_{ji.}^4}(\frac{Z_{jit}-z_{j0}}{h})^{2m}X_{jit,l}^2\sigma_\epsilon^2 = O(n^{-1})$ for $t \neq \tau$, and $V(C_{2n3,ml}) = O(n^{-1}h^{-1})$ for $t = \tau$. Furthermore, $C_{2n1} = O_p(n^{-\frac{1}{2}})$, because for $C_{2n1,ml} = \frac{1}{nh}\sum_{i=1}^{n}\frac{K_{jit}K_{ji\tau}}{K_{ji.}}(\frac{Z_{jit}-z_{j0}}{h})^m X_{jit,l}\epsilon_{i\tau}$, $EC_{2n1,ml} = 0$ and $V(C_{2n1,ml}) = O(n^{-1})$. So we obtain that $C_{2n} = C_{2n2} + O_p(n^{-\frac{1}{2}})$

By Lemma 1, $C_{3n} = O_p(n^{-1}h)\frac{1}{nh}\sum_{i=1}^{n}\sum_{l=1,l\neq i}^{n}\sum_{t=1}^{T}\sum_{\tau=1}^{T}\frac{K_{jit}K_{jl\tau}}{K_{ji.}K_{jl.}}(\tilde{R}_{jit}\otimes X_{jit})\epsilon_{l\tau}$ $= O_p(n^{-1}h)C_{3n1}$. Consider a typical element in C_{3n1} as $C_{3n1,mq} = [\frac{1}{nh}\sum_{i=1}^{n}\sum_{t=1}^{T}\frac{K_{jit}}{K_{ji.}}(\frac{Z_{jit}-z_{j0}}{h})^m X_{jit,q} * \frac{1}{nh}\sum_{l=1,l\neq i}^{n}\sum_{\tau=1}^{T}\frac{K_{jl\tau}}{K_{jl.}}\epsilon_{l\tau}]nh = [C_{3n1a,mq} * C_{3n1b,mq}]nh.$

Since $l \neq i$, we can show that $C_{3n1b,mq} = O_p((nh)^{-\frac{1}{2}})$, and $E|C_{3n1a,mq}| = O_p(1)$. Thus, $C_{3n1,mq} = O_p((nh)^{-\frac{1}{2}})nh = O_p((nh)^{\frac{1}{2}})$ and $C_{3n} = O_p(n^{-1}h)O_p((nh)^{\frac{1}{2}})$ $= O_p(n^{-\frac{1}{2}}h^{\frac{3}{2}}) = o_p(n^{-\frac{1}{2}})$.

In all, we have $\frac{1}{nh}\tilde{R}_j(z_{j0})'S_h(z_{j0})\epsilon = \frac{1}{nh}\sum_{i=1}^{n}\sum_{t=1}^{T}K_{jit}(1-\frac{K_{jit}}{K_{ji.}})(\tilde{R}_{jit}\otimes X_{jit})\epsilon_{it}$ $+o_p(n^{-\frac{1}{2}}) = C_{0n} + o_p(n^{-\frac{1}{2}})$. Now we show that $\sqrt{nh}C_{0n} \xrightarrow{d} N(0, \Omega_j(z_{j0}))$. Let λj be a $2r_j \times 1$ vector of arbitrary nonzero constants. Then $\sqrt{nh}\lambda_j'C_{0n} = \sum_{i=1}^{n}\frac{1}{\sqrt{nh}}\sum_{t=1}^{T}K_{jit}(1-\frac{K_{jit}}{K_{ji.}})\epsilon_{it}\lambda_j'(\tilde{R}_{jit}\otimes X_{jit}) = \sum_{i=1}^{n}W_{in}$. It is easy to see that $E(\sqrt{nh}\lambda_j'C_{0n}) = 0$, and $V(\sqrt{nh}\lambda_j'C_{0n}) = \lambda_j'\Omega_{jn}(z_{j0})\lambda_j$, where $\Omega_{jn}(z_{j0}) = \frac{1}{h}\sum_{t=1}^{T}EK_{jit}^2(1-\frac{K_{jit}}{K_{ji.}})^2(\tilde{R}_{jit}\tilde{R}_{jit}'\otimes X_{jit}X_{jit}')\sigma_\epsilon^2$. Now consider $S_n = \sum_{i=1}^{n}\frac{W_{in}}{(\lambda_j'\Omega_{jn}(z_{j0})\lambda_j)^{\frac{1}{2}}}$. By construction, $ES_n = 0$ and $ES_n^2 = 1$, then we have $S_n \xrightarrow{d} N(0,1)$ if we can show that $\lim_{n\to\infty}\sum_{i=1}^{n}E|\frac{W_{in}}{(\lambda_j'\Omega_{jn}(z_{j0})\lambda_j)^{\frac{1}{2}}}|^{2+\delta} = 0$ for some $\delta > 0$.

As $\lambda_j'\Omega_{jn}(z_{j0})\lambda_j \to \lambda_j'\Omega_j(z_{j0})\lambda_j$, and

$$\sum_{i=1}^{n} E|W_{in}|^{2+\delta} \le C\sum_{i=1}^{n}\frac{1}{(nh)^{1+\frac{\delta}{2}}}\sum_{t=1}^{T} EK_{jit}^{2+\delta}\left(1-\frac{K_{jit}}{K_{ji.}}\right)^{2+\delta} |\lambda_j'(\tilde{R}_{jit}\otimes X_{jit})|^{2+\delta} \; E(|\epsilon_{it}|^{2+\delta})$$
$$\le \frac{C}{(nh)^{\frac{\delta}{2}}}\sum_{t=1}^{T}\frac{1}{h} EK_{jit}^{2+\delta} |\lambda_j'(\tilde{R}_{jit}\otimes X_{jit})|^{2+\delta} \; E(|\epsilon_{it}|^{2+\delta})$$
$$\to 0 \text{ by } A1, C1, C3(2) \text{ and } A3(1).$$

By the Cramer–Rao's device, we have $\sqrt{nh}C_{0n} \xrightarrow{d} N(0,\Omega_j(Z_{j0}))$, and thus we have the claim that $\sqrt{nh}\frac{1}{nh}\tilde{R}'_{j(z_{j0})}S_h(z_{j0})\epsilon \xrightarrow{d} N(0,\Omega_j(z_{j0}))$.

(ii) We first write $\hat{\lambda}_{jl}-\lambda_{jl}=S_{jl}(\hat{\lambda}-\lambda)$, where S_{jl} is an $L_n\times(L_n r)$ selection matrix, whose elements are all zeros except that we insert an identity matrix I_{L_n} in its $L_n\left(\sum_{i=1}^{j-1} r_i + l - 1\right)+1$-th column through its $L_n\left(\sum_{i=1}^{j-1} r_i + l\right)$-th column. We note that

$$\hat{\beta}_{jl}(z_j)-\beta_{jl}(z_j)=\Phi_{L_n}(z_j)'S_{jl}(\hat{\lambda}-\lambda)+\Phi_{L_n}(z_j)'\lambda_{jl}-\beta_{jl}(z_j).$$

So we can write

$$\begin{aligned}
&\sqrt{nh}[\breve{\beta}_j(z_{j0})-\tilde{\beta}_j(z_{j0})]\\
&= e_{\cdot,2r_j}{'}\Sigma_{j0}(z_{j0})^{-1}\frac{1}{\sqrt{nh}}\tilde{R}_j(z_{j0})'S_h(z_{j0})[(X'\beta)_{(-j)}-(X'\hat{\beta})_{-j}](1+o_p(1))\\
&=\sum_{q=1,q\neq j}^{d}\sum_{l=1}^{r_q} e_{\cdot,2r_j}{'}\Sigma_{j0}(z_{j0})^{-1}\frac{1}{\sqrt{nh}}\tilde{R}_j(z_{j0})'S_h(z_{j0})[[X_{qit,l}(\beta_{ql}(z_{qit})\\
&\quad -\hat{\beta}_{ql}(z_{qit}))]_{t=1}^{T}]_{i=1}^{n}(1+o_p(1))\\
&= -(1+o_p(1))\left\{\begin{aligned}&\sum_{q=1,q\neq j}^{d}\sum_{l=1}^{r_q} e_{\cdot,2r_j}{'}\Sigma_{j0}(z_{j0})^{-1}\frac{1}{\sqrt{nh}}\tilde{R}_j(z_{j0})'S_h(z_{j0})\\ &[[X_{qit,l}\Phi_{L_n}(z_{qit})']_{t=1}^{T}]_{i=1}^{n}S_{ql}(\hat{\lambda}-\lambda)\end{aligned}\right.\\
&\quad +\sum_{q=1,q\neq j}^{d}\sum_{l=1}^{r_q} e_{\cdot,2r_j}{'}\Sigma_{j0}(z_{j0})^{-1}\frac{1}{\sqrt{nh}}\tilde{R}_j(z_{j0})'S_h(z_{j0})[[X_{qit,l}\\
&\quad (\Phi_{L_n}(z_{qit})'\lambda_{ql}-\beta_{ql}(z_{qit}))]_{t=1}^{T}]_{i=1}^{n}.
\end{aligned}$$

To obtain the claim in (ii) that $\|\sqrt{nh}[\breve{\beta}_j(z_{j0})-\tilde{\beta}_j(z_{j0})]\|=o_p(1)$, given *C1*(3), we only need to show that $\|D_{in}\|=o_p(1)$ for $i = 1, 2$, where $D_{1n}=\frac{1}{\sqrt{nh}}\tilde{R}_j(z_{j0})'S_h(z_{j0})[[X_{qit,l}\Phi_{L_n}(z_{qit})']_{t=1}^{T}]_{i=1}^{n}S_{ql}(\hat{\lambda}-\lambda)$ and $D_{2n}=\frac{1}{\sqrt{nh}}$ $\tilde{R}_j(z_{j0})'S_h(z_{j0})[[X_{qit,l}(\Phi_{L_n}(z_{qit})'\lambda_{ql}-\beta_{ql}(z_{qit}))]_{t=1}^{T}]_{i=1}^{n}\}$.

(1) By Theorem 1, we write

$$D_{1n} = \frac{1}{\sqrt{nh}} \tilde{R}_j(z_{j0})' S_h(z_{j0}) [[X_{qit,l} \Phi_{L_n}(z_{qit})']_{t=1}^{T}]_{i=1}^{n} S_{ql} \Sigma_{\Phi\Phi}^{-1} \frac{1}{n} \chi' M_D$$
$$(D_0\alpha + \epsilon + X'\beta - \chi\lambda)(1 + o_p(1))$$

Let $\xi_{1n} = \frac{1}{n}\chi' M_D D_0 \alpha$, $\xi_{2n} = \frac{1}{n}\chi' M_D \epsilon$, and $\xi_{3n} = \frac{1}{n}\chi' M_D (X'\beta - \chi\lambda)$. We first establish some preliminary results. Given the dimension of $\tilde{R}_j(z_{j0})$, we let $c = (c_1', c_2')'$ be a $2r_j \times 1$ vector of arbitrary nonzero constants, where ci is $r_j \times 1$ for $i = 1, 2$. Then

$$c' \frac{1}{nh} \tilde{R}_j(z_{j0})' S_h(z_{j0}) [[X_{qit,l} \Phi_{L_n}(Z_{qit})']_{t=1}^{T}]_{i=1}^{n}$$
$$= \frac{c'}{nh} \tilde{R}_j(z_{j0})' [W_h(z_{j0}) - W_h(z_{j0}) D_M (D_M{}' W_h(z_{j0}) D_M)^{-1} D_M W_h(z_{j0})]$$
$$[X_{qit,l} \Phi_{L_n}(Z_{qit})']_{t=1}^{T}]_{i=1}^{n}$$
$$= d_{1n} = d_{1n1} + d_{1n2}.$$

$$d_{1n1} = \frac{1}{nh} \sum_{i=1}^{n} \sum_{t=1}^{T} [c_1' X_{jit} + c_2' X_{jit} (\frac{Z_{jit} - z_{j0}}{h})] K_{jit} X_{qit,l} \Phi_{L_n}(Z_{qit})', q \neq j.$$

$$Ed_{1n1} = \sum_{t=1}^{T} \int\int\int\int K(\psi)[c_1' X_{jit} + c_2' X_{jit}\psi] X_{qit,l} \Phi_{Ln}(Z_{qit})' f_{z_{jt}, z_{qt} | x_{jt}, x_{qt}}$$
$$(z_{j0} + h\psi, Z_{qit}) \times f_{x_{jt}, x_{qt}}(X_{jit}, X_{qit}) d\psi dZ_{qit} dX_{jit} dX_{qit}$$
$$= \sum_{t=1}^{T} \int\int\int \Phi_{L_n}(Z_{qit})' f_{z_{jt}, z_{qt} | x_{jt}, x_{qt}}(z_{j0}, Z_{qit}) dZ_{qit} c_1' X_{jit} X_{qit,l} f_{x_{jt}, x_{qt}}$$
$$(X_{jit}, X_{qit}) dX_{jit} dX_{qit} + \sum_{t=1}^{T} \int\int\int\int K(\psi) \Phi_{L_n}(Z_{qit})' [f_{z_{jt}, z_{qt} | x_{jt}, x_{qt}}$$
$$(z_{j0} + h\psi, Z_{qit}) - f_{z_{jt}, z_{qt} | x_{jt}, x_{qt}}(z_{j0}, Z_{qit})] dZ_{qit} d\psi \times c_1' X_{jit} X_{qit,l} f_{x_{jt}, x_{qt}}$$
$$(X_{jit}, X_{qit}) dX_{jit} dX_{qit} + \sum_{t=1}^{T} \int\int\int\int K(\psi) \psi \Phi_{L_n}(Z_{qit})' [f_{z_{jt}, z_{qt} | x_{jt}, x_{qt}}$$
$$(z_{j0} + h\psi, Z_{qit}) - f_{z_{jt}, z_{qt} | x_{jt}, x_{qt}}(z_{j0}, Z_{qit})] d\psi$$
$$\times c_2' X_{jit} X_{qit,l} f_{x_{jt}, x_{qt}}(X_{jit}, X_{qit}) dZ_{qit} dX_{jit} dX_{qit}$$

$Ed_{1n11} + Ed_{1n12} + Ed_{1n13}$, where we use $C2$ that $K(\cdot)$ is symmetric.

$$\sup_{z_{j0} \in G_j} \| Ed_{1n11} \| \leq C \sup_{z_{j0} \in G_j} \| \sum_{t=1}^{T} \int \Phi_{L_n}(Z_{qit})' f_{z_{jt}, z_{qt}}(z_{j0}, Z_{qit})$$
$$dZ_{qit} E | c_1' X_{jit} X_{qit,l} | \| \text{ by A1(6)}$$
$$\leq C \sum_{t=1}^{T} | c_1' X_{jit} X_{qit,l} | \sup_{zj0 \in G_j} \| \int \Phi L_n$$
$$(Z_{qit})' fz_{jt}, z_{qt}(z_{j0}, z_{qit}) dZ_{qit} \|$$
$$\leq C,$$

where we obtain the last inequality with *A2*, and also follow Horowitz and Mammen (2004, p. 2435), to argue that components in $\int \Phi_{L_n}(Z_{qit})' f_{z_{jt},z_{qt}}(z_{j0}, Z_{qit}) dZ_{qit}$ are the Fourier coefficients of a function that is bounded uniformly on $z_{j0} \in G_j$, so $\sup_{z_{j0}\in G_j} \| \int \Phi_{L_n}(Z_{qit})' f_{z_{jt},z_{qt}}(z_{j0}, Z_{qit}) dZ_{qit} \| < C$.

$$\begin{aligned}
\| Ed_{1n12} \| &= \| \sum_{t=1}^{T} \int\int\int\int \Phi_{L_n}(Z_{qit})'[h\psi f^{(1)}_{z_{jt},z_{qt}|x_{jt},x_{qt}}(z_{j0}, Z_{qit}) + \frac{h^2}{2}\psi^2 f^{(2)}_{z_{jt},z_{qt}|x_{jt},x_{qt}} \\
&\quad (z^*_{j0}, Z_{qit})] K(\psi) d\psi dZ_{qit} \times c_1' X_{jit} X_{qit,l} f_{x_{jt},x_{qt}}(X_{jit}, X_{qit}) dX_{jit} dX_{qit} \| \\
&\leq \frac{h^2}{2} \sum_{t=1}^{T} \| \int \Phi_{L_n}(Z_{qit})' K(\psi)\psi^2 f^{(2)}_{z_{jt},z_{qt}|x_{jt},x_{qt}}(z^*_{j0}, Z_{qit}) \\
&\quad d\psi dZ_{qit} c_1' X_{jit} X_{qit,l} f_{x_{jt},x_{qt}}(X_{jit}, X_{qit}) dX_{jit} dX_{qit} \| \\
&= O(\sqrt{L_n} h^2),
\end{aligned}$$

where we obtain the first inequality by *C2*(3), and obtain the last equality since by *C1*(4), $| f^{(2)}_{z_{jt},z_{qt}|x_{jt},x_{qt}}(z^*_{j0}, Z_{qit}) | < C$, $\int K(\psi)\psi^2 d\psi < C$, $\Phi_{L_n}(\cdot)$ is $L_n \times 1$ and each of its elements is bounded. Similarly, $\| Ed_{1n13} \| = O(\sqrt{L_n} h)$. So in all, we obtain $\| Ed_{1n1} \| = O_p(1 + \sqrt{L_n} h)$. With Lemma 1 from Martins-Filho et al. (2018) and $| \phi_p(\cdot) | < C$, we obtain $\| d_{1n1} - Ed_{1n1} \| = O_p(\sqrt{L_n}(\frac{\log(n)}{nh})^{\frac{1}{2}})$. So we have $\| d_{1n1} \| \leq \| Ed_{1n1} \| + \| d_{1n1} - Ed_{1n1} \| = O_p(1 + \sqrt{L_n} h) + O_p(\sqrt{L_n}(\frac{\log(n)}{nh})^{\frac{1}{2}})$
$= O_p(1 + \sqrt{L_n} h)$.

$$\begin{aligned}
d_{1n2} &= -\frac{c'}{nh} \tilde{R}_j(z_{j0})' W_h(z_{j0}) D_M (D_M' W_h(z_{j0}) D_M)^{-1} D_M W_h(z_{j0}) [X_{qit,l} \Phi_{L_n}(Z_{qit})']_{t=1}^{T}]_{i=1}^{n} \\
&= -\frac{1}{nh} \sum_{i=1}^{n} q_{ii} \sum_{t=1}^{T}\sum_{\tau=1}^{T} \left(c_1' X_{jit} + c_2' X_{jit} \left(\frac{z_{jit} - z_{j0}}{h} \right) \right) K_{jit} K_{ji\tau} X_{qi\tau,l} \Phi_{Ln}'(z_{qi\tau}) \\
&\quad - \frac{1}{nh} \sum_{\substack{i=1 \\ i\neq m}}^{n} \sum_{m=1}^{n} q_{im} \sum_{t=1}^{T}\sum_{\tau=1}^{T} \left(c_1' X_{jit} + c_2' X_{jit} \left(\frac{z_{jit} - z_{j0}}{h} \right) \right) K_{jit} K_{jm\tau} X_{qm\tau,l} \Phi_{Ln}'(z_{qm\tau}) \\
&= d_{1n21} + d_{1n22}.
\end{aligned}$$

$$\begin{aligned}
d_{1n21} &= -\frac{1}{nh} \sum_{i=1}^{n} [K_{ji.}^{-1} - \frac{K_{ji.}^{-2}}{\sum_{i=1}^{n} K_{ji.}^{-1}}] \sum_{t=1}^{T}\sum_{\tau=1}^{T} \left(c_1' X_{jit} + c_2' X_{jit} \left(\frac{z_{jit} - z_{j0}}{h} \right) \right) \\
&\quad K_{jit} K_{ji\tau} X_{qi\tau,l} \Phi_{Ln}'(z_{qi\tau}) \\
&= d_{1n21a} + d_{1n21b}.
\end{aligned}$$

$$
\begin{aligned}
d_{1n21a} &= -\frac{1}{nh}\sum_{i=1}^{n} K_{ji.}^{-1} \sum_{t=1}^{T}\sum_{\tau=1}^{T}\left(c_1{}'X_{jit} + c_2{}'X_{jit}\left(\frac{z_{jit}-z_{j0}}{h}\right)\right) K_{jit}K_{ji\tau}X_{qi\tau,l}\Phi_{Ln}{}'(z_{qi\tau}) \\
&= -\frac{1}{nh}\sum_{i=1}^{n} K_{ji.}^{-1} \sum_{t=1}^{T}\left(c_1{}'X_{jit} + c_2{}'X_{jit}\left(\frac{z_{jit}-z_{j0}}{h}\right)\right) K_{jit}^{2}X_{qit,l}\Phi_{Ln}{}'(z_{qit}) \\
&\quad -\frac{1}{nh}\sum_{i=1}^{n} K_{ji.}^{-1} \sum_{t=1}^{T}\sum_{\substack{\tau=1 \\ t\neq\tau}}^{T}\left(c_1{}'X_{jit} + c_2{}'X_{jit}\left(\frac{z_{jit}-z_{j0}}{h}\right)\right) K_{jit}K_{ji\tau}X_{qi\tau,l}\Phi_{Ln}{}'(z_{qi\tau}) \\
&= d_{1n21aa} + d_{1n21ab}.
\end{aligned}
$$

With Assumption *C1*(4),

$$
\begin{aligned}
\| Ed_{1n21aa} \| &= \| -\sum_{t=1}^{T}\frac{1}{h} EK_{ji.}^{-1}\left(c_1{}'X_{jit} + c_2{}'X_{jit}\left(\frac{z_{jit}-z_{j0}}{h}\right)\right) K_{jit}^{2}X_{qit,l}\Phi'_{Ln}(z_{qit}) \| \\
&\leq C \| \sum_{t=1}^{T}\int\int |c_1{}'X_{jit}X_{qit,l}| \int\int K(\psi)\Phi'_{Ln}(z_{qit})[f_{z_{jt},z_{qt}|x_{jt},x_{qt}} \\
&\quad (z_{j0}+h\psi, Z_{q_{it}}) - f_{z_{jt},z_{qt}|x_{jt},x_{qt}}(z_{j0}, Z_{q_{it}}) \\
&\quad + f_{z_{jt},z_{qt}|x_{jt},x_{qt}}(z_{j0}, Z_{q_{it}})] dZ_{qit} d\psi f_{x_{jt},x_{qt}}(X_{jit}, X_{qit}) dX_{jit} dX_{qit} \\
&\quad + \sum_{t=1}^{T}\int\int |c_2{}'X_{jit}X_{qit,l}| \int\int K(\psi)|\psi|\Phi'_{Ln}(z_{qit})[f_{z_{jt},z_{qt}|x_{jt},x_{qt}} \\
&\quad (z_{j0}+h\psi, Z_{q_{it}}) - f_{z_{jt},z_{qt}|x_{jt},x_{qt}}(z_{j0}, Z_{q_{it}}) \\
&\quad + f_{z_{jt},z_{qt}|x_{jt},x_{qt}}(z_{j0}, Z_{q_{it}})] dZ_{qit} d\psi f_{x_{jt},x_{qt}}(X_{jit}, X_{qit}) dX_{jit} dX_{qit} \| \\
&= O(1+\sqrt{L_n}h) \text{ with similar arguments as in } d_{1n1}.
\end{aligned}
$$

With $|\phi_j(v)| < C$, we apply Lemma 1 in Martins-Filho et al. (2018) to have $\sup_{z_{j0}\in G_j} \| d_{1n21aa} - Ed_{1n21aa} \| = O_p(\sqrt{L_n}(\frac{\log(n)}{nh})^{\frac{1}{2}})$. With a similar argument and Assumption *C1*(5), we obtain $\| Ed_{1n21ab} \| = O(1+\sqrt{L_n}h)$ and $\sup_{z_{j0}\in G_j} \| d_{1n21ab} - Ed_{1n21ab} \| = O_p(\sqrt{L_n}(\frac{\log(n)}{nh})^{\frac{1}{2}})$. $\| d_{1n21b} \| = O_p(n^{-1}h)\frac{1}{nh}\| \sum_{i=1}^{n}\sum_{t=1}^{T}\sum_{\tau=1}^{T}$

$\left(c_1{}'X_{jit} + c_2{}'X_{jit}\left(\frac{z_{jit}-z_{j0}}{h}\right)\right) \frac{K_{jit}K_{ji\tau}}{K_{i.}^{2}} X_{qi\tau,l}\Phi_{Ln}{}'(z_{qi\tau}) \| = O_p(n^{-1}h\sqrt{L_n})$ as d_{1n21bp} $= \frac{1}{nh}\sum_{i=1}^{n}\sum_{t=1}^{T}\sum_{\tau=1}^{T} \left(c_1{}'X_{jit} + c_2{}'X_{jit}\left(\frac{z_{jit}-z_{j0}}{h}\right)\right) \frac{K_{jit}K_{ji\tau}}{K_{i.}^{2}} X_{qi\tau,l}\phi_p(z_{qi\tau})$ $= O_p(1+h) = O_p(1)$ given that $E|d_{1n21bp}| = O(1+h)$ and $|\phi_p(\cdot)| < C$. So to summarize

$$\begin{aligned}&\| d_{1n21} \| \leq \| Ed_{1n21aa} \| + \| Ed_{1n21ab} \| + \| d_{1n21aa} - Ed_{1n21aa} \| + \| d_{1n21ab} - Ed_{1n21ab} \| \\ &+ \| d_{1n21b} \| \\ &= O_p(1+\sqrt{L_n}h) + O_p\left(\sqrt{L_n}\left(\frac{\log(n)}{nh}\right)^{\frac{1}{2}}\right) + O_p(n^{-1}h\sqrt{L_n}) = O_p(1+\sqrt{L_n}h).\end{aligned}$$

$$\begin{aligned}d_{1n22} &= \frac{1}{nh}\sum_{\substack{i=1\\ i\neq m}}^{n}\sum_{m=1}^{n}\frac{K_{ji.}^{-1}K_{jm.}^{-1}}{\sum_{i=1}^{n}K_{ji.}^{-1}}\sum_{t=1}^{T}\sum_{\tau=1}^{T}(c_1'X_{jit} + c_2'X_{jit}(\frac{z_{jit}-z_{j0}}{h}))K_{jit}K_{jm\tau}X_{qm\tau,l}\Phi_{Ln}'(z_{qm\tau}) \\ &= O_p(n^{-1}h)\frac{1}{nh}\sum_{\substack{i=1\\ i\neq m}}^{n}\sum_{m=1}^{n}\sum_{t=1}^{T}\sum_{\tau=1}^{T}(c_1'X_{jit} + c_2'X_{jit}(\frac{z_{jit}-z_{j0}}{h}))\frac{K_{jit}K_{jm\tau}}{K_{ji.}K_{jm.}}X_{qm\tau,l}\Phi_{Ln}'(z_{qm\tau}).\end{aligned}$$

Consider $d_{1n22p} = \frac{1}{nh}\sum_{\substack{i=1\\ i\neq m}}^{n}\sum_{m=1}^{n}\sum_{t=1}^{T}\sum_{\tau=1}^{T}\left(c_1'X_{jit} + c_2'X_{jit}\left(\frac{z_{jit}-z_{j0}}{h}\right)\right)\frac{K_{jit}K_{jm\tau}}{K_{ji.}K_{jm.}}X_{qm\tau,l}\phi_p$ $(z_{qm\tau})$. Since $i \neq m$, $\frac{1}{h}E\,|\,d_{1n22p}\,| \leq \frac{(n-1)n}{n}\frac{1}{h^2}\sum_{t=1}^{T}\sum_{\tau=1}^{T}E[(|\,c_1'X_{jit}\,| + |\,c_2'X_{jit}$ $\left(\frac{z_{jit}-z_{j0}}{h}\right)|)\frac{K_{jit}K_{jm\tau}}{K_{jm.}}|\,X_{qm\tau,l}\,|\,\phi_p(z_{qm\tau})] = O(n)$, so $d_{1n22p} = O_p(nh)$. Thus, $d_{1n22} = O_p(n^{-1}h\sqrt{L_n}nh) = O_p(\sqrt{L_n}h^2)$.

So we have

$$\begin{aligned}d_{1n} &= d_{1n1} - d_{1n2} = d_{1n1} - [d_{1n21a} + d_{1n21b} + d_{1n22}] \\ &= Ed_{1n1} - Ed_{1n21a} - Ed_{1n21b} + [(d_{1n1} - Ed_{1n1}) - (d_{1n21a} - Ed_{1n21a}) \\ &\quad -(d_{1n21b} - Ed_{1n21b}) - d_{1n22}] \\ &= d_{1nA} + d_{1nB}.\end{aligned}$$

The results above imply that $\| d_{1nA} \| = O_p(1+\sqrt{L_n}h)$ and $\| d_{1nB} \| = O_p(\sqrt{L_n}(\frac{\log(n)}{nh})^{\frac{1}{2}} + \sqrt{L_n}h^2)$. Given *C4*(1), we have $\| d_{1nA} \| = O_p(1), \| d_{1nB} \| = o_p(\| d_{1nA} \|) = o_p(1)$ and $\| d_{1n} \| = O_p(1)$.

Now consider D_{1n}.

$$\begin{aligned}c'D_{1n} &= c'\frac{1}{\sqrt{nh}}\tilde{R}_j(z_{j0})'S_h(z_{j0})[[X_{qit,l}\Phi_{L_n}(z_{qit})']_{t=1}^{T}]_{i=1}^{n}S_{ql}\Sigma_{\Phi\Phi}^{-1}\frac{1}{n}\chi'M_D \\ &\quad (D_0\alpha + \epsilon + X'\beta - \chi\lambda)(1+o_p(1)) \\ &= (D_{1n1} + D_{1n2} + D_{1n3})(1+o_p(1)).\end{aligned}$$

$$\begin{aligned} D_{1n2} &= c'\frac{\sqrt{nh}}{nh}\tilde{R}_j(z_{j0})'S_h(z_{j0})[[X_{qit,l}\Phi_{L_n}(z_{qit})']_{l=1}^{T}]_{i=1}^{n}S_{ql}\Sigma_{\Phi\Phi}^{-1}\frac{1}{n}\chi'M_D\epsilon \\ &= \sqrt{nh}d_{1nA}S_{ql}\Sigma_{\Phi\Phi}^{-1}\xi_{2n} + \sqrt{nh}d_{1nB}S_{ql}\Sigma_{\Phi\Phi}^{-1}\xi_{2n} \\ &= D_{1n2,1} + D_{1n2,2}. \end{aligned}$$

Note that d_{1nA} are expectation terms. So

$$\begin{aligned} ED_{1n2,1}^2 &= nhd_{1nA}S_{ql}\Sigma_{\Phi\Phi}^{-1}E(\xi_{2n}\xi_{2n}{}')\Sigma_{\Phi\Phi}^{-1}S_{ql}{}'d_{1nA}{}' \\ &= nh\frac{d_{1nA}}{\| d_{1nA} \|}S_{ql}\Sigma_{\Phi\Phi}^{-1}E(\xi_{2n}\xi_{2n}{}')\Sigma_{\Phi\Phi}^{-1}S_{ql}{}'\frac{d_{1nA}{}'}{\| d_{1nA} \|}\| d_{1nA} \|^2 \\ &\quad \text{by the definition of a spectral norm} \\ &\le nh\| d_{1nA} \|^2 \lambda_{max}(S_{ql}\Sigma_{\Phi\Phi}^{-1}E(\xi_{2n}\xi_{2n}{}')\Sigma_{\Phi\Phi}^{-1}S_{ql}{}')\| \frac{d_{1nA}}{\| d_{1nA} \|}\|^2 \\ &= nh\| d_{1nA} \|^2 \lambda_{max}(\Sigma_{\Phi\Phi}^{-1}E(\xi_{2n}\xi_{2n}{}')\Sigma_{\Phi\Phi}^{-1}S_{ql}{}'S_{ql}) \end{aligned}$$

For symmetric matrices A, B, we have $\lambda_{max}(AB) \le \lambda_{max}(A)\lambda_{max}(B)$. By Assumption $A3(1)$, $E(\xi_{2n}\xi_{2n}{}') = \frac{1}{n^2}E(\chi'M_D\epsilon\epsilon'M_D\chi) = \frac{\sigma_\epsilon^2}{n}E\Sigma_{n,\Phi\Phi}$, so $\lambda_{max}(E(\xi_{2n}\xi_{2n}{}')) = \frac{\sigma_\epsilon^2}{n}\lambda_{max}(E\Sigma_{n,\Phi\Phi})$. As in Theorem 1(i)(1), $\lambda_{min}(\Sigma_{\Phi\Phi} - E\Sigma_{n,\Phi\Phi}) \le \lambda_{max}(\Sigma_{\Phi\Phi}) - \lambda_{max}(E\Sigma_{n,\Phi\Phi}) \le \lambda_{max}(\Sigma_{\Phi\Phi} - E\Sigma_{n,\Phi\Phi})$, and $|\lambda_{min}(\Sigma_{\Phi\Phi} - E\Sigma_{n,\Phi\Phi})| \le \| \Sigma_{\Phi\Phi} - E\Sigma_{n,\Phi\Phi} \| = O_p\left(\frac{\sqrt{L_n}}{n}\right)$, and $|\lambda_{max}(\Sigma_{\Phi\Phi} - E\Sigma_{n,\Phi\Phi})| \le \| \Sigma_{\Phi\Phi} - E\Sigma_{n,\Phi\Phi} \| = O_p(\frac{\sqrt{L_n}}{n})$, so $\lambda_{max}(E\Sigma_{n,\Phi\Phi}) = \lambda_{max}(\Sigma_{\Phi\Phi}) + \lambda_{max}(E\Sigma_{n,\Phi\Phi}) - \lambda_{max}(\Sigma_{\Phi\Phi}) = \lambda_{max}(\Sigma_{\Phi\Phi}) + O_p(\frac{\sqrt{L_n}}{n})$. Then, $\lambda_{max}(E(\xi_{2n}\xi_{2n}{}')) = \frac{\sigma_\epsilon^2}{n}\left[\lambda_{max}(\Sigma_{\Phi\Phi}) + O_p(\frac{\sqrt{L_n}}{n})\right]$. By Assumption $B2(1)$, we have $\lambda_{max}(\Sigma_{\Phi\Phi}) \le C$, and $\lambda_{min}^{-2}(\Sigma_{\Phi\Phi}) \le \frac{1}{\underline{c}^2}$. The matrix $S'_{ql}S_{ql}$ is diagonal, with either 0 or 1 on the diagonal, so its eigenvalue is 0 or 1, $\lambda_{max}S'_{ql}S_{ql} = 1$. The results above imply that

$$\begin{aligned} ED_{1n2,1}^2 &\le nh\| d_{1nA} \|^2 \lambda_{max}^2(\Sigma_{\Phi\Phi}^{-1})\lambda_{max}(E(\xi_{2n}\xi'_{2n}))\lambda_{max}(S'_{ql}S_{ql})) \\ &= nh\| d_{1nA} \|^2 \lambda_{min}^{-2}(\Sigma_{\Phi\Phi})\lambda_{max}(E(\xi_{2n}\xi'_{2n}))\lambda_{max}(S'_{ql}S_{ql})) \\ &\le Cnh\| d_{1nA} \|^2 \frac{1}{n} = ch\| d_{1nA} \|^2 = O_p(h), \text{ as } \| d_{1nA} \| = O_p(1). \end{aligned}$$

Note that $\| A \|_{sp} \le \| A \|, \| A \times B \|_{sp} \le \| A \|_{sp} \| A \|_{sp}$, we have

$$
\begin{aligned}
|D_{1n2,2}| &= |\sqrt{nh} d_{1nB} S_{ql} \Sigma_{\Phi\Phi}^{-1} \xi_{2n}| \\
&\le \sqrt{nh} \| d_{1nB} \| \| S_{ql} \|_{sp} \| \Sigma_{\Phi\Phi}^{-1} \|_{sp} \| \xi_{2n} \| \\
&= \sqrt{nh} O_p\left(\sqrt{L_n}\left(\frac{\log(n)}{nh}\right)^{\frac{1}{2}} + \sqrt{L_n} h^2 \right) O_p\left(\sqrt{\frac{L_n}{n}}\right) \\
&= O_p\left(L_n \left(\left(\frac{\log(n)}{n}\right)^{\frac{1}{2}} + \sqrt{h} h^2 \right)\right).
\end{aligned}
$$

where the second to the last equality follows because $\| S_{ql} \|_{sp} = 1, \| \Sigma_{\Phi\Phi}^{-1} \|_{sp} \le C$, and $\| \xi_{2n} \| = \| \frac{1}{n} \xi' M_D \epsilon \| = O_p\left(\sqrt{\frac{L_n}{n}}\right)$. By Assumption *C4*(1), we have $L_n \left(\frac{lnn}{n}\right)^{\frac{1}{2}} \to 0$, and $L_n h^{\frac{5}{2}} \to 0$ as $n \to \infty$. Then

$$
D_{1n2} = O_p(h^{\frac{1}{2}}) + O_p\left(L_n \left(\left(\frac{\log(n)}{n}\right)^{\frac{1}{2}} + \sqrt{h} h^2 \right)\right) = o_p(1).
$$

$$
\begin{aligned}
D_{1n3} &= c' \frac{\sqrt{nh}}{nh} \tilde{R}_j(z_{j0})' S_h(z_{j0}) [[X_{qit,l} \Phi_{L_n}(z_{qit})']_{t=1}^T]_{i=1}^n S_{ql} \Sigma_{\Phi\Phi}^{-1} \frac{1}{n} \chi' M_D (X'\beta - \chi\lambda) \\
&= \sqrt{nh} d_{1n} S_{ql} \Sigma_{\Phi\Phi}^{-1} \xi_{3n}.
\end{aligned}
$$

$|D_{1n3}| \le \sqrt{nh} \| d_{1n} \| \| S_{ql} \|_{sp} \| \Sigma_{\Phi\Phi}^{-1} \|_{sp} \| \xi_{3n} \| = \sqrt{nh} O_p(1) O_p(L_n^{-\xi}) = o_p(1)$, where we have shown that $\| \xi_{3n} \| = O_p(L_n^{-\xi})$ in Theorem 1(i)(3) and $\sqrt{nh} L_n^{-\xi} = o(1)$ as assumed in *C4*(3).

$$
\begin{aligned}
D_{1n1} &= c' \frac{\sqrt{nh}}{nh} \tilde{R}_j(z_{j0})' S_h(z_{j0}) [[X_{qit,l} \Phi_{L_n}(z_{qit})']_{t=1}^T]_{i=1}^n S_{ql} \Sigma_{\Phi\Phi}^{-1} \frac{1}{n} \chi' M_D D_0 \alpha \\
&= \sqrt{nh} d_{1n} S_{ql} \Sigma_{\Phi\Phi}^{-1} \xi_{1n}.
\end{aligned}
$$

$|D_{1n1}| \le \sqrt{nh} \| d_{1n} \| \| S_{ql} \|_{sp} \| \Sigma_{\Phi\Phi}^{-1} \|_{sp} \| \xi_{1n} \| = \sqrt{nh} O_p(1) O_p(n^{-\frac{1}{2}}) = O_p(h^{\frac{1}{2}})$, where $\| \xi_{1n} \| = O_p(n^{-\frac{1}{2}})$ is shown in Theorem 1(i)(4).

So in all,

$$
\begin{aligned}
c' D_{1n} &= (D_{1n1} + D_{1n2} + D_{1n3})(1 + o_p(1)) = O_p(h^{\frac{1}{2}}) + O_p \\
&\quad \left(L_n \left(\left(\frac{\log(n)}{n}\right)^{\frac{1}{2}} + \sqrt{h} h^2 \right)\right) + O_p(\sqrt{nh} L_n^{-\xi}) = o_p(1).
\end{aligned} \tag{2}
$$

$$D_{2n} = \frac{1}{\sqrt{nh}} \tilde{R}_j(z_{j0})' S_h(z_{j0}) [[X_{qit,l}(\Phi_{L_n}(z_{qit})'\lambda_{ql} - \beta_{ql}(z_{qit}))]_{t=1}^{T}]_{i=1}^{n}$$
$$= \sqrt{nh}[D_{2n1} - D_{2n2}].$$

By *B1*(1), we have $\sup_{z_{j0} \in G_j} | \beta_{ql}(z_{qit}) - \Phi_{L_n}(z_{qit})'\lambda_{ql} | = O(L_n^{-\xi})$. Let

$A_{it} = \Phi_{L_n}(z_{qit})'\lambda_{ql} - \beta_{ql}(z_{qit})$.

$$| c'D_{2n1} | = | \frac{1}{nh} \sum_{i=1}^{n} \sum_{t=1}^{T} (c'\tilde{R}_{jit} \otimes X_{jit}) K_{jit} X_{qit,l} A_{it} | \leq O(L_n^{-\xi})$$
$$\frac{1}{nh} \sum_{i=1}^{n} \sum_{t=1}^{T} | c'\tilde{R}_{jit} \otimes X_{jit} | K_{jit} | X_{qit,l} | = O_p(L_n^{-\xi}).$$

$$D_{2n2} = \frac{1}{nh} \sum_{i=1}^{n} \sum_{l'=1}^{n} q_{il'} \sum_{t=1}^{T} \sum_{\tau=1}^{T} (\tilde{R}_{jit} \otimes X_{jit}) K_{jit} K_{jl'\tau} X_{ql'\tau,l} A_{l'\tau}$$
$$= \frac{1}{nh} \sum_{i=1}^{n} [K_{ji.}^{-1} - \frac{K_{ji.}^{-2}}{\sum_{i=1}^{n} K_{ji.}^{-1}}] \sum_{t=1}^{T} \sum_{\tau=1}^{T} K_{jit} K_{ji\tau} (\tilde{R}_{jit} \otimes X_{jit}) X_{qi\tau,l} A_{i\tau}$$
$$+ \frac{1}{nh} \sum_{\substack{i=1 \\ i \neq l'}}^{n} \sum_{l'=1}^{n} [-\frac{K_{ji.}^{-1} K_{jl'.}^{-1}}{\sum_{i=1}^{n} K_{ji.}^{-1}}] \sum_{t=1}^{T} \sum_{\tau=1}^{T} K_{jit} K_{jl'\tau} (\tilde{R}_{jit} \otimes X_{jit}) X_{ql'\tau,l} A_{l'\tau}.$$

It is easy to bound each terms above to obtain $c'D_{2n2} = O_p(L_n^{-\xi})$.

So we have $c'D_{2n} = \sqrt{nh} O_p(L_n^{-\xi}) = o_p(1)$ by *C4*(3). So $c'D_{1n} = o_p(1)$ and $c'D_{2n} = o_p(1)$. So we have the claim that $\| \sqrt{nh}[\beta_j(z_{j0}) - \tilde{\beta}_z(z_{j0})] \| = o_p(1)$.

CHAPTER 8

THE ROLE OF MANAGEMENT IN EFFICIENT PRODUCTION: THEORETICAL AND STATISTICAL IMPLICATIONS

Mike G. Tsionas

Lancaster University Management School, Lancaster, UK

ABSTRACT

In this chapter, we consider the possibility that a firm may use costly resources to improve its technical efficiency. Results from static analyses imply that technical efficiency is determined by the configuration of factor prices. A dynamic model of the firm is developed under the assumption that managerial skill contributes to technical efficiency. Dynamic analysis shows that the firm can never be technically efficient if it maximizes profits, the steady state is always inefficient, and it is locally stable. In terms of empirical analysis, we show how likelihood-based methods can be used to uncover, in a semi-non-parametric manner, important features of the inefficiency-management relationship using a flexible functional form accounting for the endogeneity of inputs in a production function. Managerial compensation can also be identified and estimated using the new techniques. The new empirical methodology is applied in a data set previously analyzed by Bloom and van Reenen (2007) on managerial practices of manufacturing firms in the UK, US, France and Germany.

Keywords: Organization theory; firm behavior; technical inefficiency; inefficiency-management relationship; panel data econometrics

---

Essays in Honor of Subal Kumbhakar
Advances in Econometrics, Volume 46, 185–210

Published under exclusive licence by Emerald Publishing Limited
ISSN: 0731-9053/doi:10.1108/S0731-905320240000046008

Classical economic theory assumes that decision makers, whether groups or individuals, know everything about the world and use it all to calculate the optimal way to behave. Well, in the case of a firm, there are a zillion things that firm doesn't know about its environment, two zillion things it doesn't know about possible products or marketing methods that nobody's ever thought of, and more zillions of calculations it can't make, even if it had all the facts needed to dump into the calculations. This is a ridiculous view of what goes on.

Herbert A. Simon: Thinking machines,
Interviewed June 1994 by Doug Stewart

1. INTRODUCTION

Factors of production and production techniques cannot spontaneously, effortlessly and costlessly be organized, coordinated and supervised to produce the maximum possible amount of output. This activity requires resources, such as managerial skills and real resources like capital and labor. If that commonplace truth is indeed adopted, then the firm will not choose to be technically efficient[1] because it will *not*, in general, pay to do so. Instead, the firm will be at efficiency levels where the marginal revenue of managerial and real resources is no less than the marginal cost of those resources in efficiency improvement. Existing inefficiency models rely on the assumption that decision makers have perfect information that can be obtained without cost. Clearly, what is not true of information acquisition cannot be true of efficiency so it is important to develop models where efficiency is endogenously determined by the choice mechanism of the firm.[2]

It is not necessary to resort to information processing restrictions within the firm to generate inefficiencies, although it is clear that if such restrictions are indeed present, and the firm does not take any action to be efficient, then it must necessarily be inefficient. Simon (1955) for example proposes an alternative to optimizing economic models by proposing "satisficing" behavior on the part of the firm. This behavior produces outcomes that can be computed easily contrary to optimal plans of formal economic models. To the extent that optimal and satisficing plans are different, inefficiencies arise. In Simon's words:

OMNI

You've said human decision makers, instead of making the "best choice," always settle for "what's good enough." Even in choosing a spouse?

Simon

Certainly. There are hundreds of millions of eligible women in the world at any given time. I don't know anybody who's gone the rounds before making the choice. As a result of experience, you get an idea of which women will tolerate you and which women you will tolerate. I don't know how many women I looked at before I met my wife. I doubt it was even 1,000. By the way, I've stayed married for 56 years.

Simon's point is that since decision makers face severe computational and informational limitations they need to severely simplify the decision process, and follow "satisficing" principles instead of optimal plans by using heuristics and other simplifications of the decision process. That would certainly be one way to explain "X-inefficiency" if the comparison of a "satisficing" to an optimal decision makes any sense. If such comparisons do not make sense, we could compare decision makers that use the same heuristics and face the same computational and information-processing restrictions to figure out inefficiency of one decision maker relative to another. Koopmans (1951, p. 34) pointed out that:

> It has long been recognized that a concept of a production function representing a given productive technique is unnecessarily restrictive. (...) Managers choose between, or employ efficient combinations of, several processes to obtain in some sense best results (...) an efficient manager chooses that combination of productive activities which maximizes the amount produced for given available quantities of factors which have given qualitative characteristics.

Koopmans rightly argues that "[t]he production function so obtained is descriptive of reality only if and when the assumption of efficient choice is a good approximation to reality" (Koopmans, 1951, p. 34). Such normative statements place a lot of burden on managers, and require computations, choices to be made and comparisons to be performed. Such comparisons are clearly difficult to perform because of their conditioning assumptions. Moreover, conditioning assumptions can be properly taken into account only in dynamic models (Epstein, 1983 ; Rungsuriyawiboon & Stefanou, 2003[3]; Stefanou, 1989). Dynamic models of efficiency estimation have recently gained some attention, see for example Tsionas (2006). In this chapter, we try to approach the problem as follows: Suppose firms may hire inputs that can ease their computational as well as information-processing restrictions at some cost, and it is even possible to relax such restrictions completely, again at some cost. Would the firm choose to be technically efficient in this case? In other words, would it be optimal (in the classical sense) for the firm to be fully computationally and informationally efficient? We show that *the answer is, in general, negative*, and in that sense computational and information-processing restrictions bind to some extent and, therefore, inefficiencies arise because there is an optimal degree of information processing. To state it even more clearly, it is not optimal for the firm to be fully efficient in the information-processing sense even if this possibility is open. More importantly, we find that it is not optimal for the firm to be efficient even in the long-run. The purpose of this chapter is to examine the implications of endogenous efficiency in static and dynamic settings, and determine whether or not efficiency is indeed endogenously determined. The next section develops simple, static models of the firm to gain an understanding of the issues involved and develop intuition about the determination of efficiency in more general models. In Section 3, a dynamic model of the firm is developed. The firm chooses an investment plan and managerial hours to maximize the discount net present value. Managerial hours determine the amount of managerial skill which, in turn, determines the efficiency level of the firm. It is shown that there is no steady state where full technical efficiency is attained, so it is optimal for the firm to remain at an inefficient level. This steady state is always stable, and local convergence can be either monotone or cyclical depending on the underlying parameters of the problem. The speed of local convergence to the steady state is determined by the rate of depreciation of managerial capital, the form of transformation of hours to managerial skill, the way managerial skill determines efficiency, and managerial compensation itself: Along with the rate of depreciation of managerial capital, these are the critical parameters of the model, given some reasonable assumptions about the behavior of functions that are involved in the analysis. Next, we take up the question of estimating models of the firm when managerial practice is observed. The availability of such data in recent years is documented in papers by Bloom and van Reenen (2007). Models of the form that account for the presence of management pose significant challenges. First, we must allow for input endogeneity in the production function (a well-known obstacle). Second, we show how we can, in fact, uncover statistically in a semi-non-parametric manner important features of the inefficiency-management relationship. We consider this an important contribution as it is not necessary to assume a restrictive functional form between technical inefficiency and management. Third, we show how managerial compensation can, in fact, also be identified and estimated as it is, practically never, available in the data.

The chapter is organized as follows. In Section 2, we consider static models of the firm. In Section 3, we consider a dynamic model. Analysis near the steady state is taken up in Section 4. The econometric tools to uncover semi-non-parametrically important features of the inefficiency-management relation are presented in Section 5. The empirical application to the Bloom and van Reenen (2007) data is presented in Section 6. The final section summarizes the chapter.

2. STATIC MODELING OF THE FIRM

Consider a firm with a single productive input K, capital stock, and another input M, managerial skills, with production function given by $f(K)-u(M)$.[4] Here, f is a strictly increasing, concave, differentiable production function, with $f'(K)>0$, $f''(K)<0$, $\lim_{K\to 0} f'(K)=\infty$, and $u(M)$ is an inefficiency function that is assumed to be differentiable, with $u'(M)\leq 0$, and $u''(M)\geq 0$. For basic results related to the efficiency of production, see Fare and Lovell (1978) and Farrell (1957). The inefficiency function depends on the managerial input, implying that management is not productive *per se* but can be used to organize and supervise production in order to achieve higher levels of technical efficiency. We will consider that it is indeed possible to achieve full technical efficiency using managerial input up to level $\bar{M}$ in the sense that: There exists $\bar{M}>0$, and $u'(M)<0$ for all $M\in[0,\bar{M})$, and $u(M)=0$ for all $M\in[\bar{M},\infty)$ with $u'(M)=0$ for all $M\in[\bar{M},\infty)$.[5]

One problem with this formulation is that $f(K)-u(M)$ may be negative for some input levels. Since $f(K)-u(M)$ represents actual output this should not be the case, so this requires placing constraints of the following form: There exist K, $M>0$ with $K\geq \underline{K}$, $M\geq \underline{M}$, and $f(K)-u(M)\geq 0$, for all $(K,M)\in[\underline{K},\infty)\times[\underline{M},\infty)$. So, the restriction $f(K)-u(M)\geq 0$ may be violated but this will be the case only for capital stocks and/or managerial input below the lower bounds $\underline{K}$ and $\underline{M}$. It is clear that the problem of the firm is given by the following:

$$\max_{(K,M)} : f(K) - u(M) - rK - wM$$

$$K \geq \underline{K}$$

$$\underline{M} \leq M \leq \bar{M},$$

where r and w represent the price of capital and managerial compensation, respectively. This is a concave differentiable program for which the Kuhn-Tucker conditions are necessary and sufficient: There exist $\lambda_i \geq 0$ such that:

$$u'(M) + w - \lambda_2 + \lambda_3 = 0, \tag{1}$$

$$r - f'(K) - \lambda_1 = 0, \tag{2}$$

$$\lambda_1 = 0 \text{ or } K = \underline{K}, \tag{3}$$

$$\lambda_2 = 0 \text{ or } M = \underline{M}, \tag{4}$$

$$\lambda_3 = 0 \text{ or } M = \bar{M}. \tag{5}$$

We consider only the interesting case with $u(M) = 0$, for all $M \geq \bar{M}$. We have the following[6]:

Remark 1.

Suppose $u(M)$ is differentiable, with $u'(M) \leq 0$, $u''(M) \geq 0$, and there exists $\bar{M} > 0$, and $u'(M) < 0$ for all $M \in [0, \bar{M})$, $u(M) = 0$ for all $M \in [\bar{M}, \infty)$ with $u'(M) = 0$ for all $M \in [\bar{M}, \infty)$. Then we have the following:

(i) $r \leq f'(\underline{K})$ implies that $K > \underline{K}$,
(ii) $w \leq -u'(\underline{M})$ implies $M > \underline{M}$,
(iii) Since (i) and (ii) hold, and $w \geq -u'(\bar{M})$ then $M < \bar{M}$, and the firm cannot attain full production efficiency.

Conditions (i) and (ii) are reasonable provided the lower bounds are sufficiently close to zero (which is a matter of functional forms for $f(K)$ and $u(M)$) and the conditions $\lim_{K \to 0} f'(K) = \infty$ and $\lim_{M \to 0} u'(M) = \infty$ are in place. The interpretation is that if management compensation is too high, the firm will choose the lowest possible value $\underline{M}$, thus getting stuck at the highly inefficient state. If management compensation is within the bounds determined by (ii) and (iii) the firm will choose an interior solution for management, and will end up being inefficient. Although this is an extremely simple model it illustrates nicely the fundamental point of this chapter, namely that the firm is inefficient employing the lowest possible value of management. In the previous example, the firm hires the managerial input to manage and supervise the organization of production, and has to pay this resource a certain price w. Another possibility is that the firm can use its internal resources to manage production at no extra costs. In particular, part of the capital stock, that will also be called M, can be used up to monitor efficiency, in which case the problem of the firm is:

$$\max_{(K,M)}: f(K) - u(M) - r(K + M),$$

subject to $M \leq \overline{M}$.

We consider a more general firm of the following form:

$$\max_{(K,M)}: f(K,M) - u(M) - rK - wM, \tag{6}$$

subject to $M \leq \overline{M}$,

and we ignore the possibility of other corner solutions assuming the appropriate price conditions to be in place. We have the following:

Remark 2.

Let $\frac{\partial f(K(\bar{M}),\bar{M})}{\partial K} \equiv r$. If $w > \frac{\partial f(K(\overline{M}),\overline{M})}{\partial M}$, the firm cannot attain full technical efficiency.

In this case, we have $\frac{\partial f(K,M)}{\partial M} \equiv 0$, and $w = r$ so the previous proposition implies that the unmanaged firm can never be efficient if it faces strictly positive capital prices. However, one can envision the unmanaged firm in a slightly different way to allow $\frac{\partial f(K,M)}{\partial M} > 0$: The firm has two inputs one of which can be used to monitor efficiency and be productive as well. In this case, if the M-input is too expensive, the firm cannot be efficient in the spirit of Remark 1. The reader might have wondered why we have not considered the more reasonable specification $Y = \theta(M)f(K)$ for the production function, where $0 \leq \theta(M) \leq 1$, with $\theta'(M) > 0$, and $\theta''(M) < 0$. Part of the problem is that this specification complicates considerably the dynamic analysis that will be taken up in the next section. In addition, this formulation implies some strange behavior. Suppose, for example, that we have $\theta(M) = 1 - \exp(-\phi M)$, $\phi > 0$, and consider the unmanaged firm with $r = w$. Assuming $f(K) = K^{\alpha}$, the first order conditions imply that the optimal capital input satisfies the nonlinear equation:

$$\alpha K^{\alpha} - rK - (r\alpha / \phi) = 0$$

This may have zero, one or two roots. For example, let $\alpha = 0.7$, $\phi = 2$ and $r = 0.5$. Then the nonlinear equation has two solutions. The first is $K^* = 0.4478$ with $\theta(M^*) = 0.561$, and the profit of the firm is -0.110. The second is $K^* = 1.5687$ with $\theta(M^*) = 0.818$ and profit -0.221. Therefore, it is not profitable for the firm to choose the high capital and high efficiency root. The reason for the "surprising behavior" of the profit function is that it is not globally concave, but only for some of the values of M. The condition for concavity is $M < 1/\phi \, ln(1/(1-\alpha))$ which is not the case here. This condition, effectively, places an upper bound on optimal physical capital. The author is indebted to an anonymous reviewer for pointing this out.

Apparently, the reason is that the capital input is too expensive in this case, so it is more profitable for the firm to devote capital to production instead of improving its efficiency! Another point is that $\theta(M^*) = 1 - (r/\phi) \, K^{*-\alpha}$, implies that there is systematic variation of efficiency with prices.

To study this specification in more detail, consider the following problem:

$$\max : \theta(M)f(K) - rk - wM$$

subject to $M \leq \bar{M}$.

The Kuhn-Tucker conditions are:

$$\theta(M)f'(K) = r,$$

$$\theta'(M)f(K) - w = \lambda \geq 0,$$

$$\lambda(M - \bar{M}) = 0.$$

If we suppose that $M = \bar{M}$ is a solution, we have $\theta(\bar{M}) = 1$, $\theta'(\bar{M}) = 0$ and, therefore, we have $-w \geq 0$, a contradiction.

One important implication of this analysis is that the marginal product of capital must equal $r / \theta(M)$. Therefore, the firm effectively faces a higher real rate of return and will employ a lower amount of capital compared to the full efficiency case.

Next, we consider the following related problem:

$$\max : f(K,M)\theta(M) - rK - wM,$$

with the standard assumptions about f, and $M \leq \bar{M}$ with $\theta'(M) > 0$ for $M < \bar{M}$, $\theta(\bar{M}) = 1$, and $\theta'(M) = 0$ for $M \geq \bar{M}$.

This means that we have a differentiability assumption in place, since it is possible for $\theta'(M)$ to have a jump at $\bar{M}$.[7]

There are, basically, two cases that we can consider in conjunction with a given $\theta(M)$ function. One case is $\theta(M) < 1$, for all $M \geq 0$ which always implies existence of inefficiency. We will not consider this case. Therefore, the Kuhn-Tucker conditions are as follows:

$$f_K(K,M) \, \theta(M) = r,$$

$$f_M(K,M) \, \theta(M) + f(K,M) \, \theta'(M) - w = \lambda,$$

$$\lambda \, (M - \bar{M}) = 0, \ \lambda \geq 0, \ M \leq \bar{M}.$$

To examine whether perfect efficiency could be a viable solution, define $K(M)$ as the solution of the first condition, namely $f_K(K(M), M)\theta(M) = r$. Then we need to have $f_M\left(K\left(\bar{M}\right), \bar{M}\right) > w$. This condition cannot hold if M does not appear as an argument of the production function, i.e., if $f_M = 0$. The viability condition, $f_M(K(\bar{M}), \bar{M}) > w$, implies conditions on prices that must be satisfied in order for the firm to be efficient.

To see this in detail, suppose

$$f(K,M) = K^{\alpha} M^{\beta}, \alpha, \beta > 0$$

Define

$$M^*(w,r) = (r/\beta)^{\frac{1-\alpha}{\alpha+\beta-1}} \alpha^{\frac{\alpha}{1-(\alpha+\beta)}} w^{\frac{\alpha}{\alpha+\beta-1}}$$

This is the optimal value of the managerial resource from the optimization problem in this instance. Then, we can easily prove[8] the following:

Remark 3.

If $f(K,M) = K^{\alpha} M^{\beta}$, $\alpha, \beta > 0$, and the following conditions hold, perfect efficiency is incompatible with profit maximizing behavior:

$$\alpha + \beta > 1 \text{ and } M^*(w,r) > \bar{M},$$

$$\alpha + \beta < 1 \text{ and } M^*(w,r) < \bar{M},$$

$$\alpha + \beta = 1 \text{ and } w \geq (1-\alpha)(r/\alpha)^{\frac{\alpha}{\alpha-1}}.$$

These conditions show that the possibility of perfect efficiency depends on factor prices and the technology. With decreasing returns, the firm needs $\bar{M}$ to be sufficiently low so that it can be attained. With constant returns, the firm needs the managerial input to be sufficiently "cheap" independently of $\bar{M}$. A similar result has been shown in Papadopoulos (2021) who considers management as an input but one result reinforces the other. Therefore, the configuration of factor prices will determine whether the firm is efficient or not. Moreover, when the firm is inefficient (i.e., $M < \bar{M}$) its efficiency will still depend on factor prices. In that case, the optimal factor levels solve the first order conditions:

$$f_K(K^*, M^*)\theta(M^*) = r, \text{ and } f_M(K^*, M^*)\theta(M^*) + f(K^*, M^*)\theta'(M^*) = w,$$

from which we can get an explicit solution for efficiency in the form $\theta(M^*)$. The solution will, of course, depend on the particular parameterization for the function $\theta(M)$.[9]

3. A DYNAMIC PROBLEM OF THE FIRM

In this section, we consider a firm that employs capital for productive purposes, and managerial hours that can be used to build managerial skills within the firm. Managerial skills can be used to improve efficiency but, of course, they depreciate over time. The problem of the firm is to maximize the discounted net present value[10]

$$\max_{\{K(t),M(t),I(t),H(t)\}} : \int_0^\infty \exp(-rt)[f(K(t)) - u(M(t)) - q(t)I(t) - w(t)H(t)]\,dt$$

subject to

$$\dot{K}(t) = I(t) - \delta K(t), \tag{7}$$

$$\dot{M}(t) = g(H(t)) - \nu M(t), \tag{8}$$

$$K(t), M(t), I(t), H(t) \geq 0, \tag{9}$$

$$K(0), \quad M(0) > 0 \tag{10}$$

are both given,

$$H \leq \bar{H}, \tag{11}$$

where $r > 0$ is the risk-free rate, $H(t)$ denotes managerial hours, $0 < \delta, \nu < 1$ are the depreciation rates for physical and managerial capital, $K(t)$ and $M(t)$ are physical and managerial capital, $I(t)$ is investment, $w(t)$ is managerial compensation, and $q(t)$ is the price of investment. To give efficiency a fair chance, we assume (11) viz., that is there is an upper bound on hours such that $H > \bar{H}$ implies $u(M) = 0$.

The optimal control necessary and sufficient conditions for a solution (using the current-value Hamiltonian) are the following:

$$\mu g'(H) - w = \psi \geq 0, \tag{12}$$

$$H \leq \bar{H}\,(= \bar{H} \text{ if } \psi > 0), \tag{13}$$

$$\dot{q} = (r + \delta)q - f'(K), \tag{14}$$

$$\dot{\mu} = (r + \nu)\mu + u'(M), \tag{15}$$

along with (7), (8), (10) and the transversality conditions:

$$\lim_{t\to\infty} \exp(-rt)q(t)K(t) \;=\; \lim_{t\to\infty} \exp(-rt)w(t)M(t)\,/\,g'(H(t)) \;=\; 0 \tag{16}$$

where $\mu \equiv \mu(t)$ is the co-state variable (the other co-state variable turns out to be equal to $q(t)$, and $\psi \equiv \psi(t)$ is a Kuhn-Tucker multiplier. It is evident from these conditions that $\dot{\mu} - (r + \nu)\mu$ may be interpreted as the "user cost of managerial capital" just like $(r + \delta)q - \dot{q}$ has the Jorgensonian "user cost of capital" interpretation. The transversality conditions in (14) follow immediately from their original form:

$$\lim_{t\to\infty} \exp(-rt)q(t)K(t) \;=\; \lim_{t\to\infty} \exp(-rt)\mu(t)M(t) = 0.$$

Assuming that (12) is binding, so that $H(t) < \bar{H}$, differentiate (12) with respect to time, and substitute the result and (12) itself in (14) to obtain:

$$\dot{H} = \left[\frac{g'(H)}{wg''(H)}\right]\left(\dot{w} - u'(M)g'(H) - (r+\nu)w\right). \qquad (17)$$

One way to interpret this condition is to notice that if managerial compensation grows at a rate more than $r+\nu$, then $\dot{H} < 0$ so managerial hours are reduced and the firm becomes even less efficient.

Remark 4.

If $g \in C^1[0, \bar{M}]$ and $g(M) = g(\bar{M})$ for any $M > \bar{M}$, there can be no interval $[a,b](b > a \geq 0)$ such that for all $t \in [a,b]$ we have $H(t) = \bar{H}$, i.e., the firm cannot be fully efficient in any time interval of non-zero length.

Remark 5.

If for all $t \in [a,b]$ we have $\dot{w}(t)/w(t) \geq r+\nu$, then $\dot{H}(t) < 0$ and the firm becomes continually less efficient in $[a,b]$ in the sense that $u(M(t)) > u(M(\tau))$ for any $t, \tau \in [a,b], t > \tau$.

This remark, in fact, shows that efficiency can exhibit autocorrelated behavior, provided managerial compensation grows sufficiently fast in a given time interval.

Therefore, it is not possible to observe full efficiency in a time interval *continually*, no matter how small the length of the time interval is. In a sense, this implies that full efficiency is an event of measure zero, and may happen only at particular points in the time continuum. The critical assumption is that $g \in C^1$. If this is not the case, the firm may be able to exploit this fact to sustain efficiency.

Remark 6.

Suppose $u \in C^1[0,\infty)$, g is differentiable in $[0, \bar{H})$ and $H(t) = \bar{H} \Leftrightarrow M(t) = \bar{M}$ with $u(M) = u'(\bar{M}) = 0$ for all $M \geq \bar{M}$. The necessary and sufficient condition for the firm to have $H(t) = \bar{H}$, for all $t \in [a,b]$, is that $w(t) < \mu(a)\, \exp[(r+\nu)(t-a)]\, g'(\bar{H}^-)$, where $g'(\bar{H}^-)$ denotes a left derivative.

This remark shows that when g' has a jump at $\bar{H}$ for full efficiency over some time interval, then it is necessary and sufficient that managerial compensation sufficiently cheap. This result makes sense and shows the critical role of managerial compensation in determining the choice of the firm between efficiency and inefficiency.

Illustration 1. An important special case of the problem is when the function $g(H)$ is, in fact, linear. Suppose $g(H) = g \cdot H$, $g > 0$. The problem of maximizing the Hamiltonian with respect to H reduces to:

$$\max : [\mu g - w]H, \text{subject to } 0 \leq H \leq \bar{H}$$

It is clear that $\mu(t)g \geq w(t)$ implies $H(t) = \bar{H}$ as the optimal solution and, therefore, we have $M(t) = \bar{M}, u'(\bar{M}) = 0$, which implies $\dot{\mu} = (r+\nu)\mu$. It is clear that we have the following:

Remark 7.

If $g(H) = g \cdot H$, $g > 0$, the firm is fully efficient in the interval T if and only if the following condition holds:

$$w(t) \leq g\mu(0)\exp[(r+\nu)t], \text{for all } t \in T.$$

Therefore, linearity of the g function can save full efficiency as an attainable state of the firm. One implication of the remark is that managerial compensation must be low enough in order for the firm to be able to attain full efficiency. The precise bound is provided by the remark, and one implication is that managerial compensation cannot grow at a rate greater than $r + \nu$.###

To gain more insight into the problem, we focus on a steady state where prices remain unchanged ($\dot{w} = \dot{q} = 0$ and $w(t) = \bar{w}$, $q(t) = \bar{q}$). The interior steady state satisfies the following equations:

$$f'(K^*) = (r + \delta)\bar{q}, \tag{18}$$

$$u'(M^*)g'(H^*) + (r + \nu)\bar{w} = 0, \tag{19}$$

$$I^* = \delta K^*, \tag{20}$$

$$g(H^*) = \nu M^* \tag{21}$$

Can we have an efficient steady state? If $H^* = \bar{H}$ then $g(\bar{H}) = \nu M^*$. But at the efficient steady state we must have $u(M^*) = 0$ which is only possible if there exists $\bar{M} > 0$ such that $u(M) = u'(M)$ for all $M \geq \bar{M}$, so it must be the case that $M^* = \bar{M}$ and, therefore, we must have $g(\bar{H}) = \nu\bar{\bar{M}}$. Clearly, this may happen only by chance. If it does not happen, there can be no efficient steady state and the proof is completed. Suppose, however, that this is the case. Then $u'(\bar{M}) = 0$. By (15) we have $\dot{\mu}(t) = (r + \nu)\mu(t)$. This, however, violates the transversality condition (16) so there can be no efficient steady state. It is perhaps important to notice that this result is obtained under the assumption that $\dot{\mu}(t) = (r + \nu)\mu(t)$ so that there is no jump in the derivative u'. This assumption is reasonable (contrary perhaps to the assumption that $g \in C^1$). It does not seem plausible to assume that the marginal contribution of managerial skills to inefficiency suddenly jumps from a negative value to zero as $M = \bar{M}$. From the technical point of view, we need the differentiability of u to obtain (15).

The most important implication of this analysis is that if indeed $u \in C^1[0, \infty)$ we cannot observe a firm that remains efficient in time intervals of the form $[a,b]$, in other words *the* firm will be inefficient almost always under the differentiability assumption *on* g. A natural question might be: If the differentiability at $\bar{H}$ fails so that we have a jump at this point, can the firm be efficient over an interval *provided* managerial compensation is not too expensive? By a theorem of Arrow and Kurz (see Kamien & Schwarz, 1991, pp. 243–244) this cannot happen if the maximized Hamiltonian is strictly concave in the state variable for given values of the multipliers and time. In other words, this implies that *if* $u(M)$ is strictly convex, a quite natural assumption in our context, then there can be no jumps in $M(t)$. This has the additional implication that the firm cannot even be efficient at particular points because, otherwise, it would violate the no-jump implication of strict convexity of $u(M)$. Therefore, with strict convexity of $u(M)$ the firm will be efficient everywhere in $t \in (0, \infty)$. We saw that with a linear g function the firm may attain full efficiency. However, there can be no efficient steady state even when this function is linear. The reason is that we must have $\mu = 0$ but efficiency requires $w < \mu g$, which would imply negative managerial compensation. Moreover, from (17) it is evident that zero compensation is uninteresting and the steady state is well defined.

4. DYNAMIC ANALYSIS NEAR THE STEADY STATE

In the following, we will study the local dynamic behavior of the firm near the steady state with constant input prices. We will consider the system of differential equations in (8) and (17). This depends only on H and M and, therefore, two-dimensional phase space analysis can be used to study the local dynamics. The system can be linearized around the steady state to obtain the approximation:

$$\begin{bmatrix} \dot{H} \\ \dot{M} \end{bmatrix} = \begin{bmatrix} G_H^* & G_M^* \\ g_*' & -\nu \end{bmatrix} \begin{bmatrix} H - H^* \\ M - M^* \end{bmatrix} \tag{22}$$

where $G_H^* = -\frac{u_*' g_*'}{\overline{w}}$, and $G_M^* = -\frac{u_*'' g_*'^2}{\overline{w} g_*''}$ in obvious notation. Both G_M^* and G_H^* are positive. The characteristic polynomial of the dynamical system is:

$$\lambda^2 + (G_H^* - \nu)\lambda + (\nu G_H^* + g_*' G_M^*) = 0 \tag{23}$$

After some algebra, we obtain that the discriminant of the quadratic equation is:

$$D_\lambda = \nu^2 + 6u_*' g_*' \nu + \left[u_*'^2 g_*'^2 + 4 g_*'^3 u_*'' / (\overline{w} g_*'') \right]. \tag{24}$$

so, there are always two roots ν_1 and ν_2. We have

$$\nu_1 \nu_2 = u_*'^2 g_*'^2 + 4 g_*'^3 u_*'' / (\overline{w} g_*'') \equiv C, \tag{25}$$

and

$$\nu_1 + \nu_2 = 6 u_*' g_*' < 0 \tag{26}$$

If $C > 0$, it is clear that both roots are negative so $D_\nu > 0$ for all $\nu \geq 0$, which implies $D_\lambda > 0$ always, and the system has two roots λ_1 and λ_2 of the same sign. Stability requires that both roots are negative: Since $\lambda_1 + \lambda_2 = G_H^* - \nu$, stability is equivalent to $G_H^* < \nu$ or $\nu + u_*' g_*' > 0$. It may appear that this places a lower bound on the rate of depreciation of managerial capital but in fact it places no restrictions at all as we will see below. If $C < 0$, we have roots ν_1 and ν_2 of opposite sign, so $\nu > \nu_{\max} \equiv \max(\nu_1, \nu_2)$ implies $D_\lambda > 0$ and we have two roots λ_1 and λ_1. The condition for stability, as in the previous case is $\nu + u_*' g_*' > 0$. If $\nu < \nu_{\max}$ then $D_\lambda < 0$, and we have complex roots. The sum of roots is $\lambda_1 + \lambda_2 = G_H^* - \nu$ so if $\nu + u_*' g_*' > 0$ we have a converging cycle, if $\nu + u_*' g_*' < 0$ we have a diverging cycle, and if $\nu + u_*' g_*' = 0$ we have a limit cycle.

It can be shown that the condition for stability is always satisfied. Suppose first that both roots are real. Indeed, if the roots ν_1 and ν_2 are real they have to be $-3u_*'g_*' \pm 2\sqrt{2u_*'^2 g_*'^2 - g_*'^3 u_*''/(\overline{w}g_*'')}$ so the maximum root is given by

$$\nu_{\max} = -3u_*'g_*' + 2\sqrt{2u_*'^2 g_*'^2 - g_*'^3 u_*''/(\overline{w}g_*'')}.$$

The condition for stability is $\nu + u_*'g_*' > 0$. After some algebra, this implies:

$$\frac{g_*'\ u_*''}{\overline{w}\ g_*''\ u_*'^2} < 1. \tag{27}$$

The left-hand sign is always negative under the reasonable assumption that $g''<0$ so the condition holds always under the theoretical constraints on functions $u(M)$ and $g(H)$. In the case of complex roots, as was pointed out their sum is $\lambda_1 + \lambda_2 = G_H^* - \nu$, and it is required that $\nu + u_*'g_*' > 0$ for convergence, which is exactly what we have just shown. It is important to point out, perhaps, that the dynamical system is either stable in the sense that every local trajectory converges to the steady state or in the sense that we have a converging cycle. In particular, this rules out a saddle point instability, so the only allowable steady state – the inefficient one – is always locally stable. Another noteworthy property of (22) is that near a steady state, local convergence does not depend on the price of investment; the only price that affects the dynamics is managerial compensation, $\overline{w}$. If managerial compensation is large, i.e., $\overline{w} \to \infty$, both G_H^* and G_M^* converge to zero and the system has two roots, one of which is zero, and the other is $-\nu$ so in this case the speed of local convergence of both $H(t)$ and $M(t)$ to the steady state is determined *entirely* by the rate of depreciation of managerial capital. Fast local convergence would require relatively high rates of depreciation of managerial capital, due perhaps to exogenous innovations in managerial practice. Of course, since the only steady state is inefficient, it is no surprise that local convergence is higher when managerial capital depreciates fast.

5. EMPIRICAL IMPLICATIONS

5.1. Econometric Model

Consider the problem

$$\max_{X \in \mathbb{R}^k, M} : f(X)\exp\{-u(M)\} - \boldsymbol{W}'\boldsymbol{X} - mM.$$

In this problem, inefficiency appears in a multiplicative rather than an additive way as we assumed in the previous sections. The reason is that the multiplicative specification has been used extensively in empirical research, and an additive specification emerges when the production function is considered in log terms following such popular specifications as the translog.

From the first order conditions, assuming interior solution we have:

$$f_j(\mathbf{X})\exp\{-u(M)\} = W_j, j = 1,\dots,k$$

$$-f(\mathbf{X})\exp\{-u(M)\}u'(M) = m.$$

Denote $\alpha = -u'(M)M / u(M)$, the elasticity of the u-function with respect to the managerial input. From these equations, we have:

$$\frac{\partial \ln f(\mathbf{X})}{\partial \ln X_j} f(\mathbf{X}) \exp\{-u(M)\} = W_j X_j, j = 1,\ldots,k$$

$$f(\mathbf{X}) \exp\{-u(M)\} \alpha = \frac{mM}{u(M)}$$

It is possible to rewrite these equations as follows:

$$\ln\left[\frac{\partial \ln f(\mathbf{X})}{\partial \ln X_j}\right] + \ln f(\mathbf{X}) - x_j = w_j + \ln u \tag{28}$$

$$\ln f(\mathbf{X}) - \ln M = \ln m - \ln u - \ln \alpha$$

where $w_j = \ln W_j, j = 1,\ldots,k$. Since we adopt a translog form for the production function it is convenient to express $\ln f(\mathbf{X}) = F(\mathbf{x})$ where $\mathbf{x} = \ln \mathbf{X}$ from which it follows $\frac{\partial \ln f(\mathbf{X})}{\partial \ln X_j} = F_j(\mathbf{x})$. Assuming the availability of panel data and introducing error terms, we have:

$$y_{it} = F(\mathbf{x}_{it}) + v_{it,o} - u_{it}$$

$$\ln[F_j(\mathbf{x}_{it})] + F(\mathbf{x}_{it}) - x_{j,it} = w_{j,it} + \ln u_{it} + v_{it,j}, j = 1,\ldots,k \tag{29}$$

$$F(\mathbf{x}_{it}) - \ln M_{it} = \ln m_i - \ln u_{it} - \ln \alpha_i + v_{it,k+1}$$

$$i = 1,\ldots,n;\ t = 1,\ldots,T$$

Suppose $\mathbf{v}_{it} = [v_{it,o}, v_{it,1},\ldots,v_{it,k+2}]' \equiv [\mathbf{v}_{it}', v_{it,k+2}]'$ with the stochastic specification $\mathbf{v}_{it} \sim N_{k+2}(\mathbf{0}, \mathbf{\Omega})$. For the technical inefficiency process, we assume:

$\ln u_{it} = A_i - \alpha_i \ln M_{it} + \varepsilon_{it}$, where $\varepsilon_{it} \sim N(0, \sigma_\varepsilon^2)$ under the assumption that α is constant but firm-specific. The assumption is equivalent to a log-normal specification for the positive random variable u_{it}. Substituting in the equations above, we obtain:

$$y_{it} = F(\mathbf{x}_{it}) + v_{it,o} - u_{it}$$

$$\ln[F_j(\ln \mathbf{x}_{it})] + F(\mathbf{x}_{it}) - x_{j,it} = w_{j,it} + \{A_i - \alpha_i \ln M_{it} + \varepsilon_{it}\} + v_{it,j}, j = 1,\ldots,k \tag{30}$$

$$F(\mathbf{x}_{it}) - \ln M_{it} = \ln m_i - \{A_i - \alpha_i \ln M_{it} + \varepsilon_{it}\} - \ln \alpha_i + v_{it,k+2}$$

Estimating this system of equations permits (i) to identify the elasticity α_i, (ii) to estimate log managerial compensation $\ln m_i$ and (iii) estimate technical inefficiency. The error terms ε_{it} are the same across all equations so estimation of σ_ε^2 is possible. Writing the system in a somewhat simpler form, we have:

$$y_{it} = F(\mathbf{x}_{it}) + v_{it,o} - u_{it}$$

$$\ln\left[F_j(\mathbf{x}_{it})\right] + F(\mathbf{x}_{it}) - x_{j,it} + \alpha_i \ln M_{it} = A_i + w_{j,it} + \varepsilon_{it} + v_{it,j}, j = 1,\ldots,k$$

$$F(\mathbf{x}_{it}) - (1+\alpha_i)\ln M_{it} = \ln m_i - A_i - \ln \alpha_i - A_i\varepsilon_{it} + v_{it,k+2}$$

The system of equations has $k + 2$ endogenous variables (y, $\mathbf{x}$ and $\ln M$) and consists of $k + 2$ equations, so that the system is complete. To complete the specification, it remains to assume that $\ln m_i$ is fixed firm-specific effects, as we suspect that they are not uncorrelated with management or the vector of inputs. Identification rests upon particular assumptions made about the managerial input as it is unobserved. The particular assumption we use is that managerial resources or ability are time-invariant as in Section 5.2. Among the many possible specifications this is, perhaps, the most innocuous. The A_is are also fixed effects and they can be identified separately from the first set of equations. The elasticities α_i are also treated as fixed parameters and can be identified as well. Again, it is not necessary to assume that A_i s or elasticities α_i are uncorrelated with management or the vector of inputs. The system above is a simultaneous equations model which can be seen from the structure of the Jacobian. In vector notation, the system is:

$$y_{it} = F(\mathbf{x}_{it}) + v_{it,o} - u_{it}$$

$$\ln\left[\nabla F(\mathbf{x}_{it})\right] + F(\mathbf{x}_{it}) - \mathbf{x}_{it} + \alpha_i \ln M_{it}\mathbf{1}_k = A_i + \mathbf{w}_{it} + \varepsilon_{it}\mathbf{1}_k + \tilde{\mathbf{v}}_{it}$$

$$F(\mathbf{x}_{it}) - (1+\alpha_i)\ln M_{it} = \ln m_i - A_i - \ln \alpha_i - A_i\varepsilon_{it} + v_{it,k+2}$$

The Jacobian is given as follows:

$$J_{it} = \left\| \frac{\partial \mathbf{v}_{it}}{\partial(y_{it}, \mathbf{x}_{it}, \ln M_{it})'} \right\| = (1+\alpha_i)\left\{\nabla^2 F(\mathbf{x}_{it}) \odot \tilde{\nabla} F(\mathbf{x}_{it}) + \nabla^2 F(\mathbf{x}_{it}) - \mathbf{I}_k\right\}$$
$$+ \alpha_i \mathbf{1}_k' \nabla F(\mathbf{x}_{it})$$

where $\tilde{\nabla} F(\mathbf{x}) \triangleq \left[\frac{1}{\partial F(\mathbf{x}) / \partial x_j}, j = 1,\ldots,k\right]$. This can be expressed in simpler terms as:

$$J_{it} = (1+\alpha_i)\left\{\nabla^2 \ln F(\mathbf{x}_{it}) + \nabla F(\mathbf{x}_{it}) \otimes \mathbf{1}_k - \mathbf{I}_k\right\} + \alpha_i \mathbf{1}_k' \nabla F(\mathbf{x}_{it})$$

As the translog form can be expressed as:

$$F(\mathbf{x}_{it}) = \beta_o + \boldsymbol{\beta}'\mathbf{x}_{it} + \tfrac{1}{2}\mathbf{x}_{it}'\mathbf{B}\mathbf{x}_{it}$$

it is clear that

$$\nabla F(\mathbf{x}_{it}) = \boldsymbol{\beta} + \mathbf{B}\mathbf{x}_{it}$$

and

$$\nabla^2 F(\mathbf{x}_{it}) = \mathbf{B}$$

However, the Jacobian still depends on $\mathbf{x}_{it}$ although not on M_{it}. The likelihood function of the model is the following:

$$L(\boldsymbol{\theta};\mathbb{Y}) = (2\pi)^{-nT(k+1)/2} \prod_{i=1}^{n} |\boldsymbol{\Sigma}_i|^{-T/2} \prod_{t=1}^{T} J_{it} \exp\left\{-\tfrac{1}{2}\mathbf{v}_{it}(\boldsymbol{\theta})'\,\boldsymbol{\Sigma}^{-1}\mathbf{v}_{it}(\boldsymbol{\theta})\right\} \quad (31)$$

where $\boldsymbol{\Sigma}_i = \boldsymbol{\Omega} + \sigma_\varepsilon^2 \begin{bmatrix} \mathbf{J}_k & -A_i \\ -A_i & A_i^2 \end{bmatrix}$, $\mathbf{J}_k$ denotes the $k \times k$ matrix consisting of ones, and

$$\mathbf{v}_{it}(\boldsymbol{\theta}) \triangleq \begin{bmatrix} \ln[\nabla F(\mathbf{x}_{it})] + F(\mathbf{x}_{it}) - \mathbf{x}_{it} + \alpha_i \ln M_{it}\mathbf{1}_k - A_i - \mathbf{w}_{it} \\ F(\mathbf{x}_{it}) - (1+\alpha_i)\ln M_{it} - \ln m_i + A_i + \ln \alpha_i \end{bmatrix}$$

and $\boldsymbol{\theta} \in \mathbb{R}^p$ denotes the parameter vector while $\mathbb{Y}$ denotes all available data. Of course, the Jacobian is a function of both the data and the parameters, and the same is true for $\boldsymbol{\Sigma}_i$ which depends on the fixed effects A_i and, of course, σ_ε^2. With large n maximizing the likelihood function is clearly a difficult problem due to the fact that we cannot explicitly concentrate out $\boldsymbol{\Sigma}_i$. A random-effects assumption on the A_i s would make the problem easier at the cost of assuming that "maximum possible efficiency" (which is A_i) is stochastically independent of management and the inputs: This would still not permit the concentration of the likelihood function although it would reduce the number of unknown parameters. We feel, however, that such an assumption is heroic and should not be used. Thus, the peculiarity of the system is that both the covariance matrix and the system equations themselves are dependent on unknown parameters.

5.2. Time-Invariant Management

Often, time series data on management are not available. This necessitates a slight modification of the basic procedure that we introduced above. Let $\mathbf{y}_i = [y_{i1},\ldots,y_{iT}]'$ and $\mathbf{x}_i = [\mathbf{x}_{i1}',\ldots,\mathbf{x}_{iT}']'$ denote the vectors of output and inputs for unit i ($i = 1,\ldots,n$). With time-invariant management data we have the following system of equations:

$$\mathbf{y}_i - F(\mathbf{x}_i) - \alpha_i \ln M_i \mathbf{1}_T = -A_i\mathbf{1}_T + \mathbf{v}_{i,o} - \boldsymbol{\varepsilon}_i$$

$$\ln[\nabla F(\mathbf{x}_i)] + F(\mathbf{x}_i) - \mathbf{x}_{it} + \alpha_i \ln M_{it}\mathbf{1}_{kT} = A_i\mathbf{1}_T + \mathbf{w}_i + \boldsymbol{\varepsilon}_i \otimes \mathbf{1}_k + \tilde{\mathbf{v}}_i \quad (32)$$

$$F(\mathbf{x}_i)-(1+\alpha_i)\ln M_{it}\mathbf{1}_T=(\ln m_i-A_i-\ln\alpha_i)\mathbf{1}_T-A_i\boldsymbol{\varepsilon}_i+\mathbf{v}_{i,k+2}$$

The Jacobian of the system is given by

$$J_i=(1+\alpha_i)\mathbf{1}_T'\left\{\nabla^2\ln F(\mathbf{x}_i)+\nabla F(\mathbf{x}_{it})\otimes\mathbf{1}_k-\mathbf{I}\right\}+\alpha_i\mathbf{1}_{kT}'\nabla F(\mathbf{x}_i)$$

The contribution of unit i to the likelihood, namely $p(\mathbf{y}_i\mid\boldsymbol{\theta})$ can be computed as before and the likelihood function becomes $L(\boldsymbol{\theta};\mathbb{Y})=\prod_{i=1}^{n}p(\mathbf{y}_i\mid\boldsymbol{\theta})$ assuming stochastic independence of units.

6. EMPIRICAL ANALYSIS

In this chapter, we use the same data as in Bloom and van Reenen (2007): there are 620 companies from 1994 to 2004. The companies are medium-sized manufacturing firms from the US, the UK, France and Germany. Following Bloom and van Reenen (2007), management is measured using an average across 18 different practices. Data on output (deflated value of sales), capital (real assets) and labor (deflated employee expenses) are available. There are 5,336 observations in total. The data set was analyzed also, using quite different techniques and perspective, in Triebs and Kumbhakar (2014). The management variable is time-invariant as firms were interviewed about their management practices in 2004. Our interest focuses on: (i) estimating technical inefficiency and comparing with conventional techniques where it is assumed to follow a half-normal distribution. (ii) Estimating the inefficiency elasticity with respect to management (α_i) without restrictive assumptions on the functional form. Finally, (iii) estimating managerial compensation (m_i or its log). Apparently, since both the functional form of the inefficiency-management relationship as well as managerial compensation cannot be known in advance, estimating such features is extremely important. We use a translog production function which includes capital, labor and trend, as a second-order approximation to an arbitrary production function. To account for additional heterogeneity, we include country and firm-level fixed effects in the production function. We use maximum likelihood to estimate the system of equations implied by endogenous inefficiency, which is implemented using a conjugate gradients algorithm with numerical first and second derivatives.

In Fig. 8.1, we present sample distributions of technical inefficiency by country, using estimates delivered by the techniques proposed in this chapter (straight line) versus technical inefficiency based on maximum likelihood estimation of the production function using a half-normal specification. The measures are quite different confirming that the assumption of optimal inefficiency makes an important difference. Estimated measured of managerial compensation ($\log m_i$) are reported in Fig. 8.2.

Managerial elasticities (α_i) are reported in Fig. 8.3. These elasticities are positive, as expected, but also less than unity. Considerable heterogeneity exists not only among but also across countries. To our knowledge, this is the first study that estimates and reports the important features of the inefficiency–management

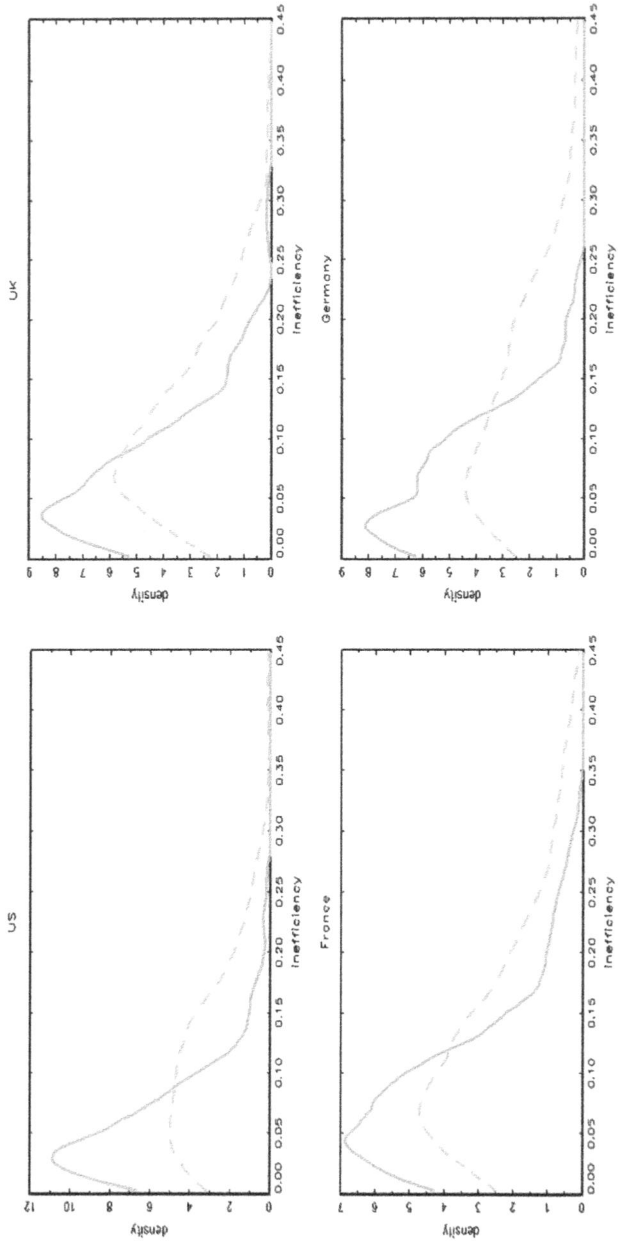

Fig. 8.1. Sample Distributions of Technical Inefficiency.

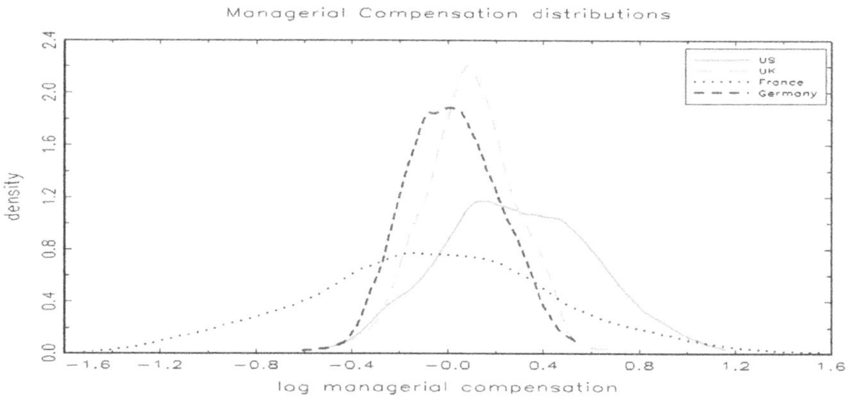

Fig. 8.2. Sample Distributions of Managerial Compensation ($\log m_i$).

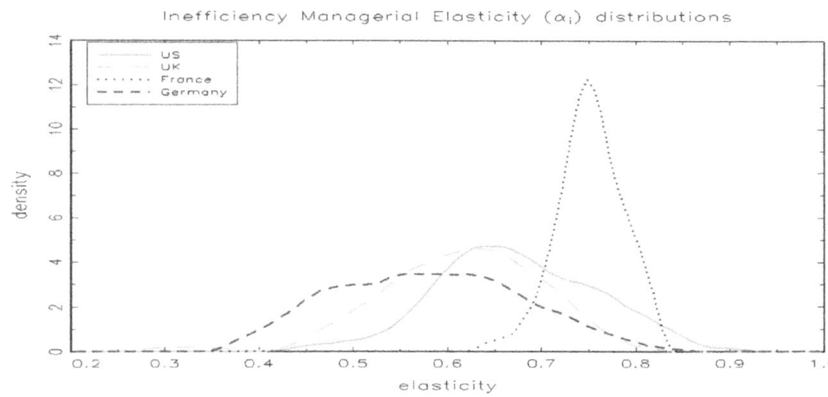

Fig. 8.3. Elasticity of Inefficiency Function with Respect to Management.

relationship at the firm-level. The techniques used here can be used, as we mentioned, to uncover such features when time-varying management data are available but also when management data, which are difficult to obtain in the first place, can only be obtained at a specific point in time thus making such data time-invariant.

Another important aspect of the analysis concerns the relationship between managerial practice or effort and estimated managerial compensation. As the units of measurement are not relevant due to the nature of the data, we normalize logs of managerial effort (M_i) and managerial compensation (m_i) based on their ranks and then in the unit interval, following standard practices introduced in efficiency measurement by Akhavein, Berger, and Humphrey (1997). The results are shown in Fig. 8.4.

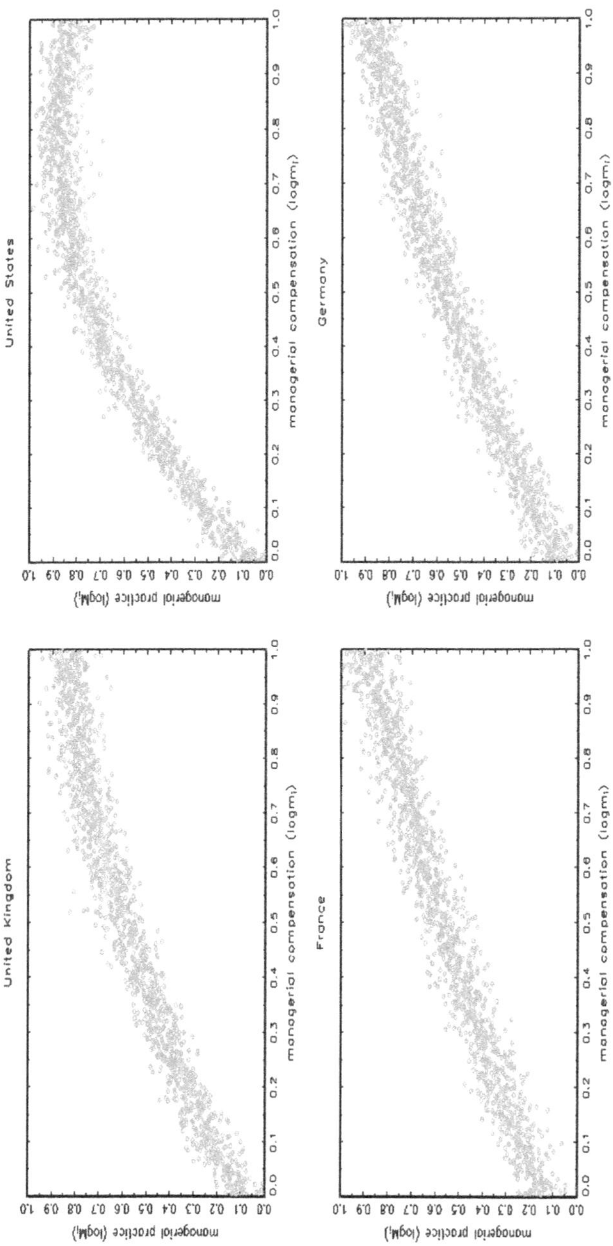

Fig. 8.4. The Relationship Between Managerial Effort and Estimated Managerial Compensation.

The results show a nonlinear but positive relationship between the two variables and, remarkably, the fit is quite accurate. Especially for the United States the relationship shows a concave relationship where, after a point corresponding approximately to 70% of managerial compensation, managerial effort begins to decrease slightly. To investigate this issue further and account for statistical uncertainty in point estimates of managerial compensation, we apply the bootstrap to the estimation of the system using maximum likelihood. With 10,000 bootstrap replications it turns out that the turning point has a 95% confidence interval [0.681, 0.754]. So, it is quite robust and somewhat asymmetric to the right. Sickles, Sun, and Triebs (2021) and Triebs and Kumbhakar (2018) propose estimation of managerial resources using different models although the concerns and motivation are the same as in this chapter. For example, Sickles et al. (2021), using the Bloom and Van Reenen (2017) data, find that the shadow price of management is, approximately, 1.3 million USD and most firms make too little use of this resource. As management is scarce and costly this finding certainly makes sense.

7. CONCLUSIONS AND IMPLICATIONS FOR EMPIRICAL WORK

In this chapter, we have examined static and dynamic models of the firm with two main implications. *First*, when attaining perfect technical efficiency requires real resources, factor prices determine the extent of technical inefficiency. *Second*, in a dynamic context, under reasonable assumptions, the firm can never be perfectly efficient, the steady state is always inefficient, and it is locally stable. It seems that technical efficiency should be the exception rather than the rule even when formal dynamic considerations are fully taken into account, and the relation between efficiency and factor prices is also taken into account. In terms of empirical analysis, we show how likelihood-based methods can be used to uncover, in a semi-nonparametric manner, important features of the inefficiency–management relationship using a flexible functional form accounting for the endogeneity of inputs in a production function. The new empirical techniques are applied in a data set previously analyzed by Bloom and van Reenen (2007) on managerial practices of manufacturing firms in the UK, US, France and Germany.

Relevant also are econometric models that try to distinguish between strictly positive and zero inefficiency (Kumbhakar, Parmeter, & Tsionas, 2013). More importantly, dynamic models of the firm are broadly inconsistent with an efficient steady state as we showed in the chapter. This necessitates more work on dynamic inefficiency models which, with some important exceptions (Rungsuriyawiboon & Stefanou, 2003, Silva & Stefanou, 2007, Stefanou, 1989), has not received the required attention in the literature. Such models could be organized around two principles. First, that inefficiency follows a dynamic process and, second, it should be possible to test the prediction that the steady state is not efficient. One obstacle is that managerial effort is often not observed directly. In some applications, this limitation is removed and the behavior of inefficiency or productivity is examined (Triebs & Kumbhakar, 2013). Clearly more work is needed in this area and this can be done by treating management as an additional latent variable whose estimation can, most likely, be facilitated in the presence of panel data, although, in this case, semi-non-parametric features of the inefficiency–management relationship will not be identifiable. When managerial effort is not observed we have shown that it can identified and estimated. As a result, it becomes clear that the joint description of inputs and inefficiency is of the utmost importance for the realistic modeling of inefficiency in a dynamic framework. In this front more empirical theory-based research along the lines of Stefanou (1989), Triebs and Kumbhakar (2018) or Silva and Stefanou (2007) would be essential. The essential tools for this undertaking (input endogeneity, time-invariant management, Jacobian of the likelihood function) have already been developed and explained in the present chapter.

NOTES

1. For econometric models of technical efficiency, see Aigner, Knox-Lovell, and Schmidt (1977) and Meeusen and van den Broeck (1977). For surveys, see Bauer (1990), Greene (1993, 2001), and Kumbhakar and Lovell (2000).
2. There is a large literature on costly information primarily in connection with auction models. Schweizer and von Ungern-Sternberg (1983) explore the role of information for two bidders using simulation. Milgrom (1981) presents a two-stage model where at the first stage the agent can choose to become perfectly informed about the value of the object. Lee (1984) proposes a two-agent model with incomplete information and costly revelation of information. In Hausch and Li (1993), there is a private signal whose accuracy is related to the amount spent to obtain it. Guzman and Kolstad (1997) provide a model with endogenous information acquisition.
3. The last paper proposes an estimable model of dynamic efficiency. A "reduced form" model is proposed in Tsionas (2006).
4. A multiplicative specification of the production function will be presented below.
5. An alternative assumption is that full efficiency is never possible in the sense that: $\lim_{M \to \infty} u(M) > 0$ his case did not yield different results.
6. Proofs for selected remarks can be found at the Appendix to this paper.
7. If we allow for a jump, the firm could be technically efficient but it is not clear that this discontinuity makes any sense and / or has practical relevance. It would require the assumption that using managerial resources more intensively (at $M > \bar{M}$, say) would instantly eliminate inefficiency. It is not obvious to us that such management technologies are available but if they are then production would be in a sense "simple enough" so that re-organization of inputs would be possible, irrespective of scale, with maximum managerial effectiveness once a certain management threshold is attained. This does not appear to be of much relevance, see for example Sickles et al. (2021).
8. The proof is omitted.
9. Similar analyses can be conducted for the monopolistic firm. If the monopolist faces a demand elasticity e, and we normalize $D(q^*) = 1$, where q^* is equilibrium output, it can be shown that it is more difficult for the monopolist to be technically efficient (relative to the competitive firm) when increasing returns, and easier with decreasing returns. The practical implication is that market structure and demand conditions affect technical inefficiency.
10. The scope for dynamic efficiency is explored in Tsionas (2006) and Murillo-Zamorano (2004, section 3.2.2). The latter is an excellent survey of theory and estimation in efficiency analysis.

ACKNOWLEDGMENTS

The author wishes to thank Spiro Stefanou for useful discussions and two anonymous reviewers for comments on an earlier version. The usual disclaimer applies.

REFERENCES

Aigner, D., Knox-Lovell, K. A., & Schmidt, P. (1977). Formulation and estimation of stochastic frontier production function models. *Journal of Econometrics*, *6*, 21–37.

Akhavein, J. D., Berger, A. N., & Humphrey, D. B. (1997). The effect of mega-mergers on efficiency and prices: Evidence from a bank profit function. *Review of Industrial Organization*, *12*, 301–322.

Bauer, P. W. (1990). Recent developments in the econometric estimation of frontiers. *Journal of Econometrics*, *46*, 39–56.

Bloom, N., & van Reenen, J. (2007). Measuring and explaining management practices across firms and countries. *Quarterly Journal of Economics*, *CXXII*(4), 1351–1408.

Epstein, L. G. (1983). Duality theory and functional forms for dynamic factor demands. *Review of Economic Studies*, *48*, 81–95.

Fare, L., & Lovell, C. A. K. (1978). Measuring the technical efficiency of production. *Journal of Economic Theory*, *19*, 150–162.

Farrell, M. J. (1957). The measurement of productive efficiency. *Journal of the Royal Statistical Society A*, *120*, 253–281.

Greene, W. H. (1993). The econometric approach to efficiency analysis. In H. O. Fried, C. A. K. Lovell, & S. S. Schmidt (Eds.), *The measurement of productive efficiency: Techniques and applications* (pp. 68–119). New York: Oxford University Press.

Greene, W. H. (2001). New developments in the estimation of stochastic frontier models with panel data, Remarks prepared for the 7th European Workshop on Efficiency and Productivity Analysis, University of Oviedo, Spain.

Guzman, R. M., & Kolstad, C. D. (1997). *Auction equilibrium with costly information acquisition*. Unpublished. Department of Economics, University of Illinois-Urbana Champaign.

Hausch, D., & Li, T. (1993). A common value auction model with endogenous entry and information acquisition. *Economic Theory*.

Kamien, M. I., & Schwarz, N. L. (1991). *Dynamic optimization* (2nd ed.). Amsterdam, North Holland.

Koopmans, T. C. (1951). Analysis of production as an efficient combination of activities. In T. C. Koopmans (Ed.), *Activity analysis of production and allocation* [Monograph No. 13]. New York: Cowles Commission for Research in Economics.

Kumbhakar, S. C., & Lovell, C. A. K. (2000). *Stochastic frontier analysis*. New York: Cambridge University Press.

Kumbhakar, S. C., Parmeter, C. & Tsionas, E. G. (2013). A zero inefficiency stochastic frontier model. *Journal of Econometrics*, *172*, 66–76.

Lee, T. K. (1984). Incomplete information, high-low bidding and public information in first price auctions. *Management Science*, *30*, 1490–1496.

Meeusen, W., & van den Broeck, J. (1977). Efficiency estimation from Cobb-Douglas production functions with composed error. *International Economic Review*, *8*, 435–444.

Milgrom, P. (1981). Rational expectations, information acquisition, and competitive bidding. *Econometrica*, *49*, 921–943.

Murillo-Zamorano, L. R. (2004). Economic efficiency and frontier techniques. *Journal of Economic Surveys*, *18*(1), 33–77.

Papadopoulos, A. (2021). Measuring the effect of management on production: A two-tier stochastic frontier approach. *Empirical Economics*, *60*(6), 3011–3041.

Rungsuriyawiboon, S., & Stefanou, S. E. (2003). *Dynamic efficiency estimation: An application to US electric utilities*. Working Paper. Center for Efficiency and Productivity Analysis, School of Economics, University of Queensland, Australia.

Schweizer, U., & von Ungern-Sternberg, T. (1983). Sealed bid auctions and the search for better information. *Economica*, *50*, 79–85.

Sickles, R. C., Sun, K., & Triebs, T. P. (2021). The optimal use of management. *Economic Inquiry*, *59*(3), 1346–1363.

Silva, E., & Stefanou, S. (2007). Dynamic efficiency measurement: Theory and application. *American Journal of Agricultural Economics*, *89*, 398–419.

Simon, H. A. (1955). A behavioral model of rational choice. *Quarterly Journal of Economics*, *LXIX*, 99–118.

Stefanou, S. E. (1989). Returns to scale in the long run: The dynamic theory of cost. *Southern Economic Journal*, *55*, 570–579.

Triebs, T. P., & Kumbhakar, S. C. (2013). Productivity with general indices of management and technical change. *Economics Letters*, *120*, 18–22.

Triebs, T. P., & Kumbhakar, S. C. (2018). Management in production: From unobserved to observed. *Journal of Productivity Analysis*, *49*(2), 111–121.

Tsionas, E. G. (2006). Inference in dynamic stochastic frontier models. *Journal of Applied Econometrics*, *21*, 669–676.

APPENDIX. PROOFS OF CERTAIN REMARKS

Remark 1.
Suppose $u(M)$ is differentiable, with $u'(M) \leq 0$, $u''(M) \geq 0$, and there exists $\bar{M} > 0$, and $u'(M) < 0$ for all $M \in [0, \bar{M})$, $u(M) = 0$ for all $M \in [\bar{M}, \infty)$ with $u'(M) = 0$ for all $M \in [\bar{M}, \infty)$. Then

(i) $r \leq f'(\underline{K})$ implies that $K > \underline{K}$.
(ii) $w \leq -u'(\underline{M})$ implies $M > \underline{M}$.
(iii) If (i) and (ii) hold, and $w \geq -u'(\bar{M})$ then $M < \bar{M}$ and the firm cannot attain full production efficiency.

Proof.
To show (i), assume $K = \underline{K}$ so that (3) implies $\lambda_1 = 0$. By (2) $r > f'(\underline{K})$, a contradiction. To show (ii) assume $M = \underline{M}$ so that (4) implies $\lambda_2 = 0$. Since $M < \bar{M}$, (5) implies $\lambda_3 = 0$. By (1) $u'(\underline{M}) + w > 0$, a contradiction. Next, we show (iii). Under (i) and (ii) we have $K > \underline{K}$ and $M > \underline{M}$, so $w(t)$ by (3) and (4). Assume $q(t)$, which implies $\lambda_3 > 0$ by (5). By (1) we have $u'(\bar{M}) + w = -\lambda_3 < 0$, a contradiction.

Remark 2.
Let $\frac{\partial f(K(\bar{M}), \bar{M})}{\partial K} \equiv r$. If $w > \frac{\partial f(K(\overline{M}), \overline{M})}{\partial M}$ the firm cannot attain full technical efficiency.

Proof.
The necessary and sufficient Kuhn-Tucker conditions for this concave differentiable program are:

$$\frac{\partial f(K, M)}{\partial K} - w = 0$$

$$\frac{\partial f(K, M)}{\partial M} - u'(M) - w \geq 0 (= 0 \, if \; M < \bar{M}),$$

$$M \leq \bar{M}$$

Suppose the firm is fully efficient, i.e., $M = \bar{M}$. Then $\frac{\partial f(K, M)}{\partial M} - u'(M) > w$, a contradiction.

Remark 3.
If $f(K, M) = K^{\alpha} M^{\beta}$, $\alpha, \beta > 0$, and the following conditions hold, perfect efficiency is incompatible with profit maximizing behavior:

$$\alpha + \beta > 1 \text{and}\, M^{*}(w, r) > \bar{M},$$

$$\alpha + \beta < 1 \text{and}\, M^{*}(w, r) < \bar{M},$$

$$\alpha + \beta = 1 \text{and}\, w \geq (1 - \alpha)(r / \alpha)^{\frac{\alpha}{\alpha - 1}}.$$

Proof.

The first order condition with respect to K gives $K(M) = \alpha^{\frac{1}{1-\alpha}} r^{\frac{1}{\alpha-1}} M^{\frac{\beta}{1-\alpha}}$, and we need to examine the implications of the first order condition with respect to M. Since $M = \bar{M}$ we have $\lambda > 0$, and the first order condition with respect to M implies $f_M(K(\bar{M}), \bar{M}) > w$ since $\theta(\bar{M}) = 1$ and $\theta'(\bar{M}) = 0$. Then we get the inequalities stated in the Remark, depending on the sign of $1-(\alpha+\beta)$. When $\alpha+\beta=1$ the first order conditions imply $K / M = \alpha^{\frac{1}{1-\alpha}} r^{\frac{1}{\alpha-1}}$. Substituting in $f_M(K(\bar{M}), \bar{M}) > w$ provides the condition $w \geq (1-\alpha)(r/\alpha)^{\frac{\alpha}{\alpha-1}}$, as stated.

Remark 4.

If $g \in C^1[0, \bar{M}]$ and $g(M) = g(\bar{M})$ for any $M > \bar{M}$, there can be no interval $[a,b]\,(b > a \geq 0)$ such that for all $t \in [a,b]$ we have $H(t) = \bar{H}$, i.e., the firm cannot be fully efficient in any time interval of positive measure.

Proof.

Suppose that for all $t \in [a,b]$ we have $H(t) = \bar{H}$ which implies $M(t) = \bar{M}$ and $u(\bar{M}) = u'(\bar{M}) = 0$. By (13) we have that $w(t) < \mu(t) g'(\bar{H})$, and by (15) we have that $\dot{\mu}(t) = (r+\nu)\mu(t)$ so that $\mu(t) = \mu(a)\exp[(r+\nu)t]$, for all $t \in [a,b]$. This provides the following bound for managerial compensation: $w(t) < \mu(a)\exp[(r+\nu)t] g'(\bar{H})$. Since $g \in C^1[0, \bar{H}]$ we have must continuity of $g'(H)$ at $\bar{H}$. Since $g'(\bar{H}^+) = 0$ this implies $g'(\bar{H}) = 0$, so we get $w(t) < 0$, a contradiction.

Remark 6.

Suppose $u \in C^1[0,\infty)$, g is differentiable in $[0, \bar{H})$ and $H(t) = \bar{H} \Leftrightarrow M(t) = \bar{M}$ with $u(M) = u'(\bar{M}) = 0$ for all $M \geq \bar{M}$. The necessary and sufficient condition for the firm to have $H(t) = \bar{H}$, for all $t \in [a,b]$ is that $w(t) < \mu(a)\exp[(r+\nu)(t-a)] g'(\bar{H}^-)$ where $g'(\bar{H}^-)$ denotes a left derivative.

Proof.

Suppose $H(t) = \bar{H}$, for all $t \in [a,b]$. Since g is not differentiable at $\bar{H}$ the necessary and sufficient condition for optimality of $\bar{H}$ is that $\mu(t) g(\bar{H}(t)) - w\bar{H} > \mu(t) g(H(t)) - wH$ for all $H(t) < \bar{H}$. After some algebra and passage to the limit as $H(t) \to \bar{H}^-$ we obtain $w(t) < \mu(t) g'(\bar{H}^-)$. Since $H(t) = \bar{H} \Leftrightarrow M(t) = \bar{M}$ with $u(M) = u'(\bar{M}) = 0$ for all $M \geq \bar{M}$, by (15) we obtain $\dot{\mu}(t) = (r+\nu)\mu(t)$, for all $t \in [a,b]$. The solution is $\mu(t) = \mu(a)\exp[(r+\nu)(t-a)]$, which proves the remark.

CHAPTER 9

A SYSTEM APPROACH TO STRUCTURAL IDENTIFICATION OF PRODUCTION FUNCTIONS WITH MULTI-DIMENSIONAL PRODUCTIVITY

Emir Malikov[a], Shunan Zhao[b] and Jingfang Zhang[c]

[a]*University of Nevada, Las Vegas, Las Vegas, NV, USA*
[b]*Oakland University, Rochester, MI, USA*
[c]*Alcorn State University, Lorman, MS, USA*

ABSTRACT

There is growing empirical evidence that firm heterogeneity is technologically non-neutral. This chapter extends the Gandhi, Navarro, and Rivers (2020) proxy variable framework for structurally identifying production functions to a more general case when latent firm productivity is multi-dimensional, with both factor-neutral and (biased) factor-augmenting components. Unlike alternative methodologies, the proposed model can be identified under weaker data requirements, notably, without relying on the typically unavailable cross-sectional variation in input prices for instrumentation. When markets are perfectly competitive, point identification is achieved by leveraging the information contained in static optimality conditions, effectively adopting a system-of-equations approach. It is also shown how one can partially identify the non-neutral production technology in the traditional proxy variable framework when firms have market power.

Essays in Honor of Subal Kumbhakar
Advances in Econometrics, Volume 46, 211–263

ISSN: 0731-9053/doi:10.1108/S0731-905320240000046009

Keywords: Production function; factor-augmenting technology; proxy variable; productivity; structural identification; endogeneity

JEL Classification: D24; L10

1. INTRODUCTION

Production function and productivity are fundamental economic concepts the importance of which requires no justification among economists. Their identification however remains a challenge. At the micro level, identifying production functions – and firm productivity, by extension – from observational data is not a trivial matter due to the endogeneity issue arising from the fact that firm "productivity" capturing such factors like tacit knowledge and managerial quality is unobserved yet must be controlled for because it is correlated with input usage. The literature focused on addressing these methodological issues is vast and uses myriad different approaches, but most consider the case of scalar productivity. Until very recently (most notably Doraszelski & Jaumandreu, 2018), few studies have considered the identification of production functions when latent firm productivity is multi-dimensional in that the productivity change may not affect marginal products of all inputs in the same proportion (i.e., neutrally) despite the strong evidence thereof in the data (e.g., Raval, 2020). In this chapter, we develop a structural framework for the proxy variable estimation of production functions with multi-dimensional productivity, including factor-augmenting and -neutral components, that does not rely on the typically unavailable cross-sectional variation in prices for instrumentation.

Among many methods to tackling endogeneity in the production function context, the proxy variable approach by Olley and Pakes (1996) and Levinsohn and Petrin (2003) has become one of the most prevalent estimators in applied productivity research in economics as evidenced, e.g., by over 15,000 Google Scholar citations (as of the time of writing) amassed by these two papers alone. A proxy variable methodology for the structural identification of production functions arguably owes its popularity to not only good empirical performance but also the relative simplicity of implementation. The conventional proxy variable estimators as well as their many refinements and extensions (e.g., Ackerberg, Caves, & Frazer, 2015; De Loecker, 2013; Flynn, Gandhi, & Traina, 2019; Gandhi, Navarro, & Rivers, 2020; Kim, Luo, & Su, 2019; Malikov & Lien, 2021; Malikov & Zhao, 2021; Wooldridge, 2009) assume that latent firm productivity is scalar and factor-neutral. Then, under some structural timing assumptions, this latent productivity can be expressed as a function of (observable) either the physical investment or intermediate inputs along with other state variables by inverting the corresponding input demand/investment function. This identification strategy relies crucially on the scalar unobservable assumption, whereby there exists a single latent productivity term, which is necessary to ensure the invertibility of demand functions to construct a proxy.

However, the usual assumption of a scalar Hicks-neutral productivity in the production function to capture technological/productivity changes remains inconsistent with many economic theories as well as may be too restrictive in many empirical applications. For example, as Doraszelski and Jaumandreu (2018) point out, the traditional theories of both exogenous and endogenous economic growth rest on the assumption that technological change is non-neutral and, in particular, labor-saving. Large cross-firm heterogeneity in variable input ratios documented in the data is at odds with the factor-neutral productivity too, and the "biased" technological change has been widely used to explain changes in the labor share of income (see Doraszelski & Jaumandreu, 2018, 2019; Oberfield & Raval, 2021; Zhang, 2019).[1] Therefore, the impetus to accommodate non-neutral productivity while estimating production functions is strong and has garnered much attention among economists.

We extend Gandhi et al.'s (2020) system-based proxy variable framework for structurally identifying production functions to a more general case when latent firm heterogeneity is multi-dimensional, consisting of factor-neutral and factor-augmenting productivities. Following Doraszelski and Jaumandreu (2018), to model non-neutral technology we augment the standard proxy variable setup by introducing labor-augmenting (Harrod-neutral) productivity in addition to the Hicks-neutral productivity. Our focus on the labor bias of productivity change is motivated by both its being a key element in growth theory and its inherently unique distinction from other traditional inputs like (physical and human) capital and intermediates, which are all producible. As such, the marginal productivity of inputs other than labor (i.e., capital and materials) is assumed to change equiproportionately at the rate determined by the Hicks-neutral productivity, whereas the (relative) productivity of labor is also affected by biased technology shift. Under separability of variable and dynamic inputs, factor-neutral productivity scales the variable input demands but does not change their ratio, which ensures that the information about Harrod-neutral productivity can be teased out and identified (separately from the Hick-neutral component) from the observed variation in firms' variable input ratios.

To disentangle the two components of firm productivity (neutral and labor-biased) and to identify the production function, we trade the fully nonparametric formulation in Gandhi et al. (2020) in favor of a parametric specification of the production technology. In doing so, we are able to explicitly utilize a known functional form of the static first-order conditions for freely varying inputs which enables us to derive a proxy for the labor-augmenting productivity in a closed form and use it to effectively concentrate this non-neutral unobservable out. Namely, we assume that the firm's production function takes a flexible log-quadratic translog specification. We then develop a three-step system-based estimation procedure that makes explicit use of static first-order conditions for flexible inputs and the Markovian properties of both productivity components for structural identification.

Our model is closely related to Doraszelski and Jaumandreu (2018, 2019) and Zhang (2019) who also use the information contained in the mix of flexible inputs to separately identify Hicks- and Harrod-neutral productivities.[2] The key and important distinction between their and our methodologies is that we develop an alternative identification scheme that does *not* require external instruments (from outside the production function) such as lagged firm-level variation in (input) prices used in these studies. While it may be suitable for their specific empirical applications, the validity and practicality of using lagged cross-sectional variation in prices for identification is not universal. Not only are such price data typically unavailable or prone to measurement errors in micro-level production datasets (Levinsohn & Petrin, 2003), but their use as valid instruments may also be problematic on theoretical grounds (see Ackerberg, Benkard, Berry, & Pakes, 2007; Ackerberg et al., 2015; Griliches & Mairesse, 1998; Malikov & Lien, 2021). Aside from the concerns about plausible exogeneity of heterogeneous input prices, their strength as instruments also implicitly relies on the strong conditions for the price evolution (see Flynn et al., 2019). In this chapter, we therefore contribute to the literature by developing a methodology that identifies the production function and multi-dimensional productivity even if prices are homogeneous. To achieve identification without external firm-level instruments, we leverage the information contained in static optimality conditions, in effect, adopting a system-of-equations approach.

Our chapter is mainly concerned with the identification of production functions for firms operating in perfectly competitive markets. Although the latter assumption continues to be maintained – implicitly or explicitly – by most productivity studies in the literature, which is partly dictated by the lack of firm-level price data, we also discuss an extension in which we relax this assumption by allowing for monopolistic competition in the output market. In contrast to many other studies that deviate from the perfect competition assumption, our setup does not rely on additional price information or a parameterization of the demand or places restrictions on the production technology in a pursuit of point identification. Instead, we show how one can *partially* identify the production function with non-neutral productivity when firms have market power in the traditional proxy variable framework.

We demonstrate the ability of our estimator to successfully identify multi-dimensional firm productivity through a small set of Monte Carlo simulations and, then, provide an empirical illustration by applying it to the firm-level data from China's leather manufacturing industry. We find that the labor-augmenting productivity behaves quite differently from its factor-neutral counterpart: it shows a larger dispersion and minor growth across years. On the other hand, we also find that foreign direct investment (FDI), which is arguably one of the most important productivity boosters available to firms in developing countries, has both economically and statistically significant effect on labor-saving productivity, whereas its effect size on Hicksian productivity is effectively zero. This suggests that the productivity-enhancing effect of FDI on domestic firms' productivity has a bias toward labor. At the same time, our estimates provide evidence that productivity change in China's leather industry is, overall, factor-neutral.

The rest of the chapter is organized as follows. Section 2 describes the model of production with multi-dimensional firm heterogeneity. We describe our identification strategy in Section 3, and the detailed estimation procedure is provided in

Section 4. We examine the finite-sample performance of our methodology using simulations and provide an empirical illustration in Section 5. The extension to imperfect competition is discussed in Section 6, and Section 7 concludes.

2. A MODEL OF FIRM PRODUCTION

This section describes a model of production decisions by a firm in the presence of multi-dimensional productivity. Our model builds upon the conceptual paradigm considered by Doraszelski and Jaumandreu (2018) although we abstract away from their many application-specific nuances with the goal of formulating a generic, versatile framework suitable for application to typical datasets.

Consider the production process of a firm i ($i = 1,\ldots,n$) in the time period t ($t = 1,\ldots,T$) in which physical capital K_{it}, labor L_{it} and an intermediate input such as materials M_{it} are being transformed into the output Y_{it} via production function $F(\cdot)$ given firm productivity. We differentiate between factor-neutral and factor-biased productivities. Namely, let the firm's production technology take the following form:

$$Y_{it} = F(K_{it}, \exp\{\varphi_{it}\}L_{it}, M_{it})\exp\{\omega_{it}\}\exp\{\eta_{it}\}, \tag{2.1}$$

where, in addition to the usual log-additive Hicks-neutral productivity ω_{it}, we also allow for Harrod-neutral productivity φ_{it} that affects firm output indirectly by "augmenting" the labor input. Both can be persistent. The error η_{it} is an *ex-post* transitory productivity shock, which is sometimes alternatively interpreted as a classical measurement error in the log-output.

In what follows, we characterize structural assumptions about the firm's technology, productivity, economic environment and its dynamic decision-making process which facilitate a structural identification of the model.

Assumption 1. Among the firm's inputs: (i) physical capital K_{it} is a dynamic input subject to adjustment frictions; (ii) labor L_{it} and intermediate inputs M_{it} are freely varying inputs with no dynamic implications.

Since physical capital is subject to adjustment costs (e.g., time-to-install), the firm optimizes K_{it} dynamically at time $t-1$ rendering it a predetermined input quasi-fixed at time t. Thus, K_{it} is a state variable with dynamic implications that follows the law of motion:

$$K_{it} = I_{it-1} + (1-\delta)K_{it-1}, \tag{2.2}$$

where I_{it} and δ are the gross investment and the depreciation rate, respectively. Labor and materials are freely varying and are therefore determined by the firm statically at time t, given the already optimized choice of K_{it}. This is a fairly standard treatment of inputs in the literature (e.g., see Olley & Pakes, 1996; Levinsohn & Petrin, 2003; Wooldridge, 2009). The setup can also be extended to allow for more inputs. The only requirement is that there be at least one freely varying input in addition to labor, which is necessary for identification of labor-augmenting productivity (more on this point below).

Assumption 2. The production relationship between inputs, Hicks- and Harrod-neutral productivities, and the output takes the form of (2.1). The production function $F(\cdot)$ is (i) continuous and satisfies the standard neoclassical assumptions, including differentiability, positive monotonicity and concavity in inputs, and (ii) strongly separable in the partition $(K_{it}, (\exp\{\varphi_{it}\} L_{it}, M_{it}))$ as follows:

$$F(K_{it}, \exp\{\varphi_{it}\} L_{it}, M_{it}) = G\left(K_{it}, H\left(\exp\{\varphi_{it}\} L_{it}, M_{it}\right)\right), \tag{2.3}$$

where $H(\cdot)$ is homogeneous of arbitrary degree, and (iii) of the known parametric functional form.

The assumption is that the dynamic inputs are separable from the remaining production-function arguments. Separability is an identifying restriction that ensures information about Harrod-neutral productivity can be teased out and identified from the variation in the firm's material-to-labor ratio which does not depend on the Hicks-neutral productivity.[3] This restriction on production technology imposes that the marginal rate of technical substitution between the two variable inputs (materials and labor) does not depend on dynamic inputs. Whether explicit or not, the same assumption is made in the majority of productivity studies using proxy variable estimators, in line with popular practice, when assuming that the technology is Cobb-Douglas or Constant Elasticity of Substitution (CES). The latter is also the case for Doraszelski and Jaumandreu (2018) and Zhang (2019).

In line with the literature, we model persistent firm productivities as first-order Markov processes which we endogenize à la Doraszelski and Jaumandreu (2013), De Loecker (2013) and Malikov and Zhao (2021) by incorporating productivity-enhancing and/or "learning" activities of the firm. To keep our model as general as possible, we denote all such activities via generic variables X_{it} and Z_{it} which, depending on the empirical application of interest, may measure the firm's R&D expenditures, FDI exposure, export status/intensity, etc. Letting Ξ_{it} be the information set available to the ith firm for making the period t decisions, the dynamics of unobservables are summarized as follows.

Assumption 3. (i) Both components of persistent firm productivity ω_{it} and φ_{it} evolve according to their respective controlled first-order Markov processes: $\mathcal{P}_{\omega}(\omega_{it} \mid \Xi_{it-1}) = \mathcal{P}_{\omega}(\omega_{it} \mid \omega_{it-1}, X_{it-1})$ and $\mathcal{P}_{\varphi}(\varphi_{it} \mid \Xi_{it-1}) = \mathcal{P}_{\varphi}(\varphi_{it} \mid \varphi_{it-1}, Z_{it-1})$, where some or all elements in X_{it-1} and Z_{it-1} may be common. (ii) The transitory productivity shock η_{it} is an *i.i.d.* white noise process: $\mathcal{P}_{\eta}(\eta_{it} \mid \Xi_{it}) = \mathcal{P}_{\eta}(\eta_{it})$.

The Markov assumptions imply the following regressions for ω_{it} and φ_{it}:

$$\omega_{it} = r_{\omega}\left(\omega_{it-1}, X_{it-1}\right) + \zeta_{\omega,it}, \tag{2.4}$$

$$\varphi_{it} = r_{\varphi}\left(\varphi_{it-1}, Z_{it-1}\right) + \zeta_{\varphi,it}, \tag{2.5}$$

where $r_{\omega}(\cdot)$ and $r_{\varphi}(\cdot)$ are the conditional-mean functions of ω_{it} and φ_{it}, respectively; and $\zeta_{\omega,it}$ and $\zeta_{\varphi,it}$ are mean-zero unanticipated random innovations: $\mathbb{E}\left[\zeta_{\omega,it} \mid \Xi_{it-1}\right] = \mathbb{E}\left[\zeta_{\omega,it} \mid \omega_{it-1}, X_{it-1}\right] = \mathbb{E}\left[\zeta_{\omega,it}\right] = 0$ and $\mathbb{E}\left[\zeta_{\varphi,it} \mid \Xi_{it-1}\right] = \mathbb{E}\left[\zeta_{\varphi,it} \mid \varphi_{it-1}, Z_{it-1}\right] = \mathbb{E}\left[\zeta_{\varphi,it}\right] = 0$. Also note that Assumption 3(i) places no restriction on the correlation between two productivity components ω_{it} and φ_{it}. The two may correlate via productivity-modifying "controls" and the innovations that may reasonably be expected to be positively correlated.

The evolution processes in (2.4) and (2.5) implicitly assume that productivity-enhancing activities and learning affect future firm productivity with a delay, which is why the dependence of productivities on their controls X_{it} and Z_{it} is lagged implying that the improvements in firm productivity take a period to materialize. In $\mathbb{E}\left[\zeta_{\omega,it} \mid \Xi_{it-1}\right] = \mathbb{E}\left[\zeta_{\varphi,it} \mid \Xi_{it-1}\right] = 0$, we effectively assume that firms do not adjust their productivity-modifying activities in light of expected *future* innovations in their productivity, which rules out their ability to systematically predict future shocks. Since random innovations $\zeta_{\omega,it}$ and $\zeta_{\varphi,it}$ represent uncertainty in productivity evolution as well as uncertainty in the success of productivity-modifying activities, the firm relies on its knowledge of *contemporaneous* productivities ω_{it-1} and φ_{it-1} when choosing the optimal level of X_{it-1} and Z_{it-1} at time $t-1$ while being unable to anticipate next period's productivity innovations. Those innovations ($\zeta_{\omega,it}$ and $\zeta_{\varphi,it}$) are realized after both X_{it-1} and Z_{it-1} have already been chosen. Analogous timing assumptions are commonly made in the production-function models with controlled productivity processes (De Loecker, 2013; Doraszelski & Jaumandreu, 2013; Malikov, Zhang, Zhao, & Kumbhakar, 2021; Malikov, Zhao, & Kumbhakar, 2020; Van Biesebroeck, 2005): they render the firm's *past* productivity-modifying activities mean-orthogonal to random innovations at time t, thereby helping the identification of the learning effects.

Assumption 4. Risk-neutral firms maximize the discounted stream of life-time profits in perfectly competitive output and factor markets with homogeneous prices.

Following the bulk of the literature, we assume perfectly competitive markets implying that firms are price-takers which, in theory, rules out any operationable firm-level variation in prices. In what follows, we therefore omit prices from the list of relevant determinants entering the firm's decision equations: they are implicitly represented by the firm-common time index. As noted earlier, we aim to develop an estimator that does *not* require firm-level price information typically unavailable in most firm- or plant-level production datasets. Having said that, we discuss ways to relax this assumption and allow for monopolistic power in the output market in Section 6.

With this structural setup, the firm's dynamic optimization problem is described by

$$\begin{aligned}\mathbb{V}_t(K_{it},\omega_{it},\varphi_{it}) = \max_{I_{it},X_{it},Z_{it}} \{ &\Pi_t(K_{it},\omega_{it},\varphi_{it}) - \mathrm{C}_t^I(I_{it},K_{it}) - \mathrm{C}_t^X(X_{it},X_{it-1}) \\ &-\mathrm{C}_t^Z(Z_{it},Z_{it-1}) + \beta\mathbb{E}[\mathbb{V}_{t+1}(K_{it+1},\omega_{it+1},\varphi_{it+1}) \mid \Xi_{it},I_{it},X_{it},Z_{it}]\},\end{aligned} \tag{2.6}$$

where β is a time discount factor; $(K_{it}, \omega_{it}, \varphi_{it})' \in \Xi_{it}$ are the state variables; $\Pi_t(\cdot)$ is the value function corresponding to the static profit-maximization problem in (3.3), i.e., a "short-run" restricted profit function; and $C_t^{\kappa}(\cdot)$ is the cost function for capital ($\kappa = I$) and productivity-enhancing activities ($\kappa = \{X, Z\}$). In the above optimization problem, albeit also with dynamic implications, the levels of productivity-enhancing activities X_{it+1} and Z_{it+1} are chosen by the firm contemporaneously at time $t+1$ unlike the level of K_{it+1} which is a delayed decision made at time t (via I_{it}). This allows for persistence in productivity-enhancing activities but does not force them to be subject to adjustment frictions that would also render them delayed and, hence, predetermined.[4] This distinction is important because it does not rule out a contemporaneous correlation between firm productivities $(\omega_{it}, \varphi_{it})'$ and $(X_{it}, Z_{it})'$. Then, solving (2.6) for I_{it}, X_{it} and Z_{it} yields their respective optimal policy functions in terms of the firm's state variables.

Technically, our methodology can be formulated without explicit formalization of the firm's dynamic decisions by only describing its static optimization. We opt to spell out the dynamics, however, to structurally contextualize the predeterminedness of fixed inputs and productivity-modifying activities with respect to the innovations in productivity which, otherwise, would have had to be assumed prima facie.

3. IDENTIFICATION

The estimation of the production function in (2.1) is not trivial because of the latent nature of firm productivity. In our case, the problem is further complicated by the fact that unobserved productivity is two-dimensional. Omitting ω_{it} and φ_{it} from the production-function regression is ill-advised because it would lead to an endogeneity problem given that firm productivities are correlated with inputs. We tackle this problem by adopting a control function approach à la Olley and Pakes (1996) and Levinsohn and Petrin (2003). Specifically, we consider the identification and estimation of the production function (2.1) by building on the Gandhi et al. (2020) methodology, which we generalize to accommodate multidimensional firm productivity.

Due to the presence of *multiple* unobservables in (2.1) and the fundamentally different manner in which they enhance inputs, to achieve the (separable) identification of ω_{it} and φ_{it} we make use of a parametric-form assumption for the production function. This makes our methodology distinct from Gandhi et al. (2020) whose approach is fully nonparametric. Forgoing a nonparametric formulation of the production function $F(\cdot)$ in favor of a parametric specification is the price of letting firm productivity not be restricted to a single factor-neutral dimension. We adopt a log-quadratic translog specification for $F(\cdot)$.[5] Namely,

$$\begin{aligned} f(\cdot) = {} & \beta_K k_{it} + \frac{1}{2}\beta_{KK} k_{it}^2 + \beta_M m_{it} + \frac{1}{2}\beta_{MM} m_{it}^2 + \beta_{KM} k_{it} m_{it} + \\ & \beta_L[\varphi_{it} + l_{it}] + \frac{1}{2}\beta_{LL}[\varphi_{it} + l_{it}]^2 + \beta_{KL} k_{it}[\varphi_{it} + l_{it}] + \beta_{ML} m_{it}[\varphi_{it} + l_{it}], \end{aligned} \tag{3.1}$$

where the lower-case variables/functions denote the logs of the respective variables/functions.

Under Assumption 2(ii), $\beta_{KM} = \beta_{KL} = 0$ and the function needs be normalized to be homogeneous of arbitrary degree in freely varying inputs. Following Doraszelski and Jaumandreu (2019), we set the degree of homogeneity to $\beta_L + \beta_M$. With this, logging both sides of (2.1), we get the following "restricted" translog form:

$$y_{it} = \underbrace{\beta_K k_{it} + \frac{1}{2}\beta_{KK}k_{it}^2 + \beta_M m_{it} + \beta_L[\varphi_{it} + l_{it}] - \frac{1}{2}\beta_0[m_{it} - \varphi_{it} - l_{it}]^2}_{\overline{y}_{it}} + \omega_{it} + \eta_{it}, \quad (3.2)$$

where $\beta_0 \equiv -\beta_{MM} = -\beta_{LL} = \beta_{ML}$.

We opt for the translog specification chiefly out of convenience given its linearity in parameters. Other functional forms could also be used; e.g., the nested CES specification preferred by Doraszelski and Jaumandreu (2018) and Zhang (2019). We describe how to implement our methodology under this alternative parameterization in Appendix 1.

3.1. A System Approach to Identification

Since freely varying inputs are non-dynamic, the risk-neutral firm's optimal choice of L_{it} and M_{it} can be modeled statically as the concentrated expected profit-maximization problem subject to the already predetermined optimal choice of the quasi-fixed input K_{it} and both components of persistent firm productivity ω_{it} and φ_{it}:

$$\max_{L_{it}, M_{it}} P_t^Y F(K_{it}, \exp\{\varphi_{it}\} L_{it}, M_{it}) \exp\{\omega_{it}\}\theta - P_t^L L_{it} - P_t^M M_{it}, \quad (3.3)$$

where P_t^Y, P_t^L and P_t^M are respectively the output, labor and material prices that, given the perfect competition assumption, are common to all firms; and $\theta \equiv \mathbb{E}[\exp\{\eta_{it}\} \mid \Xi_{it}]$. The value function corresponding to (3.3) yields $\Pi_t(\cdot)$ entering the firm's Bellman equation (2.6). The corresponding first-order conditions yield the firm's conditional demand for L_{it} and M_{it}.

Making use of the functional form in (3.2), the static optimality conditions are

$$P_t^Y \frac{\exp\{\overline{y}_{it}\}}{L_{it}} \left(\beta_L + \beta_0[m_{it} - \varphi_{it} - l_{it}]\right) \exp\{\omega_{it}\}\theta = P_t^L, \quad (3.4)$$

$$P_t^Y \frac{\exp\{\overline{y}_{it}\}}{M_{it}} \left(\beta_M - \beta_0[m_{it} - \varphi_{it} - l_{it}]\right) \exp\{\omega_{it}\}\theta = P_t^M. \quad (3.5)$$

Taking the ratio of (3.4) and (3.5), we obtain the equation for the firm's optimal labor-to-material ratio:

$$\frac{L_{it}}{M_{it}} = \frac{P_t^M}{P_t^L} \times \frac{\beta_L + \beta_0[m_{it} - \varphi_{it} - l_{it}]}{\beta_M - \beta_0[m_{it} - \varphi_{it} - l_{it}]}, \quad (3.6)$$

which, expectedly, does not depend on factor-neutral productivity ω_{it} because the latter enhances both inputs equally thereby leaving their ratio unaffected. The input ratio however is affected by the labor-augmenting productivity, since φ_{it} changes the *relative* marginal products of labor and materials.

We can solve (3.6) for Harrod-neutral productivity φ_{it} to arrive at

$$\varphi_{it} = m_{it} - l_{it} + \frac{\beta_L}{\beta_0} - \left(\frac{\beta_L + \beta_M}{\beta_0}\right) S_{it}^L, \tag{3.7}$$

where $S_{it}^L \equiv P_t^L L_{it} / \left(P_t^L L_{it} + P_t^M M_{it}\right)$ is the labor share of the firm's variable input cost. This expression is an operationable proxy for unobservable φ_{it}.

First step.—We first identify the sum of β_L and β_M coefficients as well as nuisance parameter θ and random productivity shocks $\{\eta_{it}\}$. To do so, we transform static first-order conditions in (3.4) and (3.5) by taking their logs and subtracting (3.2) from each of them to obtain the corresponding share equations in logs, i.e.,

$$\ln V_{it}^L = \ln\left(\theta\beta_0\left[\frac{\beta_L}{\beta_0} + m_{it} - \varphi_{it} - l_{it}\right]\right) - \eta_{it}, \tag{3.8}$$

$$\ln V_{it}^M = \ln\left(\theta\beta_0\left[\frac{\beta_M}{\beta_0} - m_{it} + \varphi_{it} + l_{it}\right]\right) - \eta_{it}, \tag{3.9}$$

where $V_{it}^L \equiv P_t^L L_{it} / \left(P_t^Y Y_{it}\right)$ and $V_{it}^M \equiv P_t^M M_{it} / \left(P_t^Y Y_{it}\right)$ are the nominal shares of labor and material costs in total revenue, respectively.

To operationalize these equations into the estimating regression equations, we need to tackle the unobservable φ_{it} appearing on the right-hand size of (3.8) and (3.9). Failure to control for it would lead to endogeneity due to the correlation with Harrod-neutral productivity and freely varying inputs. We control for φ_{it} using the material-to-labor ratio proxy function. That is, substituting for φ_{it} in either one of the two log-share equations using the expression in (3.7), we obtain the following variable-input-cost-to-revenue equation in logs:

$$\ln R_{it} = \ln\left(\theta[\beta_L + \beta_M]\right) - \eta_{it}, \tag{3.10}$$

where $R_{it} \equiv \left(P_t^L L_{it} + P_t^M M_{it}\right) / \left(P_t^Y Y_{it}\right)$. The cost-to-revenue ratio R_{it} is observable in the data, and the construction thereof does not require firm-level price data: the information on total flexible input expenditures and total revenue suffices.

The variable-input-cost-to-revenue equation in (3.10) is useful in that it enables us to identify $\beta_L + \beta_M$, both elements of which enter the production function of interest in (3.2), using the observable information about expenditures on flexible inputs and revenue. Specifically, we first identify a "scaled" sum of these two translog coefficients $\theta \times [\beta_L + \beta_M]$ using the moment condition $\mathbb{E}[\eta_{it} \mid \Xi_{it}] = 0$, from which we have that

$$\ln\left(\theta[\beta_L + \beta_M]\right) = \mathbb{E}[\ln R_{it}]. \tag{3.11}$$

To identify $\beta_L + \beta_M$ net of constant θ, note that θ can be identified via $\theta \equiv \mathbb{E}[\exp\{\eta_{it}\}] = \mathbb{E}[\exp\{\mathbb{E}[\ln R_{it}] - \ln R_{it}\}]$, which allows us to isolate $\beta_L + \beta_M$ as follows:

$$\beta_L + \beta_M = \frac{\exp\{\mathbb{E}[\ln R_{it}]\}}{\mathbb{E}[\exp\{\mathbb{E}[\ln R_{it}] - \ln R_{it}\}]}. \tag{3.12}$$

Let the identified $\beta_L + \beta_M$ be denoted as $\delta_{LM} = \beta_L + \beta_M$.

Second step.—Next, we show how to separate β_L and β_M and identify β_0. We utilize the Markov assumption about labor-augmenting productivity. More concretely, with δ_{LM} already identified in the first step, the proxy function for φ_{it} in (3.7) contains only two unknown parameters: β_0 and β_L. Substituting this partly identified $\varphi_{it}(\beta_0, \beta_L)$ expression for φ_{it} in the Markov productivity evolution process in (2.5) and treating δ_{LM} as an observable, we obtain

$$m_{it} - l_{it} + \frac{\beta_L}{\beta_0} - \frac{\delta_{LM}}{\beta_0} S_{it}^L = r_\varphi\left(\left[m_{it-1} - l_{it-1} + \frac{\beta_L}{\beta_0} - \frac{\delta_{LM}}{\beta_0} S_{it-1}^L\right], Z_{it-1}\right) + \zeta_{\varphi,it}, \tag{3.13}$$

which identifies $(\beta_0, \beta_L)'$ as well as the mean productivity function $r_\varphi(\cdot)$ on the basis of

$$\mathbb{E}\left[\zeta_{\varphi,it} \mid 1, m_{it-1} - l_{it-1}, S_{it-1}^L, Z_{it-1}\right] = 0. \tag{3.14}$$

Note that the nonlinear equation in (3.13) technically contains an endogenous regressor S_{it}^L which is not mean-orthogonal to the innovation $\zeta_{\varphi,it}$ because the former includes information on the choice of both L_{it} and M_{it} which are decided by the firm after $\zeta_{\varphi,it}$ is realized (i.e., after φ_{it} is updated). This however does *not* impede identification of (3.13) because S_{it}^L is not a "free" regressor but enters the equation subject to a parameter restriction whereby the coefficient thereon is the same as that on weakly exogenous S_{it-1}^L. No external instrumentation for S_{it}^L is therefore needed.

To make our identification arguments more transparent, let unknown function $r_\varphi(\cdot)$ be linear and, since it can only be identified up to a constant, normalize $r_\varphi(0) = 0$.[6] More concretely, $r_\varphi = \rho_1\left[m_{it-1} - l_{it-1} + \frac{\beta_L}{\beta_0} - \frac{\delta_{LM}}{\beta_0} S_{it-1}^L\right] + \rho_2' Z_{it-1}$. Denoting the vector of exogenous instruments $Q_{it-1} = (1, m_{it-1} - l_{it-1}, S_{it-1}^L, Z_{it-1}')'$, consider now the identification of equidimensional parameter vector $\alpha = (\beta_0, \beta_L, \rho_1, \rho_2')'$ in the following nonlinear Generalized Method of Moments (GMM) problem:

$$\alpha_0 = \arg\min_\alpha \mathbb{E}[Q_{it-1}\zeta_{\varphi,it}(\alpha)]' W \mathbb{E}[Q_{it-1}\zeta_{\varphi,it}(\alpha)], \tag{3.15}$$

where W is a symmetric positive-definite moment-weighting matrix. To see that (3.15) identifies all parameters in α, consider an information matrix

$$\Psi(\alpha)=\mathbb{E}\left[Q_{it-1}\frac{\partial\zeta_{\varphi,it}(\alpha)}{\partial\alpha'}\right]$$

$$=\mathbb{E}\left[\begin{pmatrix}1\\ m_{it-1}-l_{it-1}\\ S^L_{it-1}\\ Z_{it-1}\end{pmatrix}\begin{pmatrix}-\frac{\beta_L}{\beta_0^2}(1-\rho_1)+\frac{\delta_{LM}}{\beta_0^2}\left[S^L_{it}-\rho_1 S^L_{it-1}\right]\\ \frac{1-\rho_1}{\beta_0}\\ m_{it-1}-l_{it-1}+\frac{\beta_L}{\beta_0}-\frac{\delta_{LM}}{\beta_0}S^L_{it-1}\\ Z_{it-1}\end{pmatrix}'\right] \tag{3.16}$$

and note that it is full-rank (we unpack this expression in Appendix 2). Thus, the information matrix for the GMM problem in (3.15) when evaluated at the true parameter values $\Psi(\alpha_0)$ has a full column rank. All parameters in α are therefore locally identified (see Rothenberg, 1971).

Although, in theory, the four instruments in Q_{it-1} are enough to exactly identify the second-step parameters of interest α, there is a potential to improve the finite-sample performance if additional valid instruments are included in the estimation. Obvious candidates are the firm's dynamic quasi-fixed inputs $k_{it}, k_{it-1}, \ldots$ which are weakly exogenous with respect to the time t shocks, including $\zeta_{\varphi,it}$, and relevant for the choice of $(S^L_{it}, S^L_{it-1}, Z'_{it-1})'$ through both the static and dynamic optimization decisions. These additional instruments are to act as exclusion restrictions to strengthen the moment condition and help in identification. For instance, Kim et al. (2019) propose a similar simple strategy to robustify the Ackerberg et al. (2015) estimation procedure.

Following identification of β_L, β_M is identified from $\beta_M=\delta_{LM}-\beta_L$ as a by-product. We also achieve the identification of Harrod-neutral productivity via $\varphi_{it}=m_{it}-l_{it}+\beta_L/\beta_0-(\beta_L+\beta_M)/\beta_0\times S^L_{it}$.

Third step.—With $(\beta_0,\beta_L,\beta_M)'$ identified, we have effectively pinpointed the production function in the dimension of its endogenous freely-varying inputs L_{it} and M_{it} thereby addressing the Gandhi et al. (2020) critique, whereby the endogenous static inputs are lacking valid internal instruments when directly included as regressors in the proxied production function estimation. This is evident by rewriting (3.2) with the substitution for ω_{it} using its Markov process from (2.4) as follows:

$$y^*_{it}=\beta_K k_{it}+\frac{1}{2}\beta_{KK}k^2_{it}+r_\omega\left(\omega_{it-1},X_{it-1}\right)+\zeta_{\omega,it}+\eta_{it}, \tag{3.17}$$

where $y^*_{it}\equiv y_{it}-\beta_M m_{it}-\beta_L[\varphi_{it}+l_{it}]+\frac{1}{2}\beta_0[m_{it}-\varphi_{it}-l_{it}]^2=y_{it}-\beta_M m_{it}-\beta_L[m_{it}+\beta_L/\beta_0-(\beta_L+\beta_M)/\beta_0\times S^L_{it}]+\frac{1}{2\beta_0}[(\beta_L+\beta_M)S^L_{it}-\beta_L]^2$ is already identified and, hence, equation (3.17) now contains *no* endogenous regressors that need instrumentation. However, we still need to deal with unobservability of ω_{it-1}.

To identify the rest of the production function, i.e., $(\beta_K, \beta_{KK})'$, we proxy for latent Hicks-neutral ω_{it-1} in (3.17) by inverting the conditional material demand function implied by the static first-order condition in (3.5):

$$\omega_{it} = \begin{matrix} \overbrace{\ln\left[\frac{P_t^M}{P_t^Y}\right] - \ln\theta - \ln\left(\beta_M - \beta_0[m_{it} - \varphi_{it} - l_{it}]\right) + (1-\beta_M)m_{it}}^{m_{it}^*} \\ -\beta_L[\varphi_{it} + l_{it}] + \frac{1}{2}\beta_0[m_{it} - \varphi_{it} - l_{it}]^2 - \beta_K k_{it} - \frac{1}{2}\beta_{KK}k_{it}^2, \end{matrix} \tag{3.18}$$

where, given the already identified $(\beta_0, \beta_L, \beta_M, \theta)'$ and φ_{it} in the first two steps, m_{it}^* is observable. Substituting for ω_{it-1} using this proxy, from (3.17) we derive

$$y_{it}^* = \beta_K k_{it} + \frac{1}{2}\beta_{KK}k_{it}^2 + r_\omega\left(\left[m_{it-1}^* - \beta_K k_{it-1} - \frac{1}{2}\beta_{KK}k_{it-1}^2\right], X_{it-1}\right) + \zeta_{\omega,it} + \eta_{it}, \tag{3.19}$$

where, under our structural assumptions, all regressors are weakly exogenous because the productivity innovation $\zeta_{\omega,it}$ is realized at time t after the firm had already optimized its dynamic input K_{it} (at time $t-1$) for the period t production and, obviously, after the lagged flexible inputs contained inside m_{it-1}^* were chosen. That is, all right-hand-side variables in (3.19) can self-instrument. This identifies $(\beta_K, \beta_{KK})'$ as well as the mean productivity function $r_\omega(\cdot)$ from

$$\mathbb{E}\left[\zeta_{\omega,it} + \eta_{it} \mid k_{it}, k_{it-1}, m_{it-1}^*(m_{it-1}, l_{it-1}), X_{it-1}\right] = 0. \tag{3.20}$$

In fact, given the exogeneity of regressors, $\gamma = (\beta_K, \beta_{KK}, r_\omega(\cdot))'$ can be identified as a solution to the following nonlinear sieve M-problem:

$$\gamma_0 = \arg\min_\gamma \mathbb{E}\left[\varrho_{it}(k_{it}, k_{it-1}, m_{it-1}^*, X_{it-1}; \gamma)^2\right], \tag{3.21}$$

where $\varrho_{it}(k_{it}, k_{it-1}, m_{it-1}^*, X_{it-1}; \gamma) \equiv \zeta_{\omega,it} + \eta_{it}$ is the residual function from (3.19).

Remark 1. One can alternatively operationalize the third step using the inverted conditional *labor* demand implied by (3.4) to construct a proxy function for ω_{it} using observable l_{it}^*:

$$\omega_{it} = \begin{matrix} \overbrace{\ln\left[\frac{P_t^L}{P_t^Y}\right] - \ln\theta - \ln\left(\beta_L + \beta_0[m_{it} - \varphi_{it} - l_{it}]\right) + (1-\beta_L)l_{it}}^{l_{it}^*} \\ -\beta_M m_{it} - \beta_L\varphi_{it} + \frac{1}{2}\beta_0[m_{it} - \varphi_{it} - l_{it}]^2 - \beta_K k_{it} - \frac{1}{2}\beta_{KK}k_{it}^2, \end{matrix} \tag{3.22}$$

or using a convex combination of the two inverted static input demands. Under the model assumptions, all these proxies are numerically equivalent.

With $(\beta_K, \beta_{KK})'$ identified, we can also recover Hicks-neutral productivity either via the proxy in (3.18) or from the production function (3.2) as

$$\omega_{it} = y_{it} - \beta_K k_{it} - \frac{1}{2}\beta_{KK} k_{it}^2 - \beta_M m_{it} - \beta_L [\varphi_{it} + l_{it}] + \frac{1}{2}\beta_0 [m_{it} - \varphi_{it} - l_{it}]^2 - \eta_{it}, \quad (3.23)$$

with the translog parameters, Harrod-neutral productivity φ_{it} and the transitory shock η_{it} successfully identified in the three steps.

On a final note, our methodology is robust to the Ackerberg et al. (2015) critique that focuses on the inability of structural proxy estimators to separably identify the additive production function and Hicksian productivity proxy. Such an issue normally arises in the wake of perfect functional dependence between freely varying inputs appearing both inside the unknown production function and productivity proxy. Our third-step equation (3.19) does not suffer from such a problem because it contains no endogenous variable input on the right-hand side, the corresponding parameters of which have already been identified from the variable-input-cost-to-revenue equation and Harrodian productivity process in the first two steps.

3.2. Unidentification of the Standard Proxy Approach

We now show that, were one to pursue the standard proxy variable approach, the production function (3.2) would be unidentified in the absence of external instruments (outside the production function) for freely varying inputs.

Normally, to estimate the production function via proxy variable technique, one makes use of the Markovian nature of unobservables and proxies for them by inverting the firm's optimality conditions. Specifically, along the lines of Doraszelski and Jaumandreu (2018) empirical methodology, the estimating model consists of two *stochastic* equations: (*i*) the production function in (3.2) combined with the law of motion for Hicksian productivity in (2.4):

$$\begin{aligned} y_{it} = {} & \beta_K k_{it} + \frac{1}{2}\beta_{KK} k_{it}^2 + \beta_M m_{it} + \beta_L [\varphi_{it} + l_{it}] - \frac{1}{2}\beta_0 [m_{it} - \varphi_{it} - l_{it}]^2 + \\ & r_{\omega}(\omega_{it-1}, X_{it-1}) + \zeta_{\omega,it} + \eta_{it} \end{aligned} \quad (3.24)$$

and (*ii*) the law of motion for Harrodian productivity in (2.5):

$$\varphi_{it} = r_{\varphi}(\varphi_{it-1}, Z_{it-1}) + \zeta_{\varphi,it}, \quad (3.25)$$

in both of which the unobservables φ_{it} and ω_{it} are "controlled" for using their *deterministic* proxy expressions in (3.7) and (3.18), respectively.

The two-equation model in (3.24) and (3.25) suffers from endogeneity originating in the correlation between freely varying inputs m_{it} and l_{it} (and functions thereof) and contemporaneous random productivity innovations. The remaining covariates are predetermined and can self-instrument. To identify the model, one is to use a system of moment restrictions on the two errors $(\zeta_{\omega,it} + \eta_{it}, \zeta_{\varphi,it})'$ à la

$$\mathbb{E}\left[A_{it}\begin{pmatrix}\zeta_{\omega,it}+\eta_{it}\\ \zeta_{\varphi,it}\end{pmatrix}\right]=0, \tag{3.26}$$

where A_{it} is a block-diagonal matrix of exogenous instruments and their functions.

Following the bulk of literature, one may be tempted to make use of higher-order[7] lagged inputs $(k_{it-2}, l_{it-2}, m_{it-2}, \ldots)'$ and productivity-modifying controls $(X_{it-2}', Z_{it-2}', \ldots)'$ to instrument for m_{it} and l_{it} given that such lags meet the weak exogeneity requirement for valid instruments under the structural assumptions. However, the identification can only be achieved if these additional lags provide additional *relevant* (exogenous) variation for M_{it} after conditioning on the already included self-instrumenting variables. Intuitively, these additional lags must be relevant to meet the rank condition for identification of the model.

It happens that despite the apparent abundance of internal instruments, model (3.24) and (3.25) remains *un*identified because all such relevant instruments for m_{it} and l_{it} that were initially excluded from production function (3.2) are now used to proxy for the unobserved φ_{it-1} and ω_{it-1}. This is the key argument in the Gandhi et al. (2020) critique of the proxy estimators. More formally, consider the endogenous m_{it} input which, according to the conditional material demand implied by the first-order condition in (3.5), is given by the following implicit function:

$$\begin{aligned}0 = {} & \ln\left[P_t^Y / P_t^M\right] + \ln\theta + \ln\left(\beta_M - \beta_0\left[m_{it} - l_{it} - r_\varphi(\varphi_{it-1}, Z_{it-1}) - \zeta_{\varphi,it}\right]\right) - \\ & (1-\beta_M)m_{it} + \beta_L\left[l_{it} + r_\varphi(\varphi_{it-1}, Z_{it-1}) + \zeta_{\varphi,it}\right] - \frac{1}{2}\beta_0\left[m_{it} - l_{it} - r_\varphi\right. \\ & \left.(\varphi_{it-1}, Z_{it-1}) - \zeta_{\varphi,it}\right]^2 + \beta_K k_{it} + \frac{1}{2}\beta_{KK}k_{it}^2 + r_\omega(\omega_{it-1}, X_{it-1}) + \zeta_{\omega,it},\end{aligned} \tag{3.27}$$

where we have substituted for φ_{it} and ω_{it} using their respective laws of motion. An analogous expression exists for l_{it} which, when combined with (3.27), expectedly shows that both static inputs are a function of $(K_{it}, \varphi_{it-1}, \omega_{it-1}, X'_{it-1}, Z'_{it-1}, P_t^Y, P_t^M, P_t^L, \zeta_{\varphi,it}, \zeta_{\omega,it})'$. Comparing these determinants of m_{it} and l_{it} with the variables entering the two equations in (3.24) and (3.25), it is evident that the only sources of variation in m_{it} and l_{it}, which have not already been included as a self-instrumenting variable, are the prices $(P_t^Y, P_t^M, P_t^L)'$ and the unobservable innovations $\zeta_{\varphi,it}$ and $\zeta_{\omega,it}$.

Assuming the price-taking behavior of competitive firms, *aggregate* prices $(P_t^Y, P_t^M, P_t^L)'$ provide very little – however theoretically valid – identifying variation in practice (even in long panels) as studied by Gandhi et al. (2020). This means that, conditional on the already included predetermined variables (or their proxies), there is practically *no* other relevant exogenous variables from within the production model that may be used to instrument for the endogenous m_{it} and l_{it} because, for them to be relevant in predicting m_{it} and l_{it}, they would have to correlate with $\zeta_{\varphi,it}$ and $\zeta_{\omega,it}$, which is the only source of "free" variation left in static inputs. The correlation with these productivity innovations would however violate the exogeneity requirement thereby invaliding the instruments. Therefore, both flexible inputs lack excluded relevant internal instruments, and the model in (3.24) and (3.25) is *un*identified.

Note that, although not explicitly discussed, this unidentification problem is overcome by Doraszelski and Jaumandreu (2018) along the lines of their earlier work in Doraszelski and Jaumandreu (2013) by incorporating external instruments such as demand shifters and, importantly, lagged *firm-level* variation in input prices. However, while suitable for their empirical application, the validity and practicality of using lagged firm-level prices for identification is not universal. Not only are the price data often unavailable or prone to measurement errors (Levinsohn & Petrin, 2003), but the use of prices may also be problematic on theoretical grounds (see Ackerberg et al., 2007, 2015; Flynn et al., 2019; Griliches & Mairesse, 1998).

Specifically, the validity of input prices as exogenous instruments is normally justified by invoking the assumption of perfectly competitive markets. However, if firms were indeed price-takers, in theory, one should not observe the firm-level variation in prices and, without such a variation, prices cannot be used as operational instruments. Even with the aggregate prices varying exogenously across space, such a variation may be insufficient for identification as discussed earlier. If a researcher does observe the variation in prices across all individual firms, the latter variation may be reflecting differences in the firms' market power and/or the quality of inputs/outputs. For instance, if the firm-level variation in input prices reflects differential quality in inputs, then random updates in prices that render lagged prices usable instruments[8] are likely related to productivity innovations because a more productive firm is to use more productive, higher-quality inputs (Flynn et al., 2019). Thus, be it due to the market power or quality differentials, the variation in prices will then be endogenous to firms' decisions and hence cannot help the identification (also see Gandhi et al., 2020). Furthermore, putting the issue of exogeneity aside, Flynn et al. (2019) raise concerns about the strong conditions on the price evolution processes that must be satisfied for the lagged prices to have any strength as instruments. We therefore pursue an alternative identification strategy which does not require *firm-level* variation in prices.

To achieve identification without external firm-level instruments, we build upon Gandhi et al. (2020) ideas by effectively augmenting a system in (3.24) and (3.25) with an additional (simultaneous) equation for the optimal variable-input-cost-to-revenue ratio in (3.10).

4. ESTIMATION PROCEDURE

We now describe how to empirically implement our identification strategy outlined in Section 3.1. We estimate the unknown production-function parameters and the two components of persistent firm productivity φ_{it} and ω_{it} via a three-stage procedure. If the functional form of productivity conditional-mean functions $r_{\omega}(\cdot)$ and $r_{\varphi}(\cdot)$ in the evolution processes (2.4) and (2.5) is known, the estimation becomes fully parametric which, among other things, can streamline asymptotic inference. For instance, a go-to choice in applied productivity research involving the proxy-variable estimation of production functions is to assume that firm productivity is a linear AR(1) process (e.g., see Ackerberg, Frazer, Kim, Luo, & Yingjun, 2020; Grieco, Li, & Zhang, 2020; Kim et al., 2019; Mo, Qiu, Zhang, & Dong, 2021; Zhang, 2017, 2019). To maximize impact among practitioners, in what follows, we also assume that both $r_{\omega}(\cdot)$ and $r_{\varphi}(\cdot)$ are linear (parametric) functions.[9] We discuss a semiparametric alternative to our estimator in which the unknown functions are approximated using sieves in Appendix 3.

In the first step, we consistently estimate $\beta_L + \beta_M$ via a sample analogue of (3.12):

$$\hat{\delta}_{LM} \equiv \widehat{(\beta_L + \beta_M)} = \frac{\exp\{\frac{1}{nT}\sum_{it} \ln R_{it}\}}{\frac{1}{nT}\sum_{it} \exp\left\{\left(\frac{1}{nT}\sum_{it} \ln R_{it}\right) - \ln R_{it}\right\}}, \tag{4.1}$$

where the denominator is $\hat{\theta} = \frac{1}{nT}\sum_{it} \exp\left\{\left(\frac{1}{nT}\sum_{it} \ln R_{it}\right) - \ln R_{it}\right\}$.

We then proceed to the second-step estimation of the Harrodian productivity process in (3.13). We parameterize the unknown function $r_{\varphi}(\varphi_{it-1}, Z_{it-1})$ using a linear function,[10] with the unobservable φ_{it-1} substituted for by the proxy function from (3.7) and δ_{LM} replaced with its estimate from the first step. The second-step equation is then estimated via nonlinear GMM along the lines of (3.15):

$$\hat{\alpha} = \arg\min_{\alpha} \left[\frac{1}{nT}\sum_{it} \mathbb{Q}_{it-1}\epsilon_{it}(D_{it};\alpha)\right]' W \left[\frac{1}{nT}\sum_{it} \mathbb{Q}_{it-1}\epsilon_{it}(D_{it};\alpha)\right], \tag{4.2}$$

where $\alpha = (\beta_0, \beta_L, \rho_{\varphi,1}, \rho_{\varphi,2})'$, $D_{it} = (m_{it} - l_{it}, m_{it-1} - l_{it-1}, S^L_{it}, S^L_{it-1}, Z'_{it-1})'$, and the corresponding residual function is

$$\epsilon_{it}(D_{it};\alpha) = m_{it} - l_{it} + \frac{\beta_L}{\beta_0} - \frac{\hat{\delta}_{LM}}{\beta_0} S^L_{it} - \rho_{\varphi,1}\left[m_{it-1} - l_{it-1} + \frac{\beta_L}{\beta_0} - \frac{\hat{\delta}_{LM}}{\beta_0} S^L_{it-1}\right] - \rho_{\varphi,2} Z_{it-1}. \tag{4.3}$$

Following our earlier arguments, here we expand the instrument vector to include capital as additional instruments: $\mathbb{Q}_{it-1} = (1, m_{it-1} - l_{it-1}, S^L_{it-1}, Z'_{it-1}, k_{it}, k_{it-1}, \ldots)'$. With $(\hat{\beta}_0, \hat{\beta}_L)'$ in hand, we construct $\hat{\beta}_M = \hat{\delta}_{LM} - \widehat{\beta_L}$ as well as the estimator of Harrod-neutral productivity via $\hat{\varphi}_{it} = m_{it} - l_{it} + \hat{\beta}_L / \hat{\beta}_0 - \hat{\delta}_{LM} / \hat{\beta}_0 \times S^L_{it}$.

To estimate the third-step equation in (3.19), we first construct estimators of y^*_{it} and m^*_{it} using the results from steps one and two: $\hat{y}^*_{it} = y_{it} - \hat{\beta}_M m_{it} - \hat{\beta}_L[\hat{\varphi}_{it} + l_{it}] + \frac{1}{2}\hat{\beta}_0[m_{it} - \hat{\varphi}_{it} - l_{it}]^2$ and $\hat{m}^*_{it} = \ln\left[P^M_t / P^Y_t\right] - \ln\hat{\theta} - \ln\left(\hat{\beta}_M - \hat{\beta}_0[m_{it} - \hat{\varphi}_{it} - l_{it}]\right) + (1 - \hat{\beta}_M)m_{it} - \hat{\beta}_L[\hat{\varphi}_{it} + l_{it}] + \frac{1}{2}\hat{\beta}_0[m_{it} - \hat{\varphi}_{it} - l_{it}]^2$. Then, using a linear parameterization for $r_{\omega}(\cdot)$ with ω_{it-1} replaced by its proxy, we estimate $\gamma = (\beta_K, \beta_{KK}, \rho_{\omega,0}, \rho_{\omega,1}, \rho_{\omega_2})'$ via nonlinear sieve least squares in line with (3.21):

$$\hat{\gamma} = \arg\min_{\gamma} \sum_{it} \begin{bmatrix} \hat{y}^*_{it} - \beta_K k_{it} - \frac{1}{2}\beta_{KK} k^2_{it} - \rho_{\omega,0} \\ -\rho_{\omega,1}\left[\hat{m}^*_{it-1} - \beta_K k_{it-1} - \frac{1}{2}\beta_{KK} k^2_{it-1}\right] - \rho_{\omega,2} X_{it-1} \end{bmatrix}^2. \tag{4.4}$$

Using the obtained $(\hat{\beta}_K, \hat{\beta}_{KK})'$ estimates, we then construct Hicks-neutral productivity via $\hat{\omega}_{it} = y_{it} - \hat{\beta}_K k_{it} - \frac{1}{2}\hat{\beta}_{KK} k^2_{it} - \hat{\beta}_M m_{it} - \hat{\beta}_L[\hat{\varphi}_{it} + l_{it}] + \frac{1}{2}\hat{\beta}_0[m_{it} - \hat{\varphi}_{it} - l_{it}]^2 - \hat{\eta}_{it}$ using $\hat{\eta}_{it} = \ln\left(\hat{\theta}\hat{\delta}_{LM}\right) - \ln R_{it}$ from step one.

The outlined three-step estimator is consistent and asymptotically normal. This is easy to establish by recasting all three steps in a multiple-equation system GMM framework which, conveniently, also permits the derivation of an asymptotic variance-covariance matrix that accounts for a multi-step nature of the estimator (see Newey, 1984). Essentially, we can rewrite our sequential estimator as a simultaneous multiple-equation system of moment restrictions where the instrument sets vary across equations.

Specifically, referring to all unknown parameters collectively as $\Lambda = \left(\beta_0, \beta_L, \beta_M, \beta_K, \beta_{KK}, \theta, \rho_{\varphi,1}, \rho_{\varphi,2}, \rho_{\omega,0}, \rho_{\omega,1}, \rho_{\omega,2}\right)'$, the fully expanded third-step error after the substitutions for y^*_{it}, φ_{it} and m^*_{it} is

$$\begin{aligned} r_{it}(\Lambda) = {} & y_{it} - \beta_M m_{it} - \beta_L\left[m_{it} + \frac{\beta_L}{\beta_0} - \frac{\beta_L + \beta_M}{\beta_0} S^L_{it}\right] \\ & + \frac{1}{2\beta_0}\left[-\beta_L + (\beta_L + \beta_M) S^L_{it}\right]^2 - \beta_K k_{it} - \frac{1}{2}\beta_{KK} k^2_{it} - \rho_{\omega,0} - \rho_{\omega,1}\left\{\ln\left[\frac{P^M_t}{P^Y_t}\right]\right. \\ & - \ln\left[\theta(\beta_L + \beta_M)(1 - S^L_{it})\right] + (1 - \beta_M) m_{it} - \beta_L\left[m_{it} + \frac{\beta_L}{\beta_0} - \frac{\beta_L + \beta_M}{\beta_0} S^L_{it}\right] \\ & \left. + \frac{1}{2\beta_0}\left[-\beta_L + (\beta_L + \beta_M) S^L_{it}\right]^2 - \beta_K k_{it-1} - \frac{1}{2}\beta_{KK} k^2_{it-1}\right\} - \rho_{\omega,2} X_{it-1}, \end{aligned}$$

and we can rewrite the three estimation steps in the form of their equivalent multiple-equation moment restrictions:

$$\mathbb{E}[\mathrm{f}(\Lambda)] \equiv \mathbb{E}\begin{bmatrix} \ln R_{it} - \ln\left(\theta[\beta_L + \beta_M]\right) \\ \exp\left\{\ln\left(\theta[\beta_L + \beta_M]\right) - \ln R_{it}\right\} - \theta \\ \begin{pmatrix} m_{it} - l_{it} + \frac{\beta_L}{\beta_0} - \frac{\beta_L + \beta_M}{\beta_0} S^L_{it} - \\ \rho_{\varphi,1}\left[m_{it-1} - l_{it-1} + \frac{\beta_L}{\beta_0} - \frac{\beta_L + \beta_M}{\beta_0} S^L_{it-1}\right] - \rho_{\varphi,2} Z_{it-1} \end{pmatrix} \mathbb{Q}_{it-1} \\ r_{it}(\Lambda) \frac{\partial r_{it}(\Lambda)}{\partial(\beta_K, \beta_{KK}, \rho_{\omega,0}, \rho_{\omega,1}, \rho_{\omega_2})'} \end{bmatrix} = \mathbf{0}, \tag{4.5}$$

consisting of three blocks, where the first two moments correspond to the sample estimator of $\delta_{LM} = \beta_L + \beta_M$ and θ (first block), the middle dim($\mathbb{Q}$) moments correspond to the GMM estimation of $\alpha = (\beta_0, \beta_L, \rho_{\varphi,1}, \rho_{\varphi,2})'$ in (4.2) (second block) and the remaining five orthogonality conditions correspond to the nonlinear least-squares estimation of $\gamma = (\beta_K, \beta_{KK}, \rho_{\omega,0}, \rho_{\omega,1}, \rho_{\omega_2})'$ in (4.4) (third block).

The benefit of interpreting our sequential multi-step estimator as solving a GMM problem corresponding to a system of nonlinear moment equations in (4.5) simultaneously is that the standard large-n limit results for a class of such GMM estimators apply here. Furthermore, using the moment equivalents in (4.5) also facilitates asymptotic inference based on the optimal covariance matrix of GMM estimators $\mathbb{V}[\widehat{\Lambda}] = [\mathbb{E}\frac{\partial f(\Lambda)}{\partial \Lambda'}]^{-1}\mathbb{E}[f(\Lambda)f(\Lambda)'][\mathbb{E}\frac{\partial f(\Lambda)}{\partial \Lambda}]^{-1}$ which, if desired, can also be robustified using usual off-the-shelf methods. Having said that, should one find evaluating the analytical covariance matrix tedious or in the case when asymptotic inference is difficult to justify, bootstrap provides an alternative avenue for hypothesis testing. We discuss how to approximate the sampling distribution of our estimator via wild residual block bootstrap[11] that takes into account a sequential nature of our methodology in Appendix 4.

5. FINITE-SAMPLE PERFORMANCE

In this section, we examine the finite-sample performance of our methodology. We first demonstrate its ability to successfully identify the multi-dimensional firm productivity and the production-function parameters in a small Monte Carlo study. Then, we apply our estimator to the firm-level data to provide an empirical illustration in practice.

5.1. Simulations

We conduct simulations to evaluate the performance of our proposed estimator in finite samples. Our data generating process (DGP) draws from those used by Grieco, Li, and Zhang (2016), Gandhi et al. (2020) and Malikov and Zhao (2021). More specifically, we consider a balanced panel of $n = \{100, 200, 400, 1600\}$ firms operating during $T = 10$ time periods.[12] Each panel is simulated 1,000 times. We let that the true production technology take a (restricted) translog form with a two-dimensional firm productivity given in (3.2), where we set $\beta_K = 0.2$, $\beta_{KK} = -0.01$, $\beta_M = 0.5$, $\beta_L = 0.25$ and $\beta_0 = -0.05$. Given the DGPs for the production variables below, this choice of parameter values facilitates that the monotonicity and curvature properties of the production function are satisfied in the generated data; firms exhibit decreasing returns to scale (RTS).

The persistent firm productivity components are generated as follows. To simplify matters, we abstract away from productivity modifiers (X and Z) and model the Hicks- and Harrod-neutral productivities as exogenous linear AR(1) processes:

$$\omega_{it} = \rho_{\omega,0} + \rho_{\omega,1}\omega_{it-1} + \zeta_{\omega,it}, \tag{5.1}$$

$$\varphi_{it} = \rho_{\varphi,1}\varphi_{it-1} + \zeta_{\varphi,it}, \tag{5.2}$$

where we set $\rho_{\omega,0} = 0.2$, $\rho_{\omega,1} = 0.6$ and $\rho_{\varphi,1} = 0.9$. The innovations are drawn independently as $\zeta_{\omega,it} \sim i.i.d.\ \mathbb{N}(0,\sigma_\omega^2)$ and $\zeta_{\varphi,it} \sim i.i.d.\ \mathbb{N}(0,\sigma_\varphi^2)$, with $\sigma_\omega = \sigma_\varphi = 0.04$. The initial levels of Hicks- and Harrod-neutral productivities ω_{i1} and φ_{i1} are drawn from $\mathbb{U}(-1,1)$ identically and independently distributed over i. The random transitory productivity shocks $\{\eta_{it}\}$ entering the production function are drawn from $\eta_{it} \sim i.i.d.\ \mathbb{N}\left(0,\sigma_\eta^2\right)$ with $\sigma_\eta = 0.07$.

We assume the following about evolution of the firm's state variables. Physical capital, a dynamic predetermined input, is set to evolve according to $K_{it} = I_{it-1} + (1-\delta_i)K_{it-1}$, where the firm-specific depreciation rates $\delta_i \in \{0.05, 0.075, 0.10, 0.125, 0.15\}$ are distributed uniformly across i, and the investment function takes the following form:

$$I_{it-1} = K_{it-1}^{\iota_1}\left[\exp\{\omega_{it-1}\}\right]^{\iota_2}\left[\exp\{\varphi_{it-1}\}\right]^{\iota_3}, \tag{5.3}$$

where $\iota_1 = 0.8$ and $\iota_2 = \iota_3 = 0.1$. The initial level of capital is generated as $K_{i1} \sim i.i.d.\ \mathbb{U}(10,200)$.

The optimal labor and materials series (the freely varying inputs) are generated by numerically solving the firm's static first-order conditions in (3.4) and (3.5) after having already generated the series of $(K_{it}, \omega_{it}, \varphi_{it})'$ for each firm and time period. When doing so, we normalize $P_t^L = P_t^M = \theta\ \forall\ t$ and also intentionally assume away any temporal variation in output prices: $P_t^Y = 1$ for all t. In such a scenario, changes in the firm's labor-to-materials ratio are driven by the improvements in labor-augmenting productivity only.

We estimate our model via the three-step algorithm outlined in Section 4.[13] For each simulation repetition, we obtain point estimates of the production-function and productivity-process parameters and then report the mean, the root mean squared error (RMSE) and the mean absolute error (MAE) of these point estimates computed over 1,000 simulations. Table 9.1 reports these simulation results. The results are encouraging and show that, with a modestly large sample size, our methodology recovers the true parameters fairly well, thereby lending support to the validity of our identification strategy. Of all parameters, those obtained in the third step are the most imprecisely estimated. This is unsurprising given that their (nonlinear) estimation relies on the generated regressors estimated in not one but two previous steps all of which are measured with sampling error. But overall, as expected of consistent estimators, the estimation becomes more stable as n grows.

5.2. *Empirical Illustration*

We showcase our methodology by applying it to study the multi-dimensional productivity heterogeneity among Chinese manufacturing firms. We let the Hicks- and Harrod-neutral productivities share the same scalar productivity shifter, i.e., $X_{it-1} = Z_{it-1}$ in (2.4) and (2.5). Given the well-documented importance of inbound FDI – as a vehicle of international technological diffusion – for productivity advances among domestic firms in the recipient countries (see Malikov & Zhao,

Table 9.1. Simulation Results for the Proposed Three-Step Estimator.

	$n = 100$			$n = 200$			$n = 400$			$n = 1,600$		
	Mean	**RMSE**	**MAE**	**Mean**	**RMSE**	**MAE**	**Mean**	**RMSE**	**MAE**	**Mean**	**RMSE**	**MAE**
β_K	0.1900	0.5316	0.4115	0.1705	0.3619	0.2821	0.2077	0.2549	0.2039	0.2003	0.1277	0.1003
$\beta_{KK}(\times 10)$	−0.0856	0.8633	0.6704	−0.0518	0.5927	0.4635	−0.1123	0.4167	0.3335	−0.1006	0.2096	0.1644
β_L	0.2502	0.0038	0.0030	0.2502	0.0024	0.0019	0.2500	0.0018	0.0014	0.2500	0.0009	0.0007
β_M	0.4997	0.0038	0.0030	0.4998	0.0024	0.0019	0.4999	0.0018	0.0014	0.4999	0.0009	0.0007
$\beta_0(\times 10)$	−0.5024	0.0165	0.0124	−0.5008	0.0104	0.0081	−0.5003	0.0070	0.0056	−0.5004	0.0036	0.0029
$\rho_{\varphi,1}$	0.8990	0.0135	0.0107	0.8995	0.0094	0.0074	0.8998	0.0062	0.0050	0.8998	0.0031	0.0024
$\rho_{\omega,1}$	0.5981	0.0381	0.0305	0.5988	0.0268	0.0211	0.5996	0.0198	0.0156	0.5998	0.0095	0.0076
$\rho_{\omega,0}$	0.2082	0.6385	0.4987	0.2338	0.4380	0.3418	0.1891	0.3083	0.2475	0.1993	0.1546	0.1217

Notes: The true parameter values are $\beta_K = 0.20$, $\beta_{KK} \times 10 = -0.10$, $\beta_L = 0.25$, $\beta_M = 0.50$, $\beta_0 \times 10 = -0.50$, $\rho_{\varphi,1} = 0.90$, $\rho_{\omega,1} = 0.60$ and $\rho_{\omega,0} = 0.20$. Throughout, $T = 10$.

2021, for more discussion and references to the related literature), we use a measure of the foreign equity share as a productivity-modifying "control," with an objective to examine the potentially differential factor-neutral and labor-saving effects of FDI on firm productivity. Through their foreign investors, domestic firms gain access to intangible productive "knowledge" assets from abroad such as new technologies, proprietary know-hows, more efficient and innovative marketing and management practices, established relational networks, reputation, etc., which can help boost their productivity. Whether such knowledge/technology transfers are neutral or biased remains, however, unexamined.

Data.—Our data come from the Chinese Industrial Enterprises Database survey conducted by China's National Bureau of Statistics (NBS). We focus on the "leather, fur, feather and the related products" industry (SIC 2-digit code 19) because China is the largest leather producing country in the world, representing more than a quarter of the annual global production, and is one of the world's largest leather exporters and importers. Also, a relatively large share of firms (15.2%) in this industry are foreign-invested.

The production variables are standard. The firm's capital stock (K_{it}) is the net fixed assets deflated by the price index of investment into fixed assets. Labor (L_{it}) is measured as the total wage bill plus benefits deflated by the GDP deflator. Materials (M_{it}) are the total intermediate inputs, including raw materials and other production-related inputs, deflated by the purchasing price index for industrial inputs. The output (Y_{it}) is defined as the gross industrial output value deflated by the producer price index. The price indices are obtained from NBS and the World Bank. The four variables are measured in thousands of real RMB. Our sample period runs from 1998 to 2007, and the operational sample is an unbalanced panel of 11,167 firms with a total of 31,287 observations.[14]

The summary statistics of data are reported in Table A5.1. For all variables, the mean values are much larger than their medians, consistent with their distributions being right-skewed, and their inter-quartile ranges are wide. The large heterogeneity of variable distributions suggests that a more flexible model of the production process, such as ours, is needed to better characterize the production relationship between inputs and output. Also note that all variable statistics are larger for foreign-invested firms ($Z > 0$) compared with their wholly-domestically-owned counterparts ($Z = 0$). This difference provides a further motivation to incorporate the information about firms' exposure to foreign investment into the analysis, which we accomplish by conditioning productivity evolution processes on the foreign equity share.

Results.—We report the estimated input elasticities, RTS and the productivity-process parameters in Table 9.2. Note that, albeit parametrically, we model the production function using a log-quadratic form, which is why the estimated elasticities and RTS are observation-specific. As discussed in Section 4, we assume that both $r_{\omega}(\cdot)$ and $r_{\varphi}(\cdot)$ are linear given the wide popularity of an AR(1) assumption for productivity processes among practitioners. Therefore, the estimated productivity parameters are fixed and global. Lastly, following the discussion of our methodology, our main results are obtained using the inverted conditional material demand to proxy for Hicksian productivity. While in theory the estimator is

Table 9.2. Estimates of the Production Function and Productivity Parameters.

Panel A: Elasticities and RTS				
	Mean	**1st Qu.**	**Median**	**3rd Qu.**
Capital elasticity	0.0361	0.0213	0.0368	0.0507
	(0.0080)	(0.0094)	(0.0081)	(0.0099)
Labor elasticity	0.0950	0.0458	0.0864	0.1287
	(0.0003)	(0.0001)	(0.0002)	(0.0004)
Material elasticity	0.7377	0.7041	0.7463	0.7869
	(0.0020)	(0.0019)	(0.0021)	(0.0022)
RTS	0.8688	0.8540	0.8695	0.8834
	(0.0081)	(0.0095)	(0.0082)	(0.0100)

Panel B: Productivity Parameters			
Labor-Augmenting		**Factor-Neutral**	
$\rho_{\varphi,0}$	0.0000	$\rho_{\omega,0}$	0.6525
	–		(0.1026)
$\rho_{\varphi,1}$	0.5723	$\rho_{\omega,1}$	0.7562
	(0.0244)		(0.0307)
$\rho_{\varphi,2}$	0.0726	$\rho_{\omega,2}$	0.0020
	(0.0183)		(0.0084)

Notes: The productivity processes are parameterized as follows: $\varphi_{it} = \rho_{\varphi,1}\varphi_{it-1} + \rho_{\varphi,2}Z_{it-1} + \zeta_{\varphi,it}$ with $\rho_{\varphi,0}$ normalized to 0, and $\omega_{it} = \rho_{\omega,0} + \rho_{\omega,1}\omega_{it-1} + \rho_{\omega,2}Z_{it-1} + \zeta_{\omega,it}$. Bootstrap standard errors are in parentheses.

invariant to the choice of a variable input for the role of ω proxy, whether the latter is the case in practice or not, effectively, provides an indirect test of our model assumptions. The counterpart of Table 9.2 containing the results obtained using the labor proxy as well as the average of labor and material proxies are provided in Appendix 6. The estimates differ little and are qualitatively unchanged.

Per the results in Panel A of Table 9.2, the manufacturers of leather, fur, feather and related products in China show a large material elasticity and relatively small elasticities of capital and labor. This oversized importance of intermediate inputs (materials) compared with the capital and labor inputs in the production process of Chinese manufacturing firms is confirmed by other studies that used the same dataset (see, e.g., Brandt, Van Biesebroeck, Wang, & Zhang, 2017; Malikov et al., 2021; Malikov & Zhao, 2021; Zhao, Qian, & Kumbhakar, 2020). The implied estimates of RTS have the mean value of 0.8688 (median is 0.8695) with the rather narrow inter-quartile range of 0.029. Statistically, all firms exhibit decreasing RTS, i.e., diseconomies of scale. This inference is based on the RTS point estimate being statistically less than 1 at the 5% significance level.

Panel B of Table 9.2 reports the estimated productivity parameters for factor-netural and labor-augmenting components of firm productivity. As discussed in Section 3.1, because function $r_{\varphi}(\cdot)$ is identified only up to a constant, the intercept coefficient for φ_{it} is normalized to 0. Comparing the autoregressive coefficients $\rho_{\varphi,1}$ and $\rho_{\omega,1}$, we find that Harrod-neutral productivity is not as persistent over time as is Hicks-neutral productivity. Interestingly, we find that the foreign equity share – a productivity modifier of interest – has both economically and statistically significant marginal effect on labor-saving productivity, whereas the effect size on factor-neutral productivity is insignificant and effectively zero. From this we can conclude that, at least in China's leather industry, the productivity-boosting effect of FDI on domestic firms' productivity has a bias toward labor. Thus, better/new technologies and more efficient business practices that firms "import" and learn from abroad through their foreign investors, as commonly argued in the FDI literature, appear to be primarily labor-saving as opposed to boosting marginal productivity of all factors. This is a novel empirical finding. More concretely, our point estimate of $\rho_{\varphi,2}$ implies that a 10-percentage point increase in the firm's foreign equity share boosts its expected future labor-biased productivity by about 0.73%. While this effect size might at first appear to be too modest, it is imperative to remember that $\rho_{\varphi,2}$ only captures a short-run impact of FDI on labor-augmenting productivity (that is, $\partial\mathbb{E}[\varphi_{it+1} \mid \Xi_{it}] / \partial Z_{it}$) and does not account for dynamic effects over time. Obviously, owing to the persistence of productivity, the cumulative implications of receiving more FDI are expected to be bigger in the long run. In fact, under temporal stationarity of φ_{it} we have that the long-run effect of a 10-percentage point increase in the firm's foreign equity share on its labor-augmenting productivity is estimated at $0.73/(1-0.5723) \approx 1.7\%$.

Fig. 9.1 compares the empirical distributions of the two estimated productivities. We report box-plots of the estimated φ_{it} and ω_{it} by year in Fig. 9.1(a) and of their annual changes in Fig. 9.1(b). For the ease of comparison, the medians of both productivity terms are normalized to zero in the year 1998. We see that the distributions of Harrod- and Hicks-neutral productivities behave quite differently. First, according to Fig. 9.1(a), the labor-augmented productivity has a larger cross-sectional variation, as exhibited by wider inter-quartile ranges and longer whiskers. Second, in each year, the Hicks-neutral productivity is distributed almost symmetrically across individual firms, whereas the labor-augmented productivity is heavily skewed to the right. Third, based on the medians in each year, the Hicks-neutral productivity steadily shifts up over time, but we cannot say the same about the labor-augmented productivity. Instead, it is mainly the upper/right whiskers of the labor-augmented productivity that generally shift up over time, suggesting the presence of persistently more labor-efficient firms that keep becoming more productive.

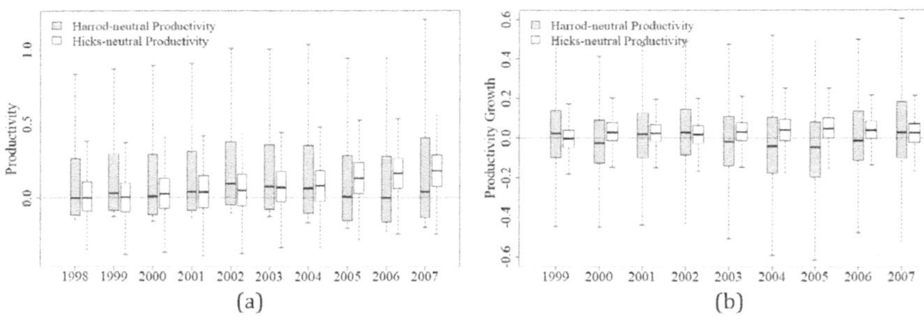

Fig. 9.1. Distributions of Hicks- and Harrod-Neutral Productivities: (a) in Levels, (b) in Growth Rates.

In Fig. 9.1(b), we plot the box-plots of annual productivity changes in logs, i.e., $\varphi_{it} - \varphi_{it-1}$ and $\omega_{it} - \omega_{it-1}$. Since both the φ_{it} and ω_{it} are attached to the log inputs and output, their changes can be approximately interpreted as the corresponding within-firm productivity growth rates. We see that, compared with factor-neutral productivity, the labor-augmenting productivity also exhibits a larger cross-sectional variation in its growth. The median growth rate of Hicks-neutral productivity is non-negative across all years, whereas that of labor-augmenting productivity oscillates around zero, with essentially a nil cumulative effect.

To see the cumulative and total impact of the growth in these two productivity components on the industry output, we calculate the aggregate industry output-weighted Harrod-neutral and Hicks-neutral productivities and plot their trends in Fig. 9.2(a). These two aggregate productivities are depicted using solid-circle and dashed-triangle lines, respectively, and for comparability, both of them are normalized to zero in the year 1998. We find that, during our sample period, the industry-level factor-neutral productivity was steadily rising and increased by around 20%. However, the aggregate labor-augmenting productivity peaked in 2002 right after China's accession to the WTO and decreased since then, although with a rebound in the last year to a level close to that of the beginning of the sample period. This trend is generally consistent with the labor-to-material ratio box-plot in Fig. 9.2(b). Were the labor-augmenting productivity to increase significantly in our sample period, we would have expected the labor-to-material ratio to decrease over time too. Such labor-saving technological advances have been documented by Doraszelski and Jaumandreu (2018) and Zhang (2019) for different countries/industries. In our case, however, the post-2002 downward trend of labor-augmented productivity is in line with the upward shift in the labor-to-material ratios observed in the data.[15] The widening whiskers over the years in Fig. 9.2(b) are also consistent with the increasing variation of labor-augmenting productivity over time documented in Fig. 9.1(a).

Now, note that, because the firm's output is log-linear in ω_{it}, the magnitude of Hicks-neutral productivity growth is directly corresponding to the output growth. However, this is not the case for the non-neutral productivity φ_{it} that affects output via labor. The marginal effect of φ_{it} on the firm's (log) output depends on the labor elasticity. Therefore, to make a fair comparison between Hicks- and

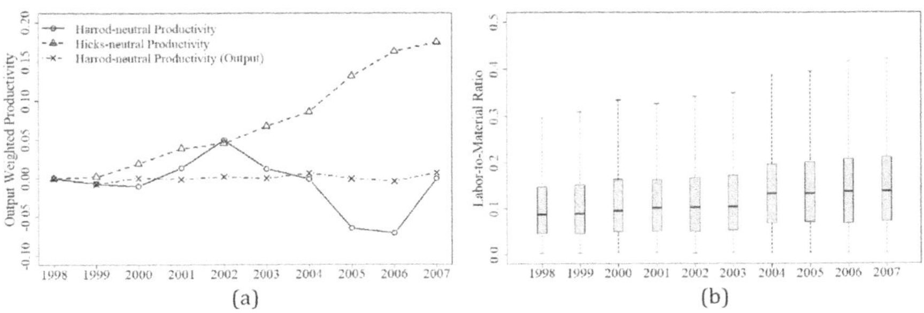

Fig. 9.2. Productivity and Flexible Input Ratio Trends.

Harrod-neutral productivities in terms of their effects on output growth, we follow Doraszelski and Jaumandreu (2018) in computing the product of the labor elasticity $\partial f_{it} / \partial l_{it}$ and φ_{it} refer to it as the labor-augmenting productivity in output terms. In Fig. 9.2(a), we plot the industry output-weighted average for it using a dot-dashed-cross line. The line is almost flat, implying that the labor-augmenting productivity had no material effect on the industry output growth during our sample period. Thus, our estimates provide evidence that the overall productivity growth in China's leather industry in 1998–2007 was factor-neutral.

6. EXTENSION TO IMPERFECT COMPETITION

As argued by Battisti, Del Gatto, and Parmeter (2022), empirical studies have so far produced very limited evidence on the magnitude of non-neutral technological change with market imperfections.[16] Our methodology and its underlying identification scheme presented above are developed under the assumption that firms operate in a perfectly competitive output market. Although this assumption continues to be maintained – implicitly or explicitly – by most productivity studies, which is partly dictated by the typical unavailability of firm-level price data,[17] there has been notable effort recently aimed at extending proxy variable production-function estimators to accommodate market power. Besides usually requiring the data on exogenous demand shifters, most such methods also tend to rely on (observable) exogenous heterogeneous input prices and/or isoelastic demand specifications for identification (e.g., see De Loecker, 2011; De Loecker, Goldberg, Khandelwal, & Pavcnik, 2016; De Loecker & Warzynski, 2012; Doraszelski & Jaumandreu, 2013, 2019). Others resort to restrictions on the production technology such as the constant RTS (see Flynn et al., 2019; Raval, 2020) or abandon the structural "proxy variable" paradigm in favor of a more "atheoretical" control function approach to handling endogeneity-inducing unobservable firm productivity (Demirer, 2020).

Motivated by this emerging literature, we show how to relax the perfect competition assumption and allow for monopolistic power in the output market. We do so while retaining the assumption of competitive homogeneous factor prices, given our earlier discussion concerning the use of firm-level variation in input prices for identification. In Appendix 7, we first show *point* non-identification of the production function in (3.2) when firms exhibit market power even if one observes exogenous demand shifters in the data. We then discuss how with some additional but quite reasonable assumptions about unobservables one can still *set* identify the production function. We derive this partial identification result without requiring that the information on demand shifters be available and rely on the same set of observables that are used in our methodology for the case of perfectly competitive markets.

7. CONCLUDING REMARKS

The literature on proxy variable identification of production functions is dominated by models that accommodate a single source of firm heterogeneity: a scalar Hicks-neutral productivity. In this chapter, we contribute to the relatively thin but emerging strand of the literature that seeks to generalize these proxy methods to allow for non-neutral production technology by considering the identification of a translog production function when latent firm productivity is multi-dimensional, with biased labor-augmenting and factor-neutral components. In contrast to the available alternatives, our model can be identified under weaker data requirements, notably, without relying on the firm-level input price information as instruments. This tremendously increases the practical value of our methodology by making it applicable to most production datasets. When markets are perfectly competitive, we achieve point identification by leveraging the information contained in static optimality conditions, in effect, adopting a system-of-equations approach. We also show how one can set identify the production function with non-neutral productivity in the traditional proxy variable framework when firms have market power.

NOTES

1. A non-Hicksian technological change is also an important feature of aggregate production functions in some recent macroeconomic studies (e.g., see Baqaee & Farhi, 2019, 2020).
2. Our chapter is also related to Demirer (2020) who also considers the problem of identifying production functions with non-neutral multi-dimensional productivity. However, unlike ours, his methodology does not take a structural "proxy variable" route but a more atheoretical "control function" approach to handling endogeneity-inducing latent firm productivities.
3. It is because of this reliance on a statically optimized input ratio that we require at least two freely varying inputs.
4. For clarity, if the optimal decision concerning production in period t is affected by its history, then that decision is said to be "dynamic." If, due to adjustment frictions, a decision concerning production in period t is effectively made at $t-1$, then we say it is "predetermined." In this nomenclature, K_{it} is dynamic and predetermined, whereas X_{it} and Z_{it} are dynamic but chosen at time t.
5. For example, see De Loecker and Warzynski (2012) and De Loecker et al. (2016) for recent applications of the translog production functions in the structural proxy estimation.
6. Since productivity/efficiency measurements are relative, this is merely a restriction which implies a "normalized" zero-mean φ and which does not affect the relative rank of firms based on efficiency of their labor. Qualitatively, this normalization is akin to the typical no-intercept restriction for production functions because an additive constant cannot be separated from the Hicksian productivity unless the latter is also normalized to have a zero mean.
7. The first-order lags are already utilized in the estimation inside Markov processes and thus self-instrument.
8. That is, not perfectly dependent with contemporaneous prices that enter estimating equations directly.
9. We can also justify this linearity as a sieve *approximation* using linear polynomials. However, in this case the estimation will no longer be "parametric" but semiparametric. See Appendix 3.
10. As noted earlier, we normalize $r_{\varphi}(0) = 0$ since φ_{it} can be identified up to a constant only. In practice, this implies that $r_{\varphi}(\cdot)$ is parameterized using a linear function with no intercept.
11. Other bootstrap procedures can also be used.

12. We have also experimented with 5 and 50 periods. The results are qualitatively unchanged.

13. Following our discussion, we include k_{it} as an additional instrument in the second-step estimation.

14. We exclude observations with missing values for production variables as well as a small number of likely erroneous observations with the foreign equity share values outside the unit interval.

15. The graph for the output-weighted average labor-to-material ratios looks similar.

16. In their study, Battisti et al. (2022) present a new approach and estimate the skill-biased technical change from the production side while allowing for labor-market inefficiencies using country-level data.

17. This is because, unless the quantity information about output/inputs is observed in the data (which is rare in practice), researchers commonly assume perfect competition with homogeneous prices to justify deflating nominal revenues and expenditures using price indices to obtain real values.

18. One can also operationalize this step using the inverted conditional labor demand instead. Both proxies are equivalent.

19. More generally, the residual demand that a firm faces can also depend on its rivals' prices. While we assume this away, one may be able to account for such substitution effects by replacing rivals' prices with an aggregate price index or dummies, although it may substantially increase the number of parameters to be estimated.

20. We can also allow for random price/demand shocks by, say, augmenting the demand equation with a log-additive unanticipated *i.i.d.* shock akin to $\eta_{it}: P_{it}^{Y} = D(Y_{it}^{Y}, U_{it})\exp\{\varepsilon_{it}\}$ with $\mathbb{E}[\varepsilon_{it} \mid \Xi_{it}] = \mathbb{E}[\varepsilon_{it}] = 0$. This would only result in an additional multiplicative constant entering the firm's static first-order conditions *in expectation* [see equations (A7.1)–(A7.2)] thereby having no material impact on the analysis.

21. θ is point identified because the random shocks $\{\eta_{it}\}$ are point identified via $\eta_{it} = \ln\left(\frac{\theta[\beta_L + \beta_M]}{\mu(P_{it}^{Y}, U_{it}^{Y})}\right) - \ln R_{it}$, where $\ln\left(\frac{\theta[\beta_L + \beta_M]}{\mu(P_{it}^{Y}, U_{it}^{Y})}\right) = \mathbb{E}[\ln R_{it} \mid P_{it}^{Y}, U_{it}^{Y}]$ is some unknown conditional mean function of $\ln R_{it}$ estimatable via least squares.

22. Assumption 5(ii) can be relaxed by making the independence be conditional on φ_{it-1} and ω_{it-1}, thereby, in effect, assuming that U_{it} is jointly independent of the contemporaneous *innovations* in firm productivities.

23. Recall that S_{it}^{L} is a deterministic function of P_{t}^{M}, P_{t}^{L}, $\exp\{m_{it}\}$ and $\exp\{l_{it}\}$.

24. Intuitively, this is akin to a restriction that variable inputs be "gross complements."

ACKNOWLEDGMENTS

We are most grateful to the editors of this volume, Chris Parmeter, Mike Tsionas, Hung-Jen Wang and Dan Millimet, and an anonymous referee for many insightful comments and suggestions that helped improve this chapter.

REFERENCES

Ackerberg, D. A., Benkard, C. L., Berry, S., & Pakes, A. (2007). Econometric tools for analyzing market outcomes. In J. J. Heckman & E. E. Leamer (Eds.), *Handbook of econometrics* (Vol. *6A*). Oxford, UK: North Holland.

Ackerberg, D. A., Caves, K., & Frazer, G. (2015). Identification properties of recent production function estimators. *Econometrica*, *83*, 2411–2451.

Ackerberg, D., Frazer, G., Kim, K., Luo, Y., & Yingjun, S. (2020). *Under-identification of structural models based on timing and information set assumptions*. Working Paper.

Baqaee, D. R., & Farhi, E. (2019). JEEA-FBBVA Lecture 2018: The microeconomic foundations of aggregate production functions. *Journal of the European Economic Association, 17*(5), 1337–1392.

Baqaee, D. R., & Farhi, E. (2020). Productivity and misallocation in general equilibrium*. *The Quarterly Journal of Economics, 135*(1), 105–163.

Battisti, M., Del Gatto, M., & Parmeter, C. F. (2022). Skill-biased technical change and labor market inefficiency. *Journal of Economic Dynamics and Control, 139*, 104428.

Brandt, L., Van Biesebroeck, J., Wang, L., & Zhang, Y. (2017). WTO accession and performance of Chinese manufacturing firms. *American Economic Review, 107*(9), 2784–2820.

Canay, I., & Shaikh, A. (2017). Practical and theoretical advances in inference for partially identified models. In B. Honoré, A. Pakes, M. Piazzesi, & L. Samuelson (Eds.), *Advances in economics and econometrics: Eleventh World Congress* (pp. 271–306). Cambridge, UK: Cambridge University Press.

Chen, X. (2007). Large sample sieve estimation of semi-nonparametric models. In J. J. Heckman & E. E. Leamer (Eds.), *Handbook of econometrics* (Vol. *6B*). Oxford, UK: North Holland.

Craven, P., & Wahba, G. (1979). Smoothing noisy data with spline functions. *Numerische Mathematik, 13*, 377–403.

De Loecker, J. (2011). Product differentiation, multiproduct firms, and estimating the impact of trade liberalization on productivity. *Econometrica, 79*, 1407–1451.

De Loecker, J. (2013). Detecting learning by exporting. *American Economic Journal: Microeconomics, 5*, 1–21.

De Loecker, J., & Eeckhout, J. (2020). *Global market power*. NBER Working Paper No. 24768.

De Loecker, J., Eeckhout, J., & Unger, G. (2020). The rise of market power and the macroeconomic implications. *Quarterly Journal of Economics, 135*, 561–644.

De Loecker, J., Goldberg, P. K., Khandelwal, A. K., & Pavcnik, N. (2016). Prices, markups, and trade reform. *Econometrica, 84*, 445–510.

De Loecker, J., & Warzynski, F. (2012). Markups and firm-level export status. *American Economic Review, 102*, 2437–2471.

Demirer, M. (2019). *Production function estimation with imperfect proxies*. Working Paper. MIT.

Demirer, M. (2020). *Production function estimation with factor-augmenting technology: An application to markups*. Working Paper. MIT.

Doraszelski, U., & Jaumandreu, J. (2013). R&D and productivity: Estimating endogenous productivity. *Review of Economic Studies, 80*, 1338–1383.

Doraszelski, U., & Jaumandreu, J. (2018). Measuring the bias of technological chance. *Journal of Political Economy, 126*, 1027–1084.

Doraszelski, U., & Jaumandreu, J. (2019). *Using cost minimization to estimate markups*. Working Paper. University of Pennsylvania.

Flynn, Z., Gandhi, A., & Traina, J. (2019). *Measuring markups with production data*. Working Paper. University of Pennsylvania.

Gandhi, A., Navarro, S., & Rivers, D. (2020). On the identification of gross output production functions. *Journal of Political Economy, 128*(8), 2973–3016

Grieco, P. L. E., Li, S., & Zhang, H. (2016). Production function estimation with unobserved input price dispersion. *International Economic Review, 57*, 665–689.

Grieco, P. L. E., Li, S., & Zhang, H. (2020). *Input prices, productivity and trade dynamics: Long-run effects of liberalization on Chinese paint manufacturers*. Working Paper.

Griliches, Z., & Mairesse, J. (1998). Production functions: The search for identification. In *Econometrics and Economic Theory in the Twentieth Century: The Ragnar Frisch Centennial Symposium* (pp. 169–203). Cambridge University Press.

Kim, K., Luo, Y., & Su, Y. (2019). A robust approach to estimating production functions: Replication of the ACF procedure. *Journal of Applied Econometrics, 34*, 612–619.

Kline, B., Pakes, A., & Tamer, E. (2021). *Moment inequalities and partial identification in industrial organization*. NBER Working Paper #29409.

Levinsohn, J., & Petrin, A. (2003). Estimating production functions using inputs to control for unobservables. *Review of Economic Studies, 70*, 317–341.

Malikov, E., & Lien, G. (2021). Proxy variable estimation of multiproduct production functions. *American Journal of Agricultural Economics, 103*(5), 1878–1902.

Malikov, E., Zhang, J., Zhao, S., & Kumbhakar, S. C. (2021). Accounting for cross-location technological heterogeneity in the measurement of operations efficiency and productivity. *Journal of Operations Management*. forthcoming.

Malikov, E., & Zhao, S. (2021). On the estimation of cross-firm productivity spillovers with an application to FDI. *Review of Economics and Statistics*. forthcoming.

Malikov, E., Zhao, S., & Kumbhakar, S. C. (2020). Estimation of firm-level productivity in the presence of exports: Evidence from China's manufacturing. *Journal of Applied Econometrics*, *35*, 457–480.

Mammen, E. (1993). Bootstrap and wild bootstrap for high dimensional linear models. *Annals of Statistics*, *21*, 255–285.

Mo, J., Qiu, L. D., Zhang, H., & Dong, X. (2021). What you import matters for productivity growth: Experience from Chinese manufacturing firms. *Journal of Development Economics*, *152*, Article 102677.

Molinari, F. (2020). *Microeconometrics with partial identification*. Working Paper CWP15/20. CEMMAP, The Institute for Fiscal Studies, Department of Economics, UCL.

Newey, W. K. (1984). A method of moments interpretation of sequential estimators. *Economics Letters*, *14*(2), 201–206.

Oberfield, E., & Raval, D. (2021). Micro data and macro technology. *Econometrica*, *89*(2), 703–732.

Olley, G. S., & Pakes, A. (1996). The dynamics of productivity in the telecommunications equipment industry. *Econometrica*, *64*, 1263–1297.

Raval, D. (2020). *Testing the production approach to markup estimation*. Working Paper. Federal Trade Commission.

Rothenberg, T. J. (1971). Identification in parametric models. *Econometrica*, *39*, 577–591.

Stoye, J. (2021). *A simple, shot, nut never-empty confidence interval for partially identified parameters*. Working Paper. Cornell University.

Van Biesebroeck, J. (2005). Exporting raises productivity in sub-Saharan African manufacturing firms. *Journal of International Economics*, *67*, 373–391.

Wooldridge, J. M. (2009). On estimating firm-level production functions using proxy variables to control for unobservables. *Economics Letters*, *104*, 112–114.

Zhang, H. (2017). Static and dynamic gains from costly importing of intermediate inputs: Evidence from Colombia. *European Economic Review*, *91*, 118–145.

Zhang, H. (2019). Non-neutral technology, firm heterogeneity, and labor demand. *Journal of Development Economics*, *140*, 145–168.

Zhao, S., Qian, B., & Kumbhakar, S. C. (2020). Estimation of productivity and markups with price dispersion: Evidence from Chinese manufacturing during economic transition. *Southern Economic Journal*, *87*(2), 666–699.

APPENDIX 1. IDENTIFICATION UNDER THE CES SPECIFICATION

In Section 3, we present our identification strategy for a restricted translog production function. To show that the same strategy can also be applied to other production function specifications, here we detail its application to a CES functional form, another widely-used specification for production technology. Specifically, let the firm's production technology $F(\cdot)$ with labor-saving productivity take the following form:

$$F(\cdot)=\left\{\beta_K K_{it}^{-\frac{1-\sigma}{\sigma}}+\left[\exp\{\varphi_{it}\}L_{it}\right]^{-\frac{1-\sigma}{\sigma}}+\beta_M M_{it}^{-\frac{1-\sigma}{\sigma}}\right\}^{-\frac{\nu\sigma}{1-\sigma}}, \tag{A1.1}$$

where ν and σ are the elasticities of scale and substitution, respectively; and β_K and β_M are the distribution parameters, with that corresponding to labor implicitly normalized to unity since it cannot be identified separately from φ_{it}.

Among others, the CES form in (A1.1) has been used by Doraszelski and Jaumandreu (2013). Besides the usual monotonicity and curvature assumptions, it is easy to confirm that it also satisfies separability per our Assumption 2(ii). Namely, $F(\cdot)$ above is a nested CES that is separable in capital as follows: $F(K_{it},\exp\{\varphi\}L_{it},M_{it})=G\left(K_{it},H\left(\exp\{\varphi_{it}\}L_{it},M_{it}\right)\right)$, where

$$G(\cdot)=\left\{\beta_K K_{it}^{-\frac{1-\sigma}{\sigma}}+H\left(\exp\{\varphi_{it}\}L_{it},M_{it}\right)^{-\frac{1-\sigma}{\sigma}}\right\}^{-\frac{\nu\sigma}{1-\sigma}},$$

$$H(\cdot)=\left\{\left[\exp\{\varphi_{it}\}L_{it}\right]^{-\frac{1-\sigma}{\sigma}}+\beta_M M_{it}^{-\frac{1-\sigma}{\sigma}}\right\}^{-\frac{\sigma}{1-\sigma}},$$

and $H(\cdot)$ is normalized to be linearly homogeneous (i.e., a unitary scale elasticity within the labor-and-materials pair of inputs), and the elasticity of substitution between capital and the labor-and-materials aggregator is the same as that between labor and materials within the aggregator.

Making use of the "known" functional form of $F(\cdot)$, from the static first-order conditions for flexible inputs L_{it} and M_{it} we obtain the following expression for the Harrod-neutral productivity φ_{it}:

$$\varphi_{it}=\frac{1}{1-\sigma}\left(m_{it}-l_{it}\right)-\frac{\sigma}{1-\sigma}\ln(\beta_M)+\frac{\sigma}{1-\sigma}\left(\ln P_t^M-\ln P_t^L\right). \tag{A1.2}$$

The above equation is the counterpart of (3.7) when the production function takes a CES functional form, and it provides a proxy for the latent φ_{it} expressed as a function of the production function parameters and observed data.

Next, we combine (A1.2) with the law of motion for labor-augmenting productivity, which is specified in (2.5), into an estimating equation for parameters of the production function in (A1.1). More concretely, substituting φ_{it} and φ_{it-1} in (2.5) with (A1.2), we have

$$\frac{1}{1-\sigma}(m_{it}-l_{it})-\frac{\sigma}{1-\sigma}\ln(\beta_M)+\frac{\sigma}{1-\sigma}\left(\ln P_t^M-\ln P_t^L\right)$$
$$= r_{\varphi}\left(\left[\frac{1}{1-\sigma}(m_{it-1}-l_{it-1})-\frac{\sigma}{1-\sigma}\ln(\beta_M)+\frac{\sigma}{1-\sigma}\left(\ln P_{t-1}^M-\ln P_{t-1}^L\right)\right],Z_{it-1}\right)+\zeta_{\varphi,it}. \tag{A1.3}$$

The above equation is the counterpart of (3.13) in the translog case. The two unknown parameters $(\sigma,\beta_M)'$ and the mean function $r_{\varphi}(\cdot)$ can be estimated via nonlinear least squares, given the exogeneity of regressors, viz., $\mathbb{E}[\zeta_{\varphi,it}\,|\,1, m_{it-1}-l_{it-1}, \ln P_t^M-\ln P_t^L, \ln P_{t-1}^M-\ln P_{t-1}^L, Z_{it-1}]=0$. Also note that, because of the particular functional form of the CES specification, we are able to recover all parameters pertaining to variable inputs in a single step, whereas in the case of translog, we do so in two steps.

With σ and β_M identified from (A1.3), we can also estimate φ_{it} following (A1.2). To see the identification of the remaining parameters in the production function, i.e., β_K and ν, take the logarithm of the production function and substitute for $F(\cdot)$ using (A1.1):

$$y_{it}=-\nu\frac{\sigma}{1-\sigma}\ln\left\{\beta_K\overbrace{K_{it}^{-\frac{1-\sigma}{\sigma}}}^{K_{it}^*}+\overbrace{\left[\exp\{\varphi_{it}\}L_{it}\right]^{-\frac{1-\sigma}{\sigma}}+\beta_M M_{it}^{-\frac{1-\sigma}{\sigma}}}^{H_{it}^*}\right\}+\omega_{it}+\eta_{it},$$
$$=-\nu\frac{\sigma}{1-\sigma}\ln\left\{\beta_K K_{it}^*+H_{it}^*\right\}+r_{\omega}\left(\omega_{it-1},X_{it-1}\right)+\zeta_{\omega,it}+\eta_{it}, \tag{A1.4}$$

where we have replaced ω_{it} with its law of motion in the second equality. The new variables $K_{it}^*\equiv K_{it}^{-\frac{1-\sigma}{\sigma}}$ and $H_{it}^*\equiv\left[\exp\{\varphi_{it}\}L_{it}\right]^{-\frac{1-\sigma}{\sigma}}+\beta_M M_{it}^{-\frac{1-\sigma}{\sigma}}$ are effectively data because they are defined using observable inputs and the already identified parameters along with labor-augmenting productivity. Also, remember that $\frac{\sigma}{1-\sigma}$ is known as well.

To address the unobservability of ω_{it-1}, we proxy for it by inverting the conditional material demand function implied by the corresponding static first-order condition for M_{it}[18]:

$$\omega_{it}=\overbrace{\ln P_t^M-\ln P_t^Y+\frac{1}{\sigma}m_{it}}^{m_{it}^*}-\ln(\beta_M)+\left(1+\nu\frac{\sigma}{1-\sigma}\right)\ln\left\{\beta_K K_{it}^*+H_{it}^*\right\}-\ln(\theta\nu) \tag{A1.5}$$

where m_{it}^* is already identified and, hence, observable. The above proxy for the latent Hicks-neutral productivity is the counterpart of (3.18). Replacing ω_{it-1} in (A1.4) with the lag of (A1.5), we have the second-step estimating equation that identifies the remaining unknown parameters $(\nu,\beta_K)'$:

$$y_{it}=-\nu\frac{\sigma}{1-\sigma}\ln\left\{\beta_K K_{it}^*+H_{it}^*\right\}+$$
$$r_{\omega}\left(\left[m_{it-1}^*+\left(1+\nu\frac{\sigma}{1-\sigma}\right)\ln\left\{\beta_K K_{it-1}^*+H_{it-1}^*\right\}-\ln(\theta\nu)\right],X_{it-1}\right)+ \tag{A1.6}$$
$$\zeta_{\omega,it}+\eta_{it}.$$

Per structural assumptions, K_{it}^{*}, K_{it-1}^{*}, H_{it-1}^{*}, m_{it-1}^{*} and X_{it-1} are all mean-orthogonal to the composite innovation $\zeta_{\omega,it}+\eta_{it}$ in (A1.6) and can self-instrument. The same cannot be said about H_{it}^{*} that also appears in the equation, since it includes information on the choice of both L_{it} and M_{it} which are decided by the firm after $\zeta_{\omega,it}$ is realized (i.e., after ω_{it} is updated). However, analogous to the case with the second-step estimation under the translog specification in (3.13) in Section 3.1, the endogeneity of H_{it}^{*} does *not* impede identification of (A1.6) because H_{it}^{*} is not a "free" regressor but enters the equation subject to a parameter restriction whereby its distribution parameter is normalized to 1 and requires no estimation. No external instruments for H_{it}^{*} are therefore needed. As such, we can identify $(\beta_K,\nu)'$ as well as the mean productivity function $r_{\omega}(\cdot)$ from (A1.6) based on the following moments:

$$\mathbb{E}\left[\zeta_{\omega,it}+\eta_{it}\mid 1,k_{it}^{*},k_{it-1}^{*},m_{it-1}^{*},H_{it-1}^{*},X_{it-1}\right]=0. \tag{A1.7}$$

APPENDIX 2. EXPANDED $\Psi(\alpha)$ FROM (3.16)

Suppressing the firm index i, we have that

$$\Psi(\alpha)=\begin{pmatrix} \left\{-\frac{\beta_L}{\beta_0^2}(1-\rho_1)+\frac{\delta_{LM}}{\beta_0^2}\left[\mathbb{E}[S_t^L]-\rho_1\mathbb{E}[S_{t-1}^L]\right]\right\} & \frac{1-\rho_1}{\beta_0} & \left\{\mathbb{E}[\breve{m}_{t-1}]+\frac{\beta_L}{\beta_0}-\frac{\delta_{LM}}{\beta_0}\mathbb{E}[S_{t-1}^L]\right\} & \mathbb{E}[Z_{t-1}{}'] \\ \left\{-\frac{\beta_L}{\beta_0^2}(1-\rho_1)\mathbb{E}[\breve{m}_{t-1}]+\frac{\delta_{LM}}{\beta_0^2}\left[\mathbb{E}[\breve{m}_{t-1}S_t^L]-\rho_1\mathbb{E}[\breve{m}_{t-1}S_{t-1}^L]\right]\right\} & \frac{1-\rho_1}{\beta_0}\mathbb{E}[\breve{m}_{t-1}] & \left\{\mathbb{E}[\breve{m}_{t-1}^2]+\frac{\beta_L}{\beta_0}\mathbb{E}[\breve{m}_{t-1}]-\frac{\delta_{LM}}{\beta_0}\mathbb{E}[\breve{m}_{t-1}S_{t-1}^L]\right\} & \mathbb{E}[\breve{m}_{t-1}Z_{t-1}{}'] \\ \left\{-\frac{\beta_L}{\beta_0^2}(1-\rho_1)\mathbb{E}[S_{t-1}^L]+\frac{\delta_{LM}}{\beta_0^2}\left[\mathbb{E}[S_{t-1}^L S_t^L]-\rho_1\mathbb{E}[(S_{t-1}^L)^2]\right]\right\} & \frac{1-\rho_1}{\beta_0}\mathbb{E}[S_{t-1}^L] & \left\{\mathbb{E}[\breve{m}_{t-1}S_{t-1}^L]+\frac{\beta_L}{\beta_0}\mathbb{E}[S_{t-1}^L]-\frac{\delta_{LM}}{\beta_0}\mathbb{E}[(S_{t-1}^L)^2]\right\} & \mathbb{E}[S_{t-1}^L Z_{t-1}{}'] \\ \left\{-\frac{\beta_L}{\beta_0^2}(1-\rho_1)\mathbb{E}[Z_{t-1}]+\frac{\delta_{LM}}{\beta_0^2}\left[\mathbb{E}[S_t^L Z_{t-1}]-\rho_1\mathbb{E}[S_{t-1}^L Z_{t-1}]\right]\right\} & \frac{1-\rho_1}{\beta_0}\mathbb{E}[Z_{t-1}] & \left\{\mathbb{E}[\breve{m}_{t-1}Z_{t-1}]+\frac{\beta_L}{\beta_0}\mathbb{E}[Z_{t-1}]-\frac{\delta_{LM}}{\beta_0}\mathbb{E}[S_{t-1}^L Z_{t-1}]\right\} & \mathbb{E}[Z_{t-1}Z_{t-1}{}'] \end{pmatrix}$$

where $\breve{m}_{t-1}=m_{t-1}-l_{t-1}$ is the logged material-to-labor ratio.

APPENDIX 3. SEMIPARAMETRIC SIEVE ESTIMATION

In what follows, we describe how to empirically implement our methodology semiparametrically, with the unknown functions $r_{\varphi}(\cdot)$ and $r_{\omega}(\cdot)$ approximated using linear sieves. Sieves globally approximate unknown nonparametric (i.e., infinite-parameter) functions using a sequence of less complex parameter spaces that are characterized by a finite number of "parameters" which effectively reduces the estimation problem to a parametric estimation when implemented in practice, with the caveat being that the complexity of such an approximation increases with the sample size to ensure consistency. For more on sieves, see an excellent review by Chen (2007).

The first-step estimation remains the same as described in Section 4. In the second step, however, we now approximate the unknown function $r_{\varphi}(\varphi_{it-1}, Z_{it-1})$ using a linear series of $[\dim(Z)+1]$-variate polynomial basis functions $\{\mathrm{B}_{r,n}(\varphi_{it-1}, Z_{it-1})\}_{r=1}^{R_n}$ without the intercept term, with the degree of approximation complexity $R_n \to \infty$ slowly with n. As before, the unobservable φ_{it-1} is replaced with a proxy function from (3.7), and $\delta_{LM} = \beta_L + \beta_M$ is replaced with its estimate from the first step. Modifying the GMM problem in (4.2) to accommodate a series approximation of $r_{\varphi}(\cdot)$, the second-step equation is now estimated for a given R_n via semiparametric nonlinear sieve GMM. Thus, letting $\alpha = (\beta_0, \beta_L, \rho_1, \ldots, \rho_{R_n})'$, we have that

$$\hat{\alpha} = \arg\min_{\alpha}\Big[\frac{1}{nT}\sum_{it}\mathbb{Q}_{it-1}\epsilon_{it}(D_{it};\alpha)\Big]'W\Big[\frac{1}{nT}\sum_{it}\mathbb{Q}_{it-1}\epsilon_{it}(D_{it};\alpha)\Big], \tag{A3.1}$$

where the approximated residual function is

$$\begin{aligned}\epsilon_{it}(D_{it};\alpha) \approx\ & m_{it} - l_{it} + \frac{\beta_L}{\beta_0} - \frac{\hat{\delta}_{LM}}{\beta_0}S_{it}^{L} - \\ & \sum_{r=1}^{R_n}\rho_r B_{r,n}\left(\left[m_{it-1} - l_{it-1} + \frac{\beta_L}{\beta_0} - \frac{\hat{\delta}_{LM}}{\beta_0}S_{it-1}^{L}\right], Z_{it-1}\right),\end{aligned} \tag{A3.2}$$

and the instrument vector $\mathbb{Q}_{it-1}$ now needs to include not only the linear terms $(m_{it} - l_{it}, Z_{it-1}, S_{it-1}^{L})'$ but also the additional higher-order terms from a polynomial expansion of $(m_{it} - l_{it}, Z_{it-1}, S_{it-1}^{L})'$.

Then, just like in a fully parametric case, with the $\left(\hat{\beta}_0, \hat{\beta}_L\right)'$ estimates in hand, we can recover $\hat{\beta}_M = \hat{\delta}_{LM} - \hat{\beta}_L$ as well as estimate Harrod-neutral productivity as $\hat{\varphi}_{it} = m_{it} - l_{it} + \hat{\beta}_L / \hat{\beta}_0 - \hat{\delta}_{LM} / \hat{\beta}_0 \times S_{it}^{L}$.

The smoothing parameter R_n can be controlled indirectly by selecting the optimal degree of polynomial expansion d_n via generalized cross-validation of Craven and Wahba (1979):

$$d_n^{*} = \arg\min_{d_n}\frac{\frac{1}{nT}\|(\mathrm{I}_{nT} - \Pi_{R_n})\widehat{\varphi}\|^2}{\left[1 - \frac{1}{nT}\mathrm{tr}\{\Pi_{R_n}\}\right]^2} \quad \text{with } R_n = R_n(d_n), \tag{A3.3}$$

where, for a given $(\beta_0, \beta_L)', \Pi_{R_n} = \mathbb{P}_{R_n}(\mathbb{P}_{R_n}'\mathbb{P}_{R_n})^{-1}\mathbb{P}_{R_n}'$ is a projection matrix defined using the matrix of basis functions $\mathbb{P}_{R_n}$ constructed by stacking up $P_{R_n}(\hat{\varphi}_{it-1}, Z_{it-1}) = [\mathrm{B}_{1,n}(\hat{\varphi}_{it-1}, Z_{it-1}), \ldots, \mathrm{B}_{R_n,n}(\hat{\varphi}_{it-1}, Z_{it-1})]'$ in the ascending order of index i first then index t. The column vector $\hat{\varphi}$ is stacked up similarly but using $\{\hat{\varphi}_{it}\}$.

To estimate the third-step equation in (3.19), we construct estimators of y^*_{it} and m^*_{it} using the results from steps one and two: $\hat{y}^*_{it} = y_{it} - \hat{\beta}_M m_{it} - \hat{\beta}_L[\hat{\varphi}_{it} + l_{it}] + \frac{1}{2}\hat{\beta}_0[m_{it} - \hat{\varphi}_{it} - l_{it}]^2$ and $\hat{m}^*_{it} = \ln\left[P^M_t / P^Y_t\right] - \ln\hat{\theta} - \ln\left(\hat{\beta}_M - \hat{\beta}_0[m_{it} - \hat{\varphi}_{it} - l_{it}]\right) + (1 - \hat{\beta}_M)m_{it} - \hat{\beta}_L[\hat{\varphi}_{it} + l_{it}] + \frac{1}{2}\hat{\beta}_0[m_{it} - \hat{\varphi}_{it} - l_{it}]^2$. Then, approximating unknown $r_\omega(\cdot)$ using $[\dim(X)+1]$-variate polynomial sieves of degree d'_n, i.e.,

$$r_\omega(\omega_{it-1}, X_{it-1}) \approx \sum_{r'=1}^{R'_n} \pi_{r'} \mathrm{B}_{r',n}\left(\left[\hat{m}^*_{it-1} - \beta_K k_{it-1} - \frac{1}{2}\beta_{KK}k^2_{it-1}\right], X_{it-1}\right), \tag{A3.4}$$

where ω_{it-1} is replaced with its proxy and $R'_n(d'_n)$ increases with the sample size, we estimate $\gamma = (\beta_K, \beta_{KK}, \pi_1, \ldots, \pi_{R'_n})'$ via semiparametric nonlinear sieve least squares in line with (4.4):

$$\hat{\gamma} = \arg\min_{\gamma} \sum_{it} \left[\begin{array}{l} \hat{y}^*_{it} - \beta_K k_{it} - \frac{1}{2}\beta_{KK}k^2_{it} - \\ \sum_{r'=1}^{R'_n} \pi_{r'} B_{r',n}\left([\hat{m}^*_{it-1} - \beta_K k_{it-1} - \frac{1}{2}\beta_{KK}k^2_{it-1}], X_{it-1}\right) \end{array}\right]^2. \tag{A3.5}$$

Analogous to the second step above, R'_n can be cross-validated indirectly by selecting the optimal degree of polynomial expansion d'_n via generalized cross-validation.

Using the obtained $(\hat{\beta}_K, \hat{\beta}_{KK})'$ estimates, we then can construct the estimates of Hicks-neutral productivity as $\hat{\omega}_{it} = y_{it} - \hat{\beta}_K k_{it} - \frac{1}{2}\hat{\beta}_{KK}k^2_{it} - \hat{\beta}_M m_{it} - \hat{\beta}_L[\hat{\varphi}_{it} + l_{it}] + \frac{1}{2}\hat{\beta}_0[m_{it} - \hat{\varphi}_{it} - l_{it}]^2 - \hat{\eta}_{it}$ using $\hat{\eta}_{it}$ from step one.

Inference.—Due to a multi-step nature of our methodology and the presence of nonparametric components, computation of the asymptotic variance of the semiparametric estimator above is not that simple. For statistical inference in this case, we therefore use bootstrap; the algorithm is described in Appendix 4.

APPENDIX 4. BOOTSTRAP INFERENCE

We approximate the sampling distribution of our estimator via wild residual block bootstrap that takes into account a panel structure of the data as well as a sequential nature of our multi-step estimation procedure. Concretely, the bootstrap algorithm is as follows.

1. Compute the three steps of our estimation procedure using the original data. Denote the obtained point estimates of all the parameters and functions using a "hat." Correspondingly, let the (negative of) first-step residuals be $\{\hat{\eta}_{it}\}$, the second-step residuals be $\{\hat{\zeta}_{\varphi,it}\}$, and the third-step residuals be $\{\widehat{\zeta_{\omega,it}+\eta_{it}}\}$. Recenter these.
2. Generate bootstrap weights ξ_i^b for all cross-sectional units $i=1,\dots,n$ from the Mammen (1993) two-point mass distribution:

$$\xi_i^b = \begin{cases} \dfrac{1+\sqrt{5}}{2} & \text{with prob. } \dfrac{\sqrt{5}-1}{2\sqrt{5}} \\ \dfrac{1-\sqrt{5}}{2} & \text{with prob. } \dfrac{\sqrt{5}+1}{2\sqrt{5}}. \end{cases} \tag{A4.1}$$

   Next, for each observation (i, t) with $i=1,\dots,n$ and $t=1,\dots,T$, jointly generate a new bootstrap first-step disturbance $\eta_{it}^b=\xi_i^b\times\hat{\eta}_{it}$, a new bootstrap second-step disturbance $\zeta_{\varphi,it}^b=\xi_i^b\times\hat{\zeta}_{\varphi,it}$, and a new bootstrap third-step disturbance $(\zeta_{\omega,it}+\eta_{it})^b=\xi_i^b\times(\widehat{\zeta_{\omega,it}+\eta_{it}})$.
3. Generate a new bootstrap first-step outcome variable via $\ln R_{it}^b = \ln\left[\hat{\theta}(\hat{\beta}_M+\hat{\beta}_L)\right]-\eta_{it}^b$ for all $i=1,\dots,n$ and $t=1,\dots,T$.
4. Generate a new bootstrap second-step outcome variable recursively as $(m_{it}-l_{it})^b = -\dfrac{\hat{\beta}_L}{\hat{\beta}_0}+\left(\dfrac{\hat{\beta}_L+\hat{\beta}_M}{\hat{\beta}_0}\right)S_{it}^L+\hat{r}_{\varphi,1}\left[(m_{it-1}-l_{it-1})^b+\dfrac{\widehat{\beta_L}}{\widehat{\beta_0}}-\left(\dfrac{\hat{\beta}_L+\hat{\beta}_M}{\hat{\beta}_0}\right)S_{it-1}^L\right]$ $+\hat{r}_{\varphi,2}Z_{it-1}+\zeta_{\varphi,it}^b$ for all $i=1,\dots,n$ and $t=1,\dots,T$. To initialize at $t=0$, we set $(m_{i0}-l_{i0})^b=(m_{i0}-l_{i0})$.
5. Generate a new bootstrap third-step outcome variable via $y_{it}^{*b}=\hat{\beta}_K k_{it}+\frac{1}{2}\hat{\beta}_{KK}k_{it}^2+\hat{r}_{\omega,0}+\hat{r}_{\omega,1}\left[\hat{m}_{it-1}^*-\hat{\beta}_K k_{it}-\frac{1}{2}\hat{\beta}_{KK}k_{it}^2\right]+\hat{r}_{\omega,2}X_{it-1}+(\zeta_{\omega,it}+\eta_{it})^b$ for all $i=1,\dots,n$ and $t=1,\dots,T$.
6. Recompute the first step using $\{\ln R_{it}^b\}$ in place of $\{\ln R_{it}\}$. Denote the obtained parameter estimates as $\left((\hat{\beta}_M+\hat{\beta}_L)^b,\hat{\theta}^b\right)'$.
7. Recompute the second step using $\{(m_{it}-l_{it})^b\}$ in place of $\{(m_{it}-l_{it})\}$ and using $\{(m_{it-1}-l_{it-1})^b\}$ in place of $\{(m_{it-1}-l_{it-1})\}$. Denote the obtained parameter and function estimates as $\left(\hat{\beta}_M^b,\hat{\beta}_L^b,\hat{\beta}_0^b,\hat{r}_\varphi^b(\cdot)\right)'$. Also obtain $\hat{\varphi}_{it}^b=m_{it}-l_{it}+\dfrac{\hat{\beta}_L^b}{\hat{\beta}_0^b}-\left(\dfrac{\hat{\beta}_L^b+\hat{\beta}_M^b}{\hat{\beta}_0^b}\right)S_{it}^L$.

8. Recompute the third step using y_{it}^{*b} in place of y_{it}^{*}. When re-estimating the equation, also use m_{it}^{*b} in place of m_{it}^{*}, where $m_{it}^{*b} = \ln\left[\frac{P_t^M}{P_t^Y}\right] - \ln\theta^b - \ln\left(\hat{\beta}_M^b - \hat{\beta}_0^b[m_{it} - \hat{\varphi}_{it}^b - l_{it}]\right) + (1-\hat{\beta}_M^b)m_{it} - \hat{\beta}_L[\hat{\varphi}_{it}^b + l_{it}] + \frac{1}{2}\hat{\beta}_0^b[m_{it} - \hat{\varphi}_{it}^b - l_{it}]^2$ for all $i = 1,\ldots,n$ and $t = 1,\ldots,T$. Denote the obtained parameter and function estimates as $\left(\hat{\beta}_K^b, \hat{\beta}_{KK}^b, \hat{r}_\omega^b(\cdot)\right)'$.
9. Repeat steps 2 through 8 of the algorithm B times.

Let the estimand of interest be denoted by $\mathcal{E}$, e.g., the firm i's capital elasticity $\epsilon_{K,it} \equiv \beta_K + \beta_{KK}k_{it}$ at time t. To perform hypothesis testing, we can use the empirical distribution of $\{\hat{\mathcal{E}}^1,\ldots,\hat{\mathcal{E}}^B\}$ to obtain a bootstrap estimator of $\mathbb{V}[\hat{\mathcal{E}}]$ following the standard methods.

APPENDIX 5. DATA SUMMARY

Table A5.1. Data Summary Statistics.

	$Z = 0$ (Obs #: 27,094)				**$Z > 0$ (Obs #: 4,193)**			
	Mean	**1st Qu.**	**Median**	**3rd Qu.**	**Mean**	**1st Qu.**	**Median**	**3rd Qu.**
Output (Y)	29,719	10,554	19,353	37,684	38,611	14,483	28,312	52,405
Capital (K)	3,863	926	2,215	4,877	4,933	1,296	3,003	6,534
Labor (L)	2,140	729	1,370	2,659	3,069	1,199	2,181	4,018
Materials (M)	20,448	7,159	13,251	25,941	26,833	9,665	19,220	36,612
Foreign equity share (Z)					0.47	0.21	0.41	0.72

Notes: The three inputs and the output are in thousands of real RMB. The foreign equity share is a unit-free proportion.

APPENDIX 6. ADDITIONAL EMPIRICAL RESULTS

The two tables below report the estimates of the production function and productivity parameters obtained when using the inverted conditional labor demand in (3.22) [Table A6.1] and the average of the inverted conditional material and labor demands in (3.18) and (3.22) [Table A6.2] to proxy for latent ω_{it}. Since this proxy is used in the third step of our estimator, only the estimates of capital elasticity and the Hicks-neutral productivity process are affected; the remaining parameters are the same as those reported in Table 9.2.

Table A6.1. Estimates of the Production Function and Productivity Parameters Using the Labor Proxy.

Panel A: Elasticities and RTS

	Mean	**1st Qu.**	**Median**	**3rd Qu.**
Capital elasticity	0.0436	0.0283	0.0443	0.0587
	(0.0053)	(0.0067)	(0.0053)	(0.0080)
Labor elasticity	0.0950	0.0458	0.0864	0.1287
	(0.0003)	(0.0001)	(0.0002)	(0.0004)
Material elasticity	0.7377	0.7041	0.7463	0.7869
	(0.0020)	(0.0019)	(0.0021)	(0.0022)
RTS	0.8763	0.8610	0.8771	0.8915
	(0.0057)	(0.0071)	(0.0058)	(0.0083)

Panel B: Productivity Parameters

Labor-Augmenting		**Factor-Neutral**	
$\rho_{\varphi,0}$	0.0000	$\rho_{\omega,0}$	0.8082
	–		(0.0928)
$\rho_{\varphi,1}$	0.5723	$\rho_{\omega,1}$	0.6840
	(0.0244)		(0.0247)
$\rho_{\varphi,2}$	0.0726	$\rho_{\omega,2}$	0.0045
	(0.0183)		(0.0084)

Notes: The productivity processes are parameterized as follows: $\varphi_{it} = \rho_{\varphi,1}\varphi_{it-1} + \rho_{\varphi,2}Z_{it-1} + \zeta_{\varphi,it}$ with $\rho_{\varphi,0}$ normalized to 0, and $\omega_{it} = \rho_{\omega,0} + \rho_{\omega,1}\omega_{it-1} + \rho_{\omega,2}Z_{it-1} + \zeta_{\omega,it}$. Bootstrap standard errors are in parentheses.

Table A6.2. Estimates of the Production Function and Productivity Parameters Using the Average of Material and Labor Proxies.

Panel A: Elasticities and RTS

	Mean	**1st Qu.**	**Median**	**3rd Qu.**
Capital elasticity	0.0392	0.0243	0.0399	0.0539
	(0.0065)	(0.0077)	(0.0066)	(0.0089)
Labor elasticity	0.0950	0.0458	0.0864	0.1287
	(0.0003)	(0.0001)	(0.0002)	(0.0004)
Material elasticity	0.7377	0.7041	0.7463	0.7869
	(0.0020)	(0.0019)	(0.0021)	(0.0022)
RTS	0.8719	0.8570	0.8726	0.8866
	(0.0068)	(0.0080)	(0.0069)	(0.0091)

Panel B: Productivity Parameters

Labor-Augmenting		**Factor-Neutral**	
$\rho_{\varphi,0}$	0.0000	$\rho_{\omega,0}$	0.7115
	—		(0.0975)
$\rho_{\varphi,1}$	0.5723	$\rho_{\omega,1}$	0.7277
	(0.0244)		(0.0279)
$\rho_{\varphi,2}$	0.0726	$\rho_{\omega,2}$	0.0033
	(0.0183)		(0.0083)

Notes: The productivity processes are parameterized as follows: $\varphi_{it} = \rho_{\varphi,1}\varphi_{it-1} + \rho_{\varphi,2}Z_{it-1} + \zeta_{\varphi,it}$ with $\rho_{\varphi,0}$ normalized to 0, and $\omega_{it} = \rho_{\omega,0} + \rho_{\omega,1}\omega_{it-1} + \rho_{\omega,2}Z_{it-1} + \zeta_{\omega,it}$. Bootstrap standard errors are in parentheses.

APPENDIX 7. EXTENSION TO IMPERFECT COMPETITION

Our methodology and its underlying identification scheme in Sections 2 and 3 are developed under the assumption that firms operate in a perfectly competitive output market. In this appendix, we discuss how to relax this assumption and allow for monopolistic power in the output market in our setup.

Let the output price be no longer $P_{it}^{Y} \neq P_{t}^{Y}\ \forall\, i$. To allow firms to have some market power, we assume they produce differentiated products and operate in a monopolistically competitive market. Let each firm face a downward-sloping (residual) inverse demand function of the following generic form[19]: $P_{it}^{Y} = D(Y_{it}^{e}, U_{it})$, where $Y_{it}^{e} = Y_{it}\exp\{-\eta_{it}\}$ is the expected, or "planned," output quantity net of an unanticipated *ex-post* productivity shock η_{it}, and U_{it} is a vector of demand shifters known to the firm at time t, i.e., $U_{it} \in \Xi_{it}$.[20] But given our discussion concerning the oft-problematic use of firm-level variation in input prices for identification in Section 3.2, we retain the assumption of competitive homogeneous factor prices.

In what follows, we fist show *point* non-identification of the production function in (3.2) when firms exhibit market power even if one observes exogenous demand shifters in the data. We then discuss how, with some additional but quite reasonable assumptions about unobservables, one can still *set* identify the production function, and we derive this result without requiring that the information on demand shifters be available: we only rely on the same set of observables that are used in our main methodology for the case of perfectly competitive markets from Section 3.

Point Non-Identification of the Production Function

For a risk-neutral firm with market power, the firm's static optimality conditions are now given by

$$\left(1+\frac{1}{\delta(P_{it}^{Y},U_{it})}\right)P_{it}^{Y}\,\frac{\exp\{\overline{y}_{it}\}}{L_{it}}\big(\beta_{L}+\beta_{0}[m_{it}-\varphi_{it}-l_{it}]\big)\exp\{\omega_{it}\}\theta = P_{t}^{L}, \quad \text{(A7.1)}$$

$$\left(1+\frac{1}{\delta(P_{it}^{Y},U_{it})}\right)P_{it}^{Y}\,\frac{\exp\{\overline{y}_{it}\}}{M_{it}}\big(\beta_{M}-\beta_{0}[m_{it}-\varphi_{it}-l_{it}]\big)\exp\{\omega_{it}\}\theta = P_{t}^{M}, \quad \text{(A7.2)}$$

where $\delta(P_{it}^{Y},U_{it}) < -1$ is the price elasticity of demand. The ratio of these optimality conditions however remains unchanged [see equation (3.6)] implying that the proxy for Harrod-neutral productivity φ_{it} is also unchanged [see equation (3.7)]. But the new proxy for Hicks-neutral productivity does need to explicitly account for the firm's market power (here we continue to use the inverted material demand):

$$\omega_{it} = \overbrace{\begin{array}{l}\ln\left[\dfrac{P_{t}^{M}}{P_{it}^{Y}}\right]-\ln\theta-\ln\big(\beta_{M}-\beta_{0}[m_{it}-\varphi_{it}-l_{it}]\big)+(1-\beta_{M})m_{it}\\ -\beta_{L}[\varphi_{it}+l_{it}]+\dfrac{1}{2}\beta_{0}[m_{it}-\varphi_{it}-l_{it}]^{2}-\beta_{K}k_{it}-\dfrac{1}{2}\beta_{KK}k_{it}^{2}+\ln\mu(P_{it}^{Y},U_{it}),\end{array}}^{m_{it}^{*}} \quad \text{(A7.3)}$$

where $\mu(P_{it}^{Y},U_{it})=\left(1+\dfrac{1}{\delta(P_{it}^{Y},U_{it})}\right)^{-1}$ is a markup (a price-to-marginal-cost ratio).

Now, consider the first step of our methodology. Because the new first-order conditions in (A7.1) and (A7.2) contain the demand elasticity, the variable input share equations will also have to account for markups:

$$\ln V_{it}^{L}=\ln\left(\theta\beta_0\left[\frac{\beta_L}{\beta_0}+m_{it}-\varphi_{it}-l_{it}\right]\right)-\ln\mu(P_{it}^{Y},U_{it})-\eta_{it}, \tag{A7.4}$$

$$\ln V_{it}^{M}=\ln\left(\theta\beta_0\left[\frac{\beta_M}{\beta_0}-m_{it}+\varphi_{it}+l_{it}\right]\right)-\ln\mu(P_{it}^{Y},U_{it})-\eta_{it}. \tag{A7.5}$$

Controlling for φ_{it} using the (unchanged) material-to-labor ratio proxy function in (3.7), we thus obtain the following variable-input-cost-to-revenue equation for a monopolistically competitive firm:

$$\ln R_{it}=\ln\left(\theta[\beta_L+\beta_M]\right)-\ln\mu(P_{it}^{Y},U_{it})-\eta_{it}, \tag{A7.6}$$

in which all regressors are weakly exogenous with respect to an *ex-post* shock η_{it}.

The two components $\ln\left(\theta[\beta_L+\beta_M]\right)$ and $\ln\mu(P_{it}^{Y},U_{it})$ in (A7.6) are however not *separably* identified. The unknown function $\mu(\cdot)$ can be identified up to a scale only. With the lack of point identification of the firm's markup $\mu(P_{it}^{Y},U_{it})$, the production-function parameters $(\beta_L,\beta_M)'$ cannot be point identified either.[21] To see this more clearly, consider the special case of isoelastic demand whereby $\mu(P_{it}^{Y},U_{it})=\mu\ \forall\, i,t$. In this case, we can only point identify $(\beta_L+\beta_M)/\mu$ from (A7.6) and, consequently, we cannot point identify $(\beta_0,\beta_L)'$ from (3.13) either, with the similar implications for $(\beta_K,\beta_{KK})'$ in the third step. Thus, all production-function parameters can only be point identified up to a scale of the firm's markup μ. More generally, the point non-identification of production function when firms exercise monopolistic power (although when productivity is unidimensional) is also discussed in Flynn et al. (2019).

Interestingly, despite the lack of point identification of both the production-function parameters and the markup, the variable-input-cost-to-revenue equation under imperfect competition in (A7.6) may nonetheless provide some useful information about *markups* if P_{it}^{Y} and U_{it} are observed in the data. Namely, oftentimes markups *per se* are of little policy relevance and, instead, economists focus on their relation with some other correlates or their distribution across firms. For instance, one might be interested in testing if exporters enjoy a greater price-setting power that do wholly domestically oriented firms (e.g., De Loecker et al., 2016; De Loecker & Warzynski, 2012). Alternatively, we may be interested in temporal dynamics of markups (e.g., De Loecker & Eeckhout, 2020; De Loecker, Eeckhout, & Unger, 2020), be it on average or in terms of their cross-firm dispersion. Such analyses of markups are customarily done by regressing the estimated (log) markups on the variables of interest such export status or time trend/dummies. We can still accomplish the latter using "scaled" markup estimates from (A7.6).

Namely, $\ln\left(\frac{\theta[\beta_L+\beta_M]}{\mu(P_{it}^Y,U_{it})}\right)$ in (A7.6) is some unknown function of $(P_{it}^Y,U'_{it})'$ easily estimable via nonparametric least squares by regressing $\ln R_{it}$ on $(P_{it}^Y,U'_{it})'$ with intercept. Then, so long as the production function is correctly specified and thus $\beta_L+\beta_M$ is a constant, we can regress the recovered scaled log-markup $\ln\left(\frac{\mu(P_{it}^Y,U_{it})}{\theta[\beta_L+\beta_M]}\right)=-\ln\left(\frac{\theta[\beta_L+\beta_M]}{\mu(P_{it}^Y,U_{it})}\right)$ on whatever variables of interest, with the only (and unimportant) implication being a bias in the intercept. Analogously, we can study the dispersion in markups or changes therein over time by analyzing the ratios of $\frac{\mu(P_{it}^Y,U_{it})}{\theta[\beta_L+\beta_M]}$ across firms or the shifts in their distributions over time.

Partial Identification of the Production Function

Although the production function is not point-identified when firms have monopolistic power in the output markets, we can still achieve its partial identification. To set identify the production-function parameters $(\beta_K,\beta_{KK},\beta_M,\beta_L,\beta_0)'$, we build upon Demirer's (2019) framework which we modify to admit multi-dimensional firm productivity.

Since most production datasets contain no information on exogenous firm demand shifters, here we can also relax the assumption that demand heterogeneity U_{it} be observable. But with the introduction of new unobservables, we need to formalize their relation to other unobservables that are known to the firm such as productivity. Defining the vector of *observable* (by an econometrician) state variables as $O_{it}=(K_{it},P_t^L,P_t^M,X'_{it},Z'_{it})'$, we augment our assumptions as follows.

Assumption 5 (Replaces Assumption 4). (i) Risk-neutral firms maximize the discounted stream of life-time profits in perfectly competitive factor markets with homogeneous prices. The output market is monopolistically competitive, and the firm's downward-sloping inverse (residual) demand function is given by $P_{it}^Y=D(Y_{it}^e,U_{it})$ and $U_{it}\in\Xi_{it}$ is a vector of unobservable (to an econometrician) demand shifters known to the firm when making time t decisions. (ii) Conditional on observable O_{it-1}, demand heterogeneity U_{it} is jointly independent of firm productivity φ_{it} and ω_{it}.[22]

In the above, $Y_{it}^e=Y_{it}\exp\{-\eta_{it}\}$ is the expected/planned output quantity as defined earlier. Since the presence of markups does not in any way affect the ratio of firm's static first-order conditions, thereby providing a deterministic proxy for labor-augmenting productivity given by (3.7), we can utilize it to substitute latent φ_{it} out of the production function (3.2) to arrive at

$$\begin{aligned} y_{it} &= \beta_K k_{it}+\frac{1}{2}\beta_{KK}k_{it}^2+(\beta_L+\beta_M)m_{it}+\frac{1}{2\beta_0}\left[\beta_L^2-(\beta_L+\beta_M)^2\left(S_{it}^L\right)^2\right]+\omega_{it}+\eta_{it} \\ &= \underbrace{\frac{\beta_L^2}{2\beta_0}+\beta_K k_{it}+\frac{1}{2}\beta_{KK}k_{it}^2+(\beta_L+\beta_M)m_{it}-\frac{(\beta_L+\beta_M)^2}{2\beta_0}\left(S_{it}^L\right)^2}_{\overline{y}_{it}(v_{it};\beta)}+\omega_{it}+\eta_{it}, \end{aligned} \quad \text{(A7.7)}$$

which now contains only *additive* unobservables and where $v_{it} = (k_{it}, m_{it}, l_{it}, P_t^M, P_t^L)'$ and $\beta = (\beta_K, \beta_{KK}, \beta_L, \beta_M, \beta_0)'$.[23] In what follows, we seek to set-identify β.

We first establish the relationship between flexible inputs and firm productivity, which facilitates the proxy variable approach to tackling unobservability of the latter. Consistent with our primary methodology, we use materials to control for productivity.

Proposition 1. Under Assumptions 1–3 & 5 and some additional regularization of the curvature of the production function and the firm's downward-sloping (residual) demand function, the firm's conditional demands for M_{it} is weakly increasing in ω_{it} and φ_{it}, conditional on all other state variables entering the expected static profit maximization problem $(K_{it}, P_t^L, P_t^M, U_{it}')'$.

The proposition signs partial derivatives of the material demand with respect to both components of firm productivity and is easy but tedious to show, which involves differentiation of first-order conditions in (A7.1) and (A7.2) with respect to productivities (see Appendix 8). Intuitively, the firm (i) substitutes materials for labor conserving the latter *ceteris paribus* as the labor input becomes more productive when φ_{it} rises and (ii) uses more materials (as well as labor) expanding the production when its overall total factor productivity ω_{it} improves increasing the marginal products of static inputs. For convenience, denote the material demand as $M_{it} = \mathcal{M}(K_{it}, P_t^L, P_t^M, U_{it}, \varphi_{it}, \omega_{it}) = \mathcal{M}(K_{it}, U_{it}, \varphi_{it}, \omega_{it})$, where we suppress input prices because they provide little operationable information due to the lack of cross-firm variation under our assumptions.

To derive moment inequalities that partially identify the firm's production function, we need to tighten our assumptions by formalizing the relationship between the two components of firm productivity. As noted in Section 2, Assumption 3(i) places no restriction on the relation between ω_{it} and φ_{it} but, to identify the production function when firms have market power, it's now needs be regulated. We do so by letting the labor-augmenting productivity φ_{it} be stochastically increasing in factor-neutral Hicksian productivity ω_{it}, conditional on productivity "controls." Thus, we extend our Assumption 3(i) as follows.

Assumption 6. Conditional on productivity-modifying controls $(X_{it-1}', Z_{it-1}')'$, the distribution of φ_{it} is stochastically increasing in ω_{it}.

More specifically, Assumption 6 means that $\mathcal{P}_\varphi(\varphi_{it} \mid \omega_{it}^H, X_{it-1}, Z_{it-1})$ first-order stochastically dominates $\mathcal{P}_\varphi(\varphi_{it} \mid \omega_{it}^L, X_{it-1}, Z_{it-1})$ if $\omega_{it}^H \geq \omega_{it}^L$. In this, we intuitively assume that the firms that are more productive in general (in all factors) are likely to also be more productive in labor. Then, the set identification of the production-function parameters β is obtained based on the following proposition, according to which the material proxy can be used to stochastically order the log-additive (and only) unobservable $\omega_{it} + \eta_{it}$ entering the production function in (A7.7).

Proposition 2. For some cutoff value $\widetilde{\mathrm{m}}$ for the materials input, let $\mathbb{S} = \{(o, \widetilde{\mathrm{m}}) : \Pr(m_{it} < \widetilde{\mathrm{m}} \mid O_{it-1} = o) \in (0,1)\}$ denote the common support. Under Assumptions 1–3 & 5–6 and by Proposition 1, for $(O_{it-1}, \widetilde{\mathrm{m}}) \in \mathbb{S}$ we have

$$\mathbb{E}\left[y_{it} - \overline{y}(v_{it};\beta) \mid O_{it-1}, m_{it} > \widetilde{\mathrm{m}}\right] \geq \mathbb{E}\left[y_{it} - \overline{y}_{it}(v_{it};\beta) \mid O_{it-1}, m_{it} < \widetilde{\mathrm{m}}\right]. \quad \text{(A7.8)}$$

The proof is in Appendix 8. By this proposition, when comparing high-materials (those with $m_{it} > \widetilde{\mathrm{m}}$) and low-materials (those with $m_{it} < \widetilde{\mathrm{m}}$) firms, the firms that use more inputs are more Hicks-productive on average. In $y_{it} - \overline{y}(v_{it};\beta) = \omega_{it} + \eta_{it}$, it is evident that the focus here is on factor-neutral productivity without the need to characterize labor-augmenting productivity. This is possible owing to the availability of a deterministic proxy of the known functional form for φ_{it} afforded to us by our parametric specification of the firm's separable production technology, which enable us to concentrate Harrod-neutral productivity from production model in (A7.7).

Conditional on o and $\widetilde{\mathrm{m}}$, partially identified β parameters are a nonlinear half-space, and the identified set $\mathcal{B}^*$ is the intersection of these half-planes:

$$\begin{aligned}\mathcal{B}^* = \Big\{\breve{\beta} \in \mathcal{B} : \cap_{(o,\widetilde{\mathrm{m}})\in\mathbb{S}} \mathbb{E}\left[y_{it} - \overline{y}(v_{it};\breve{\beta}) \mid O_{it-1} = o, m_{it} > \widetilde{\mathrm{m}}\right] \\ -\mathbb{E}\left[y_{it} - \overline{y}_{it}(v_{it};\breve{\beta}) \mid O_{it-1} = o, m_{it} < \widetilde{\mathrm{m}}\right] \geq 0\Big\},\end{aligned} \quad \text{(A7.9)}$$

which contains true $\beta \in \mathcal{B}^*$ and where $\mathcal{B}$ is a compact parameter space.

To operationalize this partial identification result, we can redefine the moment inequality in (A7.8) using inverse propensity score weighting. Consider a binary variable $1\{m_{it} > \widetilde{\mathrm{m}}\}$ which delineates high- and low-materials firms for a given cutoff $\widetilde{\mathrm{m}}$ and which corresponds to the conditioning event of interest. Noting that $\Pr(m_{it} > \widetilde{\mathrm{m}} \mid O_{it-1}) = \mathbb{E}[1\{m_{it} > \widetilde{\mathrm{m}}\} \mid O_{it-1}]$, we then have

$$\mathbb{E}\left[y_{it} - \overline{y}(v_{it};\beta) \mid O_{it-1}, m_{it} > \widetilde{\mathrm{m}}\right] = \mathbb{E}\left[\frac{\left(y_{it} - \overline{y}(v_{it};\beta)\right)1\{m_{it} > \widetilde{\mathrm{m}}\}}{\mathbb{E}[1\{m_{it} > \widetilde{\mathrm{m}}\} \mid O_{it-1}]} \,\Big|\, O_{it-1}\right], \quad \text{(A7.10)}$$

$$\mathbb{E}\left[y_{it} - \overline{y}_{it}(v_{it};\beta) \mid O_{it-1}, m_{it} < \widetilde{\mathrm{m}}\right] = \mathbb{E}\left[\frac{\left(y_{it} - \overline{y}(v_{it};\beta)\right)\left(1 - 1\{m_{it} > \widetilde{\mathrm{m}}\}\right)}{1 - \mathbb{E}[1\{m_{it} > \widetilde{\mathrm{m}}\} \mid O_{it-1}]} \,\Big|\, O_{it-1}\right], \quad \text{(A7.11)}$$

which we can further transform by integrating multi-dimensional O_{it-1} out to arrive at the unconditional moment inequality:

$$\mathbb{E}\left[\frac{\left(y_{it} - \overline{y}(v_{it};\beta)\right)1\{m_{it} > \widetilde{\mathrm{m}}\}}{\mathbb{E}[1\{m_{it} > \widetilde{\mathrm{m}}\} \mid O_{it-1}]}\right] - \mathbb{E}\left[\frac{\left(y_{it} - \overline{y}(v_{it};\beta)\right)\left(1 - 1\{m_{it} > \widetilde{\mathrm{m}}\}\right)}{1 - \mathbb{E}[1\{m_{it} > \widetilde{\mathrm{m}}\} \mid O_{it-1}]}\right] \geq 0. \quad \text{(A7.12)}$$

Propensity scores $\Pr(m_{it} > \widetilde{\mathrm{m}} \mid O_{it-1}) = \mathbb{E}[1\{m_{it} > \widetilde{\mathrm{m}}\} \mid O_{it-1}]$ can be estimated via one of many semi- or nonparametric estimators for binary outcomes. With this, a confidence set for true β whose values are restricted by the moment inequality in (A7.12) can be estimated by inverting a test corresponding to this moment condition. Essentially, one is to look for a set of β values for which one fails to reject the null that the difference in means in (A7.12) is positive. The literature on inference using moment inequalities (especially in industrial organization) is vast, and many moment inequality estimation and inference frameworks are readily available to be used here, e.g., see Canay and Shaikh (2017); Molinari (2020); Kline, Pakes, and Tamer (2021); Stoye (2021) and many citations therein.

APPENDIX 8. PROOFS

Proof of Proposition 1

We examine Proposition 1 under two scenarios: (i) a special case of the isoelastic demand function and (ii) a more general case when the demand elasticity is not constant. The idea of the proof for these two scenarios is the same, but the assumption of a constant elasticity of demand simplifies the mathematical derivation.

In what follows, the monotonicity of the firm's conditional material demand $\mathcal{M}(\cdot)$ with respect to the two components of firm productivity is derived under Assumptions 1–3 & 5 *and* assuming two additional regularity conditions on the curvature of the production function and the firm's downward-sloping (residual) demand function. Namely, we assume that (i) the cross-elasticities of variable inputs are non-negative, i.e., $\frac{\partial^2 \ln F(\cdot)}{\partial \ln L \, \partial \ln M} \geq 0$,[24] and (ii) the price elasticity of markup is within the unit interval: $0 \leq \frac{\partial \ln \mu}{\partial \ln P^Y} \leq 1$.

Let us first rewrite the firm's static optimality conditions as

$$P^Y \frac{\partial Y^e}{\partial M} \theta \mu^{-1} = P^M \quad \text{and} \quad P^Y \frac{\partial Y^e}{\partial L} \theta \mu^{-1} = P^L, \tag{A8.1}$$

where the individual and time subscripts are suppressed for the ease of notation.

Isoelastic demand.—First, we show that the conditional material demand $\mathcal{M}(\cdot)$ is weakly increasing in ω. Differentiating the first-order-condition equations in (A8.1) with respect to ω, we obtain

$$\underbrace{\left(\frac{\partial P^Y}{\partial Y^e}\left(\frac{\partial Y^e}{\partial M}\right)^2 + P^Y \frac{\partial^2 Y^e}{\partial M^2}\right)}_{a_1}\frac{\partial M}{\partial \omega} + \underbrace{\left(\frac{\partial P^Y}{\partial Y^e}\frac{\partial Y^e}{\partial M}\frac{\partial Y^e}{\partial L} + P^Y \frac{\partial^2 Y^e}{\partial M \partial L}\right)}_{b_1}\frac{\partial L}{\partial \omega}$$
$$+ \underbrace{\left(\frac{\partial P^Y}{\partial Y^e}\frac{\partial Y^e}{\partial \omega}\frac{\partial Y^e}{\partial M} + P^Y \frac{\partial^2 Y^e}{\partial M \partial \omega}\right)}_{c_1} = 0$$

$$\underbrace{\left(\frac{\partial P^Y}{\partial Y^e}\frac{\partial Y^e}{\partial M}\frac{\partial Y^e}{\partial L} + P^Y \frac{\partial^2 Y^e}{\partial M \partial L}\right)}_{a_2}\frac{\partial M}{\partial \omega} + \underbrace{\left(\frac{\partial P^Y}{\partial Y^e}\left(\frac{\partial Y^e}{\partial L}\right)^2 + P^Y \frac{\partial^2 Y^e}{\partial L^2}\right)}_{b_2}\frac{\partial L}{\partial \omega}$$
$$+ \underbrace{\left(\frac{\partial P^Y}{\partial Y^e}\frac{\partial Y^e}{\partial \omega}\frac{\partial Y^e}{\partial L} + P^Y \frac{\partial^2 Y^e}{\partial L \partial \omega}\right)}_{c_2} = 0,$$

where $b_1 = a_2$. Solving the above system of equations, we can arrive at

$$\frac{\partial M}{\partial \omega} = -\frac{c_1 b_2 - c_2 b_1}{a_1 b_2 - a_2 b_1}. \tag{A8.2}$$

We now need to show that the right-hand side of (A8.2) above is non-negative. First, consider its denominator. After some algebra, we can show that

$$a_1b_2 - a_2b_1 = P^Y \frac{\partial P^Y}{\partial Y^e}\left[\frac{\partial^2 Y^e}{\partial M^2}\left(\frac{\partial Y^e}{\partial L}\right)^2 + \left(\frac{\partial Y^e}{\partial M}\right)^2 \frac{\partial^2 Y^e}{\partial L^2} - 2\frac{\partial Y^e}{\partial M}\frac{\partial Y^e}{\partial L}\frac{\partial^2 Y^e}{\partial M \partial L}\right] + \left(P^Y\right)^2\left[\frac{\partial^2 Y^e}{\partial M^2}\frac{\partial^2 Y^e}{\partial L^2} - \left(\frac{\partial^2 Y^e}{\partial M \partial L}\right)^2\right]. \tag{A8.3}$$

This equation has two terms. Under our assumptions of a downward-sloping residual demand function (Assumption 5) and the production function satisfying the standard neoclassical regularity conditions (Assumption 2), the first term is non-negative. The second term is a second-order principle minor of the production-function Hessian matrix and, given the concavity of the production function, is non-negative too. Hence, $a_1b_2 - a_2b_1 \geq 0$.

Now, consider the numerator of (A8.2). Noting that c_1 and c_2 can be rewritten as $P^Y \frac{\partial Y^e}{\partial M}\mu^{-1}$ and $P^Y \frac{\partial Y^e}{\partial L}\mu^{-1}$, respectively, we have

$$c_1b_2 - c_2b_1 = \mu^{-1}\left(P^Y\right)^2\left(\frac{\partial Y^e}{\partial M}\frac{\partial^2 Y^e}{\partial L^2} - \frac{\partial^2 Y^e}{\partial M \partial L}\frac{\partial Y^e}{\partial L}\right) \leq 0.$$

Therefore, we have shown that $\frac{\partial M}{\partial \omega} \geq 0$.

Similarly, we can show that $\mathcal{M}(\cdot)$ is weakly increasing in φ. Specifically, by taking partial derivatives of (A8.1) with respect to φ and solving for $\frac{\partial M}{\partial \varphi}$, we have

$$\frac{\partial M}{\partial \varphi} = -\frac{d_1b_2 - d_2b_1}{a_1b_2 - a_2b_1}, \tag{A8.4}$$

where $d_1 \equiv \frac{\partial P^Y}{\partial Y^e}\frac{\partial Y^e}{\partial \varphi}\frac{\partial Y^e}{\partial M} + P^Y \frac{\partial^2 Y^e}{\partial M \partial \varphi}$ and $d_2 \equiv \frac{\partial P^Y}{\partial Y^e}\frac{\partial Y^e}{\partial \varphi}\frac{\partial Y^e}{\partial L} + P^Y \frac{\partial^2 Y^e}{\partial L \partial \varphi}$.

We have already shown that the denominator is non-negative. Then, let us consider the numerator of $\frac{\partial M}{\partial \varphi}$. Recognizing that $\frac{\partial Y^e}{\partial \varphi} = \frac{\partial Y^e}{\partial L}L$, $\frac{\partial^2 Y^e}{\partial M \partial \varphi} = \frac{\partial^2 Y^e}{\partial M \partial L}L$ and $\frac{\partial^2 Y^e}{\partial L \partial \varphi} = \frac{\partial^2 Y^e}{\partial L^2}L + \frac{\partial Y^e}{\partial L}$ and with a few steps of algebra, we have

$$d_1b_2 - d_2b_1 = -\left(P^Y\right)^2 \frac{\partial Y^e}{\partial L}\left(\frac{1}{\delta}\frac{1}{Y^e}\frac{\partial Y^e}{\partial M}\frac{\partial Y^e}{\partial L} + \frac{\partial^2 Y^e}{\partial M \partial L}\right).$$

It is simple to show that the cross-partial $\frac{\partial^2 Y^e}{\partial M \partial L} = \frac{1}{Y^e}\frac{\partial Y^e}{\partial M}\frac{\partial Y^e}{\partial L} + \frac{Y^e}{LM}\frac{\partial\left(\frac{\partial \ln Y^e}{\partial \ln L}\right)}{\partial \ln M}$. Assuming that $\frac{\partial\left(\frac{\partial \ln Y^e}{\partial \ln L}\right)}{\partial \ln M} = \frac{\partial^2 \ln F}{\partial \ln L \partial \ln M} \geq 0$, then $d_1 b_2 - d_2 b_1 = -\left(P^Y\right)^2 \frac{\partial Y^e}{\partial L}\left(\mu^{-1}\frac{1}{Y^e}\frac{\partial Y^e}{\partial M}\frac{\partial Y^e}{\partial L} + \frac{\partial^2 \ln F}{\partial \ln L \partial \ln M}\frac{Y^e}{LM}\right) \leq 0$, and we have that $\frac{\partial M}{\partial \varphi} \geq 0$.

A non-constant-elasticity demand.—In this case, μ is no longer fixed but a function of P^Y. Following the same steps as in the previous case of an isoelastic demand, differentiating the optimality conditions in (A8.1) with respect to ω, we have

$$\frac{\partial M}{\partial \omega} = -\frac{c_1{}'b_2{}' - c_2{}'b_1{}'}{a_1{}'b_2{}' - a_2{}'b_1{}'}, \tag{A8.5}$$

where $a_1{}' = a_1\mu^{-1} + P^Y\left(\frac{\partial Y^e}{\partial M}\right)^2 \frac{\partial \mu^{-1}}{\partial p^Y}\frac{\partial p^Y}{\partial Y^e}$, $b_1{}' = b_1\mu^{-1} + P^Y \frac{\partial Y^e}{\partial M}\frac{\partial Y^e}{\partial L}\frac{\partial \mu^{-1}}{\partial p^Y}\frac{\partial p^Y}{\partial Y^e}$, $c_1{}' = c_1\mu^{-1} + P^Y \frac{\partial Y^e}{\partial M}\frac{\partial \mu^{-1}}{\partial p^Y}\frac{\partial p^Y}{\partial Y^e}\frac{\partial Y^e}{\partial \omega}$, $a_2{}' = a_2\mu^{-1} + P^Y \frac{\partial Y^e}{\partial M}\frac{\partial Y^e}{\partial L}\frac{\partial \mu^{-1}}{\partial p^Y}\frac{\partial p^Y}{\partial Y^e}$, $b_2{}' = b_2\mu^{-1} + P^Y\left(\frac{\partial Y^e}{\partial L}\right)^2 \frac{\partial \mu^{-1}}{\partial p^Y}\frac{\partial p^Y}{\partial Y^e}$, and $c_2{}' = c_2\mu^{-1} + P^Y \frac{\partial Y^e}{\partial L}\frac{\partial \mu^{-1}}{\partial p^Y}\frac{\partial p^Y}{\partial Y^e}\frac{\partial Y^e}{\partial \omega}$.

First, with some algebra we can show that the denominator in the $\frac{\partial M}{\partial \omega}$ expression in (A8.5) can be written as a sum of two terms:

$$a_1{}'b_2{}' - a_2{}'b_1{}' = (a_1 b_2 - a_2 b_1)\mu^{-2} + \mu^{-1}\left(P^Y\right)^2 \frac{\partial \mu^{-1}}{\partial p^Y}\frac{\partial p^Y}{\partial Y^e} + \left[\frac{\partial^2 Y^e}{\partial M^2}\left(\frac{\partial Y^e}{\partial L}\right)^2 + \frac{\partial^2 Y^e}{\partial L^2}\left(\frac{\partial Y^e}{\partial M}\right)^2 - 2\frac{\partial^2 Y^e}{\partial M \partial L}\frac{\partial Y^e}{\partial M}\frac{\partial Y^e}{\partial L}\right].$$

Substituting $a_1 b_2 - a_2 b_1$ for (A8.3) and combining the first term of (A8.3) and the second term of $a_1{}'b_2{}' - a_2{}'b_1{}'$ together, we have

$$\left[\mu^{-2}P^Y \frac{\partial P^Y}{\partial Y^e} + \mu^{-1}\left(P^Y\right)^2 \frac{\partial \mu^{-1}}{\partial p^Y}\frac{\partial p^Y}{\partial Y^e}\right]\left[\frac{\partial^2 Y^e}{\partial M^2}\left(\frac{\partial Y^e}{\partial L}\right)^2 + \frac{\partial^2 Y^e}{\partial L^2}\left(\frac{\partial Y^e}{\partial M}\right)^2 - 2\frac{\partial^2 Y^e}{\partial M \partial L}\frac{\partial Y^e}{\partial M}\frac{\partial Y^e}{\partial L}\right]$$
$$= \mu^{-2}\frac{\left(p^Y\right)^2}{Y^e \delta}\left(1 - \frac{\partial \ln \mu}{\partial \ln P^Y}\right)\left[\frac{\partial^2 Y^e}{\partial M^2}\left(\frac{\partial Y^e}{\partial L}\right)^2 + \frac{\partial^2 Y^e}{\partial L^2}\left(\frac{\partial Y^e}{\partial M}\right)^2 - 2\frac{\partial^2 Y^e}{\partial M \partial L}\frac{\partial Y^e}{\partial M}\frac{\partial Y^e}{\partial L}\right].$$

Given that the second term of (A8.3) is non-negative, if the firm's demand function is such that $\frac{\partial \ln \mu}{\partial \ln P^Y} \leq 1$, we have that $a_1{}'b_2{}' - a_2{}'b_1{}' \geq 0$.

Next, we sign $c_1'b_2' - c_2'b_1'$, the numerator of (A8.5). Using the easy-to-establish results that $\frac{\partial Y^e}{\partial \omega} = Y^e$, $\frac{\partial^2 Y^e}{\partial M \partial \omega} = \frac{\partial Y^e}{\partial M}$ and $\frac{\partial^2 Y^e}{\partial L \partial \omega} = \frac{\partial Y^e}{\partial L}$, we can simplify the expressions of c_1' and c_2' as $P^Y \mu^{-1} \frac{\partial Y^e}{\partial M}\left[1 + (1 + \frac{\partial \ln \mu^{-1}}{\partial \ln P^Y})\frac{1}{\sigma}\right]$ and $P^Y \mu^{-1} \frac{\partial Y^e}{\partial L}\left[1 + (1 + \frac{\partial \ln \mu^{-1}}{\partial \ln P^Y})\frac{1}{\sigma}\right]$, respectively. Also, note that b_1' and b_2' can be rewritten as $b_1' = \mu^{-1} P^Y \times \left(\frac{\partial Y^e}{\partial M}\frac{\partial Y^e}{\partial L}\frac{P^Y}{Y^e}\frac{1}{\sigma}\left(1 - \frac{\partial \ln \mu}{\partial \ln P^Y}\right) + \frac{\partial^2 Y^e}{\partial M \partial L}\right)$ and $b_2' = \mu^{-1} P^Y \left(\left(\frac{\partial Y^e}{\partial L}\right)^2 \frac{P^Y}{Y^e}\frac{1}{\sigma}\left(1 - \frac{\partial \ln \mu}{\partial \ln P^Y}\right) + \frac{\partial^2 Y^e}{\partial L^2}\right)$. With this, we have

$$c_1'b_2' - c_2'b_1' = \left(P^Y \mu^{-1}\right)^2 \left[1 + \left(1 - \frac{\partial \ln \mu}{\partial \ln P^Y}\right)\frac{1}{\sigma}\right]\left(\frac{\partial Y^e}{\partial M}\frac{\partial^2 Y^e}{\partial L^2} - \frac{\partial Y^e}{\partial L}\frac{\partial^2 Y^e}{\partial M \partial L}\right).$$

Since $\left(\frac{\partial Y^e}{\partial M}\frac{\partial^2 Y^e}{\partial L^2} - \frac{\partial Y^e}{\partial L}\frac{\partial^2 Y^e}{\partial M \partial L}\right) \le 0$ as already used earlier, $c_1'b_2' - c_2'b_1' \le 0$ if the curvature of the demand function is such that $\frac{\partial \ln \mu}{\partial \ln P^Y} \ge 0$. Putting the numerator and denominator together, we have thus shown that, when $0 \le \frac{\partial \ln \mu}{\partial \ln P^Y} \le 1$, we have $\frac{\partial M}{\partial \omega} \ge 0$.

Finally, we show that the conditional material demand is weakly increasing in φ. To see that, we have

$$\frac{\partial M}{\partial \varphi} = -\frac{d_1'b_2' - d_2'b_1'}{a_1'b_2' - a_2'b_1'}, \tag{A8.6}$$

where $d_1' = d_1\mu^{-1} + P^Y \frac{\partial Y^e}{\partial M}\frac{\partial \mu^{-1}}{\partial P^Y}\frac{\partial P^Y}{\partial Y^e}\frac{\partial Y^e}{\partial \varphi}$ and $d_2' = d_2\mu^{-1} + P^Y \frac{\partial Y^e}{\partial L}\frac{\partial \mu^{-1}}{\partial P^Y}\frac{\partial P^Y}{\partial Y^e}\frac{\partial Y^e}{\partial \varphi}$. Through a few steps of simple algebraic manipulation, we can obtain

$$d_1'b_2' - d_2'b_1' = (d_1b_2 - d_2b_1) + P^Y \mu^{-2} \frac{\partial \ln \mu}{\partial \ln P^Y}\frac{\partial P^Y}{\partial Y^e},$$

which is non-positive if $(d_1b_2 - d_2b_1) \le 0$ and $\frac{\partial \ln \mu}{\partial \ln P^Y} \ge 0$. Therefore, we have shown that $\frac{\partial M}{\partial \varphi} \ge 0$.

This concludes the proof.

Proof of Proposition 2

With some necessary adaptations, our proof builds on that of Proposition 3.2 in Demirer (2019) for the case with uni-dimensional productivity.

We first show that, for $(O_{it-1}, \widetilde{\mathrm{m}}) \in \mathbb{S}$, the likelihood ratio $\frac{f_{\omega}(\omega_{it} \mid O_{it-1}, m_{it} > \widetilde{\mathrm{m}})}{f_{\omega}(\omega_{it} \mid O_{it-1}, m_{it} < \widetilde{\mathrm{m}})}$ satisfies the "monotone likelihood ratio property," i.e.,

$$\frac{\partial}{\partial \omega_{it}} \left(\frac{f_{\omega}(\omega_{it} \mid O_{it-1}, m_{it} > \widetilde{\mathrm{m}})}{f_{\omega}(\omega_{it} \mid O_{it-1}, m_{it} < \widetilde{\mathrm{m}})} \right) \geq 0.$$

Here, the interest is in ω_{it} only because φ_{it} can be concentrated out of the production function as done in (A7.7). To proceed, we rewrite the conditional pdfs inside the ratio using the Bayes rule:

$$f_{\omega}(\omega_{it} \mid O_{it-1}, m_{it} > \widetilde{\mathrm{m}}) = \frac{\Pr(m_{it} > \widetilde{\mathrm{m}} \mid O_{it-1}, \omega_{it}) f_{\omega}(\omega_{it} \mid O_{it-1})}{\Pr(m_{it} > \widetilde{\mathrm{m}} \mid O_{it-1})}, \tag{A8.7}$$

$$f_{\omega}(\omega_{it} \mid O_{it-1}, m_{it} < \widetilde{\mathrm{m}}) = \frac{\Pr(m_{it} < \widetilde{\mathrm{m}} \mid O_{it-1}, \omega_{it}) f_{\omega}(\omega_{it} \mid O_{it-1})}{\Pr(m_{it} < \widetilde{\mathrm{m}} \mid O_{it-1})}. \tag{A8.8}$$

Then, the likelihood ratio is given by

$$\begin{aligned} \frac{f_{\omega}(\omega_{it} \mid O_{it-1}, m_{it} > \widetilde{\mathrm{m}})}{f_{\omega}(\omega_{it} \mid O_{it-1}, m_{it} < \widetilde{\mathrm{m}})} &= \frac{\Pr(m_{it} > \widetilde{\mathrm{m}} \mid O_{it-1}, \omega_{it}) \Pr(m_{it} < \widetilde{\mathrm{m}} \mid O_{it-1})}{\Pr(m_{it} < \widetilde{\mathrm{m}} \mid O_{it-1}, \omega_{it}) \Pr(m_{it} > \widetilde{\mathrm{m}} \mid O_{it-1})} \\ &= \frac{\Pr(m_{it} > \widetilde{\mathrm{m}} \mid O_{it-1}, \omega_{it}) \Pr(m_{it} < \widetilde{\mathrm{m}} \mid O_{it-1})}{(1 - \Pr(m_{it} > \widetilde{\mathrm{m}} \mid O_{it-1}, \omega_{it})) \Pr(m_{it} > \widetilde{\mathrm{m}} \mid O_{it-1})}. \end{aligned} \tag{A8.9}$$

The likelihood ratio in (A8.9) depends on ω_{it} via probability $\Pr(m_{it} > \widetilde{\mathrm{m}} \mid O_{it-1}, \omega_{it})$ and, clearly, the ratio is increasing in the latter. Therefore, for the likelihood ratio to be weakly increasing in ω_{it}, $\Pr(m_{it} > \widetilde{\mathrm{m}} \mid O_{it-1}, \omega_{it})$ must be weakly increasing in ω_{it}.

Recall that the material demand function is $M_{it} = \mathcal{M}(K_{it}, U_{it}, \varphi_{it}, \omega_{it})$. Also recognize that, conditional on observable state variables O_{it-1}, which include K_{it-1}, and the productivities $(\varphi_{it}, \omega_{it})'$ that each depend on their lagged values per Markov processes, K_{it} contains no new information because it is predetermined at time $t-1$ and is a deterministic function of K_{it-1} and other past state variables. Abusing notation, we therefore write M_{it} as $M(O_{it-1}, U_{it}, \varphi_{it}, \omega_{it})$ and, correspondingly, $m(O_{it-1}, U_{it}, \varphi_{it}, \omega_{it})$ in logs. Now consider a binary variable $1\{m_{it} > \widetilde{\mathrm{m}}\} = 1\{m(O_{it-1}, U_{it}, \varphi_{it}, \omega_{it}) > \widetilde{\mathrm{m}}\}$. We can represent $\Pr(m_{it} > \widetilde{\mathrm{m}} \mid O_{it-1}, \omega_{it})$ as a conditional expectation of this dummy:

$$\begin{aligned} \Pr(m_{it} > \widetilde{\mathrm{m}} \mid O_{it-1}, \omega_{it}) &= \int\int 1\{m(O_{it-1}, U_{it}, \varphi_{it}, \omega_{it}) > \widetilde{\mathrm{m}}\} f_{U,\varphi}(U_{it}, \varphi_{it} \mid O_{it-1}, \omega_{it}) dU_{it}\, d\varphi_{it} \\ &= \int\int 1\{m(O_{it-1}, U_{it}, \varphi_{it}, \omega_{it}) > \widetilde{\mathrm{m}}\} f_U(U_{it} \mid \varphi_{it}, O_{it-1}, \omega_{it}) f_{\varphi}(\varphi_{it} \mid O_{it-1}, \omega_{it}) dU_{it}\, d\varphi_{it} \\ &= \int\int 1\{m(O_{it-1}, U_{it}, \varphi_{it}, \omega_{it}) > \widetilde{\mathrm{m}}\} f_U(U_{it} \mid O_{it-1}) f_{\varphi}(\varphi_{it} \mid O_{it-1}, \omega_{it}) dU_{it}\, d\varphi_{it} \\ &= \int \phi(O_{it-1}, \varphi_{it}, \omega_{it}) f_{\varphi}(\varphi_{it} \mid O_{it-1}, \omega_{it}) d\varphi_{it}, \end{aligned} \tag{A8.10}$$

where we have made use of the joint independence of U_{it} from $(\varphi_{it},\omega_{it})'$ conditional on O_{it-1} per Assumption 5(ii) in the third line and have introduced a conditional mean function $\phi(O_{it-1},\varphi_{it},\omega_{it}) \equiv \int 1\{m(O_{it-1},U_{it},\varphi_{it},\omega_{it}) > c\} f_U(U_{it} \mid O_{it-1}) dU_{it}$ with the demand heterogeneity U_{it} integrated out in the fourth line.

By Proposition 1, $m(O_{it-1},U_{it},\varphi_{it},\omega_{it})$ is weakly increasing in both ω_{it} and φ_{it}, which implies that $\phi(O_{it-1},\varphi_{it},\omega_{it})$ is also an increasing function of ω_{it} and φ_{it}. Now, take any $\omega_{it}^H \geq \omega_{it}^L$. Owing to the conditional first-order stochastic dominance per Assumption 6, i.e., $\mathcal{P}_\varphi(\varphi_{it} \mid \omega_{it}^H, X_{it-1}, Z_{it-1}) \leq \mathcal{P}_\varphi(\varphi_{it} \mid \omega_{it}^L, X_{it-1}, Z_{it-1})$, we have that

$$\mathbb{E}\left[\phi\left(O_{it-1},\varphi_{it},\omega_{it}^H\right) \mid \omega_{it}^H, X_{it-1}, Z_{it-1}\right] \geq \mathbb{E}\left[\phi\left(O_{it-1},\varphi_{it},\omega_{it}^H\right) \mid \omega_{it}^L, X_{it-1}, Z_{it-1}\right] \tag{A8.11}$$

because $\partial\phi(\cdot)/\partial\varphi \geq 0$. We also have that

$$\mathbb{E}\left[\phi\left(O_{it-1},\varphi_{it},\omega_{it}^H\right) \mid \omega_{it}^L, X_{it-1}, Z_{it-1}\right] \geq \mathbb{E}\left[\phi\left(O_{it-1},\varphi_{it},\omega_{it}^L\right) \mid \omega_{it}^L, X_{it-1}, Z_{it-1}\right] \tag{A8.12}$$

because $\partial\phi(\cdot)/\partial\omega \geq 0$.

Combining (A8.11) and (A8.12), we obtain

$$\mathbb{E}\left[\phi\left(O_{it-1},\varphi_{it},\omega_{it}^H\right) \mid \omega_{it}^H, X_{it-1}, Z_{it-1}\right] \geq \mathbb{E}\left[\phi\left(O_{it-1},\varphi_{it},\omega_{it}^L\right) \mid \omega_{it}^L, X_{it-1}, Z_{it-1}\right], \tag{A8.13}$$

and we can then conclude that the mean of $\phi(O_{it-1},\varphi_{it},\omega_{it})$ conditional on $(O_{it-1}{}',\omega_{it})'$ is weakly increasing in Hicks-neutral productivity ω_{it} and, therefore, so is $\Pr(m_{it} > \widetilde{\mathrm{m}} \mid O_{it-1},\omega_{it})$.

We have thus shown that the likelihood ratio $\dfrac{f_\omega(\omega_{it} \mid O_{it-1}, m_{it} > \widetilde{\mathrm{m}})}{f_\omega(\omega_{it} \mid O_{it-1}, m_{it} < \widetilde{\mathrm{m}})}$ is weakly increasing in ω_{it} thereby satisfying the "monotone likelihood ratio property." In its turn, this property implies the first-order stochastic dominance and the following weak ordering of conditional expectations:

$$\mathbb{E}[\omega_{it} \mid O_{it-1}, m_{it} > \widetilde{\mathrm{m}}] \geq \mathbb{E}[\omega_{it} \mid O_{it-1}, m_{it} < \widetilde{\mathrm{m}}]. \tag{A8.14}$$

Next, substituting for ω_{it} in (A8.14) using the production function in (A7.7) and recognizing that $\mathbb{E}[\eta_{it} \mid O_{it-1}, m_{it} > \widetilde{\mathrm{m}}] = \mathbb{E}[\eta_{it} \mid \Xi_{it}] = \mathbb{E}[\eta_{it}] = 0$ under Assumption 3(ii), we obtain

$$\mathbb{E}[y_{it} - \overline{y}_{it}(v_{it};\beta) \mid O_{it-1}, m_{it} > \widetilde{\mathrm{m}}] \geq \mathbb{E}[y_{it} - \overline{y}_{it}(v_{it};\beta) \mid O_{it-1}, m_{it} < \widetilde{\mathrm{m}}], \tag{A8.15}$$

which concludes the proof.

CHAPTER 10

THE STRUCTURAL AND PRODUCTIVITY EFFECTS OF INFRASTRUCTURE PROVISION IN DEVELOPED AND DEVELOPING COUNTRIES

Luis Orea[a], Inmaculada Álvarez-Ayuso[b] and Luis Servén[c]

[a]*Department of Economics, School of Business and Economics, University of Oviedo, Oviedo, Spain*
[b]*Universidad Autónoma de Madrid, Madrid, Spain*
[c]*Centro de Estudios Monetarios y Financieros, Madrid, Spain*

ABSTRACT

This chapter provides an empirical assessment of the effects of infrastructure provision on structural change and aggregate productivity using industrylevel data for a set of developed and developing countries over 1995–2010. A distinctive feature of the empirical strategy followed is that it allows the measurement of the resource reallocation directly attributable to infrastructure provision. To achieve this, a two-level top-down decomposition of aggregate productivity that combines and extends several strands of the literature is proposed. The empirical application reveals significant production losses attributable to misallocation of inputs across firms, especially among African countries. Also, the results show that infrastructure provision has stimulated

Essays in Honor of Subal Kumbhakar
Advances in Econometrics, Volume 46, 265–308

ISSN: 0731-9053/doi:10.1108/S0731-905320240000046010

aggregate total factor productivity growth through both within and between industry productivity gains.

Keywords: Productivity growth; resource allocation; stochastic frontier analysis; structural change; infrastructure provision; top-down TFP decomposition

1. INTRODUCTION

Differences in aggregate productivity account for the bulk of cross-country per-capita income differentials. Thus, understanding the drivers of productivity growth has long been of high interest to academics and policy makers. Much of the literature on productivity growth decomposition (see Färe, Grosskopft, & Margaritis, 2008) focuses on two key ingredients: the introduction of more productive technologies (i.e., technical change) and the barriers to diffusion and learning that prevent firms from adopting those technologies (i.e., the catching-up effect or efficiency change). Another strand of the literature (see Balk et al., 2016a, 2016b) stresses that aggregate productivity growth depends not only on industry-level productivity change (within effect [WE]), but also on the shift in industry relative size (reallocation effect). Recent papers suggest that countries can increase output and aggregate total factor productivity (TFP) substantially by reallocating resources more efficiently across firms and industries (e.g., Hsieh & Klenow, 2009). Moreover, in their summary of the literature, Restuccia and Rogerson (2008, 2013) conclude that weak public institutions may distort the allocation of resources and thus become a source of productivity and income losses. Basu, Schiantarelli, Pascali, and Serven (2021) have recently pointed out that an increase in aggregate TFP due to reallocation or better use of scale economies is as much of a welfare gain for the representative consumer as a change in technology of the same magnitude and persistence. Therefore, TFP losses due to inter-firm allocative inefficiency are of direct interest if we aim to connect TFP measures with welfare.[1]

Public investment in infrastructure has long been considered as one of the key policy levers to affect both economic development and aggregate productivity. Its relevance is reflected in the large number of studies quantifying its effects on private production (Pereira & Andraz, 2013). Investment in highways is one of the components that has generated the greatest interest, due to its uncertain effects on regional economic growth and territorial disparities (see, e.g., Crescenzi & Rodríguez-Pose, 2012). In turn, public and private investments in telecommunication infrastructure and electricity distribution are increasingly recognized as fundamental for economic and social development (see, e.g., Qiang & Rossotto, 2009; Yang, 2000). Given the uneven effect that these sorts of investments might have across the economy, it is of great interest for both academics and policy makers to examine whether such infrastructure investments have also promoted gains in aggregate productivity through a better allocation of resources across firms and industries.

In this chapter, we provide evidence on the effects of infrastructure provision on aggregate productivity using industry-level data for a set of developed and developing countries. To achieve this, we propose a two-level decomposition of aggregate productivity that combines and extends several strands of the literature. The first level is a simplified version of the top-down TFP decomposition introduced by Diewert (2015).[2] Although the first level of our productivity decomposition does not require estimating any econometric model, decomposing the computed TFP productivity index into its basic sources using Diewert's (2015) theoretical framework requires not only data on quantities and prices, but also data measuring the input and output adjustments that have taken place in the economy. The second level of our productivity decomposition allows measuring aggregate TFP improvements directly attributable to infrastructure provision, and to other productivity drivers. As pointed out by a referee, infrastructure should be understood as encompassing less-tangible dimensions, such as the protection of property rights, and both government and private provision of enhanced shared information technology. For this reason, we have done our best to include such investments into our measure of public capital, in addition to controlling for differences in the quality of institutions across countries.

A distinctive feature of this theoretical decomposition is that it traces two different channels through which infrastructure provision might promote aggregate productivity gains: (i) by raising the productivity level of each industry (the *within* effect); and (ii) by stimulating the structural transformation of the economy (the *sectoral* or *inter-industry* reallocation effect). Thus, our theoretical model allows measuring sectoral reallocation effects directly attributable to infrastructure provision, which are often ignored in the literature measuring the effect of infrastructure provision on private production.[3]

Decomposition of the so-called *within* effect into its fundamental explanatory factors requires estimating several production models. We also use the estimated production models to decompose the reallocation term capturing the output side of the adjustments taking place in the economy, as it can be written as a function of several sectoral production models. These models are estimated using stochastic frontier (SF) techniques for two reasons.[4] First, as advocated by Straub (2011), this empirical strategy allows infrastructure provision to have a *direct* effect on sectoral production as a standard input, and an *indirect* effect through the inefficiency term as a productivity externality. Second, although we use sector-level data, the technical inefficiency term of our sectoral production frontier model allows us to capture, among other factors, the production losses caused by an inefficient allocation of resources across firms operating in the same industry. By comparing sectors, we identify which ones are (not) able to produce more output with the same amounts of inputs. Obviously, our sectoral inefficiency term might be capturing production losses stemming from different sources, such as differences in technology or in technical inefficiency across firms. However, given the large empirical literature on misallocation – pioneered by Restuccia and Rogerson (2008) and Hsieh and Klenow (2009) – suggesting that within-industry misallocation of production factors across firms is at the root of poor TFP performance in many countries, we view our aggregate or industry-specific inefficiency scores as evidence of misallocation, which we attribute to barriers and distortions to the efficient allocation of resources across firms. Thus, while the theoretical model allows measuring inter-industry reallocation effects, our SF specification permits measuring within-industry reallocation effects directly attributable to infrastructure provision.

Notice that we are using here a concept of within-industry allocative inefficiency that differs from that used in production economics when, say, a firm combines two inputs to minimize (maximize) its production costs (profits) given input prices. Our concept of allocative inefficiency has to do with the allocation of the total amount of capital or labor used in a particular industry across the firms that are operating in such an industry. If the marginal products at the observed inputs for each firm are not the same, there is room for production gains in the industry by reallocating inputs from the less productive firms to the more productive ones. The empirical literature on misallocation shows that a wide variety of distorting regulations, size-dependent policies, financial constraints, trade restrictions and other market frictions (Restuccia & Rogerson, 2013) might prevent the equalization of marginal products across firms, and thereby cause aggregate output and TFP to fall short of their efficient levels.

We do not observe the allocation of resources within the industry as only sectoral-level data is available. We also do not observe the marginal products at the observed inputs for each firm. Therefore, we cannot simulate the optimal allocation of inputs within the industry, as in the empirical literature on misallocation using Hsieh and Klenow (2009)'s approach.[5] Notice, however, that the gap between the observed and efficient production levels is what a SF specification of our sectoral production model is able to capture. That is, as the final effect of within-industry allocative inefficiency is a reduction in aggregate industry output (ten Raa, 2005), we link the one-sided error term of our sectoral SF production function to a misallocation of resources across firms. In this sense, we follow the traditional literature on misallocation that typically measures the cost of misallocation in terms of aggregate output or TFP losses. Moreover, as we allow our one-sided error term to follow a heteroskedastic distribution, we will be able to measure within-industry reallocation effects attributable to infrastructure provision, in line with Asturias, García-Santana, and Ramos (2019) and Perez-Sebastian and Steinbuks (2017).

Our sectoral reallocation effect can be viewed as a traditional shift-share term that reflects changes in aggregate productivity coming from reallocation of capital and labor across sectors. For instance, it allows us to investigate whether weak TFP growth over the period of analysis can be explained by resources being systematically allocated to the "wrong" sectors, i.e., those with poor performance in terms of productivity growth. As in many bottom-up decompositions of aggregate productivity growth proposed in the literature, our top-down reallocation effect can be expressed as a function of industry shares. Although examining the connection between the two approaches – bottom-up and top-down – is beyond the scope of our chapter, our chapter thus contributes to link both approaches.[6] It is also worth mentioning that our simplification of Diewert (2015)'s decomposition consists precisely in expressing the sectoral reallocation effect as a function of industry shares. This implies that we do not need separate price data to quantify the importance of sectoral reallocation of factors in accounting for the aggregate evolution of TFP.[7]

The decomposition of our *sectoral* reallocation term is much more challenging because employment is an intrinsically complex phenomenon influenced by many factors (see Vivarelli, 2012). A proper decomposition requires "endogenizing" industry-specific input levels using a suitable theoretical framework. The choice of theoretical framework is far from obvious, however, and instead we opt for estimating a set of auxiliary regressions to examine the effect of infrastructure provision on both industry labor and capital volumes and shares.

We illustrate our decompositions using industry-level data for a set of developed and developing countries over the 1995–2010 period. The first-level decomposition shows that in many developing countries the simple aggregation of industry TFP growth rates does not properly describe aggregate TFP growth because the productivity gains attributable to reallocation of inputs across industries far exceed the poor TFP growth rates found in many industries. We also find significant production losses attributable to misallocation of inputs across firms in many industries, especially in Africa. Our most interesting result is the one concerning the role of public infrastructure capital. Not only does it improve within-firm productivity, but it also facilitates the efficient reallocation of inputs across both firms and industries, suggesting that promotion of enhanced infrastructure investments should be a public policy priority in developing countries.

The next section outlines the top-down approach used by Diewert (2015) to decompose aggregate productivity growth using a continuous-time setting. In Section 3, we develop a theoretical model that yields mutually consistent decompositions of both within and reallocation effects, once a set of production functions and auxiliary regressions are estimated. In Section 4, we discuss the data used in the empirical analysis and its sources. Section 5 presents both the parameter estimates and the computed productivity effects. This section also includes a discussion on the implications of the analysis for the design of strategies aimed at raising aggregate TFP, especially in developing countries. Finally, Section 6 presents the conclusions.

2. DIEWERT'S (2015) TFP DECOMPOSITION

This section outlines, using a continuous-time setting, the top-down approach proposed by Diewert (2015) to decompose an aggregate TFP productivity measure (M) that can be defined as aggregate real output (Y) divided by aggregate real input (X)[8]:

$$M = \frac{\sum_{n=1}^{N} P_n Y_n / P}{\sum_{n=1}^{N} W_n X_n / W} = \frac{Y}{X} \tag{1}$$

where the subscript n stands for industry or sector, Y_n is industry n real output (value-added), P_n is the corresponding industry value added output price, and

P is the aggregate output price index. On the other hand, X_n is industry n aggregate input, W_n is industry n aggregate input price, and W is the aggregate input price index. While X_n can be viewed as a weighted average of industry labor and capital volumes, X is a weighted average of industry-specific inputs.

Diewert (2015, equation 28) shows that it is possible to relate aggregate TFP level (M) to the industry TFP levels ($M_n = Y_n / X_n$) as follows:

$$M = \sum_{n=1}^{N} \left(\frac{p_n}{w_n} \right) s_{Xn} M_n \tag{2}$$

where $p_n = P_n / P$ is the industry n real output price, $w_n = W_n / W$ is the industry n real input price, and

$$s_{Xn} = \frac{W_n X_n}{\sum_{s=1}^{N} W_s X_s} = \frac{W_n X_n}{WX} \tag{3}$$

is the *nominal* input share of industry n in aggregate cost.[9] Thus, aggregate TFP is a weighted sum of industry-specific TFP productivities where the weight for each industry is its real output–input price ratio (p_n / w_n) times its input cost share (s_{Xn}). Next, Diewert (2015) develops an expression for the rate of growth of aggregate TFP. Using definition (1) and equation (2), aggregate TFP growth is equal to:[10]

$$\dot{M} = \sum_{n=1}^{N} s_{Yn} \dot{\mathrm{M}}_n + \sum_{n=1}^{N} s_{Yn} \dot{\mathrm{p}}_n - \sum_{n=1}^{N} s_{Yn} \dot{\mathrm{w}}_n + \sum_{n=1}^{N} s_{Yn} \dot{\mathrm{s}}_{Xn} \tag{4}$$

where a dot over a variable indicates its rate of growth, and s_{Yn} is the *nominal* value added or output share of industry n in total value added:

$$s_{Yn} = \frac{P_n Y_n}{\sum_{s=1}^{N} P_s Y_s} = \frac{P_n Y_n}{PY} \tag{5}$$

The first term in (4) can be interpreted as the aggregate TFP growth that would obtain if all real output and input prices and industry relative sizes were to remain constant over time. Notice that this term is just the straightforward aggregation of industry-specific TFP growth rates, and thus it can be labeled as multifactor *WE*. The second and third terms in (4) indicate that aggregate TFP growth can also change due to changes in industry real output and input prices, respectively. We shall label these two terms respectively as *OPE* and *IPE*. The last term indicates that aggregate TFP growth can also change due to changes in industry input cost shares. As this term has to do with transformation of the economy, measured by relative industry input usage, it represents an *input reallocation effect,* and thus it is labeled hereafter as *IRE*. Accordingly, if all real output and input prices remain constant, individual industries can contribute positively to aggregate productivity change in two ways: if their own TFP level increases, or if those industries with above-(below-) average input cost share increase (decrease) in relative size.

Up to this point, our analysis follows that of Diewert (2015), but now we extend his decomposition further. He links the *OPE* term to changes in the price weights of the industry output growth rates in (1), which in turn affects aggregate TFP growth. We show in Appendix 1 that Diewert's output price effect (OPE) is (the negative) of an *output reallocation effect* that measures changes in the structure of the economy using industry real output shares, instead of using relative industry input usages as *IRE*. We also show in Appendix 1 that, although the output changes in the structure of the economy might be remarkable, the *OPE* term tends to be negligible in practice as it mainly depends on the difference between real and nominal output shares. This term vanishes if both output shares coincide. Notice that this happens if all industry output prices P_n are equal to the aggregate output price P. As both prices are likely similar in applications using industry-level data, we should not expect large *OPE* values in practice.[11]

A similar conclusion can be obtained for the *IPE* and *IRE* terms. We demonstrate in Appendix 2 that the sum of these two input-based terms captures input reallocation effects, and that their combined effect (labelled hereafter as *Input Price Reallocation Effect, IPRE*) depends on how the structure of the economy differs when we compare the share of each industry in terms of outputs and inputs. As the relative size of a particular industry in output and input terms might differ notably in practice, we thus expect larger values for *IPRE* than for *OPE*.

In summary, aggregate TFP growth can alternatively be decomposed as follows:

$$\dot{M} = WE + OPE + IPRE \tag{6}$$

where

$$WE = \sum_{n=1}^{N} s_{Yn} \dot{\mathrm{M}}_n$$

$$OPE = -\sum_{n=1}^{N} s_{Yn} \dot{S}_{Yn} = \sum_{n=1}^{N} (S_{Yn} - s_{Yn}) \dot{Y}_n$$

$$IPRE = \sum_{n=1}^{N} s_{Yn} \dot{S}_{Xn} = \sum_{n=1}^{N} (s_{Yn} - S_{Xn}) \dot{X}_n$$

Several comments are in order regarding the above decomposition. First, it is a simplified version of the top-down TFP decomposition introduced by Diewert (2015) as it only includes three productivity sources. Equation (6) yields a decomposition with no price effects that instead incorporates the traditional WE and two reallocation terms that capture both the input and output sides of the adjustments taking place in the economy. In this sense, equation (6) treats symmetrically the two variables used to compute aggregate TFP productivity, total input and total output. Second, as written above, the *OPE* and *IPRE* terms and their components can be readily evaluated with the help of the sectoral production and input models that will be used in the next section to proceed with the second level of our decomposition. Third, as the output shares of the highest (lowest) productivity industries tend to be larger (smaller) than their input shares, the **IPRE** term simply suggests that to raise aggregate TFP the input share of high-productivity sectors should increase and the input share of low-productivity sectors should decrease. In this sense, the **IPRE** term has an economic interpretation similar to that of the traditional shift-share term that often appears in a bottom-up decomposition of aggregate productivity growth. Finally, Diewert (2016) shows for the case of Australia that while his real output and (real) price terms and input share augmentation factor can be quite significant, their aggregate effects were also close to zero. Thus, only the weighted average of industry TFP growth rates proved to be a significant determinant of overall multifactor productivity growth in his application. He states that this result is caused by the fact that most statistical agencies use balancing rates of return in their user costs in order to make the value of inputs equal to the value of outputs. As this implies that the industry primary input costs equal the corresponding industry net revenues, the industry (cost) share reallocations do not have a remarkable effect on aggregate TFP growth.

3. DECOMPOSING THE WITHIN AND REALLOCATION EFFECTS

We next try to decompose the above-mentioned three general productivity effects into their basic drivers using the parametric estimates of a set of production functions and auxiliary regressions.

3.1. Decomposing the WE

As is customary in regional economics, we hereafter assume that the output of industry *n* depends on its own use of private capital and labor, and on a set of country-level variables measuring the provision of different infrastructures such as transport, electricity, information, communication, etc. Moreover, in order to distinguish between an industry's pure (i.e., technological) productivity improvements and those caused by a more efficient allocation of resources among its constituent firms, we propose estimating a stochastic production frontier model for each industry, which may be written as follows:

$$\ln Y_n = \beta_{0n} + \beta_{Kn}\ln K_n + \beta_{Ln}\ln L_n + \delta_n t + \gamma_n \ln Z + v_n - u_n(\ln Z) \tag{7}$$

where for notational ease we have dropped the standard subscript *t* indicating time, and we include a country-specific fixed-effect (with the country subscript omitted) to control for unobserved cross-country heterogeneity in the estimation.[12] K_n denotes the capital stock of industry *n*, and $\ln Z$ is an indicator measuring infrastructure provision (including transport, electricity distribution, telecommunication networks, etc.). Notice that for ease of notation we have included a conventional time trend in (7) as a placeholder to summarize common shocks; it is replaced in our empirical application by a set of time dummies to capture better the effect of technological improvements, the global cycle, or any common factor that affects all countries equally. Lastly, equation (7) also includes two error terms, v_n and u_n. While the former is a symmetric error term measuring pure random shocks, the latter is a non-negative error term measuring industry inefficiency, which we link to misallocation of resources across firms. As Asturias et al. (2019) and Perez-Sebastian and Steinbuks (2017) found evidence that inter-firm resource misallocation in India and Brazil depends on (transportation) infrastructure, we allow our industry inefficiency term to depend on our indicator measuring infrastructure provision.[13]

Using the production model in (7), the changes in industry production can be decomposed as:

$$\dot{Y}_n = \beta_{Kn}\dot{K}_n + \beta_{Ln}\dot{L}_n + \theta_n\dot{Z} + \delta_n \tag{8}$$

where

$$\theta_n = \frac{\partial \ln Y_n}{\partial \ln Z} = \gamma_n - \frac{\partial u_n}{\partial \ln Z} \tag{9}$$

Equation (9) just indicates that the effect of infrastructure provision on industry output is a combination of a *direct* effect through the frontier, and an *indirect* effect through the allocative efficiency term. Alternatively, we can rewrite the changes in industry production in (8) as:

$$\dot{Y}_n = \beta_n\dot{X}_n + \theta_n\dot{Z} + \delta_n \tag{10}$$

where $\beta_n = \beta_{Kn} + \beta_{Ln}$, and

$$\dot{X}_n = \left[\frac{\beta_{Ln}}{\beta_n}\dot{L}_n + \frac{\beta_{Kn}}{\beta_n}\dot{K}_n\right] \tag{11}$$

The above equations suggest that the estimated coefficients in (7) can be used to both compute (the change of) an aggregate input measure at industry level, and decompose changes in industry production. They can also be used to decompose (the change of) an industry TFP measure if we simply subtract from both sides of equation (10) the aggregate input measure:

$$\dot{M}_n = \dot{Y}_n - \dot{X}_n = (\beta_n - 1)\dot{X}_n + \delta_n + \theta_n\dot{Z} \tag{12}$$

where $(\beta_n - 1)$ is a measure of the returns to scale at industry level. Equation (12) decomposes industry TFP changes into a size effect associated to an increase in the usage of inputs, technical change, and the overall effect of the Z variables. Using (12) we can now decompose the WE that appears in (6) as follows:

$$WE = \sum_{n=1}^{N}(\beta_n - 1)s_{Yn}\dot{X}_n + \sum_{n=1}^{N}s_{Yn}\delta_n + \sum_{n=1}^{N}s_{Yn}\theta_n\dot{Z} \tag{13}$$

3.2. Decomposing the OPE

Next, we discuss how to decompose the *OPE* term. We show in Appendix 1 that Diewert's OPE can be interpreted as an output reallocation effect that measures changes in the structure of the economy using industry real output shares. Unlike the *IPRE* term, we do not need a new theoretical framework to decompose *OPE* because the production model used in Subsection 3.1 to decompose *WE* also provides information on the industry output shares.

$$\frac{\partial \ln S_{Yn}}{\partial \ln Z} = \theta_n - \sum_{s=1}^{N} S_{Ys}\theta_s = \theta_n - \theta \tag{14}$$

This equation indicates that the effect of infrastructure provision on the relative size of industry n depends on how different the within productivity effect is with respect to the average. Recall that we have found that *OPE* can be defined as $-\sum_{n=1}^{N} s_{Yn}\dot{S}_{Yn}$. Therefore, the productivity effect of infrastructure provision through structural changes in the economy disappears if θ_n is the same for all industries.

The output share of each industry also depends on capital and labor, and the time trend. Therefore, these ingredients also generate inter-industry reallocation effects. Taking next into account that *OPE* can alternatively be defined as $\sum_{n=1}^{N}(S_{Yn} - s_{Yn})\dot{Y}_n$, the OPE can be decomposed as follows:

$$OPE = \sum_{n=1}^{N}(S_{Yn} - s_{Yn})\left[\beta_{Kn}\dot{K}_n + \beta_{Ln}\dot{L}_n + \theta_n\dot{Z} + \delta_n\right] \tag{15}$$

It should be emphasized that all decompositions in this subsection rely on the same parameters that have been used (and estimated) to decompose the WE in the previous subsection. In this sense, our decomposition of *OPE* is theoretically consistent with the decomposition of *WE*. In other words, both *WE* and *OPE* decompositions are mutually consistent.

3.3. Decomposing the Input Price Reallocation Effect

Lastly, we discuss how to evaluate the components of the *IPRE* term that appears in our TFP decomposition (6). Recall that *IPRE* is equivalent to $\sum_{n=1}^{N}(s_{Yn} - S_{Xn})\dot{X}_n$, Therefore, its decomposition requires explaining changes in the aggregate input, X_n. Using a Divisia index and our parameter estimates, the effect of infrastructure provision on X_n can be computed as follows:

$$\frac{\partial \ln X_n}{\partial \ln Z} = \frac{\beta_{Ln}}{\beta_n}\frac{\partial \ln L_n}{\partial \ln Z} + \frac{\beta_{Kn}}{\beta_n}\frac{\partial \ln K_n}{\partial \ln Z} \tag{16}$$

where $\frac{\partial \ln L_n}{\partial \ln Z}$ and $\frac{\partial \ln K_n}{\partial \ln Z}$ respectively measure the effect of infrastructure provision on labor and capital demand by industry n. Decomposing these input demands is more challenging than decomposing the industry output shares. Indeed, the decomposition of *IPRE* requires "endogenizing" the industry-specific input levels using a theoretical framework. As we do not know a priori which framework is more appropriate (e.g., cost vs profit-based), we adopt a holistic approach and propose estimating for each industry the following auxiliary regressions:

$$\ln L_n = \sum_{c=1}^{C} b_{0nc} D_c + b_{1n} t + b_{2n} t^2 + b_{zn} \ln Z + \varepsilon_{Ln} \quad (17)$$

$$\ln K_n = \sum_{c=1}^{C} a_{0nc} D_c + a_{1n} t + a_{2n} t^2 + a_{zn} \ln Z + \varepsilon_{Kn} \quad (18)$$

where $(a_{0nc}, a_{1n}, a_{2n}, a_{zn})$, $(b_{0nc}, b_{1n}, b_{2n}, b_{zn})$ are new parameters to be estimated, and D_c is a dummy variable which is equal to 1 for country c and 0 otherwise. We use industry and country-specific intercepts and a time polynomial with industry parameters to control for the net effect of an unknown set of demand drivers that vary over time and across industries and countries.[14] Using the above equations, we get:

$$\frac{\partial \ln X_n}{\partial \ln Z} = \frac{\beta_{Ln}}{\beta_n} b_{zn} + \frac{\beta_{Kn}}{\beta_n} a_{zn} \quad (19)$$

Finally, the portion of *IPRE* that can be attributed to infrastructure provision can be computed as $\sum_{n=1}^{N} (s_{Yn} - S_{Xn}) \frac{\partial \ln X_n}{\partial \ln Z}$.

4. SAMPLE AND DATA

To illustrate the proposed decompositions, we use a balanced data panel for 39 countries and 5 industries over the period 1995–2009. The industries examined in this chapter are fairly aggregated: Agriculture, Energy, Manufacturing, Construction and Services. To simplify the empirical exercise, we have aggregated mining together with electricity, gas and water supply into one sector. In addition, the services sector includes a large range of services such as wholesale and retail trade, hotels, transport, storage, and communications, finance and insurance. The dataset includes annual observations on sectoral value-added and prices, physical capital and labor, and a set of mature and technological infrastructure asset stocks, namely transportation, electricity distribution, and information and telecommunication. Except for industry value-added, output prices and labor, the remaining variables are measured at the country level.

We were forced to drop many countries from the sample given that many years suffered from missing values. Despite these data issues, we were able to work with a broad sample of countries from different world regions (see Appendix 3). As these regions exhibit different time patterns in their productivity indicators, the relative importance of the intra and inter-industry effects for the observed productivity growth rates should be expected to vary substantially across regions.

The *Groningen Growth and Development Centre (GGDC) 10-Sector Database* provides annual data for a large set of countries on real gross value added (Y_n) and nominal gross value added ($P_n Y_n$) and employment (L_n) for each industry. Aggregate real value added ($Y = \sum_{n=1}^{N} Y_n$) and aggregate nominal gross value added ($\sum_{n=1}^{N} P_n Y_n$) are also available in this database, as is total employment ($L = \sum_{n=1}^{N} L_n$). Sectoral and aggregate deflators are simply obtained by dividing each nominal value added by its corresponding real value. While nominal (real) output is measured at current (constant 2005) national prices in millions, the labor input is measured in thousands of jobs.

The aggregate private capital stock (K) was obtained from the International Monetary Fund, and it is originally measured in billions of national currencies. Notice that we do not have information on industry-specific capital input (K_n), just the aggregate stock. To address this issue, we propose modeling the gap between K_n and K econometrically. The industry-specific but unobserved capital stock can be written as $K_n = S_{Kn} K$, where S_{Kn} is the share of capital used by industry n. This variable is however not observed. As S_{Kn} is likely correlated with S_{Ln}, we will assume in our empirical application that $\ln S_{Kn} = d_n S_{Ln}$, where d_n is a new parameter that captures such a correlation.[15] Once this parameter is estimated with our production functions, all capital shares are adjusted proportionately in order to impose $\sum_{n=1}^{N} K_n = K$. As pointed out by a referee, another problem of our variable measuring capital stock is that it does not include land or inventory stocks, which are significant omissions. However, as land and many other omitted variables (e.g., the abundance of natural resources) are likely invariant over time, our country fixed effects are already capturing most of the production effects attributable to these omitted variables.[16]

We collected four indicators on aggregate infrastructure provision. From the World Bank, we use three indicators on transportation (the length of the total road network in millions of kilometers), information network (the number of internet users), and telecommunication network (the number of fixed telephone and mobile cellular subscriptions). The last infrastructure variable used in our empirical application is electric generation capacity (measured in thousands of KW), provided by the US Energy Information Administration.

Measuring infrastructure is a challenging task. While the measure we use in our analysis is admittedly not perfect, we improve upon most of the existing literature in two respects. First, we take into account the multidimensionality of infrastructure by using a variety of indicators on aggregate infrastructure provision. Much of the empirical literature on the output and/or growth effects of infrastructure has focused on a single infrastructure sector (e.g., telephone lines), but in reality the term "physical infrastructure" refers to the combined availability of several individual ingredients – such as telecommunications, transport, energy, etc. Taken in isolation, none of these ingredients is likely to provide an adequate measure of the overall availability of infrastructure. However, attempting to capture the multidimensionality of infrastructure by introducing a multitude of infrastructure indicators as inputs in our production functions could lead to imprecise and unreliable parameter estimates. For this reason, we use a principal component analysis (PCA) to build a synthetic index summarizing the above-mentioned dimensions of infrastructure: telephone lines and mobile phones, internet, road transport and power.

Second, we use physical measures of infrastructure rather than monetary ones, such as the accumulation of public infrastructure investment spending into public infrastructure capital stocks. While such monetary measures may be adequate for the private sector's capital stock, they can be badly misleading for public capital, as an abundant literature has argued. The reason is that the link between public investment spending and public capital accumulation is mediated by the extent of inefficiency and corruption surrounding project selection and implementation and government procurement practices (e.g., Collier, Kirchberger, & Söderbom, 2016; Keefer & Knack, 2007; Pritchett, 2000). These features can vary greatly across countries and over time (IMF, 2022), effectively making cumulative public infrastructure investment an error-ridden proxy for the trends in the public infrastructure capital stock, whose use in empirical estimations is likely to lead to inconsistent estimates of the output contribution of infrastructure. In contrast, the physical measures of infrastructure availability we employ (such as km of roads or the number of telephone lines) are not subject to these limitations.

As aforementioned, we use PCA to capture the many aspects of public infrastructure. A similar approach is employed by Calderón, Moral-Benito, and Servén (2015) and Sánchez-Robles (1998) to assess the output contribution of infrastructure. Our synthetic infrastructure indicator is given by the first principal component of four individual infrastructure variables: telecommunications network (PHONES), information network (INTERNET), road transport (ROADS) and power capacity (POWER). The principal component is the linear combination of the infrastructure variables in the dataset that explains the most variance.[17]

In order to facilitate the interpretation of our infrastructure composite, we first express all infrastructure variables in logs, and then we apply PCA to the logged series.[18] That is, we use $\ln Z$ to simply indicate that our synthetic infrastructure indicator is a weighted average of logged variables. In other words, $\ln Z$ is not the logarithm of a sum of individual infrastructure variables. The weights have also been rescaled to add up to one in order to impose the traditional proportionality property of the index numbers. That is, an increase by a given percentage in all four infrastructure variables raises the synthetic infrastructure indicator by the same percentage. This is an appealing property because it allows interpreting an increase of $\ln Z$ as an increase of all individual infrastructure variables when they all increase in the same proportion. Moreover, as it is mandatory in PCA to standardize the data before proceeding with the decomposition of its covariance matrix, all logged individual variables have a zero mean once they have been standardized, and hence our infrastructure indicator ($\ln Z$) is also a mean-centered variable. In addition, as in Calderón et al. (2015), all four variables enter our infrastructure index with approximately similar weights:

$$\begin{aligned} \ln Z = {} & 0.26 \ln PHONES + 0.26 \ln INTERNET + 0.23 \ln ROADS \\ & + 0.25 \ln POWER \end{aligned} \tag{20}$$

We also compute a PCA composite (Q) of four indicators of institutional quality provided by the World Bank, namely corruption (CORRUP), government effectiveness (GOVEF), quality of regulation (REG) and rule of law (LAW). This synthetic index is interacted with Z in order to allow the production effect of public investment in infrastructure to depend on the quality of institutions (see, e.g., Crescenzi, Di Cataldo, & Rodriguez-Pose, 2016; Esfahani & Ramírez, 2003).

We do not express these institutional variables in logs because they have been constructed as indices that might have both positive and negative values. Therefore, in this case, we label our institutional synthetic indicator without logs (i.e., as Q), indicating that it is a weighted average of several (again standardized) variables. In addition, like in our infrastructure composite, all four institutional variables enter our institutional index with approximately similar weights:

$$Q = 0.243 \cdot CORRUP + 0.242 \cdot GOVEF + 0.260 \cdot REG + 0.257 \cdot LAW \tag{21}$$

Computing aggregate TFP (M) requires computing the aggregate real input, X, which in turn requires computing first industry-specific real input, X_n. Diewert (2015, p. 372) states that the exact functional form for X_n does not matter for his analysis. He only assumes that $W_n X_n$ equals industry n's input cost. In his application to Australian sector data, he computes X_n using the Fisher index number formula, which is a superlative index (Diewert, 1976). We in turn propose using a Törnqvist index, the discrete counterpart of a Divisia index. As both indices are superlative indices, their results using annual data tend to converge. Using the Divisia index, the rate of growth of our aggregate input variable can be written as a weighted average of $\dot{L}_n$ and $\dot{K}_n$. In his Australian application, Diewert computed each input weight using the *observed* industry shares for both labor and capital. This is not possible in our multi-country application because we do not have such information at the industry level. To address this issue, we propose using the estimated elasticities of our industry production functions (see next section) to compute the above weights. That is, we replace *observed* weights with *estimated* weights.[19] Once we have computed $X_n = L_n^{\beta_{Ln}/\beta_n} \cdot K_n^{\beta_{Kn}/\beta_n}$ for each industry using estimated weights, labor volumes, and real capital stocks, they should be aggregated in order to compute the aggregate real input, X. We compute X simply by aggregating the industry-level real inputs (i.e., $X = \sum_{n=1}^{N} X_n$).

The corresponding input price variables are computed using the same assumption as in Diewert (2015, p. 374), i.e., that value added equals input cost for each industry,[20] so that with our industry nominal value-added volumes ($P_n Y_n$) and our estimates of aggregate input quantities by industry (X_n) we can obtain estimates of $W_n = P_n Y_n / X_n$ by industry. These implicit price indexes for each industry input were normalized to equal 1 in 2005. Finally, we compute W as a weighted average of the individual industry input price indexes, where the weights are the real input cost shares of each industry in total input, that is: $W = \sum_{n=1}^{N} W_n X_n / X$.

We also compute industry output and input shares using the above output and input volumes. While the *nominal* input share s_{Xn} of industry n is computed using equation (3), the *real* input share S_{Xn} is computed as X_n / X. The *nominal* and *real* output shares of industry n are computed equally. That is, while the *nominal* output share s_{Yn} is computed using equation (5), the *real* output share S_{Yn} is computed as Y_n / Y. The variation over time of these four industry shares provides useful information about the output and input-oriented structural changes taking place in the economy.

Fig. 10.1 depicts the average temporal evolution of these industry output and input shares for the whole set of countries of our empirical application. Two comments are in order regarding this figure. First, it shows that, on average, the structure of the sample economies has changed markedly over the 1995–2009 period. For instance, both output and input shares in agriculture and manufacturing have declined over time. The production factors (in particular, labor) released by the agricultural sector as part of the well-known rural-to-urban migrations occurred in many countries have been absorbed mostly by services and the construction sector. Second, Fig. 10.1 also shows that, while *nominal* and *real* industry shares are similar, the *output* and *input* industry shares differ notably in many cases. Therefore, we expect larger values for *IPRE* (which heavily depends on differences between the relative size of the industries in output and input terms) than for *OPE* (which mainly depends on the difference between nominal and real output shares).

Table 10.1 summarizes the descriptive statistics of the variables used in the empirical application. It also includes the annual rates of growth (or annual changes) of the key variables used to compute our TFP measures. Notice that, by construction, the rate of growth of the aggregate real input (3.19%) is a weighted average of the rate of growth of labor (1.85%) and the rate of growth of total capital (6.10%). As the increase in aggregate real output (3.78%) exceeded the increase in aggregate input (3.19%), aggregate TFP rose (0.58%) over the sample period. The growth in aggregate labor productivity was much larger (1.93%) due to the moderate expansion of the labor input, and the large accumulation of capital occurred in this period.[21] It is finally worth mentioning that our synthetic infrastructure index also exhibits a non-negligible increase during the sample

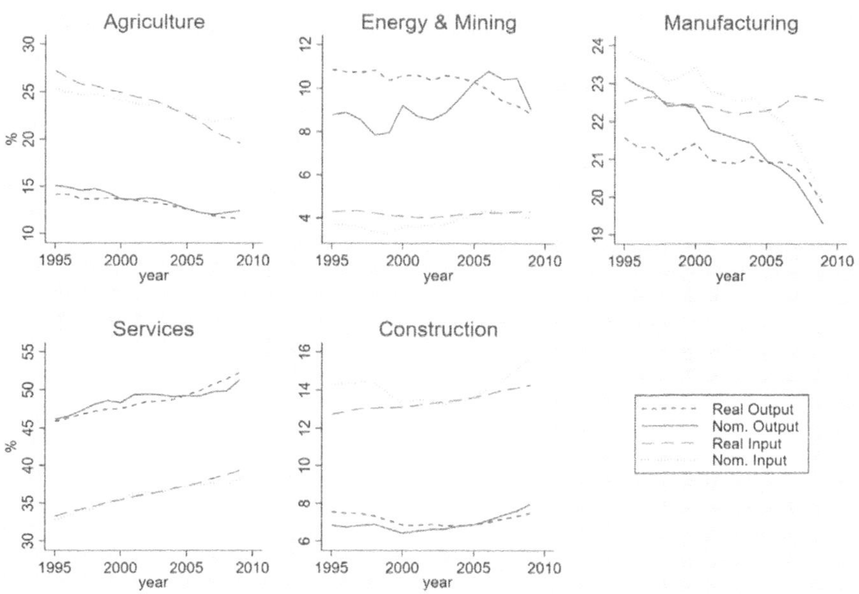

Fig. 10.1. Output and Input Shares.

Table 10.1. Descriptive Statistics.

Industry-Level Variables						Country-Level Variables					
Variable	Obs	Mean	Std. Dev.	Min	Max	Variable	Obs	Mean	Std. Dev.	Min	Max
Real gross value added (thousand million US$)[a]						*Labor and capital*					
Agriculture	585	56.41	195.15	0.05	1304.99	Private capital (thousand million US$)[a]	585	1.26	3.05	0.00	20.40
Energy	585	52.20	137.98	0.04	1464.58	Labor (Million jobs)	585	46.82	123.81	0.39	715.04
Manufacturing	585	146.63	295.90	0.18	1680.13	*Technological indicators and infrastructures*					
Services	585	413.93	1169.62	0.70	8019.36	Fixed and mobile phones (% of population)	585	60.06	54.78	0.25	241.64
Construction	585	57.64	131.51	0.07	843.52	Electricity access (% of population)	585	66.35	161.12	0.13	1000.00
Real output prices (ratio)						Internet users (% of population)	585	18.36	24.30	0.00	91.00
Agriculture	585	1.10	0.21	0.49	2.11	Roads (thousand Kms)	585	518.60	1180.58	1.72	6500.00
Energy	585	0.96	0.23	0.35	2.13	*Annual rates of growth (%)*					
Manufacturing	585	1.03	0.11	0.73	1.84	Real gross value added	546	3.78	4.02	−16.13	14.36
Services	585	1.01	0.08	0.82	1.58	Labor	546	1.85	2.17	−10.28	9.15
Construction	585	0.99	0.21	0.37	2.44	Private capital	546	6.10	8.81	−43.20	70.03
Labor (Million jobs)						Total input[b]	546	3.19	3.10	−10.12	19.00
Agriculture	585	20.44	65.60	0.01	366.40	TFP[a]	546	0.58	4.08	−17.35	12.84
Energy	585	0.64	2.14	0.00	15.73	Labor productivity	546	1.93	3.52	−16.61	13.09
Manufacturing	585	7.01	19.73	0.03	144.63	*Annual changes of synthetic indexes*					
Services	585	15.69	31.99	0.11	215.33	Infrastructure[c]	546	0.195	0.29	−0.01	3.16
Construction	585	3.04	7.89	0.02	52.41	Quality of institutions[d]	546	−0.001	0.08	−0.60	0.30

Notes: [a]The monetary variables have been expressed in US dollars for the unique purpose of issuing this table.
[b]This variable has been computed using the estimated elasticities for capital and labor of our industry production models.
[c]This index has been computed using a PCA based on the logged total value of the above technological and infrastructure variables.
[d]This index has been computed using a PCA based on four variables measuring the quality of institutions provided by the World Bank (control of corruption: government effectiveness, regulatory quality, and rule of law).

period. Therefore, it might have contributed substantially to the above increase in both aggregate TFP and labor productivity. This is one of the issues we examine in the next section. We also try to examine whether infrastructure provision has had an uneven effect across industries, and whether infrastructure development has enhanced (or weakened) aggregate productivity through a more (less) efficient allocation of resources across industries and firms.

5. RESULTS

5.1. Parameter Estimates

The proposed productivity decompositions rely on the estimation of a heteroscedastic SF production model for five industries: Agriculture, Energy & Mining, Manufacturing, Construction and Services. We have assumed that the inefficiency term u_{nt} in equation (7) is distributed as a heteroscedastic half-normal random variable, i.e., as $N^{+}\left(0,\sigma_u^2\right)$ where $ln\sigma_u$ is a linear function of a set of covariates that might affect the allocation of resources within the industry. On the other hand, the noise term v_{nt} is assumed to be distributed as a homoscedastic normal random variable, i.e., as $N^{+}\left(0,\sigma_v^2\right)$.

The five SF production models extend the specification provided by equation (7). First, all the models are estimated using a set of country-specific dummy variables to control for unobserved country heterogeneity. In this sense, our model can be viewed as a heteroscedastic version of the True Fixed Effect (TFE) SF model introduced by Greene (2005). Second, for the estimation the simple time trend in (7) is replaced by a set of time dummies in order to capture better common technological shocks that reflect shifts of the global technological frontier over time.[22]

Third, in keeping with the majority of earlier literature, constant returns to scale have been imposed. That is, we impose the restriction $\beta_{Kn}+\beta_{Ln}=1$ when we estimate our models by maximum likelihood. We decided to estimate our models imposing the constant returns to scale assumption not only because it allows using the capital/labor ratio as explanatory variable, thus reducing its collinearity with the infrastructure variable, our target production driver, but also because most national bureaus of statistics make the industry primary input costs equal to the corresponding industry revenues and the satisfaction of this equality only happens when the production process is characterized by constant returns to scale.[23]

Fourth, in the empirical implementation equation (7) is augmented adding the synthetic index of infrastructure provision (ln$Z$) times the institutional quality index (Q), to allow the production effect of public infrastructure to depend on the quality of institutions. Moreover, as equation (9) indicates, infrastructure provision not only has a *direct* or frontier effect on industry output, but also an *indirect* effect through the efficiency term. For this reason, σ_u depends on Z.

Fifth, as mentioned above, $\ln K_n$ in equation (7) is replaced with $d_n S_{Ln}+\ln K$ because we do not have industry data on capital ($\ln K_n$). This implies that our SF production models are estimated using aggregate private capital ($\ln K$) plus the industry share of labor (S_{Ln}). Moreover, lacking estimates of capital utilization by industry, we opt for using the labor-to-capital ratio of neighboring countries as a proxy of capacity utilization.[24] As labor is a variable input while capital is a quasi-fixed input, the ratio varies with the cycle of the economy. The implicit assumption here is that the cycles of neighboring economies are correlated.

Sixth, as noted by Kumbhakar and Tsionas (2011), Kumbhakar, Asche, and Tveteras (2013) and Tsionas, Kumbhakar, and Malikov (2015), endogeneity problems can arise in our SF models if firms' economic behavior affects both private capital and labor inputs. Some authors (e.g., Feng & Wu, 2018) similarly argue that public capital is likely to be an endogenous variable due to the likely reverse causality between output and infrastructure. For this reason, we treat labor, private capital, and our infrastructure indicator as endogenous variables. We deal with this issue using the two-step procedure proposed by Amsler, Prokhorov, and Schmidt (2016). They suggest estimating first a set of reduced form equations for the endogenous variables using exogenous frontier variables and a set of external instruments, and then using the reduced form residuals in the estimation of a standard SF model by maximum likelihood.[25]

We use spatial lags of the endogenous variables (and their squared values) as external instruments because they are likely good instruments in our application.[26] On the one hand, they are likely strong instruments because private and public inputs tend to follow similar time patterns across countries within the same World region (block), owing to the effect of common regional shocks, and they tend to display similar trends over time. On the other hand, they are likely valid instruments for two reasons. First, conditional on a country's own production factors, we do not expect foreign countries' infrastructure (and labor and private capital) to have a significant impact on domestic production, as most countries in our sample are poorly interconnected even within their own regions (except perhaps the European countries). Second, there is a large literature on spatial econometrics that suggests that the spatial effects attributable to infrastructure are more important at municipal or provincial level, compared to the national scale.[27]

Although researchers in political science and economics have often built spatial instruments from realizations of the endogenous variable in neighboring units (see, e.g., Acemoglu, Johnson, Robinson, & Yared, 2008; Boix, 2011; Büthe & Milner, 2008; Stasavage, 2005) to address endogeneity issues, Betz, Cook, and Hollenbach (2020) point out that this empirical strategy is problematic if there is unmodelled spatial interdependence in the outcome (dependent) variable. We recognize that our results might be biased if one country's output strongly depends on foreign countries' output, but we believe that this is not a relevant issue in our application because the spatial interdependence problem is mostly a cross-sectional issue (see, e.g., Orea & Álvarez, 2019) and we are using a FE-type estimator that only uses the temporal variation of the data to estimate the frontier and inefficiency coefficients of the model.

The existence of infrastructure spillovers is not a primary concern in our chapter, but it is at the core of Han, Ryu, and Sickles (2016).[28] They do not use sectoral data, and thus they do not examine the effect of changes in the structure of the economy on countries' productivity, nor how infrastructure provision (public capital) has contributed to this structural effect. Han et al. (2016) instead employ a spatial autoregressive SF (SARF) model to account for potential spillover effects from public infrastructure. In this sense, the two papers offer a complementary view of the effect of infrastructure provision on countries' productivity.[29]

It is finally worth mentioning that estimating a production model for each industry using country-level data proved to be troublesome because many of the production drivers exhibited similar time patterns (due to the aggregate nature of the data), and we wanted to control for unobserved country-specific fixed effects that might be correlated with both capital and labor inputs, and other production factors, such as country's infrastructure provision.[30] In this sense, we recognize that our empirical strategy based on simple but traditional constant-returns-to scale production frontier model with relatively few regressors has been highly conditioned by the data. It should be pointed out, however, that most of our parameter estimates have the expected sign and our results are sound despite (or perhaps thanks to) the lack of sophistication of our production models.

The industry-specific parameter estimates are shown in Table 10.2. The means across industries of the industry-specific elasticities of capital and labor are 0.36 and 0.64, respectively. They are close to the elasticities typically used in growth accounting – a labor elasticity around two-thirds, and a capital elasticity around one-third.[31] Notice also that the labor share coefficient is negative and highly significant for Energy & Mining and Construction. This suggests that labor replaces capital in these two industries.

We also find positive and significant coefficients for the infrastructure index, especially when it is interacted with the index measuring the quality of institutions. Like Crescenzi et al. (2016), the implication is that the effects of infrastructure depend on government quality. Moreover, in many cases, the estimated coefficients differ substantially across industries, suggesting the existence of non-negligible structural effects attributable to infrastructure provision. In addition to shifting the production frontier, infrastructure expansion tends to reduce industry inefficiency in most industries. This particularly occurs at the beginning of our sample period in Agriculture and Construction, or at the end of the period in Manufacturing and Services. The result is consistent with the view advanced by Straub (2011) of public infrastructure as an efficiency-enhancing externality. It is also consistent with the hypothesis defended by Asturias et al. (2019) that transportation infrastructure increases competition between firms, and thus helps reduce resource misallocation through a less dispersed distribution of markups in the industry.

Notice, however, that we find large (and significant) coefficients on the time trend in the inefficiency term. While the coefficient is positive in Agriculture, Energy & Mining and Construction, it is negative in Manufacturing and Services. This implies that other (unknown) factors have significantly worsened the allocation of resources between firms operating in the former three industries, whereas they have improved the allocation of resources across manufacturing and services firms. These time patterns are fully or partially offset by the estimated time effects (not shown in Table 10.2). Indeed, we find that the global technological

Table 10.2. SF Production Functions. Parameter Estimates.

	Agriculture		Energy & Mining		Manufacturing		Services		Construction	
Variables	Coef.		Coef.		Coef.		Coef.		Coef.	
Frontier function										
Intercept	9.782	***	9.502	***	10.365	***	10.631	***	8.680	***
Capital (K)	0.111	**	0.398	***	0.453	***	0.387	***	0.439	***
Labor (L)	0.889	***	0.602	***	0.547	***	0.613	***	0.561	***
Infrastructure (Z)	0.003		0.341	***	−0.014		0.043		0.282	***
Z·Quality of Inst.	0.004		0.218	***	0.061	***	0.028	*	0.099	***
Capital function										
Labor share (S_L)	0.558		−8.171	***	−0.551		−0.017		−5.874	***
Noise term										
Intercept	−5.199	***	−12.09	***	−0.798	***	−0.893	***	−2.771	***
Inefficiency term										
Intercept	−5.199	***	−12.09	***	−0.798	***	−0.893	***	−2.771	***
Infrastructure (Z)	−0.503	***	1.523		0.110	**	0.044		−0.416	***
$Z{\cdot}t$	0.006		−0.110		−0.016	*	−0.024	*	0.027	***
Time trend (t)	0.242	***	0.733	***	−0.194	***	−0.244	***	0.092	***
Fixed effects	Yes		Yes		Yes		Yes		Yes	
Time effects	Yes		Yes		Yes		Yes		Yes	
CU proxy	Yes		Yes		Yes		Yes		Yes	
1st-Stage residuals	Yes		Yes		Yes		Yes		Yes	
Mean log-likelihood	0.9760		0.7018		1.0128		1.1653		0.7988	
Observations	585		585		585		585		585	

Notes: *(**)(***) stand for statistical significance at 10%(5%)(1%) respectively.

shocks penalized production in Energy & Mining, Manufacturing, Services, and Construction (but turned positive since 2003). However, we also find that the agriculture sector experienced exogenous productivity improvements.

While our productivity decompositions provide information on changes over time in industry productivity, the estimated fixed effects provide information on country-specific differences in productivity.[32] The average industry-specific fixed effects estimates are shown in Fig. 10.2 by regions. All of them measure productivity performance relative to the US. Three comments are in order. First, the productivity gaps between Europe and the US are not large, except in Energy & Mining and Construction, where we find higher productivity levels for Europe. Second, productivity performance in the energy and mining industry in developing countries outstrips those of Europe and the US, particularly in the cases of Africa and Latin America. This result can likely be explained by the abundance of natural resources in these countries. Finally, developing countries exhibit lower productivity levels in other industries when compared with Europe and the US, especially in Agriculture. As pointed out by Calderón et al. (2022), this result likely reflects a host of adverse factors, including technological gaps, geographic disadvantages, poor infrastructure, financial market imperfections, etc. that hamper their productivity levels. Our results also corroborate some of the stylized facts found in the literature (see, e.g., Adamopoulos & Restuccia, 2014) in the sense that the productivity gap between poor and rich countries tends to be bigger in agriculture than in non-agricultural activities.

There is ample empirical evidence that firm-level misallocation of resources is an important factor behind differences in measured TFP across rich and

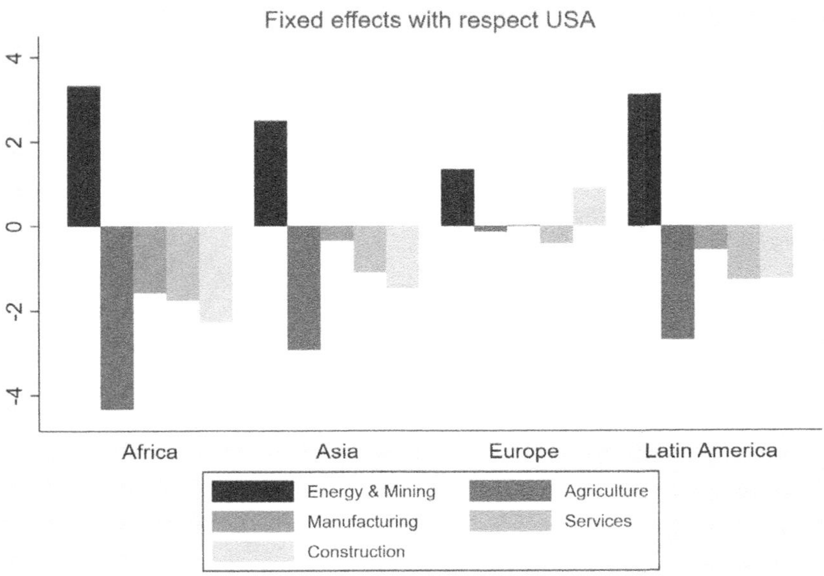

Fig. 10.2. Estimated Fixed Effects.

poor countries (e.g., Calderón et al., 2022; Hsieh & Klenow, 2009; Restuccia & Rogerson, 2008). Recall that we use the SF approach to measure the degree of misallocation across firms within the same industry because distortions in the optimal allocation of labor and capital across firms will lead to (conditional) industry production losses, and, in turn, larger industry technical inefficiency. The average production losses attributable to firm-level misallocation of resources are shown in Fig. 10.3 by industries and regions. Production losses due to misallocation are especially significant in Construction (12.3%), followed by Manufacturing (7.5%). However, it is worth highlighting that the agriculture and services sectors across African countries tend to exhibit a great degree of misallocation. Production losses are larger in Africa, especially in the agriculture sector (9.6%, compared with less than 4% in other regions). Similar results have been found in the literature. For instance, in their survey of the literature, Calderón et al. (2022) find evidence of severe misallocation in agriculture and manufacturing across sub-Saharan African countries. Like in our study, they also conclude that the dispersion of revenue productivity in these countries is larger than that of other developing countries (China and India) as well as the efficiency benchmark (US).

The decomposition of the productivity term capturing reallocation of resources across industries (i.e., what we have labeled the *IPRE* term) relies on the estimation for each industry of auxiliary regressions for both labor and capital. In Table 10.3, we show the estimated coefficients of the auxiliary regressions defined in equations (17) and (18). Notice that the fixed effects plus the two synthetic indexes of infrastructure and quality of institutions and the time polynomial

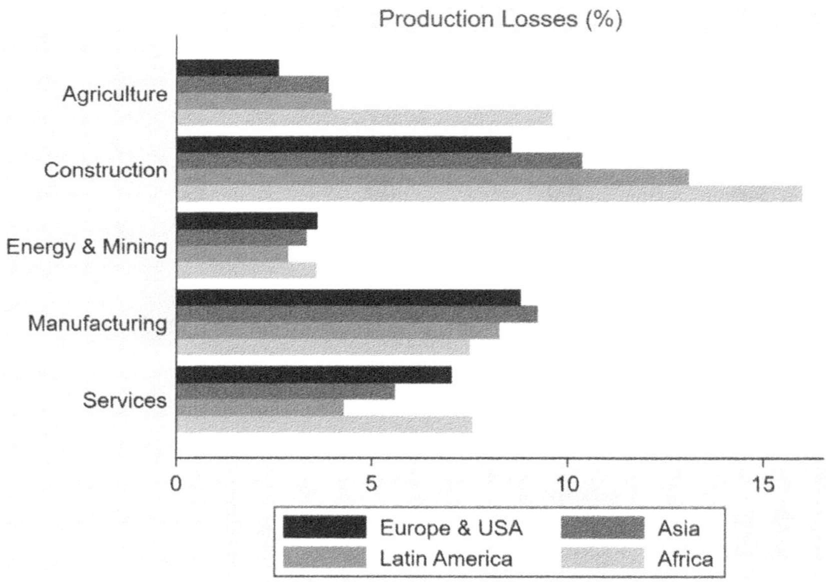

Fig. 10.3. Degree of Inter-Firm Misallocation of Resources.

Table 10.3. Labor and Capital Auxiliary Regressions. Parameter Estimates.

Labor	Agriculture			Energy & Mining			Manufacturing			Services			Construction		
	Coef.		*t*-ratio	Coef.		*t*-ratio	Coef.		*t*-ratio	Coef.		*t*-ratio	Coef.		*t*-ratio
Infrastructure (*Z*)	0.101	***	13.25	0.133	***	8.93	0.207	***	17.23	0.090	***	12.69	0.197	***	12.94
Quality of institutions (*Q*)	−0.126	***	−4.77	0.003		0.07	−0.129	***	−3.12	−0.038		−1.58	−0.102	*	−1.94
t	−0.049	***	−11.35	−0.081	***	−9.63	−0.067	***	−9.86	0.000		0.02	−0.046	***	−5.39
t^2	0.003	***	7.60	0.008	***	9.78	0.005	***	7.85	0.002	***	5.85	0.006	***	6.84
Fixed effects	Yes			Yes			Yes			Yes			Yes		
R-squared	0.999			0.991			0.995			0.998			0.992		

Capital	Agriculture			Energy & Mining			Manufacturing			Services			Construction		
	Coef.		*t*-ratio	Coef.		*t*-ratio	Coef.		*t*-ratio	Coef.		*t*-ratio	Coef.		*t*-ratio
Infrastructure (*Z*)	0.169	***	8.66	0.224	***	10.60	0.230	***	11.90	0.253	***	12.87	0.225	***	10.32
Quality of institutions (*Q*)	0.193	***	2.87	0.098		1.35	0.164	***	2.46	0.146	**	2.16	0.287	***	3.83
t	−0.079	***	−7.21	−0.062	***	−5.24	−0.080	***	−7.38	−0.091	***	−8.24	−0.080	***	−6.55
t^2	0.011	***	10.20	0.011	***	9.44	0.013	***	12.06	0.014	***	12.34	0.012	***	9.67
Fixed effects	Yes			Yes			Yes			Yes			Yes		
R-squared	0.987			0.993			0.994			0.994			0.990		

Notes: *(**)(***) stand for statistical significance at 10%(5%)(1%) respectively.

allow us to achieve an almost perfect fit. Infrastructure provision tends to increase both capital and labor usage, but the effect is slightly larger for capital than for labor. The effect of the quality of institutions on input usage is biased toward capital: while we find a positive effect on capital demand in most industries, we find a negative effect on labor demand.

5.2. First-Level Decomposition

In this subsection, we decompose the rates of growth of aggregate TFP using equation (6), i.e., our simplified version of the top-down TFP decomposition introduced by Diewert (2015). Recall that equation (6) provides a decomposition with no price effects that incorporates instead the traditional WE and two reallocation terms capturing transformations in the structure of the economy. Table 10.4 summarizes the descriptive statistics of the computed TFP growth rates and their components.[33]

Several comments are worth making. First, the aggregation of within-industry TFP growth rates (i.e., the WE term) is positive on average in Europe and the US (0.78%), but negative in other regions, especially in Latin America (−0.42%). We also find that the OPE is, on average, much smaller. As in Diewert (2015), the

Table 10.4. Diewert's TFP Growth Decomposition (%).

Asia	Mean	Std Dev	Minimum	Maximum
Aggregate TFP Growth (M)	0.66	4.09	−17.31	10.48
Within Effect (WE)	−0.10	4.23	−21.94	10.22
Output Price Effect (OPE)	−0.03	0.20	−0.84	0.84
Input Price Reallocation Effect (IPRE)	0.78	1.40	−3.22	6.69
Europe & US	Mean	Std Dev	Minimum	Maximum
Aggregate TFP Growth (M)	0.76	3.89	−11.32	12.84
Within Effect (WE)	0.78	3.93	−11.32	13.13
Output Price Effect (OPE)	−0.03	0.19	−0.80	0.62
Input Price Reallocation Effect (IPRE)	0.01	0.16	−0.33	0.60
Latin America	Mean	Std Dev	Minimum	Maximum
Aggregate TFP Growth (M)	−0.19	3.71	−11.90	10.21
Within Effect (WE)	−0.42	3.90	−10.85	10.07
Output Price Effect (OPE)	0.04	0.36	−1.02	1.67
Input Price Reallocation Effect (IPRE)	0.19	0.74	−1.60	4.43
Africa	Mean	Std Dev	Minimum	Maximum
Aggregate TFP Growth (M)	0.97	4.40	−14.76	11.60
Within Effect (WE)	−0.12	4.87	−19.27	17.28
Output Price Effect (OPE)	−0.04	0.82	−6.18	2.26
Input Price Reallocation Effect (IPRE)	1.12	2.00	−4.53	9.74
World	Mean	Std Dev	Minimum	Maximum
Aggregate TFP Growth (M)	0.58	4.08	−17.31	12.84
Within Effect (WE)	0.00	4.32	−21.94	17.28
Output Price Effect (OPE)	−0.01	0.50	−6.18	2.26
Input Price Reallocation Effect (IPRE)	0.59	1.43	−4.53	9.74

aggregate TFP contribution of changes in real output prices is practically zero (the world average is just-0.01%). As discussed before, this is an expected result because the nominal and real output shares are similar in our application (their correlation coefficient ranges between 90% and 99%).

Notice as well that while the small OPE term indicates that changes in industry output shares are of little help to explain changes in TFP, as expected, the large IPRE terms in some regions indicate that changes in labor and capital input shares do account for a remarkable proportion of aggregate TFP growth. Moreover, we find that the IPRE term is the most important TFP driver for the set of countries examined in this chapter. Indeed, the improved allocation of inputs across industries explains, on average, almost 100% of the TFP gains occurred in the world.

Table 10.4 decomposes a TFP growth measure that takes into account the growth of all inputs. If the input mix does not vary over time, both TFP and labor productivity growth should coincide. Labor productivity growth exceeds TFP growth if capital per worker increases over time.[34] While TFP grows by 0.58% annually in our empirical application, labor productivity grows by 1.93% annually. Therefore, the accumulation of capital accounts for most of the observed labor productivity growth, but the contribution of TFP growth is remarkable as well. Similar figures are found in Calderón et al. (2022), who conclude that the share due to TFP that explains labor productivity disparities is about 30%. They also find that the contribution of TFP growth has increased significantly over the past two decades. The larger TFP contribution could be attributed to an improving allocation of resources, in line with Hsieh and Klenow (2009).

5.3. Second-Level Decomposition

Next, we turn to the second level of our decomposition, where we try to measure the aggregate TFP changes that can be directly attributable to infrastructure provision and other productivity drivers. The average effects for each region, and for the whole set of countries, are shown in Table 10.5.

5.3.1. Decomposing the WE

We first decompose the WE using equation (13). As we have assumed constant returns to scale technologies, the size effect associated with an increase in the usage of inputs vanishes. The other productivity drivers are: global technological shocks, changes in infrastructure provision, changes in the quality of institutions and a residual comprising other effects not included above.

The contribution of each of these productivity drivers is shown in the first decomposition of the WE in Table 10.5. In all regions, the main factor raising within-industry TFP growth is infrastructure provision. Within-industry TFP rises on average 1.11% annually due to the expansion of both mature and technological infrastructure. Interestingly, the contribution is much larger in Africa as infrastructure provision raises TFP 1.47% per annum. These positive effects are partially offset by a deterioration in the quality of institutions. An appropriate infrastructure network that complements private capital and labor represents a

Table 10.5. Productivity Growth Decompositions by Region.

Decomposition Level	Asia	Europe & US	Latin America	Africa	World
First-Level					
TFP Growth (M)	*0.66*	*0.76*	*−0.19*	*0.97*	*0.58*
Within Effect (WE)	−0.10	0.78	−0.42	−0.12	0.00
Output Price Effect (OPE)	−0.03	−0.03	0.04	−0.04	−0.01
Input Price Reallocation Effect (IPRE)	0.78	0.01	0.19	1.12	0.59
Second-Level					
Within Effect (WE)	*−0.10*	*0.78*	*−0.42*	*−0.12*	*0.00*
Infrastructure	0.85	1.17	0.88	1.47	1.11
Quality of Institutions	0.03	−0.09	−0.02	−0.10	−0.05
Global Technological Shocks	−0.50	−0.63	−1.09	−1.06	−0.84
Other Factors	−0.47	0.32	−0.20	−0.42	−0.23
Within Effect (WE)	*−0.10*	*0.78*	*−0.42*	*−0.12*	*0.00*
Frontier Effects	−0.97	−0.89	−0.81	−0.78	−0.86
Non-frontier Effects	0.87	1.66	0.38	0.66	0.86
Output Price Effect (OPE)	*−0.03*	*−0.03*	*0.04*	*−0.04*	*−0.01*
Infrastructure	0.06	0.12	0.14	0.04	0.08
Quality of Institutions	0.00	0.00	0.00	0.01	0.00
Global Technological Shocks	−0.08	−0.18	−0.17	−0.05	−0.11
Other Factors	0.00	0.03	0.08	−0.03	0.01
Input Price Reallocation Effect (IPRE)	*0.78*	*0.01*	*0.19*	*1.12*	*0.59*
Infrastructure	0.20	−0.08	−0.06	0.36	0.13
Quality of Institutions	0.00	0.00	0.00	0.01	0.00
Other Factors	0.59	0.09	0.25	0.75	0.46

source of TFP growth (Kim & Loayza, 2019). However, as Calderón and Servén (2010, 2014) argue, it also requires an institutional framework that regulates efficiently the provision of infrastructure. In turn, as the large (negative) estimated contribution of the time effects in Table 10.5 exceeds the (positive) contribution of infrastructure, within-industry productivity changes are positive only in Europe and the US, and negative in the other regions, especially in Latin America.

It is worth mentioning that a portion of the measured within-industry productivity gains is due to reallocation of resources across firms, and therefore it does not reflect pure technological advancement. In this regard, the frontier WE can be computed and decomposed as in (12), but using frontier elasticities instead of total elasticities (e.g., using γ_n instead of θ_n). This amounts to measuring gains in industry productivity when there is no inter-firm misallocation (i.e., when $u_n = 0$) as in Asturias et al. (2019). The total WE not explained by the frontier WE is the non-frontier WE, which captures productivity gains attributable to the changing allocation of resources between firms within the industry.

Hence, the second decomposition of the WE term that appears in Table 10.5 decomposes the WE into frontier (pure) and non-frontier (misallocation) effects. Generally speaking, this second decomposition shows that the productivity growth attributable to reallocation effects within the industry is of similar magnitude to that of the productivity growth due to pure (frontier) technological improvements in the industry. However, one tends to counterbalance the other. Indeed, as we find negative technological shocks in most sectors, frontier TFP growth is negative in all regions.[35] This negative performance is partially or totally offset by improved within-industry allocation of resources. Recall that infrastructure expansion has had a catching-up effect in most industries. Thus, infrastructure provision has helped improve the allocation of resources between firms in the same fashion as in Asturias et al. (2019).

5.3.2. Decomposing the OPE

We next decompose the *OPE* using equation (15). Table 10.5 breaks down the *OPE* term into changes in infrastructure, global technological shocks and changes in other factors. This allows us to study to what extent each of these forces has contributed to improve (worsen) the output allocation across the different sectors of the economy.

Recall that Diewert's OPE can be interpreted as an output reallocation effect that depends on two factors: (i) changes in industry real output shares; and (ii) differences between real and nominal output shares. Regarding the first factor, we obtained quite different coefficients across sectors for our infrastructure index when estimating the industry production functions, suggesting non-negligible structural effects attributable to infrastructure provision, at least in some regions. In practice, however, these structural changes have little effect on aggregate TFP because real and nominal output shares are very similar in our application.

Indeed, aggregate TFP only decreases 0.01% annually on average due to the structural changes in industry production. Although the reallocation of value added across industries is not too large on average, the most relevant OPE drivers are the time effects, which we interpret as technological shocks, and infrastructure provision. The time effects generate a worsened allocation of value added across industries, whose TFP contribution is slightly negative (−0.11%). In turn, the infrastructure index does not have major output reallocation effects as aggregate TFP only increases on average 0.08% annually due to the improved allocation of value added across industries attributable to infrastructure development.

5.3.3. Decomposing the Input Price Reallocation Effect

Lastly, we decompose the so-called input price reallocation effect (*IPRE*) using the parameter estimates of our auxiliary regressions. Table 10.5 breaks the *OPE* term into changes in infrastructure, changes in the quality of institutions and changes in other factors. Given that we did not find significant output reallocation effects from infrastructure development, this decomposition allows us to study to what extent infrastructure provision has, in contrast, generated aggregate TFP improvements due to improved allocation of inputs between the different sectors of the economy.

We find much larger capital and labor reallocation effects than those found in terms of value added. Indeed, aggregate TFP rises 0.59% annually on average due to structural changes in industry input usage. The TFP gains associated to better allocation of inputs across industries are quite large in developing countries, especially those in Africa (1.12%) and Asia (0.78%). Our infrastructure indicator explains a remarkable portion (about one-fourth) of all the productivity growth attributable to sectoral input reallocation, which represents a 0.13% annual increase in aggregate TFP. While this contribution is almost negligible in Latin America (−0.06%) and Europe and the US (−0.08%), it is especially large in Africa (0.36%) and Asia (0.20%). The bottom line is that infrastructure provision has promoted aggregate TFP growth by both within- and between-industry productivity gains in these two regions. These findings highlight the importance of boosting infrastructure development in Africa and Asia. This agrees with the conclusion in Calderón et al. (2022) that adequate infrastructure can help overcome geographical disadvantages in those regions.

It should be finally mentioned that, due to lack of data, we have not been able to identify other relevant drivers that explain the remainder 0.46% annual increase in aggregate TFP associated to sectoral input reallocation effects. This is again an expected result given that employment and capital use are intrinsically complex phenomena that depend on many other factors, which in our auxiliary regressions are summarized by a simple time polynomial.

5.3.4. Discussion

This subsection draws implications of the analysis for the design of strategies aimed at promoting aggregate TFP improvements, especially in developing countries.

Fig. 10.4 summarizes the productivity growth decomposition of each country. It shows the relative importance of the two main productivity growth drivers, namely the within-industry effect (WE) and the input-oriented inter-industry reallocation effect (IPRE). The vertical and horizontal lines on the graphs show the average values for the respective regions, and thus allow us to organize the countries in each region into four quadrants. The countries located in the upper right quadrant have WE and IPRE terms above the region's averages, and hence they tend to exhibit the best TFP performance in their regions. This is the case of China, India and Hong Kong in Asia, the United Kingdom in Europe, along with the US, Peru in Latin America, and Tanzania in Africa.[36]

At the other end, countries located in the bottom left quadrant tend to be among the worst TFP performers in their respective region, with below-average WE and IPRE values. Moreover, some of these countries have simultaneously negative WE and IPRE terms, implying that their aggregate TFP fell over the

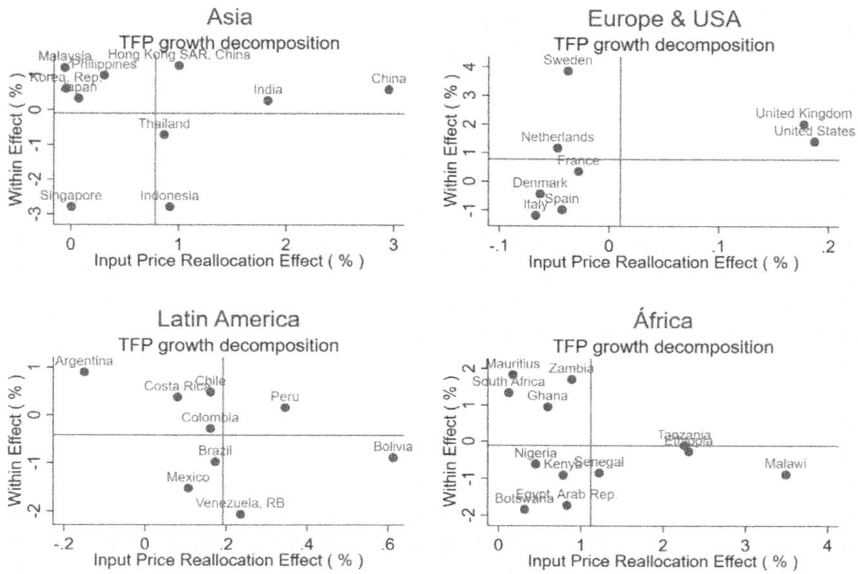

Fig. 10.4. Computed WE and IPRE Terms by Country.

sample period due to poor performance along both the WE and IPRE dimensions. Countries in the bottom left quadrant can improve their aggregate productivity by raising the TFP of some of their industries or by stimulating structural change in their economies favoring their high TFP industries.

The remaining countries, located in the bottom right and upper left quadrants, have exhibited performance above the regional average in only one of the two main productivity growth drivers. These countries therefore might improve their relative position by focusing their policy measures on the productivity driver with the poorest performance. That is, the countries located in the bottom right quadrant could try to enhance the WE productivity component by improving the TFP of some of their industries, while those located in the upper left quadrant should try instead to adopt measures that result in sectoral reallocation of capital and labor toward high TFP industries, thereby raising their aggregate TFP. Notice in this sense that most African, Latin American, and Asian countries located in these two quadrants exhibit large WE components but small IPRE components, indicating that there may be room for substantial TFP improvement, relative to the regional average, from implementing reforms that facilitate the transformation of their economies.

Two comments are in order about the aforementioned strategies to promote aggregate TFP improvements. First, adjustment costs to the mobility of labor and/or capital across firms (and sectors) could be partly responsible for the observed dispersion of marginal products, which would then be a natural part of the efficient (short-run) equilibrium rather than a symptom of misallocation (unless the adjustment costs are themselves the result of policy or other distortions). In this way, as the literature makes clear (see, e.g., Restuccia & Rogerson, 2017), ignoring adjustment costs could lead to overstating the extent of misallocation and, hence, the production gains to be achieved from the removal of distortions such as size-dependent policies and regulations, entry or exit barriers, etc., which likewise prevent equalization of marginal products even in the absence of adjustment costs. Still, the contribution of adjustment costs to the observed dispersion of marginal products appears to be quantitatively modest (e.g., David & Venkateswaran, 2019). Second, identifying the specific frictions at work and the policies to address them should be a priority for policy makers, especially in poor countries (such as those in Sub-Saharan Africa), where the literature has shown that the extent of misallocation is bigger and its welfare cost is correspondingly expected to be larger.

The next two figures help identify more specific strategies for promoting aggregate productivity growth associated to the within-industry productivity effect (WE) and the inter-industry reallocation effect (IPRE). Fig. 10.5 depicts the estimated sectoral fixed effects of our production models (equation 7) that explain most of the (persistent) differences in TFP across countries, along with the estimated degree of inter-firm misallocation of resources for each industry in terms of production losses. The estimated fixed effects capture differences not only in sectoral production conditions that are mostly out of the control of the country's economic authorities – such as the abundance of natural resources, climatic and geographic conditions – but also differences in other factors more amenable to policy action such as sectoral technology and the quality of the country's infrastructure and institutions. Fig. 10.5 thus allows us to identify two potential channels of productivity gains associated with the WE term: (i) improvements in actionable sectoral production conditions; (ii) improvements in the allocation of labor and capital among the firms operating in the same industry. The policy actions that the two channels would require are likely different. For instance, while improving sectoral technology might involve incentives to innovation activities or technology imports, enhancing the allocation of labor and capital likely demands enhancing the flexibility of labor and financial markets.

Each country might try to improve the TFP of their industries using either or both of the above-mentioned strategies. The choice should be dictated by the economic situation and the feasibility of the desired policy measures. Fig. 10.5 splits the sample countries into four groups, defined again using by the average value for their respective regions. As the initial economic situation of each group of countries is likely different, this figure thus shows areas in which there may be a chance for non-negligible sectoral productivity improvements. Countries located in the upper left quadrant exhibit above-average efficiency in the allocation of their sectoral inputs, and their sectoral production conditions (technologies) are also relatively favorable, suggesting no obvious choice of strategy to improve their TFP performance. In contrast, countries located in the bottom right quadrant exhibit relatively large production losses associated to suboptimal input across firms within the industry, and relatively poor production conditions, suggesting that either policy strategy could be helpful. Finally, countries located in the bottom

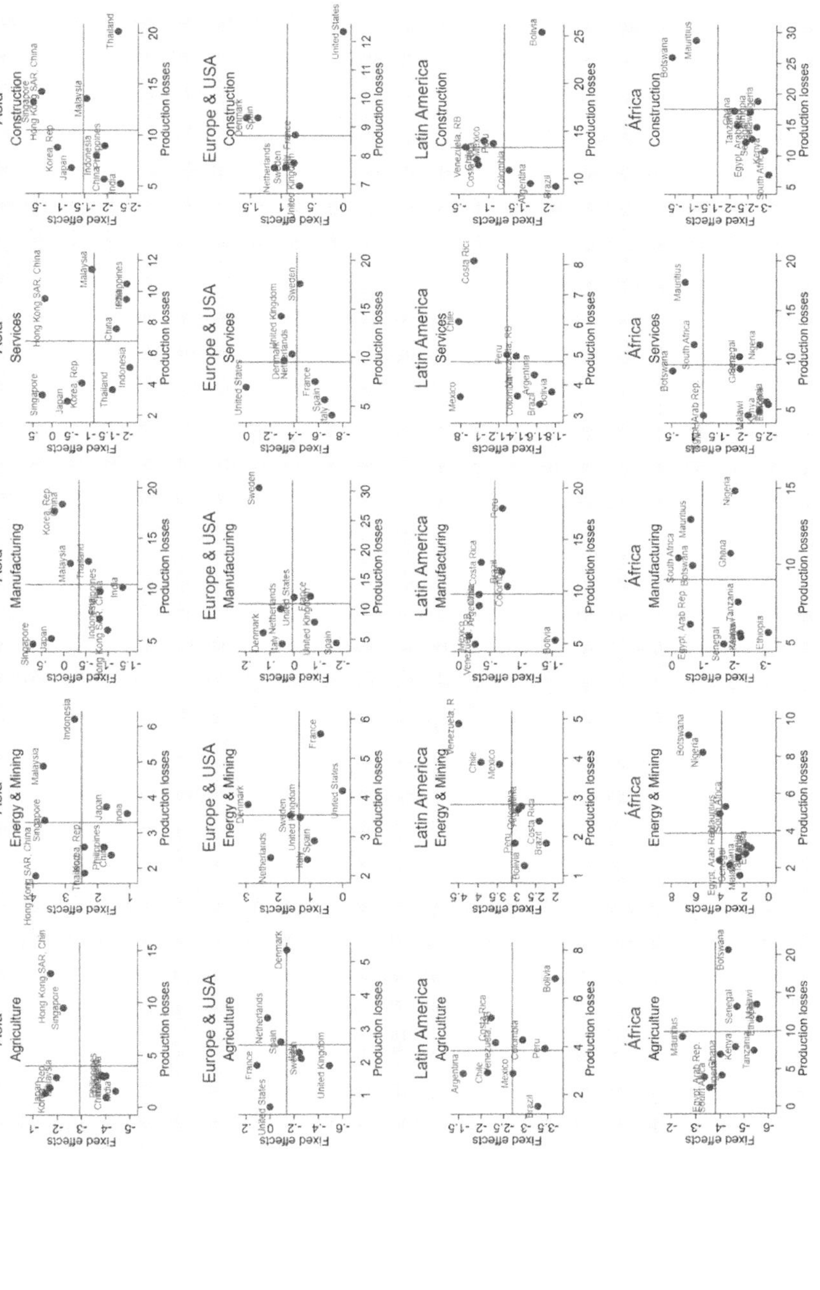

Fig. 10.5. Estimated Fixed Effects and Production Losses by Country.

right and upper left quadrants might want to give priority to the policy strategy targeting the dimension along which they underperform the regional average.

In summary, Fig. 10.5 shows that the country taxonomy is quite diverse, and hence the appropriate strategy to boost sectoral TFP should be tailored to each country's circumstances. For instance, in Fig. 10.4, we saw that Indonesia exhibits negative within-industry TFP growth during the sample period. Fig. 10.5 now suggests that Indonesia might try to remedy this situation by implementing reforms aiming to improve, say, its relatively poor production conditions in the services sector. Another interesting comparison is that between Botswana and Nigeria. Both countries exhibit a poor within-industry TFP contribution. Fig. 10.5 shows that Botswana has relatively large fixed effects (i.e., good production conditions) in most industries, and hence it might focus on policy measures aiming to reduce the relatively large degree of inter-firm misallocation of resources found in Agriculture, Energy and Mining, and Construction, which translates into above-average production losses in these industries. However, Nigeria's production conditions are much poorer in Manufacturing, Services and Construction. In this case, the priority might be to implement policy measures aiming to improve production conditions in these three industries.

Another strategy to boost aggregate TFP is through structural change that improves the allocation of inputs across industries. Recall that the IPRE term in equation (6) shows that aggregate TFP rises when the input share of high-productivity sectors increases and the input share of low-productivity sectors declines. Taking advantage of this mechanism requires implementing economy-wide reforms that facilitate the shift of resources from low-productivity (usually traditional) sectors to high-productivity (usually modern) sectors. The output shares of the highest (lowest) productivity industries tend to be larger (smaller) than their input shares, and thus Fig. 10.6 depicts the differences between industry output and input shares for each country and industry in order to identify the high-productivity industries that should capture production resources from low-productivity industries. The figure also shows the input share of each industry. If high-productivity sectors use a relatively small proportion of the aggregate input, policy should aim to increase their weight in the economy.

As in previous figures, we divide the figure into four quadrants using the average values for the regions under consideration. Notice that in many of the industries (and regions) the two variables shown are negatively correlated. For example, this is the case of the traditional agricultural and construction sectors in developing countries. We observe that several developing countries employ a relatively large proportion of their inputs in these two sectors, even though their productivity is lower than in other countries.[37] One way to raise aggregate TFP then is to reduce the weight of these industries in the economy. Hence, policy makers in these countries should focus not only on raising the productivity of these sectors, but also on facilitating the transfer of labor and capital to higher productivity sectors of their economies, thus speeding up the process of structural transformation. Finally, it is worth noting that the two variables depicted in Fig. 10.6 are positively correlated in other industries (see, e.g., Energy and Mining) and regions (see, e.g., Europe and US). In these cases, the policy objective should be to increase the weight of these industries in the economy.

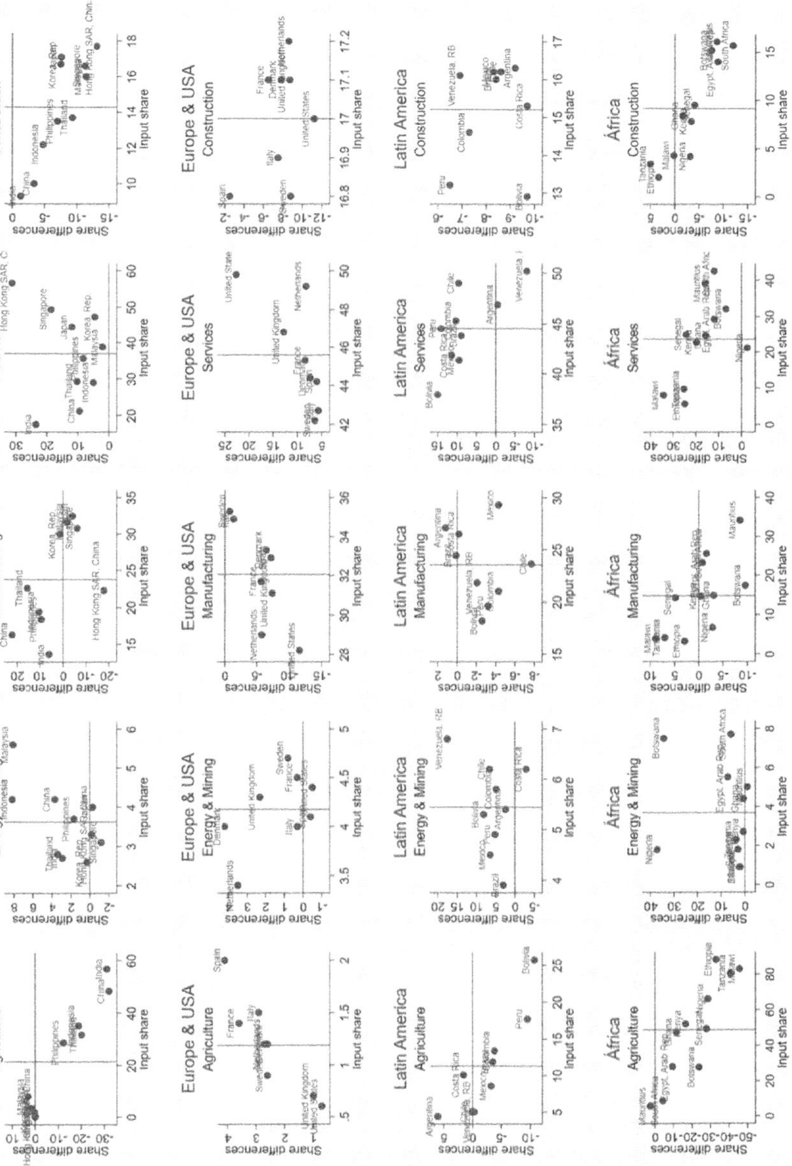

Fig. 10.6. Share Differences Versus Input Share by Country.

Previous figures suggest strategies for promoting aggregate productivity growth that may require implementing policy measures of different nature. However, this is not always the case. For instance, in our sample we have found that infrastructure provision stimulated aggregate TFP growth through both within- and between-industry productivity gains. That is, the expansion of mature and/or technological infrastructure helped raise aggregate TFP not only through improvements in sectoral technology (one of the strategies reviewed above), but also through an improved allocation of resources across both firms and industries (the other strategy reviewed above). Moreover, the TFP gains due to improved allocation of inputs were quite large in Africa and Asia, and the development of infrastructures contributed significantly to such gains.[38]

6. CONCLUSIONS

We provide novel insights about the relevance of infrastructure development as one of the policy tools exerting the greatest impact on both economic development and aggregate productivity. A distinctive feature of our empirical strategy is that it allows measurement of the resource reallocation across both firms and industries directly attributable to infrastructure provision, an effect often ignored in the literature measuring the effect of infrastructure provision on private production.

In order to achieve this objective, we propose a two-level decomposition of aggregate TFP that combines and extends several strands of the literature. The first level is a simplified version of the top-down TFP decomposition introduced by Diewert (2015) and evaluates the aggregate TFP attributable to both the aggregation of industry TFP growth rates and the reallocation of inputs from low-productivity sectors to high-productivity sectors. The second level of our decomposition analyses the impact of infrastructure on aggregate productivity by improving sectoral production technologies, allowing better within-industry allocation of capital and labor, and/or stimulating the structural transformation of the economy.

We illustrate our decompositions using industry-level data for a set of developed and developing countries over the 1995–2010 period. The first-level decomposition shows that the within-industry productivity effect was negative in most developing regions, but positive in the European Union and the US. The reallocation of inputs across industries improved overall productivity in all regions, and especially among African and Asian countries. Moreover, our results indicate that the simple aggregation of industry TFP growth rates does not portray accurately TFP performance in many developing countries.

A more detailed country-by-country analysis hints at the different strategies that different countries might try to implement to raise their TFP. In this regard, the contribution of infrastructure provision to productivity in Africa and other developing countries merits special attention. We find that expansion of mature and/or technological infrastructures did enhance aggregate TFP, as in Calderón and Servén (2010). Unlike previous literature measuring the effect of infrastructure provision on private production, we find that infrastructure provision not only helped improve within-firm productivity, but also helped improve the allocation of inputs across both firms and industries. Given the multiple positive productivity effects associated to infrastructure provision, and the key role of productivity growth in raising living standards, the implication is that infrastructure expansion and upgrading should remain a top policy priority for most developing countries.

NOTES

1. Basu et al. (2021) show that one can measure welfare using data on aggregate TFP and the capital stock per capita, provided that TFP is calculated using domestic absorption rather than GDP as the output concept. They, however, do not decompose their aggregate TFP measure into its sectoral components.
2. This top-down decomposition relies on a productivity measure that first aggregates all individual outputs and inputs and then computes the productivity of the aggregate. Petrin and Levinsohn (2012) pointed out that top-down productivity decompositions are conceptually more appealing than bottom-up decompositions that use a weighted 'mean' of individual productivities in order to get an aggregate productivity measure (see, e.g., Baily, Hulten, & Campbell, 1992; Foster et al., 2001). Indeed, Petrin and Levinsohn (2012) showed that in the latter case the computed aggregate productivity can be negatively correlated with the degree of efficiency in the allocation of resources in the economy.
3. Remarkable exceptions are Asturias et al. (2019) and Perez-Sebastian and Steinbuks (2017), who calibrate a general equilibrium model to investigate respectively the role of transportation infrastructure in explaining inter-firm resource misallocation in India (using a rich micro-level dataset), and the structural transformation of the economy attributed to public infrastructure in Brazil (using industry-level data).
4. A comprehensive summary of this literature can be found in Kumbhakar and Lovell (2000) and Parmeter and Kumbhakar (2014).
5. Hsieh and Klenow (2009) show that an increase in the dispersion of a factor's marginal revenue product across firms could reflect increasing barriers to the efficient allocation of resources and be associated with a TFP loss at the aggregate or industry level.
6. A comprehensive analysis of the connection between the bottom-up approach (aggregate productivity) and top-down approach (productivity of the aggregate) can be found in Balk (2016b). He shows that both approaches are equivalent if some restrictions are fulfilled.
7. However, as industry shares are computed using nominal magnitudes, our simplified version of Diewert's decomposition does involve prices indirectly.
8. Diewert (2015) also proposed a decomposition of an aggregate measure of labor productivity.
9. Hereafter we use lowercase "s" to denote *nominal* shares, and uppercase "S" to denote *real* shares.
10. Diewert (2016) provides the same decomposition of aggregate TFP growth in his equation (1.28), but he expresses it as a change in TFP from period 0 to 1. We write most equations using a continuous-time framework only for notational convenience. Obviously, empirical implementation of our TFP decomposition with annual data requires using a discrete-time approximation to all continuous-time definitions and decompositions, which is potentially subject to biases. However, as the rates of growth are computed in our application using a Bennet-type method, and the resulting TFP index can be viewed as a Törnqvist index, which in turn is a superlative index in the terminology coined by Diewert (1976), the approximation biases in our application are likely negligible.
11. Note that, by construction, all industry and aggregate output prices are equal to unity in the base year because they are indices. If the period examined includes (or is close

to) the base year, all output prices are not likely to differ too much in practice. This likely explains why the overall productivity contribution term due to changes in industry real output prices found in Diewert (2015) is practically zero.

12. Kumbhakar and Wang (2005) also include country-specific intercepts in their frontier-based growth model. That is, instead of assuming a single world frontier function for all the countries, they allow heterogeneity via country-specific intercepts in the frontier production function. Interestingly, they related the change in inefficiency to the literature on growth convergence as the dispersion of u_n tends to decrease when u_n decreases over time.

13. In our application we follow Kumbhakar (1990) and Battese and Coelli (1992) and include a time trend as an additional covariate of u_n in order to capture the effect of other factors on the efficiency of the allocation of resources across firms operating in the same industry.

14. Similar results are obtained if we use a time polynomial á la Cornwell, Schmidt, and Sickles (1990) with both country-specific and industry-specific parameters, which suggests that we are controlling quite well for other factors determining industry labor/capital demand (such as input prices).

15. The sign of d_n is not known a priori. If large (small) industries use not only more (less) labor but also more (less) capital, we expect a positive value for d_n. But if labor is used to replace capital, we should expect a negative value for d_n.

16. The effect of time-varying omitted variables is expected to be controlled in the estimation of our stochastic frontier models using the first-stage residuals of our set of reduced-form equations for the endogenous variables.

17. Interestingly, while this principal component is the linear combination of the (standardized) variables in the dataset that explains the most variance, the weight vector is a nonlinear transformation of these variables.

18. We used a within-transformation of the (logged) individual infrastructure indicators before implementing the principal component analysis because the production models will be estimated using a FE-type estimator that only uses the temporal variation of the data.

19. Equating elasticities and shares not only requires assuming constant returns to scale technologies, but also the existence of perfect competitive input markets and long-run equilibria.

20. Notice that this implies constant returns to scale for each industry under perfect competition.

21. The largest (smallest) increase in labor productivity growth (not shown in Table 10.1) is found in the agriculture (construction) sector. This result is mostly caused by labor mobility, from the agriculture sector to the construction sector. The services sector also saw an increase in employment, but its productivity performance outpaced that of the construction sector due to its faster output growth. Aggregating all industry outputs and labor quantities, we obtain an aggregate labor productivity growth rate of about 2%.

22. Notice that our set of time dummies will not capture accurately the trends in TFP that have occurred in all countries over the past decades if the common (global) technological shocks have impacted each country differently.

23. It should be recognized, however, that we might overestimate (underestimate) the effect of technical change or the changes in within-industry allocation of resources if underlying (dis)economies of scale are ignored, which in our TFP decomposition should appear in a separate size-related effect associated to changes in the usage of inputs (see equation (12) in Section 3.1).

24. Other countries in our sample that belong to the same region (Asia, Africa, Europe & US, or Latin America) are considered here as neighboring countries.

25. The fact that some variables may be endogenous has gained increasing attention in the SF literature. A summary of the most recent models addressing this issue in SF can be found in Orea and Zofío, (2019) and Kumbhakar, Parmeter, Zelenyuk, et al. (2021).

26. They have been constructed using a block diagonal W matrix, whose elements corresponding to countries in the same World region (block) are equal to one, and the elements corresponding to countries in different regions are zero. We use a block diagonal W matrix

because, as Han et al. (2016) point out, a contiguity matrix (relation) is not appropriate when considering a geographically incomplete dataset, which is our case.

27. For instance, Álvarez-Ayuso, Condeço-Melhorado, Gutierrez, and Zofío (2016) found in their empirical analysis of the effect of transport infrastructures in Spanish regions that the relative magnitude of the spillover effects increases with the level of territorial disaggregation, being larger for provincial than for regional data. Their findings are in line with some other previous studies (see, e.g., Cantos, Gumbau-Albert, & Maudos, 2005; Rodriguez-Pose, Psycharis, & Tselios, 2012) emphasizing that the existence of spillovers in public capital, mainly in infrastructures, predominate at the regional level.

28. We are grateful to an anonymous referee for bringing to our attention this interesting paper that also uses a SFA specification for the production function of each country.

29. Obviously, we can enrich our analysis if we develop a theoretical TFP decomposition and a SFA model aiming to account for the existence of spatial spillovers. To this end, we are currently working on a spatial autoregressive frontier (SARF) specification of the production model with sectoral input–output linkages introduced by Liu and Sickles (2021) and Liu and Cheng (2021) to simulate the compound economic effects of the COVID-19 pandemic outbreak. This model will not only account for the existence of spatial spillovers, but also for the existence of inter-sectoral spillovers and the effect of input–output linkages through international trade. Estimating a SARF model is challenging because it is not clear how to extend the stochastic frontier model with endogenous variables introduced by Amsler et al. (2016) to a setting with spatial correlation in the dependent variable. On the other hand, its implementation requires extending the two levels of our TFP decomposition, which is also not trivial because both own and foreign infrastructure will have an impact on each sectoral production and on the structure of the economy.

30. In early versions of the paper, we tried more flexible specifications of our sectoral stochastic production frontier models (using, e.g., a Translog form). We also tried to estimate our model without assuming constant returns to scale, and tried to examine the separate effect on sectoral production of several infrastructure variables, including transport, electricity distribution, telecommunication networks, etc. Unfortunately, many of the parameter estimates were not statistically significant because many of the variables are highly correlated over time. Other coefficients were difficult to interpret from an economic point of view because they had the wrong sign in some of the industries. For this reason, we decided to follow a more prudent approach and estimate simpler specifications of our models.

31. Notice that these proportions are roughly satisfied in all industries, except Agriculture. This means that the aggregate input X_n is computed using very similar weights in all sectors except Agriculture.

32. As we are assuming constant returns to scale, the fixed effects explain most of the (persistent) technological differences in TFP across countries. The main other (frontier) cross-sectional productivity driver is infrastructure provision.

33. In this chapter, we use a Bennet-type symmetric method to obtain the discrete-time counterparts of all continuous-time decompositions. For instance, following the method introduced by Bennet (1920), the discrete-time counterpart of equation (6) can be written as:

$$\ln\left(\frac{\mathrm{M}_t}{\mathrm{M}_{t-1}}\right) = \sum\nolimits_{n=1}^{N} \frac{s_{Ynt-1} + s_{Ynt}}{2} \ln\left(\frac{M_{nt}}{M_{nt-1}}\right) + \sum\nolimits_{n=1}^{N} \frac{s_{Ynt-1} + s_{Ynt}}{2} \ln\left(\frac{S_{Ynt}}{S_{Ynt-1}}\right)$$
$$+ \sum\nolimits_{n=1}^{N} \frac{s_{Ynt-1} + s_{Ynt}}{2} \ln\left(\frac{S_{Xnt}}{S_{Xnt-1}}\right)$$

Notice that we do not need to introduce in our first-level decomposition of TFP the conventional covariance (or second order) terms that appear, for instance, in Diewert (2015). The covariance-type terms disappear from the productivity decomposition because the Bennet method is symmetric (Balk et al., 2016a). Diewert (2015) proposed a simplified decomposition with only three terms as in (4) by assigning second and third order terms to corresponding first order terms in a symmetric, even-handed manner. He points out that this assignment scheme is similar to that applied by Bennet (1920).

34. Using equation (12), the changes in industry labor productivities can be decomposed as $\dot{X}_n = \dot{M}_n + (1-\beta_{Ln})(\dot{K}_n - \dot{L}_n)$. The second term measures the productivity effects of changes in the input mix. It vanishes if $\dot{K}_n = \dot{L}_n$.

35. A negative frontier effect might appear if the input elasticities are over-estimated due to our constant returns to scale assumption. We estimated our industry production models without this assumption in early versions of this paper, but we decided to impose this restriction because we got implausibly large or small returns to scale in some industries.

36. It should be pointed out, however, that being in the north-east quadrant does not guarantee top TFP performance because what matters is the sum of the two components, not that both be "high." While China is the Asian's TFP leader with a TFP growth rate of 3.52% and belongs to the upper right quadrant, the other regional leaders belong to other quadrants. This is the case of Sweden in Europe with a 3.59% increase in TFP, Chile in Latin America with a poorer TFP growth rate of 0.85%, and Malawi in Africa with a remarkable increase in TFP of 2.63%.

37. Developing countries, especially in Africa, exhibit very large shares of employment in agriculture, in contrast with the small agricultural employment share typically found in advanced economies; see, e.g., Calderón, et al. (2022).

38. This is consistent with the evidence that agricultural and manufacturing firms are often constrained by high transport cost (Diao & Yanoma, 2003), which can be attenuated by improvements in road quality. For instance, Asturias et al. (2019) and Perez-Sebastian and Steinbuks (2017) assess using rich micro-data sets the significance of transportation infrastructure in the reallocation of inputs to more productive activities in two developing countries (India and Brazil). In their models, the accumulation of infrastructure accelerates structural transformation through effects channeled by cross-sector differences in public capital intensity and entry costs. Overall, public capital formation explains about 15% of the Brazilian structural transformation process. On the other hand, Shiferaw, Söderbom, Siba, and Alemu (2015) point out that improving infrastructure provision can encourage the entry and increase the size of manufacturing firms and the mobility of factors across sectors.

REFERENCES

Acemoglu, D., Johnson, S., Robinson, J. A., & Yared, P. (2008). Income and democracy. *American Economic Review*, *98*(3), 808–842.

Adamopoulos, T., & Restuccia, D. (2014). The size distribution of farms and international productivity differences. *American Economic Review*, *104*(6), 1667–1697.

Álvarez-Ayuso, I., Condeço-Melhorado, A. M., Gutierrez, J., & Zofío, J. L. (2016). Integrating network analysis with the production function approach to study the spillover effects of transport infrastructure. *Regional Studies*, *50*(6), 996–1015.

Amsler, C., Prokhorov, A., & Schmidt, P. (2016). Endogeneity in stochastic frontier models. *Journal of Econometrics*, *150*(2), 280–288.

Asturias, J., García-Santana, M., & Ramos, R. (2019). Competition and the welfare gains from transportation infrastructure: Evidence from the Golden Quadrilateral of India. *Journal of the European Economic Association*, *17*(6), 1881–1940.

Baily, M. N., Hulten, C., & Campbell, D. (1992). Productivity dynamics in manufacturing plants. *Brookings Papers on Economic Activity: Microeconomics*, *2*, 187–249.

Balk, B. M. (2016a). The dynamics of productivity change: A review of the bottom-up approach. In W. H. Greene, L. Khalaf, R. C. Sickles, M. Veall, & M.-C. Voia (Eds.), *Productivity and efficiency analysis Proceedings in Business and Economics*. Switzerland: Springer International Publishing.

Balk, B. M. (2016b). *Aggregate productivity and productivity of the aggregate: Connecting the bottom-up and top-down approaches*. Paper prepared for the 34th IARIW General Conference Dresden, Germany, August 21-27, 2016.

Basu, S., Schiantarelli, F., Pascali, L., & Serven, L. (2021). Productivity and the welfare of nations. *Journal of the European Economic Association*, *20*(4), 1647–1682.

Battese, G. E., & Coelli, T. J. (1992). Frontier production functions, technical efficiency and panel data: With application to paddy farmers in India. *Journal of Productivity Analysis*, *3*, 153–169.

Bennet, T. L. (1920). The theory of measurement of changes in cost of living. *Journal of the Royal Statistical Society*, *83*(3), 455–462.

Betz, T., Cook, S. J., & Hollenbach, F. M. (2020). Spatial interdependence and instrumental variable models. *Political Science Research and Methods*, *8*(4), 646–661.

Boix, C. (2011). Democracy, development, and the international system. *American Political Science Review*, *105*(4), 809–828.

Büthe, T., & Milner, H. V. (2008). The politics of foreign direct investment into developing countries: Increasing FDI through international trade agreements? *American Journal of Political Science*, *52*(4),741–762.

Calderón, C. Aragón, F., Barrot, D., Cantú, C., Chen, Ch., Duarte, M., ..., Soderbom, M. (2022). *Boosting productivity in Sub-Saharan Africa*. Washington, DC: World Bank.

Calderón, C., Moral-Benito, E., & Servén, L. (2015). Is infrastructure capital productive? A dynamic heterogeneous approach. *Journal of Applied Econometrics*, *30*(2), 177–198.

Calderón, C., & Servén, L. (2010). Infrastructure and economic development in Sub-Saharan Africa. *Journal of African Economies, 19*(Suppl. 1), i13–i87.

Calderón, C., & Servén, L. (2014). *Infrastructure, growth, and inequality: An overview*. Policy Research Working Paper Series 7034, The World Bank.

Cantos, P., Gumbau-Albert, M., & Maudos, J. (2005). Transport infrastructures, spillover effects and regional growth: Evidence of the Spanish case. *Transport Reviews*, *25*, 25–50.

Collier, P., Kirchberger, M., & Söderbom, M. (2016). The cost of road infrastructure in low- and middle-income countries. *World Bank Economic Review*, *30*(3), 522–548.

Cornwell, C., Schmidt, P., & Sickles, R. C. (1990). Production frontiers with cross-sectional and time-series variation in efficiency levels. *Journal of Econometrics*, *46*, 185–200.

Crescenzi, R., Di Cataldo, M., & Rodriguez-Pose, A. (2016). Government quality and the economic returns of transport infrastructure investment in European regions. *Journal of Regional Science*, *56*(4), 555–582.

Crescenzi, R., & Rodríguez-Pose, A. (2012). Infrastructure and regional growth in the European Union. *Papers in Regional Science*, *91*(3), 487–513.

David, J. M., & Venkateswaran, V. (2019). The sources of capital misallocation. *American Economic Review*, *109*(7), 2531–2567.

Diao, X., & Yanoma, Y. (2003). *Exploring regional dynamics in Sub-Saharan African Agriculture*, No. 2. Washington, DC: International Food Policy Research Institute.

Diewert, W. E. (1976). Exact and superlative index numbers. *Journal of Econometrics*, *4*, 114–145.

Diewert, W. E. (2015). Decompositions of productivity growth into sectoral effects. *Journal of Productivity Analysis*, *43*(3), 367–387.

Diewert, W. E. (2016). Decompositions of productivity growth into sectoral effects: Some puzzles explained. In W. Greene, L. Kalaf, R. C. Sickles, M. Veall, & M.-C. Voia (Eds.), *Productivity and efficiency analysis* (Chapter 1, pp. 1–13) Switzerland: Springer International Publishing.

Esfahani, H. S., & Ramírez, M. T. (2003). Institutions, infrastructure, and economic growth. *Journal of Development Economics*, *70*, 443–477.

Färe, R., Grosskopft, S., & Margaritis, D. (2008). Efficiency and productivity: Malmquist and more. In H. Fried, K. Lovell, & S. Schmidt (Eds.), *The measurement of productive efficiency and productivity growth* (Chapter 5). Oxford University Press.

Feng, Q., & Wu, G. L. (2018). On the reverse causality between output and infrastructure: The case of China. *Economic Modelling*, *74*, 97–104.

Foster, L., Haltiwanger, J., & Krizan, C. J. (2001). Aggregate productivity growth: Lessons from microeconomic evidence. In C. R. Hulten, E. R. Dean, & M. J. Harper (Eds.), *New developments in productivity analysis*. Studies in Income and Wealth (Vol. 63). London: The University of Chicago Press.

Greene, W. (2005). Fixed and random effects in stochastic frontier models. *Journal of Productivity Analysis*, *23*(1), 7–32.

Han, J., Ryu, D., & Sickles, R. (2016). How to measure spillover effects of public capital stock: A spatial autoregressive stochastic frontier model. *Spatial Econometrics: Qualitative and Limited Dependent Variables* (Advances in Econometrics, Vol. 37, pp. 259–294). Bingley: Emerald Group Publishing Limited.

Hsieh, C.-T., & Klenow, P. J. (2009). Misallocation and manufacturing TFP in China and India. *The Quarterly Journal of Economics, 124*(4), 1403–1448.

International Monetary Fund. (2022). *Public investment management assessment*. Washington DC: International Monetary Fund.

Keefer, P., & Knack, S. (2007). Boondoggles, rent-seeking, and political checks and balances: Public investment under unaccountable governments. *Review of Economics and Statistics*, *89*, 566–572.

Kim, Y. E., & Loayza, N. V. (2019). *Productivity growth patterns and determinants across the world*. Policy Research Working Paper 8852, World Bank Group.

Kumbhakar, S. C. (1990). Production frontiers, panel data, and time-varying technical inefficiency. *Journal of Econometrics*, *46*(1–2), 201–211.

Kumbhakar, S. C., Asche, F., & Tveteras, R. (2013). Estimation and decomposition of inefficiency when producers maximize return to the outlay: An application to Norwegian fishing trawlers. *Journal of Productivity Analysis*, *40*(3), 307–321.

Kumbhakar, S. C., & Lovell, C. A. (2000). *Stochastic frontier analysis*. Cambridge: Cambridge University Press.

Kumbhakar, S. C., Parmeter, C. F., & Zelenyuk, V. (2021). Stochastic frontier analysis: Foundations and advances I. In S. C. Ray R. Chambers & S. Kumbhakar (Eds.), *Handbook of production economics*. Springer Nature Singapore Pte Ltd.

Kumbhakar, S. C., & Tsionas, E. G. (2011). Stochastic error specification in primal and dual production systems. *Journal of Applied Econometrics*, *26*, 270–297.

Kumbhakar, S. C., & Wang, H.-J. (2005). Estimation of growth convergence using a stochastic production frontier approach. *Economics Letters*, *88*(3), 300–305.

Liu, W., & Cheng, Q. (2021). Global production network, technology spillover, and shock transmission. *Applied Economics*, *53*(60), 7020–7036.

Liu, W., & Sickles, R. C. (2021). *Industry-specific productivity and spatial spillovers through input-output linkages*. Technical report, Rice University, mimeo.

Orea, L., & Álvarez, I. C. (2019). A new stochastic frontier model with cross-sectional effects in both noise and inefficiency terms. *Journal of Econometrics*, *213*(2), 556–577.

Orea, L., & Zofío, J. L. (2019). Common methodological choices in non-parametric and parametric analyses of firms' performance. In *The Palgrave handbook of economic performance analysis* (pp. 419–484). Cham: Palgrave Macmillan.

Parmeter, C. F., & Kumbhakar, S. C. (2014). Efficiency analysis: A primer on recent advances. *Foundations and Trends in Econometrics*, *7*(3–4), 191–385.

Pereira, A. M., & Andraz, J. M. (2013). On the economic effects of public infrastructure investment: A survey of the international evidence. *Journal of Economic Development*, *38*(4), 1–37.

Perez-Sebastian, F., & Steinbuks, J. (2017). *Public infrastructure and structural transformation*. Policy Research Working Paper N° 8285, World Bank Group.

Petrin, A., & Levinsohn, J. (2012). Measuring aggregate productivity growth using plant-level data. *RAND Journal of Economics*, *43*(4), 705–725.

Pritchett, L. (2000). The tyranny of concepts: CUDIE (cumulated, depreciated, investment effort) is not capital. *Journal of Economic Growth*, *5*, 361–384.

Qiang, C. Z.-W., & Rossotto, C. M. (2009). *Economic Impacts of Broadband, Information and Communications for Development 2009: Extending Reach and Increasing Impact* (pp. 35–50). Washington, DC.: World Bank.

Restuccia, D., & Rogerson, R. (2008). Policy distortions and aggregate productivity with heterogeneous establishments. *Review of Economic Dynamics*, *11*(4), 707–720.

Restuccia, D., & Rogerson, R. (2013). Misallocation and productivity. *Review of Economic Dynamics*, *16*(1), 1–10.

Restuccia, D., & Rogerson, R. (2017). The causes and costs of misallocation. *Journal of Economic Perspectives*, *31*(3), 151–174.

Rodriguez-Pose, A., Psycharis, J., & Tselios, V. (2012). Public investment and regional growth and convergence evidence from Greece. *Papers in Regional Science*, *91*, 543–568.

Sánchez-Robles, B. (1998). Infrastructure investment and growth: Some empirical evidence. *Contemporary Economic Policy*, *16*, 98–108.

Shiferaw, A., Söderbom, M., Siba, E., & Alemu, G. (2015). Road infrastructure and enterprise dynamics in Ethiopia. *Journal of Development Studies, 51*(11), 1541–1558.

Stasavage, D. (2005). Democracy and education spending in Africa. *American Journal of Political Science*, *49*(2), 343–358.

Straub, S. (2011). Infrastructure and development: A critical appraisal of the macro-level literature. *Journal of Development Studies*, *47*(05), 683–708.

ten Raa, T. (2005). *The economics of input-output analysis*. New York: Cambridge University Press.

Tsionas, E. G., Kumbhakar, S. C., & Malikov, E. (2015). Estimation of input distance functions: A system approach. *American Journal of Agricultural Economics*, *97*(5), 1478–1493.

Vivarelli, M. (2012). *Innovation, employment, and skills in advanced and developing countries: A survey of the literature*. Discussion Paper series, Forschungsinstitut zur Zukunft der Arbeit, No. 6291, Institute for the Study of Labor (IZA), Bonn.

Yang, H. (2000). A note on the causal relationship between energy and GDP in Taiwan. *Energy Economics*, *22*(3), 309–317.

APPENDIX 1

Diewert (2015) defines his output price effect (OPE) as a weighted average of industry real output prices:

$$OPE = \sum_{n=1}^{N} s_{Yn} \dot{p}_n \tag{A1.1}$$

Notice that the industry n real output price p_n is the industry output price P_n divided by the aggregate output price index P, which can be defined as:

$$P = \sum_{n=1}^{N} P_n \frac{Y_n}{Y} = \sum_{n=1}^{N} P_n S_{Yn} \tag{A1.2}$$

where $S_{Yn} = Y_n / Y$ is the *real* output share of industry n in total output. As the *nominal* output share s_{Yn} can be rewritten as $s_{Yn} = \frac{P_n}{P} S_{Yn}$, the change of aggregate output price is equal to:

$$\dot{P} = \sum_{n=1}^{n} s_{Yn} \dot{P}_n + \sum_{n=1}^{N} s_{Yn} \dot{S}_{Yn} \tag{A1.3}$$

Rearranging (A1.3), we get:

$$OPE = -\sum_{n=1}^{N} s_{Yn} \dot{S}_{Yn} \tag{A1.4}$$

Therefore, we find that Diewert's OPE is (the negative of) an *output reallocation effect* that measures changes in the structure of the economy using industry real output shares.

Notice, however, that the change in real industry output share is $\dot{S}_{Yn} = \dot{Y}_n - \sum_{s=1}^{N} S_{Ys} \dot{Y}_s$, where the second term is common to all industries. If we replace $\dot{S}_{Yn}$ with $\dot{Y}_n - \sum_{s=1}^{N} S_{Ys} \dot{Y}_s$ in (A1.4), we get:

$$OPE = \sum_{n=1}^{N} (S_{Yn} - s_{Yn}) \dot{Y}_n \tag{A1.5}$$

Therefore, equation (A1.5) finally indicates that the OPE term mainly depends on the difference between nominal and real output shares.

APPENDIX 2

Diewert (2015) defines his input price effect (IPE) as (the negative of) a weighted average of industry real input prices:

$$IPE = -\sum_{n=1}^{N} s_{Yn}\dot{w}_n \tag{A2.1}$$

Notice that the industry n real input price w_n is the industry input price W_n divided by the aggregate input price index W, which can be defined as:

$$W = \sum_{n=1}^{N} W_n \frac{X_n}{X} = \sum_{n=1}^{N} W_n S_{Xn} \tag{A2.2}$$

where $S_{Xn} = X_n / X$ is the *real* input cost share of industry n in total input. The *nominal* input price share s_{Xn} can be rewritten as $s_{Xn} = \frac{W_n}{W} S_{Xn}$. Taking into account that $\dot{W} = \sum_{n=1}^{N} s_{Xn}\dot{W}_n + \sum_{n=1}^{N} s_{Xn}\dot{S}_{Xn}$, we get:

$$IPE = \dot{W} - \sum_{n=1}^{N} s_{Yn}\dot{W}_n = \sum_{n=1}^{N} (s_{Xn} - s_{Yn})\dot{W}_n + \sum_{n=1}^{N} s_{Xn}\dot{S}_{Xn} \tag{A2.3}$$

The first term in (A2.3) indicates that Diewert's input price effect measures changes in (nominal) input prices if the structure of the economy in terms of output and inputs differ. The second term indicates that *IPE* also measures changes in the structure of the economy using (changes in) industry *real* input cost shares ($\dot{S}_{Xn}$), instead of industry *nominal* input cost shares ($\dot{s}_{Xn}$) as the *IRE* term does.

As both *IPE* and *IRE* terms are capturing input reallocation effects, it is interesting to examine their combined effects. In this sense, it is first worth highlighting that both *nominal* and *real* changes in industry input cost shares are mathematically linked, i.e., $\dot{s}_{Xn} = \dot{S}_{Xn} + \dot{W}_n - \dot{W}$. Using this equation, the *IRE* term is equivalent to:

$$IRE = \sum_{n=1}^{N} s_{Yn}\dot{s}_{Xn} = \sum_{n=1}^{N} s_{Yn}\dot{S}_{Xn} - IPE \tag{A2.4}$$

Therefore, equation (A2.4) indicates that the sum of *IPE* and *IRE* is equal to $\sum_{n=1}^{N} s_{Yn}\dot{S}_{Xn}$. That is, their combined effect is simply a weighted sum of changes in industry *real* input cost shares ($\dot{S}_{Xn}$) where the weight for each industry is its nominal output share (s_{Yn}). The change in real industry input cost share is $\dot{S}_{Xn} = \dot{X}_n - \sum_{s=1}^{N} S_{Xs}\dot{X}_s$. This equation indicates that the change in relative size of industry n depends on how different the change in $\dot{X}_n$ is with respect to the average change in the economy. As the second term is common to all industries, we get:

$$IPRE = IPE + IRE = \sum_{n=1}^{N} (s_{Yn} - S_{Xn})\dot{X}_n \tag{A2.5}$$

As the relative size of a particular industry in output and input terms might differ notably in practice, we expect larger values for *IPRE* than for *OPE*.

APPENDIX 3

Region	Countries
Africa	Botswana, Egypt, Ethiopia, Ghana, Kenya, Mauritius, Malawi, Nigeria, Senegal, Tanzania, South Africa, Zambia
Asia	China, China, Indonesia, India, Japan, Republic of Korea, Malaysia, Philippines, Singapore, Thailand
Europe and US	Denmark, Spain, France, United Kingdom, Italy, Netherlands, Sweden, US
Latin America	Argentina, Bolivia, Brazil, Chile, Colombia, Costa Rica, México, Perú, Venezuela

CHAPTER 11

IMPROVING PREDICTIONS OF TECHNICAL INEFFICIENCY

Christine Amsler[a], Robert James[b], Artem Prokhorov[b,c,d] and Peter Schmidt[a]

[a]*Department of Economics, Michigan State University, East Lansing, MI, USA*
[b]*University of Sydney Business School, Darlington, NSW, Australia*
[c]*Center for Econometrics and Business Analytics, St.Petersburg State University, St.Petersburg, Russia*
[d]*Centre interuniversitaire de recherche en économie quantitative, Montreal, Canada*

ABSTRACT

The traditional predictor of technical inefficiency proposed by Jondrow, Lovell, Materov, and Schmidt (1982) is a conditional expectation. This chapter explores whether, and by how much, the predictor can be improved by using auxiliary information in the conditioning set. It considers two types of stochastic frontier models. The first type is a panel data model where composed errors from past and future time periods contain information about contemporaneous technical inefficiency. The second type is when the stochastic frontier model is augmented by input ratio equations in which allocative inefficiency is correlated with technical inefficiency. Compared to the standard kernel-smoothing estimator, a newer estimator based on a local linear random forest helps mitigate the curse of dimensionality when the conditioning set is large. Besides numerous simulations, there is an illustrative empirical example.

Keywords: Stochastic frontier analysis; inefficiency scores; copulas; local random forest; nonparametrics; machine learning; synthetic data

JEL classification C14; C23; C53

Essays in Honor of Subal Kumbhakar
Advances in Econometrics, Volume 46, 309–328

ISSN: 0731-9053/doi:10.1108/S0731-905320240000046011

1. INTRODUCTION

The accurate prediction of technical inefficiency is one of the central goals of productivity and efficiency analysis. Estimates of technical inefficiency inform public policy and regulatory decisions that affect market competitiveness and economic growth. In this chapter, we investigate whether it is possible to obtain improved predictions of technical inefficiency in two settings, (i) when there is allocative inefficiency, and (ii) when there is temporal dependence in technical inefficiency.

The classic estimator of technical inefficiency proposed by Jondrow et al. (1982) is the conditional mean estimator $\hat{u}_i = E[u_i \mid \varepsilon_i]$, where u_i is the technical inefficiency and ε_i is the composed error term of firm i. The composed error contains both u_i and a statistical noise component. This estimator is often referred to as the JLMS estimator. Clearly, the JLMS estimator only uses information from ε_i, the (contemporaneous) composed error term. By now, it is well understood that in the settings mentioned above there are other sources of information. For example, technical inefficiency and allocative inefficiency may not be independent. In models with allocative inefficiency, this information can be used in the prediction of u_i. Amsler, Prokhorov, and Schmidt (2016, section 4.4) make this point.

Similarly, in panel settings, the composed error terms are likely to be correlated over time. For example, it is reasonable to expect that if a firm is relatively inefficient in one time period it will be inefficient in the other time periods so the values of future (and past) ε_i contain useful information about u_i. Amsler, Prokhorov, and Schmidt (2014) make this point and propose several estimators of the stochastic frontier model parameters that account for temporal dependence between composed errors.

The potential to improve the estimation accuracy comes from enlarging the conditioning set. Let ξ_i denote the additional information available to predict u_i. Then an improved estimator is $\tilde{u}_i = E[u_i \mid \varepsilon_i, \xi_i]$. To see why it is better than $\hat{u}$, recall the basic identity (for arbitrary u and z), $V(u) = V[E(u \mid z)] + E[V(u \mid z)]$. The first term on the right-hand size of this equation is the variation in u explained by z (which we want to be large) and the second term is the unexplained variation (which we want to be small). If we expand the conditioning set, we explain more variation in u. That is, $V[E(u_i \mid \varepsilon_i, \xi_i)] \geq V[E(u_i \mid \varepsilon_i)]$ and $E[V(u_i \mid \varepsilon_i, \xi_i)] \leq E[V(u_i \mid \varepsilon_i)]$, where equality holds in the unlikely case that u_i is independent of ξ_i conditional on ε_i, so that the additional information is redundant.

The discussion of the previous paragraph does not take into account parameter estimation, i.e., the fact that in practice both the form of the conditional expectation function and the values of the conditioning set will depend on estimated parameters. This will not have an effect asymptotically, because the parameter estimation error vanishes asymptotically while the intrinsic prediction error $V(u \mid \varepsilon)$ remains. However, in finite samples using estimated parameters will cause additional variance and may also cause bias. Accordingly, we evaluate the extent of the finite-sample improvement in prediction from additional information using simulations. We use two non-parametric estimators of conditional expectations to exploit the information contained in correlated error terms. Importantly, one of these non-parametric estimators uses regularization to control the variance of the estimates.

Our approach is designed to be used after estimating the stochastic frontier model using any of the applicable consistent estimators. That is, this chapter is *not* about improved estimation of the parameters of the stochastic frontier models, but rather about new ways of using available information in predicting technical inefficiency. Most of the models we consider require a copula function for both the estimation of the model parameters and for the prediction of technical inefficiency. The use of copulas in stochastic frontier analysis is relatively new but has been growing recently (see, e.g., Amsler, Prokhorov, & Schmidt, 2021; Mamonov, Parmeter, & Prokhorov, 2022). We describe the basics of copulas in Appendix 1.

First, we investigate a panel stochastic frontier model where the non-contemporaneous composed error terms are used as ξ_i. Second, we consider a copula-based cross-sectional model with allocative inefficiency which is derived from the first-order conditions for cost minimization. Here, the input-specific allocative inefficiencies are used as ξ_i. In both cases, the improved estimators are obtained using non-parametric alternatives to JLMS. Our key result is that even if the additional signal is only moderately strong, the technical inefficiency scores computed using the non-parametric estimators are substantially more accurate than those computed using the classic JLMS estimator, that is they leave much less variation unexplained.

Our approach is general and can be used with any stochastic frontier model where a joint distribution, such as a copula, is assumed for the dependent error terms. For example, our key results can be extended to models that specify the distribution of technical inefficiency as a function of exogenous variables, the so-called "determinants of inefficiency" (see, e.g., Kumbhakar, Ghosh, & McGuckin, 1991).

The application of non-parametric regression in stochastic frontier models has been studied previously (see, e.g., Kneip & Simar, 1996; Simar, Van Keilegom, & Zelenyuk, 2017). This literature has primarily focused upon estimation of the production frontier using non-parametric techniques. In contrast, we are interested in using non-parametric regression as a way to estimate the technical inefficiency scores that are allowed to depend upon additional error terms from the frontier. Moreover, we study a non-parametric regression estimator that is particularly useful in the presence of high dimensional data.

From the copula modeling perspective, our study contributes by exploring how to use estimated copulas to construct training data sets for multivariate non-parametric estimation and prediction. As such, our approach is also broadly related to literature that uses copulas to construct synthetic training data for statistical learning models (see, e.g., Meyer & Nagler, 2021; Meyer, Nagler, & Hogan, 2021).

The remainder of this chapter is structured as follows. In Section 2, we briefly described the models and estimators we consider. Details of the estimation methods are delegated to Appendices 2 and 3. In Section 3, we discuss the simulation results for the two types of models we consider. We demonstrate the applicability of the estimators using a classic dataset of US electricity-generating firms in Section 4. Finally, Section 5 concludes.

2. ESTIMATORS OF TECHNICAL INEFFICIENCY

2.1. The JLMS Estimator

Jondrow et al. (1982) [JLMS] proposed an analytical expression for the conditional mean $E(u_i \mid \varepsilon_i)$ derived under the distributional assumptions of Aigner, Lovell, and Schmidt (1977) who considered the model

$$y_i = \mathbf{x}_i^T \boldsymbol{\beta} + v_i - u_i = \mathbf{x}_i^T \boldsymbol{\beta} + \varepsilon_i, \tag{1}$$

where i indexes the firm (production unit), y_i denotes the (log) output, $\mathbf{x}_i$ denotes the (log) inputs, ε_i is the composed error, v_i is the symmetric random noise and u_i is the technical inefficiency, that is the amount by which output falls short of the production frontier. The key assumptions used by JLMS are that $u_i \sim N^+(0,\sigma_u^2)$, $v_i \sim N(0,\sigma_v^2)$ and u_i is independent of v_i.[1] Under these assumptions $u_i \mid \varepsilon_i$ is truncated normal with the conditional mean (the JLMS estimator of u_i) equal to

$$\hat{u}_i = E[u_i \mid \varepsilon_i] = \sigma_* \left[\frac{\phi(b_i)}{1-\Phi(b_i)} - b_i \right] \tag{2}$$

where $\sigma_*^2 = \dfrac{\sigma_u^2 \sigma_v^2}{\sigma^2}$, $b_i = \varepsilon_i \lambda / \sigma$, $\sigma^2 = \sigma_u^2 + \sigma_v^2$ and $\lambda = \sigma_u / \sigma_v$. The associated expression for the conditional variance $V[u_i \mid \varepsilon_i]$ is given by Bera and Sharma (1999). Similar expressions for the firm-specific technical inefficiency score have been derived under the assumption that u_i follows an exponential distribution, truncated normal distribution and a Gamma distribution (see, e.g., Kumbhakar & Lovell, 2003, pp. 82–89).

Estimates of the model parameters ($\boldsymbol{\beta}$, σ_u^2, σ_v^2) can be obtained using any conventional estimator (COLS, MLE, GMM, etc.). The estimates are then used to construct the residuals $\hat{\varepsilon}_i = y_i - \mathbf{x}_i^T \hat{\boldsymbol{\beta}}$ and to evaluate the conditional expectation in (2).

2.2. The APS14 Estimator

In a panel data setting, Amsler et al. (2014) [APS14] make the point that the past and future values of $\hat{\varepsilon}_i$ contain useful information about technical inefficiency. The stochastic frontier model they consider is

$$y_{it} = \mathbf{x}_{it}^T \boldsymbol{\beta} + v_{it} - u_{it} = \mathbf{x}_{it}^T \boldsymbol{\beta} + \varepsilon_{it}, \tag{3}$$

where $t = 1,\dots,T$ denotes time periods at which we observe the cross-section of the firms. APS14 propose to estimate technical inefficiency by conditioning on the entire composed error vector $\boldsymbol{\varepsilon}_i = (\varepsilon_{i1},\dots,\varepsilon_{iT})$, rather than the contemporaneous scalar ε_{it}. The improved estimator can be written as

$$\tilde{u}_{it} = E(u_{it} \mid \boldsymbol{\varepsilon}_i). \tag{4}$$

The idea is that, under temporal dependence, all of the values $\varepsilon_{i1}, \varepsilon_{i2}, \dots, \varepsilon_{iT}$ are informative about u_{it}. Using this additional information, we can potentially improve the precision of the predictor for each t and smooth the estimates over t.

In general, there is no analytical expression for the conditional expectation in (4) – the density $f(u_{it} \mid \varepsilon_i)$ is not known. However, APS14 point out that one can easily estimate this conditional expectation by drawing from the joint distribution of $(u_{i1},\ldots,u_{iT})$, once the panel data model in (3) is estimated. Assume as before that $u_{it} \sim N^+(0,\sigma_u^2)$, $v_{it} \sim N(0,\sigma_v^2)$ and $u_{it} \perp v_{it}$. Additionally, assume that the copula implied by the joint distribution of $(u_{i1},\ldots,u_{iT})$ is Gaussian with correlation matrix $\mathbf{\Gamma}$. Then, APS14 (Section 5) show how to construct the (simulated) likelihood and estimate the model parameters ($\boldsymbol{\beta}$, σ_u^2, σ_v^2 and $\mathbf{\Gamma}$). We provide details of this construction in Appendix 2. The Maximum Simulated Likelihood estimator (MSLE) is consistent in large samples (large in the cross-sectional dimension) under these distributional assumptions.

Once the estimates $\hat{\sigma}_u^2$, $\hat{\sigma}_v^2$ and $\widehat{\mathbf{\Gamma}}$ are available, it is easy to generate samples from the distribution of $(u_{i1},\ldots,u_{iT})$ and $(\varepsilon_{i1},\ldots,\varepsilon_{iT})$ jointly. Specifically, we first draw from the Gaussian copula with correlation matrix $\widehat{\mathbf{\Gamma}}$. This gives T uniforms. We then transform the uniforms into half-normals using the inverse of the half-normal cdf evaluated at $\hat{\sigma}_u^2$. This gives a draw of $(u_{i1},\ldots,u_{iT})$. Now we simulate T normals using the normal cdf evaluated at $\hat{\sigma}_v^2$. Finally, we obtain a vector $(\varepsilon_{i1},\ldots,\varepsilon_{iT})$, where each element is computed as $\varepsilon_{it} = v_{it} - u_{it}$. As a result, we can generate any number of draws of the vector $(u_{it},\boldsymbol{\varepsilon}_i)$ for any t.

Let S denote the number of such draws. As argued in APS14, we can now use any non-parametric estimator (e.g., kernel based) of the conditional expectation that will be consistent as $S \to \infty$.

2.3. The APS16 Estimator

A similar approach is used by Amsler et al. (2016) [APS16]. They consider the general case of endogenous input variables but we are interested in the special case where allocative inefficiency is correlated with technical inefficiency (see, e.g., Schmidt & Lovell, 1980). The stochastic frontier model with allocative inefficiency can be written as follows

$$y_i = \alpha + \sum_{j=1}^{J} \beta_j x_{ij} + v_i - u_i = \alpha + \sum_{j=1}^{J} \beta_j x_{ij} + \varepsilon_i \tag{5}$$

$$x_{i1} - x_{ij} = p_{ij} - p_{i1} + \ln\beta_1 - \ln\beta_j + \omega_{ij}, \quad j = 2,\ldots,J, \tag{6}$$

where, as before, $u_i \sim N^+(0,\sigma_u^2)$, $v_i \sim N(0,\sigma_v^2)$, and additionally, $\boldsymbol{\omega}_i = (\omega_{i2},\ldots,\omega_{iJ}) \sim \mathcal{N}(\mathbf{0},\Sigma)$ and the copula implied by the joint distribution of $(u_i, v_i, \boldsymbol{\omega}_i)$ is what Amsler et al. (2021) called a folded Gaussian copula. Here, in addition to the stochastic frontier equation (5), there is an equation for the input ratios (6), obtained from the cost minimization problem, where p_j is the natural log of the price of input j.

APS16 show (Section 4.5.2) how to obtain the MSLE estimator of the parameters of this model and describe an algorithm, similar to the one proposed by APS14, that can be used to obtain draws from the joint distribution of $(v_i, u_i, \boldsymbol{\omega}_i)$. See Appendix 3 for details of how to construct the likelihood function. By similar arguments, any non-parametric estimator of $E[u_i \mid \varepsilon_i, \boldsymbol{\omega}_i]$ based on a large number of these draws will be consistent and should permit more precise prediction of u_i when it is correlated with v_i and $\boldsymbol{\omega}_i$ than when it is uncorrelated with v_i and $\boldsymbol{\omega}_i$.

2.4. Nadaraya-Watson

For a baseline non-parametric technique to estimate the conditional expectations with expanded conditioning sets, we follow APS14 and use the Nadaraya-Watson (NW) estimator with a tensor product of univariate kernels. Let the additional variables in conditioning set be denoted by $\xi_{i1},\ldots,\xi_{id}$ and let $\mathbf{e}_i$ denote the entire p-dimensional conditioning set used to estimate u_i, i.e., $\mathbf{e}_i = (\varepsilon_i, \xi_{i1},\ldots,\xi_{id})$. Then, the improved predictor of u_i can be written as

$$\tilde{u}_i = E[u_i \mid \mathbf{e}_i]. \tag{7}$$

Assuming we have S draws from the joint distribution of $(u_s, \mathbf{e}_s)$, $s = 1,\ldots,S$, the NW estimator of the technical inefficiency score can be written as follows

$$\tilde{u}_i(\mathbf{e}_i) = \frac{\sum_{s=1}^{S} u_s \cdot K\left(\frac{\varepsilon_s - \varepsilon_i}{h_\varepsilon}\right) \cdot K\left(\frac{\xi_{s1} - \xi_{i1}}{h_{\xi_1}}\right) \cdot \ldots \cdot K\left(\frac{\xi_{s,d} - \xi_{i,d}}{h_{\xi_d}}\right)}{\sum_{s=1}^{S} K\left(\frac{\varepsilon_s - \varepsilon_i}{h_\varepsilon}\right) \cdot K\left(\frac{\xi_{s1} - \xi_{i1}}{h_{\xi_1}}\right) \cdot \ldots \cdot K\left(\frac{\xi_{s,d} - \xi_{i,d}}{h_{\xi_d}}\right)}, \tag{8}$$

where $K(\cdot)$ is a univariate kernel function and $h_{(\cdot)}$ denotes the variable-specific bandwidth parameter. We use a Gaussian kernel and with the rule-of-thumb bandwidth[2] $h_\xi = 1.06\hat{\sigma}_\xi S^{-1/5}$, where $\hat{\sigma}_\xi$ is the sample standard deviation of the variable ξ. This non-parametric regression estimator is well studied and computationally easy to implement.

However, being a tensor product kernel estimator, the NW estimator suffers from the curse of dimensionality. For example, in panel stochastic frontier models where we may wish to condition on composed error terms observed over many time periods, the performance of the NW estimator would be expected to degrade rapidly. Moreover, Gaussian kernel regression techniques are not suitable near the boundary, and more generally when local neighborhoods are asymmetric. Since regulators are likely to be particularly interested in firms with errors at the boundaries (either very large or very small), it is important that the technical inefficiency score is estimated accurately for these firms. Finally, since our estimation problem is multivariate, adaptive bandwidth kernel regression techniques are likely to be beneficial.

2.5. Local Linear Forests

In light of the issues associated with the benchmark NW estimator, we consider a recently proposed non-parametric regression technique known as the Local Linear Forest (LLF) (Friedberg, Tibshirani, Athey, and Wager, 2021). In essence, the LLF model uses the adaptive weights derived from a random forest (RF) model instead of a pre-defined kernel function in a local linear regression model that also includes a ℓ_2 regularization penalty. From the perspective of a traditional RF model, the LLF model offers an improvement in accuracy for smooth responses.[3] Since we are strictly dealing with continuous variables the LLF model is well suited to the prediction of technical inefficiency. From the point of view of a traditional local linear regression model, the LLF model can be viewed as one possible approach to extend the traditional model to settings with a large number of covariates.

RFs estimate the conditional expectation in (7) by averaging the predictions from a large number of B individual regression trees, denoted by T_b. Each individual regression tree is constructed based upon a random sub-sample of the training data and splits within the tree are constructed based upon a random sample of m different variables. This randomized construction process has the advantage of decorrelating the individual trees. Let $L_b(\mathbf{e}_i)$ denote the leaf node in tree T_b for point $\mathbf{e}_i$. The prediction from a RF is given by averaging the response over all training data points in $L_b(\mathbf{e}_i)$ for all trees, that is

$$\tilde{u}_i = \frac{1}{B}\sum_{b=1}^{B}\sum_{s=1}^{S} u_s \frac{\mathbb{1}(\mathrm{e}_s \in L_b(\mathbf{e}_i))}{|L_b(\mathbf{e}_i)|} \tag{9}$$

We refer readers to James, Witten, Hastie, and Tibshirani (2013) and Biau and Scornet (2016) for a textbook treatment of decision trees and the RF model, and Varian (2014) for a discussion of decision trees and RFs within economics and econometrics.

The LLF model views RFs as adaptive weight generating functions. The LLF model derives the adaptive weights from the RF model as

$$a_s(\mathbf{e}_i) = \frac{1}{B}\sum_{b=1}^{B} \frac{\mathbb{1}(\mathbf{e}_s \in L_b(\mathbf{e}_i))}{|L_b(\mathbf{e}_i)|} \tag{10}$$

The adaptive weights $a_s(\mathbf{e}_i)$ benefit from the RF's ability to model high dimensional non-linear functions, ignore irrelevant covariates, and naturally facilitate variable interactions. Intuitively, observations in the training data that frequently appear in the same leaf node as $\mathbf{e}_i$ receive larger weights since they are often partitioned into the same rectangular region of the feature space.

To split a parent node into two candidate child nodes within each decision tree, the traditional RF model uses a greedy classification and regression tree (CART) splitting criteria which seeks to minimize the sum of squared differences between the observed responses and the average response in each child node (see, e.g., Breiman, Friedman, Olshen, & Stone, 2017). Since the LLF model intends to use the adaptive weights, rather than the predictions, from the RF model, and because the local linear regression model in the second stage includes an ℓ_2-norm penalty, Friedberg et al. (2021) propose to construct splits that minimize the sum of residuals from the ridge regression in each child node. Friedberg et al. (2021) demonstrate that this ridge regression based splitting rule tends to grow trees that model the most complex local relationships in the data.

We follow Friedberg et al. (2021) and always grow so-called honest trees. Specifically, an honest tree is constructed by first splitting the random sub-sample of training data into two non-overlapping subsamples, denoted by $\mathcal{I}_b$ and $\mathcal{J}_b$. The subsample $\mathcal{J}_b$ is only used for deciding splits and therefore obtaining the tree structure. The subsample $\mathcal{I}_b$ is only used to define the neighbors of a point $\mathbf{e}_i$, that is only observations in $\mathcal{I}_b$ are used to define $L_b(\mathbf{e}_i)$ and hence construct the adaptive weight $a_s(\mathbf{e}_i)$. Honest trees control for over-fitting because the observations that were used to construct the adaptive weights were held out when constructing T_b. Honest trees are also necessary for establishing centered and asymptotically correct point-wise confidence intervals. Since we can effectively simulate a large training sample by drawing from our estimated copula function issues associated with growing honest trees in small samples do not apply to our work.

After fitting the RF and computing the adaptive weights, the LLF predictions are then given by

$$\begin{pmatrix} \tilde{\mu}(\mathbf{e}_i) \\ \hat{\theta}(\mathbf{e}_i) \end{pmatrix} = \arg\min_{\mu,\theta} \left\{ \sum_{s=1}^{S} a_s(\mathbf{e}_i)(u_s - \hat{\mu}(\mathbf{e}_i) - (\mathbf{e}_s - \mathbf{e}_i)^T \hat{\theta}(\mathbf{e}_i))^2 + \lambda \| \hat{\theta}(\mathbf{e}_i) \|_2^2 \right\} \quad (11)$$

where $\tilde{\mu}(\mathbf{e}_i) = \tilde{u}_i$ is the estimated technical inefficiency score, $\hat{\theta}(\mathbf{e}_i)$ is the vector of estimated coefficients measuring the local linear trend and $\|\cdot\|_2$ is the ℓ_2-norm. The ℓ_2-norm penalty is used to prevent over-fitting to the local trend. Friedberg et al. (2021) also propose a bootstrap based method of estimating the variance of $\tilde{\mu}(\mathbf{e}_i)$.

As the number of conditioning variables increases Friedberg et al. (2021) recommend to first fit a Lasso regression and only use the variables selected by the Lasso, that is the variables with a non-zero coefficient, in the local linear regression model. We always follow this approach. However, because we have already estimated the stochastic frontier model parameters the Gaussian copula correlation matrix $\widehat{\boldsymbol{\Gamma}}$ contains information about the relative importance of variables in the conditioning set. We can exploit this information to construct variable-specific weights to use with the ℓ_1 penalty, an approach known as the adaptive lasso[4] (Zou, 2006). Specifically, we use the inverse of the absolute value of correlation between each variable in the conditioning set and (contemporaneous) technical inefficiency as the adaptive weight in the ℓ_1 penalty for the lasso.

We use the out-of-bag mean squared error (MSE) to select the minimum leaf size within the set $\{5,10,25,50,100,300\}$ and the honesty subsample fraction in the set $\{0.5,0.6,0.7,0.8\}$. The ridge regression penalty in the local linear regression equation is selected using fivefold cross validation.[5] The number of trees is set to a relatively large number of 2,000, to ensure that we are always able to obtain appropriate confidence intervals. The subsample fraction is set to the default of 0.5, the ridge regression penalty used when determining tree splits is fixed at the default value of 0.1.

3. SIMULATIONS

3.1. Model with Temporal Dependence

We conduct simulations that represent a dynamic panel production frontier with auto-correlated technical inefficiency. Our simulations are similar to the setup in Lai and Kumbhakar (2020). The accuracy of technical inefficiency scores computed using information from the composed errors over all time periods, the APS14 estimator, is compared with the JLMS estimator that only uses the contemporaneous composed error. We fix $N = 100$ (the results for $N = 200$ are qualitatively identical and are available upon request), and consider values for $T \in \{3,5,7\}$.

The data generating process is

$$y_{it} = \ln\alpha + \beta_1 x_{1,it} + \beta_2 x_{2,it} + v_{it} - u_{it}$$
$$u_{it} = \rho u_{it-1} + u^*_{it},$$

where $u^*_{i0}, u^*_{it} \sim N^+(0,\sigma^2_{u^*})$, $v_{it} \sim N(0,\sigma^2_v)$ and $u^*_{it} \perp v_{it}$. The true parameter values are $\alpha = 1$, $\beta_1 = 0.3$, $\beta_2 = 0.2$, ,$\sigma^2_{u^*} = 1$ and $\sigma^2_v = 0.25$. The (log) inputs $x_{1,it}$ and $x_{2,it}$ are drawn independently from a normal distribution with standard deviations 1 and 1.5, respectively. We vary the auto-correlation parameter ρ between 0 and 0.95 with a step size of 0.05. Lai and Kumbhakar (2020) use the same AR(1) process for u_{it} but also include a time trend in the production function.

We estimate this model using the Gaussian copula for $(u_{i1},\ldots,u_{iT})$ and the simulated likelihood derived in equation (15) in Appendix 2, where we parameterize the time varying variance of the technical inefficiency as $\sigma^2_{u_{it}} = \exp(\delta_0 + \delta_1 t)$. The likelihood is evaluated using $K = 500$ Halton draws. We use $S = 10{,}000$ draws from the Gaussian copula to construct a training data set for the NW and LLF estimators of the technical inefficiency score. The total number of replications is 500. The estimation ignores the specific AR(1) structure in u_{it} (by not estimating ρ) and instead uses an unrestricted correlation matrix in the Gaussian copula that models time dependence between the marginals of u_{it}. This is similar to what Lai and Kumbhakar (2020) call Quasi Maximum Likelihood Estimation (QMLE) except they apply the Gaussian copula to $(\varepsilon_{i1},\ldots,\varepsilon_{iT})$, not to $(u_{i1},\ldots,u_{iT})$.

Fig. 11.1 plots the average MSE of u_{it} over all 500 replications for increasing levels of the auto-correlation parameter ρ. For reference, we also plot the non-parametric equivalent of the JLMS estimator, that is the NW estimator that only conditions on ε_{it}. As the degree of auto-correlation in technical inefficiency increases the accuracy of technical inefficiency scores computed using the LLF outperforms all other estimators. The NW estimator suffers from the curse of dimensionality for $T \geq 5$. As such, we recommend that practitioners apply non-parametric regression estimators designed for high dimensional data when using our approach in panel stochastic frontier settings.

As the number of time periods increases, the relative MSE of technical inefficiency grows smaller for the LLF estimator. Hence, conditioning on more than just the contemporaneous composed error term can substantially improve accuracy when technical inefficiency is correlated over time. In our setting, simulations suggest that the auto-correlation coefficient needs to be greater than 0.6 to achieve a meaningful reduction in the MSE of technical inefficiency estimates using our non-parametric estimators.

3.2. Model with Allocative Inefficiency

In this section, we report the simulation results that represent the cross-sectional production frontier system with allocative inefficiency discussed in Section 2.3.

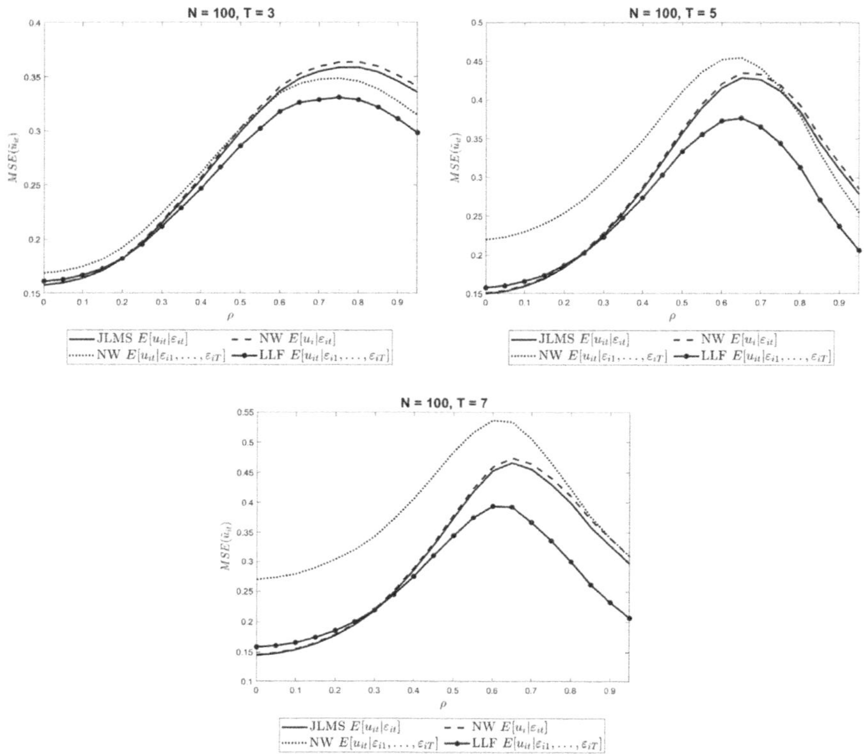

Fig. 11.1. MSE of Technical Inefficiency for Dynamic Panel Production Frontier Simulations. NW: Nadaraya-Watson Estimator. LLF: Local Linear Forest Estimator.

The accuracy of technical inefficiency scores computed with the additional allocative inefficiency terms, the APS16 estimator, is compared to the traditional JLMS estimator, which does not. We consider production systems with a varying number of inputs, $J \in \{2,3,4\}$.

The log output y_i is generated from a standard normal distribution. The log prices are generated from a standard multivariate normal distribution with the correlation between any pair $(p_i, p_j), i \neq j$, set to 0.5. The log inputs are generated using the following input demand equations (see Schmidt & Lovell, 1979, Equation (8))

$$x_{i1} = \ln q_1 + \frac{1}{r}\ln y_i + \ln\left[\prod_{g=1}^{J} P_g^{\beta_g/r} \,/\, P_1\right] - \frac{1}{r}(v_i - u_i) + \sum_{g=2}^{J}\frac{\beta_g}{r}\omega_{ig}$$

$$x_{ij} = \ln q_j + \frac{1}{r}\ln y_i + \ln\left[\prod_{g=1}^{J} P_g^{\beta_g/r} \,/\, P_g\right] - \frac{1}{r}(v_i - u_i) - \omega_{ij} + \sum_{g=2}^{J}\frac{\beta_g}{r}\omega_{ig}, \quad j = 2,\ldots,J,$$

where $q_j = \beta_j\left[\alpha\Pi_{j=1}^{J}\beta_j^{\beta_j}\right]^{-1/r}$, $r = \sum_{j=1}^{J}\beta_j$ measures the returns to scale and $P_j = \exp(p_j)$.

The true parameter values are $\alpha = 1$, $\beta_1 = \ldots = \beta_J = 0.9/J$, $\sigma_u^2 = \sigma_{\omega_2}^2 = \ldots = \sigma_{\omega_J}^2 = 1$ and $\sigma_v^2 = 0.5$. We report results for the sample size of $n = 500$ (the results for $n = 300$ are qualitatively identical and are available upon request). We vary the correlation parameter in the Gaussian copula between the pair of copula arguments $(F_u(u), F_2(\omega_2))$, denoted ρ_{u,ω_2}, between 0 and 0.9 with a step size of 0.05. Then, the correlation between the remaining pairs of copula arguments is set to $0.5\rho_{u,\omega_2}$. The correlation between any pair $(F_j(\omega_j), F_q(\omega_q)), j \neq q$, is set to 0.2. For example, the Gaussian copula correlation matrix for $J = 3$ and $\rho_{u,\omega_2} = 0.5$ is

$$\mathbf{\Gamma} = \begin{bmatrix} 1 & 0.5 & 0.25 \\ 0.5 & 1 & 0.2 \\ 0.25 & 0.2 & 1 \end{bmatrix}.$$

We estimate the model using the simulated likelihood function derived in equation (18) of Appendix 3, evaluated using $K = 500$ Halton draws. For the prediction of technical inefficiency, we use $S = 10{,}000$ draws from the Gaussian copula to construct a training data set for the NW and LLF estimators. The total number of replications is 500.

Fig. 11.2 plots the average MSE over all 500 replications for increasing levels of dependence between u and ω_2. For reference, we also plot the non-parametric regression equivalent of the JLMS estimator, that is the NW estimator that only conditions on ε_i. The simulation results show that conditioning on allocative inefficiencies can dramatically improve the estimation of the technical inefficiency score when technical and allocative inefficiency are correlated. The reduction in the MSE is similar regardless of the number of inputs in the production function, meaning that even conditioning on just a single allocative inefficiency term has the potential to substantially improve estimates of the technical inefficiency score.

When ρ_{u,ω_2} is greater than 0.5 the improvement in the MSE of both non-parametric regression estimators that condition on allocative inefficiency becomes particularly noticeable. We find that the LLF estimator is always associated with a lower MSE of the technical inefficiency score estimates than the NW estimator. This result is reasonable, since the LLF estimator uses an adaptive kernel. However, since the difference between the MSE of the NW and LLF estimators is not substantial when the number of inputs is small, practitioners may prefer the NW estimator since it is computationally easy to implement.

4. EMPIRICAL ILLUSTRATION

We consider an application of these estimators to a classic US electricity generation data set comprised of 72 firms over the period 1986–1999. The output variable is net steam electric power in megawatt-hours and the values of the three inputs (fuel, labor and maintenance, and capital) are obtained by dividing respective expenses by relevant input prices; the data are cleaned following Amsler et al. (2021). The prices associated with each input variable are also necessary to estimate the cross-sectional production system with allocative inefficiency. The price of fuel aggregate is a Tornqvist price index of fuels. The aggregate price of

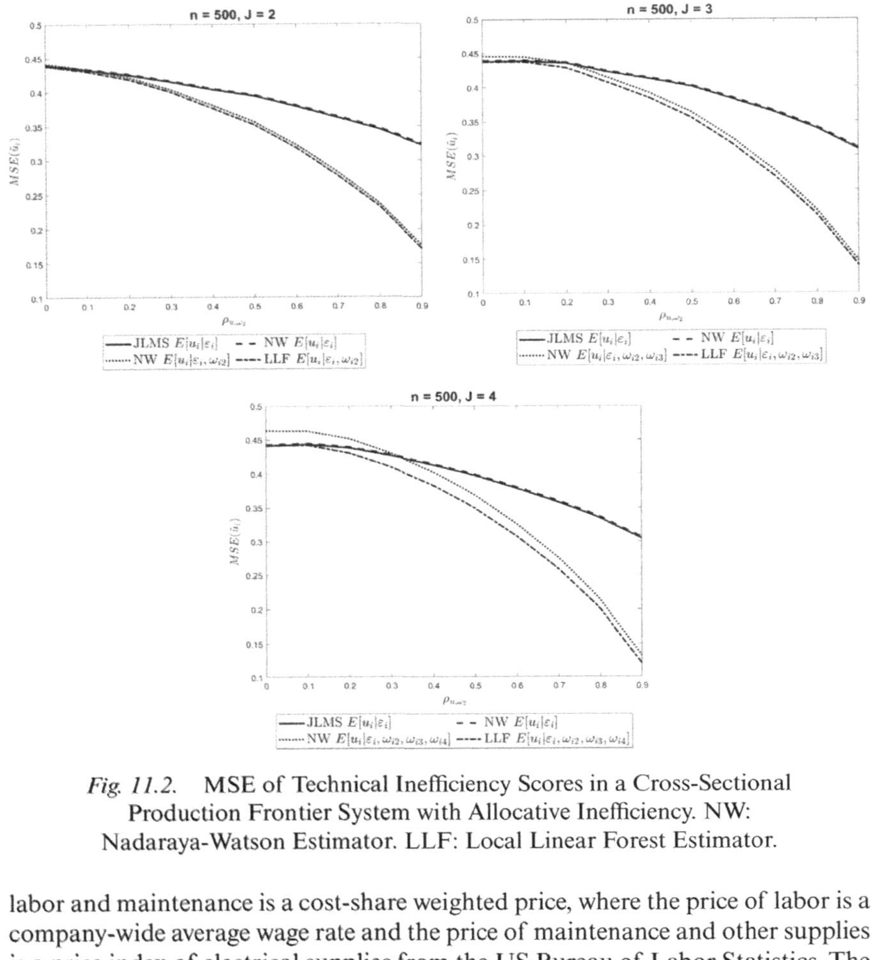

Fig. 11.2. MSE of Technical Inefficiency Scores in a Cross-Sectional Production Frontier System with Allocative Inefficiency. NW: Nadaraya-Watson Estimator. LLF: Local Linear Forest Estimator.

labor and maintenance is a cost-share weighted price, where the price of labor is a company-wide average wage rate and the price of maintenance and other supplies is a price index of electrical supplies from the US Bureau of Labor Statistics. The price of capital is the yield of the firm's latest issue of long-term debt adjusted for appreciation and depreciation. These data have recently been used by Amsler et al. (2021) and Lai and Kumbhakar (2019). Table 11.1 reports summary statistics for the electricity generation data. The output, inputs and input prices are in logs.

In Table 11.2, we report the average estimated technical inefficiencies by the year as well as the average of their estimated standard deviations, which can be viewed as measures of the unexplained variation in u. Part (i), which we call *Panel Stochastic Frontier (SF) Model* in the table, contains three predictors based on the panel model in (3) where the model parameters are estimated by MSLE as described in Appendix 2. The JLMS estimator uses only the contemporaneous ε_{it} in the conditioning set. The NW and LLF estimators use the expanded conditioning set and the APS14 approach to estimating the conditional expectation, described in Section 2.2. Part (ii) of the table, which we call *Cross Sectional SF Model*, contains three estimators

Table 11.1. Summary Statistics for the Electricity Generation Data.

	Mean	Median	Std	Min	Max
Output	2.2333	2.3853	0.9302	−0.6948	4.3786
Fuel	5.1065	5.1718	0.9777	2.4576	7.4698
Labor and Maintenance	3.9281	4.0625	0.9553	0.7046	6.2189
Capital	6.3953	6.4984	0.9648	4.1743	8.2632
Price of Fuel	0.0048	0.0069	0.0912	−1.0230	0.3549
Price of Labor and Maintenance	−0.0475	−0.0427	0.1369	−1.8879	1.8707
Price of Capital	−2.0390	−2.0377	0.1348	−2.5482	−1.5846

Table 11.2. Yearly Mean Technical Inefficiency Scores for the US Electricity Generation Data.

	(i) Panel SF Model						(ii) Cross Sectional SF Model					
	APS14 Estimator						APS16 Estimator					
	JLMS $\hat{u}$		NW $\tilde{u}$		LLF $\tilde{u}$		JLMS $\hat{u}$		NW $\tilde{u}$		LLF $\tilde{u}$	
	Est	Std Dev	Est	Std Dev	Est	Std Dev	Est	Std Dev	Est	Std Dev	Est	Std Dev
86	0.5613	0.0698	0.5014	0.0287	0.5352	0.0054	0.4521	0.1084	0.4395	0.1124	0.4484	0.0073
87	0.4508	0.0697	0.4946	0.0244	0.4673	0.0035	0.3895	0.1052	0.3848	0.1046	0.3912	0.0066
88	0.4814	0.0696	0.4872	0.024	0.4694	0.0028	0.3768	0.1053	0.3844	0.1074	0.3848	0.0062
89	0.4578	0.0698	0.4665	0.0267	0.4503	0.0036	0.3279	0.1031	0.3265	0.102	0.3334	0.0058
90	0.4424	0.0692	0.4624	0.0211	0.4342	0.0033	0.3630	0.1033	0.3675	0.1041	0.3695	0.0058
91	0.4461	0.0693	0.4565	0.0217	0.4359	0.0038	0.3686	0.1033	0.3676	0.1037	0.3731	0.0055
92	0.4426	0.0691	0.4453	0.0249	0.4334	0.003	0.3923	0.1028	0.3959	0.1036	0.3957	0.0053
93	0.4466	0.069	0.4463	0.0176	0.4395	0.0038	0.4022	0.1027	0.3948	0.1032	0.3996	0.0058
94	0.4182	0.0682	0.4354	0.0259	0.4156	0.0035	0.3792	0.1007	0.391	0.1006	0.3889	0.0057
95	0.447	0.0686	0.4431	0.0214	0.4391	0.0031	0.3949	0.1008	0.4081	0.1011	0.4061	0.0056
96	0.4048	0.0658	0.4201	0.0279	0.4165	0.0048	0.3721	0.0972	0.377	0.0984	0.3792	0.0057
97	0.3605	0.063	0.3404	0.0344	0.3533	0.0043	0.3370	0.0942	0.3424	0.0965	0.3414	0.0053
98	0.4133	0.0671	0.3892	0.0342	0.3950	0.0054	0.3450	0.0944	0.3458	0.0944	0.3504	0.0053
Average	0.4441	0.0683	0.4453	0.0256	0.4373	0.0039	0.3770	0.1016	0.3789	0.1025	0.3817	0.0058

based on the model in (5)-(6) where the parameters of the model are estimated by MSLE as described in Appendix 3. For this part, we ignore the panel nature of the data set (by viewing it as a pooled cross-section, i.e., by assuming independence over t as well as over i) and focus on the presence of the two types of inefficiency. In this case, JLMS is the estimator that does not use the ω_j's while NW and LLF include them in the conditioning set using the APS16 approach described in Section 2.3.

For the *Cross-Sectional SF Model*, the average technical inefficiency score over all firms and years is similar across estimators, regardless of whether or not we condition on the allocative inefficiency terms. Over all years, the average standard deviation of technical inefficiency scores from the LLF is considerably smaller than those from the JLMS or NW estimators. For the *Panel SF Model*, the mean

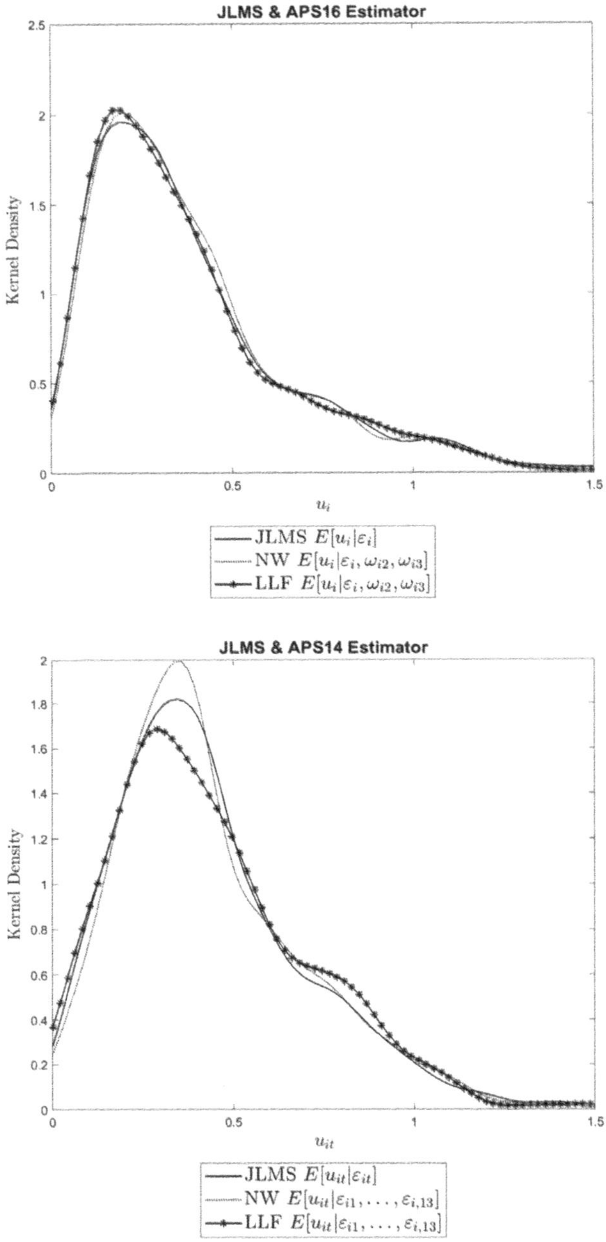

Fig. 11.3. Kernel Density Plots of the Estimated Technical Inefficiency Scores. NW: Nadaraya-Watson Estimator. LLF: Local Linear Forest Estimator.

technical inefficiency scores are always larger for all estimators and years in the data. Again, we find that the average technical inefficiency score over all firms and years is similar for all estimators. However, there are noticeable differences in the mean technical inefficiency score of estimators between years, for example in years 86, 87, 91 and 98. Finally, we note that the mean standard deviations for both non-parametric estimators are remarkably smaller than those associated with the JLMS estimator, suggesting that we explain a much larger portion of the unconditional variation in u. The technical inefficiency scores computed from the LLF estimator are always associated with the smallest standard deviations.

To complement Table 11.2, Fig. 11.3 plots the kernel density of the estimated technical inefficiency scores over all firms and years. Since the true technical inefficiency score is unobserved in applications, we do not investigate the estimation accuracy but rather, demonstrate the feasibility of estimating the different technical inefficiency scores. The kernel density plot for the LLF shows that this estimator tends to indicate that more firm-year observations have larger technical inefficiency scores and fewer firm-year observations have small technical inefficiency scores compared to the JLMS estimator.

5. CONCLUSION

In this study, we investigate improvements to the estimates of firm-specific technical inefficiency arising in cross-sectional and panel stochastic frontier models. Specifically, we focus on stochastic frontier models that use copulas to link the error terms. Our approach uses multivariate non-parametric regression techniques together with an information set comprised of dependent error terms. We consider the effect of using (i) allocative inefficiency and (ii) non-contemporaneous composed errors to improve the accuracy of estimated technical inefficiency. We apply a recently proposed non-parametric regression method, namely LLFs (Friedberg et al., 2021), that exploits a RF model's ability to fit high dimensional non-linear signals to generate adaptive weights for use in a local linear regression.

Simulations demonstrate that the estimators substantially improve the accuracy of technical inefficiency scores. In particular, when the errors in a production system are strongly correlated, our non-parametric regression estimators produce considerably more accurate estimates of the technical inefficiency than the traditional conditional mean estimator of Jondrow et al. (1982). While both the traditional NW estimator and the LLF work well for estimating technical inefficiency in cross sectional stochastic frontier models, only the LLF estimator provides more accurate inefficiency score estimates in a panel data setting. This is because the LLF is able to approximate high dimensional non-linear functions. Our study is relevant for both practitioners and regulators, since the accurate estimation of firm-specific technical inefficiency is important for maintaining competitive economies.

One might ask whether it is possible to perform a similar analysis when $\varepsilon = v - u$ and v and u are dependent, as in Smith (2008). The answer is yes, but it would be complicated. For the simplest (cross-sectional) case, Smith (2008) constructs a joint distribution for v and u by specifying the marginal distributions of u and v and a copula, and gives a generic form for the density of ε and for

$\hat{u} = E(u \mid \varepsilon)$. Only in some very special cases (e.g., logistic v, exponential u, Farlie-Gumbel-Morgenstern (FGM) copula) are analytical results possible. If we add additional variables (generically, ξ, $m \times 1$) to the conditioning set, the principle that this should improve the prediction of u must hold, but we would need to specify the m-dimensional marginal distribution of ξ and an $(m+2)$-dimensional copula to link v, u and ξ. A detailed analysis of this topic is left to future research.

NOTES

1. JLMS also consider the case of exponential u_i but we focus on the popular half-normal case here.
2. We also investigated the use of fivefold cross validation to select the bandwidth parameters and found that this generally improves the performance of our Nadaraya-Watson estimator. These results are available from the authors upon request. However, cross validation may be computationally intractable for large S and/or when there is a large number of covariates in the conditioning set, such as when T is large for the APS14 estimator.
3. We have verified numerically that the LLF always outperforms a traditional RF (where the minimum leaf size is tuned via cross validation and the sub-sample fraction is set to the same value used in the LLF model). In our simulations (not reported here for brevity), the LLF outperforms the traditional RF in terms of MSE by at least 5% and in some cases by more.
4. We thank an anonymous referee for pointing this out to us.
5. In practice, practitioners may also choose to tune the number of variables subsampled at each splitting step when building a tree. Our results are robust to tuning this parameter.

ACKNOWLEDGMENTS

Helpful comments from participants of EcoSta 2022, EWEPA 2022 and iCEBA 2022, as well as seminar participants at Florida State University, Macquarie University and Higher School of Economics are gratefully acknowledged. The use of the University of Sydney's high-performance computing cluster, Artemis, is acknowledged. James's research for this chapter was supported by a grant from the Australian Research Council (Project DP200103549). Prokhorov's research for this chapter was supported by a grant from the Russian Science Foundation (Project No. 20-18-00365).

REFERENCES

Aigner, D., Lovell, C. K., & Schmidt, P. (1977). Formulation and estimation of stochastic frontier production function models. *Journal of Econometrics*, *6*(1), 21–37.

Amsler, C., Prokhorov, A., & Schmidt, P. (2014). Using copulas to model time dependence in stochastic frontier models. *Econometric Reviews*, *33*(5–6), 497–522.

Amsler, C., Prokhorov, A., & Schmidt, P. (2016). Endogeneity in stochastic frontier models. *Journal of Econometrics*, *190*(2), 280–288.

Amsler, C., Prokhorov, A., & Schmidt, P. (2021). A new family of copulas, with application to estimation of a production frontier system. *Journal of Productivity Analysis*, *55*(1), 1–14.

Amsler, C., Prokhorov, A., & Schmidt, P. (2014). Improving predictions of technical efficiency, *Advances in Econometrics*, in press.

Archakov, I., & Hansen, P. R. (2021). A new parametrization of correlation matrices. *Econometrica*, *89*(4), 1699–1715.

Bera, A. K., & Sharma, S. C. (1999). Estimating production uncertainty in stochastic frontier production function models. *Journal of Productivity Analysis*, *12*(3), 187–210.

Biau, G., & Scornet, E. (2016). A random forest guided tour. *Test*, *25*(2), 197–227.

Breiman, L., Friedman, J. H., Olshen, R. A., & Stone, C. J. (2017). *Classification and regression trees*. New York, NY: Routledge.

Friedberg, R., Tibshirani, J., Athey, S., & Wager, S. (2021). Local linear forests. *Journal of Computational and Graphical Statistics*, *30*(2), 1–15.

James, G., Witten, D., Hastie, T., & Tibshirani, R. (2013). *An introduction to statistical learning* (Vol. 112). Springer Texts in Statistics.

Jondrow, J., Lovell, C. K., Materov, I. S., & Schmidt, P. (1982). On the estimation of technical inefficiency in the stochastic frontier production function model. *Journal of Econometrics*, *19*(2–3), 233–238.

Kneip, A., & Simar, L. (1996). A general framework for frontier estimation with panel data. *Journal of Productivity Analysis*, *7*(2), 187–212.

Kumbhakar, S. C., Ghosh, S., & McGuckin, J. T. (1991). A generalized production frontier approach for estimating determinants of inefficiency in U.S. dairy farms. *Journal of Business & Economic Statistics*, *9*(3), 279–286.

Kumbhakar, S. C., & Lovell, C. K. (2003). *Stochastic frontier analysis*. Cambridge: Cambridge University Press.

Lai, H.-P., & Kumbhakar, S. C. (2019). Technical and allocative efficiency in a panel stochastic production frontier system model. *European Journal of Operational Research*, *278*(1), 255–265.

Lai, H.-P., & Kumbhakar, S. C. (2020). Estimation of a dynamic stochastic frontier model using likelihood-based approaches. *Journal of Applied Econometrics*, *35*(2), 217–247.

Mamonov, M. E., Parmeter, C. F., & Prokhorov, A. B. (2022). Dependence modeling in stochastic frontier analysis. *Dependence Modeling*, *10*(1), 123–144.

Meyer, D., & Nagler, T. (2021). Synthia: Multidimensional synthetic data generation in python. *Journal of Open Source Software*, *6*(65), 2863.

Meyer, D., Nagler, T., & Hogan, R. J. (2021). Copula-based synthetic data augmentation for machine-learning emulators. *Geoscientific Model Development*, *14*(8), 5205–5215.

Schmidt, P., & Lovell, C. K. (1979). Estimating technical and allocative inefficiency relative to stochastic production and cost frontiers. *Journal of Econometrics*, *9*, 343–366.

Schmidt, P., & Lovell, C. K. (1980). Estimating stochastic production and cost frontiers when technical and allocative inefficiency are correlated. *Journal of Econometrics*, *13*(1), 83–100.

Simar, L., Van Keilegom, I., & Zelenyuk, V. (2017). Nonparametric least squares methods for stochastic frontier models. *Journal of Productivity Analysis*, *47*(3), 189–204.

Sklar, M. (1959). Fonctions de répartition à n dimensions et leurs marges. *Publications de l'Institut Statistique de l'Université de Paris*, *8*, 229–231.

Smith, M. D. (2008). Stochastic frontier models with dependent error components. *The Econometrics Journal*, *11*(1), 172–192.

Varian, H. R. (2014). Big data: New tricks for econometrics. *Journal of Economic Perspectives*, *28*(2), 3–28.

Zou, H. (2006). The adaptive lasso and its oracle properties. *Journal of the American Statistical Association*, *101*(476), 1418–1429.

APPENDIX 1. BASICS OF COPULAS

Copulas allow one to specify the dependence structure separately while maintaining the assumed marginal distributions for each component of a random vector. In essence, copulas are multivariate distributions with uniform marginals. Denote a d-copula function by $C(z_1,\ldots,z_d):[0,1]^d \to [0,1]$. The well-known theorem of Sklar (1959) states that any joint distribution of continuous random variables can be written as a copula function, taking as arguments the univariate marginal distributions:

$$H(z_1,\ldots,z_d) = C(F_1(z_1),\ldots,F_d(z_d))$$

If all margins $F_1,\ldots,F_d$ are continuous then the copula is unique (this is always the case in our study). In terms of densities, we have

$$h(z_1,\ldots,z_d) = c(F_1(z_1),\ldots,F_d(z_d))\prod_{i=1}^{d} f_i(z_i)$$

where f_i is the marginal density corresponding to the marginal cdf F_i, c is the d-copula density corresponding to the d-copula function C, and h is the joint density function corresponding to the joint cdf H.

As an example, a commonly used copula for stochastic frontier applications is the Gaussian copula. A d-dimensional Gaussian copula is defined as

$$C(u_1,\ldots,u_d) = \Phi_d(\Phi^{-1}(u_1),\ldots,\Phi^{-1}(u_d);\mathbf{\Gamma}) \tag{12}$$

where $\mathbf{\Gamma}$ is a $d \times d$ correlation matrix and Φ_d is the multivariate normal cdf. The Gaussian copula is comprehensive in the sense that it accommodates all values of Kendall's tau. It is also easy to sample from, which is an important consideration for our purposes. One computational difficulty in using the Gaussian copula in high dimensional cases is to estimate the correlation matrix (along with other model parameters) and we use the recently proposed unconstrained parameterization of Archakov and Hansen (2021) to ensure the matrix remains positive semi-definite in the maximum likelihood estimation.

APPENDIX 2. ESTIMATION OF MODEL (3)

Here we discuss how to construct the likelihood for the panel stochastic frontier model. The method follows Amsler et al. (2014).

Let $f_u(u)$ denote the marginal density of a one-sided technical inefficiency term and $f_{\mathbf{u}}(\mathbf{u})$ denote the joint density specified using a copula, that is

$$f_{\mathbf{u}}(\mathbf{u}) = c(F_u(u_1),\ldots,F_u(u_T))\cdot f_u(u_1)\cdots f_u(u_T) \tag{13}$$

We need the joint density of ε to form the likelihood function. As further discussed in Appendix 3 we can approximate this density using the method of simulated likelihood by making a large number of draws from the distribution of $(u_1,\ldots,u_T)$. Let $k=1,\ldots,K$ index these draws. (This notation is different from $s=1,\ldots,S$, used in the main text to denote draws from the joint distribution required for the non-parametric estimation of the conditional expectations.) The joint density of the composed error vector $\boldsymbol{\varepsilon} = (\varepsilon_1, \ldots, \varepsilon_T)$ is

$$f_\varepsilon(\boldsymbol{\varepsilon}) = \int_0^\infty \ldots \int_0^\infty f_{\mathbf{v}}(\boldsymbol{\varepsilon} + \mathbf{u}) \cdot f_{\mathbf{u}}(\mathbf{u}) du_1 \ldots du_T = \mathbb{E}_{\mathbf{u}}[f_{\mathbf{v}}(\boldsymbol{\varepsilon} + \mathbf{u})] \tag{14}$$

where $\mathbb{E}_{\mathbf{u}}$ denotes the expectation with respect to $f_{\mathbf{u}}(\mathbf{u})$ and $f_{\mathbf{v}}$ is the multivariate normal distribution with the independence covariance matrix. The simulated log-likelihood function is then

$$\ln L(\boldsymbol{\theta}) = \sum_{i=1}^{N} \ln\left(\frac{1}{K}\sum_{k=1}^{K} f_{\mathbf{v}}(\boldsymbol{\varepsilon} + \mathbf{u}^{(k)})\right), \tag{15}$$

where $\boldsymbol{\theta}$ contains all the model parameters, including the copula parameters.

APPENDIX 3. ESTIMATION OF MODEL (5)-(6)

Here, we describe the construction of the likelihood for the model with allocative inefficiency. This model was recently studied by Amsler et al. (2021) [APS21] who propose a new family of copulas to model the dependence between u and $\boldsymbol{\omega}$ in an economically realistic way. They also discuss how to construct a simulated likelihood for this model. We do not use the APS21 copula family in this chapter but closely follow the approach used for likelihood construction in that paper here.

The allocative inefficiency terms ω_{ij} measure the deviation by which the input ratios differ from their cost-minimizing values. From an economic perspective, firms that are more technically inefficient are also more allocatively inefficient and vice-versa. Therefore, we assume that u_i and ω_{ij} are dependent while v_i is independent of both u_i and ω_{ij}. This dependence structure may be modeled using a copula. While we assume a Gaussian copula in this study, any copula, including those used by APS21, can be used. Dropping the i subscript, the corresponding joint density can be written as follows

$$f_{u,\omega_2,\ldots,\omega_J}(u,\omega_2,\ldots,\omega_J) = c(F_u(u), F_{\omega_2}(\omega_2), \ldots, F_{\omega_J}(\omega_J)) \cdot f_u(u) \cdot \prod_{j=2}^{J} f_{\omega_j}(\omega_j) \tag{16}$$

To form the likelihood of the production system (5)-(6), we require the joint density of $(\varepsilon, \omega_2, \ldots, \omega_J)$. Following APS21, we start with the joint density of $(v, u, \omega_2, \ldots, \omega_J)$, which is

$$f_{v,u,\omega_2,\ldots,\omega_J}(v,u,\omega_2,\ldots,\omega_J) = f_v(v) \cdot c(F_u(u), F_{\omega_2}(\omega_2), \ldots, F_{\omega_J}(\omega_J)) \cdot f_u(u) \cdot \prod_{j=2}^{J} f_{\omega_j}(\omega_j)$$

Then, we seek to integrate u out from this joint density as follows

$$\begin{aligned} f_{\varepsilon,\omega_2,\ldots,\omega_J}(\varepsilon,\omega_2,\ldots,\omega_J) &= \int f_{v,u,\omega_2,\ldots,\omega_J}(\varepsilon + u, u, \omega_2, \ldots, \omega_J) du \\ &= \prod_{j=2}^{J} f_{\omega_j}(\omega_j) \cdot \int c(F_u(u), F_{\omega_2}(\omega_2), \ldots, F_{\omega_J}(\omega_J)) f_v(\varepsilon + u) \cdot f_u(u) du \\ &= \prod_{j=2}^{J} f_{\omega_j}(\omega_j) \cdot E_u[c(F_u(u), F_{\omega_2}(\omega_2), \ldots, F_{\omega_J}(\omega_J)) f_v(\varepsilon + u)] \end{aligned} \tag{17}$$

The expectation in (17) can be evaluated by the method of simulated likelihood, that is by taking the average over a large number of draws from the distribution of u. Specifically, letting $k = 1,\ldots,K$, index the draws from the distribution of u (again, different from S draws of $(v,u,\boldsymbol{\omega})$ required to estimate $E(u \mid \varepsilon,\boldsymbol{\omega})$), the simulated log-density can be written as follows

$$
\begin{aligned}
&\ln \hat{f}_{\varepsilon,\omega_2,\ldots,\omega_J}(\varepsilon,\omega_2,\ldots,\omega_J) \\
&= \ln\left(\prod_{j=2}^{J} f_{\omega_j}(\omega_j)\cdot\frac{1}{K}\sum_{k=1}^{K}[c(F_u(u^{(k)}),F_{\omega_2}(\omega_2),\ldots,F_{\omega_J}(\omega_J))f_v(\varepsilon+u^{(k)})]\right) \\
&= \sum_{j=2}^{J}\ln f_{\omega_j}(\omega_j)+\ln\left(\frac{1}{K}\sum_{k=1}^{K}[c(F_u(u^{(k)}),F_{\omega_2}(\omega_2),\ldots,F_{\omega_J}(\omega_J))f_v(\varepsilon+u^{(k)})]\right).
\end{aligned}
$$

Then, using the Jacobian of the transformation from $(\varepsilon,\omega_2,\ldots,\omega_J)$ to $(x_1,\ldots,x_J)$ given by Schmidt and Lovell (1980, p. 88), the simulated log-likelihood function of the copula-based cross sectional stochastic frontier model can be written as

$$
\ln L(\boldsymbol{\theta}) = n\ln r + \sum_{i=1}^{n}\ln \hat{f}_{\varepsilon,\omega_2,\ldots,\omega_J}(\epsilon_i, w_{i2},\ldots,w_{iJ}) \tag{18}
$$

where $r = \sum_{j=1}^{J}\beta_j$ and

$$
\epsilon_i = y_i - \alpha - \sum_{j=1}^{J}\beta_j x_{ij} \tag{19}
$$

$$
w_{ij} = x_{i1} - x_{ij} - p_{ij} + p_{i1} - \ln\beta_1 + \ln\beta_j, \quad j = 2,\ldots,J. \tag{20}
$$

Note that the log-likelihood parameter vector $\boldsymbol{\theta}$ includes the copula dependence parameter as well as all the other parameters of the production system in (5)-(6).

CHAPTER 12

A SEMIPARAMETRIC CONSTANT ELASTICITY OF SUBSTITUTION STOCHASTIC FRONTIER MODEL FOR PANEL DATA

Taining Wang[a] and Daniel J. Henderson[b]

[a]*International School of Economics and Management, Capital University of Economics and Business, Beijing, China*
[b]*Department of Economics, Finance and Legal Studies, University of Alabama, Tuscaloosa, AL, USA*

ABSTRACT

A semiparametric stochastic frontier model is proposed for panel data, incorporating several flexible features. First, a constant elasticity of substitution (CES) production frontier is considered without log-transformation to prevent induced non-negligible estimation bias. Second, the model flexibility is improved via semiparameterization, where the technology is an unknown function of a set of environment variables. The technology function accounts for latent heterogeneity across individual units, which can be freely correlated with inputs, environment variables, and/or inefficiency determinants. Furthermore, the technology function incorporates a single-index structure to circumvent the curse of dimensionality. Third, distributional assumptions are eschewed on both stochastic noise and inefficiency for model identification. Instead, only the conditional mean of the inefficiency is assumed, which depends on related determinants with a wide range of choice, via a positive parametric function. As a result, technical efficiency is constructed without relying on an assumed distribution on composite error. The model provides flexible structures on both the production frontier and inefficiency, thereby alleviating the risk of model

Essays in Honor of Subal Kumbhakar
Advances in Econometrics, Volume 46, 329–370

ISSN: 0731-9053/doi:10.1108/S0731-905320240000046012

misspecification in production and efficiency analysis. The estimator involves a series based nonlinear least squares estimation for the unknown parameters and a kernel based local estimation for the technology function. Promising finite-sample performance is demonstrated through simulations, and the model is applied to investigate productive efficiency among OECD countries from 1970–2019.

Keywords: Panel data; semiparametric model; CES; stochastic frontier; profile nonlinear least-square; local nonlinear kernel

JEL classifications: C14; C23

1. INTRODUCTION

The seminal works by Aigner, Lovell, and Schmidt (1977) and Meeusen and van Den Broeck (1977) evoked a myriad of studies to estimate production functions and inefficiency via stochastic frontier (SF) models.[1] The basic structure of the SF specifies a production (frontier) function $Y = m(X)$ for output Y and input vector X in the presence of a composite error $e = v - u$. Such structure is practically appealing as $m(X)$ can be specified to perform inference of economic interest and e distinguishes unobserved output variation due to stochastic noise v (e.g., production shocks, measurement error) from that due to productive inefficiency u (e.g., managerial inefficiency). The function $m(\cdot)$ is often assumed to be Cobb-Douglas (CD) or constant elasticity of substitution (CES) function. Unlike a regression model with zero mean noise, the composite error has a non-zero mean due to the one-sided nature of $u > 0$ (i.e., the shortfall of the output from its frontier). Originally, parametric distributional assumptions on v (e.g., normal) and u (e.g., half-normal, exponential, truncated normal, gamma) were required for identification.

Parametric assumptions on both $m(X)$ and e are often made via conjecture, for which violations result in inconsistent estimation and potentially invalid policy implications (Kumbhakar, Parmeter, & Zelenyuk, 2020). Effort has been made to relax these restrictive assumptions. To relax the parametric assumptions on the distribution of e, panel data methods are often employed. For example, Schmidt and Sickles (1984) consider time-invariant inefficiency, which can be bundled and eliminated with additive fixed effects. Cornwell, Schmidt, and Sickles (1990) model inefficiency as a deterministic function of a time trend. Kumbhakar (1990), Battese and Coelli (1992), Lee and Schmidt (1993), and Kumbhakar and Wang (2005a) specify a time-invariant inefficiency, scaled by a deterministic function of time with different functional forms. Alternatively, Horrace and Parmeter (2011) estimate the unknown distribution of the composite error via deconvolution, and Tran and Tsionas (2009), Parmeter, Wang, and Kumbhakar (2016), and Zhou, Parmeter, and Kumbhakar (2020) adopt a partially linear SF to estimate the mean function of inefficiency with distribution-free composite error. However, the aforementioned studies relax the parametric distributional assumption at the cost of maintaining a parametric frontier structure. A correctly specified frontier model can be paramount to provide reliable insights on many important features of the production function, such as returns to scale.

Kneip and Simar (1996) and Fan, Li, and Weersink (1996) were the first to consider a fully nonparametric frontier model $m(X)$. Martins-Filho and Yao (2015) investigate the asymptotic properties of the estimator of Fan et al. (1996), and propose a refined profile-likelihood based estimator for the nonparametric frontier. Kumbhakar, Park, Simar, and Tsionas (2007) model all parameters in the frontier and composite error distribution nonparametrically with a kernel weighted local log-likelihood approach. Park, Simar, and Zelenyuk (2015) further generalize their results to incorporate categorical data in $m(X)$. Kneip, Simar, and Van Keilegom (2015) propose a fully nonparametric frontier model when v is log-normally distributed with unknown variance. In practice, the fully nonparametric frontier can be imprecisely estimated due to the well-known *curse of dimensionality* problem. To circumvent this curse, recent studies employ semiparametric techniques: additive (Ferrara & Vidoli, 2017) or varying coefficient (Sun & Kumbhakar, 2013; Yao, Zhang, & Kumbhakar, 2018a) structures. Even with these improvements, these non/semiparametric models maintain parametric distribution assumptions on e, where violations can lead to model identification problem (Kumbhakar et al., 2020; Parmeter et al., 2016).

The restrictive parametric assumptions on e or $m(X)$ have been relaxed on one side at the expense of being maintained on the other side. In this chapter, we allow for some structure, but we relax some assumptions on both sides by proposing a semiparametric panel frontier model which unifies several attractive features. First, we do not impose distributional assumptions on v and u. We allow u to be influenced by observed determinants W through its mean function, whose structure is generally unknown.[2] As the number of inefficiency determinants rises (see, for example, Iyer, Rambaldi, & Tang, 2008), nonparametric estimation on the unknown mean function suffers from the curse of dimensionality. To improve the model's applicability, we assume the mean function of W to be positive and known up to a finite dimensional parameter vector. As emphasized by Parmeter and Kumbhakar (2014), a correct modeling on the dependence of u on W is important to avoid biasing the estimates of both frontier and technical efficiency (TE). We further provide discussion on TE measures suitable in our model without distributional assumptions. Different from existing non/semiparametric frontier models that often place restrictions on the choice of W (Ferrara & Vidoli, 2017; Sun & Kumbhakar, 2013; Yao et al., 2018a), we allow W to be chosen in a flexible fashion, which can include all, some, or none of variables in the frontier function.

Second, we begin by specifying the frontier as a semiparametric extension of CES. In a production function with two inputs K (physical capital) and L (labor), the classical (parametric) CES with constant returns to scale specifies $A\left[\pi K^{-\rho}+(1-\pi)L^{-\rho}\right]^{-\frac{1}{\rho}}$, where $A>0$ is the technology parameter, π and $(1-\pi)$ are the shares of K and L, respectively, and ρ determines the elasticity of substitution $\sigma=\frac{1}{1+\rho}$ between K and L. The flexible structure of CES receives considerable attention in the literature because, as a generalization of CD, it allows σ to differ from unity and allows non-constant factor shares (Gollin, 2002). Here, we further improve the flexibility of CES by allowing A to be an unknown function of environment variables Z (i.e., $A = A(Z)$), which are not traditional production inputs but generate facilitating impacts on Y, such as computerization (Yao et al., 2018a), human capital (Yao, Wang, Tian, & Kumbhakar, 2018b) or firm's debt (Wang, Tian, & Yao, 2020). To avoid the curse of dimensionality, we adopt a single-index structure as $A(Z^\top \gamma_z)$, where γ_z is a vector of coefficients (Ma & Song, 2015).

This general form has at least three advantages over existing models. First, parametric or semiparametric models typically involve log-transformations. Assuming e is multiplicative, the parametric CES is estimated by first logging both sides of the SF and then approximated by Taylor expansions (i.e., Kmenta approximation). Similarly, the semiparametric varying coefficient frontier can be viewed as a generalization of a log-transformed CD (Wang et al., 2020). As suggested by Sun, Henderson, and Kumbhakar (2008), log transformations on $m(\cdot)$ can lead to inconsistent estimation, since the expectation of the log error term is almost always a function of X (or (X, Z, W) in our case) (Santos Silva & Tenreyro, 2006). We avoid the conventional practice of log transformations when estimating our semiparametric CES, and follow Wang and Henderson (2022) to estimate the model directly in levels. Second, the environment variables Z can be high-dimensional, thereby facilitating investigation on the joint effects of multiple Z in the technology function without inflating estimation inaccuracy. Third, different from non/semiparametric models, our frontier allows direct estimation of some parameters of interests with important economic implications. For instance, estimating the elasticity of substitution (σ) is straightforward in our model, which can potentially explain the declining share of labor income in recent decades (Karabarbounis & Neiman, 2013). Such parameters are difficult to identify in semi/nonparametric models (Henderson, 2009). Our frontier specifies the technology function flexibility while adopting parsimonious structure on modeling certain features of the production function.

Finally, we control for unobserved and time-invariant individual heterogeneities, which is often absent in the aforementioned non/semiparametric models. It is important to incorporate fixed effects in panel SF models as it provides an efficient way to mitigate potential endogeneity. We allow the fixed effects to be arbitrarily correlated with covariates (X, Z, W), and estimate them via dummy variables in the index of the technology function $A(\cdot)$, analogous to a logged CES model where the fixed effects appear as intercept shifts.

We propose a two-step estimation procedure to estimate our semiparametric panel SF. In the first step, we employ a profile nonlinear least-square estimator (PNLS) to estimate the global parameters in the frontier and inefficiency functions, where the unknown function $A(\cdot)$ is approximated by a series estimator. In the second step, we employ a local nonlinear kernel estimator (LNK) for $A(\cdot)$, using all parameter estimates from the previous step. Our simulation study shows that the proposed estimator works fairly well in finite samples.[3] Using a panel data set of 20 OECD countries from 1970 to 2019, our model is demonstrated to be more suitable than conventional parametric SF models to uncover important features of production frontier and inefficiency.

The remainder of this chapter proceeds as follows: we present the proposed estimator and identification conditions in Section 2, illustrate the finite-sample performance through simulations studies in Section 3, demonstrate an empirical application in Section 4, and conclude in Section 5. The appendices include additional simulations (detailing the incidental parameters problem) as well as a description of the R package we created for this estimator.

2. SEMIPARAMETRIC CES STOCHASTIC FRONTIER MODEL

2.1. Model

We consider the following semiparametric CES stochastic frontier model (SF-CES-SP):

$$Y_{it} = A(Z_{it}^{\top}\gamma_z + \alpha_i)\left(\pi_1 X_{1it}^{-\rho} + \cdots + \pi_{d_x} X_{d_x it}^{-\rho}\right)^{-\frac{\nu}{\rho}} + v_{it} - u_{it}, i = 1,\ldots,n, t = 1,\ldots,T, \quad (1)$$

where n and T represent the total individual and time units, respectively. $Y_{it} \in \Re_+$ is the univariate production output and $X_{it} \in \Re_+^{d_x}$ are traditional production inputs. A linear combination of environment variables $Z_{it} \in \Re^{d_z}$ influences the technology $A(\cdot)$ by a scale effect, where $A(\cdot)$ is an unknown smooth function. We assume the fixed effects α_i appear in the SF-CES through $A(\cdot)$ such that $E(\alpha_i \mid X_{it}, Z_{it}, Q_{it}) \neq 0$ (Baltagi & Li, 2002), where $Q_{it} \in \Re^{d_q}$ are pure inefficiency determinants, such as export intensity (Iyer et al., 2008), which do not show up in the frontier. We incorporate α_i via dummy variables, and for identification purposes, we include all but the first dummy so that a total of $d_z + (n-1)$ variables are included in $A(\cdot)$. The parameter ρ $(-1 < \rho \neq 0)$ determines the elasticity of substitution $\sigma = \dfrac{1}{1+\rho}$ (assumed the same) between two production inputs X_j and X_s for $j \neq s$. $\nu > 0$ is the returns to scale and $0 \leq \pi_j \leq 1$ is the distribution parameter that explains the relative input share ($\sum_{j=1}^{p} \pi_j = 1$).[4]

In the composite error, the one-sided error $u_{it} > 0$ is the time-variant inefficiency variable, measuring the difference between the maximum output produced at the frontier and the actual output produced.[5] We do not impose a particular distribution on u_{it}, but only assume the existence of its positive conditional mean function $E(u_{it} \mid \alpha_i, X_{it}, Z_{it}, Q_{it}) \equiv \mu(W_{it};\theta) > 0$ known up to the finite dimensional parameter $\theta \in \Re^{d_w}$, with the determinants W_{it} being a subset of X_{it}, Z_{it}, and Q_{it}, so W_{it} is of dimension $d_w \leq d_x + d_z + d_q$. Finally, the two-sided error v_{it} represents random shocks in production process, which satisfies $E(v_{it} \mid \alpha_i, X_{it}, Z_{it}, Q_{it}) = 0$ for all i and t.

Our model improves existing SF models in the literature by relaxing restrictive assumptions on both the frontier and composite error. The semiparametric CES generalizes traditional parametric CD and CES by specifying the technology to be dependent on Z_{it} in an unknown fashion. Our frontier also permits large dimension of Z_{it} without affecting estimation accuracy, and allows the presence of interactive effects among inputs as opposed to other semiparametric varying coefficient frontier models (Ferrara & Vidoli, 2017; Sun & Kumbhakar, 2013; Wang et al., 2020; Yao et al., 2018a, 2018b). More importantly, the CES frontier is estimated in levels to avoid the bias due to log-transformations which exists in most parametric/semiparametric SF models. Our composite error is free of distribution misspecification as we only assume that the conditional mean of u_{it} exists. Furthermore, the choice of determinants W_{it} in $\mu(\cdot;\theta)$ is flexible as our production inefficiency may emanate from X_{it}, Z_{it} and/or Q_{it} (Parmeter & Kumbhakar, 2014). This feature contrasts, and may therefore ameliorate, the limited choices of W_{it} in existing semiparametric models ($W_{it} = \varnothing$ in additive (Ferrara & Vidoli, 2017), $W_{it} = Z_{it}$ in varying coefficient (Yao et al., 2018a), and $W_{it} = Q_{it}$ in partially linear (Parmeter et al., 2016; Tran & Tsionas, 2009; Zhou et al., 2020) models).

Our SF-CES-SP in (1) is clearly not a regression model because the conditional mean of $v_{it} - u_{it}$ is not zero. It can be readily transformed into a regression model by de-meaning u_{it} in the composite error such that $\epsilon_{it} = v_{it} - (u_{it} - \mu(W_{it};\theta))$. Thus, a regression-type SF-CES-SP is given as

$$Y_{it} = A(Z_{it}^{\top}\gamma_z + \alpha_i)\left(\pi_1 X_{1it}^{-\rho} + \cdots + \pi_{d_x} X_{d_x it}^{-\rho}\right)^{-\frac{\nu}{\rho}} - \mu(W_{it};\theta) + \epsilon_{it}, \tag{2}$$

where $E(\epsilon_{it} \mid \alpha_i, X_{it}, Z_{it}, Q_{it}) = 0$ is now satisfied by construction. Below, we discuss the identification conditions for parameters from (2) in Section 2.2, propose a two-step model estimator in Section 2.3, and list basic assumptions for establishing the estimator's consistency in Section 2.4.

2.2. *Identification*

We discuss identification of parameters in (2). Let $\alpha_{-1} = (\alpha_2, \ldots, \alpha_n)^{\top}$ be a vector that collects all but the first fixed effect. Define $\gamma = (\gamma_z^{\top}, \alpha_{-1}^{\top})^{\top}$ and $\omega = (\pi_1, \ldots, \pi_{d_x}, \rho, \nu, \theta^{\top})^{\top}$, we assume that the global parameters $\eta = (\gamma^{\top}, \omega^{\top})^{\top} \in \Theta$, where $\Theta = \{\Gamma, \Omega\}$ is a collection of compact parameter spaces in which $\gamma \in \Gamma$ and $\omega \in \Omega$.

To identify γ in $A(\cdot)$, we follow Ma and Song (2015) and let γ belong to a compact parameter space $\Gamma = \{\gamma : \| \gamma \| = 1, \gamma_1 > 0, \gamma_l \in \Re, l = 2, \ldots, d_z + n - 1\}$, where $\| m \|$ denotes the L_2 norm of any vector m. The condition $\| \gamma \| = 1$ ensures $A(\cdot)$ is identifiable by restricting the scale of γ. As a result, the true values of γ locate at the boundary points of a unit sphere, so the derivative of $A(\cdot)$ cannot be evaluated at true value of γ. Following Zhu and Xue (2006), we let all but the first element in γ be defined on the interior points of the unit sphere by assuming $\| \gamma_{-1} \| < 1$ with $\gamma_{-1} = [\gamma_{z_2}, \ldots, \gamma_{z_{d_z}}, \alpha_{-1}^{\top}]^{\top} \in \Re^{d_z + n - 2}$, so $\gamma_{z_1} = (1 - \| \gamma_{-1} \|^2)^{1/2} > 0$ is the result given in Γ.[6] We consider a "leave-one-out" parameter space for γ as

$$\Gamma_{-1} = \{\gamma_{-1} : \| \gamma_{-1} \| < 1, \gamma_{l,-1} \in \Re, l = 2, \ldots, d_z + n - 1\}$$

from which γ can be uniquely defined.

To identify ω, we assume ω belongs to a compact parameter space $\Omega = \{\rho,\nu,\theta,\pi = (\pi_j : 1 \le j \le d_x) : -1 < \rho \ne 0, \nu > 0, \theta \in \Re^{d_w}, 0 \le \pi_j \le 1, \sum_{j=1}^{d_x} \pi_j = 1\}$. Given that $\sum_{j=1}^{d_x} \pi_j = 1$ implies $\pi_1 = 1 - \sum_{j=2}^{d_x} \pi_l$, we consider a "leave-one-out" parameter space for ω as[7]

$$\Omega_{-1} = \{\rho,\nu,\theta,\pi_{-1} = (\pi_l : 2 \le l \le d_x) : -1 < \rho \ne 0, \nu > 0, \theta \in \Re^{d_w},$$
$$0 \le \pi_l \le 1, 0 \le \sum_{l=2}^{d_x} \pi_l \le 1\}.$$

The conditions above allow us to identify $\eta_{-1} = (\gamma_{-1}^{\top}, \omega_{-1}^{\top})^{\top}$ from the resulting "leave-one-out" parameter space $\Theta_{-1} = \{\Gamma_{-1}, \Omega_{-1}\}$.

We must point out that in a rare case, γ_{-1} cannot be differentiated from Θ_{-1}. Assume that $\alpha_i = 0$ for all i and that Z_{it} are deemed to generate the same effects on both the technology and inefficiency (i.e., $W_{it} = Z_{it}$ and $\gamma_z = \theta$). Then if $A(\cdot)$ takes the same functional form as $\mu(\cdot)$, we have $A(Z_{it}^{\top}\gamma_z) = \mu(W_{it};\theta)$. The frontier in (2) reduces to $A(Z_{it}^{\top}\gamma_z)\left[\left(\pi_1 X_{1it}^{-\rho} + \cdots + \pi_{d_x} X_{d_x it}^{-\rho}\right)^{-\frac{\nu}{\rho}} - 1\right]$, where γ_{-1} cannot be identified if $\left(\pi_1 X_{1it}^{-\rho} + \cdots + \pi_{d_x} X_{d_x it}^{-\rho}\right)^{-\frac{\nu}{\rho}} = 1$ for some particular values of X_j and (ρ, π_j, ν). We are less concerned about this identification problem because the probability of having zero fixed effects, identical effects of Z_{it} in frontier and inefficiency, and equivalent structures of $A(\cdot)$ and $\mu(\cdot)$, is essentially zero. Even such an event occurs, we can let $\left(\pi_1 X_{1it}^{-\rho} + \cdots + \pi_{d_x} X_{d_x it}^{-\rho}\right)^{-\frac{\nu}{\rho}} \ne 1$ by requiring $X_j > 1$ for all j, which almost always holds in applied studies.

2.3. Estimation

We employ a two-step semiparametric estimator for our model in (2). In the first step, we focus on estimating $\eta = (\gamma^{\top}, \omega^{\top})$ using series approximation. If η were known, the only unknown part in (2) is the smooth technology function $A(\cdot)$, which can be approximated via a series estimator. To avoid clustering notations below, we denote $\mathbf{Z} \in \Re^{d_z+n-1}$ as a vector including environment variables Z plus $n-1$ dummy variables for fixed effects. Let $\mathcal{Z}_j = [a_j, b_j] \in \Re$ be a compact subset of $\mathbf{Z}_j$ for some real constants a_j and b_j, with $j = 1, \ldots, d_z + n - 1$. For $\mathbf{z} = [\mathbf{z}_1, \ldots, \mathbf{z}_{d_z+n-1}]^{\top}$ with $\mathbf{z}_j \in \mathcal{Z}_j$, let $v(\gamma) = \mathbf{z}^{\top}\gamma$. We define $\phi(v(\gamma)) = [\phi_1(v(\gamma)), \ldots, \phi_L(v(\gamma))]^{\top}$ as a $L \times 1$ vector of basis functions evaluated at $v(\gamma)$, where L is a positive integer satisfying $L \to \infty$ as $nT \to \infty$. Then $A(v(\gamma)) \approx \phi(v(\gamma))^{\top}\lambda(\eta)$, where $\lambda(\eta) = [\lambda_1(\eta), \ldots, \lambda_L(\eta)]^{\top} \in \Re^L$ are unknown series coefficients. Here, we highlight the dependence of $\lambda(\cdot)$ with η because $A(\cdot)$ is not additively separable with other parametric parts in (2). Let $N = nT$, the estimator of $\lambda(\eta)$ solves the least-square problem as $\hat{\lambda}(\eta) = \underset{\{\lambda(\eta) \in \Re^L\}}{\operatorname{argmin}} \mathcal{L}_N(\lambda(\eta), \eta^{\top})$, where

$$\mathcal{L}_N(\lambda(\eta),\eta^\top)=\sum_{i=1}^{n}\sum_{t=1}^{T}\left[Y_{it}-\phi(v_{it}(\gamma))^\top\lambda(\eta)\left(\pi_1X_{1it}^{-\rho}+\cdots+\pi_{d_x}X_{d_xit}^{-\rho}\right)^{-\frac{\nu}{\rho}}+\mu(W_{it};\theta)\right]^2, \quad (3)$$

with $\phi(v_{it}(\gamma))=\phi(\mathbf{Z}_{it}^\top\gamma)$. In practice, the estimator $\hat{\lambda}(\eta)$ is infeasible because η is unknown. As mentioned above, we cannot estimate η directly through its first order condition in (3) due to the location of γ and the condition $\pi_1+\cdots+\pi_{d_x}=1$. Given the construction of $\hat{\lambda}(\eta)$, we estimate $\eta_{-1}=(\gamma_{-1},\omega_{-1})$ through a PNLS $\hat{\eta}_{-1}=\underset{\{\eta_{-1}\in\Theta_{-1}\}}{\operatorname{argmin}}\ \mathcal{L}_N(\eta_{-1})$, where

$$\mathcal{L}_N(\eta_{-1})=\sum_{i=1}^{n}\sum_{t=1}^{T}\left[Y_{it}-\phi(v_{it}(\gamma))^\top\hat{\lambda}(\eta)\left(\pi_1X_{1it}^{-\rho}+\cdots+\pi_{d_x}X_{d_xit}^{-\rho}\right)^{-\frac{\nu}{\rho}}+\mu(W_{it};\theta)\right]^2. \quad (4)$$

(4) Define the short-hand notations $\hat{A}(\mathbf{Z}_{it}^\top\gamma)=\phi(v_{it}(\gamma))^\top\hat{\lambda}(\eta)$ and $M(X_{it};\rho,\pi)=\sum_{j=1}^{d_x}\pi_jX_{jit}^{-\rho}$, the estimator in (4) is equivalent to solving the first-order conditions $\dfrac{\partial\mathcal{L}_N(\eta_{-1})}{\partial\eta_{-1}}=0$, where

$$\frac{\partial\mathcal{L}_N(\eta_{-1})}{\partial\eta_{-1}}=-\sum_{i=1}^{n}\sum_{t=1}^{T}\left[Y_{it}-\hat{A}(\mathbf{Z}_{it}^\top\gamma)M(X_{it};\rho,\pi)^{-\frac{\nu}{\rho}}+\mu(W_{it};\theta)\right]$$
$$\times\begin{bmatrix} M(X_{it};\rho,\pi)^{-\frac{\nu}{\rho}}\left(J^\top\mathbf{Z}_{it}\hat{A}'(\mathbf{Z}_{it}^\top\gamma)+\dfrac{\partial}{\partial\gamma_{-1}}\hat{A}(\mathbf{Z}_{it}^\top\gamma)\right)\\ \hat{A}(\mathbf{Z}_{it}^\top\gamma)M(X_{it};\rho,\pi)^{-\frac{\nu+\rho}{\rho}}\nu(-\rho X_{2it}^{\rho})^{-1}\\ \vdots\\ \hat{A}(\mathbf{Z}_{it}^\top\gamma)M(X_{it};\rho,\pi)^{-\frac{\nu+\rho}{\rho}}\nu(-\rho X_{d_xit}^{\rho})^{-1}\\ \hat{A}(\mathbf{Z}_{it}^\top\gamma)M(X_{it};\rho,\pi)^{-\frac{\nu}{\rho}}\dfrac{\partial}{\partial\rho}\left(\dfrac{\nu}{\rho}\ln\left(M(X_{it};\rho,\pi)\right)\right)\\ \hat{A}(\mathbf{Z}_{it}^\top\gamma)M(X_{it};\rho,\pi)^{-\frac{\nu+\rho}{\rho}}\dfrac{1}{\rho}\ln\left(M(X_{it};\rho,\pi)\right)\\ -\dfrac{\partial}{\partial\theta}\mu(W_{it};\theta)\end{bmatrix},$$

where $\hat{A}'(\mathbf{Z}_{it}^\top\gamma)$ is the series estimator for the first order derivatives (de Boor, 1978), and

$$J\equiv\frac{\partial\gamma}{\partial\gamma_{-1}}=\begin{pmatrix}-(1-\|\gamma_{-1}\|^2)^{-1/2}\gamma_{-1}^\top\\ I_{d_z+n-2}\end{pmatrix}$$

is a $(d_z+n-1)\times(d_z+n-2)$ Jacobian matrix, with I_v a $v\times v$ identity matrix for a positive integer v. We obtain $\hat{\gamma}$ via updating $\hat{\gamma}=[(1-\|\hat{\gamma}_{-1}\|^2)^{1/2},\hat{\gamma}_{z_2},\ldots,\hat{\gamma}_{z_{d_z}},\hat{\alpha}_{-1}^{\top}]^{\top}$.

In the second step, we estimate $A(\cdot)$ by a local LNK. Using the estimates $\hat{\eta}$ from the first step, let $a_0=A(v(\hat{\gamma}))$ and $a_1=A'(v(\hat{\gamma}))$ be constants in which $A(\cdot)$ and the its derivative $A'(\cdot)$ are evaluated at $\mathbf{Z}=\mathbf{z}$ with $\hat{\gamma}$. The LNK $\hat{a}=(\hat{a}_0,\hat{a}_1)^{\top}$ is obtained from

$$\hat{\alpha}^{\top}=\underset{\{a(\hat{\eta})^{\top}\}}{argmin}\sum_{i=1}^{n}\sum_{t=1}^{T}\left(Y_{it}-\left[\alpha_0+\alpha_1(\mathbf{Z}_{it}-\mathbf{z})^{\top}\hat{\gamma}\right]\left(\sum_{j=1}^{d_x}\hat{\pi}_j X_{jit}^{-\hat{\rho}}\right)^{-\frac{\hat{\nu}}{\hat{\rho}}}+\mu(W_{it};\hat{\theta})\right)^2 \times k\left(\frac{(\mathbf{Z}_{it}-\mathbf{z})^{\top}\hat{\gamma}}{h}\right). \quad (5)$$

where $k(\cdot)$ is a univariate, symmetric kernel function with a bandwidth h such that $h\to 0$ as $nT\to\infty$ (Henderson & Parmeter, 2015). The LNK is essentially a local linear estimator performed on nonlinear functions of $v_{it}(\hat{\eta})$ defined similarly in Wang and Henderson (2022).

Remark 1. The series in our estimation procedure serves only as a pilot estimator for η. The series estimator facilitates η estimation by easily imposing the structure of semiparametric CES frontier in (1). This is essentially owing to is ability to *globally* linearize $A(\cdot)$ by a number of basis functions, which grows toward infinity as $nT\to\infty$ to achieve estimation consistency. The nature of series approximation also makes it computationally efficient for the global parameters η to be estimated. It would be theoretically feasible to replace the series estimator with a modified LNK in (5) to estimate η; however, doing so becomes empirically infeasible as $nT\to\infty$, because the kernel based estimator needs to *locally* linearize $A(\cdot)$ via Taylor expansion at each sample point. Together with the nonlinear (parametric) structure in the frontier, the LNK-based estimator for η would significantly increase the computational burden that makes its applicability prohibitive with large nT. Furthermore, once η is consistently estimated at a parametric rate, LNK is employed to approximate $A(\cdot)$ and $A'(\cdot)$ because the asymptotic distribution of the kernel estimator for both the function and derivatives are more transparent than its series counterpart. Using LNK in the second step also helps for testing hypotheses regarding the technology function.

Remark 2. When including fixed-effects (α_i), our estimator suffers from the incidental parameters problem (i.e., inconsistent when n grows toward infinity while T remains fixed). In a parametric nonlinear panel model with individual fixed-effects (e.g., a panel logit model), the parameter estimator is known to have a leading bias term of order $1/T$ (Arellano & Hahn, 2007). We expect such a bias with a similar order to appear in our proposed estimator for $A(\cdot)$. We show in Appendix 1 that the incidental parameters problem indeed arises with large n and fixed T, which leads to inconsistent estimation on both parameters and the nonparametric function. To avoid the incidental parameters problem, we follow the insights of Arellano and Hahn (2007) and Fernández-Val and Weidner (2016) to consider $n, T \to \infty$ and a bounded ratio of n/T to achieve consistent estimation.

Remark 3. TE has long been an important and informative indicator in efficiency analysis. In conventional SF models with log output, a widely used measure is $TE_0 = E(\exp(-u) \mid e)$ built upon prespecified distributions for v and u with $e = v - u$ (Battese & Coelli, 1988; Lee & Tyler, 1978). In our model, TE_0 is not applicable because output is measured in level while u is an additive unobservable. Furthermore, the distributions of both v and u are eschewed. Since our model accesses the distribution of inefficiency through $E(u \mid W) = \mu(W;\theta)$, an alternative measure for TE in our model can be constructed as $TE_1 = E(\exp(-u) \mid W)$. One can employ $\exp(-\mu(W;\theta))$ as a lower bound estimate of TE_1 by Jensen's inequality, or employ $1 - \mu(W;\theta)$ as the first order approximation for TE_1. However, TE_1 does not measure TE directly in an usual sense as TE_0 does, a problem similar to recent SF models with distribution-free features (Parmeter et al., 2016; Tran & Tsionas, 2009; Zhou et al., 2020). We refer readers to see detailed discussion about TE measures in Kumbhakar et al. (2020), and left a more direct TE measure in SF models without distribution assumptions for future research.

2.4. Basic Assumptions for Estimator Consistency

In this section, we discuss basic assumptions that are useful to establish the consistency of our proposed estimator for η_{-1} and $A(\cdot)$ in SP-CES-SP. The following notation is used. For any matrix A, define the Frobenius Norm $\| A \| = [trace(A^\top A)]^{1/2}$. Let C be a generic constant with inconsequential magnitude that varies from one place to another. We denote a generic function $\zeta(w) \in C^p$ if $\zeta(w)$ and all of its partial derivatives of order less than or equal to p are continuous and uniformly bounded on its support.

Assumptions:

A1 (1) $\{(Y_{it}, X_{it}, Z_{it}, Q_{it}) : i = 1,\ldots,n, t = 1,\ldots,T\}$ is i.i.d. (identically and independently distributed) across i and stationary across t. Each $X_{jit} > 0$ for $j = 1,\ldots,d_x$ and the support of X_{jit} is a compact subset of $\Re_+$. (2) The fixed effect is α_i and $E(\alpha_i \mid X_{it}, Z_{it}, Q_{it}) \neq 0$. (3) v_{it} is $i.i.d.(0,\sigma_v^2)$ across both i and t, independent of other variables. (4) u_{it} is i.i.d. across $i = 1,\ldots,n$, $E(u_{it} \mid \alpha_i, X_{it}, Z_{it}, Q_{it}) = \mu(W_{it};\theta)$, $E(u_{it}^2 \mid \alpha_i, X_i, Z_i, Q_i) < C$ for all i, t with $X_i = \{X_{it}\}_{t=1}^T$. (5) $E(\epsilon_{it} \mid \alpha_i, X_{it}, Z_{it}, Q_{it}) = 0$ for all i and t with $\epsilon_{it} = v_{it} - (u_{it} - \mu(W_{it};\theta))$.

A2 (1) Denote the true value of $\eta_{-1} = (\gamma_{-1}^\top, \omega_{-1}^\top)^\top$ as η_{-1}^0, which uniquely minimizes the objective function $\mathcal{L}_N(\eta_{-1})$ in (4). For $\Theta_{-1} = \{\Gamma_{-1}, \Omega_{-1}\}$, a compact subset of $\Re^q$ with $q = d_z + d_x + d_w + n - 1$, η_{-1}^0 is contained in the interior of Θ_{-1}. The objective function $\mathcal{L}_N(\eta_{-1})$ is uniquely minimized at η_{-1}^0. (2) $v(\gamma) = \mathbf{Z}^\top \gamma$ is defined on its compact support $\mathcal{V}_\gamma = \{\mathbf{Z}^\top \gamma : \mathbf{Z} \in \mathcal{Z}, \gamma_{-1} \in \Gamma_{-1}\}$, where $\mathcal{Z}$ is the compact support of $\mathbf{Z}$.

A3 (1) For any $v(\gamma) \in \mathcal{V}_\gamma$ with γ_{-1} in the neighborhood of $\gamma_{-1}^0 \in \Theta_{-1}$, $\exists$ some constant $\delta > 0$ and a $L \times 1$ real vector $\lambda_A \in \Re^L$ such that

$\sup_{v(\gamma)\in\mathcal{V}_\gamma} |A(v(\gamma)) - \phi(v(\gamma))^\top \lambda_A| = O(L^{-\delta})$. (2) $L \to \infty$ as $nT \to \infty$. (3) For some nonstochastic sequences ξ_L, $\sup_{v(\gamma)\in\mathcal{V}_\gamma} \|\phi(v(\gamma))\| \le \xi_L$. (4) as $nT \to \infty$, $\xi_L^2 L / nT \to 0$.

B1 (1) For $v \equiv v(\gamma) \in \mathcal{V}_\gamma$, the kernel function $K(v): \Re \to \Re$ is symmetric and satisfies (1) $|K(v)v^j| \le C$ for all $v \in \Re$ for $j = 0,1,2,3$. (2) $\int |v^j K(v)|\, dv \le C$ for $j = 0,1,2,3$. (3) $\int K(v)dv = 1$, $\int vK(v)dv = 0$, and $\mu_{k,2} = \int v^2 K(v)dv$. (4) $K(v)$ is continuously differentiable on $\Re$ with $|v^j \frac{d}{dv} K(v)| \le C$ for all $v \in \Re$ and $j = 0,1,2,3$.

B2 (1) $A(\cdot) \in C^2$. (2) For some $\rho > 0, E|v_{it}|^{2+\rho} < C, E|u_{it}|^{2+\rho} < C$, and $E(|\epsilon_{it}|^{2+\rho} | \alpha_i, X_{it}, Z_{it}, Q_{it}) < C$. (3) $E(\epsilon_{it}^2 | \mathbf{Z}_{it}^\top \gamma = \mathbf{z}^\top \gamma) \equiv \sigma_\epsilon^2(\mathbf{z}^\top \gamma) \in C^2$. The density function $0 < f_{v(\gamma)}(\cdot) < C$ of random variable $v(\gamma) = \mathbf{Z}^\top \gamma$ is twice differentiable defined on $\mathcal{V}_\gamma$.

B3 (1) As $n, T \to \infty$, $n/T = \kappa$ for some $0 < \kappa < C$. (2) $\xi_L^2 = O(L)$. (3) $h = O((nT)^{-1/5})$.

Assumptions A1–A3 facilitate our argument on the consistency of PNLS estimator $\hat{\eta}_{-1}$ in (4). A1(1) focuses on the panel data with large n with i.i.d. assumption. We require large T to avoid incidental parameters problem when handling the fixed effects α_i. A1(2) allows α_i to be arbitrary correlated with (X_{it}, Z_{it}, Q_{it}) for all t. A1(3) imposes a mild condition on the independence of v_{it}. A1(4) assumes that the conditional mean of inefficiency u_{it} is known up to a vector of parameters θ with finite conditional variance. A1(5) specifies zero conditional mean of demeaned composite error for model identification. Assumptions A2(1) ensures the identification on parameters η_{-1}^0, which is necessary to establish the consistency of $\hat{\eta}_{-1}$ in a similar spirit to the classical assumption of D of Theorem 4.3.1 for the consistency of nonlinear least squares in Amemiya (1985). A2(2) is a common condition for the support of index value as discussed in Ma and Song (2015). A3(1) ensures that, in the first step where parameters are estimated, the series approximation errors on technology function converge to zero as $L \to \infty$, as required in A3(2). A3(3) bounds the magnitudes of the basis functions, and A3(4) gives the rates at which $L \to \infty$ as $nT \to \infty$ such that the asymptotic bias and variance generated in estimating technology are sufficiently small to achieve parametric convergence rate of $\hat{\eta}_{-1}$.

Assumptions B1–B3 are basic conditions for the consistency of LNK estimator $\hat{\alpha}(\hat{\eta})$ in (5). B1 gives conditions on kernel functions, which are frequently used in kernel-based estimation (see, for example, Yao et al., 2018a). We note that B2 allows a Gaussian kernel to be used. B2(1) assumes $A(\cdot)$ to be sufficiently smooth in order for Taylor expansions to be performed. B2(2) places boundness conditions on the conditional moment of v_{it}, u_{it}, and ε_{it} (of order slightly larger than two) to derive asymptotic distribution of LNK under Liapunov's central limit theorem. B2(3) specifically allows conditional heteroscedasticity on ε_{it}, and B3(4) assumes that the density of index value is well defined and smooth. B3(1) requires a bounded ratio of n/T when both n and T diverge toward infinity, a condition similar to recent parametric panel model with fixed effects (Fernández-Val & Weidner, 2016). Specifically, we require a large T relative to n in order to achieve accurate estimation due to the fixed effects estimation. Finally, B3(2) and B3(3) provide expected rates that the number of series basis functions (in the first step) and bandwidths (in the second step) need to be satisfied. See **Remark 4** below for detailed discussion.

With Assumptions A–B, our proposed estimator $\hat{\eta}_{-1}$ and $\hat{\alpha}(\hat{\eta})$ are expected to be consistent. This conjecture is made based on the theoretical arguments in Ma and Song (2015), whose regression model shares some similar features to our SF-CES-SP. Namely, Ma and Song (2015) consider a cross sectional (or pool) varying index coefficient model as $Y_{it} = \sum_{l=1}^{d} m_l(Z_{it}^{\top}\beta_l)X_{lit}^{0} + \epsilon_{it}$, where the coefficient of X_{lit}^{0} is an unknown function $m_l(\cdot)$, varying with an index $Z_{it}^{\top}\beta_l$ for some coefficient vector β_l. In a particular case, their model is similar to the regression type of SF-CES-SP in (2) when $d = 2$, $m_1(Z_{it}^{\top}\beta_l) \equiv -\mu(W_{it};\theta)$ with $X_{1it}^{0} = 1$, and $m_2(Z_{it}^{\top}\gamma) \equiv A(\mathbf{Z}_{it}^{\top}\gamma)$ with $X_{2it}^{0} \equiv (\pi_1 X_{1it}^{-\rho} + \cdots + \pi_{d_x} X_{d_x it}^{-\rho})^{-\frac{\nu}{\rho}}$. In other words, our proposed model can be seen as a revised version of Ma and Song (2015)'s model such that $m_1(\cdot)$ is an known function and X_{2it}^{0} (with coefficient $m_2(\cdot)$) is not directly observable because it is a scaled index of $X_{1it},\ldots,X_{d_x it}$ that depends on $(\pi_1,\ldots,\pi_{d_x},\rho,\nu)$. Owing to this similarity, Ma and Song (2015)'s model and ours share a common ground where unknown parameters are estimated by approximating unknown functions through series estimation. Therefore, following similar arguments in Ma and Song (2015), together with Assumptions A–B above, we expect that our SF-CES-SP can be consistently estimated. Following the insights from both Ma and Song (2015) and Fernández-Val and Weidner (2016), we further expect that $\hat{\eta}_{-1}$ converges at a parametric rate of $1/\sqrt{nT}$, and $\hat{\alpha}(\hat{\eta})$ at a (univariate) nonparametric rate of $1/\sqrt{nTh}$. We demonstrate below that our conjecture on the consistency and convergence rates are supported by numerical evidence through simulation study.

Remark 4. Our current assumptions do not provide specific guidance on the choice of number of basis function L and bandwidth h. Recall that $N = nT$, the regression optimal order of L satisfies $L = O(N^{\frac{1}{2p+1}})$, obtained by minimizing the integrated squared error of the technology function with p being the degree of smoothness in $A(\cdot)$ (Newey, 1997). When p is low (e.g., $p < 3$), the consistency of $\hat{\eta}_{-1}$ typically calls for an undersmoothed series estimation on $A(\cdot)$ in order for the convergence rate of $\hat{\eta}_{-1}$ to be asymptotically unaffected by the series approximation error (Ma & Song, 2015). In such a case, a larger order of L should be considered in estimating $\hat{\eta}_{-1}$, say $L = O(N^{\frac{1}{2p+1}+\varrho})$ for some $\varrho > 1/(2p(2p+1))$. When p is large (e.g., $p \geq 3$) so that $A(\cdot)$ is sufficiently smooth, we expect a similar result in Ma and Song (2015) that the regression optimal order of L can be implemented in the first step. Given that $\hat{\eta}_{-1}$ are expected to be $\sqrt{nT}$-consistent, the bandwidth h should satisfy regression optimal order $h = O(N^{-\frac{1}{5}})$ (as given in B3(3)), implying that the data-driven cross-validation can be applied in practice for optimal h.

3. FINITE-SAMPLE PERFORMANCE

We provide simulation studies to evaluate the finite-sample performance of the proposed estimator. We first illustrate the numerical property of the estimators in (4) for parameters and (5) for the technology function across different choice of T with a fixed n. Second, we investigate whether the performance of the estimators is influenced by different specifications of the inefficiency function $\mu(W_{it};\theta)$. We consider a bivariate production model with two production inputs ($d_x = 2$), and generate data via

$$Y_{it} = A(Z_{it}^{\top}\gamma_z + \alpha_i)\left(\pi X_{1it}^{-\rho} + (1-\pi)X_{2it}^{-\rho}\right)^{-\frac{\nu}{\rho}} + v_{it} - u_{it}. \tag{6}$$

We specify $d_z = 2$, so $Z_{it} = (Z_{1it}, Z_{2it})$. For $j = 1,2$, we introduce time dependence by generating $Z_{jit} = Z_{jit}^0 + \zeta_{jit}^z$, where $Z_{jit}^0 \sim U(1,4)$ and $\zeta_{jit}^z = 0.25\zeta_{jit-1}^z + \xi_{it}$ follows an AR(1) process with $\xi_{it} \sim \mathcal{N}(0, 0.25^2)$. We generate $X_{jit} = 0.5(Z_{1it} + Z_{2it}) + \zeta_{jit}^x$ to mimic possible correlations between inputs and environment variables, where $\zeta_{jit}^x = 0.5\zeta_{jit-1}^x + \xi_{it}$. Here, we rescale Z_j and X_j into the range of [1,4] to satisfy assumption A1(1) and A2(2) on the boundness of variables' support. Three specifications of the inefficiency considered. 1) (Scaling) we generate u_{it} with a scaling property $u_{it} = (\sqrt{2/\pi})^{-1}u_i^* \exp(W_{it}^{\top}\theta)$, where $u_i^* \sim |\mathcal{N}(0,1)|$ follows a half-normal distribution with $E(u_i^* \mid W_{it}) = \sqrt{2/\pi}$, so $\mu(W_{it};\theta) = \exp(W_{it}^{\top}\theta)$; 2) (Log-Probit) we consider a log of probit function in $u_{it} = -\ln(\Phi(W_{it}^{\top}\theta))$ ($\Phi(\cdot)$ being the standard CDF), so $\mu(W_{it};\theta) = -\ln(\Phi(W_{it}^{\top}\theta))$; and 3) (Log-Normal) we specify u_{it} as a log-normal random variable $u_{it} \sim Log\mathcal{N}(0, \sigma^2(W_{it}^{\top}\theta))$, where $\sigma^2(\cdot)$ is the conditional variance function and $\mu(W_{it};\theta) = \exp(0.5W_{it}^{\top}\theta)$. In each case, we draw $v_{it} \sim \mathcal{N}(0, 0.25^2)$, and specify $W_{it}^{\top}\theta = Q_{it}\theta_1 + X_{1it}\theta_2$, where $Q_{it} \sim \mathcal{U}(0,1)$. We construct the fixed effect $\alpha_i = \frac{1}{T}\sum_{t=1}^{T} c_0\left(\sum_{j=1}^{2}(X_{jit} + Z_{jit}) + Q_{it}\right) + \xi_i$, where $\xi_i \sim \mathcal{N}(0, 1.25^2)$ and $c_0 = 1$ (i.e., the fixed effects are correlated with the regressors).

We consider three data generating processes (DGPs) with different specifications for $A(\cdot)$, $\gamma = (\gamma_1, \gamma_2, \alpha_{-1})$, and $\omega = (\pi, \rho, \nu, \theta^{\top})$, with $\alpha_{-1} = [\alpha_2, \ldots, \alpha_n]$ and $\theta = (\theta_1, \theta_2)$. In DGP_1, $A(v) = sin(v\pi/2)$, $\gamma = (2, 4, \alpha_{-1}^{\top})^{\top}$, $\omega = (0.7, 0.5, 0.8, 1.5, -0.5)$; in DGP_2, $A(v) = \sqrt{v\pi}$, $\gamma = (3, 5, \alpha_{-1}^{\top})^{\top}$, $\omega = (0.5, 0, 1, 2, 1)$; and in DGP_3, $A(v) = \exp(v/2)$, $\gamma = (4, 6, \alpha_{-1}^{\top})^{\top}$, and $\omega = (0.3, -0.5, 2, -1, 0.5)$. We rescale γ empirically to satisfy $\|\gamma\| = 1$. The values of ρ and ν are chosen to reflect a production function with complementary elasticity of substitution ($\rho > 0$) and decreasing return to scale ($\nu < 1$) in DGP_1; unit elasticity of substitution ($\rho = 0$) and constant return to scale ($\nu = 1$) in DGP_2; and substitutable elasticity of substitution ($\rho < 0$) and increasing return to scale ($\nu > 1$) in DGP_3.

In our first step estimation, we implement cubic B-spline basis functions (of order $m = 3$) in (4) and place a total of $L = J + m + 1$ knots on the support of $v_{it}(\gamma)$, where J refers to the number of (strictly) interior knots of $v_{it}(\gamma)$. Since the function $A(\cdot)$ under each DGP is sufficiently smooth, we follow the arguments in **Remark 3** to select $J = [(nT)^{1/5}]$ as a *rule-of-thumb* (ROT) approach, where $[v]$ is the integer part of a real number v. We place the lth interior knot on the $(l/J+1)^{th}$ percentile of $v_{it}(\gamma)$ for $l = 1, \ldots, J$. In the second step, we use a second-order Gaussian kernel function in (5) with a ROT bandwidth $h_j = \hat{\sigma}_j(nT)^{-1/5}$ satisfying B3(3), where $\hat{\sigma}_j$ is the standard deviation of $\{v_{it}(\hat{\gamma})\}_{i=1,t=1}^{n,T}$. Throughout the experiment, we fix $n = 10$, set $T = (10, 20, 40)$, and conduct 500 repetitions. We evaluate the performance of the PNLS estimator $\hat{\gamma}$ by root mean squared error (RMSE), (absolute) bias (BIAS), and standard deviation (STD). We evaluate the performance of LNK estimator $\hat{A}(\cdot)$ via root average MSE (RAMSE), average BIAS (ABIAS), and average STD (ASTD).

Table 12.1 summarizes simulation results for our SF-CES-SP estimator by considering a scaling distribution of inefficiency in DGP_{1-3}. Given that the performance of each coefficient estimate in $\hat{\gamma}_z$ and $\hat{\theta}$ is similar, we only report the statistic measures for $\hat{\gamma}_{z_1}$ and $\hat{\theta}_1$ to save space. Conditioning on each sample, the parametric estimator uniformly outperforms the nonparametric estimator (as expected) with different DGPs. Both parameter and function estimator are consistent in that all measures decay toward zero as T doubles regardless of the DGP. More specifically, the estimators converge at their expected rates as our conjecture in Section 2.4. To clearly demonstrate the convergence rates, we re-estimate our model in (6) by fixing $n = 10$, raising $T = (5, 10, 20, 40, 80, 160)$, and compute RMSE and RAMSE given each sample size. Fig. 12.1 plots the RMSE of one frontier parameter $\hat{\pi}$ in panel (a), one technology parameter $\hat{\gamma}_{z_1}$ in panel (b), and one inefficiency parameter $\hat{\theta}_1$ in panel (c). In each panel, the RMSE under DGP_1 (dashed line with $\triangle$), DGP_2 (dot line with $+$), and DGP_3 (dot-dashed line with $\Diamond$) is plotted against the parametric rate of $1/\sqrt{nT}$ (solid line with *). Clearly, each parameter estimate decays at a rate quite close to the theoretical rate. Similar observation is made on RAMSE of $\hat{A}(\cdot)$, which closely resembles the univariate nonparametric rate of $1/\sqrt{nTh}$ in panel (d) of Fig. 12.1. The numerical properties of our estimator support our conjecture that the parameter (function) estimator is $\sqrt{nT}$ ($\sqrt{nTh}$)-consistent.

To clearly demonstrate the performance of function estimator, Fig. 12.2 plots LNK estimates $\hat{A}(\cdot)$ with a large sample $(n,T) = (20, 50)$ in Panels (a)–(c) for DGP_1, DGP_2, and DGP_3, respectively. Each LNK function estimate (dot line with $\triangle$) is plotted against its point-wise 95% wild bootstrap confidence interval (CI) with 399 repetitions (dashed line), true function (solid line), and oracle estimates in which η is assumed to be known (dot-dashed line with *). Consistent with Table 12.1, the estimates sufficiently reveal the shape of each function, and closely resemble the corresponding oracle estimates and true functions across all DGPs. We note that the bias is smaller for functions with a lower degree of curvature (i.e., DGP_1).

Table 12.2 investigates the performance of our proposed estimator under three different specifications for $\mu(W_{it};\theta)$. We report the estimation results with different sample sizes in DGP_1 under Scaling (upper panel), Log-Probit (middle panel), and Log-Normal (lower panel). The performance of both parameters and function estimator are relatively similar under the cases of Scaling and Log-Probit, but slightly worsen in the case of Log-Normal when the sample size is moderate.

Table 12.1. Simulation Results for SF-CES-SP with Scaling Inefficiency in DGP_{1-3}.

	(n,T)		RMSE	BIAS	STD		RAMSE	ABIAS	ASTD
DGP_1	(10,10)	$\hat{\gamma}_{z_1}$	0.1032	0.0820	0.0630	$\hat{A}$	0.2056	0.1568	0.1931
		$\hat{\pi}$	0.1393	0.1079	0.0886				
		$\hat{\rho}$	0.0687	0.0550	0.0413				
		$\hat{\nu}$	0.1426	0.1031	0.0989				
		$\hat{\theta}_1$	0.0883	0.0701	0.0539				
	(10,20)	$\hat{\gamma}_{z_1}$	0.0616	0.0474	0.0396	$\hat{A}$	0.1505	0.1173	0.1376
		$\hat{\pi}$	0.1127	0.0903	0.0677				
		$\hat{\rho}$	0.0423	0.0330	0.0266				
		$\hat{\nu}$	0.0995	0.0795	0.0602				
		$\hat{\theta}_1$	0.0583	0.0448	0.0375				
	(10,40)	$\hat{\gamma}_{z_1}$	0.0432	0.0350	0.0254	$\hat{A}$	0.1044	0.0868	0.0906
		$\hat{\pi}$	0.0823	0.0638	0.0524				
		$\hat{\rho}$	0.0300	0.0244	0.0176				
		$\hat{\nu}$	0.0685	0.0562	0.0395				
		$\hat{\theta}_1$	0.0449	0.0342	0.0292				
DGP_2	(10,10)	$\hat{\gamma}_{z_1}$	0.1463	0.1105	0.0964	$\hat{A}$	0.2948	0.2092	0.2774
		$\hat{\pi}$	0.0653	0.0506	0.0415				
		$\hat{\rho}$	0.1043	0.0781	0.0695				
		$\hat{\nu}$	0.1192	0.0987	0.0673				
		$\hat{\theta}_1$	0.0996	0.0749	0.0659				
	(10,20)	$\hat{\gamma}_{z_1}$	0.1091	0.0871	0.0660	$\hat{A}$	0.1992	0.1550	0.1812
		$\hat{\pi}$	0.0465	0.0354	0.0303				
		$\hat{\rho}$	0.0848	0.0658	0.0537				
		$\hat{\nu}$	0.0797	0.0666	0.0439				
		$\hat{\theta}_1$	0.0704	0.0569	0.0417				
	(10,40)	$\hat{\gamma}_{z_1}$	0.0881	0.0726	0.0502	$\hat{A}$	0.1381	0.1075	0.1326
		$\hat{\pi}$	0.0333	0.0269	0.0198				
		$\hat{\rho}$	0.0679	0.0542	0.0411				
		$\hat{\nu}$	0.0596	0.0479	0.0357				
		$\hat{\theta}_1$	0.0523	0.0420	0.0313				
DGP_3	(10,10)	$\hat{\gamma}_{z_1}$	0.0781	0.0653	0.0432	$\hat{A}$	0.3466	0.2625	0.3042
		$\hat{\pi}$	0.0631	0.0505	0.0380				
		$\hat{\rho}$	0.0964	0.0798	0.0544				
		$\hat{\nu}$	0.1258	0.1026	0.0731				
		$\hat{\theta}_1$	0.0951	0.0731	0.0611				
	(10,20)	$\hat{\gamma}_{z_1}$	0.0580	0.0463	0.0350	$\hat{A}$	0.2688	0.2040	0.2381
		$\hat{\pi}$	0.0417	0.0337	0.0246				
		$\hat{\rho}$	0.0718	0.0563	0.0449				
		$\hat{\nu}$	0.0943	0.0796	0.0510				
		$\hat{\theta}_1$	0.0804	0.0653	0.0471				
	(10,40)	$\hat{\gamma}_{z_1}$	0.0415	0.0327	0.0258	$\hat{A}$	0.1984	0.1435	0.1746
		$\hat{\pi}$	0.0323	0.0265	0.0187				
		$\hat{\rho}$	0.0517	0.0395	0.0335				
		$\hat{\nu}$	0.0721	0.0594	0.0411				
		$\hat{\theta}_1$	0.0566	0.0433	0.0366				

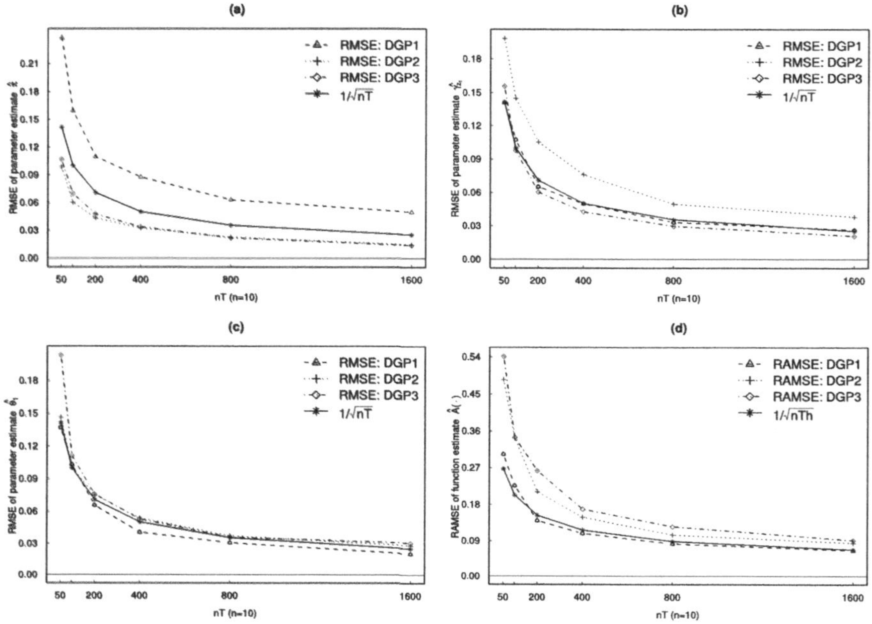

Fig. 12.1. Convergence Rates of Parameter (a)–(c) and Function (d) Estimators in DGP_{1-3}.

The estimator is qualitatively similar across all three specifications in $\mu(W_{it};\theta)$, again illustrating its consistency property. Using the sample size $(n,T)=(20,50)$, Fig. 12.2 plots in panel (d) the function estimates under Scaling (dot line with $\triangle$) against these under Log-Probit (dot short-dashed line with $\Diamond$) and Log-Normal (dot long-dashed line with *), together with 95% bootstrap CI under the Scaling case and true function. It is clear that the estimation difference under different specifications of inefficiency function becomes negligible with a larger sample size. Overall, our proposed estimator demonstrates appealing numerical performance in estimating unknown parameters and functions in SF-CES-SP, which is fairly robust to different specifications of the inefficiency.

4. EMPIRICAL APPLICATION

A number of studies have investigated country productive efficiency through SF models. For instance, Iyer et al. (2008) evaluate the roles of trade variables among developed (OECD) countries. Yao et al. (2018a, 2018b) focus specifically on the effect of human capital among both developed and developing countries. The SF models adopted by the aforementioned studies are similar

Table 12.2. Simulation Results for SF-CES-SP with Different Distribution of Inefficiency in DGP_1.

	(n,T)		RMSE	BIAS	STD		RAMSE	ABIAS	ASTD
Scaling	(10,10)	$\hat{\gamma}_1$	0.1071	0.0822	0.0629	$\hat{A}$	0.2086	0.1565	0.1915
		$\hat{\pi}$	0.1376	0.1085	0.0887				
		$\hat{\rho}$	0.0679	0.0561	0.0408				
		$\hat{\nu}$	0.1431	0.1010	0.1006				
		$\hat{\theta}_1$	0.0919	0.0710	0.0536				
	(10,20)	$\hat{\gamma}_1$	0.0601	0.0482	0.0394	$\hat{A}$	0.1511	0.1207	0.1407
		$\hat{\pi}$	0.1152	0.0884	0.0664				
		$\hat{\rho}$	0.0428	0.0339	0.0275				
		$\hat{\nu}$	0.0979	0.0778	0.0619				
		$\hat{\theta}_1$	0.0586	0.0442	0.0368				
	(10,40)	$\hat{\gamma}_1$	0.0432	0.0332	0.0252	$\hat{A}$	0.1051	0.0854	0.0904
		$\hat{\pi}$	0.0830	0.0643	0.0532				
		$\hat{\rho}$	0.0306	0.0254	0.0180				
		$\hat{\nu}$	0.0684	0.0561	0.0393				
		$\hat{\theta}_1$	0.0456	0.0336	0.0290				
Log-Probit	(10,10)	$\hat{\gamma}_1$	0.0951	0.0723	0.0621	$\hat{A}$	0.2705	0.2147	0.2611
		$\hat{\pi}$	0.0974	0.0781	0.0585				
		$\hat{\rho}$	0.1428	0.1072	0.0947				
		$\hat{\nu}$	0.1526	0.1238	0.0896				
		$\hat{\theta}_1$	0.1508	0.1193	0.0927				
	(10,20)	$\hat{\gamma}_1$	0.0589	0.0474	0.0351	$\hat{A}$	0.2113	0.1598	0.1819
		$\hat{\pi}$	0.0688	0.0575	0.0380				
		$\hat{\rho}$	0.1068	0.0838	0.0688				
		$\hat{\nu}$	0.0995	0.0766	0.0638				
		$\hat{\theta}_1$	0.0911	0.0684	0.0606				
	(10,40)	$\hat{\gamma}_1$	0.0425	0.0339	0.0257	$\hat{A}$	0.1812	0.1407	0.1330
		$\hat{\pi}$	0.0577	0.0476	0.0328				
		$\hat{\rho}$	0.0688	0.0458	0.0381				
		$\hat{\nu}$	0.0699	0.0558	0.0424				
		$\hat{\theta}_1$	0.0656	0.0523	0.0399				
Log-Normal	(10,10)	$\hat{\gamma}_1$	0.1423	0.1107	0.0899	$\hat{A}$	0.3228	0.2499	0.3077
		$\hat{\pi}$	0.1267	0.1039	0.0729				
		$\hat{\rho}$	0.1000	0.0781	0.0628				
		$\hat{\nu}$	0.1722	0.1305	0.1129				
		$\hat{\theta}_1$	0.0322	0.0251	0.0203				
	(10,20)	$\hat{\gamma}_1$	0.1083	0.0886	0.0627	$\hat{A}$	0.2704	0.1997	0.2346
		$\hat{\pi}$	0.0721	0.0579	0.0432				
		$\hat{\rho}$	0.0745	0.0618	0.0420				
		$\hat{\nu}$	0.1116	0.0937	0.0609				
		$\hat{\theta}_1$	0.0269	0.0209	0.0170				
	(10,40)	$\hat{\gamma}_1$	0.0702	0.0595	0.0374	$\hat{A}$	0.2216	0.1643	0.1664
		$\hat{\pi}$	0.0639	0.0470	0.0334				
		$\hat{\rho}$	0.0513	0.0486	0.0310				
		$\hat{\nu}$	0.0791	0.0587	0.0533				
		$\hat{\theta}_1$	0.0205	0.0161	0.0127				

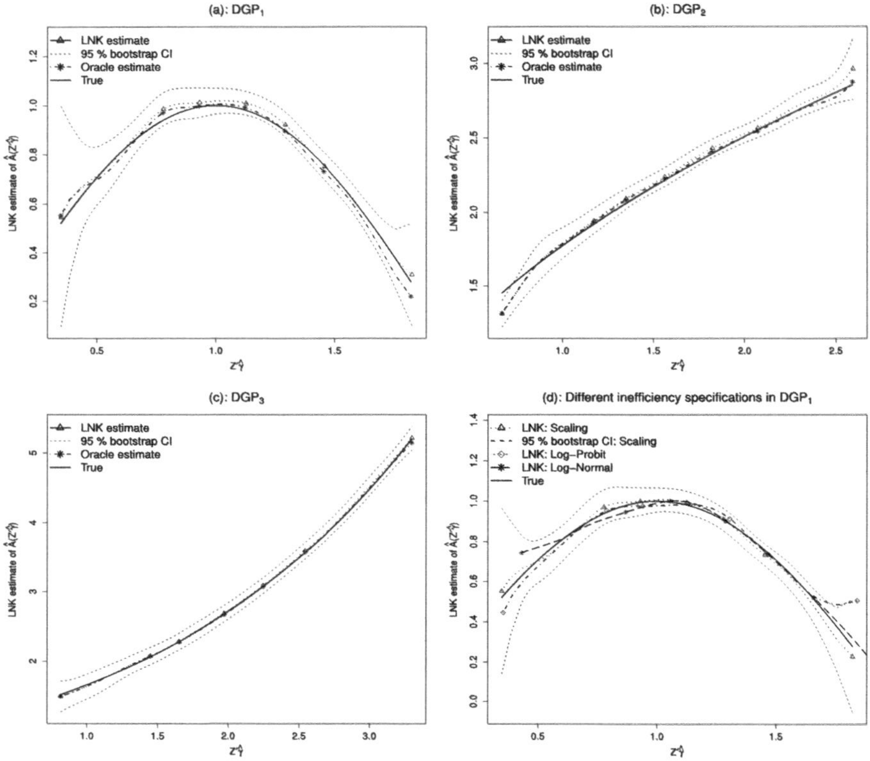

Fig. 12.2. Technology Function Estimation (LNK) with $(n,T)=(20,50)$.

in three aspects that could be potentially restrictive for the efficiency analysis. First, the frontier is specified as logged CD with either parametric or semiparametric structure. The implied unit elasticity of inputs substitution may not necessarily hold in countries with different technology bias and, as shown below, applying log transformation on a SF model would bias estimation on both CD frontier and inefficiency. Second, the composite error is assumed to follow specific distributions for the purpose of model identification, but the justification of correct distributional assumptions can be difficult with a real data set. Finally, the unobserved heterogeneities (or fixed effects) in countries are not controlled, which can lead to inconsistent model estimation due to their potential correlation with covariates appearing in the frontier and/or inefficiency.

We are therefore motivated to illustrate our semiparametric SF model with flexible features on both the frontier and inefficiency while properly handling country fixed effects. Following the insights from our simulation results, we are encouraged to employ a panel data set with small n and large T. To this end, we narrow our scope to consider OECD countries with membership since 1962 in North America and Europe from 1970 to 2019. This gives us 20 countries over 5 decades, so $n = 20$ and $T = 50$ (i.e., equivalent to the sample size used to generate Fig. 12.2). We source our data from the tenth version of Penn World Table (PWT) and United Nations Conference on Trade and Development (UNCTAD), which are by far the most complete panel data sources with aggregate production and trade variables at the country level. Using PWT, we collect data on output Y as the output side real GDP in millions; two inputs K as real capital stock in millions and HL as the human capital augmented labor[8]; and one environment variable EXS as export share of a country's real GDP, which is likely to generate non-trivial impacts on technology (Malikov, Zhao, & Kumbhakar, 2020). Given that inefficiency plays an important role in influencing productivity change (Kumbhakar & Lovell, 2000), we further include EXS as one inefficiency determinant to capture a possible indirect effect of EXS on technology through affecting productive inefficiency. Using UNCTAD, we follow the arguments by Iyer et al. (2008) to collect the share of foreign direct investment inward flows ($FDI\text{-}INS$) and outward flows ($FDI\text{-}OUTS$) relative to real GDP as two additional inefficiency determinants. All variables (except for HL) are adjusted at 2017 US dollars to facilitate estimation comparison across countries and time.

In sum, we perform production efficiency analysis among OECD countries through our SF-CES-SP (in regression form (2)) as

$$Y_{it} = A\left(EXS_{it}\gamma_{exs} + \alpha_i\right)\left[\pi K_{it}^{-\rho} + (1-\pi)HL_{it}^{-\rho}\right]^{-\frac{\nu}{\rho}} - \mu\left(W_{it};\theta\right) + \epsilon_{it}, \tag{7}$$

where $i = 1,\ldots,20$ is the OECD country index, $t = 1,\ldots,50$ represents years from 1970 to 2019, and $\epsilon_{it} = v_{it} - \left(u_{it} - \mu\left(W_{it};\theta\right)\right)$. Here, we have inputs $X = (K, HL)$, environment variables Z with EXS plus $n-1 = 19$ dummies (controlling for country fixed effects), and inefficiency determinants $W = (Cont, EXS, FDI\text{-}INS, FDI\text{-}OUTS)$, where $Cont$ is a constant term. Table 12.3 summarizes the distribution of each variable by reporting their corresponding average (Mean), standard deviation (SD), minimum (Min), and maximum (Max). We highlight that the USA exhibits the highest level of Y, K, and HL. Belgium has the largest EXS and Luxembourg tops the list of both FDI variables. In contrast, Iceland and Turkey show the lowest values in production variables (Y, K, HL) and trade variables ($EXS, FDI\text{-}INS, FDI\text{-}OUTS$), respectively.

To facilitate comparison between our SF-CES-SP and conventional models in the SF literature, we further estimate four benchmark parametric SF panel models with different frontier structures. The first benchmark model considers a parametric CD frontier in level (SF-CD-P-Level) as

Table 12.3. Data Descriptive Summary Statistics.

Variables	Description	Mean	SD	Min	Max
Y	Output-side real GDP	1285441	2787333	3647.29	20860506
K	Capital stock	5335775	10301105	18818.94	69059088
HL	Human capital-augmented labor, the product of human capital index (HC) and number of persons engaged (L)	51.54	97.72	0.20	593.52
EXS	Share of merchandise exports	0.37	0.25	0.02	1.39
FDI-INS	FDI: Inward flows and stocks	0.03	0.09	−0.66	0.83
FDI-OUTS	FDI: Outward flows and stocks	0.05	0.16	−0.38	1.59
(*n*,*T*)	(20,50)				

Notes: Variables *Y*, *K*, *HL*, and *EXS* are obtained from the 10th version of PWT, measured in millions at 2017 US dollars. Variables *FDI-INS* and *FDI-OUTS* are constructed using FDI inward and outward flows (in millions) from UNCTAD, which are adjusted at 2017 US dollar and divided by *Y*. All data are collected for 20 OECD countries during 1970–2019.

$$Y_{it} = A_p\left(EXS_{it}\gamma_{exs} + \alpha_i\right)K_{it}^{\beta_K}HL_{it}^{\beta_{HL}} - \mu\left(W_{it};\theta\right) + \epsilon_{it}, \tag{8}$$

where the technology function $A_p(v) = \exp(v)$ has a known exponential structure, and parameters β_K and β_{HL} are the output elasticity of K and HL, respectively. The second benchmark model considers a log-transformed CD frontier (SF-CD-P-Log), which has been commonly employed in applied works. Compared to SF-CD-P-Level, the structure of SF-CD-P-Log is more delicate due to logging in the presence of productive inefficiency. To see this, we define $F_{it} \equiv A_p\left(EXS_{it}\gamma_{exs} + \alpha_i\right)K_{it}^{\beta_K}HL_{it}^{\beta_{HL}}$ as the frontier and $\zeta_{it} = 1 + \left(v_{it} - u_{it}\right)/F_{it}$ as an error term, so (8) is equivalently to $Y_{it} = F_{it}\zeta_{it}$. Since $\ln\left(Y_{it}\right) = \ln\left(F_{it}\right) + \ln\left(\zeta_{it}\right)$, a first-order Taylor expansion on $\ln\left(\zeta_{it}\right)$ gives an approximation $\ln\left(1 + \left(v_{it} - u_{it}\right)/F_{it}\right) \approx \frac{v_{it} - u_{it}}{F_{it}} - \frac{\left(v_{it} - u_{it}\right)^2}{2F_{it}^2} = -\frac{\mu\left(W_{it};\theta\right)}{F_{it}} + \frac{\epsilon_{it}}{F_{it}} - \frac{\left(v_{it} - u_{it}\right)^2}{2F_{it}^2}$. Thus, the explicit form of SF-CD-P-Log is

$$\ln\left(Y_{it}\right) = EXS_{it}\gamma_{exs} + \alpha_i + \ln\left(K_{it}\right)\beta_K + \ln\left(HL_{it}\right)\beta_{HL} - \mu^*\left(W_{it};\theta\right) + \epsilon_{it}^*, \tag{9}$$

where $\mu^*\left(W_{it};\theta\right) = \mu\left(W_{it};\theta\right)/F_{it}$ and $\epsilon_{it}^* = \frac{\epsilon_{it}}{F_{it}} - \frac{\left(v_{it} - u_{it}\right)^2}{2F_{it}^2}$. As a result, the log transformation on (8) introduces non-negligible estimation bias on parameters in (9) because $\mu^*\left(W_{it};\theta\right) \neq \mu\left(W_{it};\theta\right)$ and $E\left(\epsilon_{it}^* \mid EXS_{it}, \alpha_i, K_{it}, HL_{it}, W_{it}\right) \neq 0$ in general. The third benchmark model specifies a CES frontier in level (SF-CES-P-Level) as

$$Y_{it} = A_p\left(EXS_{it}\gamma_{exs} + \alpha_i\right)\left[\pi K_{it}^{-\rho} + (1-\pi)HL_{it}^{-\rho}\right]^{-\frac{\nu}{\rho}} - \mu\left(W_{it};\theta\right) + \epsilon_{it}, \tag{10}$$

which differs from SF-CES-SP in (7) in terms of the exponential form of technology. The final benchmark model is the log-transformed version of SF-CES-P-Level through Kmenta's approximation (SF-CES-P-Log). Namely, let the frontier be $F_{it} = A_p\left(EXS_{it}\gamma_{exs} + \alpha_i\right) f_{it}(\rho)$, with $f_{it}(\rho) = \left[\pi K_{it}^{-\rho} + (1-\pi) HL_{it}^{-\rho}\right]^{-\frac{\nu}{\rho}}$. Since $\ln(F_{it}) = EXS_{it}\gamma_{exs} + \alpha_i + \ln(f_{it}(\rho))$, a first-order Taylor expansion on $\ln(f_{it}(\rho))$ around $\rho = 0$ gives an approximation $\ln(f_{it}(\rho)) \approx \ln(K_{it})b_1 + \ln(HL_{it})b_2 + \left[\ln(K_{it}) - \ln(HL_{it})\right]^2 b_3$, where $b_1 = \nu\pi, b_2 = \nu(1-\pi)$, and $b_3 = -\nu\rho(1-\pi)$. Our interested parameters in the frontier can be readily recovered as $\nu = b_1 + b_2, \pi = b_1 / \nu$, and $\rho = b_3\nu / b_1 b_2$. Thus, taking log on both sides gives an explicit form of SF-CES-P-Log as

$$\begin{aligned}\ln(Y_{it}) = {} & EXS_{it}\gamma_{exs} + \alpha_i + \ln(K_{it})b_1 + \ln(HL_{it})b_2 \\ & + \left[\ln(K_{it}) - \ln(HL_{it})\right]^2 b_3 - \mu^*(W_{it};\theta) + \epsilon_{it}^*,\end{aligned} \tag{11}$$

where $\mu^*(W_{it};\theta)$ and ϵ_{it}^* are defined similarly as in (9), except that F_{it} now takes CES form and, more importantly, ϵ_{it}^* now contains Taylor's expansion error not only from $\ln(\zeta_{it})$ but also $\ln(f_{it}(\rho))$. Due to this reason, we expect to observe severer estimation bias from SF-CES-P-Log than that from SF-CD-P-Log. As discussed below, our conjecture is indeed supported by our empirical results.

To implement SF-CES-SP, we follow the insights from our simulation study to employ ROT interior knots $J = [(nT)^{1/5}]$ for estimating η_{-1} and cross-validation bandwidth h for estimating $A(\cdot)$. To provide a fair comparison, all four benchmark models (8)–(11) are estimated without imposing distributional assumptions on v_{it} and u_{it}. Given that the estimation results remain qualitatively similar when different functional forms of $\mu(W_{it};\theta)$ are considered, we report the empirical results below for $\mu(W_{it};\theta) = \exp\left(W_{it}^{\top}\theta\right)$.

We first compare several important metrics regarding the production frontier across different models. *Panel A* of Table 12.4 reports estimated parameters $(\hat{\pi}, \hat{\rho}, \hat{\nu})$ in models with CES frontiers and parameters $(\hat{\beta}_K, \hat{\beta}_{HL})$ in models with CD frontiers. All parameters' estimates (except for $\hat{\pi}$ in SF-CES-P-Log) are significant at the 1% level. Our SF-CES-SP reveals a production function with about 2/3 uses of K as indicated by $\hat{\pi} = 0.673$, consistent with conventional wisdom that developed countries are commonly capital intensive. The estimate of $\hat{\rho}$ is 0.044, suggesting that K and HL in OECD countries are complementary given that the implied elasticity of input substitution is $\hat{\sigma} = 1/(1+\hat{\rho}) = 0.958$. The underlying production is also suggested to exhibit increasing returns to scale (RTS) as indicated by $\hat{\nu} = 1.143$, significantly larger than unity at the 1% level. Compared to SF-CES-SP, parameters (π, ρ) are slightly overestimated under SF-CES-P-Level but largely underestimated under SF-CES-P-Log which, in particular, suggests that K accounts for less than 1/3 of total inputs ($\hat{\pi} = 0.269$). In contrast to SF-CES-SP, both parametric CES models suggest a substitutable relationship between K and HL, with $\hat{\sigma} = 1.095$ in SF-CES-P-Level and $\hat{\sigma} = 1.107$ in SF-CES-P-Log. We highlight that the estimate $\hat{\rho}$ across all three SF models with CES frontier significantly differs from zero at the 1% level, indicating that a CD production frontier is restrictive in our study. Finally, the constant

Table 12.4. Summary of Estimation Results in Frontier.

Panel A	SF-CES-SP		SF-CD-P-Level		SF-CD-P-Log		SF-CES-P-Level		SF-CES-P-Log	
$\hat{\pi}$	0.6730***	(0.1487)	–	–			0.6889***	(0.1425)	0.2689**	(0.1324)
$\hat{\rho}$	0.0441***	(0.0103)	–	–			0.0870***	(0.0097)	−0.0967***	(0.0325)
$\hat{\nu}$	1.1432***	(0.0540)	–	–			1.3587***	(0.0514)	1.0225***	(0.0740)
$\hat{\beta}_K$	–	–	0.6061***	(0.0118)	0.5003***	(0.0116)	–	–	–	–
$\hat{\beta}_{HL}$	–	–	0.5143***	(0.0124)	0.5217***	(0.0120)	–	–	–	–
Panel B	**Elas(*K*)**	**Elas(*HL*)**	**Elas(*K*)**	**Elas(*HL*)**	**Elas(*K*)**	**Elas(*HL*)**	**Elas(*K*)**	**Elas(*HL*)**	**Elas(*K*)**	**Elas(*HL*)**
0.10	0.5766	0.4675	–	–	–	–	0.5073	0.4517	0.5006	0.3380
0.25	0.5856	0.4707	–	–	–	–	0.5137	0.4578	0.5123	0.3447
0.50	0.5889	0.4755	–	–	–	–	0.5196	0.4638	0.5350	0.3529
0.75	0.5940	0.4806	–	–	–	–	0.5277	0.4696	0.5427	0.3606
0.90	0.5994	0.4848	–	–	–	–	0.5332	0.4768	0.5629	0.3698
Mean	0.5889	0.4757	0.6061	0.5143	0.5003	0.5217	0.5201	0.4640	0.5326	0.3532
Panel C	**Mean**	**Median**	**Mean**	**Median**	**Mean**	**Median**	**Mean**	**Median**	**Mean**	**Median**
RTS	1.0646	1.0641	1.1204	1.1204	1.0220	1.0220	1.3429	1.3382	0.9841	0.9842

Notes: Standard errors are reported in parenthesis beneath the estimated coefficients in Panel A. ***, **, and * stand for the statistically significant level at 1%, 5%, and 10%, respectively.

estimate for RTS ($\hat{\nu}$) is relatively over (under) estimated in SF-CES-P-Level (SF-CES-P-Log).

With the parameter estimates above, we compute the estimated output elasticity (i.e., the share) of K (Elas(K)) and HL (Elas(HL)) in models with CES frontier, where

$$\text{Elas}(K) = \frac{\hat{\pi}K^{-\hat{\rho}}}{\left[\hat{\pi}K^{-\hat{\rho}} + (1-\hat{\pi})HL^{-\hat{\rho}}\right]^{\hat{\nu}}}, \quad \text{Elas}(HL) = \frac{(1-\hat{\pi})HL^{-\hat{\rho}}}{\left[\hat{\pi}K^{-\hat{\rho}} + (1-\hat{\pi})HL^{-\hat{\rho}}\right]^{\hat{\nu}}}.$$

Clearly, the output elasticity of each input is country-year specific under CES as opposed to constants ($\hat{\beta}_K, \hat{\beta}_{HL}$) under CD. *Panel B* of Table 12.4 reports Elas(K) and Elas(HL) evaluated at five different percentiles (0.1, 0.25, 0.5, 0.75, 0.9) and the mean. In SF-CES-SP, the mean of output elasticity of K (HL) takes 0.59 (0.48), which is lower than the conventional value of 2/3 (1/3) possibly due to the effect of human capital through HL. Compared to SF-CES-SP, both SF-CES-P-Level and SF-CES-P-Log yield a lower Elas(K) with means of 0.52 and 0.53, respectively. Although Elas(HL) remains quantitatively similar under SF-CES-P-Level with a mean of 0.46, the log approximation on CES leads to a significant reduction on Elas(HL) in SF-CES-P-Log, with a mean of 0.35. Across all models, the largest Elas(K) and Elas(HL) stem from SF-CD-P-Level with 0.61 and 0.51, respectively. When the log-transformation is applied, we note that SF-CD-P-Log discloses a more even share of two inputs.

Fig. 12.3 provides a more vivid picture of the dispersion of Elas(K) and Elas(HL) across different models in panels (a) and (b), respectively. In each panel, we plot the kernel density of elasticity of K or HL by SF-CES-SP (solid curve) against those by SF-CD-P-Level (vertical dashed line with $\wedge$), SF-CD-P-Log (vertical dot line with $\diamond$), SF-CES-P-Level (dot-dashed curve with *), and SF-CES-P-Log (long-dashed curve with $\boxplus$). We find that the nonparametric technology

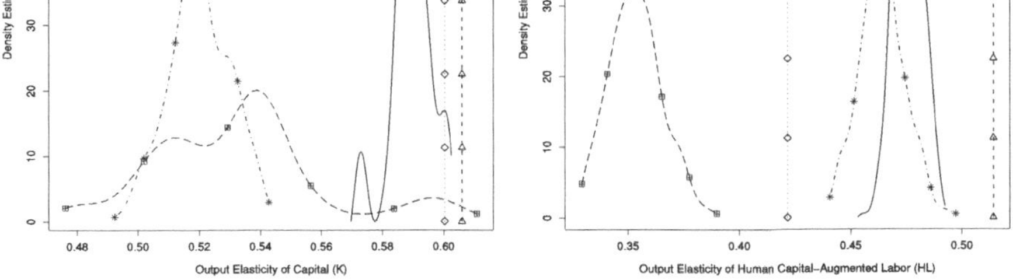

Fig. 12.3. Density of Output Elasticity of Capital (a) and Augmented Labor (b).

under SF-CES-SP makes the magnitude of Elas(HL) roughly similar to, yet Elas(K) quite distinguishable from, its parametric counterparts by SF-CES-P-Level. Furthermore, the log-approximation on CES results in a notably larger variation in Elas(K) and smaller magnitude in Elas(HL) under SF-CES-P-Log. The impact of log-transformation can also be observed from SF models with CD, from which the Elas (HL) differs significantly across SF-CD-P-Level and SF-CD-P-Log. As a result, the large difference in estimated elasticity of inputs across different models constitutes different estimates of (observation specific) return to scale as RTS = Elas(K) + Elas(HL). *Panel C* of Table 12.4 reports the mean and median of the RTS, which imply a production function with increasing RTS under SF-CES-SP, SF-CES-P-Level, and SF-CD-P-Level; constant RTS under SF-CD-Log; and decreasing RTS under SF-CES-P-Log.[9]

We next compare several results regarding the technology function. *Panel A* of Table 12.5 reports estimated coefficients of EXS (i.e., $\hat{\gamma}_{exs}$) in the technology function across different SF models. By controlling for country fixed effects, we observe a significant positive impact of export share on technology at the 1% level across all models, albeit in different magnitudes. The estimate is given by 0.671 under SF-CES-SP (assuming unknown structure of $A(\cdot)$), about 12% lower than the estimate of 0.751 under SF-CES-P-Level (assuming known structure of $A_p(\cdot)$ being exponential). However, applying log-transformation on CES significantly reduces the magnitude of estimate toward 0.058 under SF-CES-P-Log. A similar observation is made on SF models with CD, where the estimate 0.367 in SF-CD-P-Level drops by almost threefold to 0.092 in SF-CD-P-Log.

To evaluate how countries' export share evolve technology in the presence of latent heterogeneities, *Panel B* of Table 12.5 reports our LNK estimates $\hat{A}(\cdot)$ at five percentiles of the estimated index $EXS_{it}\hat{\gamma}_{exs} + \hat{\alpha}_i$. The function estimates are all significant at 1% level, with the mean given on the bottom of the panel. We observe that technology is not increased monotonically when $EXS_{it}\hat{\gamma}_{exs} + \hat{\alpha}_i$ exceeds about its 25% percentile. To better visualize the estimated technology function, panel (a) of Fig. 12.4 plots $\hat{A}(\cdot)$ (solid line) along with its 95% wild bootstrap confidence interval (dashed line) using 399 repetitions. Our estimated index $EXS_{it}\hat{\gamma}_{exs} + \hat{\alpha}_i$ is positive for all observations, given that $\hat{\gamma}_{exs}$ and 17 out of 19 fixed effects estimates are significantly positive.[10] As indicated by Table 12.5, an initial increase in index (driven by increasing export share) from 0.752 to 0.847 (about 25% percentile) significantly improves the technology from 2.793 toward 3.735, or a 33.7% increase. A further rise in the index toward 1.167 (about 88% percentile), however, steadily declines $\hat{A}$ until it reaches a local trough at 3.356 (about 11.3% decrease). The technology is improved again with export share plus fixed effects continuously rising, although this upward moving trend is driven by less than 10% country-year observations (mostly from the Netherlands and Belgium with high export shares).

Our SF-CES-SP reveals a significant nonlinear structure of the technology function, which clearly deviates from a commonly assumed exponential form. For comparison purpose, *Panel B* of Table 12.5 reports estimated exponential technology $\hat{A}_p(\cdot) = \exp(\cdot)$ from all four benchmark models. As expected, $\hat{A}_p(\cdot)$

Table 12.5. Summary of Estimation Results on Technology.

Panel A	SF-CES-SP		SF-CD-P-Level		SF-CD-P-Log		SF-CES-P-Level		SF-CES-P-Log	
EXS	0.6705***	(0.2314)	0.3671***	(0.1442)	0.0922***	(0.0201)	0.7505***	(0.1955)	0.058***	(0.0214)
Panel B	$\hat{A}(EXS\hat{\gamma}_{exs}+\hat{\alpha})$		$\hat{A}_p(EXS\hat{\gamma}_{exs}+\hat{\alpha})$		$\hat{A}_p(EXS\hat{\gamma}_{exs}+\hat{\alpha})$		$\hat{A}_p(EXS\hat{\gamma}_{exs}+\hat{\alpha})$		$\hat{A}_p(EXS\hat{\gamma}_{exs}+\hat{\alpha})$	
0.10	3.4983***	(0.0395)	2.1057***	(0.0208)	1.9943***	(0.0305)	3.6512***	(0.0208)	4.8434***	(0.0219)
0.25	3.7041***	(0.0444)	2.1837***	(0.0212)	2.0126***	(0.0314)	3.9331***	(0.0224)	4.8665***	(0.0289)
0.50	3.5753***	(0.0536)	2.2855***	(0.0325)	2.0358***	(0.0324)	4.3174***	(0.0344)	4.8956***	(0.0482)
0.75	3.5353***	(0.0632)	2.4752***	(0.0258)	2.077***	(0.0342)	5.0816***	(0.0336)	4.9469***	(0.0348)
0.90	3.4549***	(0.0823)	2.6030***	(0.0514)	2.1034***	(0.0354)	5.6328***	(0.0623)	4.9795***	(0.0790)
Mean	3.6291		2.3436		2.0470		4.5896		4.9162	
Panel C	**Mean**	**Median**	**Mean**	**Median**	**Mean**	**Median**	**Mean**	**Median**	**Mean**	**Median**
Elas(*EXS*)	0.3239	0.0293	0.0572	0.058	0.3637	0.3637	0.7794	0.7794	0.3693	0.3273

Notes: Standard errors are reported in parenthesis beneath the estimated coefficients in *Panel A* and *Panel B*. ***, **, and * stand for the statistically significant level at 1%, 5%, and 10%, respectively.

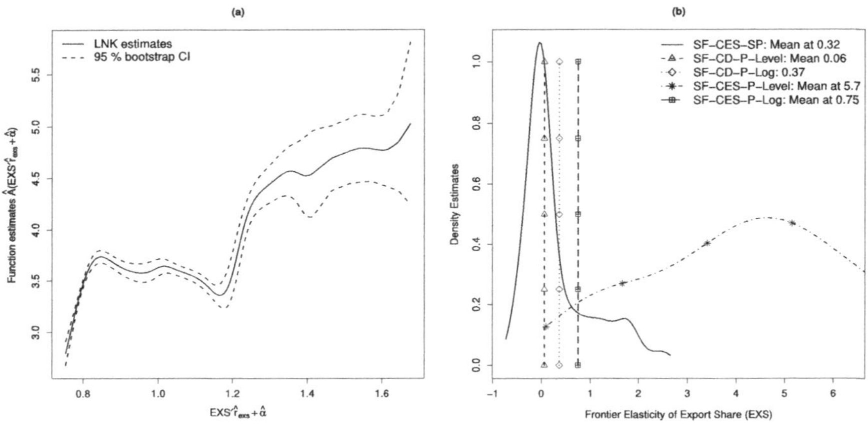

Fig. 12.4. Technology Function Estimate (a) and Frontier Elasticity of Export Share (b).

differs from its semiparametric counterpart both in magnitude and rate of change because, in this case, the index $EXS_{it}\hat{\gamma}_{exs} + \hat{\alpha}_i$ is assumed *a priori* to rise technology monotonically at an exponential rate. As a result, different implications are drawn for the role of EXS in technology. The SF-CES-SP implies that, for the majority of the estimated index (< 90% percentiles), the technology is significantly increased only when the export share (plus fixed effects) rises toward a moderate level. Given our sample, it suggests that countries with relatively low EXS, such as Turkey, USA, and Greece, are likely to witness technology improvement if export becomes more intensive. This is in contrast to the implication from all benchmark models, suggesting that the technology can be improved at an increasing rate by rising export share. Compared to benchmark models, therefore, modeling technology nonparametrically is vital to avoid misleading inference on the effect of environment variables due to model misspecification.

Given that EXS significantly influences the frontier (F) through technology, we further compute the frontier elasticity of export share, or Elas(EXS), defined as $\frac{dF / F}{dEXS}$ (i.e., the percentage change in frontier due to one unit change in export share).[11] *Panel C* of Table 12.5 reports the mean and median of Elas(EXS) under each model, which shows a small variation in SF-CD-P-Level but wide dispersion in SF-CES-SP and SF-CES-P-Level. This can be vividly seen from panel (b) of Fig. 12.4, which plots kernel densities of Elas(EXS) under models in levels against constants of Elas(EXS) under models in logs. Here, we only plot the average of Elas(EXS) under SF-CD-P-Level because the estimates are highly centered around the mean. The estimates of Elas(EXS) across all models (except for SF-CES-P-Level) are less than unity with the lowest mean of 0.06 in SF-CD-P-Level, followed by 0.32 in SF-CES-SP, 0.37 in SF-CD-P-Log and 0.75 in SF-CES-P-Log. Different from benchmark models, our SF-CES-SP yields 35.6% negative estimates due to the downward moving trend of $\hat{A}(\cdot)$ depicted in panel (a) of

Fig. 12.3. Different from the rest of the models, the Elas(*EXS*) under SF-CES-P-Level are exceptionally large with a mean of 5.7 and a notable variation. Overall, we observe a significant positive effect of export share on improving country's production frontier.

We finally compare estimation results regarding the inefficiency function. *Panel A* of Table 12.6 reports the coefficient estimates (i.e., $\hat{\theta}$) under each model. Recall that $\mu(\cdot) = \exp(\cdot)$ is positive, a coefficient with negative sign indicates that a rise in the corresponding inefficiency determinant reduces the mean inefficiency. In fact, the exponential structure of $\mu(\cdot)$ implies that each $\hat{\theta}_j$ is the estimated inefficiency elasticity of its (percentage measured) determinant W_j, because $\frac{d\mu(W;\theta)/\mu(W;\theta)}{dW_j} = \theta_j$ for $j \in \{EXS, FDI\text{-}INS, FDI\text{-}OUTS\}$. Our SF-CES-SP shows that, all else constant, the marginal impact of export share on reducing a country's mean inefficiency (or shrinks the averaged gap between a country's frontier and actual output) is 29.5% at the 1% significance level. Combined with our above results on the frontier elasticity of *EXS*, our model reveals that a higher (yet not excessive) export share is beneficial for not only improving a country's frontier but facilitating the country to produce closer to its frontier. The inefficiency elasticity of *EXS* remains qualitatively similar in SF-CD-P-Level (−0.376) and SF-CES-P-Level (−0.206), but becomes indifferent from zero once log transformation is applied in SF-CD-P-Log and SF-CES-P-Log.

Similar to the findings in Iyer et al. (2008), we observe opposite roles of FDI inflows and outflow shares in determining the mean inefficiency. On one hand, a one percentage increase in FDI inflows under SF-CES-SP shrinks mean inefficiency by 10.5%, quantitatively similar to all benchmark models but SF-CD-P-Level. On the other hand, a one unit (or fraction) increase in *FDI-OUTS* under SF-CES-SP significantly enlarges the mean inefficiency (or widens the averaged gap between a country's frontier and actual output) by 12.8%, fairly close to 13.4% under SF-CES-P-Level. One possible underlying cause for the effect of *FDI-OUTS* is that capital outflow may induce producers to opt for low-cost facilities overseas, which deteriorates a country's manufacturing sector, depletes the capital market, and thus lowers the country's efficiency (Iyer et al., 2008). Similar to the effect of *EXS* in $\mu(\cdot)$, the impact of *FDI-OUTS* turns to be either amplified under SF-CD-P-Level or insignificant in log-transformed benchmark models.

The estimated inefficiency function facilitates our analysis on the country-specific productive efficiency. We evaluate the efficiency by ranking countries based on the yearly average of the inefficiency function estimates as $\bar{\hat{\mu}}(W_i;\hat{\theta}) = \frac{1}{T}\sum_{t=1}^{T}\hat{\mu}(W_{it};\hat{\theta})$. Thus, a more efficient country is indicated by a lower magnitude of $\bar{\hat{\mu}}(\cdot)$.[12] We also compute the yearly average of percentage change in inefficiency function estimates as $\%\Delta\bar{\hat{\mu}}(W_i;\hat{\theta}) = \frac{1}{T-1}\sum_{t=2}^{T}(\hat{\mu}(W_{it};\hat{\theta}) - \hat{\mu}(W_{it-1};\hat{\theta}))/\hat{\mu}(W_{it-1};\hat{\theta})$. The first four columns in Table 12.7 report the rank of OECD countries based on an ascending order of $\bar{\hat{\mu}}(\cdot)$ under SF-CES-SP, along with the corresponding $\%\Delta\bar{\hat{\mu}}(\cdot)$.

Table 12.6. Summary of Estimation Results on Inefficiency.

	SF-CES-SP		SF-CD-P-Level		SF-CD-P-Log		SF-CES-P-Level		SF-CES-P-Log	
Cons	0.5478***	(0.1232)	0.5094***	(0.1432)	0.9856***	(0.1697)	0.1615*	(0.0932)	1.094***	(0.0924)
EXS	−0.2949***	(0.0985)	−0.376***	(0.0623)	−0.0377	(0.0535)	−0.2055**	(0.0853)	−0.0501	(0.5155)
FDI-INS	−0.1052***	(0.0524)	−0.4273***	(0.0448)	−0.1137*	(0.0640)	−0.1138***	(0.0417)	−0.1004*	(0.0532)
FDI-OUTS	0.1276***	(0.0677)	−0.4893***	(0.0572)	−0.0534	(0.0587)	0.1339**	(0.0604)	−0.0482	(0.0312)

Notes: Standard errors are reported in parenthesis beneath the estimated coefficients in *Panel A* and *Panel B*. ***, **, and * stand for the statistically significant level at 1%, 5%, and 10%, respectively.

Table 12.7. Country Ranking Based on SF-CES-SP Yearly Averaged Inefficiency Function Estimates.

Ranking	SF-CES-SP	$\bar{\hat{\mu}}(\cdot)$	$\%\Delta\bar{\hat{\mu}}(\cdot)$	SF-CD-P-Level	SF-CD-P-Log	SF-CES-P-Level	SF-CES-P-Log
1	USA	1.3261	−0.04%	USA	USA	Luxembourg	Luxembourg
2	Luxembourg	1.4397	0.02%	Luxembourg	Luxembourg	USA	USA
3	Belgium	1.4469	−0.06%	Belgium	Belgium	Belgium	Belgium
4	Netherlands	1.4784	−0.35%	Netherlands	Ireland	Netherlands	Ireland
5	Ireland	1.5153	−0.21%	Ireland	Netherlands	Ireland	Netherlands
6	Norway	1.5174	0.09%	Norway	Norway	Norway	Norway
7	Denmark	1.5282	−0.18%	Switzerland	Switzerland	Denmark	Switzerland
8	Sweden	1.5332	−0.11%	Denmark	Sweden	Sweden	Denmark
9	Switzerland	1.5430	−0.30%	Sweden	Denmark	Switzerland	Sweden
10	Iceland	1.5453	−0.08%	Iceland	Iceland	Iceland	Iceland
11	Austria	1.5514	−0.22%	Austria	Austria	Austria	Austria
12	Germany	1.5712	−0.26%	Germany	Germany	Germany	Germany
13	Canada	1.6144	−0.06%	Canada	Canada	Canada	Canada
14	France	1.6154	−0.10%	UK	UK	France	UK
15	UK	1.6211	−0.06%	France	France	UK	France
16	Italy	1.6328	−0.11%	Italy	Italy	Italy	Italy
17	Portugal	1.6496	−0.14%	Portugal	Portugal	Portugal	Portugal
18	Spain	1.6773	−0.14%	Spain	Spain	Spain	Spain
19	Greece	1.6863	−0.10%	Greece	Greece	Greece	Greece
20	Turkey	1.6927	−0.46%	Turkey	Turkey	Turkey	Turkey

The USA is ranked the most efficient country over the past five decades, in line with observations in Henderson and Russell (2005) that USA produces on the frontier in 1965 and 1990. Luxembourg, Belgium, and the Netherlands are also fairly efficient, but the Netherlands discloses a faster decreasing rate of inefficiency of $\%\Delta\bar{\hat{\mu}}(\cdot) = -0.35\%$. Spain and Greece are more inefficient, placed at the third and second to last of the ranking, respectively. Although Turkey is ranked the most inefficient country, it catches up the frontier (or decreases inefficiency) at the fastest average rate of 0.46% compared to all other OECD countries. As reported in the last four columns of Table 12.7, we do not observe significant differences in the ranking across all four benchmark models, particular for the top and bottom three countries.

All comparisons above disclose notable estimation differences across SF-CES-SP and benchmark models. The differences may be driven by two sources of estimation bias in benchmark models. The first source is the log approximation on a SF model, which impedes the identification of parameters in the frontier and inefficiency function (see (9) and (11)). The log-induced bias is larger in SF-CES-P-Log because, as shown in (11), the log-approximation error stems from both frontier and composite error that are not asymptotically negligible. This may explain our findings that SF-CES-P-Log differs significantly from all other models in terms of frontier and inefficiency estimation. The second source is the exponential function imposed *a priori* on technology, which masks an important non-monotonic effect (and thus implication) of export share as revealed by our SF-CES-SP. To provide statistical evidence on the potential misspecification of $A_p(\cdot) = \exp(\cdot)$, we implement a nonparametric test for the null hypothesis $H_0 : Pr(A(v) = \exp(v)) = 1$ for almost all $v = EXS\gamma_{exs} + \alpha$. Following the insights of Ullah (1985), we construct the F-type test statistic $J = (SSR_0 - SSR_1) / SSR_1$, where SSR_0 is the sum of squared residuals (SSR) of SF-CES-P-Level under H_0 and SSR_1 the SSR of SF-CES-SP under the alternative.[13] Notice that SF-CES-SP properly nests SF-CES-P-Level as a special case. We employ a bootstrap version of J with 399 repetitions, and obtain $J = 64.952$ with empirical p-value of 0.0000. Thus, we reject the null of a correctly specified $A_p(\cdot) = \exp(\cdot)$ at 1% level, indicating that an exponential function is inadequate to capture the evolvement of technology. Overall, our empirical findings highlight the importance of considering a semiparametric CES frontier in level, as the case in SF-CES-SP, for productive efficiency analysis.

5. CONCLUSION

We propose a panel SF model (SF-CES-SP) to alleviate parametric restrictions on both the frontier and composite error. Our frontier specifies a semiparametric form of the CES production function, which improves the conventional CES by avoiding log-induced estimation bias and allowing unknown functional form of technology. The semiparametric CES frontier specifies the technology as a smooth single-index function of environment variables, and within the index, the fixed effects are accounted for individual unobserved, time-invariant heterogeneity. The frontier further retains certain parameters of interests to be directly estimated, including distribution of inputs, elasticity of inputs substitution, and returns to scale. Our composite error requires no distributional assumptions on either the stochastic noise or inefficiency, and allows the conditional mean of the inefficiency to depend on a wide range of determinants. The structure of our proposed frontier model is flexible in modeling the complex nonlinear structure of a production function, free of the curse of dimensionality, and robust to different distributions of inefficiency. The appealing finite-sample performance of the proposed estimator is demonstrated through simulation studies.

We showcase the empirical applicability of SF-CES-SP by investigating productive efficiency among 20 OECD countries from 1970 to 2019. Our model provides reasonable estimation on several metrics of the frontier, suggesting the increasing returns to scale production function, and complementary relationship between capital and (human capital augmented) labor. The flexible structure of our model uncovers a significantly nonlinear technology function. We find that moderate increase in export share significantly rises a country's frontier and reduces productive inefficiency. The inefficiency can be also reduced by a higher FDI inflow and lower FDI outflow share. Compared to our proposed model, we observe large different (and perhaps unreasonable in some cases) estimation from conventional parametric SF models. Through results comparison, we show that a SF model with semiparametric CES frontier in level is more robust to estimation bias due to model misspecification and log-transformation.

NOTES

1. For comprehensive reviews of SF models, see Kumbhakar and Lovell (2000), Parmeter and Kumbhakar (2014), and Kumbhakar et al. (2020). For the illustration of SF empirical studies, see Kumbhakar, Wang, and Horncastle (2015).
2. Tran and Tsionas (2009), Parmeter et al. (2016), and Zhou et al. (2020) estimate the mean function nonparametrically, which is appealing.
3. Similar to the findings in Wang and Henderson (2022), we will suggest, in Section 2.3, large n and T in practice in order to avoid the incidental parameters problem.
4. Note that π_j in (1) is not the output elasticity of the jth input as is the case in CD.
5. We mention that our model specification does not account for time invariant, or persistent, inefficiency such that $u_{it} = c_i^* + u_{it}^*$ with $c_i^*, u_{it}^* > 0$. Such decomposition receives increasing attention in parametric SF panel models. See Kumbhakar et al. (2020) for more details.
6. In practice, one can set any element in γ to be positive for $j = 1, 2, ..., d_z + n - 1$, or to be negative by setting $\gamma_j = -(1 - \| \gamma_{-j} \|^2)^{1/2} < 0$.
7. We note that the condition $\sum_{j=1}^{\pi_{d_x}} \pi_j = 1$ is not necessary for ω in (1) to be identified. Rather, the condition is commonly made in the literature to provide economic interpretation on the distribution parameters (Masanjala & Papageorgiou, 2004).
8. We follow Henderson and Russell (2005) to construct $HL = HC \times L$, where HC is the human capital index based on years of schooling and returns to education from PWT, and L the millions of persons engaged in employment.
9. Note that the observation-specific RTS is consistent with the implication from constant RTS estimate $\hat{\nu}$ in *Panel A* of Table 12.4. The increasing RTS is suggested under both SF-CES-SP and SF-CES-P-Level, equivalently to the result that $\hat{\nu}$ is significantly larger than one at 1% level. Similarly, the decreasing RTS in SF-CES-P-Log is in line with the result that $\hat{\nu}$ is insignificantly different from one.
10. The fixed effect being dropped as a reference point corresponds to Turkey.
11. Earlier we defined the frontier as the production function without inefficiency. That is, we have $F = A(EXS\gamma_{exs} + \alpha)\left[\pi K^{-\rho} + (1-\pi)HL^{-\rho}\right]^{-\frac{\nu}{\rho}}$ under SF-CES-SP; $F = A_p(EXS\gamma_{exs} + \alpha)K^{\beta_K} HL^{\beta_{HL}}$ under SF-CD-P-Level; and $F = A_p(EXS\gamma_{exs} + \alpha)\left[\pi K^{-\rho} + (1-\pi)HL^{-\rho}\right]^{-\frac{\nu}{\rho}}$ under SF-CES-P-Level. Notice that under SF-CD-P-Log and SF-CES-P-Log, $\frac{dF / F}{dEXS} = d\ln(F) / dEXS = \gamma_{exs}$. Thus, Elas($EXS$) are observation-specific under three models in level but constant under two models in logs.
12. See **Remark 3** for alternative measures for technical efficiency in our model.
13. We construct the SSR under H_0 as $SSR_0 = \frac{1}{nT}\sum_{i=1}^{n}\sum_{t=1}^{T}\left[Y_{it} - \hat{F}_{it} + \mu(W_{it};\hat{\theta})\right]^2$, where $\hat{F}_{it} = A_p(EXS_{it}\hat{\gamma}_{exs} + \hat{\alpha}_i)\left[K_{it}^{-\hat{\rho}} + HL_{it}^{-\hat{\rho}}\right]^{-\frac{\hat{\nu}}{\hat{\rho}}}$ is the estimated CES frontier in SF-CES-P-Level. The construction of SSR_1 is similar to SSR_0, except that $\hat{F}_{it}$ is replaced with estimated frontier from SF-CES-SP assuming unknown structure of $A(\cdot)$.

ACKNOWLEDGMENTS

The authors would like to thank the co-editor, Chris Parmeter, and two anonymous referees for helpful comments and suggestions. An R package which can be used to apply the methods developed in this chapter is available from the authors' websites and discussed in Appendix 2.

REFERENCES

Aigner, D., Lovell, C. A. K., & Schmidt, P. (1977). Formulation and estimation of stochastic frontiers production function models. *Journal of Econometrics*, *6*, 21–37.

Amemiya, T. (1985). *Advanced econometrics*. Cambridge, MA: Harvard University Press.

Arellano, M., & Hahn, J. (2007). Understanding bias in nonlinear panel models: Some recent developments. *Econometric Society Monographs*, *43*, 381.

Baltagi, B. H., & Li, D. (2002). Series estimation of partially linear panel data models with fixed-effects. *Annals of Economics and Finance*, *3*, 103–116.

Battese, G. E., & Coelli, T. J. (1988). Prediction of firm-level technical efficiencies with a generalized frontier production function and panel data. *Journal of Econometrics*, *38*(3), 387–399.

Battese, G. E., & Coelli, T. J. (1992). Frontier production functions, technical efficiency and panel data: with application to paddy farmers in India. *Journal of Productivity Analysis*, *3*, 153–169.

Cornwell, C., Schmidt, P., & Sickles, R. C. (1990). Production frontiers with cross-sectional and time-series variation in efficiency levels. *Journal of Econometrics*, *46*(2), 185–200.

de Boor, C. R. (1978). *A practical guide to splines*. New York, NY: Springer-Verlag.

Fan, Y., Li, Q., & Weersink, A. (1996). Semiparametric estimation of stochastic production frontier models. *Journal of Business and Economic Statistics*, *14*, 460–468.

Ferrara, G., & Vidoli, F. (2017). Semiparametric stochastic frontier models: A generalized additive model approach. *European Journal of Operational Research*, *258*(2), 761–777.

Fernández-Val, I., & Weidner, M. (2016). Individual and time effects in nonlinear panel models with large N, T. *Journal of Econometrics*, *192*(1), 291–312.

Gollin, D. (2002). Getting income shares right. *Journal of Political Economy*, *110*, 458–474.

Henderson, D. J. (2009). A non-parametric examination of capital-skill complementarity. *Oxford Bulletin of Economics and Statistics*, *71*(4), 519–538.

Henderson, D. J., & Russell, R. R. (2005). Human capital and convergence: A production-frontier approach. *International Economic Review*, *46*(4), 1167–1205.

Henderson, D. J., & Parmeter, C. F. (2015). *Applied nonparametric econometrics*. New York, NY: Cambridge University Press.

Horrace, W. C., & Parmeter, C. F. (2011). Semiparametric deconvolution with unknown error variance. *Journal of Productivity Analysis*, *35*(2), 129–141.

Iyer, K. G., Rambaldi, A. N., & Tang, K. K. (2008). Efficiency externalities of trade and alternative forms of foreign investment in OECD countries. *Journal of Applied Econometrics*, *23*(6), 749–766.

Jondrow, J., Lovell, C. A. K., Materov, I. S., & Schmidt, P. (1982). On the estimation of technical inefficiency in the stochastic frontier production function model. *Journal of Econometrics*, *19*, 233–238.

Karabarbounis, L., & Neiman, B. (2013). The global decline of the labor share. *The Quarterly Journal of Economics*, *129*(1), 61–103.

Kneip, A., & Simar, L. (1996). A general framework for frontier estimation with panel data. *Journal of Productivity Analysis*, *7*(2), 187–212.

Kneip, A., Simar, L., & Van Keilegom, I., (2015). Frontier estimation in the presence of measurement error with unknown variance. *Journal of Econometrics*, *184*(2), 379–393.

Kumbhakar, S. C. (1990). Production frontiers, panel data, and time-varying technical inefficiency. *Journal of Econometrics*, *46*(1–2), 201–211.

Kumbhakar, S. C., & Lovell, C. A. K. (2000). *Stochastic frontier analysis*. Cambridge, UK: Cambridge University Press.

Kumbhakar, S. C., & Wang, H.-J. (2005a). Estimation of growth convergence using a stochastic production frontier approach. *Economics Letters*, *88*(3), 300–305.

Kumbhakar, S. C., Park, B. U., Simar, L., & Tsionas, E. (2007). Nonparametric stochastic frontiers: A local maximum likelihood approach. *Journal of Econometrics*, *137*, 1–27.

Kumbhakar, S. C., Wang, H. J., & Horncastle, A. P. (2015). *A practitioner's guide to stochastic frontier analysis using STATA*. Cambridge, UK: Cambridge University Press.

Kumbhakar, S. C., Parmeter, C. F., Zelenyuk, V. (2020). Stochastic frontier analysis: Foundations and advances I-II. In S. C. Ray, R. G. Chambers & S. C. Kumbhakar (Eds.), *Handbook of production economics* (pp. 1–40). Singapore: Springer

Lee, L. F., & Tyler, W. G. (1978). The stochastic frontier production function and average efficiency: An empirical analysis. *Journal of Econometrics*, *7*(3), 385–389.

Lee, Y., & Schmidt, P. (1993). A production frontier model with flexible temporal variation in technical efficiency. In L. H. Fried & S. Schmidt (Eds.), *The measurement of productive efficiency* (pp. 237–255). Oxford: Oxford University Press.

Ma, S., & Song, P. X. (2015). Varying index coefficient models. *Journal of the American Statistical Association*, *110*, 341–356.

Malikov, E., Zhao, S., & Kumbhakar, S. C. (2020). Estimation of firm-level productivity in the presence of exports: Evidence from China's manufacturing. *Journal of Applied Econometrics*, *35*(4), 457–480.

Martins-Filho, C., & Yao, F. (2015). Nonparametric stochastic frontier estimation via profile likelihood. *Econometric Reviews*, *34*(4), 413–451.

Masanjala, W. H., & Papageorgiou, C. (2004). The Solow model with CES technology: Nonlinearities and parameter heterogeneity. *Journal of Applied Econometrics*, *19*(2), 171–201.

Meeusen, W., & van Den Broeck, J. (1977). Efficiency estimation from Cobb-Douglas production functions with composed error. *International Economic Review*, *18*, 435–444.

Newey, W. K. (1997). Convergence rates and asymptotic normality for series estimators. *Journal of Econometrics*, *79*, 147–168.

Park, B. U., Simar, L., & Zelenyuk, V. (2015). Categorical data in local maximum likelihood: Theory and applications to productivity analysis. *Journal of Productivity Analysis*, *43*, 199–214.

Parmeter, C. F., & Kumbhakar, S. C. (2014). Efficiency analysis: A primer on recent advances. *Foundations and Trends[textregistered] in Econometrics*, *7*(3–4), 191–385.

Parmeter, C. F., Wang, H.-J., & Kumbhakar, S. C., (2016). Nonparametric estimation of the determinants of inefficiency. *Journal of Productivity Analysis.*

Santos Silva, J. M. C., & Tenreyro, S. (2006). The log of gravity. *Review of Economics and Statistics*, *88*, 641–658.

Schmidt, P., & Sickles, R. C. (1984). Production frontiers and panel data. *Journal of Business & Economic Statistics*, *2*(2), 367–374.

Sun, K., Henderson, D. J., & Kumbhakar, S. (2008). Biases in approximating log production. *Journal of Applied Econometrics*, *26*, 708–714.

Sun, K., & Kumbhakar, S. C. (2013). Semiparametric smooth-coefficient stochastic frontier model. *Economics Letters*, *120*(2), 305–309.

Tran, K. C., & Tsionas, E. G. (2009). Estimation of nonparametric inefficiency effects stochastic frontier models with an application to British manufacturing. *Economic Modelling*, *26*, 904–909.

Ullah, A. (1985). Specification analysis of econometric models. *Journal of Quantitative Economics*, *1*(2), 187–209.

Wang, T., Tian, J., & Yao, F. (2020). Does high leverage ratio influence Chinese firm performance? A semiparametric stochastic frontier approach with zero-inefficiency. *Empirical Economics*, 1–50.

Wang, T., Tian, J., & Yao, F. (2021). Does high debt ratio influence Chinese firms' performance? A semiparametric stochastic frontier approach with zero inefficiency. *Empirical Economics*, *61*, 587–636.

Wang, T., & Henderson, D. J. (2022). Estimation of a varying coefficient, fixed-effects Cobb-Douglas production function in levels. *Economics Letters*, *213*, 1–6.

Yao, F., Zhang, F., & Kumbhakar, S. C. (2018a). Semiparametric smooth coefficient stochastic frontier model with panel data. *Journal of Business & Economic Statistics*, *37*(3), 556–572.

Yao, F., Wang, T., Tian, J., & Kumbhakar, S. C. (2018b). Estimation of a smooth coefficient zero-inefficiency panel stochastic frontier model: A semiparametric approach. *Economics Letters*, *166*, 25–30.

Yao, F., Zhang, F., & Kumbhakar, S. C. (2019). Semiparametric smooth coefficient stochastic frontier model with panel data. *Journal of Business & Economic Statistics*, *37*(3), 556–572.

Zhu, L., & Xue, L. (2006). Empirical likelihood confidence regions in a partially linear single-index model. *Journal of the Royal Statistical Society, Series B*, *68*, 549–570.

Zhou, J., Parmeter, C. F., Kumbhakar, S. C. (2020). Nonparametric estimation of the determinants of inefficiency in the presence of firm heterogeneity. *European Journal of Operational Research*, *286*(3), 1142–1152.

APPENDIX 1. INCIDENTAL PARAMETERS PROBLEM

From our SF-CES-SP in (1), the estimation of individual fixed effects α_i, appearing in $A(\cdot)$, can be challenging with large n and fixed T (i.e., the incidental parameters problem). We expect worse numerical performance of our proposed estimator as α_i is not consistently estimated. To investigate the impact of incidental parameters problem on our model estimation, we repeat the same exercise for our simulation studies in Section 3, except that we fix $T = 10$ and let $n = (10, 20, 40)$.

Table A1.1 reports the simulation results, which shows a clear negative impact of the incidental parameters problem on the estimator's performance. We note that a large $n = 40$ with a small $T = 10$ leads to a much worse estimation of the fixed effects, causing parameter estimates, such as $\hat{\gamma}_{z_1}$, fail to converge. For

Table A1.1. Incidental Parameters Problem in SF-CES-SP with Scaling Inefficiency in DGP_{1-3}.

	(n,T)		RMSE	BIAS	STD		RAMSE	ABIAS	ASTD
DGP_1	10, 10	$\hat{\gamma}_{z_1}$	0.2442	0.1931	0.1502	$\hat{A}$	2.5605	1.4440	2.5348
		$\hat{\pi}$	0.1610	0.1299	0.0955				
		$\hat{\rho}$	0.1012	0.0922	0.0421				
		$\hat{\nu}$	0.0872	0.0750	0.0449				
		$\hat{\theta}_1$	0.0946	0.0750	0.0580				
	10, 20	$\hat{\gamma}_{z_1}$	0.2355	0.1833	0.1486	$\hat{A}$	3.3007	1.1071	3.1073
		$\hat{\pi}$	0.1207	0.0978	0.0712				
		$\hat{\rho}$	0.1139	0.0919	0.0676				
		$\hat{\nu}$	0.0774	0.0705	0.0322				
		$\hat{\theta}_1$	0.0736	0.0625	0.0390				
	10, 40	$\hat{\gamma}_{z_1}$	0.2799	0.2345	0.1536	$\hat{A}$	1.3053	0.1829	0.6652
		$\hat{\pi}$	0.1106	0.0831	0.0734				
		$\hat{\rho}$	0.0851	0.0820	0.0228				
		$\hat{\nu}$	0.0702	0.0672	0.0206				
		$\hat{\theta}_1$	0.0660	0.0582	0.0313				
DGP_2	10, 10	$\hat{\gamma}_{z_1}$	0.1275	0.0914	0.0893	$\hat{A}$	4.5039	1.8774	4.3394
		$\hat{\pi}$	0.0971	0.0788	0.0570				
		$\hat{\rho}$	0.1004	0.0825	0.0575				
		$\hat{\nu}$	0.0813	0.0656	0.0483				
		$\hat{\theta}_1$	0.0788	0.0656	0.0439				
	10, 20	$\hat{\gamma}_{z_1}$	0.1383	0.0963	0.0997	$\hat{A}$	14.8140	2.7401	14.4186
		$\hat{\pi}$	0.0696	0.0538	0.0444				
		$\hat{\rho}$	0.1069	0.0935	0.0521				
		$\hat{\nu}$	0.0613	0.0477	0.0387				
		$\hat{\theta}_1$	0.0645	0.0530	0.0369				
	10, 40	$\hat{\gamma}_{z_1}$	0.1591	0.1133	0.1123	$\hat{A}$	2.3722	2.3582	1.9548
		$\hat{\pi}$	0.0536	0.0427	0.0327				
		$\hat{\rho}$	0.0905	0.0852	0.0304				
		$\hat{\nu}$	0.0585	0.0501	0.0305				
		$\hat{\theta}_1$	0.0599	0.0510	0.0317				
DGP_3	10, 10	$\hat{\gamma}_{z_1}$	0.1023	0.0730	0.0721	$\hat{A}$	2.2381	1.2774	2.2072

Table A1.1. (*Continued*)

(n,T)		RMSE	BIAS	STD		RAMSE	ABIAS	ASTD
	$\hat{\pi}$	0.0831	0.0664	0.0501				
	$\hat{\rho}$	0.1570	0.1216	0.0997				
	$\hat{\nu}$	0.0962	0.0720	0.0642				
	$\hat{\theta}_1$	0.0855	0.0719	0.0466				
10, 20	$\hat{\gamma}_{z_1}$	0.1301	0.1013	0.0820	$\hat{A}$	5.8606	2.0761	5.7200
	$\hat{\pi}$	0.0636	0.0497	0.0399				
	$\hat{\rho}$	0.1035	0.0887	0.0536				
	$\hat{\nu}$	0.0527	0.0443	0.0286				
	$\hat{\theta}_1$	0.0653	0.0553	0.0349				
10, 40	$\hat{\gamma}_{z_1}$	0.1939	0.1686	0.0963	$\hat{A}$	1.0532	0.9806	1.0077
	$\hat{\pi}$	0.0511	0.0400	0.0320				
	$\hat{\rho}$	0.0907	0.0811	0.0408				
	$\hat{\nu}$	0.0555	0.0486	0.0269				
	$\hat{\theta}_1$	0.0621	0.0532	0.0321				

instance, the RMSE of $\hat{\gamma}_{z_1}$ under DGP_1 with $(n,T)=(40,10)$ increases by more than fivefold compared to that with $(n,T)=(10,40)$ in Table 12.1. This observation is consistent with conventional result in nonlinear parametric panel models, where the incidental parameters impact not only fixed effects but other coefficients when the fixed effects enter the model nonlinearity (Arellano & Hahn, 2007; Fernández-Val & Weidner, 2016). Since the LNK estimator $\hat{A}(\cdot)$ depends crucially on the accurate measure of the index $Z_{it}^{\top}\gamma_z+\alpha_i$, the approximation error on technology is evidently inflated as n doubles across all DGPs due to the poor estimation of α_i.

As a consequence, the model estimator becomes inconsistent due to the presence of incidental parameters. We demonstrate it by repeating our simulations with $T = 10$ and $n=(5,10,20,40,80,160)$, and compute RMSE (RAMSE) of parameter (function) estimates. Similar to Fig. 12.1, we plot in Fig. A1.1 the RMSE of $\hat{\pi}$, $\hat{\gamma}_{z_1}$, and $\hat{\theta}_1$ against the parametric rate in panels (a), (b), and (c), respectively, under DGP_{1-3}. Clearly, each parameter estimator no longer converges at a rate of $1/\sqrt{nT}$ as n doubles, regardless of which DGP being considered. Panel (d) of Fig. A1.1 plots the RAMSE of function estimates against the nonparametric rate under each DGP. In contrast to our observation in Fig. 12.1, the LNK estimator is now largely biased without converging at a rate of $1/\sqrt{nTh}$.

Overall, our results should be taken as numerical evidence for applied researchers to avoid having a large n with small T for a panel data model with fixed-effects (i.e., a large ratio of n/T) in order to achieve reasonable estimation for our SP-CES-SP.

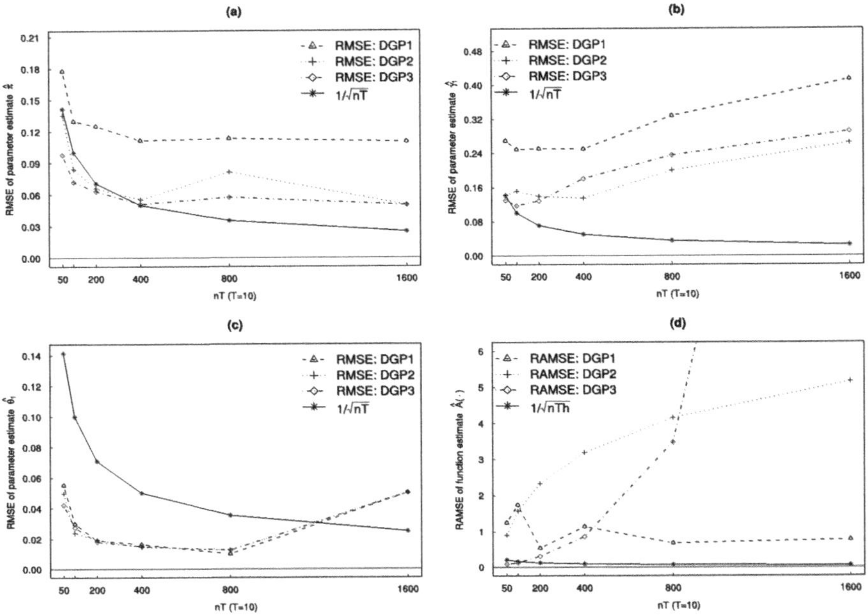

Fig. A1.1. Incidental Parameters Problem in Convergence Rates of Estimators in DGP_{1-3}.

APPENDIX 2. DEMONSTRATION OF OUR R PACKAGE

The proposed estimation procedure for SF-CES-SP in (1) is implemented in an **R** package with user-friendly design. The package is available at https://694160821.wixsite.com/taining, and navigate to the top panel of **R code**. The code is stored in a text file and needs to be copy-pasted into an R script for it to run. The file contains five packages (on the top of the file) that need to be pre-installed before running the code for SF-CES-SP estimation. Below these packages, there are a total of 12 functions defined: Function [8.1] generates simulated panel data for demonstration purpose; function [8.2] generates simulated pool data; function [9], which uses functions [1]–[7], performs estimation for SF-CES-SP; and function [10] summarizes the estimation result by a table and several figures.

As an example, we use function [8.1] to generate a panel data set according to a simple *DGP* as

$$Y_{it} = A(Z_{it}^{\top}\gamma_z + \alpha_i)\left(\pi X_{1it}^{-\rho} + (1-\pi)X_{2it}^{-\rho}\right)^{-\frac{\nu}{\rho}} + v_{it} - u_{it}, \tag{A2.1}$$

where $Z_{it} = (Z_{1it}, Z_{2it})$ and X_{jit} are drawn independently from $U(1, 4)$. The parameters in the coefficient functions are $\gamma = (2, 4, \alpha_{-1}^{\top})$, with $\alpha_{-1} = (\alpha_2, ..., \alpha_n)^{\top}$. We empirically rescale γ to satisfy $\| \gamma_0 \| = 1$. We specify $\mu(W_{it};\theta) = \exp(W_{it}^{\top}\theta)$, where $W_{it} = (Z_{1it}, Q_{it})$ with $Q_{it} \sim U(1,4)$. We generate the fixed effects as $\alpha_i = \frac{1}{T}\sum_{t=1}^{T}(X_{1it} + Z_{1it}) + \xi_i$, where $\xi_i \sim \mathcal{N}(0,1)$. Finally, $v_{it} \sim \mathcal{N}(0, 0.5^2)$ is drawn independently from all *X*, *Z*, and *Q*. We specify the technology function $A(v) = \sqrt{v\pi}$. To reduce computational cost in this demonstration, we simply set $(n, T) = (5, 50)$ and generate data as

```
> set.seed(03)
> n=5; t=50
> Dgp<-psudo.data.panel(n=n,t=t,a=1,b=4,c=1,d=4,u.dist=1)
> y<-Dgp$y; x<-Dgp$x; z<-Dgp$z[,c(1:2)]; w<-Dgp$w
```

In the first line, a random seed is specified for results replication; in the second line, n and t represent the number of individual and time units, respectively; in the third line, (a,b) are the lower and upper bound of a uniform distribution (i.e., $\mathcal{U}(a,b)$) for each X_j. Similarly, (c,d) are the lower and upper bound of a uniform distribution (i.e., $\mathcal{U}(c,d)$) for all Z_j and *Q*; in the fourth line, we extract data from Dgp, including a $nT \times 1$ vector y, a $nT \times 2$ matrix x; a $nT \times 2$ matrix z; and a $nT \times 2$ matrix w. The specification u.dist=1 assumes a scaling function of u_{it}, and u.dist=2 sets u_{it} to be Log-Probit (see our specification in Section 3). Running the following code performs estimation for SF-CES-SP in (A2.1):

```
> sf.ces.sp.panel<-WH.SF.CES(y=y,x=x,z=z,w=w,n=n,t=t,Kernel=TRUE,
Jn.zr.pos = 'quantile',method='fe',u.dist='scaling')
```

```
> country.id<-paste0('country',c(1:n))
> result.WH.SF.CES(sf.ces.sp.panel,country.id = country.id)
```

where WH.SF.CES() estimates the SF-CES-SP and saves it as sf.ces.sp.panel, and result.WH.SF.CES() reports the summary of empirical results. Namely, WH.SF. CES() is implemented using data from Dgp above, with 99 wild bootstraps for 95% point-wise confidence interval for LNK estimator. The default number of bootstrap repetitions is boot.num = 99. We purposely set a small boot.num in this example to increase computational speed, but it should be a large integer in practice, such as 399. Notice that WH.SF.CES() reports LNK estimation if Kernel=TRUE, but it also reports series estimation on $A(\cdot)$ if Kernel=FALSE. Therefore, given a large sample data in practice, one can take advantage of series estimator to quickly obtain preliminary results without spending much longer time for the LNK estimator. Within WH.SF.CES(), the command Jn.zr.pos = 'quantile' requires the interior knots to be placed on different percentiles of the index $Z_{it}^{\top}\gamma_z + \alpha_i$. If method='fe', a total of $n-1$ dummy variables will be added into the matrix z to control for individual fixed effects. Alternatively, one can perform a pool estimation by setting method='pool', n=nT, and t=1. In this way, the fixed effects are assumed zero. The exponential structure of $\mu(\cdot) = \exp(\cdot)$ is specified through u.dist='scaling', and the Log-Probit structure of $\mu(\cdot) = -\ln(\Phi(\cdot))$ through u.dist='log-probit'. All additional arguments in WH.SF.CES() are listed with explanation in the script.

Function result.WH.SF.CES() in turn summarizes the estimation results from sf.ces.sp.panel. It automatically returns numerical results as a table with panels A–D, printed in the console panel of R. Panel A summarizes the estimated parameters in the CES function, technology and inefficiency mean function. Panel B summarizes the distribution of output elasticity of inputs and return to scales. Panel C reports the summary for estimated technology function and its derivative. Below it are distribution summaries of partial effect of environment variables on frontier.[14] Panel D summarizes different metrics on the estimated inefficiency function. On the bottom of Panel D, a ranking (in ascending order) on individual units based on the magnitude of yearly averaged $\hat{\mu}(\cdot)$ is displayed, provided that the name of the individual units are given in result.WH.SF.CES(). Here, we simply name them as "country 1,...,country 5" for illustration by generating country.id above, and insert it in result.WH.SF.CES(). The very last panel in the table provides data information, tuning parameters, kernel function type, and nonparametric R-square $(corr(Y_{it}, \hat{Y}_{it})^2$, with $\hat{Y}_{it}$ being the fitted SF-CES-SP by LNK estimation.)

Function result.WH.SF.CES() also prints out several figures by default (figure=TRUE). There are four sets of figures to be printed. Each set of figures will be displayed one at a time, and the next set is printed by hitting <Enter>. The first figure is given in Fig. A2.1, which plots the estimated technology function (red solid line) against its point-wise 95% wild bootstrap confidence interval (black dash line). The second set of figures plots output elasticity of inputs (of size $2 \times d_x$), as shown in Fig. A2.2. In the current example, the first column shows the kernel density of output elasticity of

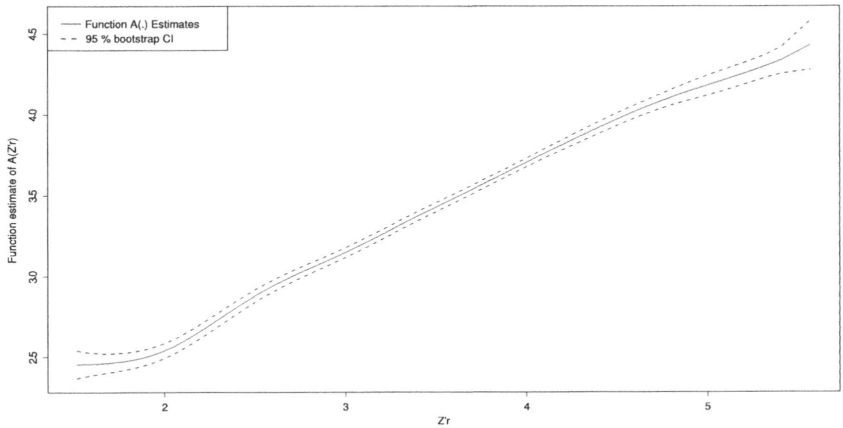

Fig. A2.1. Kernel Estimation of $A(\cdot)$ in the Package.

X_1 (first row) and of X_2 (second row). The mean and median of the elasticity of inputs are labeled as vertical dot or dashed lines, respectively, and reported in the legend. The second column of Fig. A2.2 plots the partial elasticity of inputs by holding all other variables in X at their respective medians. Again, the mean and median are labeled as horizontal lines. The third set of figures is of size $1 \times d_z$, which plots the kernel density of estimated partial effect of Z on frontier as shown in Fig. A2.3. These estimates are computed by holding all other environment variables in Z at median. The last set of figures is of size $2 \times d_w$, which summarizes the partial effect of W on inefficiency mean function as in Fig. A2.4. Similar to Fig. A2.2, the first (second) column reports the kernel density of estimated $d\mu(W_{it};\hat{\theta}) / dW_j$ without (by) holding all else variables in W at certain level (median).

All other arguments in result.WH.SF.CES() are given with explanations in the script.

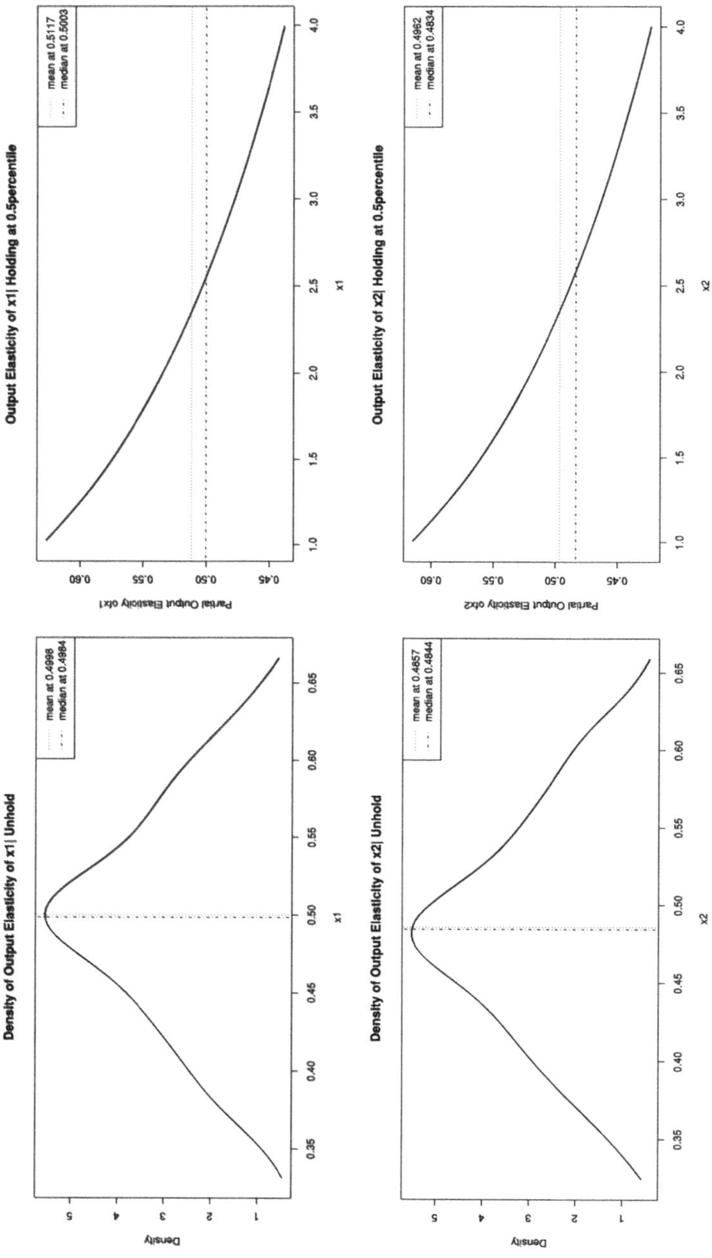

Fig. A2.2. Output Elasticity of Inputs in the Package.

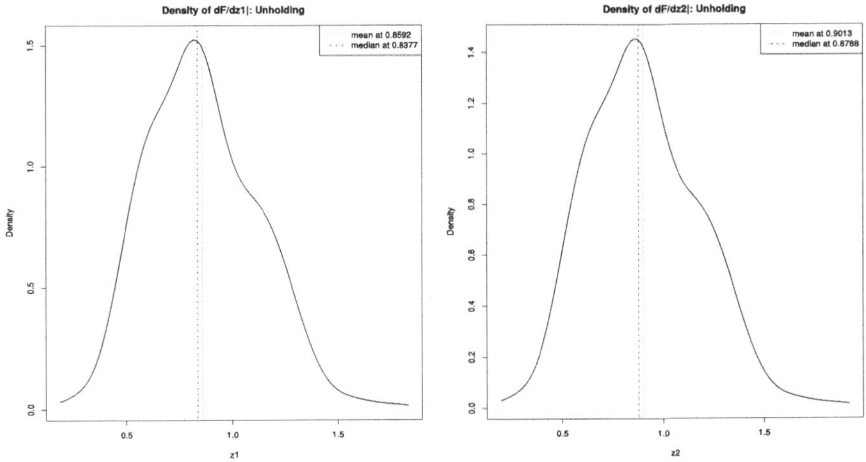

Fig. A2.3. Partial Effects of environment Variables on Frontier in the Package.

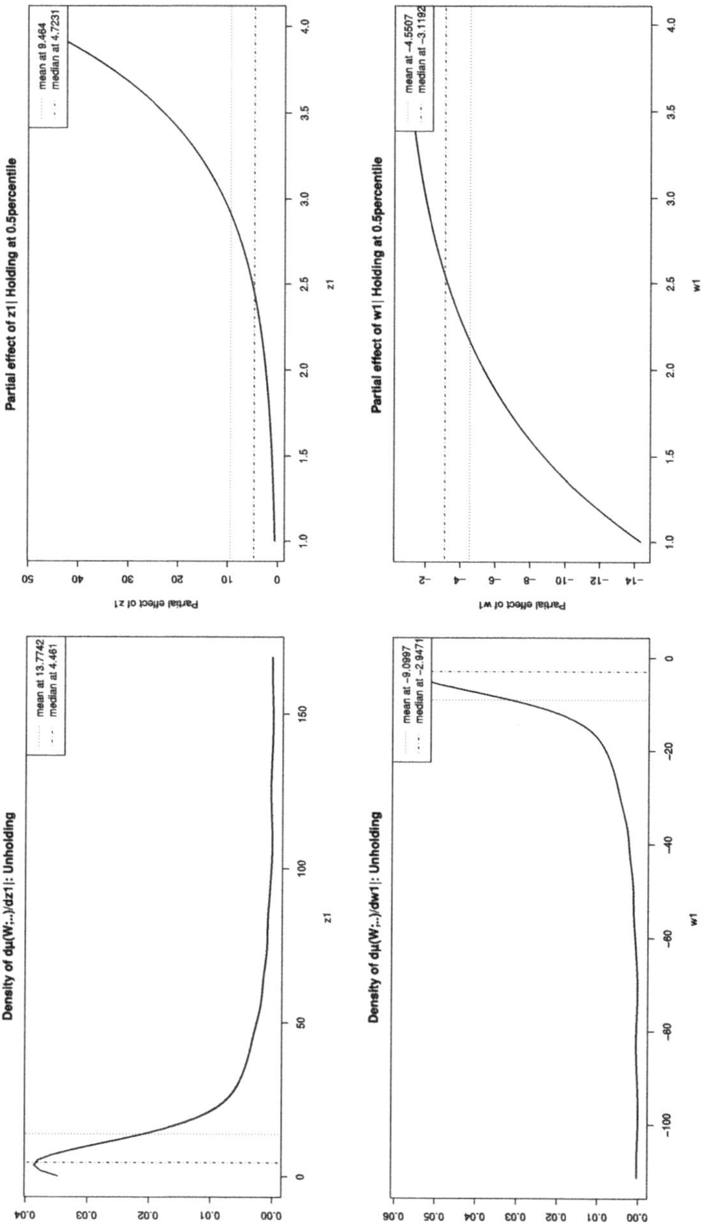

Fig. A2.4. Partial Effects of Inefficiency Determinants in the Package.

CHAPTER 13

RANDOM VERSUS EXPLAINED INEFFICIENCY IN STOCHASTIC FRONTIER ANALYSIS: THE CASE OF QUEENSLAND HOSPITALS

Zhichao Wang[a] and Valentin Zelenyuk[b]

[a]*School of Economics, University of Queensland, Brisbane, QLD, Australia*
[b]*School of Economics and Centre for Efficiency and Productivity Analysis, University of Queensland, Brisbane, QLD, Australia*

ABSTRACT

Estimation of (in)efficiency became a popular practice that witnessed applications in virtually any sector of the economy over the last few decades. Many different models were deployed for such endeavors, with Stochastic Frontier Analysis (SFA) models dominating the econometric literature. Among the most popular variants of SFA are Aigner, Lovell, and Schmidt (1977), which launched the literature, and Kumbhakar, Ghosh, and McGuckin (1991), which pioneered the branch taking account of the (in)efficiency term via the so-called environmental variables or determinants of inefficiency. Focusing on these two prominent approaches in SFA, the goal of this chapter is to try to understand the production inefficiency of public hospitals in Queensland. While doing so, a recognized yet often overlooked phenomenon emerges where possible dramatic differences (and consequently very different policy implications) can be derived from different models, even within one paradigm of SFA models. This emphasizes the importance of exploring many alternative models, and scrutinizing their assumptions, before drawing policy implications, especially when

Essays in Honor of Subal Kumbhakar
Advances in Econometrics, Volume 46, 371–413

Published under exclusive licence by Emerald Publishing Limited
ISSN: 0731-9053/doi:10.1108/S0731-905320240000046013

such implications may substantially affect people's lives, as is the case in the hospital sector.

Keywords: Efficiency; hospitals; stochastic frontier analysis; environmental variables; determinants of inefficiency; Queensland; Australia

JEL Codes: C14; C61; D24; I11

1. INTRODUCTION

Measuring the efficiency of organizations has attracted a lot of interest from researchers and policy makers in various fields, e.g., banking, healthcare, transportation, energy, etc. The roots of the many approaches and applications for such measurements can be traced back to Debreu (1951), Shephard (1953), Farrell (1957), Shephard, Gale, and Kuhn (1970), to mention a few. Based on these seminal works, Stochastic Frontier Analysis (SFA) was first proposed by Aigner, Lovell, and Schmidt (1977) and Meeusen and van den Broeck (1977).[1] The other mainstream approach, branded as Data Envelopment Analysis (DEA) by Charnes, Cooper, and Rhodes (1978), who generalized the approach proposed in the seminal work of Farrell (1957). Both approaches have been further developed in many ways in past decades and have been applied in various research fields and industries.[2]

Comparisons between the two approaches, DEA and SFA, and specifically, the choice for hospital efficiency evaluation have also been widely discussed in the past decades. Usually, the SFA approach is parametric and thus requires more assumptions on production technology than the non-parametric DEA method. On the other hand, the SFA approach is capable of disentangling the inefficiency term from statistical noise (albeit at the cost of additional assumptions). Various studies applied the two approaches as a comparison or robust test to each other, e.g., Linna (1998), Jacobs (2001), Varabyova and Schreyögg (2013) for the case of healthcare/hospitals.[3]

Focusing on the two prominent approaches in SFA, Aigner et al. (1977) and Kumbhakar, Ghosh, and McGuckin (1991), in this chapter, we try to understand the production inefficiency of public hospitals in Queensland. As the seminal work in the SFA paradigm and the canonical model in the vein of SF models with determinants of inefficiency, these two classic models still exhibit vitality in the literature. The current analysis, therefore, may also provide some additional insights and references for further applications with more advanced SFA variants on this and other related topics.

During the analysis, we run into a known yet often overlooked phenomenon, where dramatically different results and hence divergent policy implications can be derived from different models, even within the paradigm of SFA models. Specifically, the estimates of the Aigner et al. (1977) model indicate nearly full efficiency among all the hospitals, while when the determinant variables are taken into account, the Kumbhakar et al. (1991) model exhibits substantial inefficiency estimates with significant disparity between different groups of hospitals. Therefore, we conduct a sequence of model selection processes among the alternative model specifications. The selected model is further tested with a recovery test to gain more confidence in the model estimates.

The remainder of the chapter is organized as follows. In Section 2, we give some background on healthcare and hospital efficiency in general and for Australia and Queensland in particular. In Section 3, we briefly describe the SFA models we intend to apply. Section 4 describes the data and model specified for analysis and Section 5 reports the results. Concluding remarks are summarized in Section 6. Further details are also provided in Appendices 1–6.

2. BACKGROUND ON HEALTHCARE AND HOSPITAL EFFICIENCY

Healthcare is an indispensable foundation of a "healthy society," as it is a solid pillar of both a healthy population and a prosperous economy. Yet, the cost of an effective healthcare system can be incredibly high. In the US, the total expenditure on healthcare accounted for around 16.8% of GDP in 2019, which is about 11,000 US dollars per capita. During the same period, the proportion of healthcare expenditure to GDP in Australia and on average among the OECD countries is about 9.3% and 8.3%, respectively (OECD, 2021).

Beyond the enormous and still rapidly growing spending, the resources supplied for health services are limited, while the wishes of patients pursuing better quality services, longer lives, and lower costs, may be infinite. Hence, how to provide more health services with limited resources has become a key concern of the policymakers, academia, and the whole society when discussing the healthcare system.

The hospital, as the main provider of health services and as a central component of the healthcare system, is naturally a popular subject of study in this context. Evaluating hospital efficiency and finding possible ways of improvement have been discussed by many studies in past decades, along with the development of the efficiency analysis approaches, e.g., the seminal works using DEA by Sherman (1984); Grosskopf and Valdmanis (1987), and those with SFA models by Wagstaff (1989); Zuckerman, Hadley, and Iezzoni (1994); Rosko (2001); Street (2003); Brown (2003), and more applications with their derived models, such as Chowdhury and Zelenyuk (2016) with the two-stage double-bootstrap DEA method proposed by Simar and Wilson (2007), and the studies analyzing panel data with SFA models, e.g., Bosmans and Fecher (1995) using Schmidt and Sickles (1984), Linna (1998) with Battese and Coelli (1992), Colombi, Martini, and Vittadini (2017) applying Colombi, Kumbhakar, Martini, and Vittadini (2014), and Herr (2008) with Greene (2005a), to mention a few.

The empirical focus of this chapter is on public hospitals in Queensland, Australia, to be precise. While one may say or think this part of the world is relatively too far from almost anywhere on Earth, we believe there are a lot of valuable lessons to learn from it. Indeed, in their inspiring chapter, comparing the performance of healthcare in the US to other countries, Schneider et al. (2021, p. 14) concluded:

> International comparisons allow the public, policymakers, and health care leaders to see alternative approaches to delivering health care, ones that might be borrowed to build better health systems that yield better health outcomes. Lessons from the three top performers we highlight in this report – Norway, the Netherlands, and Australia – can inform the United States and other countries seeking to improve.

Despite this and other high rankings of Australian healthcare, relatively few studies focused on the (in)efficiency of hospitals in Australia. In particular, several studies for Australian hospitals were reported by Australia's Productivity Commission (2009, 2010), in which a wide range of SFA models were deployed and a nationwide 10% to 20% technical inefficiency level was concluded, on average, between financial year (FY) 2004/05 to FY 2006/07. At about the same time, Gabbitas and Jeffs (2009) evaluated the public acute hospital efficiency in Australia from FY 1995/96 to FY 2005/06 with SFA models (i.e., Pitt & Lee, 1981; Battese & Coelli, 1995 for random effects and Schmidt & Sickles, 1984; Greene, 2005a for fixed effects), and reported an achievable productivity improvement of 10% in aggregate nationwide. Meanwhile, the estimated efficiency levels of the States and Territories presented mild variations.

Regarding the hospitals in Queensland, Nghiem, Coelli, and Barber (2011) evaluated the efficiency change and the influential factors of 35 public hospitals from 1996 to 2004 with Malmquist Productivity Index (MPI) and SFA. They found a 1.6% growth of the total factor productivity (TFP) on average in Queensland public hospitals, where the number of nurses performs as the most influential factor to the output in SFA estimates. Meanwhile, O'Donnell and Nguyen (2013) estimated the efficiency level of 116 Queensland public hospitals during the same period later with a conventional SFA model. The average level of inefficiency, compared to a benchmark large general hospital at the beginning of the study period (FY 1995/96), was estimated at 32.9%, in further decomposition of which, the scale effect was found as the most influential factor associated with the inefficiency.

More recently, using DEA and partial quantile frontier models, Nguyen and Zelenyuk (2021b, in Daouia and Ruiz-Gazen (Eds.)) estimated the efficiency level of 15 Queensland Hospital and Health Service districts in FY 2016/17. One notable conclusion was that more hospitals of small size and in a remote area could partially explain the low efficiency level of some districts. It is also worth noting that nationwide studies like Gabbitas and Jeffs (2009) also had some findings for Queensland. Specifically, Gabbitas and Jeffs (2009) indicated that the inefficiency level of the Queensland public hospital system was estimated at about 20%, which is one of the highest among the States and Territories in Australia.[4]

To contribute to this interesting literature, in this chapter, our main interest is in analyzing not only the existence of inefficiency of Queensland public hospitals during FY 2012/13 to FY 2015/16, but also its potential determinants, i.e., variables that may explain its variation. For this reason, we will focus on the Kumbhakar et al. (1991) approach, which appears to be the most widely used for this purpose, and contrast it to the Aigner et al. (1977) approach. Markedly different results are obtained via different models with different specifications (e.g., using the Cobb-Douglas or Translog production function). Specifically, models based on Aigner et al. (1977) suggest nearly efficient performance of most hospitals. Meanwhile, models based on Kumbhakar et al. (1991) reveal a 20% to 30% inefficiency level of Queensland public hospitals on average during the study period. Meanwhile, the estimated inefficiency levels also evidently present that better performance is achieved by large, non-remote, and teaching hospitals in comparison with their reference groups. We also find evidence for a strong negative statistical association between inefficiency and the occupancy and turnover rates of beds.

3. SFA MODELS

3.1. Basic SFA Model

The stochastic frontier model (SFM) can be formulated as

$$Y_i = \psi(X_i \mid \beta)\exp(v_i)\exp(-u_i), \quad i = 1,\ldots,n, \tag{1}$$

where $X_i \in \Re_+^p$ is the vector of p inputs that can be used to produce the output, measured by $Y_i \in \Re_+^1$, via technology characterized by the production frontier $\psi(X_i \mid \beta)$, where β is the unknown vector of parameters (corresponding to X_i), and $\exp(v_i)$ stands for statistical noise, while $\exp(-u_i)$ represents the efficiency of unit i.

Rearranging Equation (1), the efficiency term is given by

$$\exp(-u_i) = Y_i / \left(\psi(X_i \mid \beta)\exp(v_i)\right), \tag{2}$$

which is the reciprocal of Farrell-type output-oriented technical efficiency (i.e., the observed output over the maximal attainable or frontier output) with an additional stochastic term, $\exp(v_i)$, in the denominator that makes the frontier stochastic. Let $y_i = \ln(Y_i)$ and $x_i = \ln(X_i)$, then a linear form of Equation (1) can be obtained as

$$y_i = f(x_i \mid \beta) + \varepsilon_i, \quad i = 1,\ldots,n, \tag{3}$$

where ε_i is the error term composed as

$$\varepsilon_i = v_i - u_i, \tag{4}$$

where v_i is the noise term, and u_i is the technical inefficiency term, both of which are in logarithmic form.

Different assumptions about these two terms, as well as about $f(x_i \mid \beta)$, and consequently on how they are estimated (parametrically, semi-parametrically, or non-parametrically) yield different variants of SFMs.

Here, we will start with the classical (which still appears to be the most popular[5]) SFM developed by Aigner et al. (1977) (hereafter ALS77), where $f(x_i \mid \beta)$ is assumed to have some known functional form (usually Cobb-Douglas, Translog, etc.), while v_i and u_i are assumed to be independent from each other and from x_i, and such that

$$v_i \sim iid\mathcal{N}(0,\sigma_v^2), \tag{5}$$

$$u_i \sim iid\mathcal{N}^+(0,\sigma_u^2). \tag{6}$$

The model can then be estimated with the maximum likelihood estimation (MLE). Using the estimated parameters, the expected level of efficiency ($E[\exp(-u)] \approx 1 - E(u)$) and expected inefficiency $\left(E(u) = \sqrt{\frac{2}{\pi}}\sigma_u\right)$ can be further estimated. Meanwhile, the individual level of (in)efficiency of unit i, can be estimated following Jondrow, Lovell, Materov, and Schmidt (1982) (hereafter JLMS), by estimating $E(u_i \mid \varepsilon_i)$ or, analogously by estimating $E[\exp(-u_i \mid \varepsilon_i)]$, where note that $E[\exp(-u_i \mid \varepsilon_i)] \approx 1 - E(u_i \mid \varepsilon_i)$.

3.2. SFA Models with Determinants of Inefficiency

An attractive advancement of the basic SFM is to consider whether some exogenous variables (also referred to as the "environmental factors") are associated with (in)efficiency. The model introduced in Kumbhakar et al. (1991) (hereafter KGM91) appears to be the pioneer and among the most popular in this vein (although sometimes overlooked),[6,7] and can be formulated (in the log-log linear form) as

$$\begin{aligned} y_i &= x_i'\beta + v_i - u_i, \quad i = 1,\ldots,n, \\ v_i &\sim iid\mathcal{N}(0,\sigma_v^2), \\ u_i &\sim iid\mathcal{N}^+(\tau_i,\sigma_u^2), \\ \tau_i &= z_i'\gamma, \end{aligned} \tag{7}$$

where the notation is as in the previous section, with a new vector $z_i \in \Re^m$ that represents m exogenous (also called "environmental") variables that are expected to "determine" the pre-truncation mean of the distribution of u_i, via γ, the vector of corresponding parameters to be estimated. Moreover, since τ_i is varying across units, it not only takes account of the unit-related factors in inefficiency, but also introduces more flexibility into the distributional assumptions of inefficiency.[8]

Following the likelihood function derived in Kumbhakar et al. (1991), one can estimate parameters consistently with a one-step MLE, and then the expected inefficiency (i.e., $E(u_i)$) accordingly. The inefficiency of an individual unit can also be estimated using the JLMS approach with the estimated parameters.

It is worth noting that while the models above are described in a cross-sectional setting, they can be adapted in various ways to panel data contexts, for example, with the seminal model by Pitt and Lee (1981); Schmidt and Sickles (1984), and the further developed variants with different functional specifications or assumptions. Other alternative models are also available in the wide spectrum of SFMs, which are worth considering for further study of this topic. One example is the Battese and Coelli (1992) model and others in the vein that take account of time-variant inefficiency.[9] The more recent Kumbhakar, Lien, and Hardaker (2014) model introduced a framework to separate the transitory and persistent inefficiency. The local least squares method proposed in Simar, Van Keilegom, and Zelenyuk (2017) extended the non-parametric method into the estimation of SFM.[10] We leave the extensive applications of these methods as fruitful directions for this topic for future endeavors. Meanwhile, as a matter of further exploration, we also conduct an analysis of the Queensland hospitals with some recently developed prominent panel data SFMs in Appendix 6.

4. DATA, VARIABLES, AND MODEL SPECIFICATION

4.1. Data Sources

The sample data include 388 records of 97 public hospitals in Queensland, Australia in a four-year period from FY 2012/13 to FY 2015/16. We obtained the data about hospital performance, expenditure, human resource, classification, etc., from the collections of Queensland Health (QH), and several characteristic factors, such as the location and peer group code, from the Australian Institute of Health and Welfare (AIHW).

The hospitals can be intuitively classified in three dimensions of characteristics: (i) size, (ii) location, and (iii) teaching status. The size of the hospital can be categorized by the peer group code, defined by AIHW (2015), where hospitals are divided into five groups, i.e., the principal referral and public acute groups A, B, C, and D. The latter two groups are usually much smaller in size than the other groups so they are labeled as "small hospitals" in this analysis, while the others are "large hospitals" (Nguyen & Zelenyuk, 2021a). The location code collected by AIHW, as defined by Australian Bureau of Statistics (2006), categorizes hospitals into six types regarding their physical distance to the nearest urban center. The hospitals in our sample belong to five categories, i.e., major cities, inner regional, outer regional, remote, and very remote, in which the latter two types are labeled as "remote hospitals," while the others are "non-remote hospitals." Finally, the teaching status, recorded by QH, divides hospitals into "teaching" and "non-teaching hospitals." The distributions of these characteristics of the 97 hospitals are illustrated in Fig. 13.1.

From a quantitative perspective as in Panel (a) of Fig. 13.1, the number of hospitals in non-remote areas is more than twice those in remote areas. Though "small hospitals" are the majority of the sample in all areas, very few "large hospitals" are located in remote areas. "Teaching hospitals" are usually of a large size. More specifically, in a percentage perspective as in Panel (b) of Fig. 13.1, 75% and 100% of "large hospitals" in non-remote and remote areas are teaching hospitals, respectively, while the proportions of "small hospitals" with teaching functions are below 10% in both areas.

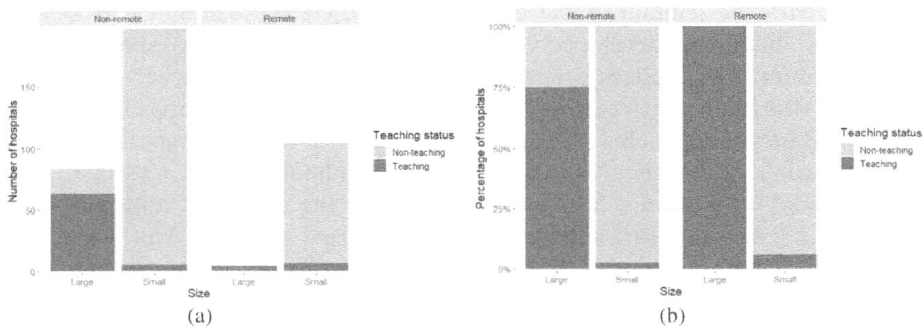

Fig. 13.1. Characteristics of Queensland Public Hospitals, FY 2012/13 to FY 2015/16.

4.2. Variables and Data Processing

Following the studies on hospital efficiency, e.g., Grosskopf and Valdmanis (1987); Zuckerman et al. (1994); Rosko (2001); Chowdhury and Zelenyuk (2016), as well as more practices in the literature as reviewed by, Hollingsworth (2008); O'Neill, Rauner, Heidenberger, and Kraus (2008); Hussey et al. (2009) among others, and the more recent work focusing on Queensland hospital efficiency, e.g., Nguyen and Zelenyuk (2021a), we choose three inputs with one aggregate output variable and use seven indicators to represent the determinant factors.

The three inputs are (i) Labor, (ii) Consumable expenditure, and (iii) Capital. Specifically, to construct an aggregate variable that represents Labor, we consider six categories of Full-Time Equivalent (FTE) staff, including medical officers, nurses, diagnostic professionals, personal care staff, administrative staff, and domestic staff, and reduce these six dimensions to one aggregated variable (AGGLABOR) using Principal Component Analysis (PCA).[11] The information explained by the first principle component accounts for 95.26% of the total, as a result, AGGLABOR could express most of the information for the six labor categories.[12]

Two categories of expenditures on supplies, i.e., drug supplies and surgical and medical supplies, are considered to reflect the aggregate variable measuring consumables (SUPP), which are deflated by the consumer price index (CPI) to the constant price of FY 2012/13. For capital input, the number of beds is the most commonly applied proxy of capital investment and utilization in the literature (BEDS), which is therefore, used in this study.

The output of a hospital comprises two categories, the inpatient and the outpatient service. The admitted patients belong to different Diagnosis-Related Groups (DRGs), where substantial variations exist in the treatment and resources needed. Thus, to aggregate the number of inpatient episodes by hospital, the episodes are weighted by the case-mix weight of year 2013 published by the Independent Hospital Pricing Authority (2013). Meanwhile, the outpatient service is directly accounted for by the number of visits, which is based on the availability of data, and contains emergency visits and non-admitted occasions. Finally, using the

PCA procedure as for the labor inputs, the two output indicators are aggregated into one variable (AGGOUT), where 98.75% of information is explained by the first component.[13]

According to the distribution of these four input and output variables, we identified eight outliers that are substantially higher than the others in each dimension. After trimming these outliers, the data set for further analysis contains 380 observations of 95 hospitals, which is 98% of the data.[14]

Besides the three hospital features (i.e., size, location, and teaching status), we derive four more Key Performance Indicators (KPIs) from the original data to further explore the potential explanatory factors, which are: (i) Occupancy rate (OCCUP): the ratio of the number of inpatient days to the number of available bed days, (ii) Inpatient–outpatient ratio (INOUT): the ratio of inpatient episodes to outpatient visits, (iii) Average length of stay (AVELOS): the number of total inpatient days divided by the number of admitted episodes, and (iv) Turnover rate (TOVER): the number of inpatient episodes divided by the number of available beds.[15]

Finally, dummy variables for different years (i.e., Y2013, Y2014, Y2015) are also included to estimate the time-related effects. Descriptive statistics of all the selected variables are as shown in Table 13.1.

4.3. Model Specification

Various production functions are possible candidates for the implementation of SFA, with the Cobb-Douglas and the Translog (transcendental logarithmic) functions being the most widely used (Rosko & Mutter, 2008).[16]

To be precise, the SFA with the Cobb-Douglas production function is given by

$$\ln Y_i = \beta_0 + \sum_{j=1}^{p} \beta_j \ln X_{ji} + v_i - u_i, \quad i = 1, \ldots, n, \tag{8}$$

while the SFA with the Translog form can be expressed as

$$\ln Y_i = \beta_0 + \sum_{j=1}^{p} \beta_j \ln X_{ji} + \frac{1}{2} \sum_{k=1}^{p} \sum_{h=1}^{p} \beta_{kh} \ln X_{ki} \ln X_{hi} + v_i - u_i, \quad i = 1, \ldots, n. \tag{9}$$

The Translog function is usually favored in the literature (e.g., Hjalmarsson, Kumbhakar, & Heshmati, 1996; Greene, 2004; Kumbhakar, 2010) for its flexibility. However, due to many more parameters, it may lose a lot of degrees of freedom, compared to the Cobb-Douglas function, potentially overfitting the data. In addition, the Translog function as in Equation (9) also requires imposing homogeneity, i.e., $\sum_{j=1}^{p} \beta_j = 1$ and $\sum_{h=1}^{p} \beta_{kh} = 0$, as well as symmetry that i.e., $\beta_{kh} = \beta_{hk}$.[17]

As indicated by Rosko and Mutter (2008), a hypothesis test of the nested relationship between these two functions is widely accepted for the decision between them, for which a likelihood ratio (LR) test is usually deployed. The null hypothesis here would be $H_0 : \beta_{kh} = 0, k = 1, \ldots, p; h = 1, \ldots, p$, i.e., the Cobb-Douglas form

Table 13.1. Descriptive Statistics of Queensland Public Hospitals, FY 2012/13 to FY 2015/16.

Variables	Description	Mean	Std Dev	Min	Q1	Q3	Max
Input							
AGGLABOR	Aggregated labor input	0.76	1.57	0.01	0.07	0.42	8.71
MEO	Salaried medical officers[a]	49.18	109.62	0.00	2.18	14.75	630.91
TNUR	Nurses[a]	147.94	297.45	2.28	15.19	82.43	1641.75
DHP	Diagnostic and health professionals[a]	30.09	74.40	0.00	0.00	15.18	468.00
ACS	Administrative and clerical staff[a]	46.54	101.53	0.18	2.11	22.66	627.80
OPCS	Other personal care staff[a]	7.39	17.55	0.00	0.01	4.00	125.42
DOS	Domestic and other staff[a]	49.31	85.62	0.00	8.62	42.45	509.30
SUPP	Consumable input[b]	7.83	19.20	0.03	0.16	2.53	164.00
DSUP	Drug supplies expenditure[b]	2.16	5.48	0.00	0.04	0.81	36.60
MSSUP	Medical and surgical supplies[b]	5.95	15.00	0.02	0.12	1.74	148.00
BEDS	Number of beds	74.92	133.78	3.00	11.00	48.50	680.00
Output							
AGGOUT	Aggregated output	0.54	1.03	0.01	0.04	0.32	5.05
WEPISODES	Case-mix weighted episodes	8012.15	16837.94	31.08	341.26	4001.78	82815.42
OUT	Number of outpatient visits	77741.66	137870.60	1248.00	6361.50	48525.50	677604.00
Environmental							
Continuous							
OCCUP	Occupancy rate	0.56	0.29	0.05	0.33	0.76	2.31
INOUT	Inpatient–outpatient ratio	0.09	0.04	0.01	0.05	0.11	0.29
AVELOS	Average length of stay	3.54	4.04	1.28	2.21	3.62	54.24
TOVER	Bed turn-over rate	71.05	41.05	7.79	38.16	99.84	189.59
Binary		**Number**	**Percentage**				
REMOTE	Located in remote areas	108	28.42%				
SMALL	Small hospitals	300	78.95%				
TEACH	Teaching hospitals	70	18.42%				

Notes: [a]Full-time equivalent staffs.
[b]AUD 1,000,000 in constant price of FY2012/13.

is the correct specification, versus the alternative Translog function. Hence, the LR statistic would be

$$LR = -2\ln\left(\frac{L(m_R)}{L(m_U)}\right) = 2(ll(m_U) - ll(m_R)), \tag{10}$$

where $L(m_.)$ and $ll(m_.)$ are the likelihood and log-likelihood functions of model $m_.$, and m_U and m_R are the unrestricted and restricted models, respectively. It is worth noting that the usual caveats of statistical testing apply here. In particular, if the null hypothesis is not rejected, it does not mean it is correct, rather it means there is not enough evidence (e.g., due to data limitations or due to various maintained assumptions, such as distributional assumptions, etc.) to reject the null hypothesis at the specified significance level. On the other hand, if the null hypothesis is rejected, it does not necessarily mean that the Translog functional form is the correct specification and further diagnostics and simplification (e.g., by dropping some of the variables with statistically insignificant coefficients to attain greater parsimony) may still be needed.

5. RESULTS AND DISCUSSION

5.1. Benchmark Models

The estimated parameters for the parametric models are as reported in Table 13.2. To start with, we conduct ordinary least squares (OLS) regression with robust standard errors (s.e.) to preliminarily study the production relationship. As a result, the coefficients of capital, expenditure, and the dummy variables of the year indicate significant positive relationships between the variables and the output, when the Cobb-Douglas function is deployed. In comparison, the coefficients estimated in the Translog function are all statistically insignificant, except those of the year dummies. Besides, the estimation results, including the coefficients and standard errors, of the ALS77 model, are quite close to those of the OLS regression.

In the latter estimation of hospital-level inefficiency, as reported by the statistics in Table 13.5 as well as the kernel density plot in Fig. 13.3,[18] the estimation of ALS77 apparently runs into some sort of degeneracy.[19] One possible reason for the degeneracy or overfitting phenomenon is that the basic ALS77 model is too simple to represent the reality, possibly due to substantial heterogeneity embedded in the inefficiency term, which violates the half-normal assumption of the ALS77.[20] Therefore, we deploy the more advanced KGM91 model as discussed ahead for more elaborate estimations and further explorations of the explanatory factors.

5.2. Production Relationship

In Table 13.2, the regressors of KGM91 in the Cobb-Douglas function representing the capital and expenditure inputs show statistically significant relationships with the output in the estimation, while the regressor for the labor input is not significantly associated with the output. In practice, healthcare is a labor-intensive industry and so the labor input is generally believed to be quite an influential factor in the hospital production relationship. Hence, it is expected that a suitable model should reflect this importance via the significance of the coefficient representing labor. As a result, the insignificant coefficient estimated for the labor in the KGM91 model in the Cobb-Douglas function, as well as the insignificant coefficients in the ALS77 model in both production functions, suggest possible

Table 13.2. Parameter Estimates of Selected Models.

Model Production function	OLS (robust s.e.)		ALS77		KGM91		
	Cobb-Douglas	Translog	Cobb-Douglas	Translog	Cobb-Douglas	Translog	Parsimonious-Translog
Frontier function							
ln BEDS	0.25***	2.27	0.25***	2.27	0.52***	5.40***	4.83***
	0.07	1.85	0.06	1.64	0.05	1.12	1.02
ln AGGLABOR	0.03	2.35	0.03	2.35	0.04	2.76***	3.53***
	0.06	1.85	0.05	1.59	0.04	1.04	1.02
ln SUPP	0.60***	−0.92	0.60***	−0.92	0.33***	−4.03***	−4.30***
	0.05	1.63	0.04	1.28	0.03	0.89	0.87
ln BEDS * ln AGGLABOR		0.08		0.08		0.20**	0.29***
		0.17		0.15		0.09	0.09
ln BEDS * ln SUPP		−0.21		−0.21		−0.39***	−0.27***
		0.16		0.14		0.1	0.07
ln AGGLABOR * ln SUPP		−0.16		−0.16		−0.21***	−0.29***
		0.12		0.1		0.06	0.06
$(\ln BEDS)^2$		0.34		0.34		0.28*	
		0.25		0.25		0.15	
$(\ln SUPP)^2$		0.14		0.14		0.38***	0.36***
		0.13		0.11		0.07	0.07
$(\ln AGGLABOR)^2$		0.19		0.19		0.24**	0.26**
		0.19		0.17		0.11	0.11
Y2013	0.17***	0.14**	0.17***	0.14***	0.06	0.04	
	0.06	0.06	0.05	0.05	0.04	0.03	
Y2014	0.14**	0.11**	0.14***	0.11**	0.06*	0.04	
	0.06	0.06	0.05	0.05	0.04	0.03	

Y2015	0.13**	0.11**	0.13**	0.11**	0.05	0.04	
	0.06	0.05	0.05	0.05	0.04	0.03	
Constant	−11.10***	−1.58	−11.09***	−1.58	−7.91***	17.02***	20.52***
	0.69	11.03	0.61	8.93	0.44	6.04	6.03
τ_i							
TEACH					−6.89	0.06	
					(.)	0.09	
REMOTE					0.17*	0.06	
					0.09	0.04	
SMALL					−1.60***	3.64	
					0.4	(.)	
OCCUP					−0.67**	−0.42***	−0.45***
					0.27	0.12	0.11
INOUT					13.28	7.67***	7.55***
					(.)	0.41	0.4
AVELOS					0.02**	0.03***	0.03***
					0.01	0.01	0.00
TOVER					−0.03***	−0.02***	−0.02***
					0.00	0.00	0.00
Constant					2.37***	−2.77***	0.99***
					0.49	0.09	0.07
σ_u			0.01	0.01	0.27***	0.15***	0.16***
			0.36	0.24	0.03	0.02	0.02
σ_v			0.36***	0.34***	0.22***	0.16***	0.16***
			0.01	0.01	0.01	0.01	0.01

Notes: Standard errors beneath.
* $p < 0.10$; ** $p < 0.05$; *** $p < 0.01$.

substantial misspecification (e.g., oversimplification) of those models. In the Translog function, on the other hand, the coefficients of all three inputs and most coefficients of their cross-product and squared terms are significant, which suggest a non-linear relationship between the inputs and output.

Importantly, the signs of the coefficients of the three input categories in the Cobb-Douglas function are all positive, indicating positive relationships between the inputs and the output, as one would expect. However, when accounting for the squared and cross-product regressors in the Translog function, the coefficient of the expenditure input is negative, while the coefficient of the squared expenditure input (in natural logarithm) is positive. This implies a non-monotonic relationship between the expenditure input and the output. We may leave the exploration of this interesting relationship, whether for the case of Queensland hospitals or for hospitals in general, for future studies. Finally, all three dummy variables for time are reported as positively related to the output in each function, though most of the coefficients are not statistically significant.

All in all, the estimation of the production function is different across the models. The coefficient of the expenditure input is positive in the Cobb-Douglas function, while it is negative when the Translog function is applied. Besides, the coefficients of the inputs are all insignificant when we estimate the ALS77 model in the Translog function, while most of the coefficients are significant when the KGM91 model is estimated instead. Consequently, different interpretations would result in different conclusions about the production relationships, which in turn may lead to different policy implications. To explore this aspect more carefully, we perform a model selection process with statistical tests in the next subsection.

5.3. *Model Selection*

To select the model for further analysis, we deploy the LR-test following the literature (e.g., see the review in Rosko & Mutter, 2008) and the results are reported in Table 13.3. The selection process is concisely illustrated in Fig. 13.2. Specifically, we first compare the two production functions with both SFMs. As indicated in the first two rows of Table 13.3, we reject the null hypothesis in both models, which implies that some of the coefficients of the eliminated squared and cross-product terms are not zero. Therefore, we will mainly focus on the results of the Translog function as well as its restricted versions in our further analysis and discussion.

We then test the KGM91 model with two restricted forms where the first one assumes all coefficients for the inefficiency function are zero (except the constant term) in the Translog function. As a result, we reject the null hypothesis and would not replace the unrestricted KGM91 model with this restricted form.

In the other restricted form, we exclude the variables (in both production and inefficiency functions) with insignificant coefficients estimated in the unrestricted model (as indicated in Table 13.2). As reported in the last two rows of Table 13.3, the KGM91 model for the Cobb-Douglas function with such restrictions is rejected in favor of the unrestricted model. Meanwhile, we cannot

Table 13.3. LR Test Results Between Various Restricted and Unrestricted Models.

Model			*LR*	*p*-Value	Decision
Restricted		Unrestricted			
Production functions					
ALS77-CD	vs	ALS77-Translog	34.322	0	Reject***
KGM91-CD	vs	KGM91-Translog	190.531	0	Reject***
SFMs					
ALS77-CD	vs	KGM91-CD	259.563	0	Reject***
ALS77-Translog	vs	KGM91-Translog	415.772	0	Reject***
Parsimonious KGM91					
KGM91-Translog-$\gamma = 0$[a]	vs	KGM91-Translog	414.369	0	Reject***
KGM91-CD-Restricted[b]	vs	KGM91-CD	210.117	0	Reject***
KGM91-Translog-Restricted[b]	vs	KGM91-Translog	6.899	0.440	Not Reject

Notes: Not reject: $p > 0.10$; Reject: * $p < 0.10$; ** $p < 0.05$; *** $p < 0.01$.
[a]Assuming all coefficients of environmental factors, except the constant term, as zero.
[b]Dropping variables with insignificant coefficient estimates in the unrestricted model.

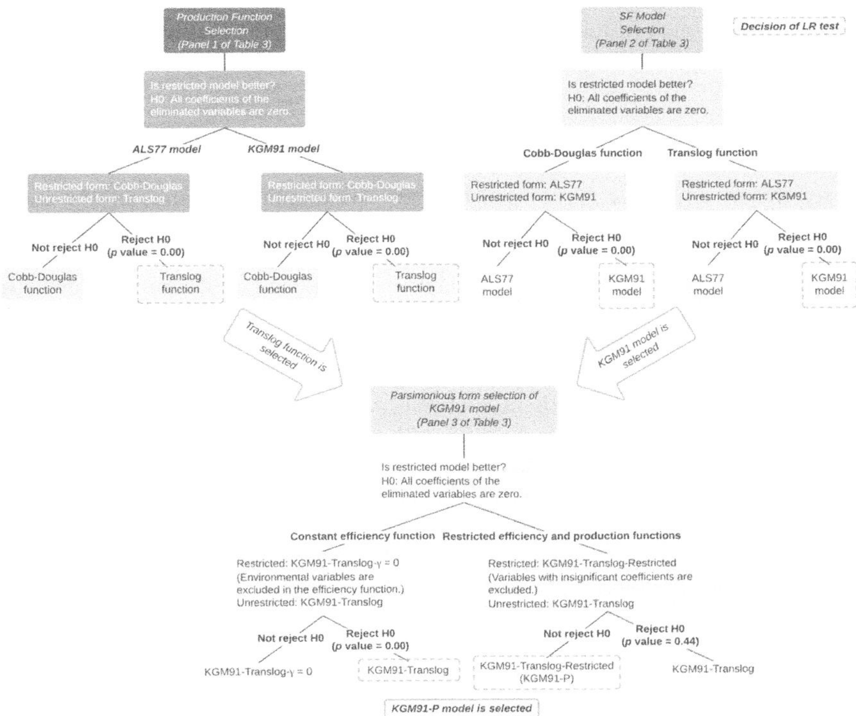

Fig. 13.2. Model Selection Process.

Table 13.4. AIC and BIC of Unrestricted and Restricted Models.

Models	*AIC*	*BIC*	Models	*AIC*	*BIC*
Unrestricted			*Restricted models*		
ALS77-CD	312.02	347.48	KGM91-Translog-$\gamma = 0$	290.29	353.33
ALS77-Translog	289.69	348.80	KGM91-CD-Restricted	260.57	292.09
KGM91-CD	64.45	123.56	KGM91-Translog-Restricted	−117.18	−54.14
KGM91-Translog	−112.08	−25.39			

reject the analogous null hypothesis for this restriction form with the Translog function. Consequently, we will focus more on this parsimonious form of the KGM91 model (hereafter KGM91-P), particularly in the Translog function, for further analysis.

The model selection with Akaike's Information Criteria (AIC) and Bayesian Information Criteria (BIC) may run into the same result as we obtain with the series of LR tests. As reported in Table 13.4, most of the rejected models in the LR tests have higher AIC and BIC values than their counterparts.

As reported in the last two columns of Table 13.2, the parameter estimates of KGM91-P, for the production function, as well as for the inefficiency function, are quite similar to those of the unrestricted KGM91 model in the Translog function.[21]

5.4. *Inefficiency Function*

A significant difference is reported between the estimation results of the three dummy variables for the environmental factors in different production functions of KGM91. In the Cobb-Douglas function, the teaching status and size of hospitals are negatively associated with the inefficiency term u_i, while the remoteness is positively related to u_i. Accordingly, the teaching, small, or non-remote hospitals would perform more efficiently than their reference groups (i.e., the non-teaching, large, or remote hospitals). It is also suggested in Chua, Palangkaraya, and Yong (2010) that teaching hospitals in Victoria, Australia tended to perform better between FY 2000/01 and FY 2004/05, although larger hospitals in their study were found to perform more efficiently. On the other hand, in the Translog function, all three coefficients are positive, indicating that non-teaching, large, or non-remote hospitals tend to be more efficient. A similar conclusion was obtained for Queensland in Nguyen and Zelenyuk (2021b, in Daouia and Ruiz-Gazen (Eds.)) that large and non-remote hospitals performed relatively more efficiently in FY 2016/17.

It is worth noting that only the coefficient of size in the Cobb-Douglas function is reported to be statistically significant. Consequently, these three dummy variables are removed in KGM91-P.

The signs of the coefficients of all the four KPI variables are found to be consistent across the KGM91 and KGM91-P models. Besides, the coefficients of the four KPIs are all significant among the three KGM91 models at a 95% confidence level, except the inpatient–outpatient ratio in the Cobb-Douglas function. The negative signs of the coefficients of occupancy rate and turnover rate suggest that the higher rates of occupancy or bed turnover are associated with a lower inefficiency term. Such a relationship between occupancy rate and the efficiency level was also found in Canadian hospitals (e.g., Fixler, Paradi, & Yang, 2014; Chowdhury & Zelenyuk, 2016). Meanwhile, the signs of the coefficients of the average length of stay and the inpatient–outpatient ratio are positive, indicating that longer stays or a higher proportion of inpatient services would be associated with higher inefficiency estimates, on average and ceteris paribus.

5.5. Recovery Test of the Selected Model

To strengthen the confidence in the estimated SF model, we construct a recovery test for the KGM91-P model, which would be the mainly discussed specification in our later analysis.[22]

According to the estimated production and inefficiency functions of the KGM91-P model in Table 13.2, we generate a new dependent variable y_i^* with the input variables in our analysis, such that

$$\begin{aligned} y_i^* = {} & 20.52 + 4.83 \ln \text{BEDS}_i + 3.53 \ln \text{AGGLABOR}_i \\ & - 4.3 \ln \text{SUPP}_i + 0.29 \ln \text{BEDS}_i \ln \text{AGGLABOR}_i \\ & - 0.27 \ln \text{BEDS}_i \ln \text{SUPP}_i - 0.29 \ln \text{SUPP}_i \ln \text{AGGLABOR}_i \\ & + 0.36 \ln \text{SUPP}_i^2 + 0.26 \ln \text{AGGLABOR}_i^2 - u_i^* + v_i^*, \quad i = 1, \ldots, n, \end{aligned} \tag{11}$$

where the artificial inefficiency u_i^* is generated as

$$\begin{aligned} & u_i^* \sim iid\mathcal{N}^+(\tau_i^*, \sigma_u^{*2}), \quad i = 1, \ldots, n, \\ & \tau_i^* = 0.99 - 0.45\text{OCCUP}_i + 7.55\text{INOUT}_i + 0.03\text{AVELOS}_i - 0.02\text{TOVER}_i, \\ & \sigma_u^* = 0.16, \end{aligned} \tag{12}$$

and the random error term v_i^* is generated as

$$\begin{aligned} & v_i^* \sim iid\mathcal{N}(0, \sigma_v^{*2}), \quad i = 1, \ldots, n, \\ & \sigma_v^* = 0.16. \end{aligned} \tag{13}$$

We then estimate the KGM91-P model again with the simulated output y_i^* and the other variables from the original data set to recover the coefficients and generated inefficiency. Consequently, the estimated coefficients of both the production and inefficiency functions are close to the predetermined ones as above in both magnitude and direction. The Pearson correlation between the recovered and specified coefficients is about 90.11% (on average, over 1,000 replications). Meanwhile, the mean correlation between the recovered and simulated inefficiency is about 97.58%.

5.6. Inefficiency Estimation of Individual Hospitals

To understand the performance of our sample hospitals and explore the possible improvements, we first estimate the inefficiency level of individual hospitals. Following the general practice in the literature, we apply the JLMS approach to estimate the inefficiency term by unit in the selected SFMs. Specifically, the inefficiency term of unit i in the ALS77 and KGM91 models could be represented by u_i as discussed in Section 3. In JLMS, by defining

$$\begin{aligned} \sigma^2 &= \sigma_v^2 + \sigma_u^2, \\ \sigma_*^2 &= \sigma_v^2 \sigma_u^2 / \sigma^2, \\ u_{i*} &= -\sigma_u^2 \varepsilon_i / \sigma^2, \end{aligned} \tag{14}$$

as well as the composed error ε_i given in Equation (4), the expected value of u_i given the condition of ε_i can be estimated as

$$E(u_i \mid \varepsilon_i) = u_{i*} + \sigma_* \frac{\phi(-u_{i*} / \sigma_*)}{1 - \Phi(-u_{i*} / \sigma_*)}, \tag{15}$$

where $\phi(\cdot)$ and $\Phi(\cdot)$ are the probability density and cumulative distribution functions of the standard normal distribution, respectively.

Since the estimated $\hat{u}_i$ is the technical inefficiency in logarithm scale, to derive a more interpretable inefficiency level, we may use

$$\hat{\theta}_i = 1 - \exp(-\hat{u}_i), \tag{16}$$

where $\exp(-\hat{u}_i)$ is the estimation of the technical efficiency as derived in Equation (2). The descriptive statistics of the estimated inefficiency scores ($\hat{\theta}_i \times 100\%$) are reported in Table 13.5.

For the Cobb-Douglas function, the inefficiency scores estimated by KGM91 have a mean of 21.44% and a median of 9.52%, while the inefficiency estimated under the Translog function is substantially higher on average (median) at 30.24% (27.13%). Meanwhile, the Pearson correlation matrix indicates that the estimates of the same SFM under different production functions are highly correlated

Table 13.5. Descriptive Statistics for the Individual Inefficiency Estimated by Equation (16).

Models	Mean	Std Dev	Min	Q1	Q2	Q3	Max
Cobb-Douglas							
ALS77	0.81%	0.01%	0.77%	0.80%	0.81%	0.81%	0.85%
KGM91	21.44%	23.09%	0.67%	3.19%	9.52%	38.42%	77.79%
Translog							
ALS77	0.66%	0.01%	0.63%	0.65%	0.66%	0.66%	0.69%
KGM91	30.24%	25.95%	0.42%	3.45%	27.13%	52.49%	82.52%
KGM91-P	32.48%	25.39%	1.20%	6.49%	30.48%	53.30%	83.57%

Table 13.6. Correlation Matrix of Individual Inefficiency Estimated by Equation (16).

	ALS77-CD	KGM91-CD	ALS77-Translog	KGM91-Translog	KGM91-P-Translog
ALS77-CD	1				
KGM91-CD	0.6835	1			
ALS77-Translog	0.9559	0.6500	1		
KGM91-Translog	0.6203	0.9565	0.6013	1	
KGM91-P-Translog	0.6250	0.9535	0.6059	0.9992	1

(i.e., higher than 0.95 as shown in Table 13.6). The correlations between different SFMs are lower than 0.7 with or without the same production function.

Meanwhile, the estimation of the more parsimonious KGM91-P model is close to the result of the unrestricted KGM91 model in the Translog function.[23] The estimates of the individual inefficiency scores of KGM91 and KGM91-P are quite right-skewed with a long tail up to about 80%. The high level of similarity between these two models can also be found in kernel density estimates in Fig. 13.3. Moreover, it is also worth noting that the standard deviations of the estimates by KGM91 and KGM91-P are relatively high, compared to their means, so cautiousness is needed when interpreting their mean inefficiency levels.

The different results of the same model in different production functions indicate the importance of an appropriate model specification. For instance, one may conclude that the mean inefficiency of the Queensland hospitals in our study period is about 20% when applying the KGM91 model in the Cobb-Douglas function, while the mean could be reported as about 30% when using the same model in the Translog function. Meanwhile, in this sample, the impact of the selection of the SFM is even more substantial on policy implications. As will be discussed in more detail later, the estimates of KGM91-P indicate that teaching, non-remote, or large hospitals generally perform better than their reference groups, yet this tendency is not exhibited in the results of ALS77.

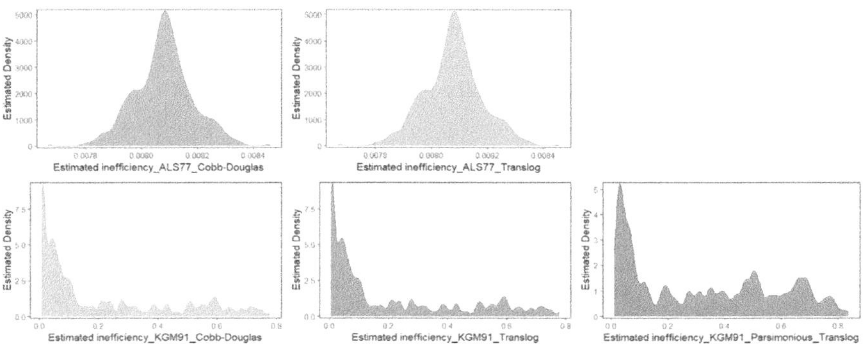

Fig. 13.3. Estimated Kernel Densities of the Inefficiency Level of Selected Models.

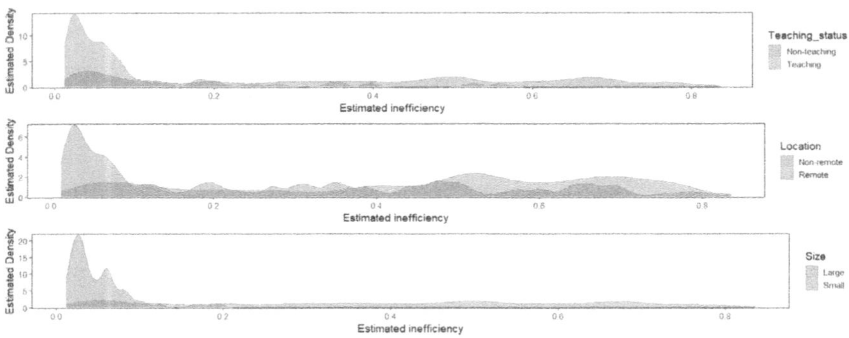

Fig. 13.4. Estimated Kernel Densities of the Inefficiency Level (with KGM91-P model) of Hospitals Grouped by Characteristics.

5.7. Impact of the Environmental Variables

As discussed in the previous section, the further analysis of the explanatory factors is conducted with the estimation of the KGM91-P model in the Translog function. Though all three coefficients of the hospital characteristics are reported as insignificantly associated with the inefficiency term u_i in KGM91, and thus removed in KGM91-P, the kernel density estimates of the inefficiency scores estimated via KGM91-P of Queensland public hospitals grouped by different characteristics show a significant difference. As shown in Fig. 13.4, "teaching hospitals" tend to have estimates with lower inefficiency scores than "non-teaching hospitals." Similarly, hospitals in non-remote areas and in large sizes are more likely to be estimated with lower inefficiency. The differences in distributions of the three pairs of groups are also concluded as significant in the Li (1996) test. As shown in Table 13.7, the null hypotheses of every pair of groups that the distributions of their inefficiency level are equal are all rejected at a 0.01 level of significance.[24]

To further explore this interesting phenomenon, we examine the KPIs, which are also explanatory variables in KGM91 and KGM91-P models. As illustrated in Fig. 13.5, the hospital groups with a possibly lower level of inefficiency, i.e., large, non-remote, or teaching hospitals, are relatively higher in occupancy, inpatient–outpatient, and turnover rates. Meanwhile, though the average length of stay is not substantially different among different groups, we can still observe a similar trend of more upper outliers for small or non-teaching hospitals.

Table 13.7. Li-Test for Distributions of Estimated Inefficiency Level by Different Groups.

Groups	Li-Test Statistics	Bootstrap *p*-Value	Decision
Non-teaching & Teaching	32.0051	0	Reject H_0
Non-remote & Remote	15.4081	0	Reject H_0
Large & Small	42.0575	0	Reject H_0

Notes: H_0 for each test: The distributions of individual hospital inefficiency are equal between the two groups.

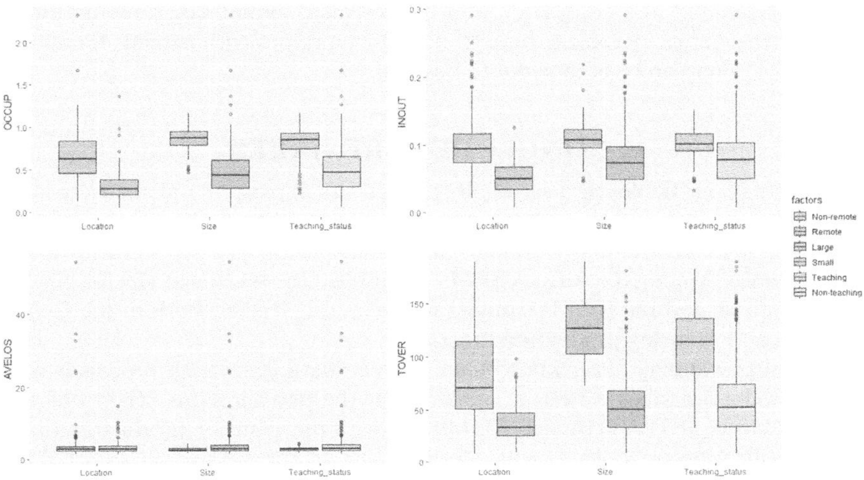

Fig. 13.5. KPIs by Characteristics of Queensland Public Hospitals, FY 2012/13 to FY 2015/16. See description of variables in Table 13.1.

Recall that the conclusions of the explanatory variables in KGM91-P were that the occupancy rate and the turnover rate are negatively related to inefficiency, and hence the higher these two ratios are, the better the hospitals would perform. In contrast, the inpatient-outpatient ratio and average length of stay are positively related to the inefficiency term, as a result, the higher these two values are, the lower hospital inefficiency level is expected to be, on average and ceteris paribus.

Therefore, according to the SFA approach based on KGM91-P, the more efficient groups in Queensland are the large, teaching, and non-remote hospitals, whose occupancy rate and turnover rate are substantially higher, which helps in improving their performance.[25] Their average length of stay, though not markedly different, still shows a tendency toward a lower level than their reference groups, which should also be helpful for better performance. Interestingly, the better performing groups present a significantly higher inpatient-outpatient ratio, which is not beneficial to their level of efficiency, yet it does not dominate the other factors that influence their efficiency.[26]

Consequently, the results suggest that to improve performance (as measured in this study), small, non-teaching, and remote hospitals can be encouraged to increase their occupancy and turnover rates, while maintaining the length of stay (and quality of services). Meanwhile, all hospitals, especially the large and teaching hospitals in urban areas can be encouraged to try to decrease their inpatient-outpatient ratio, through, for example, decentralizing a proportion of inpatient care from large hospitals to smaller and local hospitals (assuming the same type and quality of services can be provided in the latter, which may require additional investments). While improving the utilization of bed resources in small and remote hospitals, the larger regional hospitals may also be relieved from the high inpatient demand and congestion and the so-called ambulance ramping problems, when emergency vehicles have to stand by on ramps with patients for a long time before they can be accepted into hospital.[27]

6. CONCLUDING REMARKS

In this study, we deployed a set of SFA models to explore the inefficiency level of public hospitals in Queensland in a recent period and further evaluated the variables that can potentially explain (in a predictive analytic sense) the hospital performance. Among the various SFMs, we applied the ALS77 model for benchmark analysis and the KGM91 model for advanced studies, both in the Cobb-Douglas and Translog production functions.

Although we may never know what the true data generating process is and which model describes it best, it appears that the parsimonious version of the Kumbhakar et al. (1991) model (KGM91-P) with the Translog production function specification provides us with more reliable estimates than the other alternatives. This appears to be the case for both the production frontier and the inefficiency estimation, as well as the analysis of the influence of the explanatory variables.

Specifically, we found most input variables (i.e., labor, expenditure, and capital) are statistically significantly related to the output, represented by the inpatient and outpatient service of hospitals. However, the coefficients and the significance levels are different across the different models in different production functions. The significant difference in the estimated parameters (especially opposite signs of the coefficients) would lead to a different explanation of the inefficiency level and ultimately different policy suggestions, which in turn emphasizes the necessity of careful selection of the model and production function specification.

In the estimation of the inefficiency function, the three hospital characteristics (i.e., size, location, and teaching status) are generally not significantly related to the inefficiency term u_i. Meanwhile, the coefficients of all four KPIs (i.e., occupancy rate, bed turnover rate, inpatient-outpatient ratio, and average length of stay) are all found statistically significant. Specifically, the occupancy and turnover rates are found to be negatively related to the inefficiency term u_i, while the inpatient–outpatient ratio and average length of stay are positively related to u_i.

We then estimated the individual inefficiency scores of the 95 public hospitals in Queensland with the selected models. The obtained results of different SFMs in each production function also show dramatic differences, leading to divergent policy implications. The estimation of ALS77 may suggest most hospitals performed efficiently, yet the results of KGM91-P indicated that large, non-remote, and teaching hospitals had a significantly lower inefficiency level than their reference groups. Consequently, more specific policy suggestions could be derived from the analysis of the more differentiated results by the KGM91-P model.

In conclusion, according to the estimation in KGM91-P, the inefficiency of Queensland public hospitals shows a high level of divergence. In general, hospitals in the large size category, in non-remote areas, or with teaching functions, tend to be estimated with lower inefficiency scores than their reference groups, which indicates a scale effect existing in the hospital performance. The better performing hospital groups in the case of Queensland may benefit from their higher occupancy and bed turnover rates, while their inefficiency level can be further lowered if they could reduce the proportion of inpatient admissions. Accordingly, one possible solution is to encourage further decentralization of the inpatient care from large hospitals to more local hospitals (assuming the same level and quality of care can be provided, which may require additional investments). The small and regional hospitals could then reduce their inefficiency (as measured in this study) by increasing the occupancy and turnover rates of beds, while the large major hospitals may also benefit from a lowering proportion of inpatient care (and hence reducing congestion and related issues).[28]

Among the broad spectrum of SFMs, we deployed only two classical (and most popular) models in this study, while there are many other alternatives in the literature. In particular, much effort has been made to release the parametric assumptions on the functional form and disturbances defined in the classical SFM. One of the pioneering attempts was by Fan, Li, and Weersink (1996), in which a semi-parametric approach, combining the non-parametric kernel regression and parametric MLE, was proposed for estimating SFMs. An important further development is the non-parametric framework introduced in Kumbhakar, Park, Simar, and Tsionas (2007), where a local maximum likelihood method was used instead of MLE. The local likelihood estimation, compared to the parametric MLE method, comprises a kernel function based on the local inputs. In further developments, Park, Simar, and Zelenyuk (2015) extended the local likelihood method into allowing discrete regressors, and more recently, Simar et al. (2017) suggested a non-parametric least squares method as an alternative to the local likelihood method for SFM with simpler and more robust computations and fewer assumptions. Another solution consolidating the non-parametric production and SFMs was recently proposed by Tsionas, Parmeter, Zelenyuk (2023), in which the estimation could be done by Bayesian compression, while the determinants could be modeled in an artificial neural network framework. All such methods are worth more exploration in future research for the performance of Queensland hospitals, or hospitals in a wider range.[29]

ACKNOWLEDGMENTS

The authors acknowledge the support from Australian Research Council (grant FT170100401) and The University of Queensland. We thank the editors and anonymous referees of Advances in Econometrics for their constructive comments. We thank Queensland Health and AIHW for providing the hospital data sets we utilized in this paper. We are also thankful for the valuable feedback from Peter Bogetoft, David Du, Bao Hoang Nguyen, Hong Ngoc Nguyen, Evelyn Smart, Laya Venkataramanan, Jongsay Yong, and the audience of Australian Conference of Economists (2022), CEPA Conference (2022), PEARL meetings, etc. These organizations and individuals are not responsible for the views expressed in this chapter.

NOTES

1. For a recent review of the key developments of SFA, see Sickles and Zelenyuk (2019) and Kumbhakar, Parmeter, and Zelenyuk (2021a, 2021b).

2. For a recent review of major models developed in decades, see Sickles and Zelenyuk (2019).

3. For a more detailed discussion on the application of the two mainstream approaches in healthcare efficiency, see the reviews by Worthington (2004), Hollingsworth (2008), Hussey et al. (2009), and more recently See, Grosskopf, Valdmanis, and Zelenyuk (2021).

4. See more details of hospital efficiency analysis in Australia and peer regions in Wang and Zelenyuk (2021b).

5. For example, Aigner et al. (1977) received more than 14,000 citations on Google Scholar by the end of 2022.

6. For example, Kumbhakar et al. (1991) received more than 1,700 citations on Google Scholar by the end of 2022.

7. See Appendix 3 for bibliometric analysis regarding ALS77 and KGM91 in the literature.

8. For further extensions and discussions, see, e.g., Battese and Coelli (1995), Caudill, Ford, and Gropper (1995), Wang and Schmidt (2002), and Sickles and Zelenyuk (2019, Ch. 12–16).

9. In the perspective of unit-specific technical inefficiency, Ahn, Good, and Sickles (2000) proposed a dynamic SF approach to capture the evolution of inefficiency with a first-order autoregressive (AR(1)) process (Lai & Kumbhakar, 2020). Tsionas (2006) introduced another path with a Bayesian method using Markov chain Monte Carlo (MCMC) to provide inference of unit-specific inefficiency.

10. See the reviews by Kumbhakar et al. (2021a, 2021b) for more SFA models and a text-book style discussion in Sickles and Zelenyuk (2019).

11. Similarly to the analysis of Queensland public hospitals in Nguyen and Zelenyuk (2021a), the PCA aggregation used here is based on the approach proposed by Daraio and Simar (2007).

12. For more details of the PCA applications, see Appendix 1.

13. For more details of the aggregation process, see Appendix 1.

14. For more details of the outlier trimming, see Appendix 2.

15. See more discussions on the environmental factors of hospital performance in Chowdhury and Zelenyuk (2016). Also see Wang and Zelenyuk (2021a) for more details of KPIs used for hospital efficiency evaluation.

16. It is worth noting that the input distance function is also widely applied in the hospital efficiency literature. For the purpose of comparison with the previous studies for Queensland hospitals, we choose the production function approach.

17. The consistency of stochastic frontiers (e.g., monotonicity and convexity for production functions) is also widely discussed and various approaches were developed to impose these features (e.g., O'Donnell & Coelli, 2005; Henningsen & Henning, 2009) or to test their satisfaction after the estimation.

18. The kernel density hereafter is estimated with Gaussian kernel and bandwidth selected by cross-validation.

19. According to the estimation of σ_u in the Cobb-Douglas and Translog functions, we cannot reject the null hypothesis of $\sigma_u = 0$ at the 99% confidence level.

20. We further illustrate this inference in Appendix 4 with an artificial sample.

21. The time effect is accounted for via the dummy variables in the reported models. The alternative models with the trend component, the quadratic trend, and its interactions with the three inputs are rejected by the LR test. We thank the anonymous referee for their feedback on this aspect and provide more details in Appendix 5.

22. We thank the anonymous referee for the suggestions on performing this recovery test.

23. The mean inefficiency of the selected KGM91-P model (32.48%) is close to the average level of inefficiency estimated by O'Donnell and Nguyen (2013), where an SFM was

applied to Queensland public hospitals in an earlier period between FY 1995/96 and FY 2003/04. Meanwhile, the mean inefficiency of Queensland public hospitals in a similar period (FY 1996/97 to FY 2005/06) estimated by panel data SFMs (Gabbitas & Jeffs, 2009) is about 10 percentage points lower than the results reported by the KGM91-P model.

24. The effects of characteristics of hospitals, e.g., location, size, teaching status, ownership, etc., on the (in)efficiency are discussed in a variety of studies. For example, in the studies of Australian hospitals, Chua et al. (2010) indicated that teaching and large hospitals in Victoria tend to perform better, while more recently, Nguyen and Zelenyuk (2021b) concluded that smaller size and remoteness of hospitals could partially explain the low efficiency level of some districts in Queensland. In the perspective of cost efficiency, Wang, Zhao, and Mahmood (2006) also estimated a lower cost inefficiency of large hospitals, on average. Teaching hospitals in the US were also reported as statistically significantly more efficient with a DEA model (Grosskopf, Margaritis, & Valdmanis, 2004). Nevertheless, different relationships were suggested, e.g., Färe, Grosskopf, and Valdmanis (1989) found no significant difference between urban and remote hospitals, while Wang, Ozcan, Wan, and Harrison (1999) suggested that large hospital markets are more inefficient, due to the excess and not fully utilized beds and labor in the US.

25. The excess capacity of hospitals in remote areas may contribute to higher inefficiency through the correspondingly lower occupancy rate. In the performance analysis of 360 rural hospitals in the US, Ferrier and Valdmanis (1996) also indicated excess capacity as one of the cases that would lead to higher inefficiency. The reason for excess capacity may vary across different regions (e.g., the example of the New York State in Pasley, Lagoe, & Marshall, 1995), while for the rural hospitals, the lower competition and the less flexible labor market are some of the reasons (Magnussen & Mobley, 1999).

26. Similarly, Yong and Harris (1999) suggested that occupancy rate is negatively related to inefficiency, based on an SFA study on public hospitals in Victoria, Australia. Similar findings on occupancy rate were also concluded by the studies on hospitals in America, e.g., Zuckerman et al. (1994); Ferrier and Valdmanis (1996); Chowdhury and Zelenyuk (2016), where the latter two also found the negative impact of the higher inpatient-outpatient ratio on efficiency. In the study of the National Health Service (NHS) in the UK, Ali, Salehnejad, and Mansur (2019) suggested reducing the length of stay as an approach for improving hospital efficiency, which is consistent with our findings, although we note that this reduction should not be done at the expense of the quality of care.

27. For example, see Miles (2021).

28. It is worth noting that the outcome of the healthcare, e.g., the health improvement of the discharged patients, is not identical to the output analyzed in this study. A more comprehensive evaluation of the hospitals' performance may be conducted with a quality-adjusted output or by considering the quality of the healthcare as an explanatory variable (e.g., Ferrier & Valdmanis, 1996) or as an input and/or output directly (e.g., Ferrier & Trivitt, 2013). We leave this fruitful direction for the further development of this topic.

29. See Nguyen, Sickles, and Zelenyuk (2022); Sickles, Wang, and Zelenyuk (2022) for more detailed discussions of various SFA models and implementations in statistical software.

REFERENCES

Ahn, S. C., Good, D., & Sickles, R. C. (2000). Estimation of long-run inefficiency levels: A dynamic frontier approach. *Econometric Reviews*, *19*(4), 461–492.

Aigner, D., Lovell, C., & Schmidt, P. (1977). Formulation and estimation of stochastic frontier production function models. *Journal of Econometrics*, *6*(1), 21–37.

Ali, M., Salehnejad, R., & Mansur, M. (2019). Hospital productivity: The role of efficiency drivers. *The International Journal of Health Planning and Management*, *34*(2), 806–823.

Australian Bureau of Statistics. (2006). Australian standard geographical classification (ASGC). ABS Catalogue No. 1216.0. Retrieved from http://www.abs.gov.au/AUSSTATS/abs@.nsf/DetailsPage/1216.0July. Accessed on March 2023.

Australian Institute of Health and Welfare. (2015). Australian hospital peer groups. Health services series No. 66. Catalogue No. HSW 170. Retrieved from https://www.aihw.gov.au/getmedia/79e7d756-7cfe-49bf-b8c0-0bbb0daa2430/14825.pdf.aspx?inline=true. Accessed on March 2023.

Battese, G., & Coelli, T. (1992). Frontier production functions, technical efficiency and panel data: With application to paddy farmers in India. *Journal of Productivity Analysis*, *3*(1–2), 153–169.

Battese, G. E., & Coelli, T. J. (1995). A model for technical inefficiency effects in a stochastic frontier production function for panel data. *Empirical Economics*, *20*(2), 325–332.

Bosmans, N., & Fecher, F. (1995). Performance of Belgian hospitals: A frontier approach. *Health Economics*, *4*(5), 389–397.

Brown, H. S. (2003). Managed care and technical efficiency. *Health Economics*, *12*(2), 149–158.

Caudill, S. B., Ford, J. M., & Gropper, D. M. (1995). Frontier estimation and firm-specific inefficiency measures in the presence of heteroscedasticity. *Journal of Business & Economic Statistics*, *13*(1), 105–111.

Charnes, A., Cooper, W., & Rhodes, E. (1978). Measuring the efficiency of decision making units. *European Journal of Operational Research*, *2*(6), 429–444.

Chen, Y.-Y., Schmidt, P., & Wang, H.-J. (2014). Consistent estimation of the fixed effects stochastic frontier model. *Journal of Econometrics*, *181*(2), 65–76.

Chowdhury, H., & Zelenyuk, V. (2016). Performance of hospital services in Ontario: DEA with truncated regression approach. *Omega*, *63*, 111–122.

Chua, C. L., Palangkaraya, A., & Yong, J. (2010). A two-stage estimation of hospital quality using mortality outcome measures: An application using hospital administrative data. *Health Economics*, *19*(12), 1404–1424.

Colombi, R., Kumbhakar, S. C., Martini, G., & Vittadini, G. (2014). Closed-skew normality in stochastic frontiers with individual effects and long/short-run efficiency. *Journal of Productivity Analysis*, *42*(2), 123–136.

Colombi, R., Martini, G., & Vittadini, G. (2017). Determinants of transient and persistent hospital efficiency: The case of Italy. *Health Economics*, *26*, 5–22.

Cornwell, C., Schmidt, P., & Sickles, R. C. (1990). Production frontiers with cross-sectional and time-series variation in efficiency levels. *Journal of Econometrics*, *46*(1), 185–200.

Daraio, C., & Simar, L. (2007). Economies of scale, scope and experience in the Italian motor-vehicle sector. In C. Daraio & L. Simar (Eds.), *Advanced robust and nonparametric methods in efficiency analysis: Methodology and applications* (Chapter 6, pp. 135–165). New York, NY: Springer.

Debreu, G. (1951). The coefficient of resource utilization. *Econometrica*, *19*(3), 273–292.

Fan, Y., Li, Q., & Weersink, A. (1996). Semiparametric estimation of stochastic production frontier models. *Journal of Business & Economic Statistics*, *14*(4), 460–468.

Färe, R., Grosskopf, S., & Valdmanis, V. (1989). Capacity, competition and efficiency in hospitals: A nonparametric approach. *Journal of Productivity Analysis*, *1*(2), 123–138.

Farrell, M. J. (1957). The measurement of productive efficiency. *Journal of the Royal Statistical Society: Series A (General)*, *120*(3), 253–281.

Ferrier, G. D., & Trivitt, J. S. (2013). Incorporating quality into the measurement of hospital efficiency: A double DEA approach. *Journal of Productivity Analysis*, *40*(3), 337–355.

Ferrier, G. D., & Valdmanis, V. (1996). Rural hospital performance and its correlates. *Journal of Productivity Analysis*, *7*(1), 63–80.

Fixler, T., Paradi, J. C., & Yang, X. (2014). A data envelopment analysis approach for measuring the efficiency of Canadian acute care hospitals. *Health Services Management Research*, *27*(3–4), 57–69.

Gabbitas, O., & Jeffs, C. (2009). *Assessing productivity in the delivery of public hospital services in Australia: Some experimental estimates*. Productivity Commission conference paper.

Greene, W. H. (2004). Distinguishing between heterogeneity and inefficiency: Stochastic frontier analysis of the World Health Organization's panel data on national health care systems. *Health Economics*, *13*(10), 959–980.

Greene, W. H. (2005a). Fixed and random effects in stochastic frontier models. *Journal of Productivity Analysis*, *23*(1), 7–32.

Greene, W. H. (2005b). Reconsidering heterogeneity in panel data estimators of the stochastic frontier model. *Journal of Econometrics*, *126*(2), 269–303.

Grosskopf, S., Margaritis, D., & Valdmanis, V. (2004). Competitive effects on teaching hospitals. *European Journal of Operational Research*, *154*(2), 515–525.
Grosskopf, S., & Valdmanis, V. (1987). Measuring hospital performance: A non-parametric approach. *Journal of Health Economics*, *6*(2), 89–107.
Henningsen, A., & Henning, C. H. (2009). Imposing regional monotonicity on translog stochastic production frontiers with a simple three-step procedure. *Journal of Productivity Analysis*, *32*(3), 217–229.
Herr, A. (2008). Cost and technical efficiency of German hospitals: Does ownership matter? *Health Economics*, *17*(9), 1057–1071.
Hjalmarsson, L., Kumbhakar, S. C., & Heshmati, A. (1996). DEA, DFA and SFA: A comparison. *Journal of Productivity Analysis*, *7*(2), 303–327.
Hollingsworth, B. (2008). The measurement of efficiency and productivity of health care delivery. *Health Economics*, *17*(10), 1107–1128.
Hussey, P. S., De Vries, H., Romley, J., Wang, M. C., Chen, S. S., Shekelle, P. G., & McGlynn, E. A. (2009). A systematic review of health care efficiency measures. *Health Services Research*, *44*(3), 784–805.
Independent Hospital Pricing Authority (2013). *National efficient price determination 2013–2014*. Independent Hospital Pricing Authority.
Jacobs, R. (2001). Alternative methods to examine hospital efficiency: Data envelopment analysis and stochastic frontier analysis. *Health Care Management Science*, *4*(2), 103–115.
Jondrow, J., Lovell, C. K., Materov, I. S., & Schmidt, P. (1982). On the estimation of technical inefficiency in the stochastic frontier production function model. *Journal of Econometrics*, *19*(2–3), 233–238.
Kumbhakar, S. C. (2010). Efficiency and productivity of world health systems: Where does your country stand? *Applied Economics*, *42*(13), 1641–1659.
Kumbhakar, S. C., Ghosh, S., & McGuckin, J. T. (1991). A generalized production frontier approach for estimating determinants of inefficiency in US dairy farms. *Journal of Business & Economic Statistics*, *9*(3), 279–286.
Kumbhakar, S. C., Lien, G., & Hardaker, J. B. (2014). Technical efficiency in competing panel data models: A study of Norwegian grain farming. *Journal of Productivity Analysis*, *41*(2), 321–337.
Kumbhakar, S. C., Park, B. U., Simar, L., & Tsionas, E. G. (2007). Nonparametric stochastic frontiers: A local maximum likelihood approach. *Journal of Econometrics*, *137*(1), 1–27.
Kumbhakar, S. C., Parmeter, C. F., & Zelenyuk, V. (2021a). Stochastic frontier analysis: Foundations and advances I. In S. C. Ray, R. G. Chambers, & S. C. Kumbhakar (Eds.), *Handbook of production economics*. (pp. 331–370) Singapore: Springer.
Kumbhakar, S. C., Parmeter, C. F., & Zelenyuk, V. (2021b). Stochastic frontier analysis: Foundations and advances II. In S. C. Ray, R. G. Chambers, & S. C. Kumbhakar (Eds.), *Handbook of production economics*. (pp. 371–408) Singapore: Springer.
Lai, H.-p., & Kumbhakar, S. C. (2020). Estimation of a dynamic stochastic frontier model using likelihood-based approaches. *Journal of Applied Econometrics*, *35*(2), 217–247.
Li, Q. (1996). Nonparametric testing of closeness between two unknown distribution functions. *Econometric Reviews*, *15*(3), 261–274.
Linna, M. (1998). Measuring hospital cost efficiency with panel data models. *Health Economics*, *7*(5), 415–427.
Magnussen, J., & Mobley, L. R. (1999). The impact of market environment on excess capacity and the cost of an empty hospital bed. *International Journal of the Economics of Business*, *6*(3), 383–398.
Meeusen, W., & van den Broeck, J. (1977). Efficiency estimation from Cobb-Douglas production functions with composed error. *International Economic Review*, *18*(2), 435–444.
Miles, J. (2021). Fatigued workers, ambulance ramping rise as Qld public health staff face 'unsustainable' workloads. *ABC News*. Retrieved from https://www.abc.net.au/news/2021-12-16/qld-coronavirus-covid-hospital-workloads-auditor-general-report/100699752?utm_campaign=abc_news_web&utm_content=link&utm_medium=content_shared&utm_source=abc_news_web. Accessed on March 2023.
Nghiem, S., Coelli, T., & Barber, S. (2011). Sources of productivity growth in health services: A case study of Queensland public hospitals. *Economic Analysis and Policy*, *41*(1), 37–48.

Nguyen, B. H., Sickles, R. C., & Zelenyuk, V. (2022). Efficiency Analysis with stochastic frontier models using popular statistical softwares. In D. Chotikapanich, A. Rambaldi, & N. Rohde (Eds.), *Advances in economic measurement*. A Volume in Honour of D.S. Prasada Rao. Singapore: Palgrave-Macmillan.

Nguyen, B. H., Wang, Z., and Zelenyuk, V. (2023). *Efficiency of Queensland public hospitals via spatial panel stochastic frontier models*. CEPA Working Paper Series No. WP10/2023, School of Economics, University of Queensland.

Nguyen, B. H., & Zelenyuk, V. (2021a). Aggregate efficiency of industry and its groups: The case of Queensland public hospitals. *Empirical Economics*, *60*(6), 2795–2836.

Nguyen, B. H., & Zelenyuk, V. (2021b). Robust efficiency analysis of public hospitals in Queensland, Australia. In A. Daouia & A. Ruiz-Gazen (Eds.), *Advances in contemporary statistics and econometrics* (pp. 221–242). Springer.

O'Donnell, C., & Nguyen, K. (2013). An econometric approach to estimating support prices and measures of productivity change in public hospitals. *Journal of Productivity Analysis*, *40*(3), 323–335.

O'Donnell, C. J., & Coelli, T. J. (2005). A Bayesian approach to imposing curvature on distance functions. *Journal of Econometrics*, *126*(2), 493–523.

OECD. (2021). OECD Statistics. Retrieved from https://stats.oecd.org/Index.aspx?ThemeTreeId=9#. Accessed on March 2023.

O'Neill, L., Rauner, M., Heidenberger, K., & Kraus, M. (2008). A cross-national comparison and taxonomy of DEA-based hospital efficiency studies. *Socio-Economic Planning Sciences*, *42*(3), 158–189.

Park, B. U., Simar, L., & Zelenyuk, V. (2015). Categorical data in local maximum likelihood: Theory and applications to productivity analysis. *Journal of Productivity Analysis*, *43*(2), 199–214.

Pasley, B. H., Lagoe, R. J., & Marshall, N. O. (1995). Excess acute care bed capacity and its causes: The experience of New York State. *Health Services Research*, *30*, 115.

Pitt, M. M., & Lee, L.-F. (1981). The measurement and sources of technical inefficiency in the Indonesian weaving industry. *Journal of Development Economics*, *9*(1), 43–64.

Productivity Commission. (2009). *Public and private hospitals. Research report*.

Productivity Commission. (2010). *Public and private hospitals: Multivariate analysis. Supplement to Research Report*.

Rosko, M. D. (2001). Cost efficiency of US hospitals: A stochastic frontier approach. *Health Economics*, *10*(6), 539–551.

Rosko, M. D., & Mutter, R. L. (2008). Stochastic frontier analysis of hospital inefficiency: A review of empirical issues and an assessment of robustness. *Medical Care Research and Review*, *65*(2), 131–166.

Schmidt, P., & Sickles, R. C. (1984). Production frontiers and panel data. *Journal of Business & Economic Statistics*, *2*(4), 367–374.

Schneider, E. C., Shah, A., Doty, M. M., Tikkanen, R., Fields, K., & Williams II, R. D. (2021). Mirror, mirror 2021: Reflecting poorly: Health care in the US compared to other high-income countries. Fund reports. Retrieved from https://www.commonwealthfund.org/publications/fund-reports/2021/aug/mirror-mirror-2021-reflecting-poorly. Accessed on March 2023.

See, K., Grosskopf, S., Valdmanis, V., & Zelenyuk, V. (2024). *What do we know from the vast literature on efficiency and productivity in healthcare? A systematic review and bibliometric analysis*. In S. Grosskopf, V. Valdmanis, & V. Zelenyuk (Eds.), *The Cambridge Handbook of Productivity, Efficiency and Effectiveness in Health Care*. Cambridge, UK: Cambridge University Press.

Shephard, R. (1953). *Cost and production functions*. Princeton, NJ: Princeton University Press.

Shephard, R. W., Gale, D., & Kuhn, H. W. (1970). *Theory of cost and production functions*. Number 4 in Princeton studies in mathematical economics. Princeton, NJ: Princeton University Press.

Sherman, H. D. (1984). Hospital efficiency measurement and evaluation: Empirical test of a new technique. *Medical Care*, *22*(10), 922–938.

Sickles, R. C., Wang, Z., & Zelenyuk, V. (2024). *Stochastic frontier analysis for healthcare, with illustrations in R*. In S. Grosskopf, V. Valdmanis, & V. Zelenyuk (Eds.), *The Cambridge Handbook of Productivity, Efficiency and Effectiveness in Health Care*. Cambridge, UK: Cambridge University Press.

Sickles, R. C. & Zelenyuk, V. (2019). *Measurement of productivity and efficiency: Theory and practice*. New York, NY: Cambridge University Press.

Simar, L., Van Keilegom, I., & Zelenyuk, V. (2017). Nonparametric least squares methods for stochastic frontier models. *Journal of Productivity Analysis*, *47*(3), 189–204.
Simar, L. & Wilson, P. W. (2007). Estimation and inference in two-stage, semi-parametric models of production processes. *Journal of Econometrics*, *136*(1), 31–64.
Street, A. (2003). How much confidence should we place in efficiency estimates? *Health Economics*, *12*(11), 895–907.
Tsionas, E. G. (2006). Inference in dynamic stochastic frontier models. *Journal of Applied Econometrics*, *21*(5), 669–676.
Tsionas, M., Parmeter, C. F., Zelenyuk, V. (2023). Bayesian artificial neural networks for frontier efficiency analysis. *Journal of Econometrics, 236*(2), 105491. https://www.sciencedirect.com/science/article/abs/pii/S0304407623002075?via%3Dihub.
Varabyova, Y. & Schreyögg, J. (2013). International comparisons of the technical efficiency of the hospital sector: Panel data analysis of OECD countries using parametric and non-parametric approaches. *Health Policy*, *112*(1–2), 70–79.
Wagstaff, A. (1989). Estimating efficiency in the hospital sector: a comparison of three statistical cost frontier models. *Applied Economics*, *21*(5), 659–672.
Wang, B. B., Ozcan, Y. A., Wan, T. T., & Harrison, J. (1999). Trends in hospital efficiency among metropolitan markets. *Journal of Medical Systems*, *23*(2), 83–97.
Wang, H.-J. & Schmidt, P. (2002). One-step and two-step estimation of the effects of exogenous variables on technical efficiency levels. *Journal of Productivity Analysis*, *18*(2), 129–144.
Wang, J., Zhao, Z., & Mahmood, A. (2006). *Relative efficiency, scale effect, and scope effect of public hospitals: Evidence from Australia*. IZA Discussion Papers.
Wang, Z., & Zelenyuk, V. (2024). *Overview of performance analytics for healthcare with examples in R*. In S. Grosskopf, V. Valdmanis, & V. Zelenyuk (Eds.), *The Cambridge Handbook of Productivity, Efficiency and Effectiveness in Health Care*. Cambridge, UK: Cambridge University Press.
Wang, Z., & Zelenyuk, V. (2021b). *Performance analysis of hospitals in Australia and its peers: A systematic review*. CEPA Working Paper Series No. WP01/2021.
Worthington, A. C. (2004). Frontier efficiency measurement in health care: A review of empirical techniques and selected applications. *Medical Care Research and Review*, *61*(2), 135–170.
Yong, K., & Harris, A. H. (1999). *Efficiency of hospitals in Victoria under casemix funding: A stochastic frontier approach*. Number 92. Centre for Health Program Evaluation.
Zuckerman, S., Hadley, J., & Iezzoni, L. (1994). Measuring hospital efficiency with frontier cost functions. *Journal of Health Economics*, *13*(3), 255–280.

APPENDIX 1. AGGREGATION OF VARIABLES

We aggregate the group of corresponding original variables to proxy the labor, consumable expenditure, and output, respectively. As the aggregated input or output proxies contain most information of the original variables, we use them in further estimation to reduce the dimensions and simplify the production function and interpretation of the SFMs.

The correlation among each pair of input and output variables presents a high level, most of which, as in Fig. A1.1, is above 0.8. Such correlations, as indicated in Daraio and Simar (2007), often exist in productivity analysis, which also suggests a reliable aggregation is possible.

The consumable expenditure can simply be the sum of the two representing variables (i.e., DSUP, MSSUP) deflated by the CPI of FY 2012/13. For the labor and output, following Daraio and Simar (2007) and the study for Queensland hospitals by Nguyen and Zelenyuk (2021b), we apply the PCA-based approach for aggregation, where the eigenvectors are obtained based on the second order moment matrix, rather than the standardized correlation or covariance matrix as usual, to keep eigenvalues positive for the latter productivity analysis.

	MEO	TNUR	OPCS	DHP	ACS	DOS	DSUP	MSSUP	OUT	BEDS	Wepisodes
MEO	1	1	0.95	0.97	0.98	0.91	0.92	0.92	0.97	0.99	0.99
TNUR	1	1	0.95	0.98	0.98	0.92	0.94	0.92	0.97	0.99	0.99
OPCS	0.95	0.95	1	0.96	0.94	0.82	0.94	0.94	0.92	0.96	0.96
DHP	0.97	0.98	0.96	1	0.97	0.89	0.94	0.91	0.92	0.97	0.97
ACS	0.98	0.98	0.94	0.97	1	0.92	0.94	0.89	0.95	0.97	0.97
DOS	0.91	0.92	0.82	0.89	0.92	1	0.79	0.73	0.89	0.9	0.89
DSUP	0.92	0.94	0.94	0.94	0.94	0.79	1	0.92	0.89	0.92	0.93
MSSUP	0.92	0.92	0.94	0.91	0.89	0.73	0.92	1	0.9	0.93	0.94
OUT	0.97	0.97	0.92	0.92	0.95	0.89	0.89	0.9	1	0.98	0.98
BEDS	0.99	0.99	0.96	0.97	0.97	0.9	0.92	0.93	0.98	1	0.99
Wepisodes	0.99	0.99	0.96	0.97	0.97	0.89	0.93	0.94	0.98	0.99	1

(Colour scale: 1, 0.8, 0.6, 0.4, 0.2, 0, -0.2, -0.4, -0.6, -0.8, -1)

Fig. A1.1. Correlation Matrix of Original Inputs and Outputs.

Table A1.1. Eigenvalues of PCA-Based Aggregation of Inputs and Outputs.

Component	Eigenvalue	Information Explained (%)	Cumulative (%)
Aggregated labor			
1	5.7154	95.2561	95.2561
2	0.1919	3.1984	98.4546
3	0.0364	0.6075	99.0621
4	0.0309	0.5157	99.5778
5	0.0229	0.3809	99.9587
6	0.0025	0.0413	100.0000
Aggregated output			
1	1.9751	98.7539	98.7539
2	0.0249	1.2461	100.0000

Table A1.2. Correlations Between the Aggregated Variable and Original Variables.

Labor						
	MEO	TNUR	OPCS	DHP	ACS	DOS
AGGLABOR	0.9925	0.9955	0.9593	0.9846	0.9898	0.9327
Output						
	OUT	WEPISODES				
AGGOUT	0.9940	0.9935				

The eigenvalues and the percentage of information explained are reported in Table A1.1. The first component of labor and output can evidently explain most of the variation in the original data, which is also indicated by the correlations between the first component (i.e., AGGLABOR and AGGOUT) and their original multi-dimensional data as in Table A1.2.

Consequently, we obtain a production relationship with three inputs and one output.

APPENDIX 2. TRIMMING OUTLIERS

According to the distributions of the input and output variables in Fig. A2.1, each variable displays a narrow range compared to the long upper tail. The upper outliers are generally large hospitals in major cities, consuming much more resources while providing plenty of services. Specifically, the top 2% observations of every variable are mostly for two hospitals, which are trimmed as outliers in further analysis.

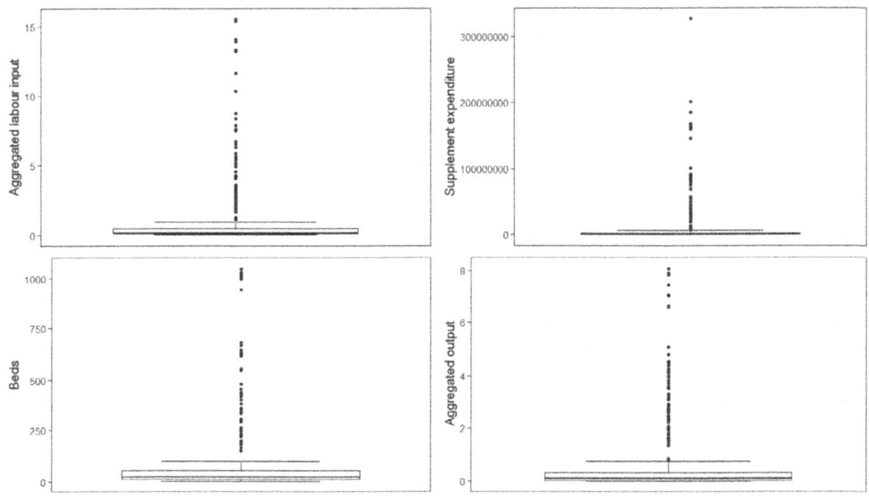

Fig. A2.1. Boxplots of Inputs and Output.

APPENDIX 3. BIBLIOMETRIC ANALYSIS OF SELECTED SFMs

The ALS77 and KGM91 models are classical SFMs, which are also popular in the literature in past decades. In this illustration, we collected the bibliometric data of papers citing ALS77 or KGM91 in Scopus.[30] The left panel is an analysis for the ALS77-related studies, while the right panel is for studies related to KGM91.

The three types of plots by row in Fig. A3.1 illustrate the following:

(i) The number of studies published by year, in which ALS77 or KGM91 is cited;
(ii) The number of studies published by country, where the deeper colored countries have more papers; and
(iii) The collaboration network by country, where the red line represents a collaborated work between the two countries.

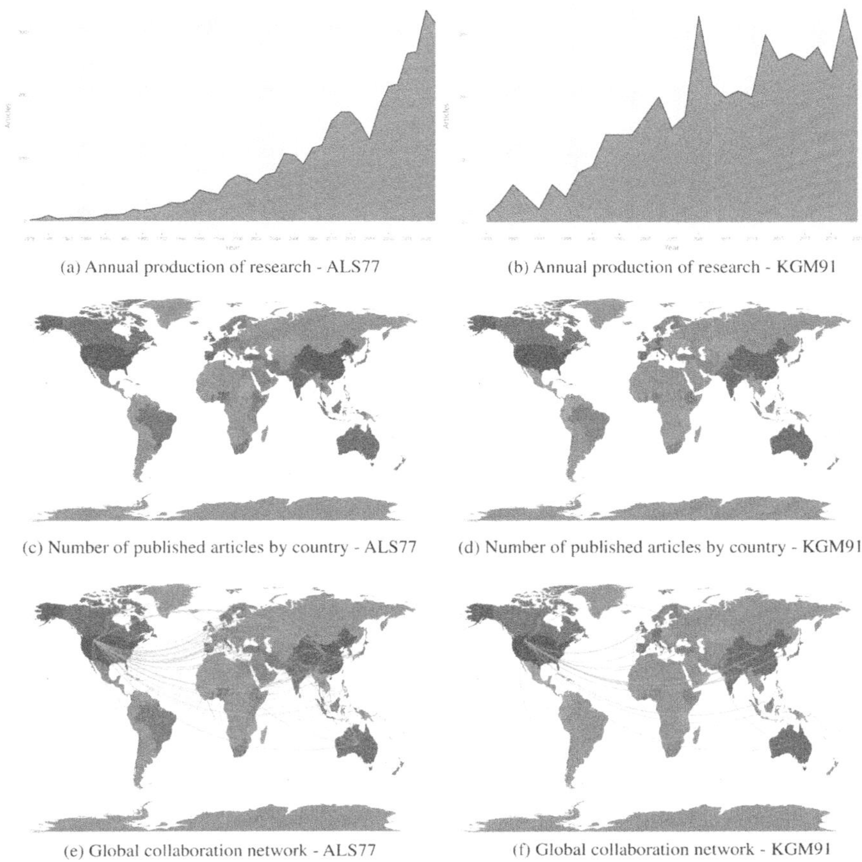

(a) Annual production of research - ALS77 (b) Annual production of research - KGM91

(c) Number of published articles by country - ALS77 (d) Number of published articles by country - KGM91

(e) Global collaboration network - ALS77 (f) Global collaboration network - KGM91

Fig. A3.1. Bibliometric Analysis of ALS77 and KGM91 in the Literature.

A clear upward trend appears in the number of articles citing the two SFMs since they were introduced in the literature. In 2020, more than 300 papers and 30 papers cited ALS77 and KGM91, respectively. As shown in (c) to (f) in Fig. A3.1, the two models are also widely applied in global research. For example, researchers from the US collaborated in 1,848 and 221 articles citing ALS77 and KGM91, respectively. The most frequent collaborations, regarding ALS77 or KGM91, are 33 times between the US and the UK, and 8 times between the US and China, respectively.

APPENDIX 4. DEGENERACY DIAGNOSTICS

As indicated by the estimation results, the ALS77 model with either production function shows a possible degeneracy phenomenon, which does not appear in the KGM91 model. The distribution of the inefficiency in KGM91 is assumed to be truncated-normal with the mean to be "determined" by the environmental variables, while the inefficiency in ALS77 is assumed to be half-normal distributed. These characteristics differentiate the models, which can lead to quite different estimation results.

We infer that the possible degeneracy of ALS77 may be due to the sample not conforming to the specifications of the model (e.g., the half-normal distribution). As we cannot obtain the true efficiency, we generate an artificial sample as follows to further investigate the possible reason of this phenomenon.

For a simplified scenario, we generate 100 units in a 4-year period (i.e., 400 observations) in a production process with three inputs (X^1, X^2, and X^3) and one output Y. As shown in the snippet of R code below, the three inputs and the optimal output (i.e., Y^0) are $iid\mathcal{N}(\mu,\sigma^2)$ and we may specify them as, i.e., $\mu_{X^1}=1$, $\sigma_{X^1}=1$, $\mu_{X^2}=2$, $\sigma_{X^2}=2$, $\mu_{X^3}=3$, $\sigma_{X^3}=3$, $\mu_{Y^0}=2$, $\sigma_{Y^0}=4$. Two continuous environmental variables (Z^1 and Z^2) are also generated as iid normal distribution that $\mu_{Z^1}=0.1$, $\sigma_{Z^1}=0.1$, $\mu_{Z^2}=0.2$, $\sigma_{Z^2}=0.2$. Besides, one binary environmental variable Z^3 is generated as 80% of the units are 0 and the other 20% are 1. Following the KGM91 model in Equation (7), we also predefine the inefficiency term u_i as $iid\mathcal{N}^+(\tau,\sigma_u^2)$, where $\tau=0.5-0.1Z^1+0.2Z^2-0.3Z^3$ and $\sigma_u=0.2$.

In this sample, the arbitrary parameters generate the inefficiency term from a truncated-normal distribution, which is also quite distinguished from a half-normal distribution. Consequently, we can observe a similar degeneracy phenomenon of the ALS77 model in some trials (e.g., as the case in Fig. A4.1), while the KGM91 model estimates a result close to the generated inefficiency.[31]

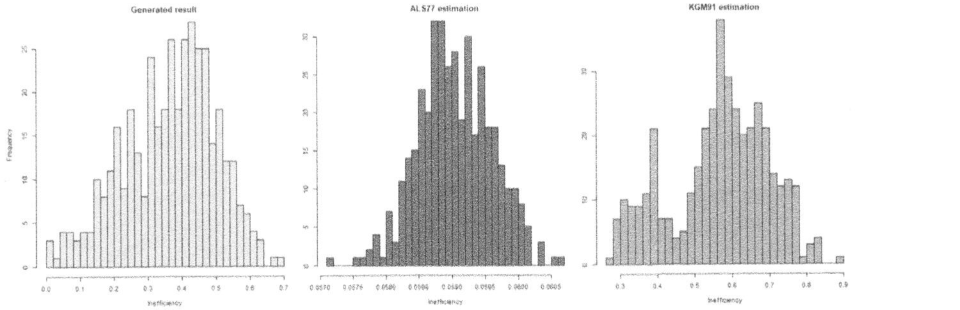

Fig. A4.1. Example Histogram of Generated and Estimated Individual Inefficiency.

```
########################## Degeneracy Diagnosis ##########################
rm(list = ls())
graphics.off()

# Define parameters
units = 100
time = 4
n = units*time
# Unit ID and time
ID = sort(rep(1:units, times = time))
Year = rep(1:time, times = units)

Year1<-rep(0,n)
Year1[Year == 1] = 1
Year2<-rep(0,n)
Year2[Year == 2] = 1
Year3<-rep(0,n)
Year3[Year == 3] = 1
Year4<-rep(0,n)
Year4[Year == 4] = 1

# Generate original Y, X, and Z
library(sn)
Yo = rnorm (n, mean = 2, sd = 4)

X1 = rnorm(n, mean = 1, sd = 1)
X2 = rnorm(n, mean = 2, sd = 2)
X3 = rnorm(n, mean = 3, sd = 3)

Z1 = rnorm(n, mean = 0.1, sd = 0.1)
Z2 = rnorm(n, mean = 0.2, sd = 0.2)
Z3 = rep(c(1, 0), times = c(0.2*units, 0.8*units))[order(runif(units))] # Assume 20% of units are 1 in Z3
Z3 = rep(Z3, each = time)

# Generate inefficiency follow KGM91
mui = 0.5-0.1*Z1+0.2*Z2-0.3*Z3

# Generate ui with mui and usigma of the estimation of u
library("truncnorm")
u = rtruncnorm(n, a=0, b=Inf, mean = mui, sd = 0.2)
ineffori = 1-exp(-u)

# Generate Y (ALS degenerate when using lAggout)
Y = Yo-u

```

```
# Composed data set
data = as.data.frame(cbind(ID, Year, Year1, Year2, Year3, Year4, Y, X1, X2, X3, Z1, Z2, Z3))

# Convert to panel data
library(plm)
paneldata <- pdata.frame(data, c(“ID”, ”Year“))

# Formulas
form = Y ~ X1 + X2 + X3 + Year1 + Year2 + Year3
formz = Y ~ X1 + X2 + X3 + Year1 + Year2 + Year3 | Z1 + Z2 + Z3

library(frontier)
# ALS77
als77 <- sfa (form, data = data, ineffDecrease = T, truncNorm = F, timeEffect = F)
summary(als77, effic = F, logDepVar = T, effMinusU = T)
ineff <- 1-efficiencies (als77, asInData = T, logDepVar = T, minusU = T)
summary(ineff)

# KGM91
K91 <- sfa(formz, data = data, ineffDecrease = T, truncNorm = T, timeEffect = F)
summary(K91, effic = F, logDepVar = T, effMinusU = T)
ineffz <- 1-efficiencies (K91, asInData = T, logDepVar = T, minusU = T)
summary(ineffz)

# Plot
par(
  mfrow=c(1,3),
  mar=c(4,4,1,0)
)
hist(ineffori, breaks=30, col=rgb(1,0,0,0.5), xlab=”Inefficiency“, ylab=”Frequecy“, main=”Generated result“)
hist(ineff, breaks=30, col=rgb(0,0,1,0.5), xlab=”Inefficiency“, ylab=””, main=”ALS77 estimation“)
hist(ineffz, breaks=30, col=rgb(0,0.5,1,0.5), xlab=”Inefficiency“, ylab=””, main=”KGM91 estimation“)
```

Listing 1. R code Snippet for Degeneracy Diagnostics.

APPENDIX 5. MODEL SELECTION WITH TREND VARIABLES

In the reported models, the effect of time is accounted for by a set of year dummies, which focus on the shocks to the output in each year. In the preliminary analysis, we also considered the specifications of SFA models with the trend variables (i.e., the trend, the quadratic trend, and its interactions with the three inputs), which represent the movement of the output over time. According to the results of the LR tests, we chose the dummy variables for the reported models. The process is not described in the main text due to the limited space, and so we report more details below as a complement.[32]

Taking the Cobb-Douglas function as an example, the model without time variables can be denoted as Equation (8) as

$$\ln Y_i = \beta_0 + \sum_{j=1}^{p} \beta_j \ln X_{j,i} + v_i - u_i, \quad i = 1,\ldots,n, \tag{17}$$

while the model with the dummy variables can be

$$\ln Y_i = \beta_0 + \sum_{j=1}^{p} \beta_j \ln X_{j,i} + \sum_{r=1}^{T} \delta_r D_{r,i} + v_i - u_i, \quad i = 1,\ldots,n, \tag{18}$$

where $D_r, r = 1,\ldots,T$, is the dummy variable for each year and δ_r is the corresponding parameters. Then the alternative model by adding the trend variables would be

$$\begin{aligned} \ln Y_i = \beta_0 + \sum_{j=1}^{p} \beta_j \ln X_{j,i} + \sum_{r=1}^{T} \delta_r D_{r,i} + \zeta_1 t_i + \zeta_2 t_i^2 \\ + \sum_{j=1}^{p} \eta_j t_i \ln X_{j,i} + v_i - u_i, \quad i = 1,\ldots,n, \end{aligned} \tag{19}$$

where t is the trend variable and ζ_1, ζ_2, and η_j, $j = 1,\ldots,P$ are the parameters of the trend, the quadratic trend, and the interactions with the inputs, respectively.

The results of the LR tests between the unrestricted and nested models of the two SFMs and two production functions are as listed in Table A5.1. In the first panel, the null hypothesis is rejected in all cases, which indicates the unrestricted form with dummy variables is likely to be more suitable than the restricted model without time variables. Instead, the results in the second panel indicate that the models with additional trend variables do not show a significant advantage. The null hypothesis that the coefficients (i.e., ζ_1, ζ_2, and η_j, $j = 1,\ldots, p$) of the additional variables are all equal to zero is not rejected in all cases.

If we reorder the sequence of adding the time variables, a similar conclusion can be reached, i.e., the models with the trend variables show an advantage over

Table A5.1. LR Test for Time Variables.

Model			*LR*	*p*-value	Decision
Restricted		Unrestricted			
No time variable vs With dummy variables					
ALS77-CD	vs	ALS77-CD-D	11.4272	0.0096	Reject***
ALS77-Translog	vs	ALS77-Translog-D	8.1798	0.0424	Reject**
KGM91-CD	vs	KGM91-CD-D	11.1670	0.0109	Reject**
KGM91-Translog	vs	KGM91-Translog-D	7.6120	0.0547	Reject*
With dummy variables vs With both dummy and trend variables					
ALS77-CD-D	vs	ALS77-CD-D&T	7.0406	0.2176	Not reject
ALS77-Translog-D	vs	ALS77-Translog-D&T	7.5906	0.1803	Not reject
KGM91-CD-D	vs	KGM91-CD-D&T	6.928	0.2261	Not reject
KGM91-Translog-D	vs	KGM91-Translog-D&T	7.0906	0.2140	Not reject

Notes: Not reject: $p > 0.10$; Reject: * $p < 0.10$; ** $p < 0.05$; *** $p < 0.01$.
Suffix -D: With year dummies.
Suffix -D&T: With both dummy and trend variables.

the initial models, while the models with both dummy and trend variables are not preferred relative to the models with the trend variables alone. Consequently, the models with year dummies are applied in the analysis, which is also in the consideration of the preference for a more parsimonious model specification.

APPENDIX 6. RESULTS FOR THE SELECTED PANEL DATA SFMs[33]

Extensive efforts have been devoted to the development of SFA in the panel data settings. Shortly after the proposition of the canonical model, Pitt and Lee (1981) and Schmidt and Sickles (1984) introduced their SFMs under a panel data framework. Cornwell, Schmidt, and Sickles (1990) and Battese and Coelli (1992) extended these models to take account of time-variant inefficiency. Many other variants of panel data SFA have been introduced since then (see, e.g., Kumbhakar et al. (2021b)). In this section, we conduct two approaches that were recently developed in the vein of panel data SFM: the "true random effect" model (hereafter TRE) proposed by Greene (2005a, 2005b) and the four-component error term model by Kumbhakar et al. (2014).

Building upon the models incorporating time-variant inefficiency (e.g., Cornwell et al., 1990; Battese & Coelli, 1992), Greene (2005a, 2005b) proposed two models to disentangle the individual technical efficiency from the fixed effect and random effect individual heterogeneity, respectively, dubbed as the "true fixed effect" and "true random effect" models. The TRE model can be denoted as

$$\begin{aligned} y_{it} &= a + x_{it}'\beta + \omega_i + v_{it} - u_{it}, \quad i = 1,\ldots,N; t = 1,\ldots,T, \\ v_{it} &\sim iid\mathcal{N}(0,\sigma_v^2), \\ u_{it} &\sim iid\mathcal{N}^+(0,\sigma_u^2), \end{aligned} \tag{20}$$

where x_{it} and y_{it} are in a panel data setting with N units over T periods, the intercept a is treated as a random variable, the individual specific heterogeneity is reflected by ω_i, and u_{it} and v_{it} are the time-variant inefficiency and noise terms, respectively.

Greene (2005a, 2005b) suggested using the simulated maximum likelihood estimator for (20) and proposed a dummy variable MLE for the "true fixed effect" model. The dummy variable MLE is intensive in computation and faces the "incidental parameter" problem especially when there is a high volume of individuals and a relatively short period. Alternatively, as suggested by Chen, Schmidt, and Wang (2014), the within transformed TFE model can be estimated with a standard MLE to circumvent this problem.

The disentangled inefficiency in Greene (2005a, 2005b) is the transitory technical inefficiency. In the more recently introduced KLH14 model, the persistent inefficiency can be further distinguished, i.e.,

$$\begin{aligned} y_{it} &= a + x_{it}'\beta + v_{it} - u_{it} + s_i - \eta_i, \quad i = 1,\ldots,N; t = 1,\ldots,T, \\ v_{it} &\sim iid\mathcal{N}(0,\sigma_v^2), \\ u_{it} &\sim iid\mathcal{N}^+(0,\sigma_u^2), \\ s_i &\sim iid\mathcal{N}(0,\sigma_s^2), \\ \eta_i &\sim iid\mathcal{N}^+(0,\sigma_\eta^2), \end{aligned} \tag{21}$$

where other than the transitory inefficiency u_{it}, the individual persistent inefficiency term η_i is also contained. Besides, the unobserved individual heterogeneity is also taken into account by s_i, and the noise is represented by v_{it}. Following Kumbhakar et al. (2014), (21) can be rewritten as

$$y_{it} = a^* + x_{it}'\beta + a_i + \varepsilon_{it}, \quad i = 1,\ldots,N; t = 1,\ldots,T, \tag{22}$$

where

$$\begin{aligned} a^* &= a - E(\eta_i) - E(u_{it}), \\ a_i &= s_i - \eta_i + E(\eta_i), \\ \varepsilon_{it} &= v_{it} - u_{it} + E(u_{it}), \end{aligned} \tag{23}$$

and where following the distributional assumptions in (21), we have $E(\eta_i) = \sqrt{2/\pi}\sigma_\eta$ and $E(u_{it}) = \sqrt{2/\pi}\sigma_u$.

Accordingly, the transformed KLH14 model (22) can be first estimated with a standard random effect panel regression approach. The estimated individual effect $\hat{a}_i$ and error term $\hat{\varepsilon}_{it}$ in the random effect model can be applied in the succeeding estimation of the last two equations in (23), which are in a standard SFA form, containing an inefficiency term and random error, respectively. Therefore, the individual persistent inefficiency η_i and the transitory inefficiency u_{it} can be then estimated through the JLMS approach as discussed above. Moreover, the estimate of the total inefficiency level can be obtained as $\hat{\theta}_{it} = 1 - \exp(-\hat{\eta}_i - \hat{u}_{it})$.*

ESTIMATES OF MODEL AND INEFFICIENCY

A similar model selection procedure as the one used in the main text for ALS77 and KGM91 is conducted for the panel data models. For the TRE model, the Cobb-Douglas production function is preferable to the Translog production function according to the LR test. Meanwhile, the Hausman-type test also indicates using the more parsimonious Cobb-Douglas function in the first-stage panel data regression in the KLH14 model. The parameters estimated for the two panel data models are as shown in Table A6.1. The estimated coefficients are statistically significant with a similar confidence level across the two models. The coefficients of the three inputs have a *priori* expected signs (indicating a strong positive association with the output). Their magnitudes are also similar across the two models, yet fairly different relative to most specifications of the ALS77 and KGM91 models we tried, which were summarized in the main text. (There is some similarity for the Cobb-Douglas specifications (except for the labor variable), which however were rejected for ALS77 and KGM91 in our tests.)

* In the context of panel data SFA, for a further advancement, one may refer to Nguyen et al. (2023), where spatial effects are incorporated into the panel data SFMs.

Table A6.1. Parameter Estimates of the Selected Panel Data Models.

Parameters	TRE-CD		KLH14-CD	
	Estimate	Standard Error	Estimate	Standard Error
Frontier function				
ln BEDS	0.40***	0.06	0.45***	0.06
ln AGGLABOR	0.25***	0.04	0.25***	0.04
ln SUPP	0.27***	0.04	0.28***	0.03
Y2013	0.09***	0.02	0.10***	0.02
Y2014	0.06**	0.03	0.07***	0.02
Y2015	0.05**	0.02	0.06***	0.02
Constant	−6.54***	0.45	−6.94***	0.41
Distribution parameters				
$\sigma_{u_{it}}$	0.18***	0.06	0.00	0.10
$\sigma_{v_{it}}$	0.11***	0.03	0.14***	0.01
σ_{η_i}			0.31***	0.08
σ_{s_i}			0.29***	0.03

* $p < 0.10$; ** $p < 0.05$; *** $p < 0.01$.

Table A6.2. Descriptive Statistics for the Inefficiency Estimation of the Selected Models.

Models	Mean	Std Dev	Min	Q1	Q2	Q3	Max
KGM91-P	32.48%	25.39%	1.20%	6.49%	30.48%	53.30%	83.57%
TRE	13.53%	6.32%	3.31%	9.77%	12.07%	15.29%	50.54%
KLH14	21.77%	7.88%	7.63%	16.31%	19.88%	24.17%	45.22%
KLH14-Persistent	21.65%	7.89%	7.48%	16.17%	19.75%	24.05%	45.13%
KLH14-Transitory	0.16%	0.00%	0.16%	0.16%	0.16%	0.16%	0.17%

The inefficiency scores ($\hat{\theta}_{it} \times 100\%$) are estimated accordingly, and the descriptive statistics are as shown in Table A6.2. The transitory inefficiency estimated by the KLH14 model is close to zero for all the observations, and hence the overall inefficiency is mainly determined by the persistent inefficiency of each individual hospital. In comparison to the estimates of the KGM91-P model, the inefficiency estimated by the panel data models is lower on average and has a relatively smaller standard deviation. Besides, the highest level of inefficiency is around 50% in the estimation of the two panel data models, which is lower than that of the KGM91-P model (where it was higher than 80%).

The kernel density estimates of the estimated inefficiency are plotted in Fig. A6.1 and they are quite different across the three models. Compared to the KGM91-P model, the panel data models show a higher concentration in the low inefficiency region and a shorter right tail.

In conclusion, it is worth reminding that a more flexible specification was used in the KGM91-P model, relative to the Cobb-Douglas specification used for the panel data SFMs. Also, note that the inefficiency level of KGM91 with Cobb-Douglas specification (see Table 13.5) is fairly similar to KLH14,

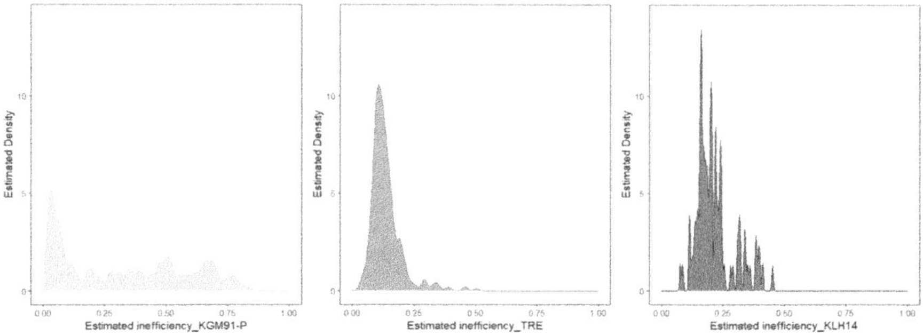

Fig. A6.1. Estimated Kernel Densities of the Inefficiency Level of Selected Models.

however, recall that Cobb-Douglas specification was rejected for KGM91, while it was not rejected for our panel data SFMs. This phenomenon of obtaining substantially different results with quite different implications again illustrates some dependency of conclusions on the model specification and, therefore, a need for trying different specifications, diagnostics, as well as expert judgment regarding the relevance of a chosen model for the context and for the research questions of interest.

CHAPTER 14

INDIRECT INFERENCE OF STOCHASTIC FRONTIER MODELS

Hung-pin Lai[a,b]

[a]*Department of Economics, National Chung Cheng University, Chiayi, Taiwan*
[b]*Research Center of Humanities and Social Sciences, Academia Sinica, Taipei, Taiwan*

ABSTRACT

The standard method to estimate a stochastic frontier (SF) model is the maximum likelihood (ML) approach with the distribution assumptions of a symmetric two-sided stochastic error v *and a one-sided inefficiency random component* u. *When* v *or* u *has a nonstandard distribution, such as* v *follows a generalized* t *distribution or* u *has a* χ^2 *distribution, the likelihood function can be complicated or untractable. This chapter introduces using indirect inference to estimate the SF models, where only least squares estimation is used. There is no need to derive the density or likelihood function, thus it is easier to handle a model with complicated distributions in practice. The author examines the finite sample performance of the proposed estimator and also compare it with the standard ML estimator as well as the maximum simulated likelihood (MSL) estimator using Monte Carlo simulations. The author found that the indirect inference estimator performs quite well in finite samples.*

Keywords: Stochastic frontier; maximum likelihood estimation; indirect inference; maximum simulated likelihood estimation; ordinary least squares; characteristic function

JEL classifications: C15; D24

Essays in Honor of Subal Kumbhakar
Advances in Econometrics, Volume 46, 415–438

Published under exclusive licence by Emerald Publishing Limited
ISSN: 0731-9053/doi:10.1108/S0731-905320240000046014

1. INTRODUCTION

Since the pioneering work of Aigner, Lovell, and Schmidt (1977, ALS), ML estimation has been the most widely used approach to estimate SF models. Let y denote the log-output variable and x be the log-input variable. A typical stochastic production frontier model can be represented as

$$y_i = \alpha + x_i^{\top}\beta + v_i - u_i,\ i = 1,\ldots,N, \tag{1}$$

where v_i is a symmetric stochastic error and $u_i > 0$ represents the one-sided random inefficiency. Let θ denote the vector of the parameters, including α, β, and the parameters contained in v and u. With the distribution assumptions on v and u, one can then derive the probability density function (pdf) of $\varepsilon = v - u$ and estimate θ by the ML approach. To implement the ML estimation, it is necessary to assume parametric distributions on both the two-sided stochastic error v and also the inefficiency term u. Given these distributions, one can then derive the distribution of the composite error $\varepsilon = v - u$. However, if v or u has a nonstandard distribution, the pdf of ε can be complicated or difficult to derive. In this case, implementation of the ML estimation will be difficult. The main objective of this chapter is to propose an easy to implement approach that can be used to estimate a SF model that may have a complicated or intractable likelihood function.

The most common distribution assumptions imposed on u include the half normal (ALS, 1977), exponential (Meeusen & van Den Broeck, 1977), and truncated normal (Stevenson, 1980) distributions. Baccouche and Kouki (2003) conducted a sensitivity analysis for the above distributions and showed that the estimates of TE depend heavily on the assumed distribution. The key empirical issue to implement the ML approach is to derive the density for the composite error. Since not all distributional assumptions will provide closed form solutions for the composite error distribution, the ML estimation is infeasible in some cases. One solution to this problem is to use the MSL estimation as discussed in Greene (2003). In the MSL estimation, one first treats u as observed and works on the conditional distribution $f_{\varepsilon}(\varepsilon \mid u)$, which is equivalent to $f_v(\varepsilon + u)$. By integrating out u, one can then obtain the marginal pdf of ε and formulate the log simulated likelihood function. The MSL approach has been widely applied in the estimation of SF models that have nonstandard distribution assumptions, such as in Greene (1990), Wheat, Stead, and Greene (2019), and others. Further extensions include applications of the MSL estimation of panel SF models, such as in Greene (2005a, 2005b), Greene (2010), and Lai and Kumbhakar (2018).

In this chapter, I propose using the indirect inference (II) method to estimate the SF model under various distribution assumptions on v and u. Similar to the MSL estimation, the indirect inference method is also a simulation-based approach. When an initial model leads to a complicated or intractable likelihood function, the II approach replaces the model with an approximated one that is easier to handle or estimate. One can then use simulations performed under the initial model to correct for the asymptotic estimation bias from the approximated model. In contrast with the standard ML estimation, there is no need to derive the marginal distribution of ε in the II estimation. Compared with the MSL estimation, there is no need to have as many Halton draws in the II estimation to achieve a similar finite sample performance. I use simulation to investigate the issue.

In addition to the computation advantage of the II estimation, it is well known that the ML and MSL estimations may have difficulties in converging to a result for some distributions and complicated models. For instance, the ML estimation of a SF model with the Laplace-truncated normal distribution could be difficult to estimate. A further extension of this model to a panel model by incorporating the firm-specific persistent inefficiency and fixed or random effects makes convergence in the ML or MSL estimation of the model even more difficult. Another possibility occurs when we consider a SF model with restrictions on the coefficients. Restrictions of the coefficients may come from the properties of the cost/production function or economic theory, and thus they may result in discontinuous regions in the maximization process. Since the II estimator is obtained by minimizing the distance function constructed from the ordinary least squares (OLS) estimators using the observed and simulated data, the objective function of the II estimation is much easier to evaluate than the log-likelihood function in the ML or MSL estimation. Therefore, the issue of convergence is less of a problem in the II estimation compared with the ML and MSL approaches.

The rest of the chapter is organized as follows. I briefly discuss the MSL estimation of a SF model under various distribution assumptions in Section 2. I then introduce an estimation procedure of the same model using the II approach in Section 3. The asymptotic properties of the II estimator are discussed in Section 4, and the predictions of technical efficiency (TE) and inefficiency are given in Section 5. In Section 6, I conduct simulations to investigate the finite sample performance of the II estimator and I also compare it with the ML and MSL estimators. I conclude the chapter in Section 7.

2. MSL ESTIMATION

In this section, I briefly discuss MSL estimation. I consider the SF model specified in (1) and allow various combinations of the distribution assumptions on v and u. For the ML estimation, the distribution of ε may be difficult to derive for some nonstandard distributions of v and u. For instance, v follows a generalized student t distribution or Laplace distribution, and u follows a χ^2 distribution or a truncated normal distribution. Although the combinations of some nonstandard distributions on v and u have been considered in the literature, there are still various potential distributions of ε that have never been considered in the literature due to the complexity of the marginal pdf of ε.

For the MSL estimation, the marginal pdf of ε is established in the following way. First, one may represent the marginal pdf of ε as the expectation of the conditional pdf $f_\varepsilon(\varepsilon \mid u)$:

$$f_\varepsilon(\varepsilon) = \int f_\varepsilon(\varepsilon \mid u) f_u(u) du = \mathbb{E}_u\left[f_\varepsilon(\varepsilon \mid u)\right]. \tag{2}$$

Since $f_\varepsilon(\varepsilon \mid u) = f_v(\varepsilon + u)$, (2) suggests that $f_\varepsilon(\varepsilon)$ can be evaluated by the simulated pdf

$$f_\varepsilon^s(\varepsilon) = \frac{1}{R}\sum_{r=1}^{R} f_v(\varepsilon - u^r), \tag{3}$$

where u^r denotes the rth draw from the parametric distribution $f_u(u)$ and $r = 1,\ldots,R$. It follows from (2) and (3) that there is no need to derive the closed form of $f_\varepsilon(\varepsilon)$ in the MSL estimation because the simulated $f_\varepsilon^s(\varepsilon)$ is used instead in the likelihood-based estimation. Once the simulated pdf of ε is obtained, the remaining estimation procedure is exactly the same as the standard ML estimation.

In the MSL estimation, it is well known that using the Halton sequence is an effective way to simulate u from its parametric distribution, and this approach has been used widely in the MSL estimation of SF models since Greene (2005a, 2005b). For a small sample size, such as the sample size $N = 200$ or 300, the number of Halton draws $R = 300$ may provide quite good finite sample performance. For instance, Wheat et al. (2019) consider a student t-half normal distribution and estimate a SF model by MSL. They use 100 Halton draws. Lai and Kumbhakar (2018, LK hereafter) use 200 draws to estimate a panel SF model with transient and persistent inefficiency by MSL estimation. In addition, LK also compare the computation time when $R = 200$, 300, and 500 in order to get some idea of how much CPU time is consumed by alternative choices of replication numbers, sample size, and Halton draws. Based on 100 successful convergences, they found that as R increases from 200 to 500 the computation time approximately doubles for their model when $N = 10$ and $T = 15$; and it increases by 150% for the model with $N = 10$ and $T = 30$. For data with a larger sample size or models with some specific distributions, a larger number of draws may be needed in order to achieve a more satisfactory result, in terms of bias and RMSE. In the simulation section, I will also investigate the finite sample performance of the MSL estimator under different numbers of draws.

3. THE INDIRECT INFERENCE

Let θ denote the vector of the parameters of the true model in (1), so it contains the parameters in the frontier equation as well as the parameters contained in the distributions of v and u. Instead of working on the ML or MSL estimation, I consider using the II estimation that uses the linear regression model as the approximated model of the true model, and the model is estimated by the least squares approach. This approximated model is also referred to as the instrument model in my following discussion. Therefore, the SF model given in (1) can also be represented as

$$y_i = a + x_i^{\mathsf{T}}\beta + v_i - u_i^*,\ i = 1,\ldots,N, \tag{4}$$

where $a = \alpha - \mathbb{E}u_i$, $u_i^* = u_i - \mathbb{E}u_i$, and the composite error $\left(v_i - u_i^*\right)$ has zero mean. Let $\hat{a}_N$ and $\hat{\beta}_N$ denote the OLS estimators of the intercept a and the slope β. It can be shown that $\hat{\beta}_N$ is a consistent estimator of β, but $\hat{a}_N$ is not a consistent estimator of α because $\mathbb{E}u_i \neq 0$.

Define $e_i = y_i - a - x_i^{\mathsf{T}}\beta$ and $\xi_i = a + v_i - u_i^* = \alpha + v_i - u_i$. Although the OLS estimator from (4) is not a consistent estimator of α, the OLS estimators $\hat{a}_N$ and $\hat{\beta}_N$ and the characteristic functions of $\hat{\xi}_i$ are functions of the true parameter θ. The moments of the residual $\hat{\xi}_i$ contain enough information for identifying the parameters of the distributions of v_i and u_i. For instance, Chen and Wang (2012) use the moment function of the OLS residual to formulate the test statistics of the distribution of ε. The characteristic function of ξ is defined as

$$\varphi_\xi(t) = \mathbb{E}\left(e^{it\xi}\right) = \mathbb{E}\left(e^{it(\alpha+v-u)}\right) = e^{it\alpha}\cdot\varphi_v(t)\cdot\varphi_u(t), \text{ where } t \in \mathbb{R}.$$

Using the observed sample, we may obtain the OLS residual

$$\hat{e}_i = y_i - \hat{a}_N - x_i^{\mathsf{T}}\hat{\beta}_N$$

and also

$$\hat{\xi}_i = \hat{e}_i + \hat{a}_N = y_i - x_i^{\mathsf{T}}\hat{\beta}_N.$$

Given the points $t = t_1, \ldots, t_q$, we can also compute the empirical characteristic function via

$$\hat{\varphi}_{N,\xi}(t) = \frac{1}{N}\sum_{i=1}^{N} e^{it\hat{\xi}_i}. \tag{5}$$

I use $\hat{b}_N = \left(\hat{a}_N, \hat{\beta}_N^{\mathsf{T}}\right)^{\mathsf{T}}$ to represent the OLS estimator.

By collecting the OLS estimator $\hat{b}_N$ and the estimators of the characteristic function at the points $t_1, \ldots, t_q$, I define the estimator $\hat{\gamma}_N$ based on the approximated model as

$$\hat{\gamma}_N = \begin{pmatrix} \hat{b}_N \\ \hat{\varphi}_{N,\xi}(t_1) \\ \vdots \\ \hat{\varphi}_{N,\xi}(t_q) \end{pmatrix}.$$

The moment conditions of the instrument model used to estimate $\hat{\gamma}_N$ are the following:

$$\mathbb{E}(e_i) = \mathbb{E}(\xi_i - a) = 0, \tag{6}$$

$$\mathbb{E}(e_i \cdot x_i) = \mathbb{E}\left[(\xi_i - a)\cdot x_i\right] = 0, \tag{7}$$

$$\mathbb{E}\left(e^{it\xi_i}\right) = \varphi_\xi(t), \text{ where } t = t_1, \ldots, t_q. \tag{8}$$

Equations (6) and (7) come from the first order conditions (FOC) of the OLS estimation, and (8) is the characteristic function $\mathbb{E}\left(e^{it\xi_i}\right)$, which is estimated by its sample counterpart. The OLS estimators together with the moments based on the characteristic functions provide a link between the auxiliary parameters γ of the instrument model and θ of the true model. Thus, the vector γ is a function of the parameter θ and can be denoted as

$$\gamma = \mathbb{B}(\theta), \tag{9}$$

where $\mathbb{B}(\theta)$ is called the binding function. For the method of moment, (8) is used to solve for the parameters contained in the distributions of v and u. For the II estimation, these parameters are estimated by matching the empirical characteristic functions from the simulated and observed data in the II estimation. Therefore, we only need to evaluate the empirical characteristic function at the given points and there is no need to derive the closed form of the characteristic function. I will discuss more details about II estimation later.

In Table 14.1, I summarize some characteristic functions of the distributions. Table 14.2 provides some examples of the binding functions for the combinations of the distributions in Table 14.1.

As shown in Table 14.2, the characteristic function of ξ is a function of α and also the parameters contained in the distributions of v and u. Since the characteristic function is unique and $t \in \mathbb{R}$, we can find infinite moment conditions for solving the true parameter θ. I then match the estimate of the instrument model from the real data and the estimate of the instrument model from the simulated data. Given the model specification, one can simulate values of $(y_1, \ldots, y_N)$ for a given value of θ, conditional on the exogenous variables $(x_1, \ldots, x_N)$. This is done by drawing v and u from their distributions. It is worth mentioning that the characteristic function contained in the binding function is evaluated by the empirical characteristic function, so it doesn't matter what the form of the characteristic function is under the true distributions of v and u. In order to identify the parameter θ, it is required that the binding function $\mathbb{B}(\cdot)$ be a function of the

Table 14.1. The Characteristic Functions of Some Distributions.

Distribution	Characteristic Function	Expectation
The symmetric random component v:		
$N(0, \sigma_v^2)$	$e^{-\frac{1}{2}t^2\sigma_v^2}$	0
$\text{Laplace}(b)$	$\frac{1}{1+b^2t^2}$	0
The one-sided random component u:		
$\chi^2(k)$	$(1-2\mathbf{i}t)^{-\frac{k}{2}}$	k
$\exp(\lambda)$	$\frac{\lambda}{\lambda-\mathbf{i}t}$	$\frac{1}{\lambda}$
$N^+(0, \sigma_u^2)$	$2 \cdot e^{-\frac{1}{2}t^2\sigma_u^2} \cdot \Phi(\mathbf{i}\sigma_u \cdot t)$	$\sqrt{\frac{2}{\pi}} \cdot \sigma_u$

Table 14.2. Some Examples of the Binding Functions.

Distribution of ε	$\mathbb{B}(\theta)$		
	$a(\theta)$	$\beta(\theta)$	$\varphi_{\xi}(t;\theta)=\mathbb{E}\left(e^{\mathbf{i}t\xi(\theta)}\right)^{a}$
Normal-half normal	$\alpha-\sqrt{\frac{2}{\pi}}\sigma_u$	β	$2e^{\mathbf{i}t\alpha}\cdot e^{-\frac{1}{2}t^2(\sigma_v^2+\sigma_u^2)}\cdot\Phi(-\mathbf{i}\sigma_u t)$
Normal-exponential	$\alpha-\frac{1}{\lambda}$	β	$e^{\mathbf{i}t\alpha}\cdot e^{-\frac{1}{2}t^2\sigma_v^2}\cdot\frac{\lambda}{\lambda+\mathbf{i}t}$
Normal- $\chi^2(k)$	$\alpha-k$	β	$e^{\mathbf{i}t\alpha}\cdot e^{-\frac{1}{2}t^2\sigma_v^2}\cdot(1+2\mathbf{i}t)^{-k/2}$
Laplace-half normal	$\alpha-\sqrt{\frac{2}{\pi}}\sigma_u$	β	$e^{\mathbf{i}t\alpha}\cdot\frac{2}{1+b^2t^2}\cdot e^{-\frac{1}{2}t^2\sigma_u^2}\cdot\Phi(-\mathbf{i}\sigma_u t)$
Laplace-exponential	$\alpha-\frac{1}{\lambda}$	β	$e^{\mathbf{i}t\alpha}\cdot\frac{1}{1+b^2t^2}\cdot\frac{\lambda}{\lambda+\mathbf{i}t}$

Note: [a] $t=t_1,t_2,\ldots,t_q\in\mathbb{R}$.

true parameters θ and the dimension of the auxiliary parameter γ must be larger than or equal to the dimension of θ. Fig. 14.1 gives a graph of the procedure, and I discuss the details below.

Step 1: Given the approximate or instrumental model, we estimate γ by OLS estimation using the observed data and denote

$$\hat{\gamma}_N=\left(\hat{b}_N^{\mathsf{T}},\hat{\varphi}_{N,\xi}(t_1),\ldots,\hat{\varphi}_{N,\xi}(t_q)\right)^{\mathsf{T}}, \tag{10}$$

where $\hat{b}_N$ is the OLS estimate from (4) using the observed data and $\hat{\varphi}_{N,\xi}(t)$ is given in (5) for $t=t_1,t_2,\ldots,t_q$.

Step 2: For a given θ, we can simulate values of the endogenous variable $\{y_i^m(\theta)\}_{i=1}^{N}$ using the true model given in (1). We then replicate M times such simulations and estimate the parameter γ. The estimator of γ of the mth replication is denoted as

$$\hat{\gamma}_N^m(\theta)=\left(\hat{b}_N^{m\,\mathsf{T}}(\theta),\hat{\varphi}_{N,\xi}^m(t_1),\ldots,\hat{\varphi}_{N,\xi}^m(t_q)\right)^{\mathsf{T}}, \tag{11}$$

where $\hat{b}_N^m(\theta)=\left(\hat{a}_N^m,\ \hat{\beta}_N^{m\,\mathsf{T}}\right)^{\mathsf{T}}$ is the solution of the problem

$$\min_b Q_N^m(b),\ \text{with}\ Q_N^m(b)=\frac{1}{N}\sum_{i=1}^{N}\left(y_i^m-a-x_i^{\mathsf{T}}\beta\right)^2, \tag{12}$$

which is estimated using the mth simulated data. Using the predicted OLS residual $\hat{\xi}^m=y_i-x_i^{\mathsf{T}}\hat{\beta}_N^m$, we can obtain the empirical characteristic function $\hat{\varphi}_{\xi}^m(t)=\frac{1}{N}\sum_{i=1}^{N}e^{\mathbf{i}t\hat{\xi}^m}$ in (11) at the points $t=t_1,t_2,\ldots,t_q$.

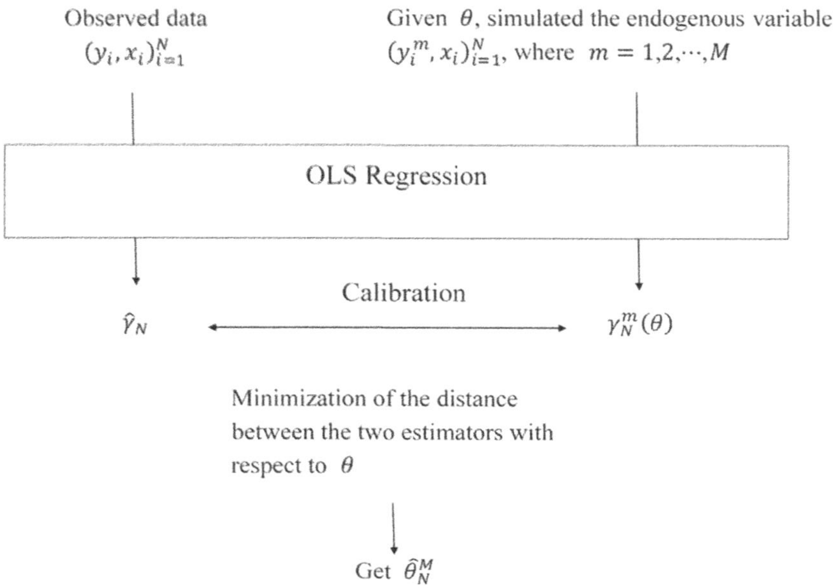

Fig. 14.1. Procedure of the Indirect Inference.

Step 3: The indirect inference estimator of θ is defined as

$$\hat{\theta}_N^M(\Omega) = \arg\min_{\theta\in\Theta} \left(\hat{\gamma}_N - \frac{1}{M}\sum_{m=1}^{M}\hat{\gamma}_N^m(\theta)\right)^{\mathrm{T}} \Omega \left(\hat{\gamma}_N - \frac{1}{M}\sum_{m=1}^{M}\hat{\gamma}_N^m(\theta)\right), \tag{13}$$

where Ω is a symmetric non-negative matrix.

In Steps 1 and 2, it is required to determine the number of discrete points q and also decide which discrete points should be used. These correspond to how many and which moments conditions should be used for the estimation of the instrument model. For the II estimation, it is required that $q/2$ should be greater than the number of the parameters contained in the distributions of v and u so that we have enough identification conditions. Since the empirical characteristic function contains the real part and imaginary part, each point t gives two moment conditions. Moreover, Schmidt (1982) considered selecting the grid that minimizes the determinant of the asymptotic covariance matrix and found that it is best to select all the points close together. Feuerverger and McDunnough (1981) suggest that the grid should be chosen to be equally spaced. If $\mathbb{E}|\xi|^k < \infty$, then $\frac{d^k}{(dt)^k}\varphi_\xi(t;\theta)$ exists for all t and

$$\frac{d^k}{(dt)^k}\varphi_\xi(t;\theta) = \mathbb{E}\left[e^{\mathbf{i}t\xi(\theta)}\left(\mathbf{i}\xi(\theta)\right)^k\right]$$

and, in particular,

$$\mathbb{E}\left(\xi(\theta)^k\right) = (-\mathbf{i})^k \frac{d^k}{(dt)^k}\varphi_\xi(0;\theta).$$

For k even, the existence of $\frac{d^k}{(dt)^k}\varphi_\xi(0;\theta)$ implies the finiteness of the kth moment $\mathbb{E}\left(\xi(\theta)^k\right)$. Thus, finer estimates of the tails of a probability distribution can be obtained by finer analysis of the behavior of $\varphi_\xi(t)$ around 0; we can pick a set of t's equally dispersed over an interval around 0. Therefore, one can select the q points that are equally spaced over an interval around 0. Moreover, in Step 2 we need to draw v and u from their distributions. This can be done by generated Halton sequences for v and u, respectively. It is worth mentioning that once the two Halton sequences are generated, they are fixed in the estimation. This procedure is quite similar to that of the MSL estimation. The main difference is that we draw both v and u in the II estimation, but we draw only u for the MSL estimation.

The main idea of the indirect inference is to use simulations performed under the "true" model to correct for the asymptotic bias of the instrument model $\hat{\gamma}_N$. It is worth mentioning that there is no need to evaluate the likelihood function in the above procedure. Steps 1 and 2 require the OLS estimation and Step 3 requires nonlinear least squares estimation. Since the characteristic function is the Fourier transform of the pdf, it completely defines the probability distribution of this random variable. The characteristic function provides an alternative route to estimate the distribution of the random variable. Therefore, $\hat{\gamma}_N$ is the binding function used in the estimation of the SF model.

4. PROPERTIES OF THE INDIRECT INFERENCE ESTIMATOR

In this section, I discuss the asymptotic properties of the II estimator. Let θ_0 denote the true parameter of the SF model in (1), and let γ denote the parameter of the instrument model. Taking the normal-half normal case as an example, we have $\theta_0 = \left(\beta_0^\top, \sigma_{v,0}^2, \sigma_{u,0}^2\right)$ and $\gamma_0 = \mathbb{B}(\theta_0) = \left(b_0^\top, \varphi_\xi(t_1;\theta_0), \ldots, \varphi_\xi(t_q;\theta_0)\right)^\top$, where $b_0 = (a_0, \beta_0^\top)^\top$, $a_0 = \alpha_0 - \sqrt{\frac{2}{\pi}}\sigma_{u,0}$ and $\varphi_\xi(t;\theta_0) = 2e^{it\alpha_0}\cdot e^{-\frac{1}{2}t^2\left(\sigma_{v,0}^2+\sigma_{u,0}^2\right)}\cdot\Phi\left(-\mathbf{i}\sigma_{u,0}t\right)$.

By the law of large numbers, it can be shown that the OLS estimator of the instrument model is a consistent estimator of γ_0, that is,

$$\lim_{N\to\infty}\hat{\gamma}_N = \gamma_0 = \mathbb{B}(\theta_0). \tag{14}$$

On the other hand, the law of large numbers implies that the estimator of the instrument model based on the simulated data for a given θ satisfies

$$\lim_{N\to\infty}\hat{\gamma}_N^m(\theta) = \mathbb{B}(\theta). \tag{15}$$

Since the binding function $\mathbb{B}(\theta)$ is a continuous function of θ and $\partial\mathbb{B}(\theta)/\partial\theta^\top$ is of full-column rank, the unique solution that minimizes the distance between $\mathbb{B}(\theta)$ and $\mathbb{B}(\theta_0)$ is θ_0. Therefore, the solution $\hat{\theta}_N^M(\Omega)$ of (12) that minimizes the distance between these two estimators $\frac{1}{M}\sum_{m=1}^{M}\hat{\gamma}_N^m(\theta)$ and $\hat{\gamma}_N$ is a consistent estimator of θ_0, that is,

$$\lim_{N\to\infty}\hat{\theta}_N^M(\Omega)=\theta_0. \tag{16}$$

See also Proposition 1 of Gourieroux, Monfort, and Renault (1993) for a similar discussion.

For notation simplicity, I define $\hat{\Psi}_N(\mathbf{t})=\left(\hat{\varphi}_{N,\xi}(t_1),\ldots,\hat{\varphi}_{N,\xi}(t_q)\right)^{\top}$, where $\mathbf{t}=\left(t_1,t_2,\ldots,t_q\right)^{\top}$. The estimators $\hat{\gamma}_N$ and $\hat{\gamma}_N^m(\theta)$ of the instrument model based on the observed data and simulated data, respectively, are

$$\hat{\gamma}_N=\begin{pmatrix}\hat{b}_N\\ \hat{\Psi}_N(\mathbf{t})\end{pmatrix} \text{ and } \hat{\gamma}_N^m(\theta)=\begin{pmatrix}\hat{b}_N^m(\theta)\\ \hat{\Psi}_N^m(\mathbf{t};\theta)\end{pmatrix}.$$

The asymptotic distribution of $\hat{\theta}_N^M(\Omega)$ depends on the asymptotic distribution of $\sqrt{N}\left(\hat{\gamma}_N-\frac{1}{M}\sum_{m=1}^{M}\hat{\gamma}_N^m(\theta)\right)$, which contains the OLS estimator and the empirical characteristic function. Below, I discuss the asymptotic distributions of these two elements separately.

Define $\mathbf{x}_i=(1,x_i^{\top})^{\top}$, then it can be shown that

$$\sqrt{N}\left(\hat{b}_N-b_0\right)=\left(\frac{1}{N}\sum_{i=1}^{N}\mathbf{x}_i\mathbf{x}_i^{\top}\right)^{-1}\left(\frac{1}{\sqrt{N}}\sum_{i=1}^{N}\mathbf{x}_ie_i\right) \tag{17a}$$

$$=\left(\frac{1}{N}\sum_{i=1}^{N}\mathbf{x}_i\mathbf{x}_i^{\top}\right)^{-1}\left(\sqrt{N}\frac{\partial Q_N(b)}{\partial b}\right), \tag{17b}$$

where $\partial Q_N(b)/\partial b=N^{-1}\sum_{i=1}^{N}\mathbf{x}_ie_i$ is the FOC of the OLS objective function. Therefore,

$$\sqrt{N}\frac{\partial Q_N(b_0)}{\partial b}\xrightarrow{d}N(0,B_0), \tag{18}$$

where

$$B_0=\lim_{N\to\infty}\operatorname{Var}\left(\sqrt{N}\frac{\partial Q_N(b_0)}{\partial b}\right)=\mathbb{E}\left(e_i^2\mathbf{x}_i\mathbf{x}_i^{\top}\right). \tag{19}$$

Define

$$A_0=\lim_{N\to\infty}\left(\frac{1}{N}\sum_{i=1}^{N}\mathbf{x}_i\mathbf{x}_i^{\top}\right). \tag{20}$$

Then

$$\sqrt{N}\left(\hat{b}_N-b_0\right)=A_0^{-1}\left(\sqrt{N}\frac{\partial Q_N(b)}{\partial b}\right)\xrightarrow{d}N(0,A_0^{-1}B_0A_0^{-1}). \tag{21}$$

Similarly, for the estimator based on the simulated data we have

$$\sqrt{N}\left(\hat{b}_N^m(\theta)-b_0\right)=\left(\frac{1}{N}\sum_{i=1}^{N}\mathbf{x}_i^{\mathsf{T}}\mathbf{x}_i\right)^{-1}\left(\sqrt{N}\frac{\partial Q_N^m(b)}{\partial b}\right). \tag{22}$$

Therefore, it follows from (17b) and (22) that

$$\sqrt{N}\left(\hat{b}_N-\frac{1}{M}\sum_{m=1}^{M}\hat{b}_N^m(\theta)\right)=A_0^{-1}\left(\sqrt{N}\frac{\partial Q_N(b)}{\partial b}-\sqrt{N}\frac{1}{M}\sum_{m=1}^{M}\frac{\partial Q_N^m(b)}{\partial b}\right). \tag{23}$$

Define the matrix

$$C_0=\lim_{N\to\infty}\operatorname{Cov}\left(\sqrt{N}\frac{\partial Q_N^m(b_0)}{\partial b},\sqrt{N}\frac{\partial Q_N^{m'}(b_0)}{\partial b}\right), \tag{24}$$

where $m\neq m'$. Since $\sqrt{N}\frac{\partial Q_N^m(b_0)}{\partial b}$ and $\sqrt{N}\frac{\partial Q_N^{m'}(b_0)}{\partial b}$ are conditionally independent given $\mathbf{x}$ and they have the same asymptotic distribution, we have

$$C_0=\lim_{N\to\infty}\operatorname{Var}\left(\mathbb{E}\left(\sqrt{N}\frac{\partial Q_N^{m'}(b_0)}{\partial b}\right)\right), \tag{25}$$

and

$$B_0-C_0=\lim_{N\to\infty}\operatorname{Var}\left(\sqrt{N}\frac{\partial Q_N(b_0)}{\partial b}-\mathbb{E}\left(\sqrt{N}\frac{\partial Q_N^m(b_0)}{\partial b}\right)\right). \tag{26}$$

Therefore, the asymptotic variance of (23) is

$$\lim_{N\to\infty}\operatorname{Var}\left(\sqrt{N}\left(\hat{b}_N-\frac{1}{M}\sum_{m=1}^{M}\hat{b}_N^m(\theta)\right)\right)$$

$$=A_0^{-1}\left[\left(1+\frac{1}{M}\right)B_0-2C_0+\frac{M(M-1)}{M^2}C_0\right]A_0^{-1} \tag{27a}$$

$$=\left(1+\frac{1}{M}\right)A_0^{-1}(B_0-C_0)A_0^{-1}. \tag{27b}$$

Next, I consider the vector of the empirical characteristic functions. By the central limit theorem, it can be shown that it is asymptotically normal, that is,

$$\sqrt{N}\left(\hat{\Psi}_N(\mathbf{t})-\Psi(\mathbf{t};\theta_0)\right)\xrightarrow{d}N(0,E_0), \tag{28}$$

where

$$E_0=\lim_{N\to\infty}\operatorname{Var}\left(\sqrt{N}\left(\hat{\Psi}_N(\mathbf{t})-\Psi(\mathbf{t};\theta_0)\right)\right). \tag{29}$$

Define

$$F_0 = \lim_{N\to\infty} \operatorname{Cov}\left(\sqrt{N}\hat{\Psi}_N^m(\mathbf{t};\theta_0), \sqrt{N}\hat{\Psi}_N^{m'}(\mathbf{t};\theta_0)\right).$$

Similar to (23), by applying the central limit theorem we obtain

$$\sqrt{N}\left(\hat{\Psi}_N(\mathbf{t}) - \frac{1}{M}\sum_{m=1}^{M}\hat{\Psi}_N^m(\mathbf{t};\theta)\right) = \sqrt{N}\left(\begin{pmatrix} \hat{\varphi}_{N,\xi}(t_1) \\ \vdots \\ \hat{\varphi}_{N,\xi}(t_q) \end{pmatrix} - \frac{1}{M}\sum_{m=1}^{M}\begin{pmatrix} \hat{\varphi}_{N,\xi}^m(t_1;\theta) \\ \vdots \\ \hat{\varphi}_{N,\xi}^m(t_q;\theta) \end{pmatrix}\right), \tag{30}$$

which is asymptotically normal with the asymptotic variance matrix

$$\lim_{N\to\infty} \operatorname{Var}\left(\sqrt{N}\left(\hat{\Psi}_N(\mathbf{t}) - \frac{1}{M}\sum_{m=1}^{M}\hat{\Psi}_N^m(\mathbf{t})\right)\right) = \left[\left(1+\frac{1}{M}\right)E_0 - 2F_0 + \frac{M(M-1)}{M^2}F_0\right] \tag{31a}$$

$$= \left(1+\frac{1}{M}\right)(E_0 - F_0). \tag{31b}$$

Next, define

$$G_0 = \lim_{N\to\infty} \operatorname{Cov}\left(\sqrt{N}\frac{\partial Q_N^m(b_0)}{\partial b}, \sqrt{N}\hat{\Psi}_N^{m'}(\mathbf{t};\theta_0)\right);$$

then it can be shown that the asymptotic covariance matrix of $\sqrt{N}\left(\hat{b}_N - \frac{1}{M}\sum_{m=1}^{M}\hat{b}_N^m(\theta)\right)$ and $\left(\sqrt{N}\hat{\Psi}_N(\mathbf{t}) - \frac{1}{M}\sum_{m=1}^{M}\hat{\Psi}_N^m(\mathbf{t};\theta)\right)$ is

$$\begin{aligned} &\lim_{N\to\infty} \operatorname{Cov}\left(\sqrt{N}\left(\hat{b}_N - \frac{1}{M}\sum_{m=1}^{M}\hat{b}_N^m(\theta)\right), \left(\sqrt{N}\hat{\Psi}_N(\mathbf{t}) - \frac{1}{M}\sum_{m=1}^{M}\hat{\Psi}_N^m(\mathbf{t};\theta)\right)\right) \\ &= \left(1+\frac{1}{M}\right)A_0^{-1}G_0. \end{aligned} \tag{32}$$

By summarizing the above results in (27b), (31b), and (32), we obtain the asymptotic variance of $\sqrt{N}\left(\hat{\gamma}_N - \frac{1}{M}\sum_{m=1}^{M}\hat{\gamma}_N^m(\theta)\right)$, which is

$$\lim_{N\to\infty} \operatorname{Var}\left(\sqrt{N}\hat{\gamma}_N - \sqrt{N}\left(\frac{1}{M}\sum_{m=1}^{M}\hat{\gamma}_N^m(\theta)\right)\right) = \left(1+\frac{1}{M}\right)\Sigma_0, \tag{33}$$

where

$$\Sigma_0 = \begin{pmatrix} A_0^{-1}(B_0 - C_0)A_0^{-1} & A_0^{-1}G_0 \\ G_0^{\mathsf{T}}A_0^{-1\mathsf{T}} & E_0 - F_0 \end{pmatrix}. \tag{34}$$

Now, consider the FOC of the objective function (13), which is

$$\left(\frac{1}{M}\sum_{m=1}^{M}\frac{\partial\hat{\gamma}_N^m(\theta)}{\partial\theta}\right)\Omega\left(\hat{\gamma}_N - \frac{1}{M}\sum_{m=1}^{M}\hat{\gamma}_N^m(\theta)\right) = 0. \tag{35}$$

The first-order expansion of (35) around θ_0 gives

$$\left(\frac{1}{M}\sum_{m=1}^{M}\frac{\partial\hat{\gamma}_N^m(\theta)}{\partial\theta}\right)\Omega\left(\hat{\gamma}_N-\frac{1}{M}\sum_{m=1}^{M}\left[\hat{\gamma}_N^m(\theta)+\frac{\partial\hat{\gamma}_N^m(\theta)}{\partial\theta^{\mathsf{T}}}\left(\hat{\theta}_N^M-\theta_0\right)\right]\right)\simeq 0. \tag{36}$$

It follows that

$$\begin{aligned}\sqrt{N}\left(\hat{\theta}_N^M-\theta_0\right)=&\left[\left(\frac{1}{M}\sum_{m=1}^{M}\frac{\partial\hat{\gamma}_N^m(\theta)}{\partial\theta}\right)\Omega\left(\frac{1}{M}\sum_{m=1}^{M}\frac{\partial\hat{\gamma}_N^m(\theta)}{\partial\theta^{\mathsf{T}}}\right)\right]^{-1}\\ &\times\left(\frac{1}{M}\sum_{m=1}^{M}\frac{\partial\hat{\gamma}_N^m(\theta)}{\partial\theta}\right)\Omega\sqrt{N}\left[\hat{\gamma}_N-\left(\frac{1}{M}\sum_{m=1}^{M}\hat{\gamma}_N^m(\theta)\right)\right].\end{aligned} \tag{37}$$

Since $\lim_{N\to\infty}\partial\hat{\gamma}_N^m(\theta)/\partial\theta=\partial\mathbb{B}(\theta)/\partial\theta$, the above equation can also be written as

$$\begin{aligned}\sqrt{N}\left(\hat{\theta}_N^M-\theta_0\right)=&\left[\left(\frac{\partial\mathbb{B}(\theta)}{\partial\theta}\right)\Omega\left(\frac{\partial\mathbb{B}(\theta)}{\partial\theta^{\mathsf{T}}}\right)\right]^{-1}\\ &\times\frac{\partial\mathbb{B}(\theta)}{\partial\theta}\Omega\sqrt{N}\left[\hat{\gamma}_N-\left(\frac{1}{M}\sum_{m=1}^{M}\hat{\gamma}_N^m(\theta)\right)\right].\end{aligned} \tag{38}$$

Therefore, we have

$$\sqrt{N}\left(\hat{\theta}_N^M-\theta_0\right)\xrightarrow{d}N(0,\Gamma_0(\Omega)), \tag{39}$$

where

$$\begin{aligned}\Gamma_0(\Omega)=&\left(1+\frac{1}{M}\right)\left[\left(\frac{\partial\mathbb{B}(\theta)}{\partial\theta}\right)\Omega\left(\frac{\partial\mathbb{B}(\theta)}{\partial\theta^{\mathsf{T}}}\right)\right]^{-1}\frac{\partial\mathbb{B}(\theta)}{\partial\theta}\Omega\Sigma_0\Omega\frac{\partial\mathbb{B}(\theta)}{\partial\theta^{\mathsf{T}}}\\ &\times\left[\left(\frac{\partial\mathbb{B}(\theta)}{\partial\theta}\right)\Omega\left(\frac{\partial\mathbb{B}(\theta)}{\partial\theta^{\mathsf{T}}}\right)\right]^{-1}.\end{aligned} \tag{40}$$

I summarize my results below.

Proposition 1. For a fixed M, as N goes to infinity the indirect inference estimator $\hat{\theta}_N^M(\Omega)$ defined in (13) is consistent and asymptotically normal:

$$\sqrt{N}\left(\hat{\theta}_N^M(\Omega)-\theta_0\right)\xrightarrow{d}N\left(0,\Gamma_0(\Omega)\right), \tag{41}$$

where $\Gamma_0(\Omega)$ is given in (40).

Note that the asymptotic variance matrix $\Gamma_0(\Omega)$ of the estimator $\hat{\theta}_N^M(\Omega)$ depends on the weighting matrix Ω, and the optimal choice of this matrix is the one that minimizes $\Upsilon_0(\Omega)$. Applying the delta method to derive the model parameter's asymptotic distribution requires the binding function's first derivative to satisfy the condition in Theorem 1 of Phillips (2012). Following a similar discussion in section 5.1 of Phillips (2012), one can show that this condition holds.

Proposition 2. For the optimal matrix $\Omega^* = \Sigma_0^{-1}$, the asymptotic variance–covariance matrix of the indirect inference estimator is simplified as

$$\Gamma_0^* = \left(1+\frac{1}{M}\right)\left[\left(\frac{\partial \mathbb{B}(\theta)}{\partial \theta}\right)\Sigma_0^{-1}\left(\frac{\partial \mathbb{B}(\theta)}{\partial \theta^{\top}}\right)\right]^{-1}. \tag{42}$$

The above results suggest the effect of simulations is summarized by the multiplicative factor $\left(1+\frac{1}{M}\right)$, but the effect will vanish as $M \to \infty$. A consistent estimator of Γ_0^* can be obtained by replacing $\frac{\partial \mathbb{B}(\theta)}{\partial \theta^{\top}}$ and Σ_0 by their sample counterparts. However, as (42) suggested evaluation of them requires computing the numerical derivative $\frac{\partial \mathbb{B}(\theta)}{\partial \theta^{\top}}$ as well as the terms contained in the matrix Σ_0, which also involve computing the numerical derivatives. Given that the computation is tedious, one can use the bootstrapped standard error instead.

5. PREDICTION OF INEFFICIENCIES AND TEs

Let $g(u)$ be an integrable function of u, such as $g(u) = u$ or $\exp(-u)$. We are interested in the conditional expectation $\mathbb{E}[g(u) \mid \varepsilon]$, where $\varepsilon = v - u$. Thus, $\mathbb{E}[g(u) \mid \varepsilon] = \mathbb{E}[u \mid \varepsilon]$ if $g(u) = u$; and $\mathbb{E}[g(u) \mid \varepsilon] = \mathbb{E}[e^{-u} \mid \varepsilon]$ if $g(u) = e^{-u}$. By the definition of conditional expectation, we can write

$$\mathbb{E}[g(u) \mid \varepsilon] = \int_0^\infty g(u) \cdot f_{u|\varepsilon}(u \mid \varepsilon)\, du \tag{43a}$$

$$= \int_0^\infty g(u) \cdot \frac{f_{u,\varepsilon}(u,\varepsilon)}{f_\varepsilon(\varepsilon)}\, du \tag{43b}$$

$$= \int_0^\infty g(u) \cdot \frac{f_{\varepsilon|u}(\varepsilon \mid u) f_u(u)}{\int_0^\infty f_{\varepsilon|u}(\varepsilon \mid u) \cdot f_u(u)\, du}\, du. \tag{43c}$$

Therefore, it follows from (43c) that $\mathbb{E}[g(u) \mid \varepsilon]$ can be estimated by the simulated estimator

$$\mathbb{E}^s[g(u) \mid \varepsilon] = \frac{1}{R}\sum_{r=1}^{R} g(u^r)\left(\frac{f_v(\varepsilon + u^r)}{\sum_{r=1}^{R} f_v(\varepsilon + u^r)}\right). \tag{44}$$

Let $W_i^r = \frac{f_v(\varepsilon + u^r)}{\sum_{r=1}^{R} f_v(\varepsilon + u^r)}$ denote the weight based on the simulated probability. Then the simulated estimator $\mathbb{E}^s[g(u) \mid \varepsilon]$ takes the form of a weighted average of $g(u^r)$'s. Below, I summarize some pdfs of v:

(i) If $v \sim N(0, \sigma_v^2)$,

$$f_v(v) = \frac{1}{\sqrt{2\pi}\sigma_v} e^{-\frac{1}{2}v^2}. \tag{45}$$

(ii) If $v \sim \sigma_v \cdot t(a)$,

$$f_v(v) = \frac{\Gamma\left(\frac{a+1}{2}\right)}{\Gamma\left(\frac{a}{2}\right)\sqrt{\pi a}\sigma_v}\left(1 + \frac{1}{a}\left(\frac{v}{\sigma_v}\right)^2\right)^{-\frac{a+1}{2}}. \tag{46}$$

(iii) If $v \sim$ Laplace(b),

$$f_v(v) = \frac{1}{2b} e^{-\frac{|v|}{b}}. \tag{47}$$

Thus, prediction of the inefficiencies and TEs can be easily done using (44) together with a pdf given in (45), (46), or (47).

6. MONTE CARLO SIMULATIONS

In this section, I conduct simulations under various specifications of the distributions of v and u. In Section 6.1, I examine the finite sample performance of the II estimator under different sample sizes. Moreover, I conduct some experiments to investigate the performance of the proposed estimator when we change the number of replications M and the number of points q. In Section 6.2, I compare the estimation efficiencies of the ML, MSL, and II estimators by comparing their biases and root mean squared errors (RMSEs) for some commonly used distribution assumptions.

6.1. Finite Sample Performance of the II Estimator

Performance of the II estimator under different distribution assumptions: In my experiments, the data generating process (DGP) is specified as

$$y_i = \alpha + x_i^{\intercal}\beta + v_i - u_i.$$

The true parameters of the frontier equation are set as $\alpha = 0.5$ and $\beta = 1$. I consider several different distribution combinations of v and u in the DGP:

I. The distribution of v:
  (i) Normal distribution: $v \sim N(0, \sigma_v^2)$.
  (ii) Generalized student t distribution: $v \sim \sigma_u \cdot t(k)$, where k is the degree of freedom.
  (iii) Laplace distribution: $v \sim \text{Laplace}(b)$, where $b > 0$ is the scale parameter.

II. The distribution of u:
  (i) Half normal : $u \sim N^+(0, \sigma_u^2)$.
  (ii) Exponential distribution: $u \sim \exp(\lambda)$, $\lambda > 0$ is the rate (inverse of the scale) parameter.
  (iii) χ^2 distribution: $u \sim \sigma_u \cdot \chi^2(h)$, where h is the degree of freedom.
  (iv) Truncated normal: $u \sim N^+(\mu, \sigma_u^2)$.

The parameters in the above distributions of v and u are set as $\sigma_v = 0.15$, $k = 2$, $b = 0.15$, $\sigma_u = 0.3$, $\mu = 0.1$, $\lambda = 5$, and $h = 2$ in all the simulations. For the indirect inference estimation, I picked the 10 points that equally lie between $[-0.1, 0.1]$ as $t_1, \ldots, t_{10}$.[1] So, we have $q = 10$. For simplicity, I choose the weighting matrix Ω as a diagonal matrix, which signs 1 for each element of the OLS estimators and $1/(2q)$ for each element of the empirical characteristic functions. The number of replications (M) for the indirect inference is set as $M = 50$ for all cases in Table 14.3. I use the Halton sequence to draw v and u from the DGPs and then generate the endogenous variable y. Once the Halton sequences are drawn, they are fixed in the minimization process. For the MSL estimation, I simulate u in the same way, but there is no need to draw v. I consider the cases when sample size $N = 250$, 500, and 1,000. The number of replications is 1,000 in all simulations.

Since scenarios under standard assumptions of v and u can be easily estimated by econometric software, such as Stata or LIMDEP, in Table 14.1, I summarize some nonstandard combinations of the distributions of v and u, such as student t-χ^2, student t-half normal, student t-exponential, student t-truncated normal, and Laplace-truncated normal distributions. I report the biases and RMSEs of the II estimators. As shown in the table, all biases are in small magnitudes and almost all RMSEs decrease as I increase the sample size. A few exceptions in Panel I are that the RMSEs of σ_v, df_v, and σ_u slightly increase by 0.0001, 0.0004, and 0.0028 as we increase the sample size from 500 to 1,000, which could be due to the outliers in the generated random sample. The extreme value appears more frequently in the student t distribution than in the normal distribution. The distribution combinations of v and u I consider here are not commonly used in the SF studies because the marginal distributions of ε are too difficult to derive.

Panels IV and V summarize the results when the composite error has the student t-truncated normal and Laplace-truncated normal distributions. For the ML estimation, it is relatively difficult to estimate the model when u follows a truncated normal distribution. Here, I found that the indirect inference estimator performs quite well in terms of the biases and RMSEs. It also suggests that the

Table 14.3. Biases and RMSEs of the II Estimators Under Various Combinations of v and u When $q = 10$ and $M = 50$.

Model	Bias			RMSE		
N	250	500	1,000	250	500	1,000
Panel I.: $v \sim \sigma_v \cdot t(df_v)$ and $u \sim \sigma_u \cdot \chi^2(df_u)$						
α	−0.0159	−0.0189	−0.0196	0.1283	0.1081	0.1020
β	−0.0013	−0.0027	−0.0048	0.0816	0.0580	0.0416
σ_v	0.0015	0.0029	0.0021	0.0178	0.0167	0.0168
df_v	0.0086	0.0077	0.0062	0.0551	0.0506	0.0510
σ_u	0.0685	0.0551	0.0620	0.2306	0.2257	0.2285
df_u	−0.0084	−0.0163	−0.0123	0.2215	0.1929	0.1981
Panel II. $v \sim \sigma_v \cdot t(df_v)$ and $u \sim N^+(0,\sigma_u^2)$						
α	0.0052	−0.0019	0.0018	0.0730	0.0861	0.0439
β	−0.0013	0.0013	−0.0014	0.0557	0.0465	0.0209
σ_v	0.0010	0.0007	0.0007	0.0169	0.0163	0.0160
df_v	0.0361	0.0425	0.0330	0.2094	0.2164	0.2183
σ_u	0.0069	0.0043	0.0043	0.0344	0.0348	0.0321
Panel III. $v \sim \sigma_v \cdot t(df_v)$ and $u \sim \exp(\lambda)$						
α	−0.0299	−0.0101	−0.0155	0.0608	0.0578	0.0396
β	0.0059	−0.0006	0.0049	0.0342	0.0316	0.0298
σ_v	0.0013	0.0009	0.0010	0.0033	0.0021	0.0013
df_v	0.0703	0.0655	0.0641	0.0307	0.0949	0.0199
λ	0.0401	0.0319	0.0172	0.0946	0.0775	0.0621
Panel IV. $v \sim \sigma_v \cdot t(df_v)$ and $u \sim N^+(\mu,\sigma_u^2)$						
α	−0.0103	−0.0112	−0.0104	0.0873	0.0784	0.0720
β	−0.0017	0.0003	0.0000	0.0444	0.0337	0.0216
σ_v	0.0024	0.0027	0.0028	0.0167	0.0164	0.0159
df_v	0.0615	0.0573	0.0459	0.2246	0.2251	0.2187
μ	−0.0215	−0.0179	−0.0177	0.0927	0.0928	0.0873
σ_u	0.0092	0.0061	0.0073	0.0327	0.0337	0.0312
Panel V. $v \sim$ Laplace(b) and $u \sim N^+(\mu,\sigma_u^2)$						
α	0.0094	0.0105	0.0111	0.0606	0.0524	0.0514
β	0.0009	−0.0004	−0.0001	0.0207	0.0149	0.0105
b	−0.0040	−0.0037	−0.0038	0.0500	0.0526	0.0514
μ	0.0166	0.0169	0.0175	0.0962	0.0950	0.0954
σ_u	0.0055	0.0041	0.0046	0.0296	0.0302	0.0313

Note: The total number of replications is 1,000.

binding functions I use here provide enough useful information to identify the true parameters.[2]

Performance of the II estimator under different number of replications M: In order to investigate the finite sample performance of the II estimator for different choices of M, I focus on the specifications considered in Panels I and II of Table 14.3. I set $v \sim \sigma_u \cdot t(k)$ and have u follows either (i) a χ^2 distribution $\sigma_u \cdot \chi^2(h)$ or (ii) a HN distribution $N^+(0,\sigma_u^2)$. The number of replications (M) in each of the II estimations is set as $M = 10$, 50, and 100. I summarize the biases and RMSEs of the estimators in Table 14.4. As shown in the table, all biases of the estimators

Table 14.4. Biases and RMSEs of the II Estimators When $q = 10$ and $M = 10$, 50, and 100.

Parameter	Bias			RMSE		
N	250	500	1,000	250	500	1,000
Panel I. $v \sim \sigma_v \cdot t(df_v)$ and $u \sim \sigma_u \cdot x^2(df_u)$						
I.A: $M = 10$						
α	−0.0704	−0.0707	−0.0685	0.1347	0.1093	0.1075
β	0.0109	0.0071	0.0001	0.0820	0.0582	0.0416
σ_v	0.0020	0.0028	0.0026	0.0177	0.0169	0.0171
df_v	0.0409	0.0324	0.0386	0.2288	0.2214	0.2221
σ_u	0.0188	0.0178	0.0134	0.0515	0.0484	0.0487
df_u	0.0560	0.0446	0.0545	0.2266	0.1986	0.2067
I.B: $M = 50$						
α	−0.0159	−0.0189	−0.0196	0.1283	0.1081	0.1020
β	−0.0013	−0.0027	−0.0048	0.0816	0.0580	0.0416
σ_v	0.0015	0.0029	0.0021	0.0178	0.0167	0.0168
df_v	0.0086	0.0077	0.0062	0.0551	0.0506	0.0510
σ_u	0.0685	0.0551	0.0620	0.2306	0.2257	0.2285
df_u	−0.0084	−0.0163	−0.0123	0.2215	0.1929	0.1981
I.C: $M = 100$						
α	−0.0085	−0.0139	−0.0145	0.1295	0.1069	0.1026
β	−0.0019	−0.0014	−0.0033	0.0816	0.0580	0.0416
σ_v	0.0013	0.0028	0.0022	0.0174	0.0165	0.0169
df_v	0.0737	0.0617	0.0633	0.2354	0.2254	0.2259
σ_u	0.0081	0.0068	0.0053	0.0551	0.0508	0.0512
df_u	−0.0233	−0.0286	−0.0228	0.2181	0.1938	0.1975
Panel II. $v \sim \sigma_v \cdot t(df_v)$ and $u \sim N^+(0, \sigma_u^2)$						
II.A: $M = 10$						
α	0.0132	0.0028	0.0053	0.0723	0.0859	0.0436
β	−0.0070	−0.0020	−0.0040	0.0558	0.0465	0.0210
σ_v	0.0012	0.0008	0.0008	0.0169	0.0161	0.0160
df_v	0.0331	0.0415	0.0341	0.2060	0.2189	0.2198
σ_u	0.0064	0.0036	0.0040	0.0346	0.0351	0.0320
II.B: $M = 50$						
α	0.0052	−0.0019	0.0018	0.0730	0.0861	0.0439
β	−0.0013	0.0013	−0.0014	0.0557	0.0465	0.0209
σ_v	0.0010	0.0007	0.0007	0.0169	0.0163	0.0160
df_v	0.0361	0.0425	0.0330	0.2094	0.2164	0.2183
σ_u	0.0069	0.0043	0.0043	0.0344	0.0348	0.0321
II.C: $M = 100$						
α	0.0093	0.0006	0.0048	0.0704	0.0870	0.0440
β	−0.0009	0.0024	−0.0007	0.0557	0.0470	0.0209
σ_v	0.0008	0.0027	0.0008	0.0171	0.0158	0.0162
df_v	0.0326	0.0155	0.0291	0.2095	0.2215	0.2137
σ_u	0.0067	0.0037	0.0037	0.0353	0.0343	0.0320

Note: The number of replications is 1,000.

under $M = 10$, 50, and 100 are all small in magnitude. Most of the biases decrease as I increase the sample size N or the number of replications M. On the other hand, the RMSEs for a fixed N and $M = 10$, 50, and 100 are quite similar.

According to these results, I found the finite sample performance of the II estimator performs quite well for a small number of replications such as $M = 10$. Increasing M is more helpful in reducing the estimation bias, instead of the RMSE.

Performance of the II estimator under different choice of q: My next experiment intends to focus on the practical issue of how many points (q) to choose for the II estimation. Here, I consider the normal-half normal distribution for the composite error and summarize the results in Table 14.5. Since the empirical characteristic function contains the real and imaginary parts, choosing q points gives $2q$ restrictions. Given that Table 14.4 has shown the II estimator performs quite well for a small value of M, I set $M = 10$ in the estimation. The estimation results for $q = 5$, 10, 20 and 100 are summarized in Table 14.5. According to the table, I found that all biases are small in magnitude. Some of them slightly decrease and some of them stay at the same level when I increase q from 5 to 100. A similar pattern is also found in the RMSEs. The results show that the improvement in the estimation efficiency is insignificant as I increase the number of points q from 5 to 100. The II estimator with $q = 5$ already performs quite well. It is worth mentioning that the normal-half normal assumption is also considered in Panel I.A of Table 14.6, so we are able to compare the estimation efficiency of the II estimator with the ML and MSL estimators. I discuss it in the next subsection.

Table 14.5. Biases and RMSEs for the II Estimator for the SF Model with Normal-Half Normal Distribution When $M = 10$ and $q = 5$, 10, 20, and 100.

Parameter	Bias			RMSE		
N	250	500	1,000	250	500	1,000
Panel I: $q = 5$						
α	−0.0031	−0.0021	−0.0008	0.0158	0.0119	0.0085
β	0.0026	0.0010	−0.0011	0.0284	0.0207	0.0151
σ_v	0.0109	0.0122	0.0099	0.0183	0.0201	0.0171
λ	0.0025	0.0024	0.0023	0.0027	0.0023	0.0023
Panel II: $q = 10$						
α	−0.0031	−0.0021	−0.0008	0.0158	0.0119	0.0085
β	0.0025	0.0009	−0.0014	0.0284	0.0206	0.0151
σ_v	0.0103	0.0100	0.0083	0.0182	0.0175	0.0164
λ	0.0024	0.0023	0.0021	0.0027	0.0021	0.0023
Panel III: $q = 20$						
α	−0.0031	−0.0021	−0.0008	0.0158	0.0119	0.0085
β	0.0025	0.0008	−0.0014	0.0284	0.0206	0.0149
σ_v	0.0091	0.0097	0.0080	0.0176	0.0176	0.0153
λ	0.0024	0.0022	0.0020	0.0025	0.0022	0.0020
Panel IV: $q = 100$						
α	−0.0031	−0.0021	−0.0008	0.0158	0.0119	0.0085
β	0.0024	0.0008	−0.0015	0.0283	0.0205	0.0148
σ_v	0.0083	0.0089	0.0082	0.0177	0.0176	0.0157
λ	0.0023	0.0021	0.0019	0.0024	0.0020	0.0022

Note: The number of replications is 1,000.

Table 14.6. Biases and RMSEs of the ML, II and MSL Estimators Under the Normal-Half Normal and Normal-Exponential Distributions.

Model	Bias			RMSE			RE		
N	250	500	1,000	250	500	1,000	250	500	1,000
Panel I. $v \sim N(0,\sigma_v^2)$ and $u \sim N^+(0,\sigma_u^2)$									
I.A: MLE									
α	−0.0017	−0.0007	−0.0006	0.0424	0.0287	0.0202	1	1	1
β	−0.0007	−0.0006	−0.0001	0.0152	0.0113	0.0082	1	1	1
σ_v	−0.0021	−0.0006	−0.0005	0.0237	0.0163	0.0108	1	1	1
σ_u	−0.0047	−0.0031	−0.0015	0.0434	0.0288	0.0195	1	1	1
I.B: Indirect inference ($M = 50$ and $q = 10$)									
α	−0.0016	−0.0013	−0.0026	0.0281	0.0207	0.0153	0.6627	0.7213	0.7574
β	−0.0007	−0.0008	−0.0001	0.0158	0.0119	0.0085	1.0395	1.0531	1.0366
σ_v	−0.0025	0.0059	0.0063	0.0480	0.0339	0.0263	2.0253	2.0798	2.4352
σ_u	0.0020	0.0023	0.0024	0.0055	0.0043	0.0040	0.1267	0.1493	0.2051
I.C: MSL ($R = 300$)									
α	−0.0038	−0.0023	−0.0013	0.0382	0.0256	0.0169	0.9009	0.8920	0.8366
β	−0.0001	−0.0001	−0.0000	0.0026	0.0020	0.0014	0.1711	0.1770	0.1707
σ_v	−0.0012	−0.0001	0.0005	0.0235	0.0162	0.0114	0.9916	0.9939	1.0556
σ_u	−0.0048	−0.0020	−0.0013	0.0454	0.0308	0.0209	1.0461	1.0694	1.0718
Panel II. $v \sim N(0,\sigma_v^2)$ and $u \sim \exp(\lambda)$									
II.A: MLE									
α	−0.0031	−0.0011	−0.0003	0.0319	0.0227	0.0167	1	1	1
β	0.0002	−0.0002	−0.0001	0.0150	0.0108	0.0081	1	1	1
σ_v	−0.0007	−0.0009	−0.0003	0.0164	0.0109	0.0080	1	1	1
λ	0.1625	0.0804	0.0340	0.7270	0.4555	0.3118	1	1	1
II.B: Indirect inference ($M = 50$ and $q = 10$)									
α	−0.0048	−0.0031	−0.0040	0.0285	0.0212	0.0165	0.8934	0.9339	0.9980
β	0.0002	−0.0004	0.0002	0.0169	0.0122	0.0094	1.1267	1.1296	1.1605
σ_v	0.0051	0.0100	0.0108	0.0574	0.0340	0.0335	3.5000	3.1193	4.1875
λ	−0.0294	−0.0419	-0.0395	0.1033	0.0747	0.0672	0.1421	0.1640	0.2155
II.C: MSL ($H = 300$)									
α	0.0016	0.0003	0.0023	0.0257	0.0172	0.0119	0.8056	0.7577	0.7126
β	0.0000	−0.0001	0.0000	0.0027	0.0019	0.0013	0.1800	0.1759	0.1605
σ_v	−0.0023	−0.0005	−0.0004	0.0165	0.0113	0.0081	1.0061	1.0367	1.0125
λ	0.0091	−0.0212	0.0884	0.7628	0.5119	0.3496	1.0492	1.1238	1.1212

Note: The total number of replications is 1,000.

6.2. Comparison of the II, ML, and MSL Estimators

In order to investigate the loss of estimation efficiency when the II estimation is used instead of the ML or MSL estimation, I consider two SF models with commonly used distribution assumptions on v and u: (i) the normal-half normal distribution and (ii) the normal-exponential distribution. In my experiments, the same generated data are separately estimated by the ML, MSL and II estimation techniques. The ML estimation is implemented using the Stata estimation command "frontier." In the MSL estimation, the Halton sequence is generated and used to evaluate the simulated pdf and the number of Halton draws (denoted as R)

is set as 300. For the II estimator, I set $M = 50$ and 10 points equally spaced between -0.1 and 0.1 are used. I compare the finite sample performance of the three estimators under the two distribution assumptions. Moreover, I summarize the relative efficiency (RE), which is defined as the ratio of RMSEs, where the denominator is the RMSE of the ML estimator. Therefore, RE > 1 (< 1) means the ML estimator is more (less) efficient. I listed the REs in the last three columns of Table 14.6.

Panel I of Table 14.6 summarizes the results of the three estimators when the composite error has a normal-half normal distribution. I found that all biases are quite small for all sample sizes. Regarding RE, 50% of the REs are greater than one and 50% are less than one. By comparing the RMSEs, I found that the II estimators of the parameters α and σ_u are more efficient than the ML and MSL estimators. The II estimators of β and σ_v are less efficient compared with the ML and MSL estimators. Moreover, the RMSEs of the MSL estimators of α and σ_u are smaller than those of the ML estimator. For the normal-exponential case in Panel II, the biases of all estimators are also small in magnitude. The patterns of the RMSEs of the ML, II, and MSL estimators are quite similar to what we have found in the normal-half normal case. In summary, there is no significant evidence showing that the II and MSL estimators are less efficient than the ML estimator.

Next, I further investigate two nonstandard distribution assumptions of the composite error: (i) the student t-half normal distribution and (ii) the normal-χ^2 distribution. Since the marginal pdf of ε is complicated in these two cases, I only compare the finite sample performance of the MSL and the II estimators. In the same manner, I also compare their RE using ratios of RMSEs, where the denominator of the ratios is the RMSE of the II estimator. The results are summarized in Panels I and II of Table 14.7. For case (i), we found the biases of the II estimator are small. Although most biases of the MSL estimator are also small in magnitude, we found that the bias of df_v from the MSL estimation is relatively larger than that of the II estimator. Regarding RE, we found that the MSL estimator is more efficient in estimating the parameters of the frontier part (α and β) but is less efficient in estimating the parameters contained in the distributions of v and u.

For case (ii), the biases of the II estimator are also small, but the biases of the MSL estimators of σ_u and df_u are much larger when the number of Halton draws (R) is 300. Although the REs in case (ii) are quite similar to those in case (i), the biases of the estimators of σ_u and df_u in the MSL estimation are quite large. Therefore, I increase the number of Halton draws from 300 to 1,000 and 2,000 and see whether we can reduce the biases of the MSL estimator by increasing the Halton draws. I summarize the results in Panels II.C and II.D. As shown in the table, increasing the number of draws R can effectively decrease the estimation biases of the MSL estimator and also improve the estimation efficiency at the same time. For the case $N = 1{,}000$, the bias of σ_u decreases from 0.1621 to 0.0297 and the bias of df_u decreases in magnitude from 0.4224 to 0.0666 as I increase R from 300 to 2000. On the other hand, the biases of the II estimators of σ_u and df_u when $N = 1{,}000$, $M = 50$, and $q = 10$ are 0.0084 and -0.0018, respectively.

Table 14.7. Biases and RMSEs of the Indirect Inference and MSL Estimators.

Model	Bias			RMSE			RE		
N	250	500	1,000	250	500	1,000	250	500	1,000
Panel I. $v \sim \sigma_v \cdot t(df_v)$ and $u \sim N^+(0,\sigma_u^2)$									
I.A: Indirect inference ($M = 50$ and $q = 10$)									
α	0.0052	−0.0019	0.0018	0.0730	0.0861	0.0439	1	1	1
β	−0.0013	0.0013	−0.0014	0.0557	0.0465	0.0209	1	1	1
σ_v	0.0010	0.0007	0.0007	0.0169	0.0163	0.0160	1	1	1
df_v	0.0361	0.0425	0.0330	0.2094	0.2164	0.2183	1	1	1
σ_u	0.0069	0.0043	0.0043	0.0344	0.0348	0.0321	1	1	1
I.B: MSL ($R = 300$)									
α	−0.0151	−0.0074	−0.0034	0.0647	0.0432	0.0258	0.8863	0.5017	0.5877
β	0.0001	−0.0001	−0.0001	0.0033	0.0024	0.0018	0.0592	0.0516	0.0861
σ_v	0.0029	0.0020	0.0016	0.0392	0.0281	0.0192	2.3195	1.7239	1.2000
df_v	0.1844	0.0755	0.0516	0.6980	0.3962	0.2683	3.3333	1.8309	1.2290
σ_u	−0.0191	−0.0088	−0.0045	0.0866	0.0588	0.0351	2.5174	1.6897	1.0935
Panel II. $v \sim N(0,\sigma_v^2)$ and $u \sim \sigma_u \cdot \chi^2(df_u)$									
II.A: Indirect inference ($M = 50$ and $q = 10$)									
α	−0.0160	−0.0188	−0.0198	0.1269	0.1081	0.1040	1	1	1
β	−0.0007	0.0020	0.0026	0.0730	0.0492	0.0378	1	1	1
σ_v	0.0055	0.0037	0.0051	0.0171	0.0166	0.0163	1	1	1
σ_u	0.0105	0.0081	0.0084	0.0486	0.0469	0.0459	1	1	1
df_u	−0.0095	−0.0035	−0.0018	0.1874	0.1815	0.1775	1	1	1
II.B: MSL ($R = 300$)									
α	−0.0208	−0.0496	−0.0765	0.1039	0.0770	0.0640	0.8188	0.7123	0.6154
β	0.0000	−0.0001	−0.0000	0.0057	0.0037	0.0028	0.0781	0.0752	0.0741
σ_v	−0.0040	0.0198	0.0371	0.0582	0.0416	0.0344	3.4035	2.5060	2.1104
σ_u	0.0842	0.1233	0.1621	0.1801	0.1979	0.1917	3.7058	4.2196	4.1765
df_u	−0.1272	−0.2860	−0.4224	0.5314	0.4078	0.3468	2.8356	2.2469	1.9538
II.C: MSL ($R = 1000$)									
α	0.0155	−0.0066	−0.0238	0.1013	0.0687	0.0557	0.7983	0.6355	0.5356
β	−0.0000	−0.0001	−0.0001	0.0057	0.0036	0.0027	0.0781	0.0732	0.0714
σ_v	−0.0233	−0.0037	0.0078	0.0587	0.0357	0.0279	3.4327	2.1506	1.7117
σ_u	0.0117	0.0352	0.0572	0.1188	0.1090	0.1197	2.4444	2.3241	2.6078
df_u	0.1093	−0.0465	−0.1481	0.5708	0.3858	0.3124	3.0459	2.1256	1.7600
II.D: MSL ($R = 2000$)									
α	0.1670	0.0040	−0.0101	0.0949	0.0677	0.0493	0.7478	0.6263	0.4740
β	−0.0001	−0.0001	−0.0001	0.0056	0.0036	0.0027	0.0767	0.0732	0.0714
σ_v	−0.0237	−0.0082	0.0012	0.0587	0.0358	0.0242	3.4327	2.1566	1.4847
σ_u	−0.0001	0.0140	0.0294	0.0976	0.0974	0.0889	2.0082	2.0768	1.9368
df_u	0.1273	0.0250	−0.0666	0.5367	0.3803	0.2827	2.8639	2.0953	1.5927

Note: The total number of replications is 1,000.

However, we only need $M = 50$ for the indirect inference estimation to achieve a similar or better estimation result. It is clear that the indirect inference estimator has some advantage over the MSL estimator in terms of the computational burden and computation time.

The simulation results in Tables 14.6 and 14.7 show that there are some trade-offs between these approaches. It seems that the II estimation is more efficient in estimating the parameters of the inefficiency (u) distribution than the ML and MSL estimation. On the other hand, both the ML and MSL estimators of the slope parameter (β) perform slightly better than the II estimator. Although I only compare the three estimators under the normal-half normal and normal-exponential assumptions in Table 14.6, a similar result is also found by comparing the II and MSL estimators in Table 14.7.

Based on my simulation results in Tables 14.3–14.7, we may conclude that the II estimator performs quite well in finite samples. The main advantage of the II estimation is that it can be easily applied to various combinations of the distributions of v and u without requiring derivation of the marginal pdf of the composite error. Although both II and MSL estimation can be applied to SF models with nonstandard distributions or a complicated marginal pdf of ε, the II estimation can effectively alleviate computation burden.

7. CONCLUSION

In this chapter, I propose using II estimation as an alternative approach to ML and MSL estimation. The indirect inference alleviates the computational burden of MSL estimation and does not require a derivation of the marginal pdf of the composite error as in ML estimation. Similar to the MSL estimation, the indirect inference method is also a simulation-based approach. When an initial model leads to a complicated or intractable likelihood function, the II approach replaces the model by an approximated one that is easier to handle or estimate. One can then use simulations performed under the initial model to correct for the asymptotic estimation bias from the approximated model. Compared with the MSL estimation, there is no need to have as many Halton draws in the II estimation to achieve a similar finite sample performance. Implementation of the II method requires only the ordinary least squares and nonlinear least squares methods. The II estimator is obtained by minimizing the distance function constructed from the OLS estimators using the observed and simulated data. The objective function of the II estimation is easier to evaluate than the log-likelihood of the ML or MSL estimation. Thus, the issue of convergence is less of a problem in the II estimation. The only drawback of the II estimator is that the computation of its asymptotic variance is tedious, thus one can use the bootstrapped standard error instead. Overall, my simulations show that the II estimator gives quite satisfactory finite sample performance.

NOTES

1. I have tried picking the 10 points between $[-0.5,0.5]$. The simulation results are quite similar.
2. One referee pointed out that some of the II estimators in Table 14.3 have slower rates of convergence. This may be due to the long tail of v or u. A similar finding also appears in the MSL estimator in Panel II of Table 14.7, where the normal-χ^2 distribution is assumed.

The rates of convergence of the MSL parameters of σ_u and df_u are also slower than $\sqrt{N}$. This issue may be worth investigating further, and we leave it for future study.

REFERENCES

Aigner, D. J., Lovell, C. A. K., & Schmidt, P. (1977). Formulation and estimation of stochastic frontier production models. *Journal of Econometrics*, *6*, 21–37.

Baccouche, R., & Kouki, M. (2003). Stochastic production frontier and technical inefficiency: A sensitivity analysis. *Econometric Reviews*, *22*, 79–91.

Chen, Y.-T., & Wang, H.-J. (2012). Centered-residuals-based moment estimator and test for stochastic frontier models. *Econometric Reviews*, *31*(6), 625–653.

Feuerverger, A., & McDunnough, P. (1981). On the efficiency of empirical characteristic function procedures. *Journal of the Royal Statistical Society. Series B (Methodological)*, *43*(1), 20–27.

Gourieroux, C., Monfort, A., & Renault, E. (1993). Indirect inference. *Journal of Applied Econometrics*, *8*(S1), S85–S118.

Greene, W. H. (1990). A gamma distributed stochastic frontier model. *Journal of Econometrics*, *46*, 141–163.

Greene, W. H. (2003). Simulated likelihood estimation of the normal-gamma stochastic frontier function. *Journal of Productivity Analysis*, *19*(2), 179–190.

Greene, W. H. (2005a). Fixed and random effects in stochastic frontier models. *Journal of Productivity Analysis*, *23*(1), 7–32.

Greene, W. H. (2005b). Reconsidering heterogeneity in panel data estimators of the stochastic frontier model. *Journal of Econometrics*, *126*(2), 269–303.

Greene, W. H. (2010). A sample selection corrected stochastic frontier model. *Journal of Productivity Analysis*, *34*(1). 15–24.

Lai, H.-p., & Kumbhakar, S. C. (2018). Panel data stochastic frontier model with determinants of persistent and transient inefficiency. *European Journal of Operational Research*, *271*(2), 746–755.

Meeusen, W., & van Den Broeck, J. (1977). Efficiency estimation from Cobb–Douglas production functions with composed error. *International Economic Review*, *18*, 435–444.

Phillips, P. (2012). Folklore theorems, implicit maps, and indirect inference, *Econometrica*, *80*(1), 425–454.

Schmidt, P. (1982). An improved version of the Quandt–Ramsey MGF estimator for mixtures of normal distributions and switching regressions. *Econometrica*, *50*, 501–524.

Stevenson, R. (1980). Likelihood functions for generalized stochastic frontier estimation. *Journal of Econometrics*, *13*, 58–66.

Wheat, P., Stead, A., & Greene, W. H. (2019). Robust stochastic frontier analysis: a Student's *t*-half normal model with application to highway maintenance costs in England. *Journal of Productivity Analysis*, *51*, 21–38.

CHAPTER 15

THE NASH BARGAINING TWO-TIER STOCHASTIC FRONTIER MODEL*

Alecos Papadopoulos

Athens University of Economics and Business, Athens, Greece

ABSTRACT

The author develops a bilateral Nash bargaining model under value uncertainty and private/asymmetric information, combining ideas from axiomatic and strategic bargaining theory. The solution to the model leads organically to a two-tier stochastic frontier (2TSF) setup with intra-error dependence. The author presents two different statistical specifications to estimate the model, one that accounts for regressor endogeneity using copulas, the other able to identify separately the bargaining power from the private information effects at the individual level. An empirical application using a matched employer–employee data set (MEEDS) from Zambia and a second using another one from Ghana showcase the applied potential of the approach.

Keywords: Nash bargaining; asymmetric information; two-tier stochastic frontier; copula; matched employer–employee data set; identification

JEL classifications J30; C78; D82; C21

---

* This chapter is partly based on research included in the PhD thesis of the author. A summary description of a less developed version of the model was published in Papadopoulos (2021b).

Essays in Honor of Subal Kumbhakar
Advances in Econometrics, Volume 46, 439–476

ISSN: 0731-9053/doi:10.1108/S0731-905320240000046015

1. INTRODUCTION

The 2TSF model was introduced by Polachek and Yoon (1987), in order to account for and measure the effects of incomplete information on both sides of the labor market, that can explain the observed heterogeneity of wage outcomes.[1] The defining property of the 2STF model is its three-component regression error, $\varepsilon = v + w - u$, that includes a symmetric zero-mean "noise" v, and two one-sided components $w, u \geq 0$, the one entering positively and the other negatively in the relation. With it, we can estimate two latent forces, one having a positive and the other having a negative effect on the dependent variable.

In its first 20 years, the 2TSF approach was rather sparingly used although in very diverse situations that demonstrated its flexibility and potential. For example, Gaynor and Polachek (1994) applied it on the market for physician services, while Groot and van den Brink (2007) used it to measure the effects of psychological internal conflicts, as regards the assessment of quality of life, in patients with cardiovascular disease.

Kumbhakar and Parmeter (2009, 2010) reinvigorated the model, by interpreting it as an applied incarnation of bilateral Nash bargaining for wage determination (in the 2009 paper), and also by using it in a hedonic-pricing context (in the 2010 article). In the last decade, the model has seen an accelerating rate of published applications that continue to extend its reach. For example, Kinukawa and Motohashi (2016) used it to study corporate alliances in the biotechnology sector, Wang (2018) applied it to bilateral aid in the International Relations field, Zhang, Zhang, Yang, and Zhou (2018) to bargaining in tourist shopping, and Tauer (2021) to the bull semen market. A detailed exposition and review of the 2TSF model and literature can be found in Papadopoulos (2021b), but already there are dozens of 2TSF papers that have been published since then.

In this chapter, we revisit the bargaining field, which appears to have become one of the most popular 2TSF applications, and we develop from first principles and in detail a bilateral Nash bargaining 2TSF model under uncertainty and asymmetric information, that goes deeper and beyond what can be found in Kumbhakar and Parmeter (2009). The model we build synthesizes elements from axiomatic and strategic bargaining theory, combines static and dynamic aspects of bargaining, and keeps relative bargaining power distinct from the effects of private information, something that allows us eventually to construct a method for their separate econometric identification and estimation. Our bargaining model can be properly estimated only if the regressor matrix includes variables for both sides of the bargaining game. It is already applicable to a cross-sectional sample, but it can be extended to a panel-data setting.

The model provides empirical quantitative answers to important questions about observed bargaining outcomes, where latent factors are never available as data and are known to play a decisive role. Under uncertainty, private information and bargaining power become instrumental for the outcome, and our model provides a structured framework to estimate the strength and influence on the outcome of these latent forces. This contributes to our understanding of how (and of how much) informational factors and external constraints influence real-world outcomes beyond the textbook determinants of economic transactions, and can also have policy implications.

The rest of the chapter is organized as follows: in Section 2, we start by summarily presenting the Nash bargaining model in a deterministic setting. Then, we show why the introduction of uncertainty and private information cannot be satisfactorily dealt with by simply substituting predictors for previously deterministic variables. We proceed to reformulate the model from scratch in a stochastic environment, and we obtain an expression for the equilibrium outcome that is based on the *common-information* set, alongside the effects of bargaining power and private information. This leads organically to the 2TSF model, and so its observed and unobserved components become estimable by maximum likelihood. Section 3 presents a statistical specification (and a related application) that handles endogeneity through the use of copulas, but cannot estimate separately the bargaining power from the private information effects. In Section 4, we develop a conditioning method to do just that and we provide another empirical illustration. Section 5 concludes. A short Appendix includes some mathematical derivations and formulas.

2. THE NASH BARGAINING FRAMEWORK IN BILATERAL NEGOTIATIONS

The Nash bargaining model and equilibrium were introduced by Nash (1950) as a solution concept in the context of axiomatic bargaining theory, for situations where self-interested parties have an opportunity to gain through collaboration, and they must agree on how to split these gains. It is a powerful concept, being fully consistent with fundamental pillars of economic theory: it emerges as the unique equilibrium when the parties involved have preferences that satisfy the basic axioms of expected utility theory (complete, transitive, and continuous preferences, satisfaction of the independence axiom), and it is Pareto-optimal. The concept was developed using a game-theoretic framework, and while it can be extended to a game with many players, by far its most frequent use is in situations with two players and we will keep that.[2] Simply put, to achieve an optimal (and unique) split of the gains from collaboration, the decision variable according to which the gains are to be split must be set so as to maximize the *product* of the utility functions (or any weighted geometric average thereof) that the two parties have in relation to the game. Binmore, Rubinstein, and Wolinsky (1986) is a seminal paper on how the Nash bargaining concept can be used for economic modeling.[3]

To focus on ideas, we will present the model in the context of wage negotiations, but we will also show that it can be applied to essentially all bilateral bargaining situations that eventually led to an agreement and collaboration. This is important to stress because our model needs not to incorporate or elaborate on the conditions required to reach an agreement, aspects that would be the main concern in a game-theoretic model. What it does is to rationalize and decompose, in a consistent and meaningful manner, already observed equilibrium outcomes.

We also stress that our focus is on bilateral, non-collective negotiations. While this is the norm between firms or between sellers and buyers in many product/services markets, since we will use the labor market as our canvas one could wonder how widespread is such kind of "personal" wage bargaining, that is, the non-unionized/non-trade-association kind. Iregui, Melo, and Ramírez (2014), working with survey data from Colombian firms, report that the bigger the firm the less willing it is to engage in individual wage bargaining with new hires, having instead in place a predefined wage structure. This makes sense because larger organizations require structure to operate, and an internally consistent (and so largely predefined) wage structure manages notions of fairness and reduces frictions on this matter, for which nobody ever agrees (what their wage should be). This implies that for medium sized and smaller firms, wage bargaining is more likely to happen. On the other hand, experience has shown that large firms with structured wage systems tend to define wage *intervals* rather than wage *points*. In this way, an employee is placed in an interval based on certain "objective" characteristics, but their actual wage will depend on bargaining, with the bargaining space delimited by the boundaries of the specific interval. Hall and Krueger (2012) report, again from survey data, that one-third of respondents bargained over pay before accepting the jobs they had during the survey. So individual bargaining, even in the labor market, appears to be widespread enough to merit our attention. We focus on that, and we do not discuss aspects and literature relevant to collective bargaining.

2.1. The Deterministic Setup

For the wage negotiation game, the players are the worker/employee (indexed here by "e") and the firm (indexed by "f"). The employee has a no-agreement payoff, which is their reservation wage, $s_0(e) \equiv \omega_r$. This may reflect unemployment benefits or another job offer that the employee has already secured. The agreement payoff of the employee is the wage $s(e) \equiv \omega$. So the "surplus function" for the employee, that here represents gains over what they would get in case of no-agreement, is

$$S_e \equiv s(e) - s_0(e) = \omega - \omega_r.$$

The no-agreement payoff of the firm is $s_0(f) = b_f \in \mathbf{R}$. Binmore et al. (1986) proposed treating b_f as strictly positive, being the gain for the firm if it were to collaborate with some other worker. But it can also be negative, if, for example, the firm wants to hire for a specific project that will experience delays if the hire is not made immediately, with contractual penalties for the firm. The agreement payoff of the firm is the value it will get from employing the worker minus the wage it will pay them. Denoting the value of the employee's output p (a magnitude that is certain in a deterministic setup), we have the surplus function for the firm,

$$S_f \equiv s(f) - s_0(f) = (p - \omega) - b_f.$$

Note that, reasonably, $p - b_f$ is the "maximum willingness to pay" from the part of the firm. With this setup, Nash proved in his distinctive intuitive and graphical way that the equilibrium would be the arg max of the product $(\omega - \omega_r) \cdot (p - \omega - b_f)$.[4]

But asymmetries may arise. As Binmore et al. (1986, p. 186) write, these asymmetries may come from preferences, disagreement points, and the bargaining procedure; or perhaps there are also asymmetries in the parties' beliefs about some determinants of the environment. Therefore, the model is endowed with a parameter $0 \leq \eta \leq 1$ which in our setting is translated as the "relative bargaining power" of the worker. We assume that $\omega_r < p - b_f$, so that a strictly positive bargaining space exists (for observed agreements, i.e., actual employment contracts, this holds *ipso facto*). Then the Nash bargaining equilibrium wage is obtained as

$$\omega^* : \arg\max(\omega - \omega_r)^{\eta}\left(p - \omega - b_f\right)^{1-\eta}, \; 0 < \eta < 1, \; \omega \in [\omega_r, p - b_f].$$

The solution is

$$\omega^* = \eta(p - b_f) + (1-\eta)\omega_r. \tag{1}$$

The higher η is, the higher the wage will be and this validates the treatment of η as the "relative bargaining power" of the worker side. We turn now to examine what modifications are needed when we introduce uncertainty around the value of the employee's productivity, as well as asymmetric and private information of the worker and the firm.

2.2. Nash Bargaining Under Productivity Uncertainty and Asymmetric Information

Bargaining under incomplete information/uncertainty is of course not a new subject, and it has been extensively studied, especially in a game-theoretic context. Indicatively, we mention Harsanyi and Selten (1972), where uncertainty is about the "type" of each player, and where they obtain a generalized Nash objective function that has a similar structure: it is the product of surpluses per type, raised to their respective probabilities of being the actual type. Ausubel, Cramton, and Deneckere (2002) examine in detail a framework with one-sided incomplete information, using mechanism design.

For our purposes, we now enhance the previous setup with two assumptions – acknowledgments really: first, that the value of the worker's productivity is no longer a certain, deterministic magnitude, neither for the firm nor for the worker. This requires that the parties form expectations about the value of this future output, and expectations are based on information: our second assumption is that the two parties do not have the same information set. There are common elements, information known to both, but also, each party holds private information, so we have an asymmetric information environment. We define the information sets $I_f \neq I_e$, $I_c \equiv I_f \cap I_e \neq \varnothing$. It follows that, except in unlikely situations, we will have $E\left(p \mid I_f\right) \neq E\left(p \mid I_e\right) \neq E\left(p \mid I_c\right)$, where we adopt the conditional expectation as our chosen predictor.

It may appear that the only thing we have to do is to modify the equilibrium wage expression in the deterministic setup, eq. (1), by substituting $E\left(p \mid I_f\right)$ for the deterministic p. The argument in favor of such an approach is that the presence of p in the deterministic setup relates to the gains of the firm only, and it is natural to redefine the "maximum willingness to pay" of the firm in this uncertain environment as its expectation about the net value of the worker's output minus the no-agreement payoff. According to this view, the equilibrium wage would be

$$\omega^* = \eta\left[E\left(p \mid I_f\right) - b_f\right] + (1-\eta)\omega_r.$$

But this is unsatisfactory and problematic in many ways. Looking at it as a possible base for econometric estimation, it has the following issues: first, over a sample of observed wage agreements the relative bargaining power η should realistically be treated as a variable, not as a constant, reflecting different bargaining power per worker. Since η enters multiplicatively, its variability will contaminate whatever expressions we may use to approximate $E\left(p \mid I_f\right)$ and ω_r, leaving essentially no hope of estimating marginal effects over the available sample, especially if it is cross-sectional. Second, the information set in the conditional expected value is the full information set of the firm, including private information, which will not be available to the econometrician as data. This intensifies the "omitted-variable" bias that is always a threat in applied studies. Third, the no-agreement payoff b_f would be unobservable and unavailable as data, and if it goes into the error term of a regression model multiplied by η, it will make *all* regressors endogenous, leading to inconsistent estimation.

These would be our problems to solve, not the real world's, but, thankfully, the above formulation is also unsatisfactory as regards its conceptual relation to the actual situation that it attempts to model: the expectations of the worker as regards their own productivity do not appear, and this does not align with real-world experience that tells us that people bargain over their wage based not only on their fall-back option, the reservation wage ω_r, but also on how they perceive their own "value in economic terms." The information set of the worker enters the picture only as the determinant of their reservation wage. Moreover, the above formulation does not take into account how the surplus functions of the two parties change during the negotiation process, and how they look at the point of agreement/equilibrium, which is the point for which we will have data.

It follows that in an environment with uncertain worker productivity and asymmetric information, we must go beyond substituting conditional expected values for previously deterministic variables in order to arrive at a conceptually satisfactory model for wage determination in a bilateral bargaining setting.

2.2.1. The Surplus Functions of the Parties During the Negotiation Process and the Modified Nash Bargaining Solution

Assume that we are in the process of wage bargaining *that will eventually turn into a realized match*, as is always the case when we look ex post at wage-related data sets. The firm makes some specific offer to the worker, denoted as ω_f^o. Since we look at realized matches, we can picture a notional sequence of such offers converging to the equilibrium point (and converging monotonically, since in such situations concessions to the other party are not reversed). Since the feasible space is constrained by the initial reservation wage of the worker, ω_r, and so the equilibrium wage will be higher than that, it follows that eventually some element of the sequence of the firm's offers, say the aforementioned ω_f^o, is above ω_r, $\omega_f^o > \omega_r$. If we freeze momentarily the process at this point, we realize that the options of the worker now are *not* "don't agree and get the fall-back payoff ω_r, or continue bargaining," but "agree now-get payoff ω_f^o, or continue bargaining." Since $\omega_f^o > \omega_r$, *their reservation wage has become the firm's offer*. Therefore, the, relevant to the moment, surplus function changes into

$$S_e^{\eta} = \left(\omega - \omega_f^o\right)^{\eta}.$$

The worker is now in a better position because the interval $[\omega_r, \omega_f^o)$ no longer belongs to the outcome space, and they can continue the effort to improve their position, since the higher the wage above the firm's current offer, the higher the gains for the worker. Note that the value of the possible "surplus extraction" tends to be *reduced*, exactly because the "reservation wage" is now higher. But this represents a benefit to the worker because what previously was uncertain surplus has now become certain payoff. Essentially we follow here the thoughtful remark of Hall and Milgrom (2008, p. 1654) who write:

> In the alternating offer wage-bargaining environment, so long as reaching an agreement creates value, a bargainer who gets a poor offer continues to bargain, because that choice has a strictly higher payoff than taking the outside option. Threats to exercise the outside option simply are not credible.

The "outside option" being the "no-agreement" situation in our case.[5]

Consider now a sequence of counteroffers by the worker. For realized hires, an element of this sequence, ω_e^o, will eventually be below the firm's maximum willingness to pay $E\left(p|I_f\right) - b_f$ so we will have

$$E\left(p \mid I_f\right) - \omega_e^o > b_f.$$

At this point, the options of the firm are no longer "don't agree and get payoff b_f, or continue bargaining." Instead they have become "agree now – get expected payoff $E\left(p \mid I_f\right) - \omega_e^o$, or continue bargaining." As in the case of the worker, the firm finds itself in a better position compared to the beginning of the game, since the no-agreement payoff b_f, like the reservation wage before, has been dominated out of the game. The firm's surplus function is now

$$S_f^{1-\eta} = \left(\left[E\left(p \mid I_f\right) - \omega\right] - \left[E\left(p \mid I_f\right) - \omega_e^o\right]\right)^{1-\eta} = \left(\omega_e^o - \omega\right)^{1-\eta}.$$

The firm is in a better position because the interval $[\omega_e^o, E\left(p \mid I_f\right)]$ no longer belongs to the outcome space. Moreover, it can continue the attempt to improve its position, since the lower the wage compared to the worker's current demands, the higher the gains for the firm. As with the case of the worker, the firm has now secured payoff $E\left(p \mid I_f\right) - \omega_e^o$ that is greater than its original no-agreement payoff b_f.

Note how these new surplus functions reflect the interaction between the parties: the gain for the worker S_e^{η} depends now on the distance of the wage ω from the firm's offer, and the gain of the firm $S_f^{1-\eta}$ depends on the distance of the wage from the worker's demands. This already is a substantial improvement over the previous model, where the surplus functions of each party depended each on their own unilateral information and expectations. But the above analysis points toward a sequential, dynamic game for which we will have no data. For Hall and Milgrom (2008), this is equivalent to abandoning the Nash bargaining framework and replacing it with a "noncooperative alternating offer model." While strictly speaking this is correct, they also write (p. 1653) "Once a qualified worker meets an employer, a threat to walk away, permanently terminating the bargain, is not credible." This is exactly what will allow us to maintain the structure of the Nash bargaining solution, albeit modified as regards the factors that express and quantify it.

First, we stress again that we build a model not to explore theoretically the factors and the conditions under which an agreement will be reached, but to meaningfully estimate and interpret the results from a data sample that represents realized matches of employer and worker. We already know that the parties have reached an agreement; our aim is to reveal ex post how was the wage determined and why it was at the level observed, not how the collaboration was achieved. Therefore, all the intricacies present in a formal modeling of a dynamic-sequential game, related to aspects such as discount factors, time between counteroffers, risk of breakdown, etc., need not concern us.

In addition, we can take into consideration the fact that, while wage offers and counteroffers may form a sequence of "tactical positions" of the parties, *they are realizations of a rationally formed strategy*, that guides them in the negotiation process. This aspect is validated because every offer made has the possibility of being accepted by the other party, and so it automatically represents a *credible commitment* of the party that makes it. Therefore, under a hypothesis of rationality, it has to be linked to some general, pivotal strategy of the party that makes the offer.

Moreover, the belief that target-setting improves outcomes has become a world-wide mantra, while, more seriously, it has also been documented scientifically (see, e.g., Huber & Neale, 1987; Northcraft, Neale, & Early, 1994, but also the summary of decades of research in Locke & Latham, 2002).

Finally, as an "approximation" argument, at least for the labor market, we invoke also the observed reality that the rounds of offers and counteroffers in individual bilateral wage bargaining usually are not numerous. For example, Lombera (2007) documents a tendency from the part of the workers to not even negotiate but accept the firm's first offer. Hall and Milgrom (2008) write:

> the parties do not actually spend any time bargaining. They think through the consequences of a sequence of offers and counteroffers and then move immediately to an agreement at the unique subgame perfect equilibrium of the bargaining game. They do not waste time and resources haggling over the wage.

In practice, they do "waste" time, but only a little.

All the above allow us to represent the sequence of surplus functions with a single one, where now the payoffs do not depend on any single offer during the process but on the aforementioned pivotal strategy, which we can simply call the "wage-target" of each party in the negotiation. Importantly, note that these targets do not necessarily coincide with the outcome, the agreed-upon wage. Denoting them as (ω_e^T, ω_f^T) we have that the target-based Nash bargaining solution is characterized by

$$\omega^* : \arg\max\left(\omega - \omega_f^T\right)^{\eta}\left(\omega_e^T - \omega\right)^{1-\eta},\ 0 < \eta < 1,\ \omega \in \left[\omega_f^T, \omega_e^T\right],$$

and it is

$$\omega^* = \eta\omega_e^T + (1-\eta)\omega_f^T. \tag{2}$$

We note that the Nash bargaining equilibrium concept is inherently a static one, formulated from a technical point of view as the solution to a game in normal form. It describes the situation before the game starts, and then it provides the solution. What we do here, by the use of our "pivotal" factors, the wage-targets, is to compact the dynamics of the strategic bargaining sequential extensive-game analysis of the model with offers, counteroffers, and tactical positions, into the static axiomatic framework of Nash bargaining. Apart from the reasons given earlier for such a transformation, this is legitimate also because we work with situations where the employer–worker match has happened, so we already know that any sequential procedure has converged to an equilibrium point.

What remains now is to formulate consistent and implementable expressions for ω_e^T and ω_f^T.

2.2.2. The Common-information Expectation, and the Target Wages of the Worker and the Firm

Since targets are rationally formed, they will depend on the information possessed by each party. We argued earlier that the intersection of the two information sets $I_c \equiv \{I_f \cap I_e\}$ is not empty: it contains characteristics (of the worker, of the firm, of the socioeconomic environment) that are commonly used to assess/predict the output of a worker. Then, the conditional expectation $E(p \mid I_c)$ is a magnitude that is obtained based only on shared information. It is a "common-information" magnitude, an expected value based on an information set that deliberately excludes all information that is not known to both parties. Typical elements of this information set are worker characteristics such as gender, age, education, professional experience, as well as publicly available information about the firm and the market conditions. The conditional expectation $E(p \mid I_c)$ forms a common base for the two parties. It can be considered a mutually accepted base because it helps keep expectations and target-setting in a reasonable range, increasing the chances of reaching an agreement. After all, the bargaining parties came in communication with the intent to strike a deal. But even if we wanted to challenge that such a base is "mutually accepted," alleging a more adversarial environment in wage negotiations, the concept remains valid as a notional device to separate those elements of the model that are known to both parties (and to the researcher), from those that are privy to each party, and unobservable for the researcher.

This productivity predictor will most likely change during the negotiation process, as information is exchanged and the set of common knowledge is altered. Therefore, when looking at realized matches, we distinguish between the ex ante and the ex post/equilibrium symmetric-information expectation. We assume that such alterations of the common-information set merge into a zero-mean random variable v ("some news increase the expectation, some decrease it"), and we write the *equilibrium* common-information expected productivity as

$$\mu_p(\mathbf{x}, v) \equiv E(p \mid I_c) + v, \quad E(v) = 0,$$

where $\mathbf{x}$ represents compactly the elements in I_c.

While this interpretation of the variable v is plausible and theoretically sound, it is also a fragile one in empirical applications: the possible existence of omitted variables will contaminate v. On top of that, in a regression setting, we expect that $E(p \mid I_c)$ will be formulated as a linear function of the vector $\mathbf{x}$, likely becoming an approximation to the actual conditional expectation, resulting in approximation errors to reside in v. Then, we will no longer be able to treat its effect on the outcome as being strictly the effect of learning during the negotiation.

We turn now to obtain an explicit expression for the wage-target of the worker, ω_e^T. The following statement is a very realistic one, and also critically unsuitable for our model: "My wage-target is ω', but I need the job so I may ask for less in the process to secure the job." The problem is that this statement mixes the wage-target with its adjustment due to the bargaining power of the worker. The worker faces an external financial constraint; they need the job and the income; hence they are prepared to "compromise," and so they may eventually adjust downwards their target wage. Perfectly rational, but incompatible with our formulation because in eq. (2) *we have kept the bargaining power and the wage-target separate*. So, in our setup, the wage-target is set without regard for the relative bargaining power (or "conditional on $\eta = 1$"), and then the actual value of the latter enters explicitly in the solution expression to co-determine the equilibrium wage. It follows that in considering how to define the wage-target, we should ignore any factors that reduce the bargaining power of the worker.[6]

We now ask, what is the target wage that the worker is after, ω_e^T? It *cannot* just be $E(p \mid I_c)$ because it does not use all the (relevant) information set of the worker. Moreover, we argue that individuals, being individuals, take the individualistic approach: "I am not just these characteristics. I am *more* than that." So one force that increases the wage-target above the common-information expected product is private information on the worker's productivity. Moreover, *beneficial particulars* to the time and place can affect the worker's target wage, like for example a tip that the firm's payroll policy is "generous" or that the firm is pressed to hire fast because of rising demand. These are strategic elements that if known to the worker should rationally tend to increase their wage-target.

In contrast, any detrimental specifics that could force the worker to accept a "low" wage (e.g., a pressing need for cash inflows in light of existing financial commitments) should not affect, in our model, their target wage, but rather, their relative bargaining power, as already discussed. So the wage-target is increased above the common-information expected productivity by all the things that could *increase* the wage above $E(p \mid I_c)$, not decrease it.[7] We capture all these in a non-negative random variable $g \geq 0$, which we will call the *self-evaluation premium*, or more generally, the "own-evaluation premium" to cover other bargaining situations. Moreover, we are interested in the ex post target wage, the target that was when the wage was agreed, so we use the equilibrium common-information expected output $\mu_p(\mathbf{x}, v)$ and we arrive at the worker's equilibrium target wage,

$$\omega_e^T \equiv \mu_p(\mathbf{x}, v) + g = E(p \mid I_c) + v + g,\ g \geq 0. \tag{3}$$

Firms, on the other hand, have sometimes disappointing experiences from how capable individuals may not succeed in being productive in collaborative environments due to organizational inefficiencies, personality and cultural clashes, and lack of guidance and direction: the reasons why internally occurring inefficiency exists in businesses in the first place. Such situations are more frequent than pleasant efficiency surprises, probably because of the fundamental entropic asymmetry that makes collaboration harder than non-collaboration. So we argue that firms tend to systematically discount $E(p \mid I_c)$, when formulating their target wage ("it always looks better than it actually proves to be"). A firm could call that figuratively "an insurance policy," we will call it the *prudential discount.* As a further indication of this systematic discount, we note the not-infrequent use of "fixed/variable pay" or "fixed pay plus bonus" schemes by firms, which is a way to offset the consequences of a possibly unsuccessful match while at the same time accommodating the "I am more than that" stance of the worker ("prove it and you will be rewarded," is the firm's answer). Moreover, certain current situations (external or internal) that the firm knows privately may affect what the firm can expect from the match (like an imminent re-organization that will initially cost in terms of efficiency). This discount persists even as the common-knowledge expected productivity is altered because it does not depend on the specific characteristics of the worker, it is a form of "statistical bias," a guard against Knightian uncertainty, not against quantifiable risk. Analogously with the worker, here we have the equilibrium target wage of the firm,

$$\omega_f^T \equiv \mu_p(\mathbf{x}, v) - d = E(p \mid I_c) + v - d, \quad d \geq 0. \tag{4}$$

The variable $d \geq 0$ is the "prudential discount" component. In reverse analogy to the worker side, and for the same fundamental reason, d captures only those elements that tend to decrease the target wage of the firm, and not specifics that may force the firm to accept a higher wage. To use the same example as before, if the firm is pressed to hire fast for some reason, this will affect the firm's bargaining power, while, if known to the worker, it will affect their target-wage, as we have said. So keeping the relative bargaining power as a separate factor in the model, allows us to view g and d, the self-evaluation premium and the prudential discount, as non-negative, which is crucial for what follows.

2.2.3. The Nash Bargaining Solution
Inserting the expressions for the target wages, eqs. (3) and (4) into the Nash bargaining solution (2) we obtain

$$\omega^* = \eta\left[E(p \mid I_c) + v + g\right] + (1-\eta)\left[E(p \mid I_c) + v - d\right]$$
$$\Rightarrow \omega^* = E(p \mid I_c) + [v + \eta g - (1-\eta)d]. \tag{5}$$

We have managed to decompose the equilibrium wage into two parts: the one is $E(p \mid I_c)$, the ex ante, initial common-information part of the wage, on which we expect that we will have data. The other component, in brackets, contains all the unobservables: The term v captures shifts in the symmetric-information expected productivity during negotiations, and other unobserved elements. The term tending to increase the equilibrium wage, ηg, is the self-evaluation premium of the worker weighted by the worker's relative bargaining power. That product can be labeled the "bargaining *performance*" of the worker. The term $(1-\eta)d$ that tends to decrease the wage (due to the negative sign) is the prudential discount by the firm, weighted by its own relative bargaining power. Correspondingly, this term can be labeled the "bargaining performance" of the firm.

Equation (5) represents a rich combination of actual aspects of economic transactions with bargaining: there is a common ground of rational thinking, $E(p|I_c)$; there are the "subjective views of the world" of the two parties through the terms g and d; and there is the allocation of bargaining power between them, $(\eta, 1-\eta)$ that reflects their constraints under which they operate, constraints that force them to accept an outcome less than "their wish," yet another instance of the Aristotelian distinction between will and choice.

Note that the equilibrium wage will not in general equal the equilibrium common-information expected productivity $E(p \mid I_c) + v$ because the one-sided components will not, in general, be equal. And the higher the self-evaluation premium of the worker the higher the agreed wage, while the higher the prudential discount by the firm the lower the agreed wage. This conforms with the real-world observation that such subjective elements do matter in an economic negotiation, in addition to the allocation of bargaining power, which has a more objective flavor: in fact eq. (5) tells us that, regarding the worker, for example, a low bargaining power (low η) can be mitigated by a higher self-evaluation premium (higher g), which we can picture as a situation where the workers actively promote themselves in the negotiations, showing self-confidence and belief in their abilities, productivity, and prospects with the firm, even though they are, say, young workers with little to show in terms of accomplishments. It follows that any deviation of the equilibrium wage above or below $E(p|I_c)$ is not just "surplus extraction due to bargaining power": it is a mixed effect of the allocation of bargaining power and of how the parties conduct themselves in the negotiations, and this is why (net) "bargaining performance" is an appropriate label for such deviations. Finally, as already noted, the existence of an agreed wage does not imply that at the time of agreement, targets coincide with it: agents can very consciously agree to a wage level as long as it does not violate their fall-back option, even though they would want for the agreement to be more in their favor. Still, they agree because they recognize the limits of their bargaining power and the constraints they face.

Contrast our model with the core model in Abowd, Kramarz, and Margolis (1999): there the authors specified "pure person" and "pure firm" effects on earnings. These represented unobservable heterogeneity/individual effects, and the fundamental purpose of their study was to estimate both. One of the main purposes of our work here was to give these effects a plausible and specific behavioral and situational content, apart from estimating their magnitude: they exist due to private information and rational self-interest, and they are shaped also by bargaining power.

We close the construction of the 2TSF Nash bargaining model by returning to the origin in response to which it arose: the 2TSF wage bargaining model of Kumbhakar and Parmeter (2009). Comparing our eq. (5) with their eq. (4), we see that their "expected productivity" observable term is largely identical to our "common-information expectation." The critical difference lies in how the composed error term is represented. There, in place of the self-evaluation premium g they have the "worker surplus," expressed as the positive difference between the firm's maximum wage offer and the expected productivity of the worker, while in place of our prudential discount d they have the "surplus of the firm," expressed as the difference between the worker's expected productivity and their reservation wage.

We detect the following issues with their formulation: there is a conceptual one, in that they distinguish between the expected productivity of the worker, and the firm's maximum wage offer. But this maximum wage offer could be *higher* than the expected productivity of the worker, only if the firm faces *immediate direct costs* if the position is left empty. It is not very often that firms face such emergency pressure coupled with lack of alternatives, so in most applied cases, the maximum wage offer should be equal to the expected productivity, for most if not all firms in the sample. But then their model stops having the two-tier structure, since the positive component of their composed error term becomes zero. There is also a statistical issue because one needs to assume that these surpluses are independent from the expected productivity (but which participates in their formulation), in order to avoid full-blown endogeneity in the model.

2.3. Applicability in Other Bargaining Situations

In order for our bilateral Nash bargaining framework to be conceptually applicable in other situations, the real-world phenomenon under study must have the following four characteristics:

(1) Asymmetric and heterogeneous information.
(2) Formulation of guiding targets by the negotiating parties.
(3) Systematic mark-up from the seller (own-evaluation premium) and systematic discount from the buyer (prudential discount), pivoting off the common-information expected value.
(4) Uncertainty about the total gain over which bargaining takes place.

Properties 1 and 2 exist in almost all cases of bargaining. Property 3 is also observed, either as an "honest" position of each party or just as a bargaining tactic (which links the axiomatic and strategic bargaining approaches). Such tactics are the oldest trick in the book, almost an obligatory ritual in flea-market transactions, and still widely used around the world in all sorts of trades. Property 4 is more subtle but it is expected to hold. It can reflect genuine uncertainty linked to the future, but it may also reflect diverging assessments of the potential gain due to informational heterogeneity, free of the time-aspect. It can also represent Stackelberg-leader thinking, where each party assesses the value that the other party assigns to the object of negotiation. So the applicability of the model becomes almost universal, not just as a measure but also as an interpretational tool.

We turn now to the task of transforming eq. (5) into an econometric model.

2.4. The Two-tier Bilateral Nash Bargaining Stochastic Frontier Model

Accommodating standard (but not universal) empirical practice, we now look at our equilibrium relation in logarithmic terms,

$$\ln \omega^* = \ln\left[E(p \mid I_c)\right] + v + \eta g - (1-\eta)d.$$

We show in the Appendix how we can formally arrive at this formulation that essentially changes the reference scale of the components of the composite error. Approximating the conditional expectation with a linear function of available covariates **x**, and applying familiar econometric regression notation, while assuming the existence of an i.i.d. cross-sectional sample of size $i = 1,\dots,n$, the model can be written as

$$\begin{aligned} &y_i = \mathbf{x}'_i\beta + \varepsilon_i, \\ &y_i = \ln \omega_i,\ \mathbf{x}'_i\beta = \ln\left[E(p_i \mid I_{c,i})\right],\ \varepsilon_i = v_i + w_i - u_i, \\ &w_i = \eta_i g_i,\ u_i = (1-\eta_i)d_i,\ E(v_i) = 0,\ w_i \geq 0,\ u_i \geq 0. \end{aligned} \tag{6}$$

This model has the 2TSF structure. It is important at this point to stress that the observable component of the regression $\mathbf{x}'_i\beta$ *must* contain variables that characterize both sides of the transaction, since it attempts to reflect an expectation based on the intersection of the individual information sets of the parties. For the case of a wage regression therefore, this model can be properly estimated only if we have a MEEDS available.[8] If we attempt to specify a typical "earnings" equation, we will not really be estimating $E(p \mid I_c)$ but some other conditional expected value. That this was the case for decades, where econometrics estimated earnings equations of the Mincerian variety, has mostly to do with the unavailability of MEEDS, which Rosen (1986) called "critical for precise measurement" while lamenting their absence. But worker's productivity does have a strong effect on earnings, and its level depends on the other factors of production as well as on the micro-environment of the firm and the market into which it operates.[9] As put simply by Jensen (2010, p. 210), "to ignore the effects of the one would be to overstate the effects of the other." His paper includes also an overview of available MEEDS, an availability that keeps growing. For our case, leaving the firm characteristics in the error term will generally contaminate the estimates and the interpretation of the latent effects that we have modeled.

3. STATISTICAL SPECIFICATION I: INTRA-ERROR DEPENDENCE AND REGRESSOR ENDOGENEITY

We have modeled the relative bargaining power of the workers η_i as a random variable, whose realization may differ from worker to worker. This creates intra-error dependence, since w_i and u_i will be correlated. Based on what these components represent, we may assume that η_i itself is independent of g_i, d_i.[10] Then, using μ to denote the mean, we have

$$\begin{aligned}\mathrm{Cov}(w,u) &= E[\eta g(1-\eta)d] - E[\eta g]E[(1-\eta)d] \\ &= E[\eta(1-\eta)]\mu_g\mu_d - E(\eta)E(1-\eta)\mu_g\mu_d \\ &= \mathrm{Cov}(\eta, 1-\eta)\mu_g\mu_d,\end{aligned}$$

while

$$\mathrm{Cov}(\eta, 1-\eta) = E(\eta - \eta^2) - E(\eta)E(1-\eta) = -\sigma_\eta^2 < 0.$$

The model incorporates a negative correlation between w_i and u_i, which is a testable prediction or at least it can become a diagnostic tool. The existence of intra-error dependence should be reflected in the statistical specification of the error term.

3.1. The 2TSF Bivariate Truncated Normal Specification

For the composite error term $\varepsilon = v + w - u$, we will use the 2TSF bivariate truncated Normal specification of Papadopoulos, Parmeter, and Kumbhakar (2021), abbreviated to 2TSF-BTN or just BTN. Here, the dependence between the terms w, u is represented by assuming that they follow jointly a bivariate Normal distribution truncated from below zero,

$$(w,u) \sim \text{i.i.d.} N_+(\mathbf{0}, D), \qquad D = \begin{bmatrix} \sigma_w^2 & \rho\sigma_w\sigma_u \\ \rho\sigma_w\sigma_u & \sigma_u^2 \end{bmatrix}.$$

The parameters σ_w, σ_u, ρ, are the standard deviations and the correlation coefficient of the underlying full-support Normals. The marginal distributions corresponding to this joint distribution are truncated Skew Normal, studied by Jamalizadeh, Pourmousa, and Balakrishnan (2009). The marginal density, say for w, is

$$f(w) = \frac{2\pi}{\cos^{-1}(-\rho)} \frac{1}{\sigma_w} \phi(w/\sigma_w) \Phi\left(\frac{\rho}{\sqrt{1-\rho^2}} (w/\sigma_w) \right), \quad w \geq 0. \tag{7}$$

Here 'ϕ' represents the standard Normal density while 'Φ' the standard Normal distribution function. For u, we just have to change the symbol. When $\rho < 0$, the density is monotonically decreasing with its mode at zero. The mean and variance are

$$E(w) = \frac{(\pi/2)(1+\rho)}{\cos^{-1}(-\rho)} \sqrt{\frac{2}{\pi}} \sigma_w, \quad \mathrm{Var}(w) = \left[1 + \frac{\rho\sqrt{1-\rho^2}}{\cos^{-1}(-\rho)} - \frac{(\pi/2)(1+\rho)^2}{(\cos^{-1}(-\rho))^2} \right] \sigma_w^2. \tag{8}$$

Their covariance and correlation coefficient are

$$\mathrm{Cov}(u,w)=\frac{\cos^{-1}(-\rho)\left[\rho\cos^{-1}(-\rho)+\sqrt{1-\rho^2}\right]-(\pi/2)(1+\rho)^2}{\left[\cos^{-1}(-\rho)\right]^2}\sigma_u\sigma_w, \tag{9}$$

$$\mathrm{corr}(w,u)=\frac{\cos^{-1}(-\rho)\left[\rho\cos^{-1}(-\rho)+\sqrt{1-\rho^2}\right]-(\pi/2)(1+\rho)^2}{\cos^{-1}(-\rho)\left[\cos^{-1}(-\rho)+\rho\sqrt{1-\rho^2}\right]-(\pi/2)(1+\rho)^2}. \tag{10}$$

From this expression, we can deduce the range of $\mathrm{corr}(w,u)$: as $\rho\to 1$ it also tends to unity, while as $\rho\to -1$ we obtain $\mathrm{corr}(w,u)\approx -0.217$. This is the maximum negative correlation that the BTN distribution can accommodate. A restricted interval as regards negative correlation is to be expected, since, as Moran (1967) has shown, Pearson's correlation coefficient of two non-negative random variables cannot reach its theoretical lower limit of -1.

The distributional specification for the composite error is completed by assuming that the v component follows a zero-mean Normal distribution, $v\sim N(0,\sigma_v^2)$. Then, the density of the composite error term is given by the authors as

$$f_\varepsilon(\varepsilon)=\frac{2\pi}{\cos^{-1}(-\rho)}\frac{1}{\sigma_\varepsilon}\phi(\varepsilon/\sigma_\varepsilon)\cdot\Phi_2\left(a_w\varepsilon,-a_u\varepsilon;\ r\right). \tag{11}$$

We use $\Phi_2(,\ ;\ \delta)$ for the bivariate standard Normal distribution function with correlation coefficient δ.

The primal parameters of the error term are $\sigma_v,\sigma_w,\sigma_u,\rho$, with the shorthands

$$\sigma_\varepsilon^2=\sigma_v^2+\sigma_u^2+\sigma_w^2-2\rho\sigma_u\sigma_w,\quad r=\frac{\rho\sigma_v^2+(1-\rho^2)\sigma_u\sigma_w}{\psi_u\psi_w},$$

$$\psi_u^2=\sigma_v^2+(1-\rho^2)\sigma_u^2,\quad \psi_w^2=\sigma_v^2+(1-\rho^2)\sigma_w^2,\quad a_w=\frac{\rho\sigma_w-\sigma_u}{\sigma_\varepsilon\psi_w},\quad a_u=\frac{\rho\sigma_u-\sigma_w}{\sigma_\varepsilon\psi_u}.$$

3.2. Handling Regressor Endogeneity Through Copulas

The realities of empirical research can induce endogeneity due to correlation, if a regressor known to usually be "common knowledge" in the transaction under study is not available to the researcher as data, and it is thought to be correlated with the available regressors. Another reason to fear endogeneity is the fact that each private information term, *g* and correspondingly *d*, may be correlated with the regressors. For example, the usually observable "Age" may be correlated with the self-evaluation premium *g*, since the higher the age of the worker the more details and accomplishments of their professional past may have been excluded from their resumé, which will then increase the self-evaluation premium. Correspondingly a firm's size may be negatively correlated with the prudential discount *d* because larger firms tend to have more robust systems of input collaboration in place, fearing less any unknown idiosyncrasies of each individual worker. Other reasons to expect endogeneity is the existence of structural unobservables with which regressors correlate, like for example "Education" with the latent "Ability" or the use of imperfect proxies like "Potential Experience" in place of actual experience. Finally, since the component v also represents changes in the information set $\{I_c\}$ during the negotiations, it may be correlated with the regressors.

Given the many different sources of possible endogeneity, it is doubtful whether an Instrumental Variables (IV) approach could cover all possibilities. Therefore we will use a copula-based method. Specifically, we will use the Gaussian copula, as has been proposed by Tran and Tsionas (2015) and developed in detail by Papadopoulos (2022), where the reader is directed for the foundations and all the particulars of the approach. The use of copulas to model regressor endogeneity has another advantage over IV estimation: apart from not needing instruments, we can formally test for endogeneity jointly with the estimation procedure. In principle, in this approach all regressors can be treated as potentially endogenous, continuous, or discrete. In the empirical application that will follow, we will treat two regressors as potentially endogenous, and one of them will be found to behave like a discrete random variable. So we narrow our presentation here to these specifics.

Let F_ε be the distribution function of the composite error term, θ the related vector of parameters, and F_j the distribution function of the j-th endogenous regressor. Let

$$\mathbf{q}_i = \left(\Phi^{-1}\left(\tilde{x}_{1i}\right), \Phi^{-1}\left(\tilde{x}_{2i}\right), \Phi^{-1}\left(F_\varepsilon\left(y_i - \mathbf{x}_i{}'\beta;\theta\right)\right)\right)',$$

where

$$\tilde{x}_{ji} \equiv \hat{F}_j\left(x_{ji}\right) = \frac{1}{n+1}\sum_{k=1}^{n} I\left\{x_{jk} \leq x_{ji}\right\},\ i = 1,\ \ldots,\ n,\ j = 1,2.$$

Namely, it is the value of the empirical distribution function at each point in the sample. Finally, define the correlation matrix

$$R = \begin{bmatrix} 1 & \hat{\rho}_{12} & \rho_{1\varepsilon} \\ \hat{\rho}_{12} & 1 & \rho_{2\varepsilon} \\ \rho_{1\varepsilon} & \rho_{2\varepsilon} & 1 \end{bmatrix},$$

where $\hat{\rho}_{ji} = \operatorname{corr}\left(\Phi^{-1}\left(\tilde{x}_j\right), \Phi^{-1}\left(\tilde{x}_i\right)\right)$. This correlation coefficient between the regressors can be estimated from the sample and be treated as a fixed number, during maximum likelihood estimation (MLE) of the (θ, β) parameters and of the unknown correlation coefficients $\rho_{j\varepsilon} = \operatorname{corr}\left(\Phi^{-1}\left(\tilde{x}_j\right), \Phi^{-1}\left(F_\varepsilon(\varepsilon)\right)\right)$.

In our application, one of the endogenous variables will have to be treated as discrete, say x_1. Let its *empirically observed* support be the increasing-ordered finite set $\{d_1, \ldots, d_j, \ldots d_L\}$, and let K_3 be the kernel of the trivariate standard Normal density,

$$K_{3,i}\left(x_{1i}^*, x_{2i}^*, \varepsilon_i^*; R\right) = \exp\left\{-\frac{1}{2}\mathbf{q}_i{}'(R)^{-1}\mathbf{q}_i\right\},$$

where $x_{1i}^{*} = \Phi^{-1}(\hat{F}_1(x_{1i}))$ and likewise for the other variables. We show in the Appendix that in such a case, the log-likelihood is (for observation *i*, and without its constants or terms that do not include parameters of interest),

$$\ell_i = -\frac{1}{2}\ln\det\left(\breve{R}\right) + \frac{1}{2}\left[\Phi^{-1}\left(F_{\varepsilon}\left(y_i - \mathbf{x}_i{}'\beta;\theta\right)\right)\right]^2 + \ln\left(\int_{x_{1i}^{*}(d_{j-1})}^{x_{1i}^{*}(d_j)} K_{3,i}\left(s, x_{2i}^{*}, \varepsilon_i^{*}; \breve{R}\right) ds\right) + \ln f_{\varepsilon}\left(y_i - \mathbf{x}_i{}'\beta;\theta\right). \quad (12)$$

The term $x_{1i}^{*}(d_{j-1}) = \Phi^{-1}(\hat{F}_1(d_{j-1}))$ is the transformed variable evaluated at that value in the empirical range of F_1 that is immediately smaller than the value associated with x_{1i}^{*}. This has nothing to do with lags. For example, suppose that in the empirical support of the variable x_1 we observe the (ordered) values $\{\ldots,2.5,3,\ldots\}$. No value is observed between 2.5 and 3. If for the *i*th observation, we have $x_{1i} = 3 = d_j$ and so $x_{1i}^{*}(d_j) = \Phi^{-1}(\hat{F}_1(3))$, then the immediately smaller value in the observed support is $d_{j-1} = 2.5$, and we will have $x_{1i}^{*}(d_{j-1}) = \Phi^{-1}(\hat{F}_1(2.5))$.

With an i.i.d. sample, summing over the observation index gives the log-likelihood of the sample. This likelihood contains two integrals that require numerical integration, the second being the distribution function F_{ε} of the composite error term, which is not available in closed form, while the density f_{ε} is eq. (11). The Appendix contains some related technical notes.

The MLE with the copula-likelihood has all the desirable properties of an MLE, like consistency and asymptotic efficiency, subject to the standard set of regularity conditions. We are now ready to put the model to work with a MEEDS.

3.3. Empirical Application: Zambia Wages in the Early 1990s

We will implement the model using part of a MEEDS that has been originally used in Bigsten et al. (2000).[11] The purpose of their study was to examine the rates of return on physical and human capital in Africa's manufacturing sector. The data were collected in three survey waves from the early 1990s and came from five African countries. We will use the data related to Zambia that refer to the years 1993–1995. For Zambia, the full sample size was 2,477 observations, but the number of observations with no missing data for all covariates deemed relevant for our purposes was 1,545 and this is our sample size. Its composition as regards the number of employees and firms per survey wave is presented in Table 15.1.

Table 15.1. Composition of the Zambia Sample.

Wave	Number of Firms	No. of Employees (Observations)	Distribution of Firm Sizes (%)			
			Up To 10	11–50	51–250	>250
1 (1993)	144	698	14.2	33.5	40.5	11.7
2 (1994)	106	492	15.7	37.8	36.2	10.4
3 (1995)	85	355	14.1	42.5	23.9	19.4
	Sample size	1,545	14.6	37.0	35.3	13.1

From all firms, 1–10 employees were surveyed, with a single exception in wave 3 that had 19 employees surveyed. "Distribution of firm-sizes" is based on number of employed, but relative frequencies are based on counts of all observations as unique. This is because we are specifically interested in the relative frequencies of wage negotiations taking place in different firm-sizes. There is some variability across survey waves.

We pooled the data and used a linear trend $t = 0, 1, 2$, to capture the possible time-effect. The dependent variable is the log of monthly earnings (basic wages plus allowances) expressed in US-PPP dollars as calculated in the original study. Descriptive statistics of the dependent variable and the explanatory variables are presented in Table 15.2.

Except for the covariates appearing in Table 15.2, the regression specification included also a constant term and the time trend mentioned earlier, as well as the squares of the variables Tenure and Education, to capture a possibly non-linear relation. We will treat as potentially endogenous two variables: Education, to acknowledge its possible correlation with the unobservable "Ability," and "Potential Experience," since it is by design an inaccurate (specifically, maximal) proxy for actual experience, and so the related measurement error resides in the error term. The estimation results are presented in Table 15.3, where we have also estimates from the simpler 2TSF Normal-Half Normal (NHN) specification of Papadopoulos (2015) that ignores intra-error dependence and regressor endogeneity. We provide either the direct estimates when they are comparable, or computed magnitudes based on them, when they are not. This is the case with the σ_w, σ_u scale parameters that have different roles in the two specifications and their magnitude differs wildly by design. But the resulting mean values for w, u can be meaningfully compared. In brackets we present p-values rather than standard errors. Estimating the variance-covariance (VCV) matrix in the 2TSF-BTN model using clustered standard errors (with the firm ID being the clustering variable), gave largely the same results.

The estimation results show that the two specifications lead to different conclusions in many aspects. Starting from the basic statistics of the residuals, already the differences are visible: the NHN model does not have room for the noise component v estimating its standard deviation σ_v as zero, while the BTN model estimates it as of mediocre strength but existent. While it is not unusual for 2TSF models to have $\sigma_v = 0$, the two models do not agree. The residuals in the BTN model have much larger variance, positive skewness instead of roughly zero, and much lower excess kurtosis (hence fewer outliers). Moreover, the mean value of the self-evaluation premium w and the prudential discount u is visibly lower in the NHN model (although we note that the *ratio* of these two expected values is essentially the same in the two models).

But also for the regression coefficients, we have certain variables whose coefficient or statistical significance changes visibly (most appear in bold letters). With the NHN model, we would likely conclude that male workers do not enjoy a premium due to their sex; not so with the BTN model. The Education variables have unusual signs in their coefficients in both models, and we provide an explanation in the next sub-section. Being in the wood industry sector as well as working in

Table 15.2. Descriptive Statistics.

Type	Label	Description	Mean	S.D.	Min	Max
Dep var	LMEARNPP	Log monthly earnings in US PPP dollars	4.55	0.97	−1.88	10.22
Employee characteristics	MALE	Binary sex dummy (1= male)	0.81	0.39		
	TENURE	Tenure in the firm in years	6.54	6.60	0.00	36.00
	EDUC	Formal Education in years	10.02	3.22	0.00	16.00
	PEXP	Potential Experience (maximum possible)	17.89	10.48	1.00	58.00
	MGMT	Binary hierarchical dummy (1=management)	0.10	0.30		
	SUPER	Binary hierarchical dummy (1=supervisor)	0.13	0.34		
	ADMIN	Binary functional dummy (1=administration)	0.07	0.26		
	SALES	Binary functional dummy (1=sales)	0.14	0.34		
	TECH	Binary functional dummy (1=technician)	0.18	0.38		
Firm characteristics	CAPCITY	Socioeconomic dummy (1 = firm in country's capital)	0.43	0.50		
	WOOD1	Industry sector (1= wood sector)	0.15	0.36		
	TEXTILE1	Industry sector (1= textile and clothing sector)	0.27	0.44		
	METAL1	Industry sector (1= metal and machinery sector)	0.28	0.45		
	ANYFOR	Ownership dummy (1= some foreign equity)	0.18	0.38		
	ANYSTAT	Ownership dummy (1= some state equity)	0.12	0.32		
	LEMP	Log of number of employees	3.86	1.39	0.69	8.01
	LVADEMPPPP	Log of value-added/ employee in US PPP dollars	7.84	1.48	−0.69	11.34
	LCAPEMPPPP	Log of physical capital/employee in US PPP dollars	8.84	1.68	0.11	12.64

Table 15.3. Obtained Estimates.

Regressor	2TSF NHN	2TSF-BTN with Copula	Regressor	2TSF NHN	2TSF-BTN with Copula
MALE	0.0376	0.0714	CAPCITY	0.0950	0.1353
	[0.435]	[0.086]		[0.005]	[0.002]
TENURE	0.0242	0.0275	**WOOD1**	0.1788	0.2949
	[0.001]	[0.032]		[0.001]	[0.000]
TENSQ	−0.0008	−0.0009	TEXTILE1	0.0951	0.1283
	[0.005]	[0.030]		[0.033]	[0.014]
EDUC	−0.0172	−0.1226	METAL1	0.2789	0.2741
	[0.397]	[0.0753]		[0.000]	[0.000]
EDUCSQ	0.0053	−0.0077	ANYFOR	0.1671	0.2192
	[0.000]	[0.040]		[0.000]	[0.000]
PEXP	0.0082	0.0059	ANYSTAT	0.2080	0.2458
	[0.000]	[0.251]		[0.000]	[0.000]
MGMT	0.9023	0.8984	LEMP	0.1235	0.0969
	[0.000]	[0.000]		[0.000]	[0.000]
SUPER	0.2199	0.2630	LVADEMPPPP	0.0851	0.0785
	[0.000]	[0.000]		[0.000]	[0.000]
ADMIN	0.3830	0.4891	**LCAPEMPPPP**	−0.0243	−0.0054
	[0.000]	[0.000]		[0.011]	[0.771]
SALES	0.1644	0.2088	Trend	0.0834	0.0769
	[0.005]	[0.009]		[0.000]	[0.001]
TECH	0.0545	0.1487	Constant	2.1933	4.5732
	[0.245]	[0.420]		[0.000]	[0.000]
σ_ε	0.6485	1.5274	$E(w)$	0.7433	1.3314
Resid. Skew	−0.0396	0.1541	$E(u)$	0.4292	0.7896
Resid. Excess Kurt	15.373	2.4867			
σ_v	0.000	0.3455	Corr(EDUC, ε)	n/a	0.8964
	[1.000]	[0.062]			[0.000]
ρ	n/a	−0.9958	Corr(PEXP, ε)	n/a	−0.2823
		[0.000]			[0.000]

Country: Zambia. Dependent variable: log monthly earnings. Sample size: 1,545. Asymptotic p-values are given in brackets, based on the outer-product matrix for 2TSF-NHN model, and on the sandwich VCV estimator for 2TSF-BTN. Estimates are truncated at the fourth decimal.

administration appear to have stronger effects on the BTN model. Overall, the results validate the anticipation that the wage is affected by the triad "worker–firm–socioeconomic environment."

A way to assess the quality of the 2TSF-BTN model is to examine whether the distributional assumptions made can be accepted. Using the residuals and the estimated parameters we can formally test whether the numerically evaluated distribution function of the error term, that is based on the assumed distributional specification, behaves like a Uniform(0,1) when viewed as a random variable or equivalently whether $\Phi^{-1}\left(F_\varepsilon(\varepsilon)\right)$ is distributed as standard Normal. We implemented the Doornik and Hansen (2008) test using $\hat{F}_\varepsilon(\hat{\varepsilon})$ for the null hypothesis $H_0 : \Phi^{-1}\left(F_\varepsilon(\varepsilon)\right) \sim N(0,1)$. For rejection of the null we obtained a p-value of 0.245, which does not strongly object to the chosen distributional specification.

3.4. Results on Endogeneity and Intra-error Dependence

The correlation coefficients between the endogenous regressors and the error term (both doubly transformed) are non-zero, and high for the Education variable. As Klaassen and Wellner (1997) have shown, these values approximate (in absolute terms) the maximum linear correlation between the original untransformed variables. This is a direct formal test for whether the suspected regressors are indeed endogenous, and in this case, endogeneity is supported.

Further, in the NHN model, the Education coefficients have both opposite signs from those usually obtained, while in the BTN model, *both* coefficients have negative signs, which appears counterintuitive since it implies that formal education tends to have a negative effect on the wage (and the more the years of education, the stronger the negative marginal effect). To make sense of this result we must interpret it together with the high positive correlation between Education and the error term. First, this compromises the reliability of the estimates obtained in the NHN model. Second, in the BTN model, the correlation link is assumed to be the unobservable "Ability," and ability is expected to have a direct positive effect on the wage, and we do obtain a positive correlation of Education with the error, and a strong one at that. Combined we get a clear message: education without ability is not really valued by the firms in the sample, maybe because it is then viewed as years wasted away from on-the-job training and experience.

Regarding Potential Experience, we also get the anticipated correlation (negative). In generic notation, let x denote Potential Experience, and, since it is a maximal estimation of actual experience x^*, their relation can be written as $x = x^* + \xi$, $\xi \geq 0$, $\text{Cov}(x,\xi) > 0$. Then the true regression relation is

$$y = \ldots + x^*\beta + \varepsilon^* = (x - \xi)\beta + \varepsilon^* \Rightarrow y = x\beta + \varepsilon,\ \varepsilon = -\beta\xi + \varepsilon^*.$$

So $\text{Cov}(x,\varepsilon) = -\beta\text{Cov}(x,\xi)$. Since the regression coefficient of Potential Experience is positive, we anticipate $\text{Cov}(\text{PEXP},\varepsilon) < 0$, which is what we got. Moreover, note that the direct effect of Potential Experience reduces and becomes statistically insignificant in the BTN copula model, compared to the NHN specification. Essentially it is overshadowed by the correlation with the error term, and this tells us that Potential Experience is not really a good proxy variable for actual experience.

Turning to the estimates related to the error term, we obtain a negative estimate for the parameter ρ, indicating negative correlation between w and u, $\text{corr}(w,u) = -0.216$, that is consistent with the theoretical model. In fact, ρ is very close to its boundary, which is an indication that the variables w and u may be more strongly correlated than the specification can reflect.

3.5. Bargaining and Negotiation Effects

Focusing on the BTN model, of particular interest are the model's predictions as regards the bargaining and negotiation effects. We report that the original estimates of the scale parameters are $\hat{\sigma}_w = 23.207$ and $\hat{\sigma}_u = 13.763$. With this, we obtain that the standard deviations of bargaining performances are $SD(w) = 1.1117$ and $SD(u) = 0.6593$.

We see that the variable w related to the bargaining performance of the worker side has higher mean than the employers' variable u, but also higher standard deviation, something that may reflect the higher number of unique workers than unique firms in the sample.

In relation to the relative bargaining power η, we cannot disentangle it from the self-evaluation premium and the prudential discount variables, but we can compute an upper bound for its variability. Specifically, we have obtained before that $\mathrm{Cov}(w,u) = -\sigma_\eta^2 \mu_g \mu_d$, while also we have $\mu_g = \mu_w / \mu_\eta$ and $\mu_d = \mu_u / (1-\mu_\eta)$. Combining, we obtain

$$\sigma_\eta^2 = \mu_\eta (1-\mu_\eta) \cdot \frac{-\mathrm{Cov}(w,u)}{E(w)E(u)}.$$

The term $\varphi \equiv -\mathrm{Cov}(w,u) / E(w)E(u)$ can be computed from the estimates. Moreover, the term $\mu_\eta(1-\mu_\eta)$ has a maximum 1/4 since μ_η ranges in (0, 1). It follows that

$$\max \sigma_\eta^2 = \hat{\varphi}/4, \quad \max SD(\eta) = \sqrt{\hat{\varphi}}/2.$$

Using eq. (9) we obtain $SD(\eta) \leq 0.1941$, for a variable that ranges in (0, 1). A reasonable way to model such a random variable is to assume that it follows the Beta distribution (we will exploit this in the next section). In the Beta distribution family, the Uniform (0, 1) has a standard deviation $1/\sqrt{12} \approx 0.2887$. So in our sample, relative bargaining power has a standard deviation no bigger than 2/3 of the variability it would have if it was distributed uniformly. This indicates a degree of concentration and consequently unequal distribution of relative bargaining power among workers.

Turning to wage determination, since we have estimated a model with the dependent variable in logarithms, ultimately we need exponentiated magnitudes,

$$\omega_i = E(p_i \mid I_{c,i}) \cdot \exp\{v_i + w_i - u_i\}. \tag{13}$$

We can obtain series for these exponentiated components, and then compute concentration measures like the empirical mean or median. Exponentiation magnifies estimation inaccuracy, possibly leading to outliers that can unduly affect sample means, so we chose to use the empirical medians.

We look first at the relation between the common-information expected productivity and the actual wage. Bargaining effects are implicitly present here, since we stratify the sample according to whether the total negotiation effect was positive ($\hat{\varepsilon} > 0$) or negative. The results are presented in Table 15.4.

The overall conclusion from Table 15.4 is how much the agreed wage depended on the negotiation process and the private information sets of the parties, relative to the formal qualifications of the worker as well as the main financial and structural indicators for the firm. Actual monthly earnings (AME) differ a lot from the common-information expectation for the worker's productivity. This strong effect

Table 15.4. Winners and Losers from Wage Negotiations.

USD PPP (Levels)	$\hat{\varepsilon}_i < 0$	$\hat{\varepsilon}_i > 0$	Full Sample
Median Values	$n = 692$	$n = 853$	$n = 1{,}545$
$\hat{E}(p_i \mid I_{c,i})$	110.08	44.43	66.89
AME ω_i	53.94	127.53	82.63
%Δ	−50.1	+187.0	+23.5
Association measures between $\hat{E}(p_i \mid I_{c,i})$ and AME			
Pearson's correlation coefficient	0.3715	0.0225	−0.05
	(0.000)	(0.510)	(0.046)
Kendall's tau	0.3408	0.1694	−0.1069
	(0.000)	(0.000)	(0.000)
Spearman's rho	0.4742	0.2332	−0.1619
	(0.000)	(0.000)	(0.000)

p-Values for no-association hypothesis in parentheses

of atypical forces on wage determination is an indication that structured payroll and remuneration policy was largely absent in the firms sampled.

As regards the statistical association of the two, the Pearson's correlation coefficient as well as the non-parametric measures, Kendall's tau and Spearman's rho, show a positive association in the sub-samples, which turns negative when measured over the whole sample. This is an occurrence of the well-known "Simpson's paradox," since the relation that accords with reason is the positive one, but it is revealed only when we decompose the sample.

3.6. Wage Frontiers and Evolution Over Time

The Nash bargaining 2TSF model provides four dimensions of the bargaining space and outcomes. Equation (13) is the actual observed level, henceforth denoted by ω_i^{A}. The "balanced" outcome would be the wage without bargaining effects ($w = u = 0$), or with exactly balanced ones ($w = u \neq 0$), the wage being determined solely from the common-information expected productivity and any random elements:

$$\omega_i^{\mathrm{B}} = E\left(p_i \mid I_{c,i}\right) \cdot \exp\{v_i\}.$$

We can then express the actual wage relative to the balanced wage,

$$\frac{\omega_i^{\mathrm{A}}}{\omega_i^{\mathrm{B}}} = \exp\{w_i - u_i\},$$

and we can do the same for the upper (U) and lower (L) wage frontier,

$$\frac{\omega_i^{\mathrm{U}}}{\omega_i^{\mathrm{B}}} = \exp\{w_i\}, \quad \frac{\omega_i^{\mathrm{L}}}{\omega_i^{\mathrm{B}}} = \exp\{-u_i\}.$$

The upper frontier gives us the wage (in relative terms, the mark-up from the balanced wage) if it were the case that $u = 0$ (no prudential discount from the part of

Table 15.5. Relative Wage Frontiers. Sample Medians.

	1993	1994	1995
Upper frontier $E(\exp\{w_i\} \mid \varepsilon_i)$	2.867	2.383	2.624
Actual wage $E(\exp\{w_i - u_i\} \mid \varepsilon_i)$	1.40	1.076	1.243
Balanced wage	1	1	1
Lower frontier $E(\exp\{-u_i\} \mid \varepsilon_i)$	0.591	0.546	0.574

the firm and/or zero bargaining power). The lower frontier gives the wage if $w = 0$ (no self-evaluation premium from the part of the worker and/or zero bargaining power). Predicted series at observation level for these expressions can be based on the residuals, by estimating $E(\exp\{w_i\} \mid \varepsilon_i), E(\exp\{w_i - u_i \mid \varepsilon_i\}), E(\exp\{-u_i \mid \varepsilon_i\})$ (the mathematical expressions are included in the Appendix). Seeing how these magnitudes evolve over time provides a quantified sense of the bargaining space, as in Table 15.5.

The main information we get from Table 15.5 is that the median wage was above the balanced wage in all three years, showing a favorable bargaining outcome for the workers. But also that the upper wage frontier fell visibly in the second year of the survey, and with it the observed mark-up that is incorporated in the actual wage. On the other hand, the lower wage frontier remained stable, indicating again the relatively higher stability in the attitudes of the firms. Also, the fact that the bargaining performance of workers impacts the outcome more strongly is in line with the conclusion of Abowd et al. (1999) that "person effects" appear to matter more than "firm effects."

To understand better the intertemporal evolution, in Table 15.6 we combine the common-information expected productivity prior to negotiations (1st column), the net effect of bargaining performance (2nd column), the actual observed wage (3rd column), while the last column records the proportion of times $\hat{E}(\exp\{w_i - u_i\} | \varepsilon_i) > 1$ and so it tended to positively affect the wage. The effect of the random component v_i is rather negligible: only for 39 observations over the whole sample did it reverse the net negotiation effect from positive to negative (which in any case was very close to neutral for these observations), and in no case did it transform a negative effect to a positive one.

From Table 15.6, we see that the common-information expected productivity tended to increase over time, but actual earnings dived in the middle year due to deterioration of the positive effect that the bargaining stage had on the wage, both as regards its sample median mark-up value but also as regards the proportion of times that it was positive. We note that in 1994, Zambia experienced a large macroeconomic contraction (–8.6% negative growth), and rebounded in 1995 (2.9% growth), and our results align with such a picture.[12] While such large fluctuations from year to year are not frequent, it is possible that we have captured here an echo of the political and social environment of the country at the time: in 1992 Zambia had just exited a 20-year single-party government system and had entered multi-party democracy. Our sample comes from these first transitional years, where the "rules of the game," any game, are expected to be in flux.

Table 15.6. Intertemporal Evolution. Sample Medians.

Year	$\hat{E}(p_i \mid I_{c,i})$ (USD PPP)	$\hat{E}(\exp\{w_i - u_i\} \mid \varepsilon_i)$ (Gross Mark-up)	AME (USD PPP)	Percentage of Positive Bargaining Effects
1993	64.03	1.400	83.80	60.74
1994	66.47	1.076	73.34	52.03
1995	76.21	1.243	100.10	59.72
Full sample	66.89	1.230	82.63	57.73

4. STATISTICAL SPECIFICATION II: IDENTIFICATION OF RELATIVE BARGAINING POWER

The main thing left to be desired from the previous statistical specification is the disentanglement and separate identification of the relative bargaining power η from the private information effects g and d. In this section, we provide a method to accomplish that.

Since the relative bargaining power η ranges in (0, 1) we assume that it follows a Beta distribution with density:

$$f_\eta(\eta; \gamma, \delta) = \frac{\eta^{\gamma-1}(1-\eta)^{\delta-1}}{\mathrm{B}(\gamma, \delta)}.$$

The great advantage of the Beta distribution is that with only two parameters it is extremely flexible: it nests "standard-looking" unimodal densities with or without positive or negative skewness, it includes the Uniform with its flat density but also the family of the arcsine distributions (symmetric or asymmetric) that have a minimum in the middle values and rising probability mass at the extremes. It can also become monotonic (increasing or decreasing). In fact, the only inflexibility of the Beta distribution is that it cannot represent populations with multiple finite modes.

Most of the available 2TSF composed error densities spring from the convolution of three single-parameter random variables, $f_\varepsilon(\varepsilon, \sigma_v, \sigma_w, \sigma_u)$ for $\varepsilon = v + w - u$. In our model, we have that $w = \eta g$, $u = (1-\eta)d$. In particular w, u are almost always assumed to be Exponentials, but we have available closed form densities where these components are Half Normals or Generalized Exponentials.[13] These distributions have support in $(0, \infty)$, and this makes them "closed under scaling," in the sense that, for D a distribution and θ the distribution parameter, we have

$$X \sim D_X(\theta) \Rightarrow Z = aX \sim D_X(a\theta).$$

This property is not universal. Multiplying a random variable by a scalar does not always mean that we can just insert the scaled parameters in the exact same density expression. For example, if the support of the distribution has a finite *non-zero* boundary, it is not closed under scaling. But when the property holds, the conditional density $f_{\varepsilon|\eta}(\varepsilon \mid \eta)$ will have the exact same form as the marginal over (v, w, u), where η and $(1-\eta)$ will operate as scaling factors of g, d to arrive correspondingly at w, u, multiplying the parameters of their distributions:

$$f_{\varepsilon|\eta}(\varepsilon \mid \eta;\ \sigma_v,\ \sigma_g,\ \sigma_d) = f_\varepsilon(\varepsilon;\ \sigma_v,\ \eta\sigma_g,\ (1-\eta)\sigma_d).$$

Then the composed error marginal density is obtained by integrating out η from the joint density,

$$f_{\varepsilon}(\varepsilon) = \int_0^1 f(\varepsilon, \eta)d\eta = \int_0^1 f_{\varepsilon|\eta}(\varepsilon \mid \eta) f_{\eta}(\eta)d\eta.$$

It follows that the sample log-likelihood for the regression model eq. (6) based on the marginal distribution of the composite error term can be written as

$$\begin{aligned}\mathcal{L}_n &= \sum_{i=1}^{n} \ln\left(\int_0^1 f_{\varepsilon|\eta}(y_i - \mathbf{x}_i'\beta \mid \eta) f_{\eta}(\eta)d\eta\right)\\ &= -n\ln \mathrm{B}(\gamma, \delta) + \sum_{i=1}^{n} \ln\left(\int_0^1 f_{\varepsilon|\eta}(y_i - \mathbf{x}_i'\beta \mid \eta) \cdot \eta^{\gamma-1}(1-\eta)^{\delta-1}d\eta\right).\end{aligned}$$

We can implement MLE of the unknown parameters using numerical integration by Gauss–Legendre quadrature, with weights adjusted for the [0,1] limits, that give

$$\int_0^1 F(\eta)d\eta \approx \frac{1}{2}\sum_{j=1}^{m} \xi_j F(\eta_j),$$

where (η_j, ξ_j) are Gauss–Legendre nodes and weights for the interval (0, 1). If the value of the likelihood is of separate importance (e.g., for non-nested goodness-of-fit tests and criteria like AIC and BIC), one should not forget to include in the sample log-likelihood the $-n\ln 2$ factor. But apart from that there is no need to apply any other transformation of the log-likelihood due to the numerical integration.

For the information effects g and d we will be able to obtain sample level moments based on σ_g, σ_d, although not individual measures per observation. But for the relative bargaining power, apart from characterizing the distribution through the estimates of γ, δ, we can also obtain estimates of its individual magnitude at observation level as follows: By Bayes' theorem for densities,

$$\begin{aligned}E(\eta_i \mid \varepsilon_i) &= \int_0^1 \eta f_{\eta|\varepsilon}(\eta \mid \varepsilon_i)d\eta = \int_0^1 \eta \frac{f_{\varepsilon|\eta}(\varepsilon_i \mid \eta) \cdot f_{\eta}(\eta)}{f_{\varepsilon}(\varepsilon_i)}d\eta\\ &= \frac{\int_0^1 \eta \cdot f_{\varepsilon}(\varepsilon_i \mid \eta) f(\eta)d\eta}{\int_0^1 f_{\varepsilon}(\varepsilon_i \mid \eta) f(\eta)d\eta}.\end{aligned} \tag{14}$$

We can apply the same numerical integration as before, separately for the numerator and the denominator, to compute this conditional expectation predictor, using the estimated parameters and the value of the residual $\hat{\varepsilon}_i$ for each observation. Note that the 1/2 factor from the Gauss–Legendre quadrature as well as the normalizing Beta function cancel out here.

Contrast this with, for example, the model of Harding, Rosenthal, and Sirmans (2003) where, in a standard hedonic-pricing regression for the housing market, the authors include linearly a vector of buyer and seller characteristics as proxies for idiosyncratic bargaining power, and they have to assume a priori symmetric bargaining power to identify the effects of these characteristics on the observed price (p. 182).

4.1. Empirical Illustration: Wage Bargaining in Ghana

To contain the size of this study, we will focus here on illustrating only the results of the estimation of relative bargaining power. We will employ the Normal-Exponential 2TSF composite error density, where in $\varepsilon = v + w - u$, v is assumed $N(0, \sigma_v)$, $w \mid \eta = \eta g$ and $u \mid \eta = (1-\eta)d$ are (conditionally) Exponential with scale parameters $\sigma_w = \eta\sigma_g$, $\sigma_u = (1-\eta)\sigma_d$, so g and d are assumed to have Exponential marginals.[14] Then, the density of ε conditional on η is,

$$f_\varepsilon(\varepsilon \mid \eta) = \frac{\exp\{a_1\}\Phi(b_1) + \exp\{a_2\}\Phi(b_2)}{\sigma_w + \sigma_u},$$

$$a_1 = \frac{\sigma_v^2}{2\sigma_u^2} + \frac{\varepsilon}{\sigma_u}, \quad b_1 = -\left(\frac{\varepsilon}{\sigma_v} + \frac{\sigma_v}{\sigma_u}\right), \quad a_2 = \frac{\sigma_v^2}{2\sigma_w^2} - \frac{\varepsilon}{\sigma_w}, \quad b_2 = \frac{\varepsilon}{\sigma_v} - \frac{\sigma_v}{\sigma_w}.$$

The conditioning variable η lives inside the scale parameters σ_w and σ_u. The log-likelihood for this particular specification is

$$\mathcal{L}_n = -n \ln \mathrm{B}(\gamma, \delta) + \sum_{i=1}^{n} \ln\left(\int_0^1 \frac{\exp\{a_1\}\Phi(b_1) + \exp\{a_2\}\Phi(b_2)}{\eta\sigma_g + (1-\eta)\sigma_d} \cdot \eta^{\gamma-1}(1-\eta)^{\delta-1} d\eta\right),$$

to be maximized over $(\beta, \sigma_v, \sigma_g, \sigma_d, \gamma, \delta)$. The copula density extension can be incorporated also in this likelihood.

We used another part of the data set from Bigsten et al. (2000) that relates to Ghana. Here too data were collected in three waves, but for the years 1992–1994. We also used the same regressor set (plus squared Potential Experience). The usable sample size was $n = 1{,}910$. We ignored the endogeneity issue in this case. Table 15.7 has the estimated distribution parameters of the composed error and the resulting moments.

The average prudential discount from the part of the firms, $\sigma_d = E(d)$, is much stronger than the self-evaluation premium of the workers $\sigma_g = E(g)$. The parameters γ, δ of the Beta distribution of relative bargaining power η are both higher

Table 15.7. Composed Error Parameters from the Ghana Sample.

Parameter	Estimate	Std. Dev.	Moments	
σ_v	0.4315	0.0551		
σ_g	0.3735	0.0728	$E(w)$	0.1926
σ_d	0.6437	0.0650	$E(u)$	0.3117
γ	1.3046	0.0406	$E(\eta)$	0.5158
δ	1.2246	0.0169	$SD(\eta)$	0.2660

Table 15.8. Distribution of η and of $E(\eta \mid \varepsilon)$.

	η	$E(\eta \mid \varepsilon)$	Quantiles of	$E(\eta \mid \varepsilon)$
Mean	0.516	0.516	0.1	0.3629
Median	0.521	0.523	0.3	0.4737
Std. Dev.	0.266	0.111	0.5	0.5229
Minimum	0.000	0.192	0.7	0.5705
Maximum	1.000	0.877	0.9	0.6460

than unity and so assign declining probability mass to the (0, 1) extremes. Being small in value, they signal that there is no significant concentration of probability mass near the middle. They are also close, indicating a roughly symmetric distribution around the 0.5 value.

Combining the expected values of g, d, η we obtain the expected values of the bargaining performance w, u. Contrary to the Zambia sample, here $E(u) > E(w)$: the bargaining performance of firms is stronger.

Turning to individual measures, we computed $E(\eta \mid \varepsilon)$ using 7-point Gauss–Legendre quadrature. We compare the postulated marginal distribution with the empirical distribution of $E(\eta \mid \varepsilon)$ in Table 15.8.

That the distribution of $E(\eta \mid \varepsilon)$ is more concentrated than the marginal should not come as a surprise: the conditional expectation is a shrinkage estimator. It does not go below 0.2 or above 0.88, and 80% of the predictions for worker relative bargaining power range close to the middle $(0.35-0.65)$. We close this illustration with the empirical relative frequency and kernel density estimation of the distribution of $E(\eta \mid \varepsilon)$, presented in Fig. 15.1.

5. CONCLUSIONS AND FURTHER RESEARCH

In this chapter, we modified the standard bilateral Nash bargaining framework to take into account value uncertainty and information asymmetry. Focusing on wage bargaining, the goal was to obtain an earnings-determination model that rationalizes and provides structural content to the unobserved individual firm and worker effects, which are thought to produce the large dispersion in earnings observed in labor markets. We arrived at a two-tier stochastic frontier model that treats these effects as being composites of private information on the uncertain productivity and of relative bargaining power, while the common base of the parties negotiating is the expected productivity of the worker based on the common-information set, and can be properly estimated by the use of MEEDS. We enhanced maximum likelihood with a copula density method to account for regressor endogeneity, and we applied a conditioning technique to separately identify relative bargaining power from private information effects. The empirical applications provided insights into how the bargaining performance of each party affected the agreed wage. The model can be applied to any bargaining situation for which we have data for both parties involved.

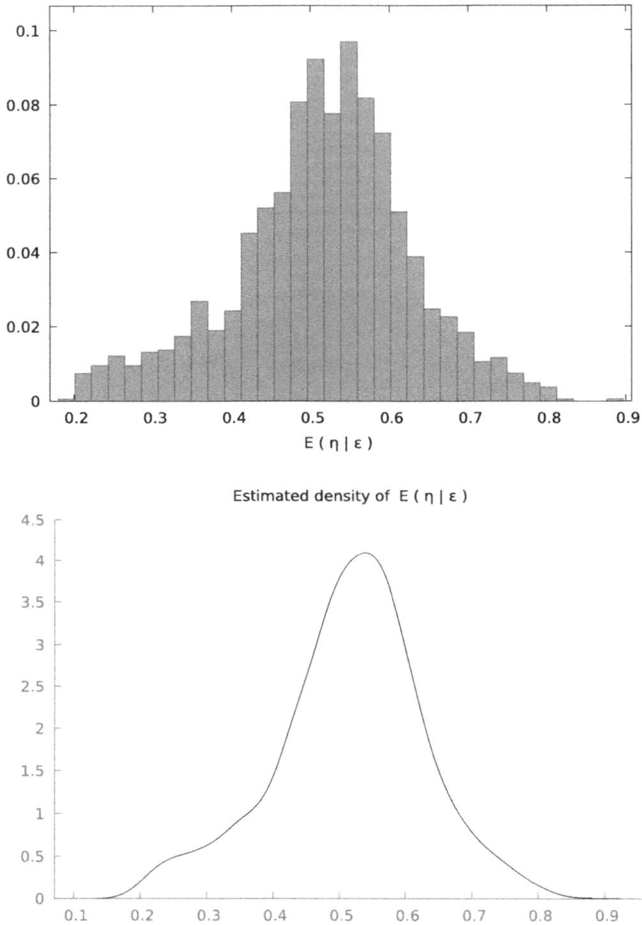

Fig. 15.1. Empirical Density Estimates of $E(\eta \mid \varepsilon)$.

There are various ways in which the 2TSF Nash bargaining model can be extended, both in theory and in applied research. While one of its advantages is that it can work with a cross-sectional sample, it certainly can be extended to a panel-data setting that could enhance its identification potential. 2TSF models have been developed for that purpose (Das & Polachek, 2017; Papadopoulos, 2021b; Polachek & Yoon, 1996). Stratification of the sample to subgroups of interest, is a potential applied extension. For example, one would want to see whether differences in bargaining performance exist between men and women, between degree-holders and non-holders, or between workers at or near a legislated minimum wage, if one exists.[15]

Another extension could be to reformulate the model in the presence of determinants of bargaining power, if they are available as data, following the method suggested by Parmeter (2018). We are skeptical though that such an extension can be implemented also for the private information components: while variables proxying financial commitments of the parties could explain well bargaining power, it is difficult to think of variables that could explain the own-evaluation premium and the prudential discount, these being too idiosyncratic.[16] Perhaps the "turn-over rate" of a firm, that is, the number of separations in a year as a percentage of its labor force, could be linked to a higher prudential discount. Finally, even if we did not touch the issue of collective bargaining, there are several features in the 2TSF Nash bargaining model that appear transferable to that environment.

NOTES

1. Abowd et al. (1999) called "extremely heterogeneous labor market outcomes," an "enduring feature of empirical analyses of labor markets in many countries."
2. Nash bargaining setups with many players should not be confused with collective bargaining.
3. And it has been used extensively in labor economics, see for example Pissarides (2000).
4. Roth (1979) contains the formal mathematical treatment.
5. See also Keniston et al. (2021) for, as they write, "a robust-inference argument to explain why agents may view the two most recent offers as corresponding to the potential surplus."
6. This has also its stochastic counterpart: if the joint distribution function of the wage-target and the relative bargaining power is, say $F\left(\omega_e^T, \eta\right)$, then the marginal distribution of ω_e^T is obtained as $F\left(\omega_e^T\right) = \lim_{\eta \to 1} F\left(\omega_e^T, \eta\right)$, which is our case.
7. Note that the "truthfulness" of the information related to the worker is not relevant here. If a rational worker has decided to "beautify" their resumé, resulting in a higher projected expectation, they will still go on and add on top of that their own-evaluation premium. Rationality does not rule out cheating or strategic/manipulative actions.
8. See Abowd and Kramarz (1999).
9. For an empirical study that links wage bargaining with what happens in the market of the firm, see Forslund, Gottfries, and Westermark (2008).
10. This independence assumption may be jeopardized in the case where both parties know privately the same piece of relevant information, that is, without knowing that the other party also knows. The possibility that a firm is pressed to hire fast, that was mentioned earlier, is a case in point.
11. The data were collected as part of the Regional Program on Enterprise Development, organized by the World Bank. The project received support from the Swedish, Norwegian, United Kingdom, Canadian, and Dutch governments. The full data set was downloaded from the website of the Centre for the Study of African Economies at the University of Oxford: http://www.csae.ox.ac.uk.
12. Data come from the World Development Indicators of the World Bank, accessed June 12, 2022.
13. See Papadopoulos (2015) for the former and Papadopoulos (2021a) for the latter.
14. This does not mean that the *marginal* distributions of $w = \eta g$ or $u = (1-\eta)d$ are Exponentials. The related integral convolution has an expression in terms of the Whittaker

function $W_{\lambda,\mu}(z)$, but it is rather unmanageable. We note that recently a family of distributions based on the Whittaker function has emerged, see Omair, Tashkandy, Askar, and Alzaid (2022).

15. In introducing the *Handbook of Research in Negotiation*, Olekalns and Adair (2013), summarizing the relevant literature mention that "meta-analyses showed small but reliable gender differences in negotiation outcomes and strategies."

16. For the universe of "individual effects/differences in negotiation," see the review by Elfenbein (2013).

REFERENCES

Abowd, J. M., & Kramarz, F. (1999). The analysis of labor markets using matched employer–employee data. In O. C. Ashenfelter & D. Card (Eds.), *Handbook of labor economics* (Vol. 3, pp. 2629–2710). Amsterdam: Elsevier.

Abowd, J., Kramarz, F., & Margolis, D. N. (1999). High wage workers and high wage firms. *Econometrica*, *67*(2), 251–333.

Ausubel, L. M., Cramton, P., & Deneckere, R. J. (2002). Bargaining with incomplete information. In R. J. Aumann & S. Hart (Eds.), *Handbook of game theory with economic applications* (Vol. 3, pp 1897–1945). Amsterdam: Elsevier.

Bigsten, A., Isaksson, A., Söderbom, M., Collier, P., Zeufack, A., Dercon, S., ... Pattillo, C. (2000). Rates of return on physical and human capital in Africa's manufacturing sector. *Economic Development and Cultural Change*, *48*(4), 801–827.

Binmore, K., Rubinstein, A., & Wolinsky, A. (1986). The Nash bargaining solution in economic modeling. *The RAND Journal of Economics*, *17*(2), 176–188.

Das, T., & Polachek, S. W. (2017). Estimating labor force joiners and leavers using a heterogeneity augmented two-tier stochastic frontier. *Journal of Econometrics*, *199*(1), 156–172

Doornik, J. A., & Hansen, H. (2008). An omnibus test for univariate and multivariate normality. *Oxford Bulletin of Economics and Statistics*, *70*, 927–939.

Elfenbein, H. A. (2013). Individual differences in negotiation. In M. Olekalns & W. L. Adair (Eds.), *Handbook of research on negotiation* (pp. 25–45). Cheltenham: Edward Elgar Publishing Limited.

Forslund, A., Gottfries, N., & Westermark, A. (2008). Prices, productivity and wage bargaining in open economies. *Scandinavian Journal of Economics*, *110*(1), 169–195.

Gaynor, M., & Polachek, S. W. (1994). Measuring information in the market: An application to physician services. *Southern Economic Journal*, *60*(4), 815–831.

Groot, W., & van den Brink, H. M. (2007). Optimism, pessimism and the compensating income variation of cardiovascular disease: A two-tiered quality of life stochastic frontier model. *Social Science & Medicine*, *65*(7), 1479–1489.

Hall, R. E., & Krueger, A. B. (2012). Evidence on the incidence of wage posting, wage bargaining, and on-the-job search. *American Economic Journal: Macroeconomics*, *4*(4), 56–67.

Hall, R. E., & Milgrom, P. R. (2008). The limited influence of unemployment on the wage bargain. *American Economic Review*, *98*(4), 1653–1674.

Harding, J. P., Rosenthal, S. S., & Sirmans, C. F. (2003). Estimating bargaining power in the market for existing homes. *Review of Economics and Statistics*, *85*(1), 178–188.

Harsanyi, J. C., & Selten, R. (1972). A generalized Nash solution for two-person bargaining games with incomplete information. *Management Science*, *18*(5-part-2), 80–106.

Huber, V. L., & Neale, M. A. (1987). Effects of self-and competitor goals on performance in an interdependent bargaining task. *Journal of Applied Psychology*, *72*(2), 197.

Iregui, A. M., Melo, L. A., & Ramírez, M. T. (2014). Wage-setting decisions on newly hired employees: Survey evidence from Colombian firms. *Managerial and Decision Economics*, *35*(3), 231–246.

Jamalizadeh, A., Pourmousa, R., & Balakrishnan, N. (2009). Truncated and limited skew-normal and skew-*t* distributions: Properties and an illustration. *Communications in Statistics – Theory and Methods*, *38*(16–17), 2653–2668.

Jensen, P. H. (2010). Exploring the uses of matched employer–employee datasets. *Australian Economic Review*, *43*(2), 209–216.

Joe, H. (2015). *Dependence modelling with copulas*. Boca Raton, FL: CRC Press.

Keniston, D., Larsen, B. J., Li, S., Prescott, J. J., Silveira, B. S., & Yu, C. (2021). *Fairness in incomplete information bargaining: Theory and widespread evidence from the field*. Technical Report 29111, National Bureau of Economic Research.

Kinukawa, S., & Motohashi, K. (2016). What determines the outcome of licensing deals in market for technology? Empirical analysis of sellers and buyers in biotechnology alliances. *International Journal of Technology Management*, *70*(4), 257–280.

Klaassen, C., & Wellner, J. (1997). Efficient estimation in the bivariate normal copula model: Normal margins are least favourable. *Bernoulli*, *3*(1), 55–77.

Kumbhakar, S. C., & Parmeter, C. F. (2009). The effects of match uncertainty and bargaining on labor market outcomes: Evidence from firm and worker specific estimates. *Journal of Productivity Analysis*, *31*(1), 1–14.

Kumbhakar, S. C., & Parmeter, C. F. (2010). Estimation of hedonic price functions with incomplete information. *Empirical Economics*, *39*(1), 1–25.

Locke, E. A., & Latham, G. P. (2002). Building a practically useful theory of goal setting and task motivation: A 35-year odyssey. *American Psychologist*, *57*(9), 705.

Lombera, D. C. (2007). Analysis of two-party salary negotiations: Factors impeding a mutually-beneficial joint agreement. Rio de Janeiro: Getúlio Vargas Foundation.

Moran, P. A. P. (1967). Testing for correlation between non-negative variates. *Biometrika*, *54*(3–4), 385–394.

Nash, J. F. J. (1950). The bargaining problem. *Econometrica*, *18*(2), 155–162.

Northcraft, G. B., Neale, M. A., & Early, P. C. (1994). Joint effects of assigned goals and training on negotiator performance. *Human Performance*, *7*(4), 257–272.

Olekalns, M., & Adair, W. L. (2013). The complexity of negotiating: From the individual to the context, and what lies between. In M. Olekalns & W. L. Adair (Eds.), *Handbook of research on negotiation* (pp. 3–22). Cheltenham: Edward Elgar Publishing Limited.

Omair, M. A., Tashkandy, Y. A., Askar, S., & Alzaid, A. A. (2022). Family of distributions derived from Whittaker function. *Mathematics*, *10*(7), 1–23.

Papadopoulos, A. (2015). The half normal specification for the two tier stochastic frontier model. *Journal of Productivity Analysis*, *43*(2), 225–230.

Papadopoulos, A. (2021a). Stochastic frontier models using the generalized exponential distribution. *Journal of Productivity Analysis*, *55*(1), 15–29.

Papadopoulos, A. (2021b). The two-tier stochastic frontier framework (2TSF): Measuring frontiers wherever they may exist. In C. F. Parmeter & R. C. Sickles (Eds.), *Advances in efficiency and productivity analysis* (pp. 163–194). Cham: Springer International Publishing.

Papadopoulos, A. (2022). Accounting for endogeneity in regression models using copulas: A step-by-step guide for empirical studies. *Journal of Econometric Methods*, *11*(1), 127–154.

Papadopoulos, A., Parmeter, C. F., & Kumbhakar, S. C. (2021). Modeling dependence in two-tier stochastic frontier models. *Journal of Productivity Analysis*, *56*(2–3), 85–101.

Parmeter, C. F. (2018). Estimation of the two-tiered stochastic frontier model with the scaling property. *Journal of Productivity Analysis*, *49*(1), 37–47.

Pissarides, C. A. (2000). *Equilibrium unemployment theory*. London: MIT Press.

Polachek, S. W., & Yoon, B. J. (1987). A two-tiered earnings frontier estimation of employer and employee information in the labor market. *The Review of Economics and Statistics*, *69*(2), 296–302.

Polachek, S. W., & Yoon, B. J. (1996). Panel estimates of a two-tiered earnings frontier. *Journal of Applied Econometrics*, *11*(2), 169–178.

Rosen, S. (1986). The theory of equalizing differences. In O. Layard & R. (Eds.), *Handbook of labor economics* (pp. 641–692). Amsterdam: North Holland.

Roth, A. E. (1979). *Axiomatic models of bargaining*. Berlin: Springer Verlag.

Song, P. X. K., Li, M., & Yuan, Y. (2009). Joint regression analysis of correlated data using Gaussian copulas. *Biometrics*, *65*(1), 60–68.

Tauer, L. W. (2021). Determining the accuracy of Holstein bull semen prices with a two-tier efficiency model. *Journal of Applied Farm Economics*, *4*(1), 50–58.

Tran, K., & Tsionas, E. (2015). Endogeneity in stochastic frontier models: Copula approach without external instruments. *Economics Letters*, *133*, 85–88.

Wang, Y. (2018). Bargaining matters: An analysis of bilateral aid to developing countries. *Journal of International Relations and Development*, *21*, 1–21.

Zhang, H., Zhang, J., Yang, Y., & Zhou, Q. (2018). Bargaining power in tourist shopping. *Journal of Travel Research*, *57*(7), 947–961.

APPENDIX

A1. THE NASH BARGAINING EQUILIBRIUM IN LOGARITHMIC TERMS

To obtain the Nash bargaining equilibrium relation in logarithmic terms, we re-write the optimization problem that precedes eq.(2) as

$$\ln\omega^* : \arg\max\left(\ln\omega - \ln\omega_f^T\right)^{\eta}\left(\ln\omega_e^T - \ln\omega\right)^{1-\eta}$$

$$\Rightarrow \ln\omega^* : \arg\max\left\{\left(\ln\left[\frac{\omega}{\omega_f^T}\right]\right)^{\eta}\cdot\left(\ln\left[\frac{\omega_e^T}{\omega}\right]\right)^{1-\eta}\right\}.$$

Here, the gains are measured as mark-ups (or mark-downs), which is a relativistic approach often encountered in actual transactions. Solving for the maximum, we obtain

$$\ln\omega^* = \eta\ln\omega_e^T + (1-\eta)\ln\omega_f^T \Rightarrow \omega^* = \left(\omega_e^T\right)^{\eta}\cdot\left(\omega_f^T\right)^{1-\eta}.$$

The optimal wage is a weighted geometric average instead of a weighted arithmetic average. Defining the targets in a multiplicative way,

$$\omega_e^T \equiv E(p \mid I_c)e^{v}e^{g} \Rightarrow \ln\omega_e^T \equiv \ln E(p \mid I_c) + v + g,$$
$$\omega_f^T \equiv E(p \mid I_c)e^{v}e^{-d} \Rightarrow \ln\omega_f^T \equiv \ln E(p \mid I_c) + v - d.$$

Note that we took the logarithm of the conditional expectation and not the conditional expectation of the logarithm because, prior to deciding on the evaluation scale, the players have to face the inherent uncertainty of the situation. So it is first $E(p \mid I_c)$ instead of p, and then we consider the logarithms.

From these, we see that the components of the error term v, g, d now refer to the logarithmic scale as said in the main text. Then, we obtain the expression for the wage

$$\omega^* = \left[E(p \mid I_c)e^{v}e^{g}\right]^{\eta}\cdot\left[E(p \mid I_c)e^{v}e^{-d}\right]^{1-\eta}$$
$$\Rightarrow \omega^* = E(p \mid I_c)\cdot e^{v}\cdot e^{\eta g}\cdot e^{-(1-\eta)d}$$
$$\Rightarrow \ln\omega^* = \ln E(p \mid I_c) + v + \eta g - (1-\eta)d.$$

A2. THE GAUSSIAN COPULA DENSITY WITH DISCRETE REGRESSORS

We adjust to the case of one discrete endogenous regressor the general results in Song, Li, and Yuan (2009), specifically their eqs. (8) and (9). See also Joe (2015, p. 226). Let a collection of random variables $\{x_k \mid k = 1, \ldots, m\}$ with marginal distribution functions $F_1, \ldots F_m$. Suppose that x_1 is discrete with its support being the increasing-ordered finite set $\{d_1, \ldots, d_j, \ldots d_L\}$, while the other variables are continuous. Denote $x_k^* = \Phi^{-1}(F_k(x_k))$, while for the discrete random variable write $x_1^*(d_j) = \Phi^{-1}(F_1(d_j))$. Let $\phi_m(\mathbf{z};\ R)$ be the multivariate standard Normal density in m dimensions with correlation matrix R,

$$\phi_m(\mathbf{z};\ R) = (2\pi)^{-m/2}[\det(R)]^{-1/2} \cdot \exp\left\{-\frac{1}{2}\mathbf{z}'R^{-1}\mathbf{z}\right\},$$

and let $K_m(\mathbf{z};\ R)$ denote its kernel. Denote $\mathbf{q}' = \{x_1^*(d_j), x_2^*, \ldots, x_m^*\}$. Then the Gaussian copula is

$$C^G(F_1, \ldots F_m) = (2\pi)^{-m/2}[\det(R)]^{-1/2} \times$$
$$\times \int_{-\infty}^{x_1^*(d_j)} \ldots \int_{-\infty}^{x_m^*} K_m(s_1, s_2, \ldots, s_m; R)ds_m \ldots ds_1.$$

Note that $x_1^*(d_L) = +\infty$, and so the expression integrates to unity over the joint support.

To arrive at the copula density, we first differentiate the copula with respect to its arguments that are related to the $m-1$ continuous variables. By the Inverse Function Theorem, we have

$$\frac{\partial x_k^*}{\partial F_k} = \frac{\partial \Phi^{-1}(F_k)}{\partial F_k} = \frac{1}{\phi(x_k^*)}, \quad k = 2, \ldots, m.$$

So, differentiating under the integral sign,

$$\frac{\partial^{m-1} C}{\partial F_2 \cdots \partial F_m} = (2\pi)^{-m/2}[\det(R)]^{-1/2} \cdot \left[\phi(x_2^*) \cdots \phi(x_m^*)\right]^{-1} \times$$
$$\times \int_{-\infty}^{x_1^*(d_j)} K_m(s_1, x_2^*, \ldots, x_m^*;\ R)ds_1.$$

The copula density is then obtained by taking the proportional change in the copula as F_1 changes,

$$c^G = \frac{\Delta_{F_1}\left(\dfrac{\partial^{m-1} C}{\partial F_2 \cdots \partial F_m}\right)}{\Delta F_1} = \frac{(2\pi)^{-m/2}[\det(R)]^{-1/2} \cdot \left[\phi(x_2^*) \cdots \phi(x_m^*)\right]^{-1}}{F_1(d_j) - F_1(d_{j-1})} \times$$
$$\times \left[\int_{-\infty}^{x_1^*(d_j)} K_m(s_1, x_2^*, \ldots, x_m^*;\ R)ds_1 - \int_{-\infty}^{x_1^*(d_{j-1})} K_m(s_1, x_2^*, \ldots, x_m^*;\ R)ds_1\right]$$
$$\Rightarrow c^G = \frac{(2\pi)^{-m/2} \cdot \left[\phi(x_2^*) \cdots \phi(x_m^*)\right]^{-1}}{F_1(d_j) - F_1(d_{j-1})} \times$$
$$\times [\det(R)]^{-1/2} \cdot \int_{x_1^*(d_{j-1})}^{x_1^*(d_j)} K_m(s_1, x_2^*, \ldots, x_m^*; R)ds_1.$$

Writing this to include the error term in place of one of the continuous variables and for $m = 3$, omitting the components that do not include parameters of interest, and using Sklar's theorem that links joint distribution functions with copulas and consequently joint densities with marginal densities and the copula density, leads, after taking the natural logarithm, to the expression presented in the main text,

$$\ell_i = -\frac{1}{2}\ln\det\left(\breve{R}\right) + \frac{1}{2}\left[\Phi^{-1}\left(F_\varepsilon\left(y_i - \mathbf{x}_i{}'\beta;\theta\right)\right)\right]^2$$
$$+\ln\left(\int_{x^*_{1i}(d_{j-1})}^{x^*_{1i}(d_j)} K_{3,i}\left(s,\ x^*_{2i},\ \varepsilon^*_i;\ \breve{R}\right)ds\right) + \ln f_\varepsilon\left(y_i - \mathbf{x}_i{}'\beta;\theta\right).$$

This likelihood contains two integrals that require numerical evaluation. The first appears explicitly above, and in the empirical application, we evaluate it by 3-point Gauss–Legendre quadrature.** We also note that when $x^*_{1i}(d_j) = \Phi^{-1}(\hat{F}_1(d_1))$, namely, it is associated with the minimum value of the empirical support of x_1, then while in theory we have $\forall d < d_1 \Rightarrow F_1(d) = 0$, for use in empirical studies we set $j = 1 \rightarrow x^*_{1i}(d_{j-1}) = \Phi^{-1}(\epsilon)$, for some small $0 < \epsilon << \hat{F}_1(d_1)$, since $\Phi^{-1}(0) = -\infty$ and the estimation algorithm would abort.

The second integral in need of numerical evaluation is F_ε, the distribution function of the composite error term, which is not available in closed form. Here we apply the transformation

$$F_\varepsilon(\varepsilon_i) = \int_{-\infty}^{\varepsilon_i} f_\varepsilon(t)dt = 1 - \int_{\varepsilon_i}^{\infty} f_\varepsilon(t)dt = 1 - \int_0^{\infty} e^{-t}\cdot[e^t f_\varepsilon(t+\varepsilon_i)]dt$$

and for each i, we evaluate it using 15-point Gauss–Laguerre quadrature.

A3. INDIVIDUAL MEASURES FOR THE BARGAINING EFFECT

The conditional expected values used in the empirical application associated with the 2TSF-BTN specification were computed by the formulas given in Papadopoulos et al. (2021) (we suppress the observation index):

$$E(e^w \mid \varepsilon) = \frac{\exp\left\{(-\sigma_w a_u / b_w)\varepsilon + \sigma_w^2 / 2b_w^2\right\}\cdot\Omega_2}{\Phi_2\left(a_w\varepsilon, -a_u\varepsilon; r\right)}$$

** Note that the interval over which the quadrature is applied changes per observation.

with

$$\Omega_2 = 1 - \Phi(-\gamma_w \varepsilon) \cdot \Phi\left(a_u \varepsilon - \frac{\sigma_w}{b_w}\right)$$

$$- \Phi_2\left(\gamma_w \varepsilon, \frac{(a_u \lambda_w + b_w \gamma_w)\varepsilon - \sigma_w \lambda_w / b_w}{\sqrt{\lambda_w^2 + b_w^2}}; \frac{b_w}{\sqrt{\lambda_w^2 + b_w^2}}\right),$$

$$b_w = \frac{\sigma_\varepsilon}{\psi_u}, \quad \lambda_w = \frac{\sigma_v^2 \rho + \sigma_w \sigma_u (1-\rho^2)}{\psi_u \sigma_v \sqrt{1-\rho^2}}, \quad \gamma_w = \frac{\sigma_u \sqrt{1-\rho^2}}{\psi_u \sigma_v}.$$

$$E(e^{-u} \mid \varepsilon) = \frac{\exp\left\{(-\sigma_u a_w / b_u)\varepsilon + \sigma_u^2 / 2b_u^2\right\} \cdot \Omega_4}{\Phi_2(a_w \varepsilon, -a_u \varepsilon; r)},$$

with

$$\Omega_4 = \Phi(\gamma_u \varepsilon) \Phi\left(a_w \varepsilon - \frac{\sigma_u}{b_u}\right) + \Phi\left(\frac{(-\sigma_u \lambda_u / b_u) + (b_u \gamma_u + a_w \lambda_u)\varepsilon}{\sqrt{b_u^2 + \lambda_u^2}}\right)$$

$$- \Phi_2\left(\gamma_u \varepsilon, \frac{(-\sigma_u \lambda_u / b_u) + (b_u \gamma_u + a_w \lambda_u)\varepsilon}{\sqrt{b_u^2 + \lambda_u^2}}; \frac{b_u}{\sqrt{\lambda_u^2 + b_u^2}}\right),$$

$$b_u = \frac{\sigma_\varepsilon}{\psi_w}, \quad \lambda_u = \frac{\sigma_v^2 \rho + \sigma_w \sigma_u (1-\rho^2)}{\psi_w \sigma_v \sqrt{1-\rho^2}}, \quad \gamma_u = \frac{\sigma_w \sqrt{1-\rho^2}}{\psi_w \sigma_v}.$$

Finally,

$$E(\exp\{w-u\} \mid \varepsilon) = \exp\left\{\frac{s_{wu}^2}{\sigma_\varepsilon^2}\varepsilon + \frac{\sigma_v^2 s_{wu}^2}{2\sigma_\varepsilon^2}\right\} \cdot \frac{\Omega_5}{\Phi_2(a_w \varepsilon, -a_u \varepsilon; r)},$$

with

$$\Omega_5 = \Phi_2\left(-a_u(\sigma_v^2 + \varepsilon), -\frac{(\sigma_v^2 + \varepsilon)s_{wu}}{\sigma_v \sigma_\varepsilon}; \frac{\sigma_v \sigma_\varepsilon}{s_{wu}} a_u\right) + \Phi\left(a_w(\sigma_v^2 + \varepsilon)\right)$$

$$- \Phi_2\left(a_w(\sigma_v^2 + \varepsilon), -\frac{(\sigma_v^2 + \varepsilon)s_{wu}}{\sigma_v \sigma_\varepsilon}; -\frac{\sigma_v \sigma_\varepsilon}{s_{wu}} a_w\right),$$

$$s_{wu}^2 = \sigma_w^2 + \sigma_u^2 - 2\rho \sigma_w \sigma_u.$$

Printed and bound by CPI Group (UK) Ltd, Croydon, CR0 4YY
22/07/2024
14531126-0005